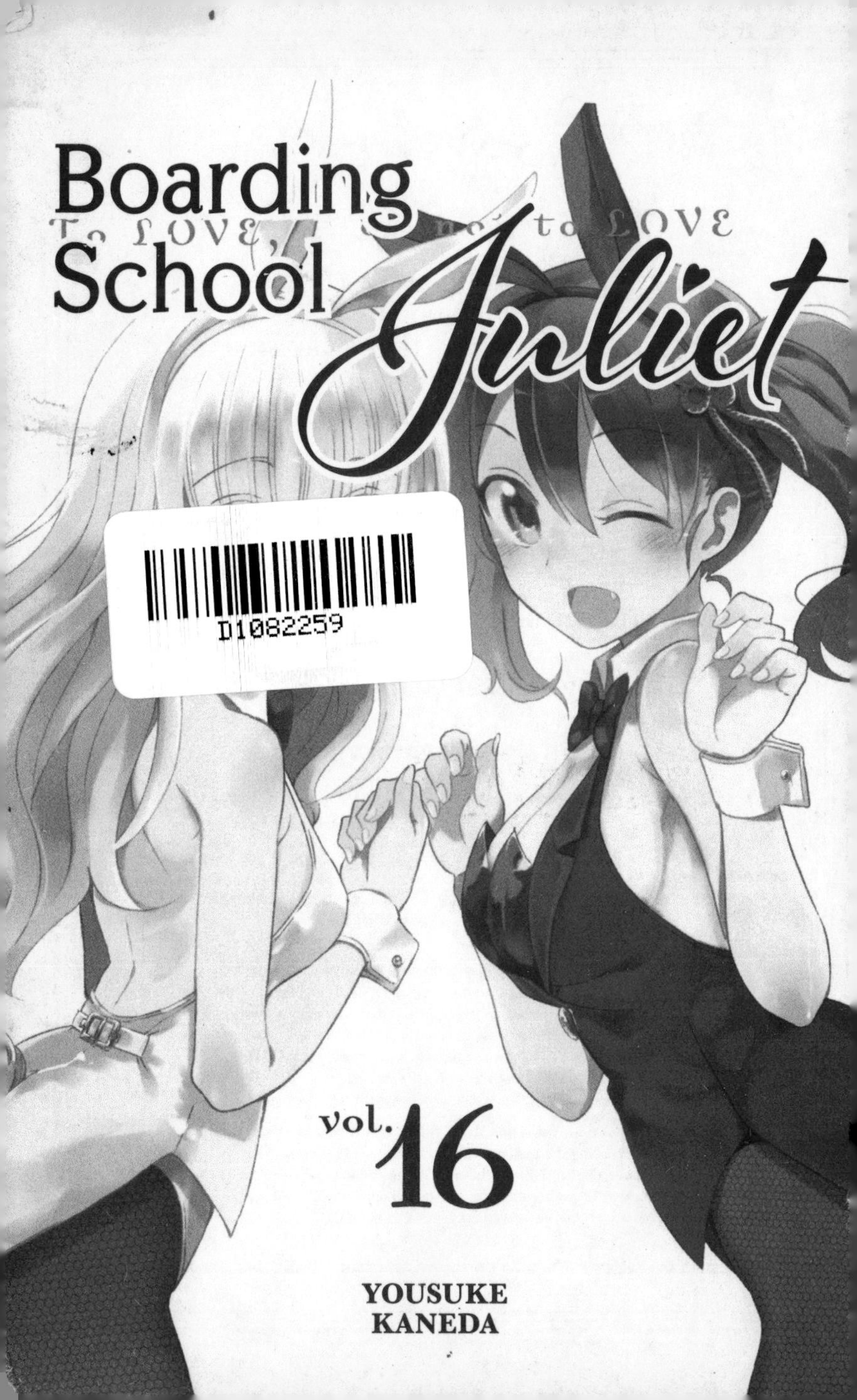

Boarding School
To LOVE, or not to LOVE
Juliet

vol.16

YOUSUKE KANEDA

D1082259

contents

story

At boarding school Dahlia Academy, attended by students from two feuding countries, one first-year longs for a forbidden love. His name: Romio Inuzuka, leader of the Black Doggy House first-years. The apple of his eye: Juliet Persia, leader of the White Cat House first-years. It all begins when Inuzuka confesses his feelings to her. This is Inuzuka and Persia's star-crossed, secret love story...

Now second-years and Head Prefects, Inuzuka and Persia are leading the first mixed Black-White class trip to West. But on the final day of the trip, Persia is taken away by her father! To get her back, White and Black have teamed up— and stormed the Persia estate!

ACT 112: ROMIO & JULIET & TURKISH I

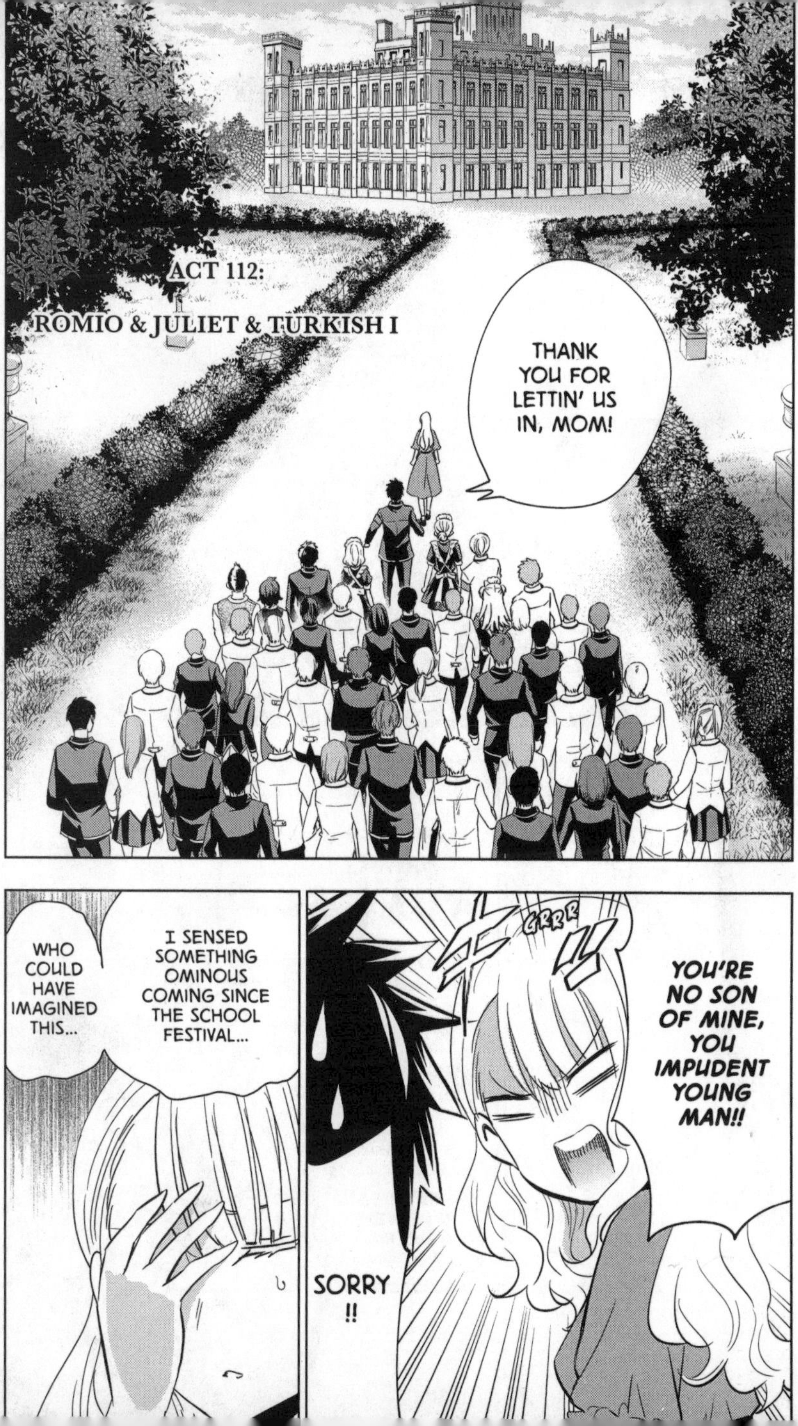
THANK YOU FOR LETTIN' US IN, MOM!
GRRR
YOU'RE NO SON OF MINE, YOU IMPUDENT YOUNG MAN!!
SORRY !!
I SENSED SOMETHING OMINOUS COMING SINCE THE SCHOOL FESTIVAL...
WHO COULD HAVE IMAGINED THIS...

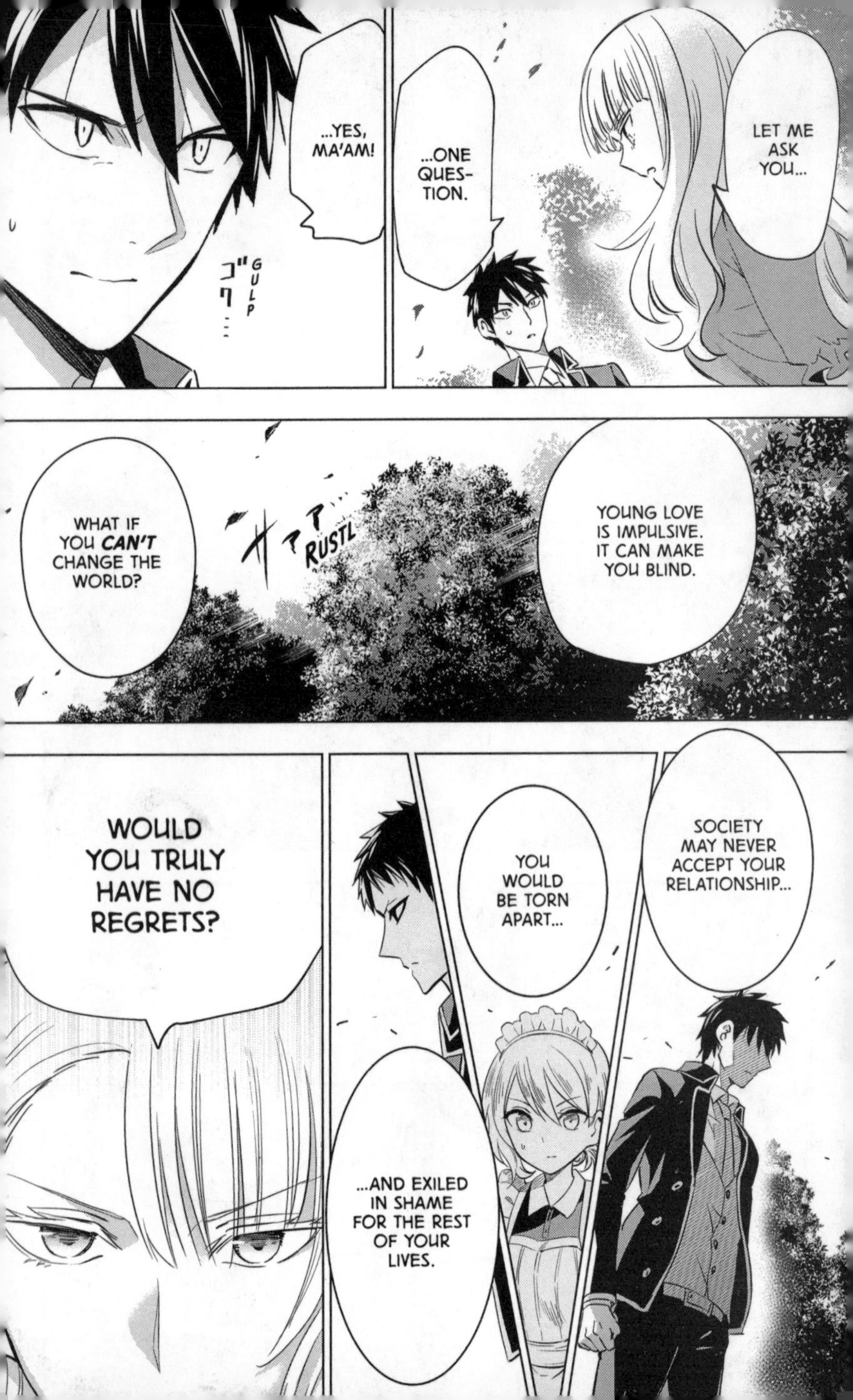

LET ME ASK YOU...
...ONE QUESTION.
...YES, MA'AM!
GULP
YOUNG LOVE IS IMPULSIVE. IT CAN MAKE YOU BLIND.
RUSTL
WHAT IF YOU CAN'T CHANGE THE WORLD?
SOCIETY MAY NEVER ACCEPT YOUR RELATIONSHIP...
YOU WOULD BE TORN APART...
...AND EXILED IN SHAME FOR THE REST OF YOUR LIVES.
WOULD YOU TRULY HAVE NO REGRETS?

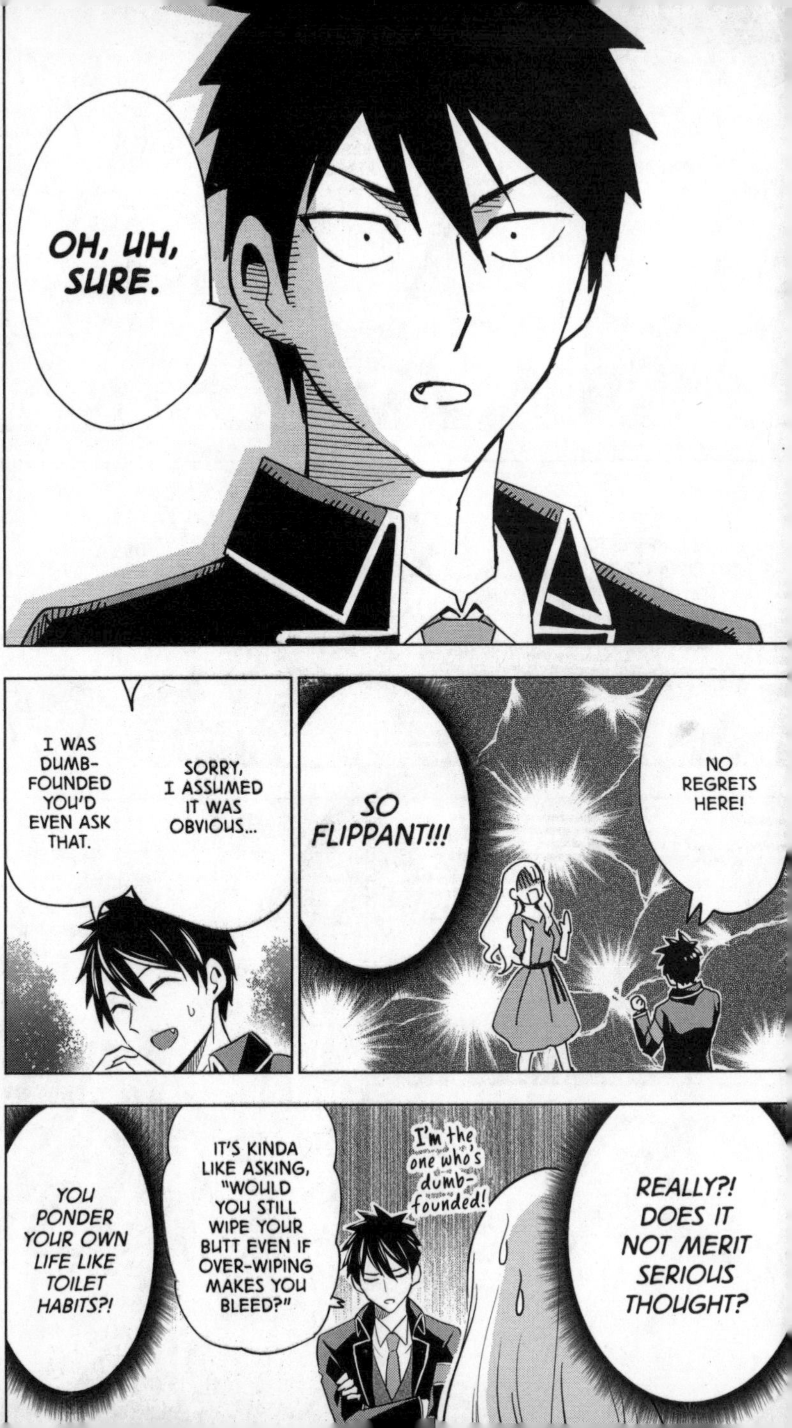
OH, UH, SURE.
NO REGRETS HERE!
SO FLIPPANT!!!
SORRY, I ASSUMED IT WAS OBVIOUS...
I WAS DUMB-FOUNDED YOU'D EVEN ASK THAT.
REALLY?! DOES IT NOT MERIT SERIOUS THOUGHT?
I'm the one who's dumb-founded!
IT'S KINDA LIKE ASKING, "WOULD YOU STILL WIPE YOUR BUTT EVEN IF OVER-WIPING MAKES YOU BLEED?"
YOU PONDER YOUR OWN LIFE LIKE TOILET HABITS?!

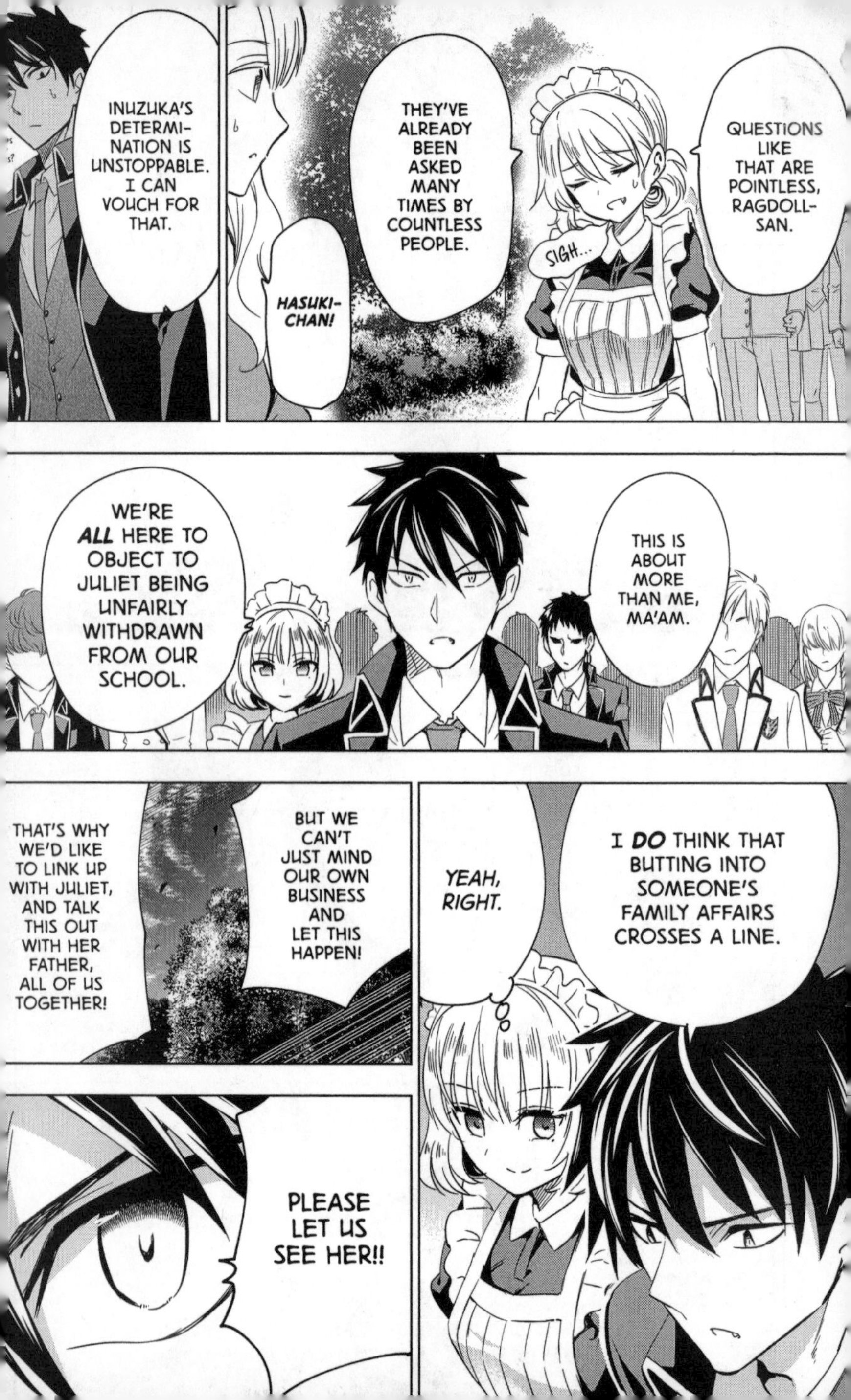
QUESTIONS LIKE THAT ARE POINTLESS, RAGDOLL-SAN.
SIGH...
THEY'VE ALREADY BEEN ASKED MANY TIMES BY COUNTLESS PEOPLE.
HASUKI-CHAN!
INUZUKA'S DETERMINATION IS UNSTOPPABLE. I CAN VOUCH FOR THAT.
THIS IS ABOUT MORE THAN ME, MA'AM.
WE'RE ALL HERE TO OBJECT TO JULIET BEING UNFAIRLY WITHDRAWN FROM OUR SCHOOL.
I DO THINK THAT BUTTING INTO SOMEONE'S FAMILY AFFAIRS CROSSES A LINE.
YEAH, RIGHT.
BUT WE CAN'T JUST MIND OUR OWN BUSINESS AND LET THIS HAPPEN!
THAT'S WHY WE'D LIKE TO LINK UP WITH JULIET, AND TALK THIS OUT WITH HER FATHER, ALL OF US TOGETHER!
PLEASE LET US SEE HER!!

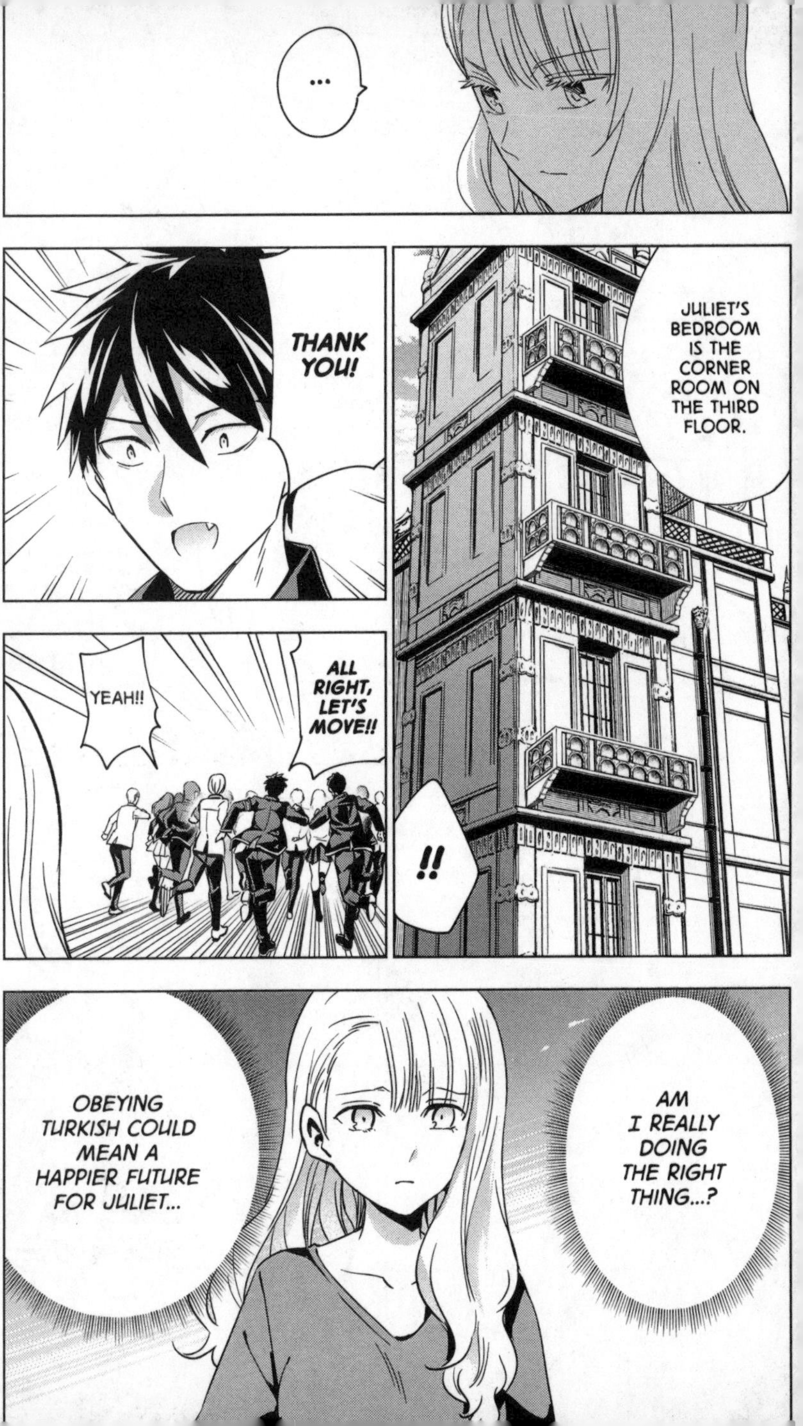
...
JULIET'S BEDROOM IS THE CORNER ROOM ON THE THIRD FLOOR.
!!
THANK YOU!
ALL RIGHT, LET'S MOVE!!
YEAH!!
AM I REALLY DOING THE RIGHT THING...?
OBEYING TURKISH COULD MEAN A HAPPIER FUTURE FOR JULIET...

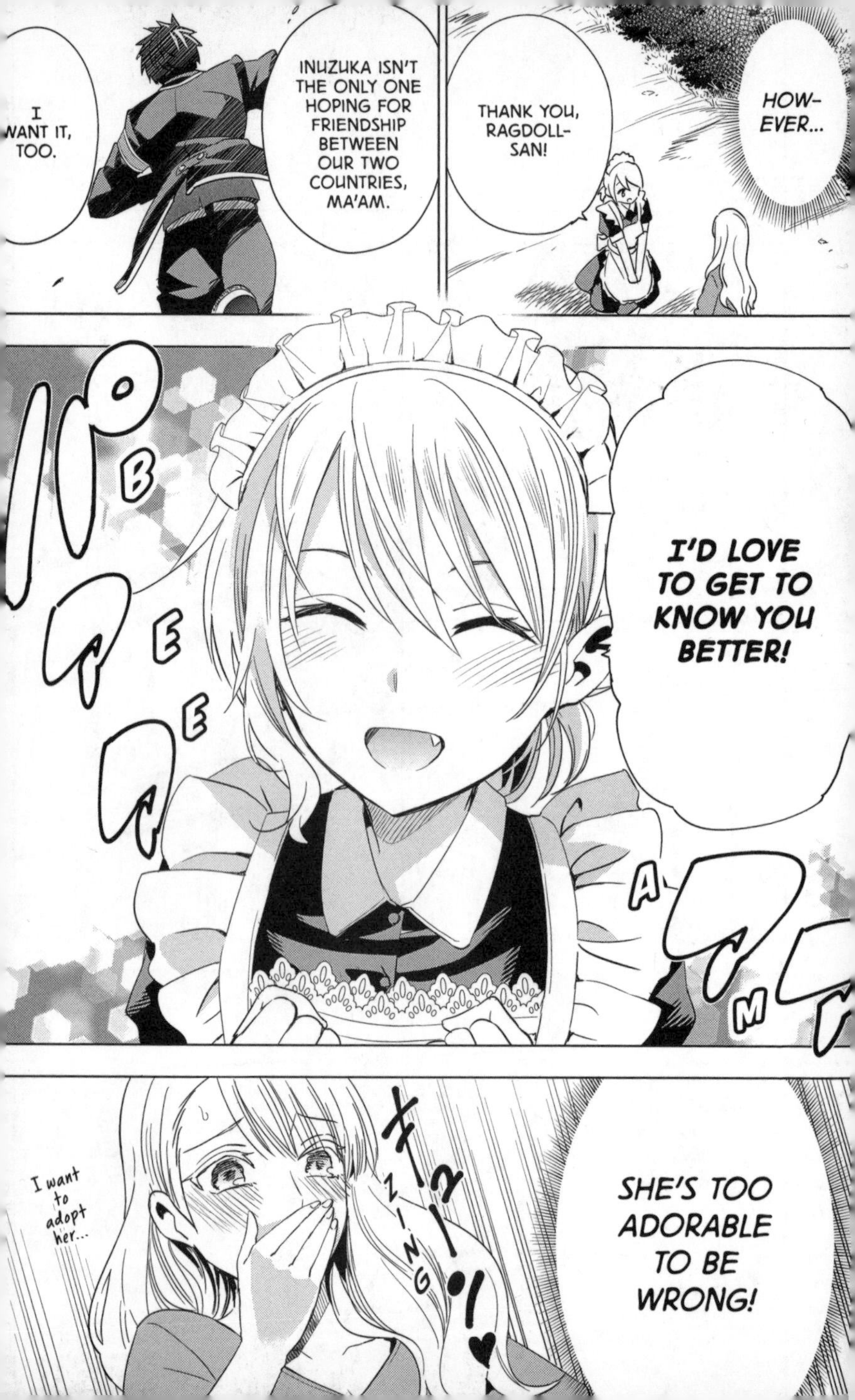
HOW-EVER...
THANK YOU, RAGDOLL-SAN!
INUZUKA ISN'T THE ONLY ONE HOPING FOR FRIENDSHIP BETWEEN OUR TWO COUNTRIES, MA'AM.
I WANT IT, TOO.
I'D LOVE TO GET TO KNOW YOU BETTER!
AM
BEE
SHE'S TOO ADORABLE TO BE WRONG!
ZING
I want to adopt her...

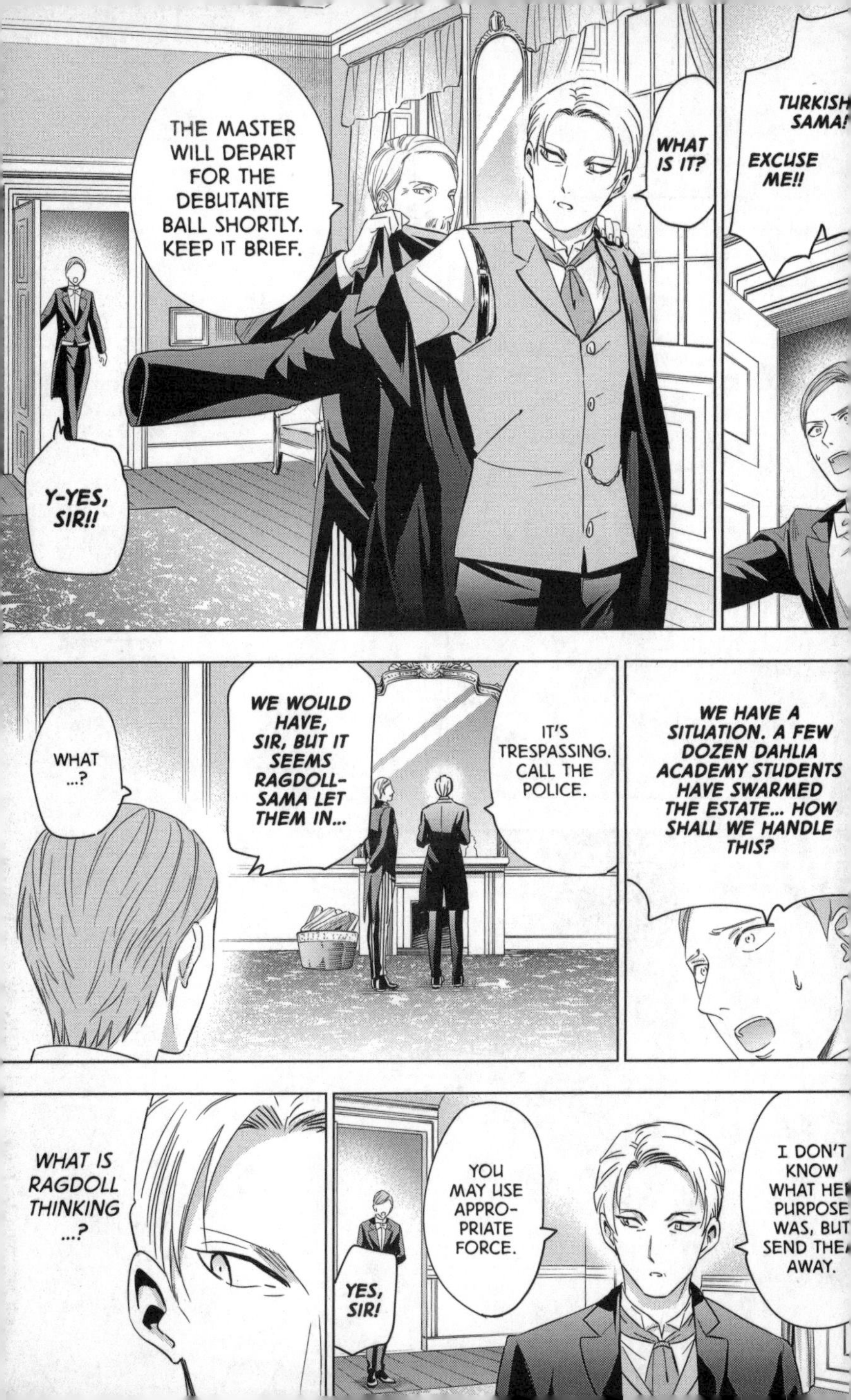
TURKISH SAMA!
EXCUSE ME!!
WHAT IS IT?
THE MASTER WILL DEPART FOR THE DEBUTANTE BALL SHORTLY. KEEP IT BRIEF.
Y-YES, SIR!!
WE HAVE A SITUATION. A FEW DOZEN DAHLIA ACADEMY STUDENTS HAVE SWARMED THE ESTATE... HOW SHALL WE HANDLE THIS?
IT'S TRESPASSING. CALL THE POLICE.
WE WOULD HAVE, SIR, BUT IT SEEMS RAGDOLL-SAMA LET THEM IN...
WHAT ...?
I DON'T KNOW WHAT HE PURPOSE WAS, BUT SEND THE AWAY.
YOU MAY USE APPRO-PRIATE FORCE.
YES, SIR!
WHAT IS RAGDOLL THINKING ...?

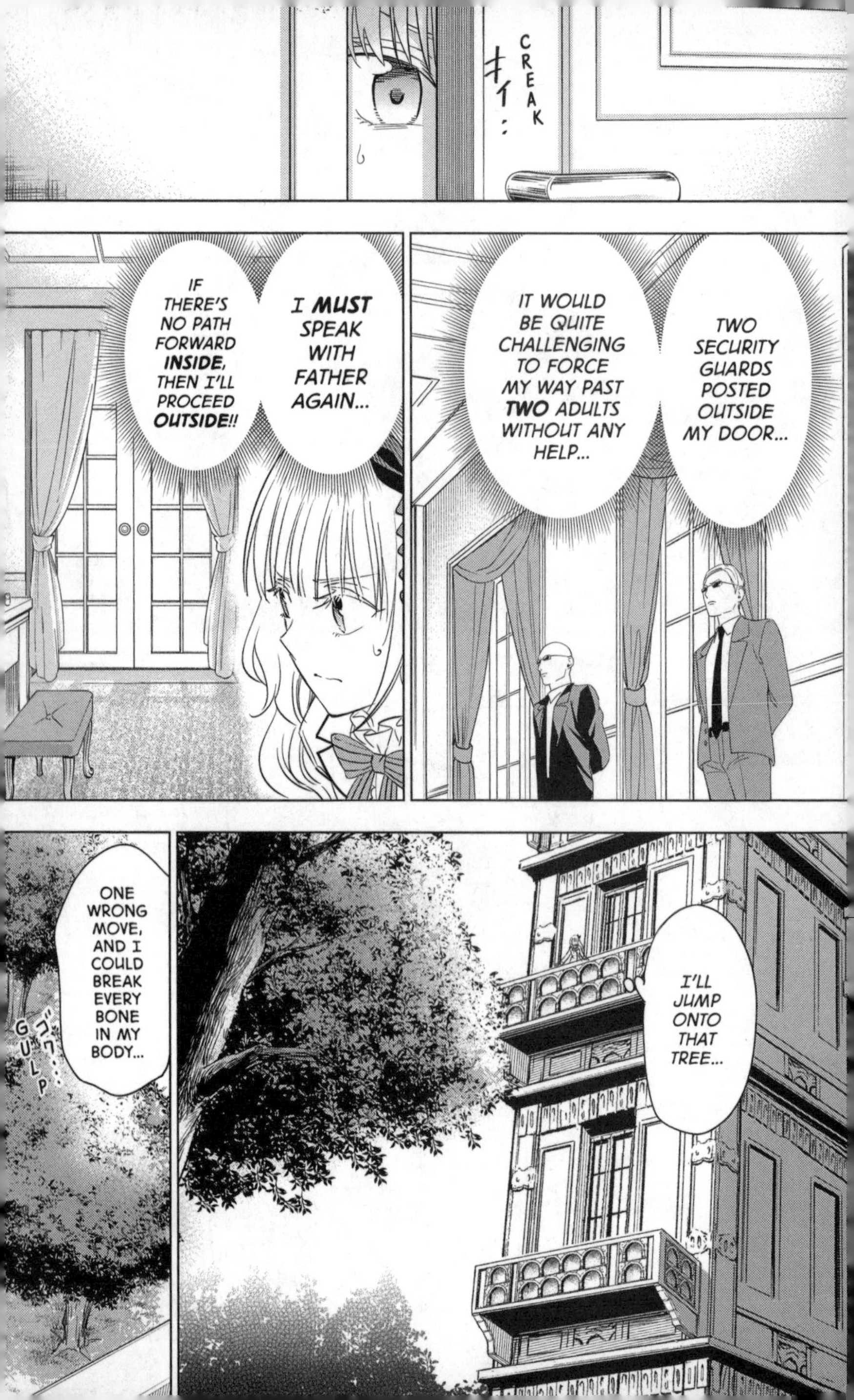

キィ…
CREAK
TWO SECURITY GUARDS POSTED OUTSIDE MY DOOR...
IT WOULD BE QUITE CHALLENGING TO FORCE MY WAY PAST **TWO** ADULTS WITHOUT ANY HELP...
I **MUST** SPEAK WITH FATHER AGAIN...
IF THERE'S NO PATH FORWARD **INSIDE**, THEN I'LL PROCEED **OUTSIDE**!!
I'LL JUMP ONTO THAT TREE...
ONE WRONG MOVE, AND I COULD BREAK EVERY BONE IN MY BODY...
ゴク…
GULP

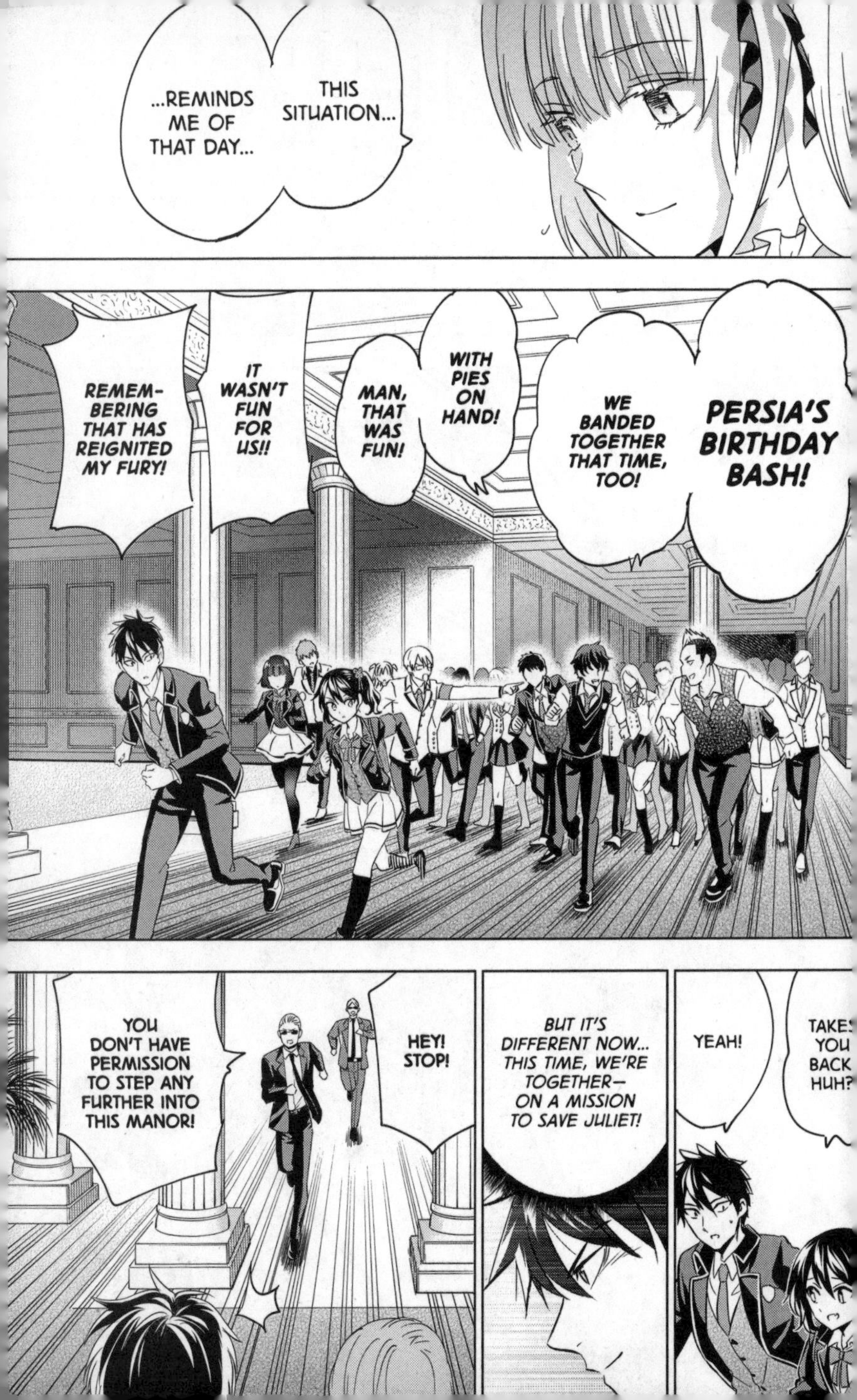
THIS SITUATION...
...REMINDS ME OF THAT DAY...
PERSIA'S BIRTHDAY BASH!
WE BANDED TOGETHER THAT TIME, TOO!
WITH PIES ON HAND!
MAN, THAT WAS FUN!
IT WASN'T FUN FOR US!!
REMEMBERING THAT HAS REIGNITED MY FURY!
TAKES YOU BACK HUH?
YEAH!
BUT IT'S DIFFERENT NOW... THIS TIME, WE'RE TOGETHER— ON A MISSION TO SAVE JULIET!
HEY! STOP!
YOU DON'T HAVE PERMISSION TO STEP ANY FURTHER INTO THIS MANOR!

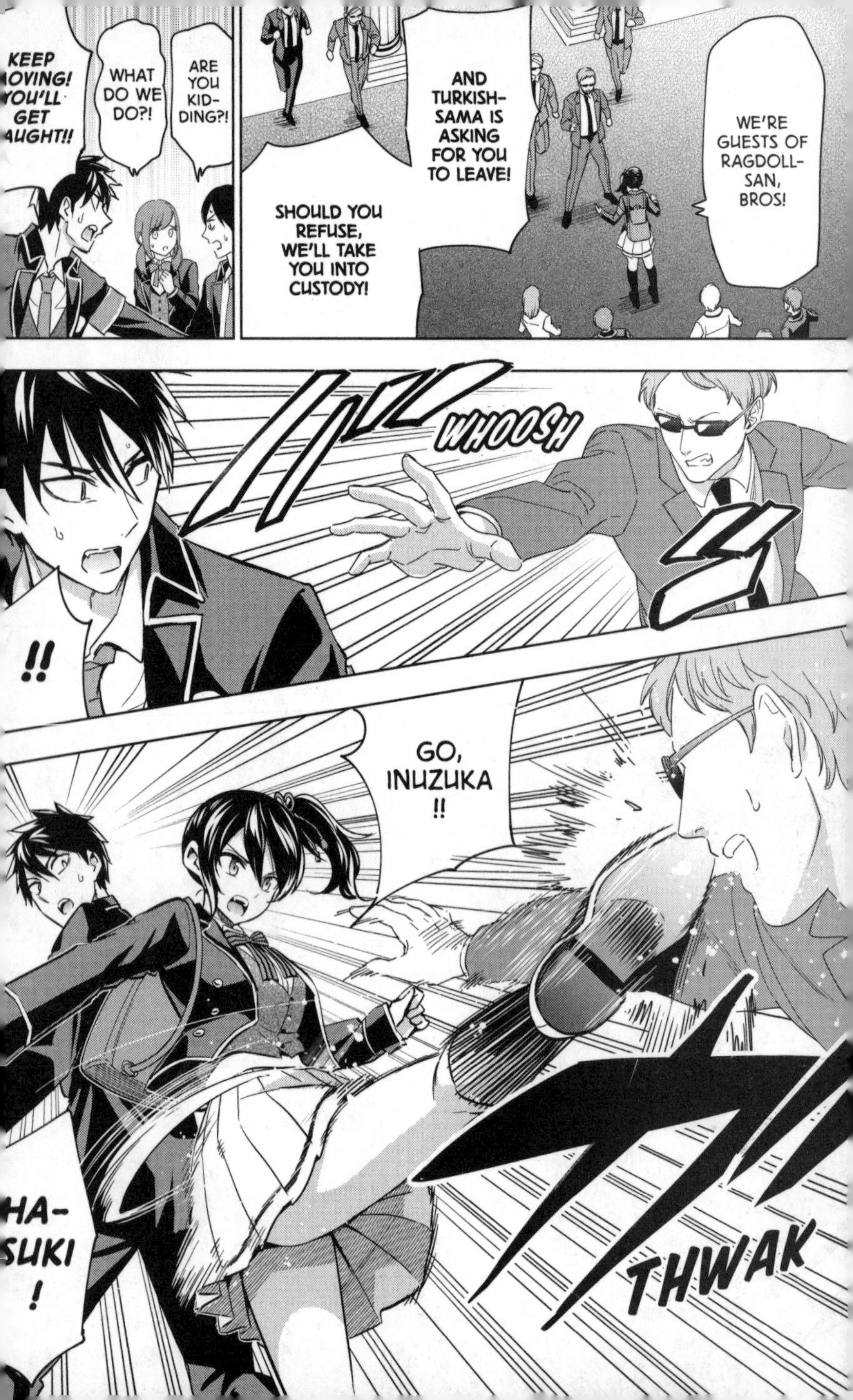
WE'RE GUESTS OF RAGDOLL-SAN, BROS!
AND TURKISH-SAMA IS ASKING FOR YOU TO LEAVE!
SHOULD YOU REFUSE, WE'LL TAKE YOU INTO CUSTODY!
ARE YOU KID-DING?!
WHAT DO WE DO?!
KEEP OVING! YOU'LL GET AUGHT!!
WHOOSH
!!
GO, INUZUKA!!
THWAK
HA-SUKI!

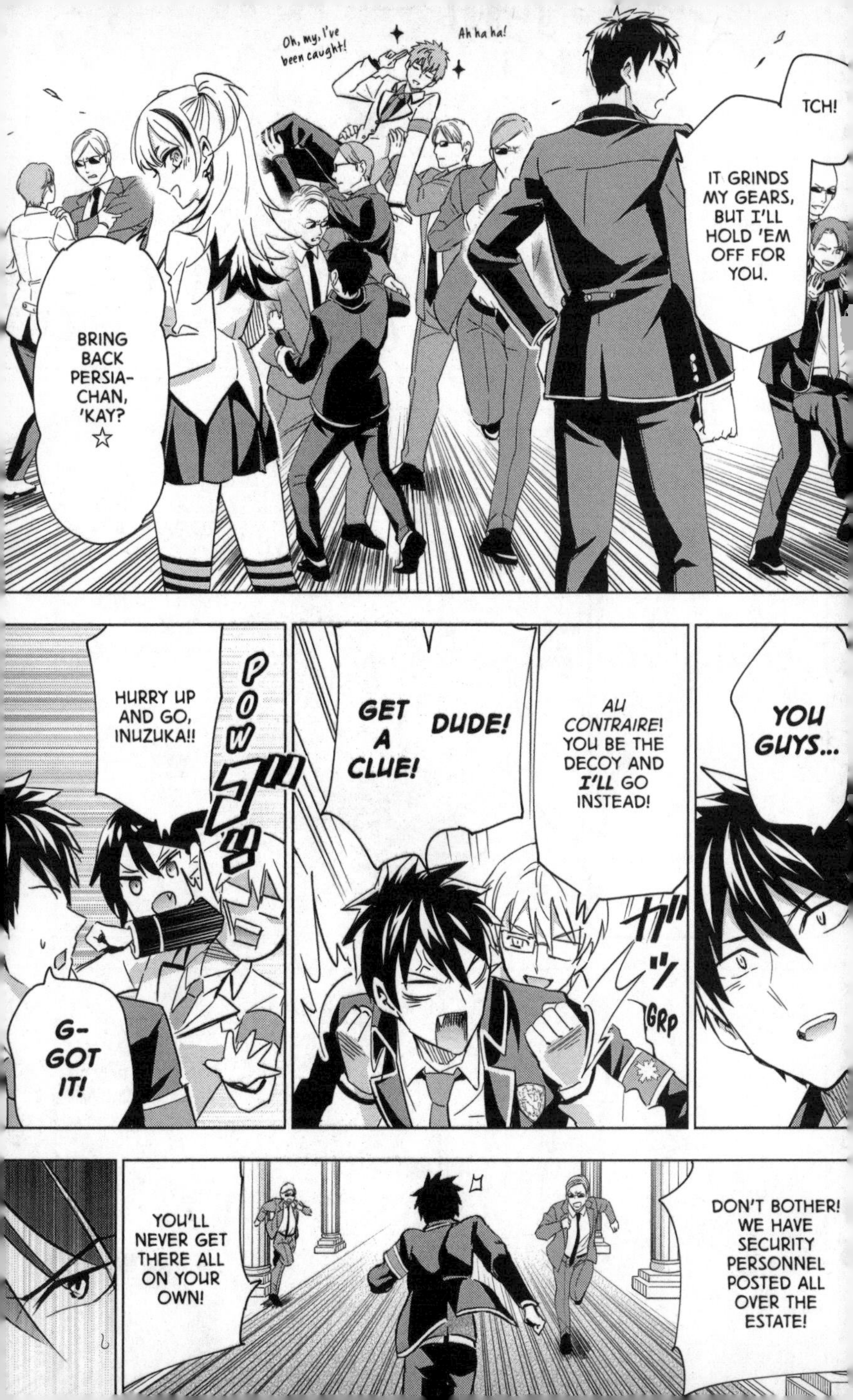
TCH!
IT GRINDS MY GEARS, BUT I'LL HOLD 'EM OFF FOR YOU.
Ah ha ha!
Oh, my, I've been caught!
BRING BACK PERSIA-CHAN, 'KAY? ☆
YOU GUYS...
AU CONTRAIRE! YOU BE THE DECOY AND I'LL GO INSTEAD!
DUDE!
GET A CLUE!
GRP
HURRY UP AND GO, INUZUKA!!
POW
G-GOT IT!
DON'T BOTHER! WE HAVE SECURITY PERSONNEL POSTED ALL OVER THE ESTATE!
YOU'LL NEVER GET THERE ALL ON YOUR OWN!

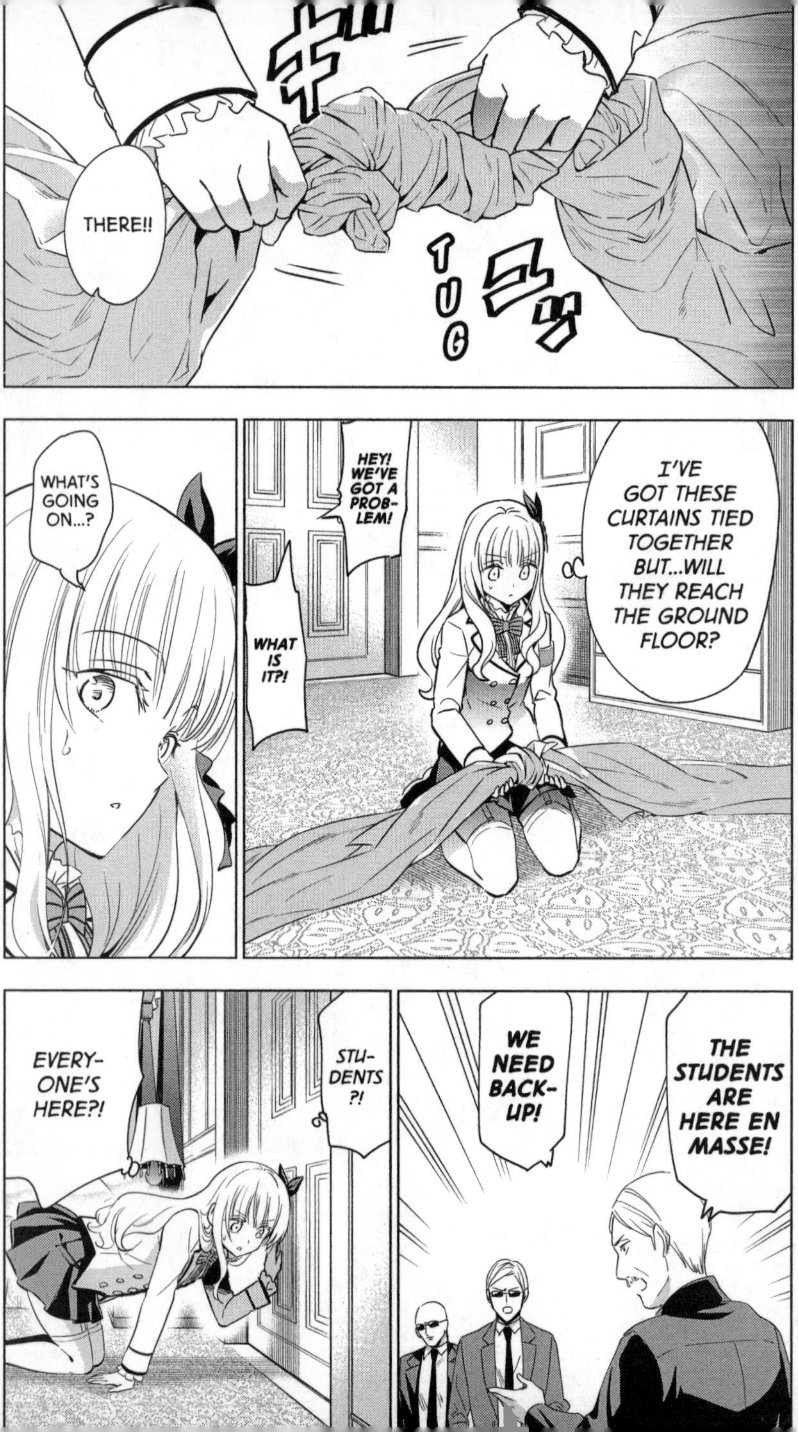
THERE!!
TUG
I'VE GOT THESE CURTAINS TIED TOGETHER BUT...WILL THEY REACH THE GROUND FLOOR?
HEY! WE'VE GOT A PROB-LEM!
WHAT IS IT?!
WHAT'S GOING ON...?
THE STUDENTS ARE HERE EN MASSE!
WE NEED BACK-UP!
STU-DENTS?!
EVERY-ONE'S HERE?!

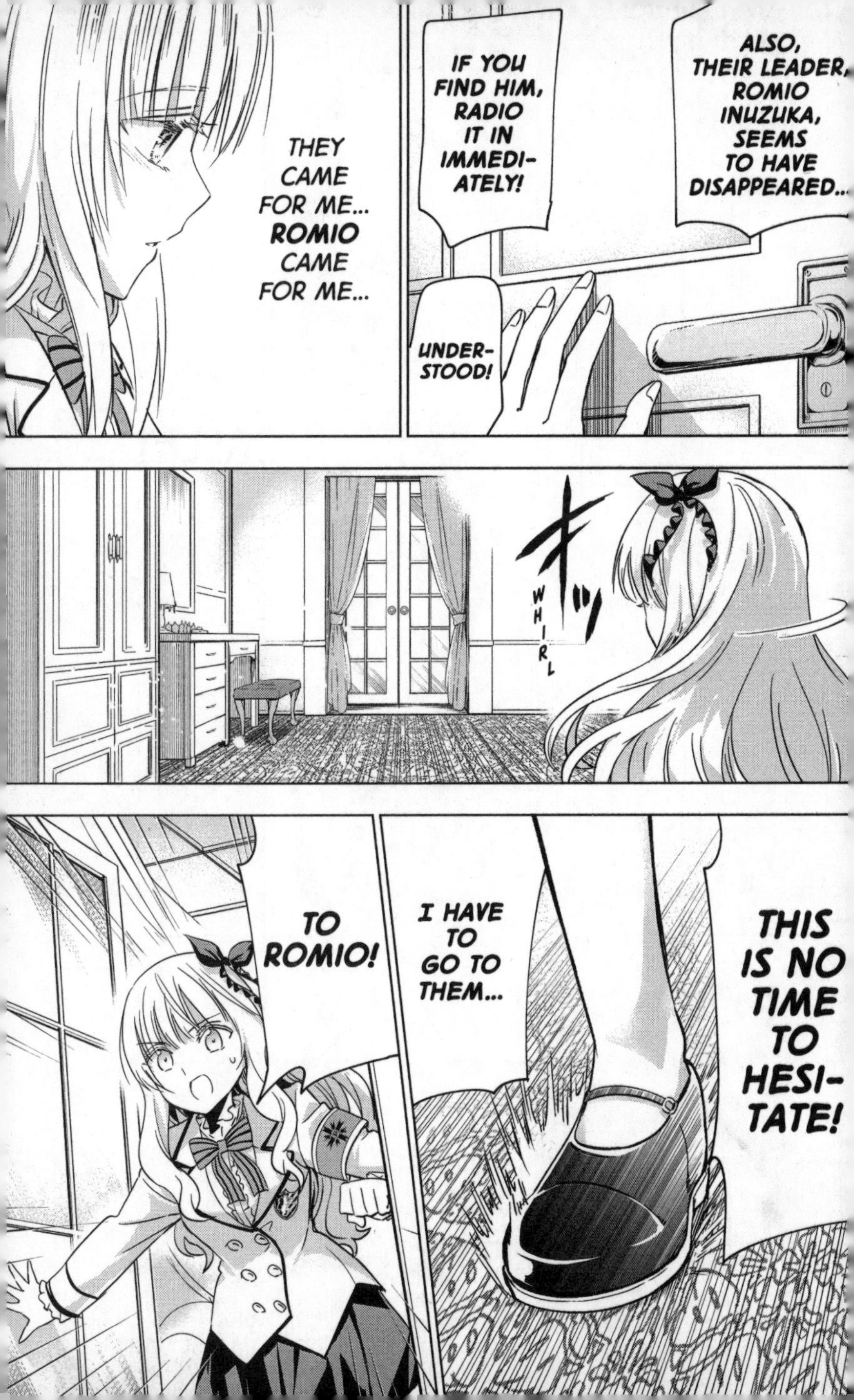
ALSO, THEIR LEADER, ROMIO INUZUKA, SEEMS TO HAVE DISAPPEARED...
IF YOU FIND HIM, RADIO IT IN IMMEDIATELY!
UNDERSTOOD!
THEY CAME FOR ME... ROMIO CAME FOR ME...
WHIRL
THIS IS NO TIME TO HESITATE!
I HAVE TO GO TO THEM...
TO ROMIO!

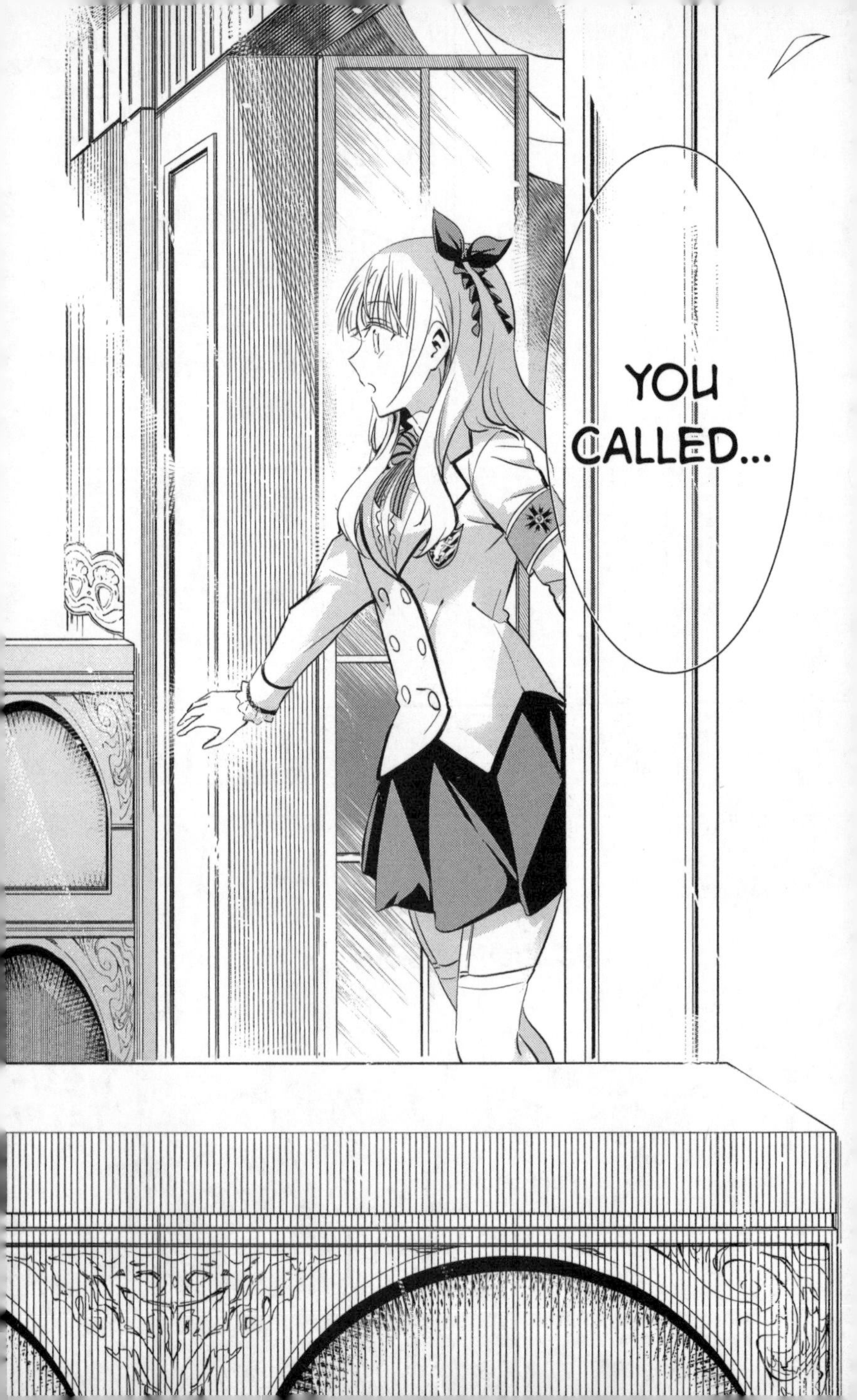
YOU CALLED...

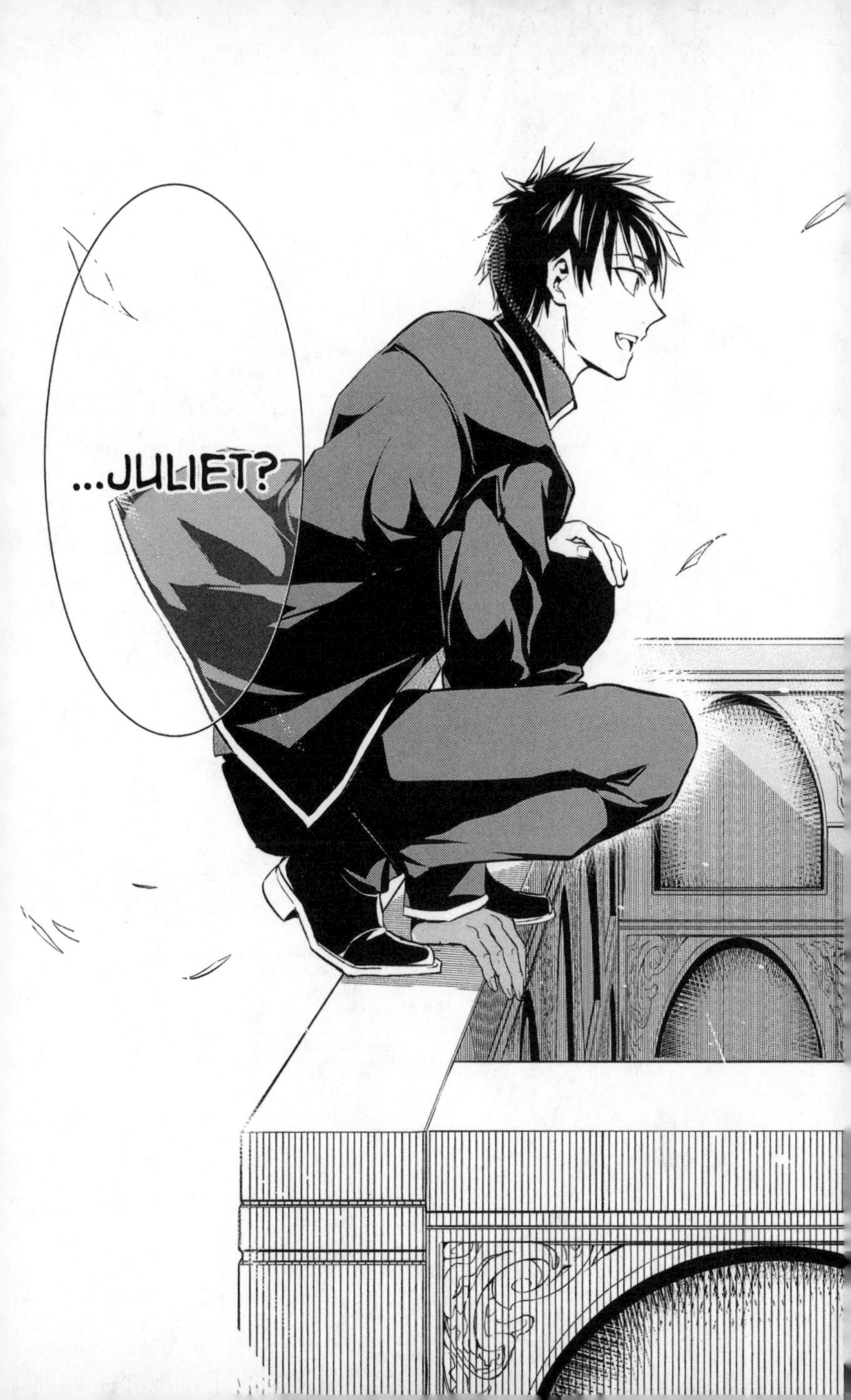
...JULIET?

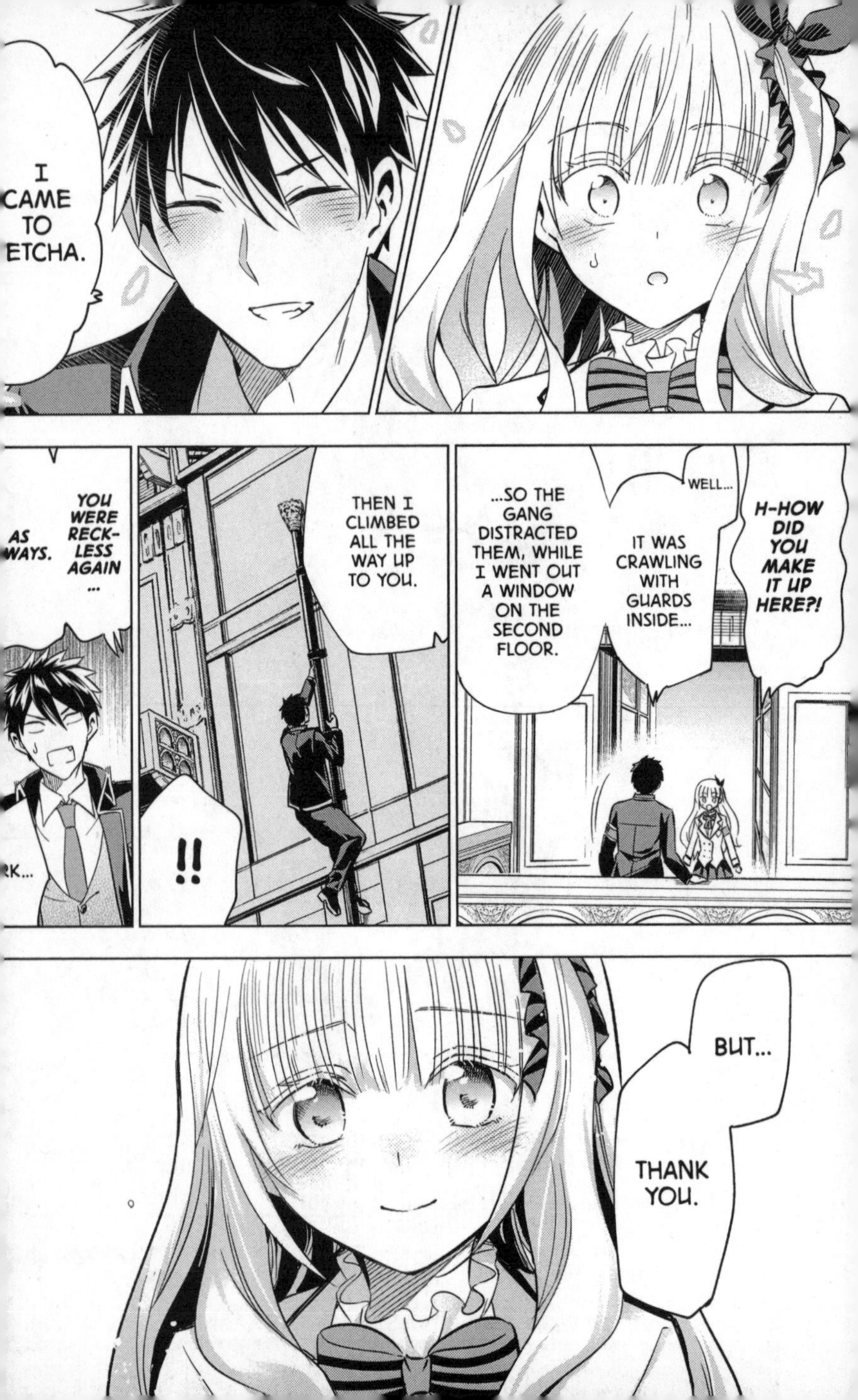
I CAME TO ETCHA.
H-HOW DID YOU MAKE IT UP HERE?!
WELL...
IT WAS CRAWLING WITH GUARDS INSIDE...
...SO THE GANG DISTRACTED THEM, WHILE I WENT OUT A WINDOW ON THE SECOND FLOOR.
THEN I CLIMBED ALL THE WAY UP TO YOU.
!!
YOU WERE RECK-LESS AGAIN ...
AS
WAYS.
BUT...
THANK YOU.

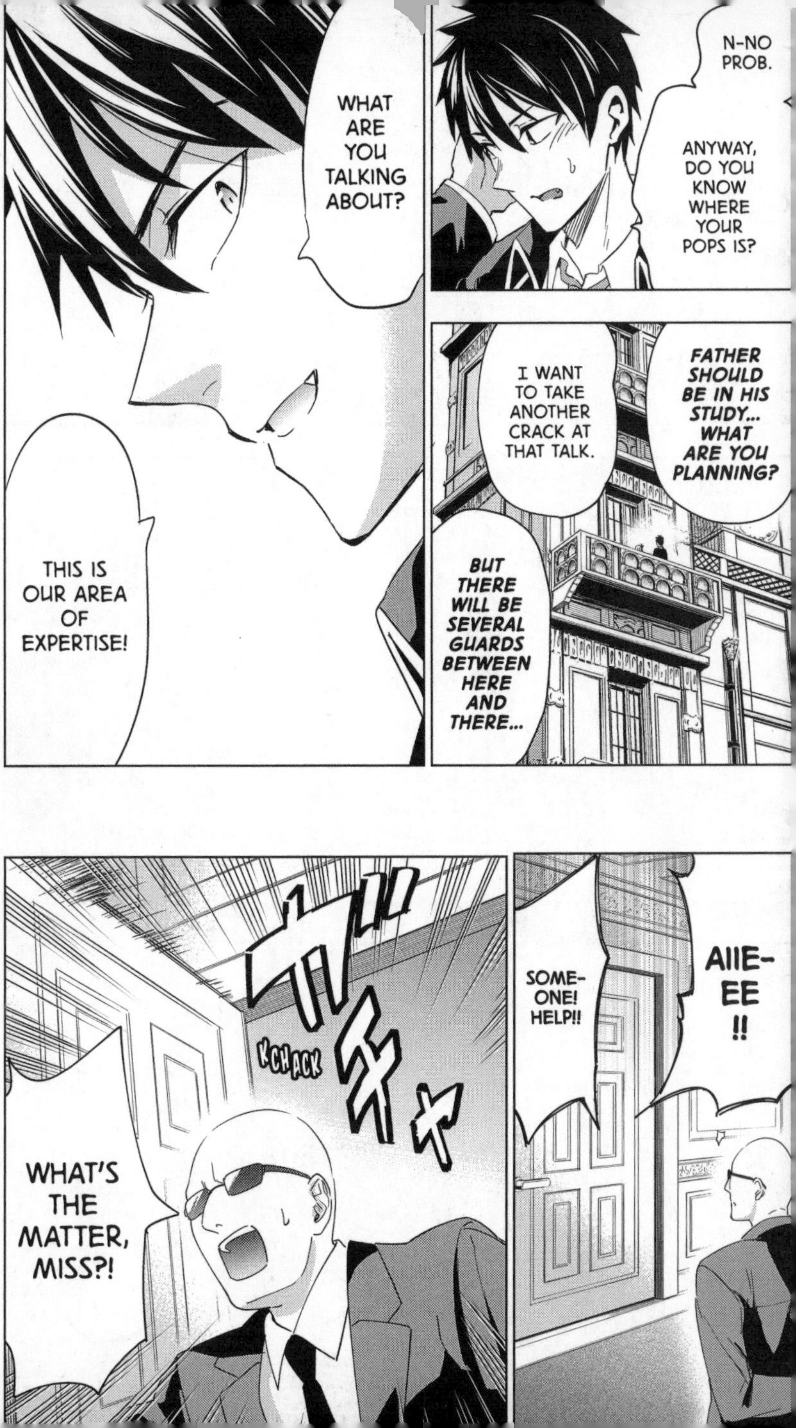
N-NO PROB.
ANYWAY, DO YOU KNOW WHERE YOUR POPS IS?
FATHER SHOULD BE IN HIS STUDY... WHAT ARE YOU PLANNING?
I WANT TO TAKE ANOTHER CRACK AT THAT TALK.
BUT THERE WILL BE SEVERAL GUARDS BETWEEN HERE AND THERE...
WHAT ARE YOU TALKING ABOUT?
THIS IS OUR AREA OF EXPERTISE!
AIIE-EE !!
SOME-ONE! HELP!!
KCHACK
WHAT'S THE MATTER, MISS?!

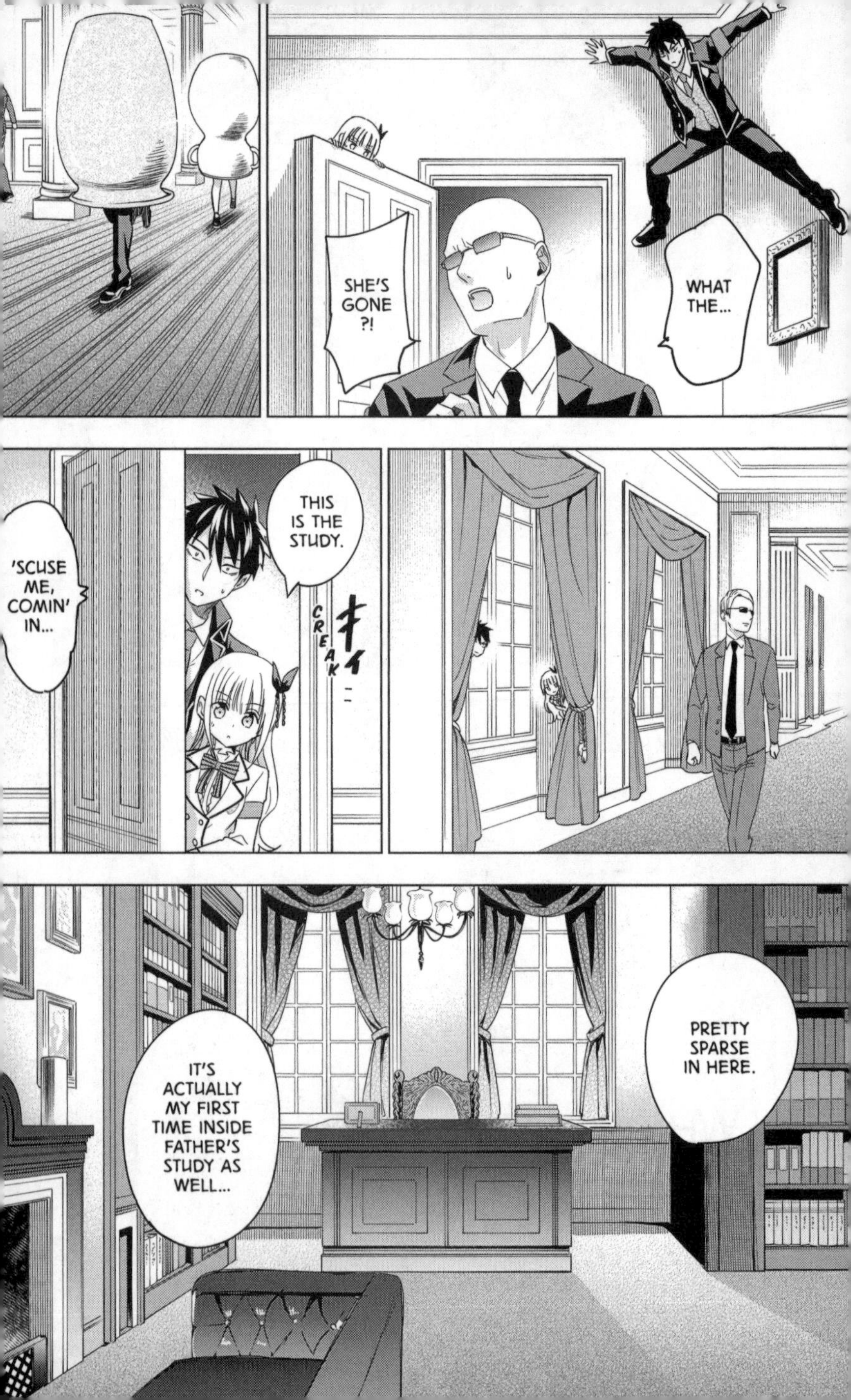
WHAT THE...
SHE'S GONE ?!
THIS IS THE STUDY.
CREAK
'SCUSE ME, COMIN' IN...
PRETTY SPARSE IN HERE.
IT'S ACTUALLY MY FIRST TIME INSIDE FATHER'S STUDY AS WELL...

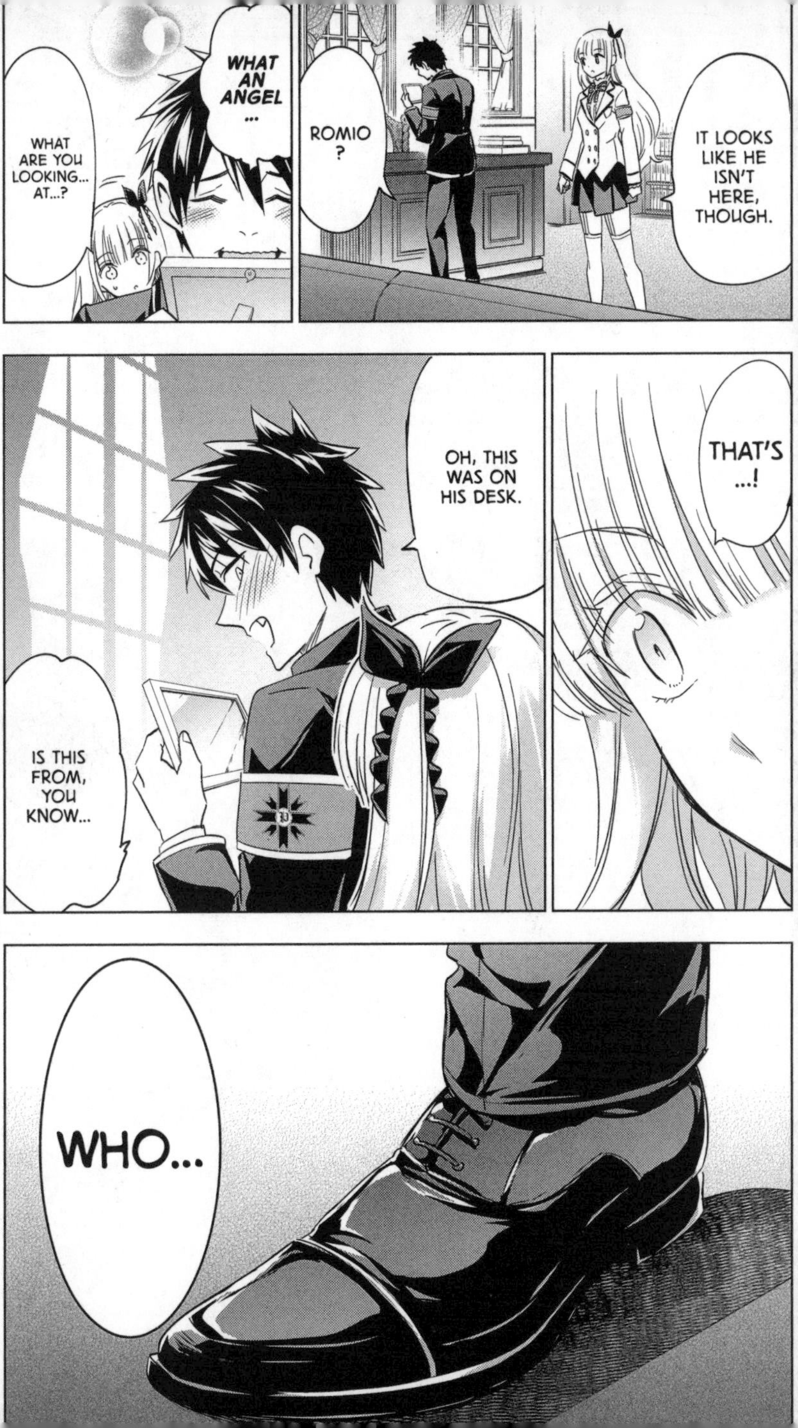
IT LOOKS LIKE HE ISN'T HERE, THOUGH.
ROMIO?
WHAT AN ANGEL...
WHAT ARE YOU LOOKING... AT...?
THAT'S...!
OH, THIS WAS ON HIS DESK.
IS THIS FROM, YOU KNOW...
WHO...

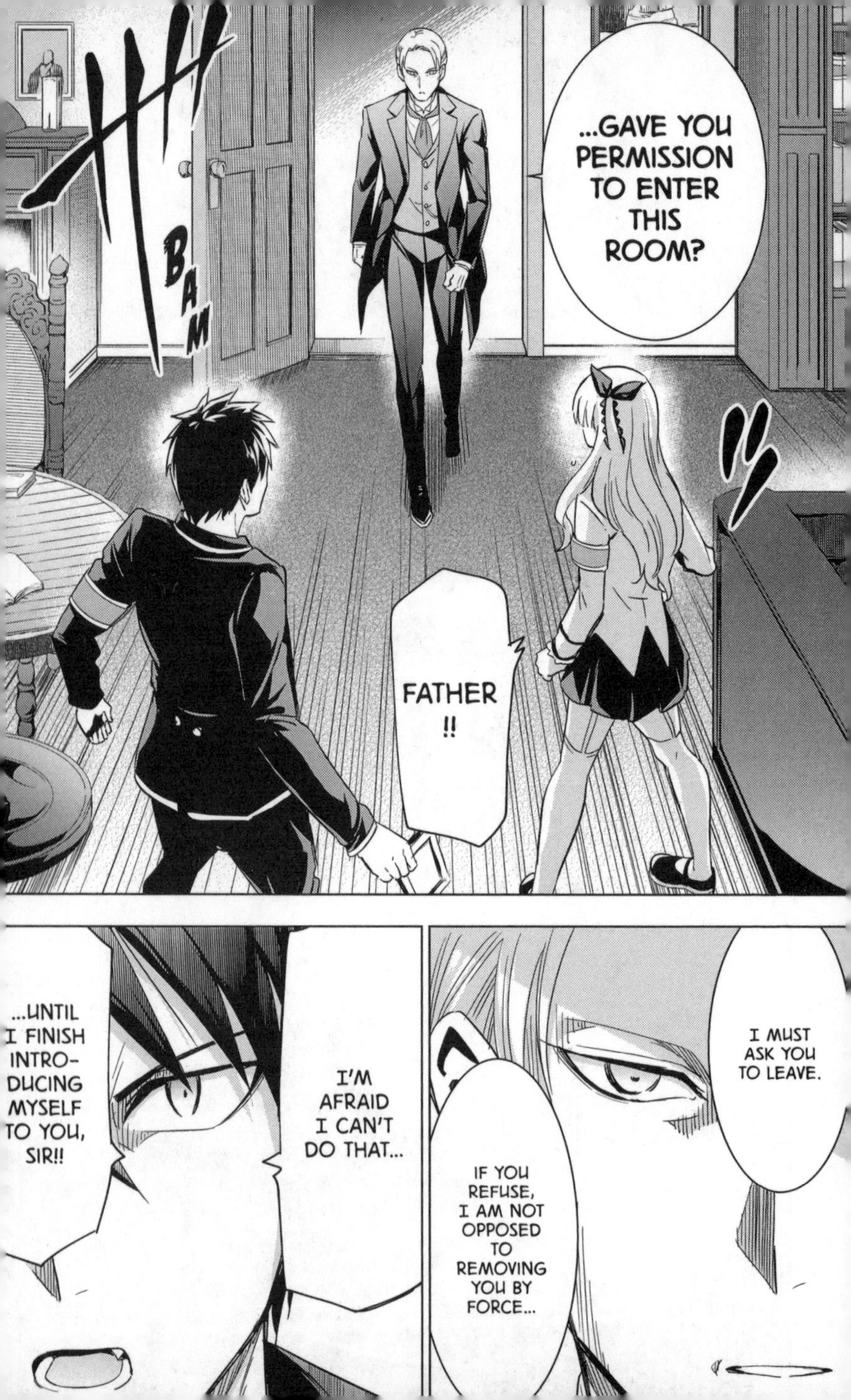
...GAVE YOU PERMISSION TO ENTER THIS ROOM?
BAM
FATHER !!
I MUST ASK YOU TO LEAVE.
IF YOU REFUSE, I AM NOT OPPOSED TO REMOVING YOU BY FORCE...
I'M AFRAID I CAN'T DO THAT...
...UNTIL I FINISH INTRO-DUCING MYSELF TO YOU, SIR!!

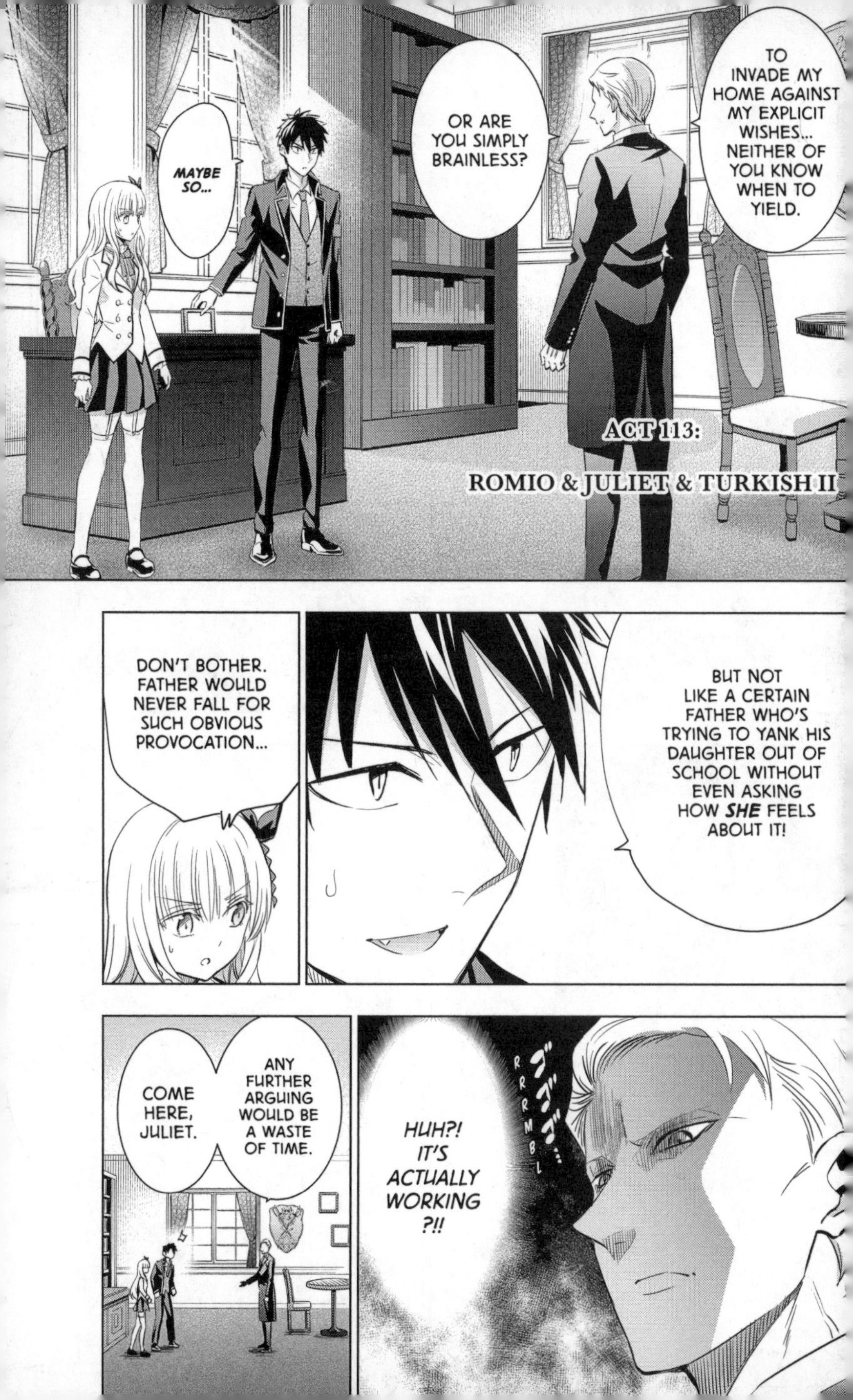
TO INVADE MY HOME AGAINST MY EXPLICIT WISHES... NEITHER OF YOU KNOW WHEN TO YIELD.
OR ARE YOU SIMPLY BRAINLESS?
MAYBE SO...
ACT 113:
ROMIO & JULIET & TURKISH II
BUT NOT LIKE A CERTAIN FATHER WHO'S TRYING TO YANK HIS DAUGHTER OUT OF SCHOOL WITHOUT EVEN ASKING HOW SHE FEELS ABOUT IT!
DON'T BOTHER. FATHER WOULD NEVER FALL FOR SUCH OBVIOUS PROVOCATION...
RRRMBL
HUH?! IT'S ACTUALLY WORKING?!!
ANY FURTHER ARGUING WOULD BE A WASTE OF TIME.
COME HERE, JULIET.

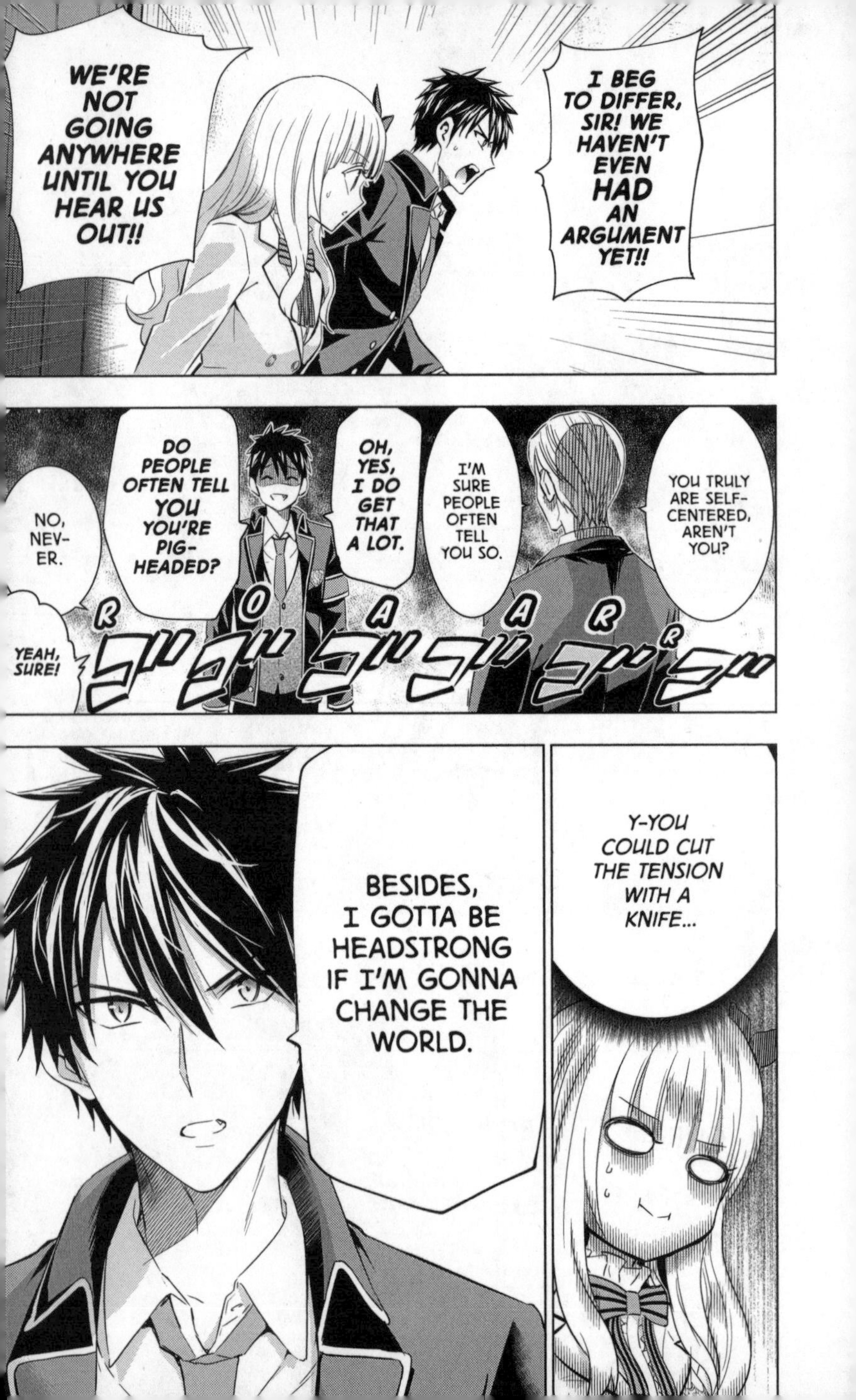
I BEG TO DIFFER, SIR! WE HAVEN'T EVEN HAD AN ARGUMENT YET!!
WE'RE NOT GOING ANYWHERE UNTIL YOU HEAR US OUT!!
YOU TRULY ARE SELF-CENTERED, AREN'T YOU?
I'M SURE PEOPLE OFTEN TELL YOU SO.
OH, YES, I DO GET THAT A LOT.
DO PEOPLE OFTEN TELL YOU YOU'RE PIG-HEADED?
NO, NEVER.
YEAH, SURE!
ROAARR
Y-YOU COULD CUT THE TENSION WITH A KNIFE...
BESIDES, I GOTTA BE HEADSTRONG IF I'M GONNA CHANGE THE WORLD.

CHILDREN BELIEVE THEY CAN DO ANYTHING.

THAT IS WHY THEY RISK EVERYTHING WITHOUT A SECOND THOUGHT.

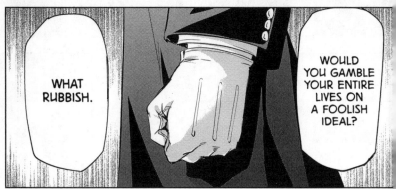

WHAT RUBBISH.

WOULD YOU GAMBLE YOUR ENTIRE LIVES ON A FOOLISH IDEAL?

GROW UP— BOTH OF YOU.

GIVE UP YOUR CHILDISH DREAMS.

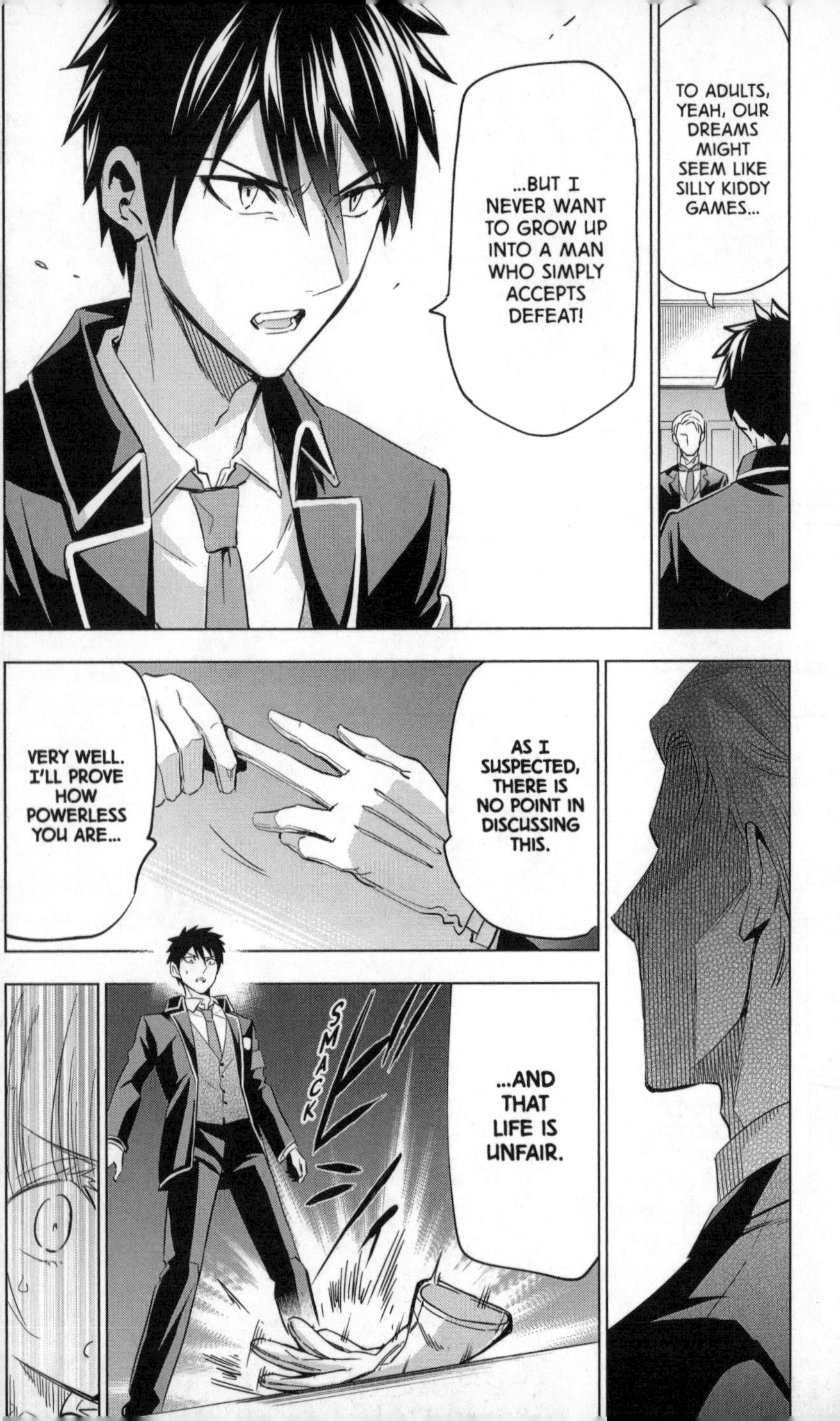
TO ADULTS, YEAH, OUR DREAMS MIGHT SEEM LIKE SILLY KIDDY GAMES...
...BUT I NEVER WANT TO GROW UP INTO A MAN WHO SIMPLY ACCEPTS DEFEAT!
AS I SUSPECTED, THERE IS NO POINT IN DISCUSSING THIS.
VERY WELL. I'LL PROVE HOW POWERLESS YOU ARE...
...AND THAT LIFE IS UNFAIR.
SMACK

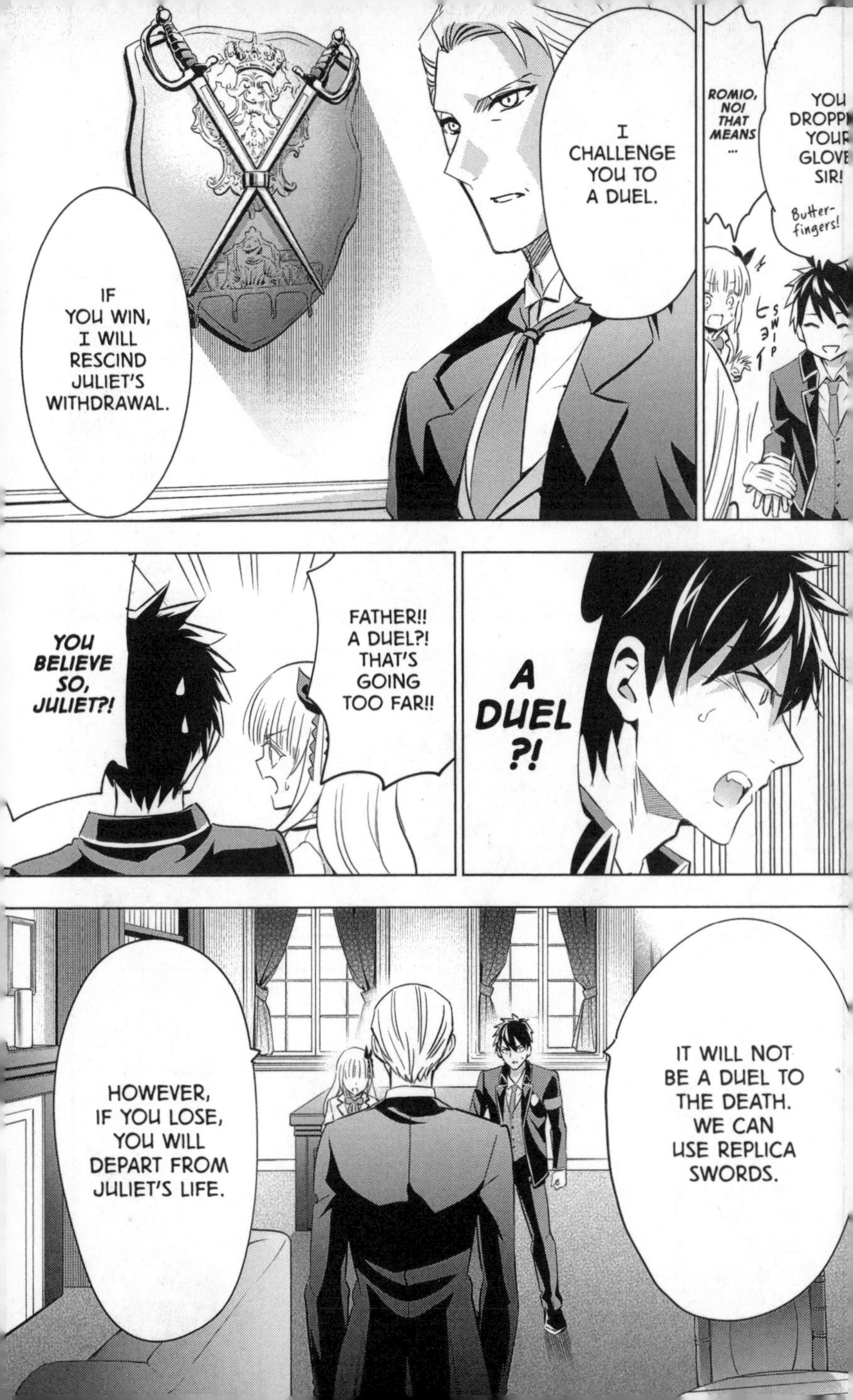
YOU DROPP YOUR GLOVE SIR!
ROMIO, NO! THAT MEANS ...
Butter-fingers!
SWIP
I CHALLENGE YOU TO A DUEL.
IF YOU WIN, I WILL RESCIND JULIET'S WITHDRAWAL.
A DUEL ?!
FATHER!! A DUEL?! THAT'S GOING TOO FAR!!
YOU BELIEVE SO, JULIET?!
IT WILL NOT BE A DUEL TO THE DEATH. WE CAN USE REPLICA SWORDS.
HOWEVER, IF YOU LOSE, YOU WILL DEPART FROM JULIET'S LIFE.

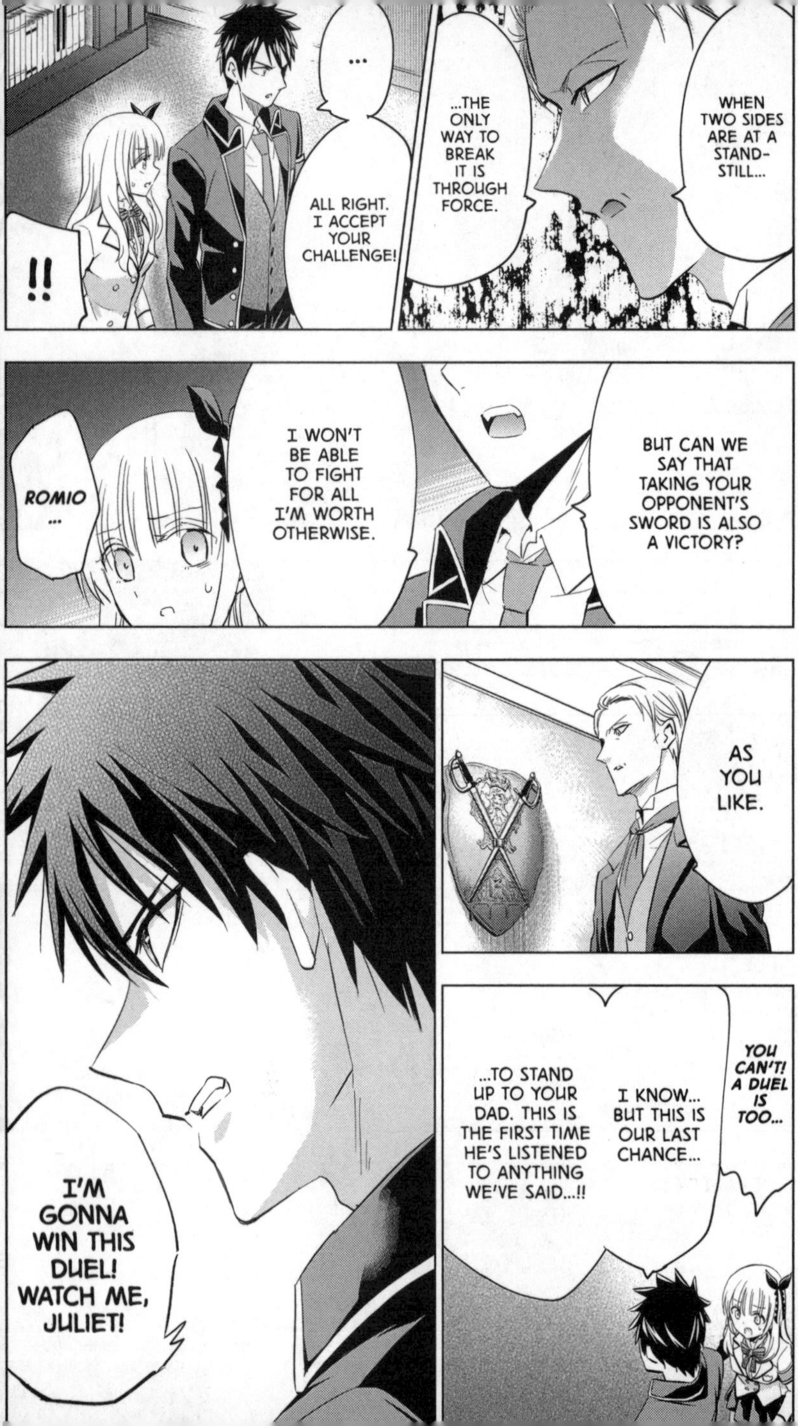

WHEN TWO SIDES ARE AT A STANDSTILL...
...THE ONLY WAY TO BREAK IT IS THROUGH FORCE.
...
ALL RIGHT. I ACCEPT YOUR CHALLENGE!
!!
BUT CAN WE SAY THAT TAKING YOUR OPPONENT'S SWORD IS ALSO A VICTORY?
I WON'T BE ABLE TO FIGHT FOR ALL I'M WORTH OTHERWISE.
ROMIO...
AS YOU LIKE.
YOU CAN'T! A DUEL IS TOO...
I KNOW... BUT THIS IS OUR LAST CHANCE...
...TO STAND UP TO YOUR DAD. THIS IS THE FIRST TIME HE'S LISTENED TO ANYTHING WE'VE SAID...!!
I'M GONNA WIN THIS DUEL! WATCH ME, JULIET!

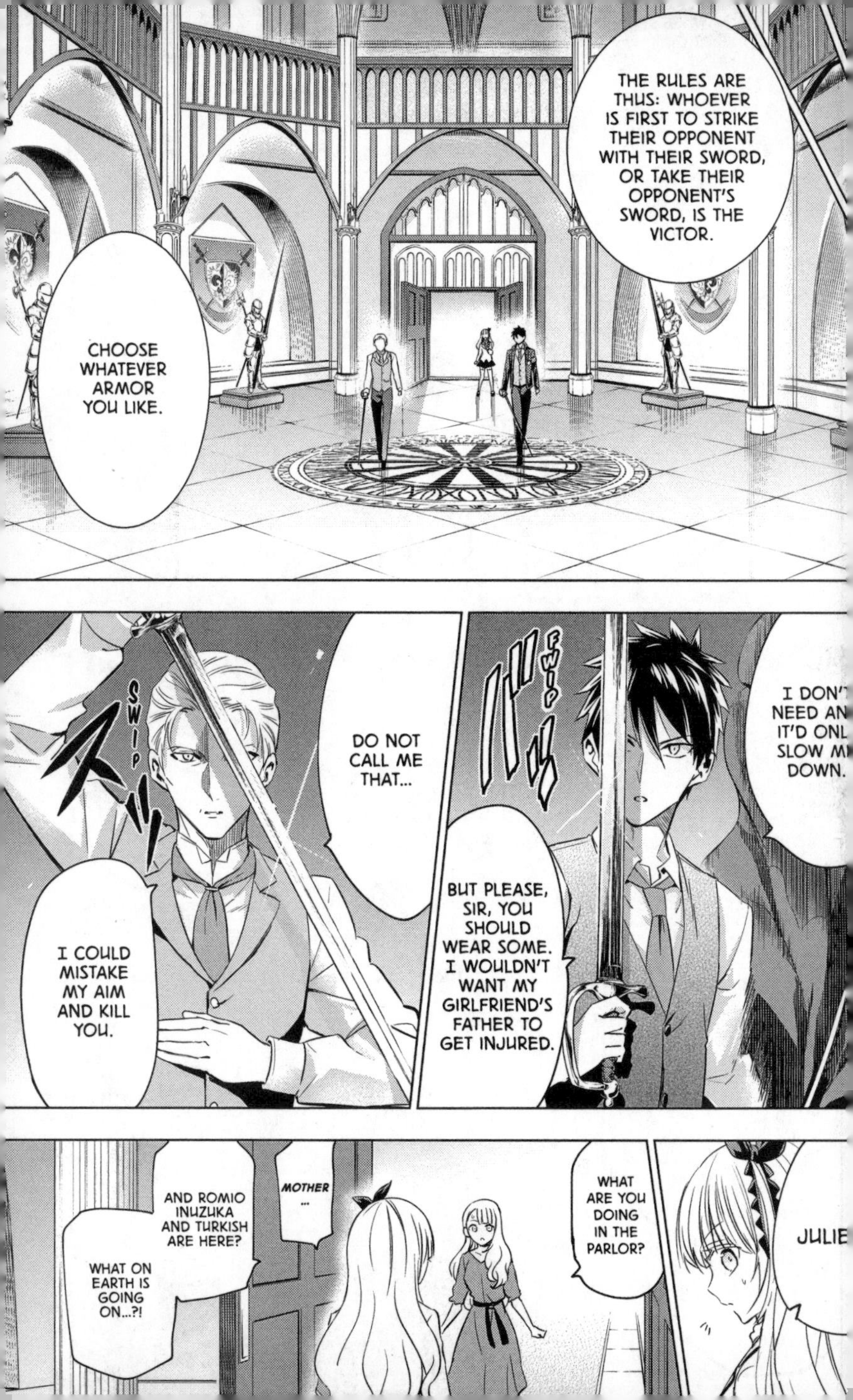
THE RULES ARE THUS: WHOEVER IS FIRST TO STRIKE THEIR OPPONENT WITH THEIR SWORD, OR TAKE THEIR OPPONENT'S SWORD, IS THE VICTOR.
CHOOSE WHATEVER ARMOR YOU LIKE.
I DON'T NEED AN IT'D ONL SLOW M DOWN.
FWIP
BUT PLEASE, SIR, YOU SHOULD WEAR SOME. I WOULDN'T WANT MY GIRLFRIEND'S FATHER TO GET INJURED.
DO NOT CALL ME THAT...
SWIP
I COULD MISTAKE MY AIM AND KILL YOU.
JULIE
WHAT ARE YOU DOING IN THE PARLOR?
MOTHER...
AND ROMIO INUZUKA AND TURKISH ARE HERE?
WHAT ON EARTH IS GOING ON...?!

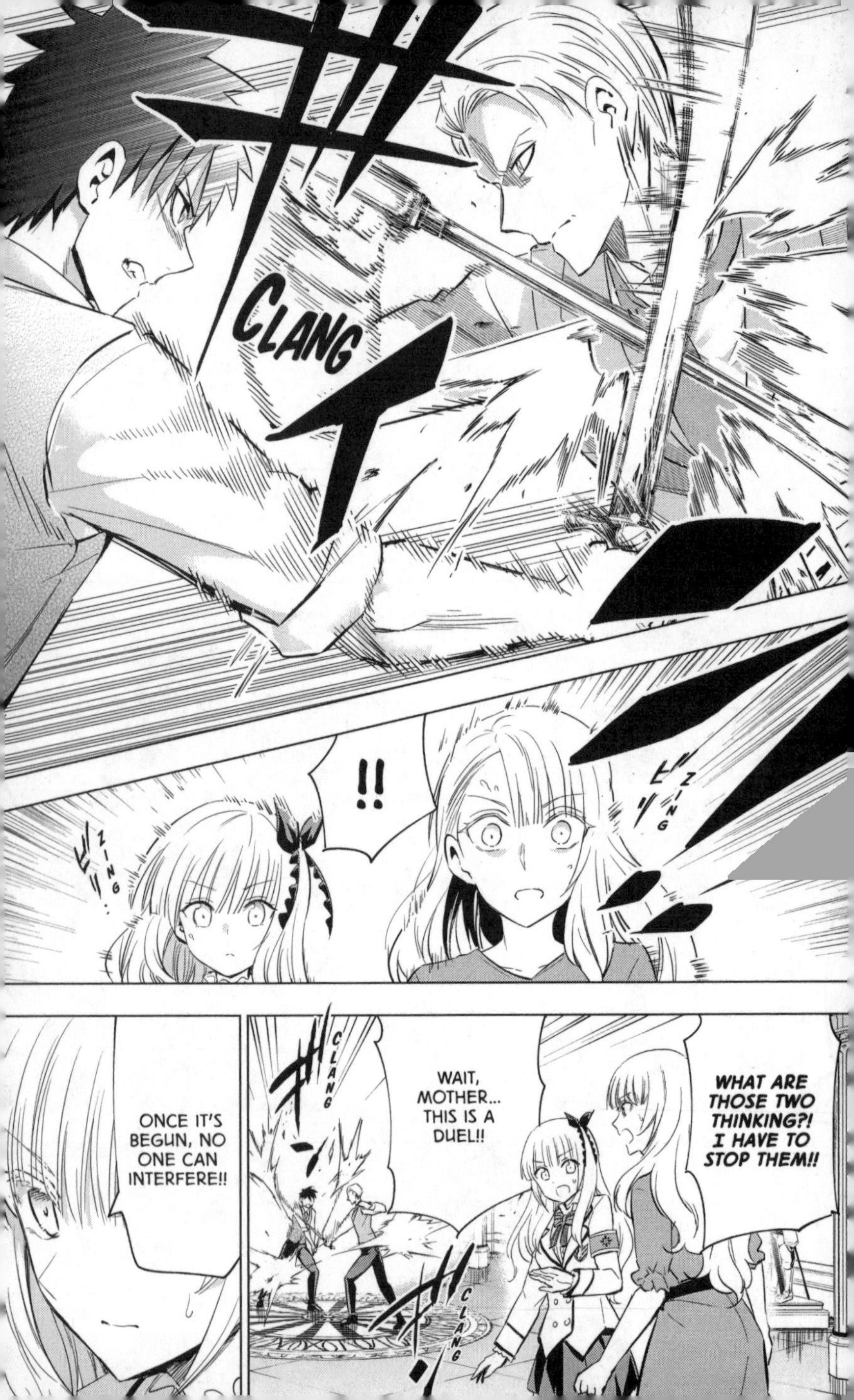
CLANG
ZING
!!
ZING
WHAT ARE THOSE TWO THINKING?! I HAVE TO STOP THEM!!
WAIT, MOTHER... THIS IS A DUEL!!
CLANG
CLANG
ONCE IT'S BEGUN, NO ONE CAN INTERFERE!!

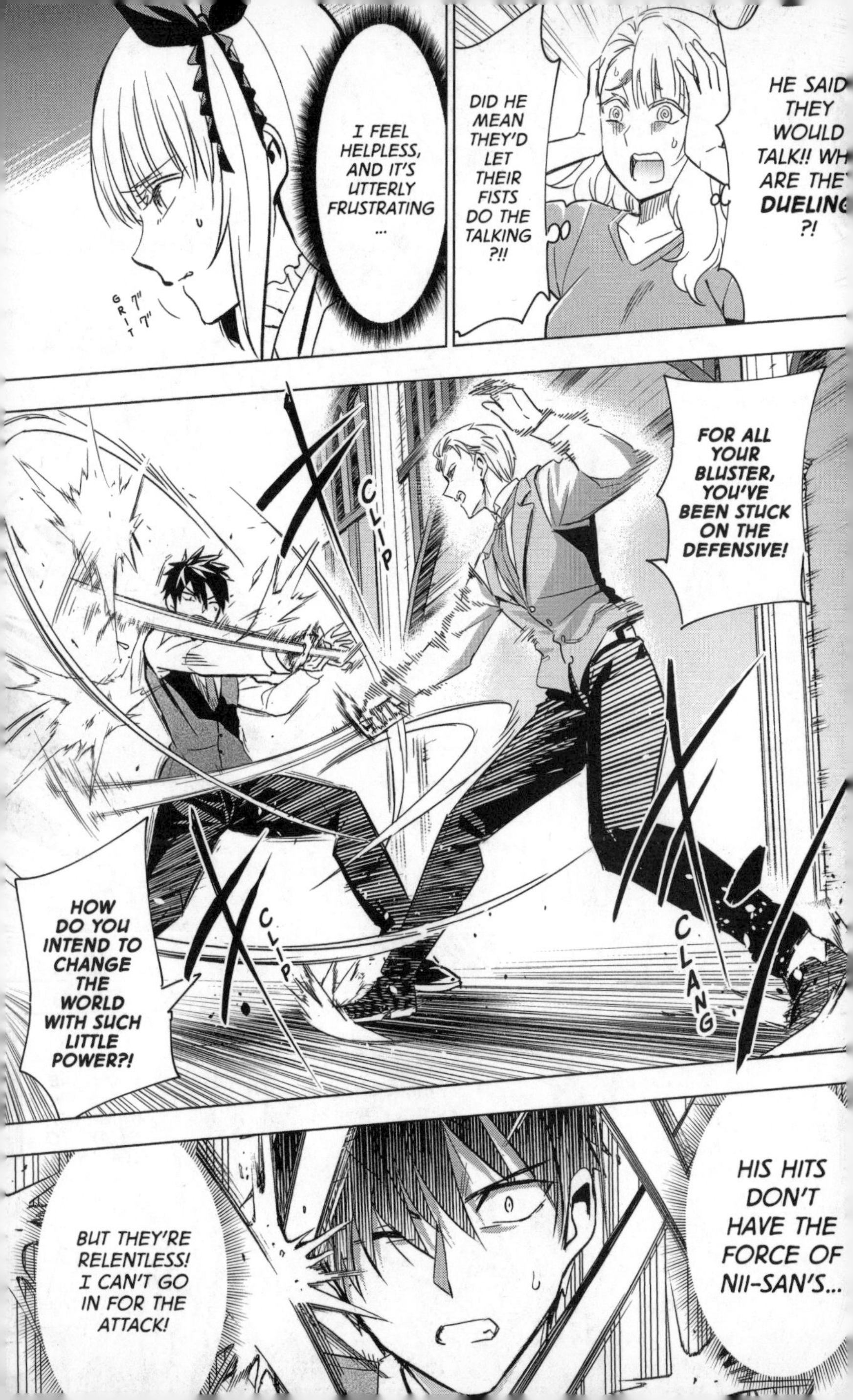
HE SAID THEY WOULD TALK!! WH ARE THE DUELIN ?!
DID HE MEAN THEY'D LET THEIR FISTS DO THE TALKING ?!!
I FEEL HELPLESS, AND IT'S UTTERLY FRUSTRATING ...
GRIT
FOR ALL YOUR BLUSTER, YOU'VE BEEN STUCK ON THE DEFENSIVE!
CLANG
CLIP
CLIP
HOW DO YOU INTEND TO CHANGE THE WORLD WITH SUCH LITTLE POWER?!
HIS HITS DON'T HAVE THE FORCE OF NII-SAN'S...
BUT THEY'RE RELENTLESS! I CAN'T GO IN FOR THE ATTACK!

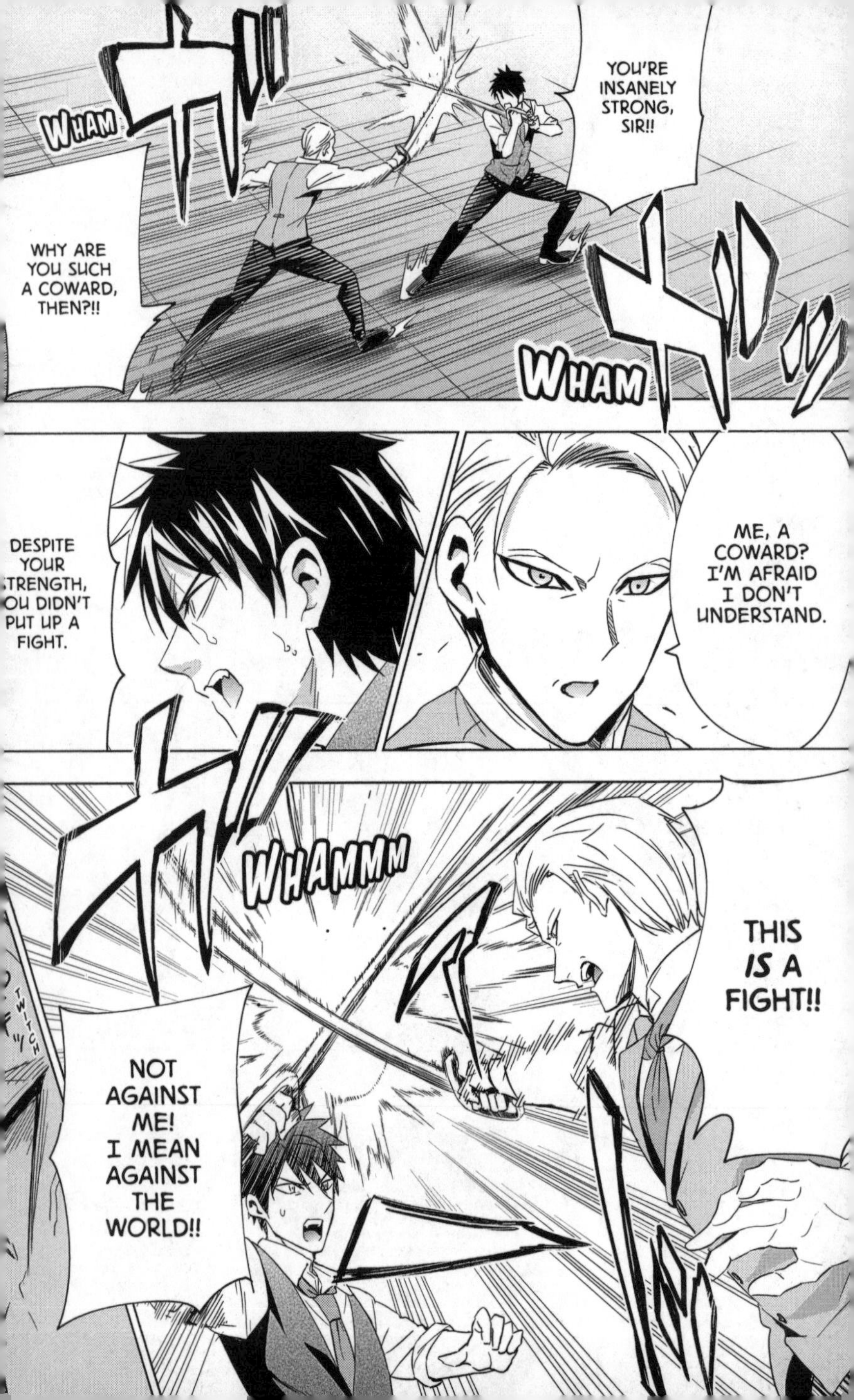
YOU'RE INSANELY STRONG, SIR!!
WHAM
WHY ARE YOU SUCH A COWARD, THEN?!!
WHAM
ME, A COWARD? I'M AFRAID I DON'T UNDERSTAND.
DESPITE YOUR TRENGTH, OU DIDN'T PUT UP A FIGHT.
THIS *IS* A FIGHT!!
WHAMMM
TWITCH
NOT AGAINST ME! I MEAN AGAINST THE WORLD!!

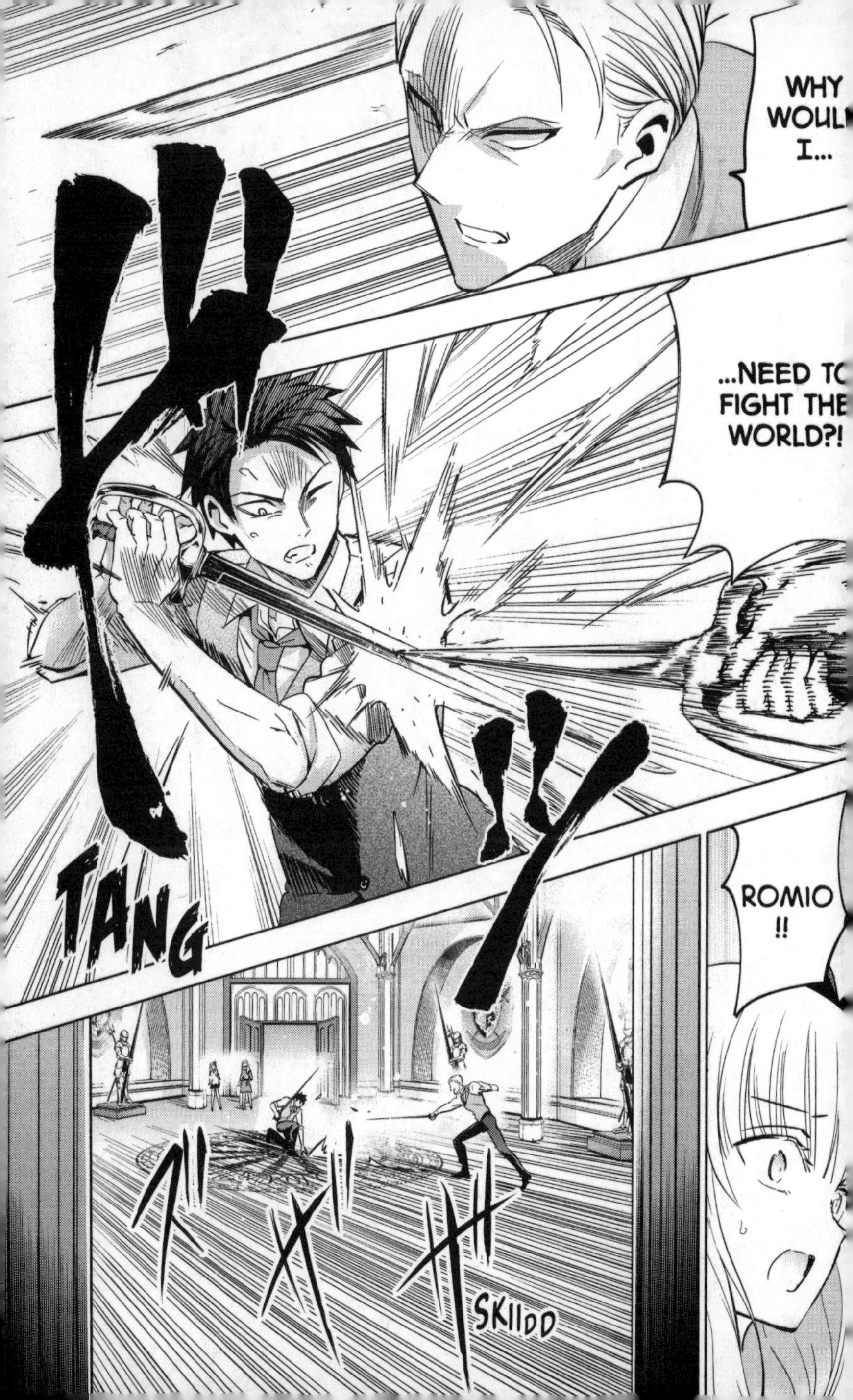
WHY WOUL I...
...NEED TO FIGHT THE WORLD?!
TANG
ROMIO !!
SKIIDD

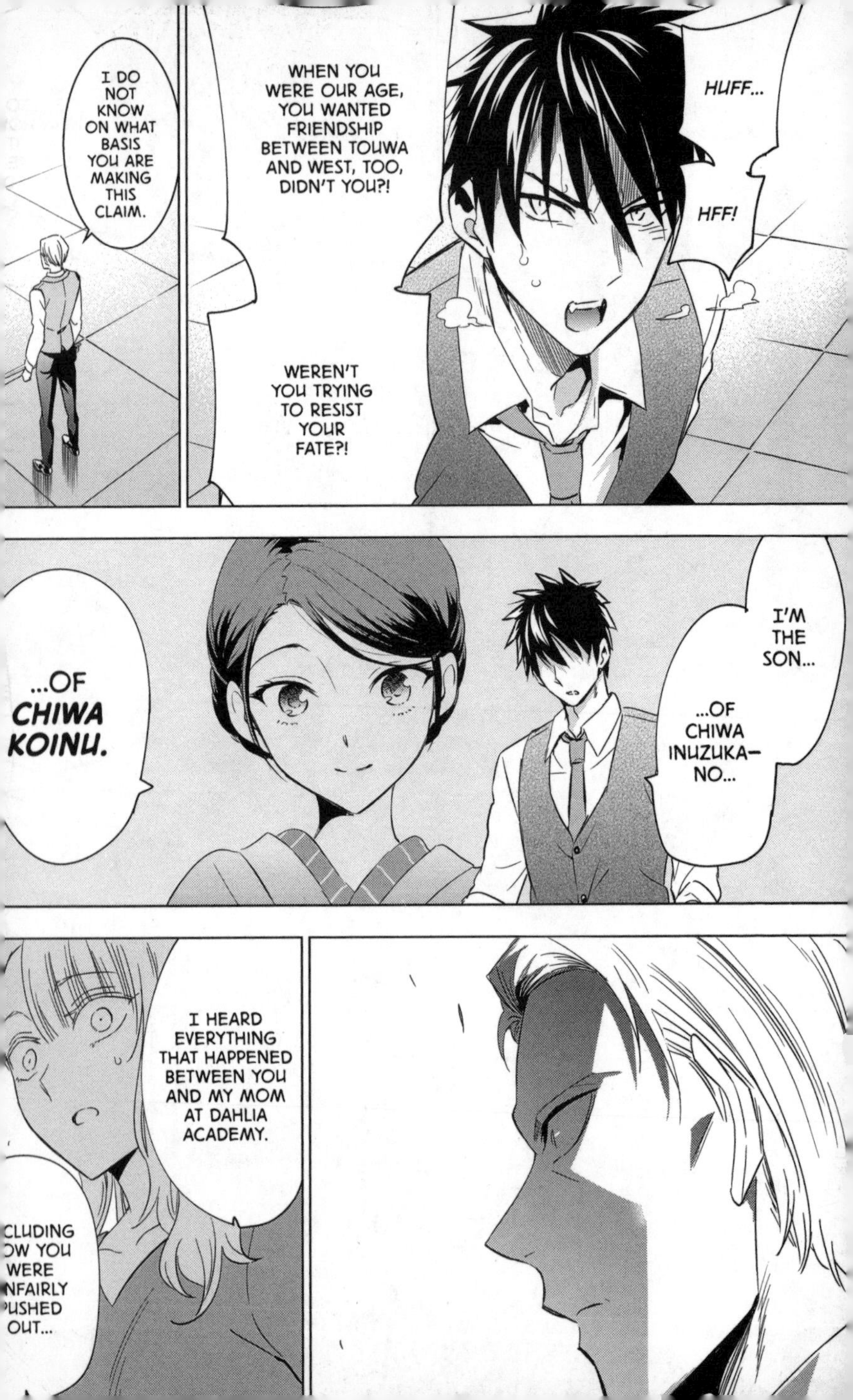
HUFF...
HFF!
WHEN YOU WERE OUR AGE, YOU WANTED FRIENDSHIP BETWEEN TOUWA AND WEST, TOO, DIDN'T YOU?!
WEREN'T YOU TRYING TO RESIST YOUR FATE?!
I DO NOT KNOW ON WHAT BASIS YOU ARE MAKING THIS CLAIM.
I'M THE SON...
...OF CHIWA INUZUKA—NO...
...OF ***CHIWA KOINU.***
I HEARD EVERYTHING THAT HAPPENED BETWEEN YOU AND MY MOM AT DAHLIA ACADEMY.
CLUDING OW YOU WERE NFAIRLY USHED OUT...

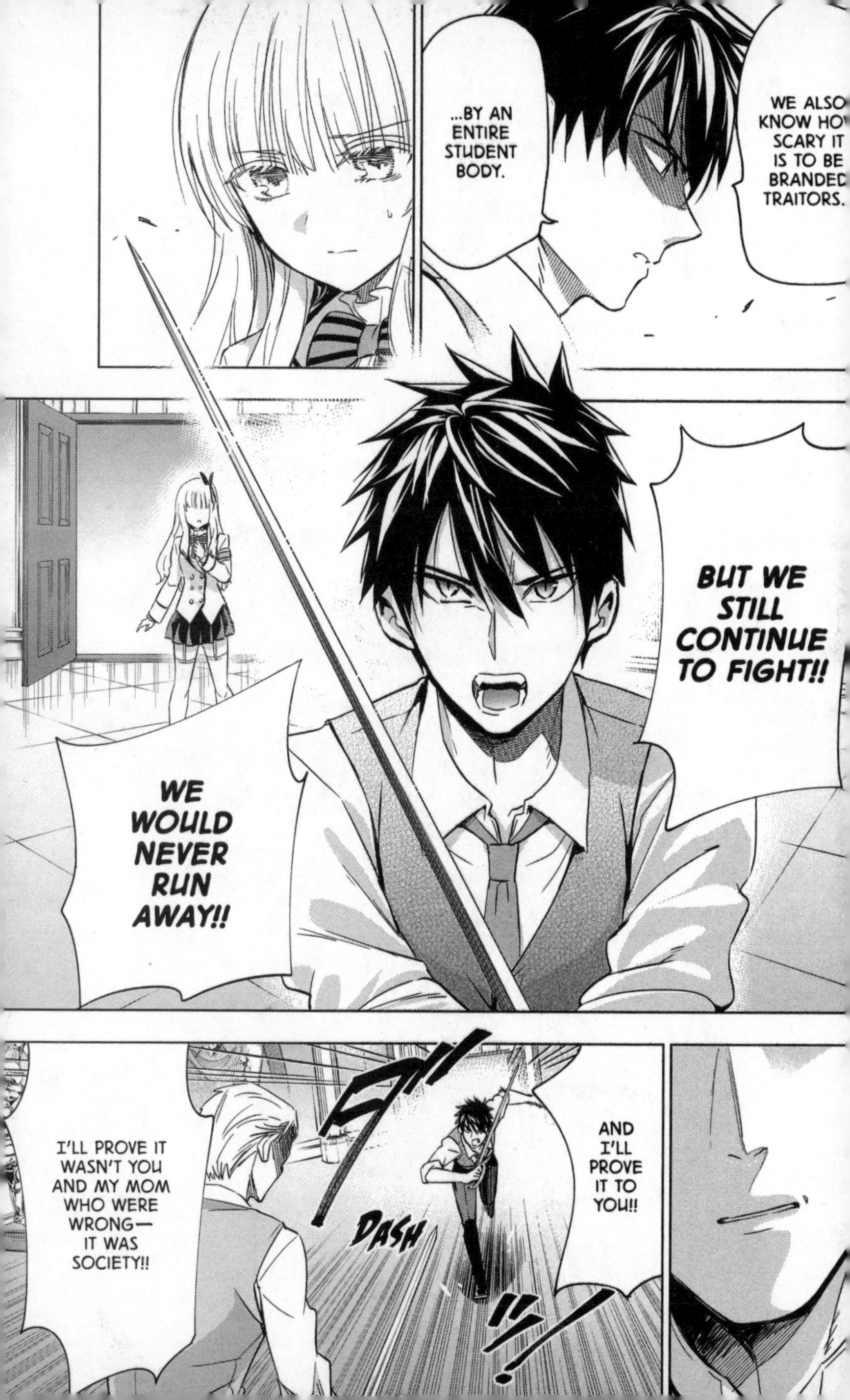
WE ALSO KNOW HO SCARY IT IS TO BE BRANDED TRAITORS.
...BY AN ENTIRE STUDENT BODY.
BUT WE STILL CONTINUE TO FIGHT!!
WE WOULD NEVER RUN AWAY!!
AND I'LL PROVE IT TO YOU!!
DASH
I'LL PROVE IT WASN'T YOU AND MY MOM WHO WERE WRONG— IT WAS SOCIETY!!

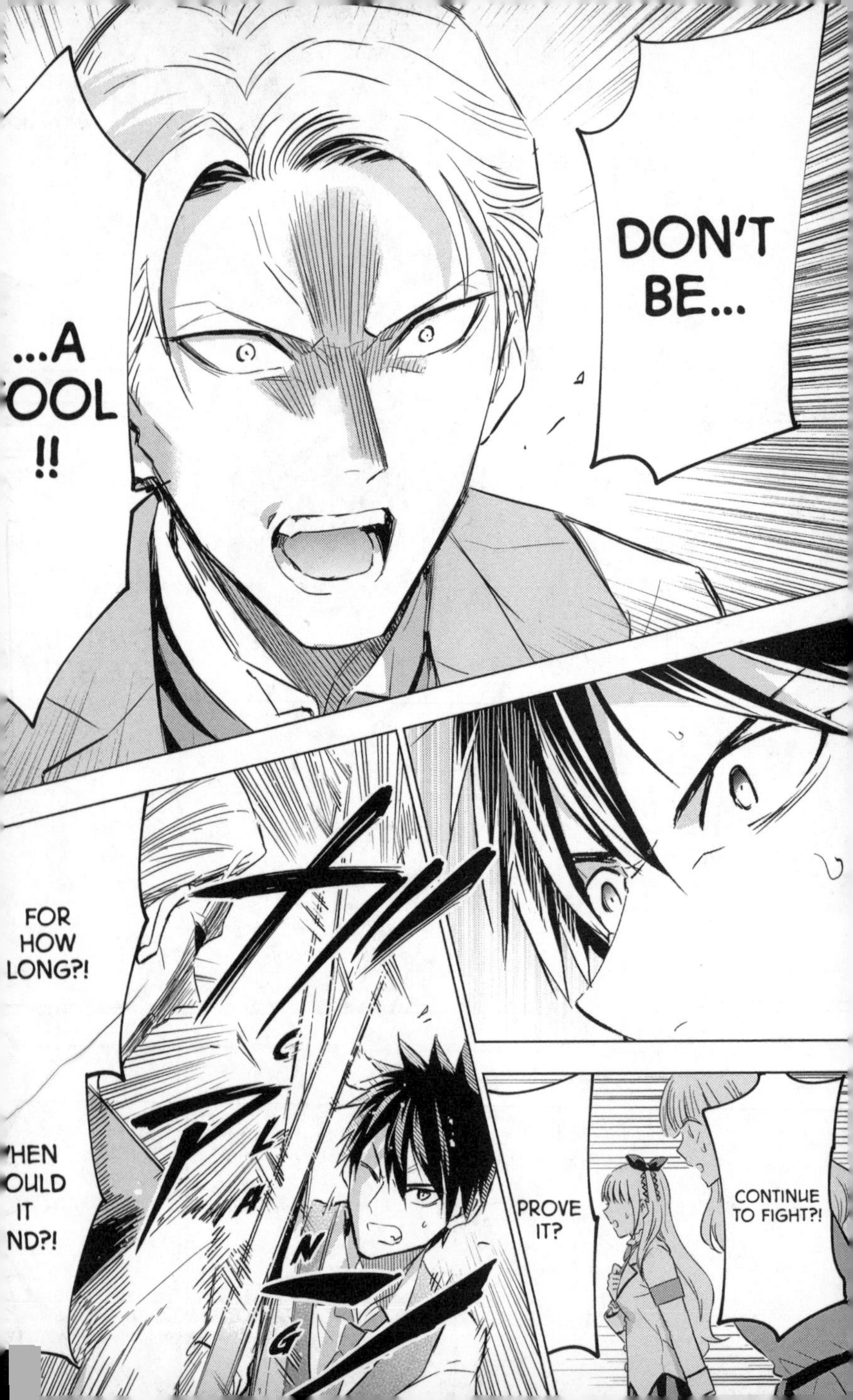
DON'T BE...
...A OOL !!
CONTINUE TO FIGHT?!
PROVE IT?
FOR HOW LONG?!
HEN OULD IT ND?!
CLANG

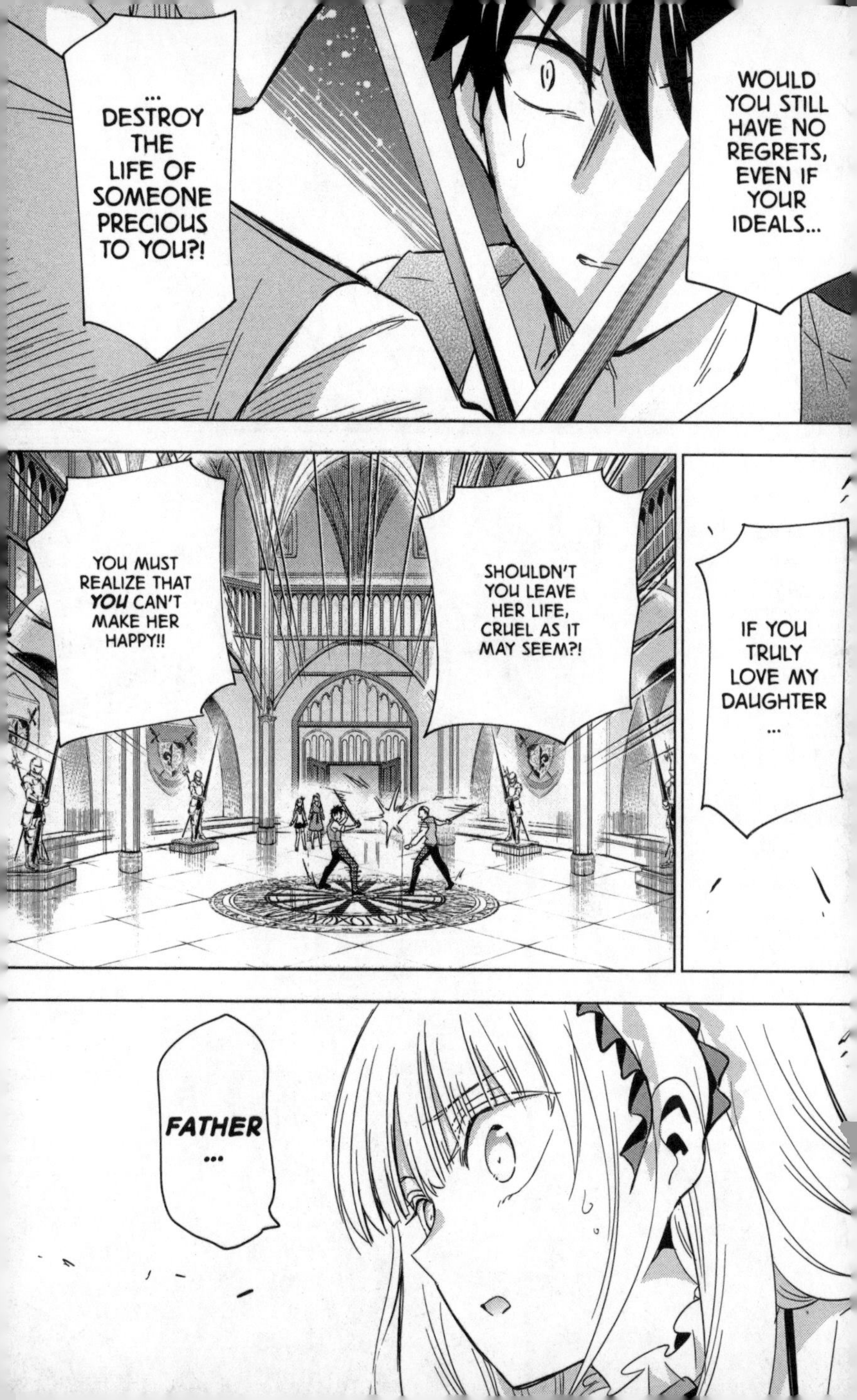
WOULD YOU STILL HAVE NO REGRETS, EVEN IF YOUR IDEALS...
... DESTROY THE LIFE OF SOMEONE PRECIOUS TO YOU?!
IF YOU TRULY LOVE MY DAUGHTER ...
SHOULDN'T YOU LEAVE HER LIFE, CRUEL AS IT MAY SEEM?!
YOU MUST REALIZE THAT *YOU* CAN'T MAKE HER HAPPY!!
FATHER ...

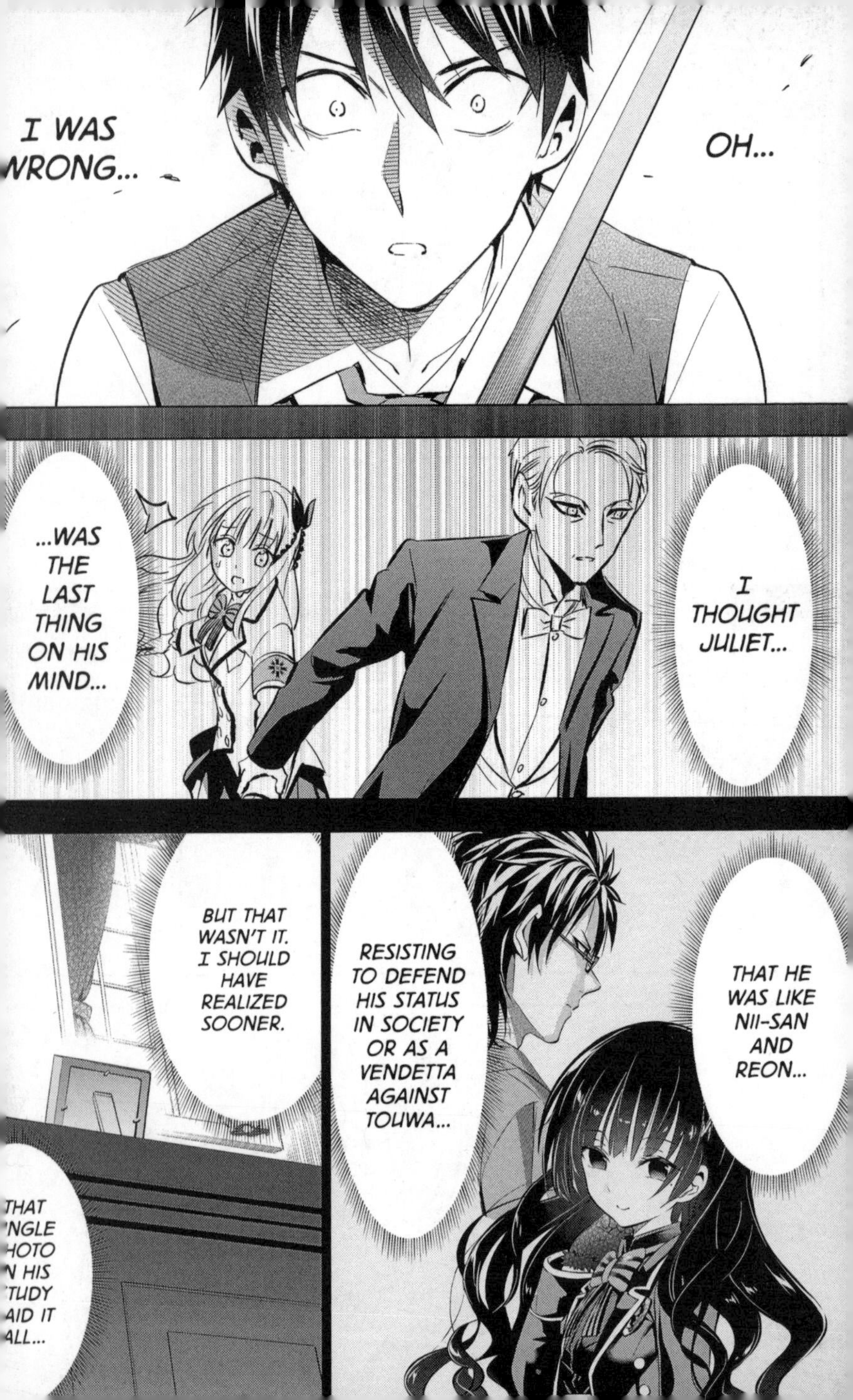

OH...
I WAS WRONG...
I THOUGHT JULIET...
...WAS THE LAST THING ON HIS MIND...
THAT HE WAS LIKE NII-SAN AND REON...
RESISTING TO DEFEND HIS STATUS IN SOCIETY OR AS A VENDETTA AGAINST TOUWA...
BUT THAT WASN'T IT. I SHOULD HAVE REALIZED SOONER.
THAT NGLE HOTO N HIS TUDY AID IT ALL...

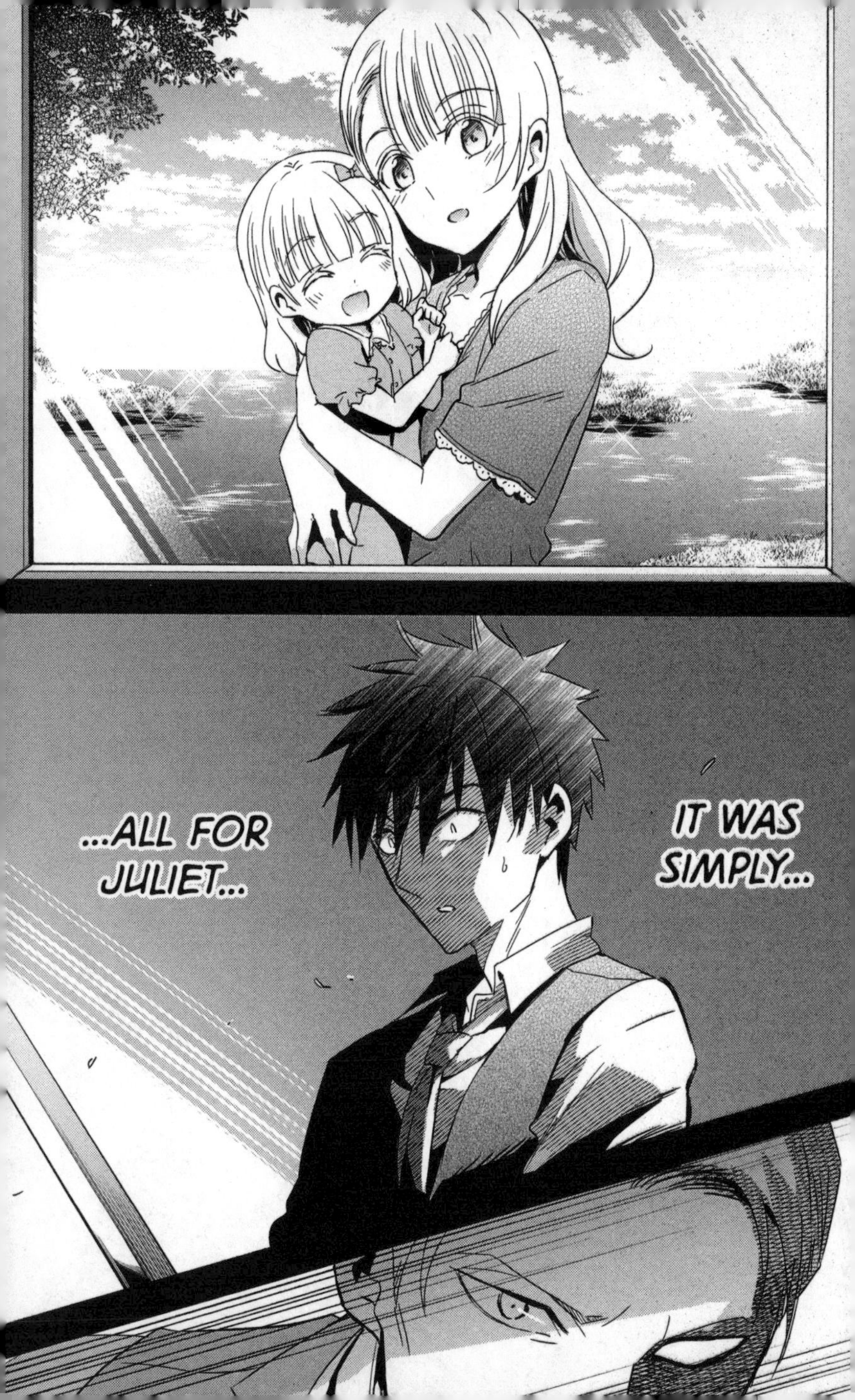
IT WAS SIMPLY...
...ALL FOR JULIET...

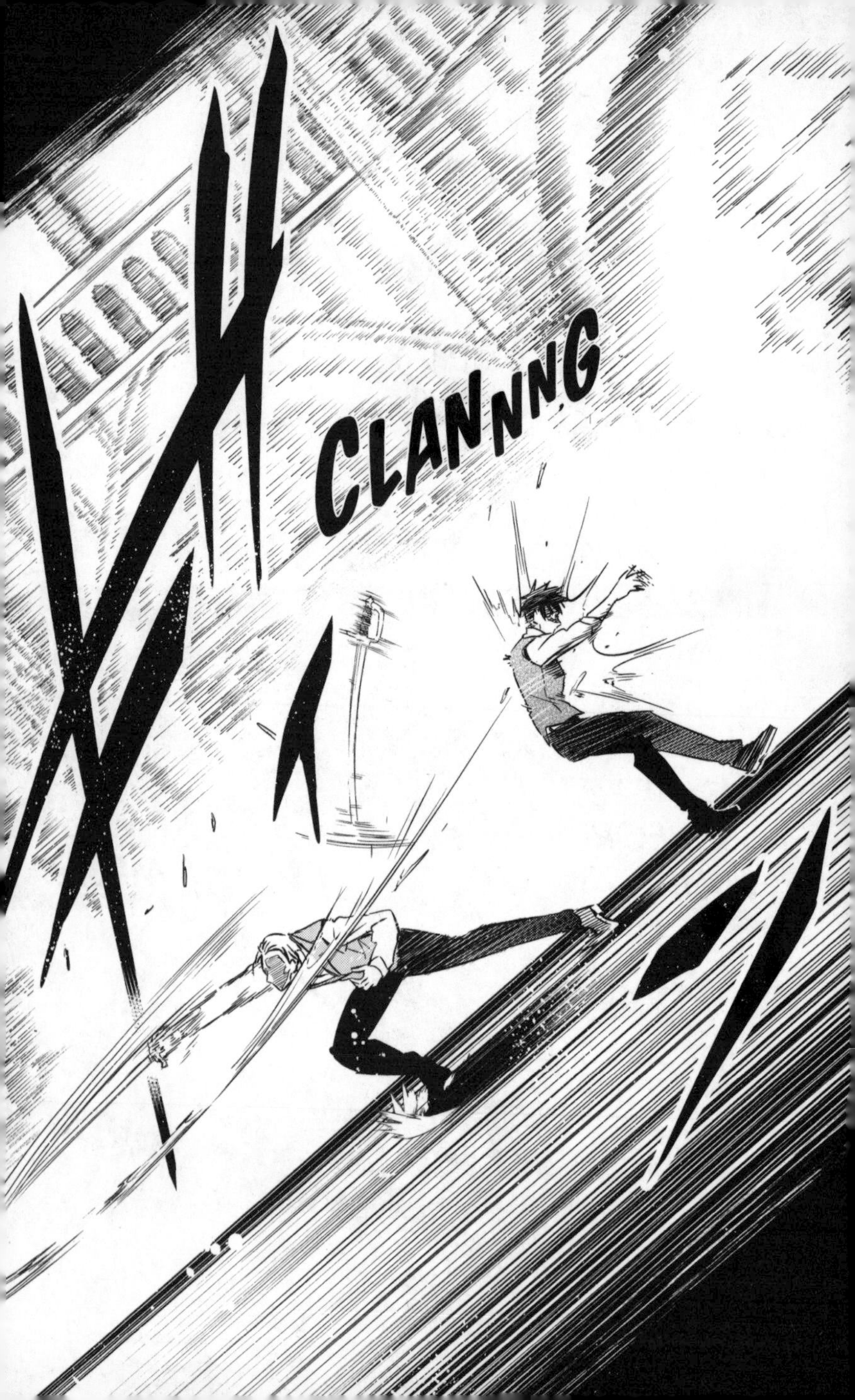
CLANNNG

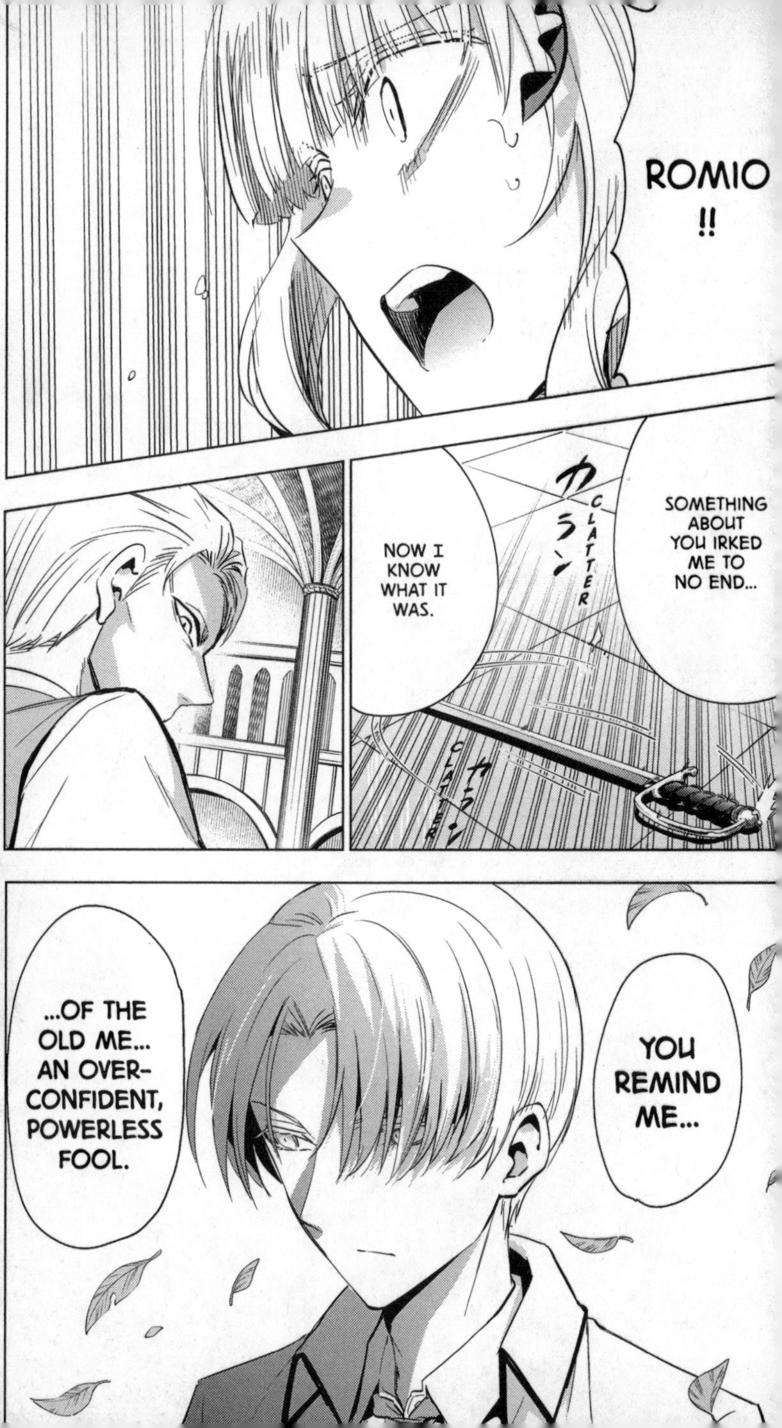
ROMIO !!
SOMETHING ABOUT YOU IRKED ME TO NO END...
NOW I KNOW WHAT IT WAS.
カラン
CLATTER
カラン
CLATTER
YOU REMIND ME...
...OF THE OLD ME... AN OVER-CONFIDENT, POWERLESS FOOL.

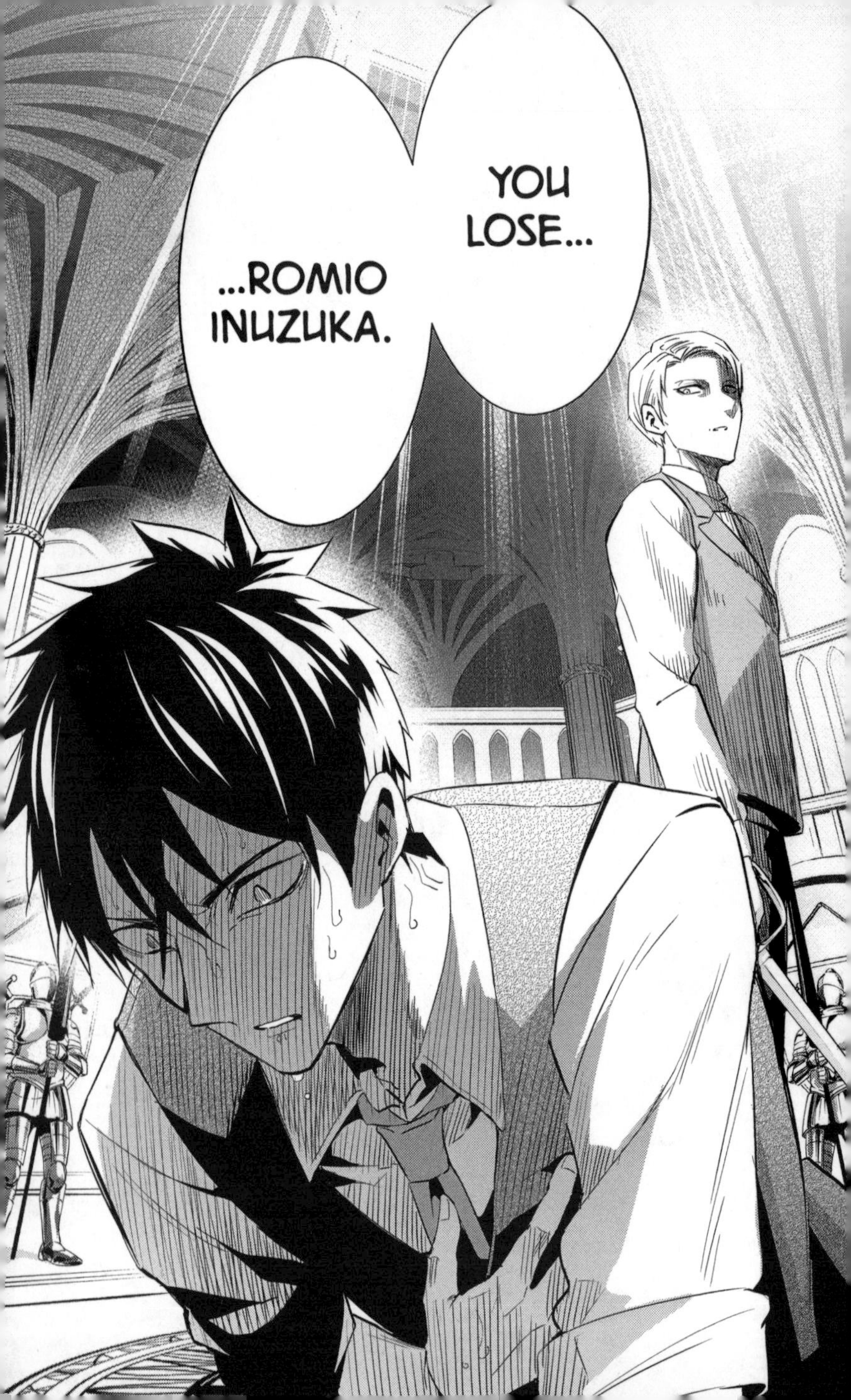
YOU LOSE...
...ROMIO INUZUKA.

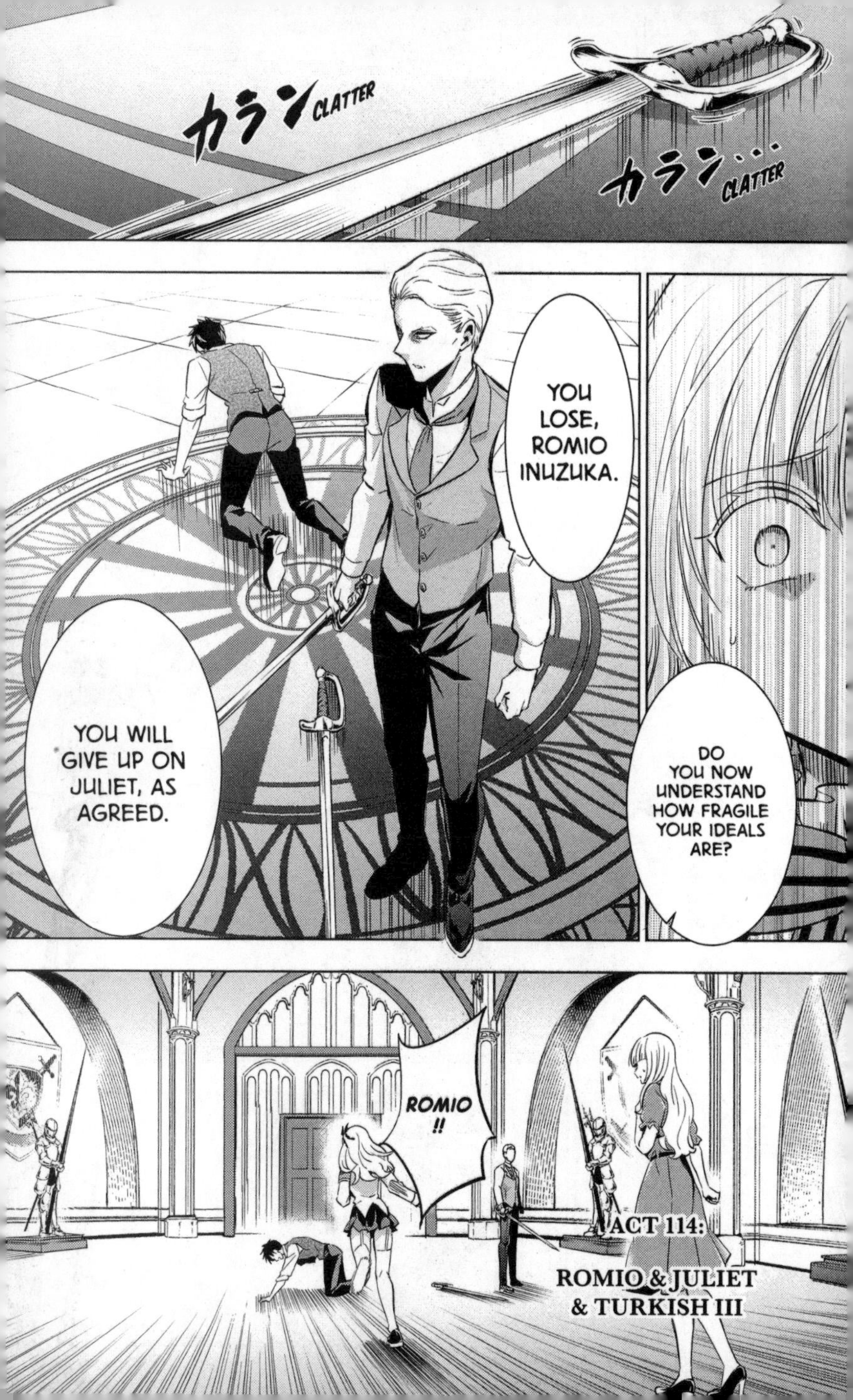
カラン CLATTER
カラン… CLATTER
DO YOU NOW UNDERSTAND HOW FRAGILE YOUR IDEALS ARE?
YOU LOSE, ROMIO INUZUKA.
YOU WILL GIVE UP ON JULIET, AS AGREED.
ROMIO !!
ACT 114:
ROMIO & JULIET & TURKISH III

WHAM

JULIET... I...

I...

ROMIO...

I...

...LOST...

I'M SORRY...

JULIET.

I LOST THE ONE BATTLE I ABSOLUTELY COULDN'T AFFORD TO LOSE!!

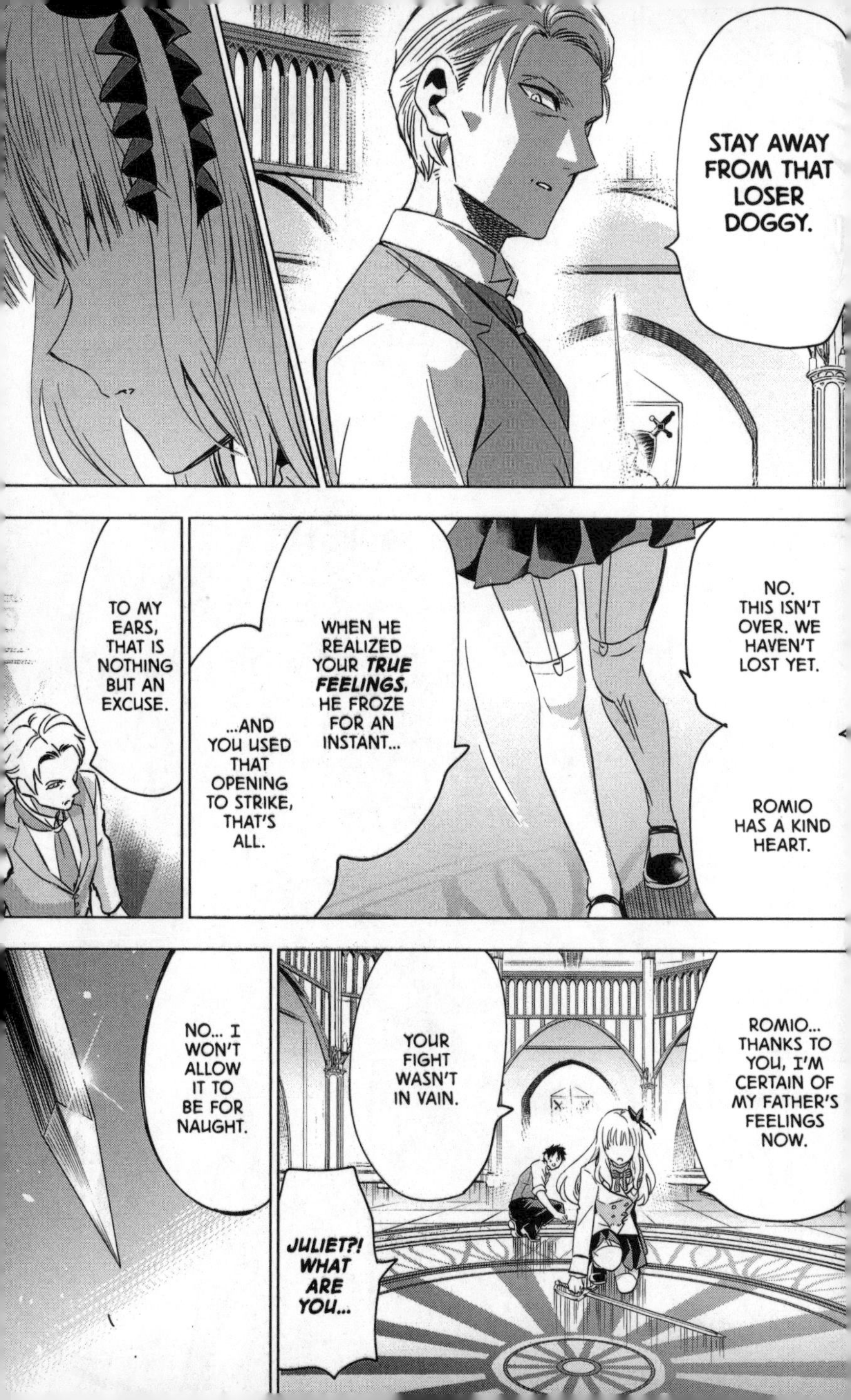
STAY AWAY FROM THAT LOSER DOGGY.
NO. THIS ISN'T OVER. WE HAVEN'T LOST YET.
ROMIO HAS A KIND HEART.
WHEN HE REALIZED YOUR ***TRUE FEELINGS***, HE FROZE FOR AN INSTANT...
...AND YOU USED THAT OPENING TO STRIKE, THAT'S ALL.
TO MY EARS, THAT IS NOTHING BUT AN EXCUSE.
ROMIO... THANKS TO YOU, I'M CERTAIN OF MY FATHER'S FEELINGS NOW.
YOUR FIGHT WASN'T IN VAIN.
JULIET?! WHAT ARE YOU...
NO... I WON'T ALLOW IT TO BE FOR NAUGHT.

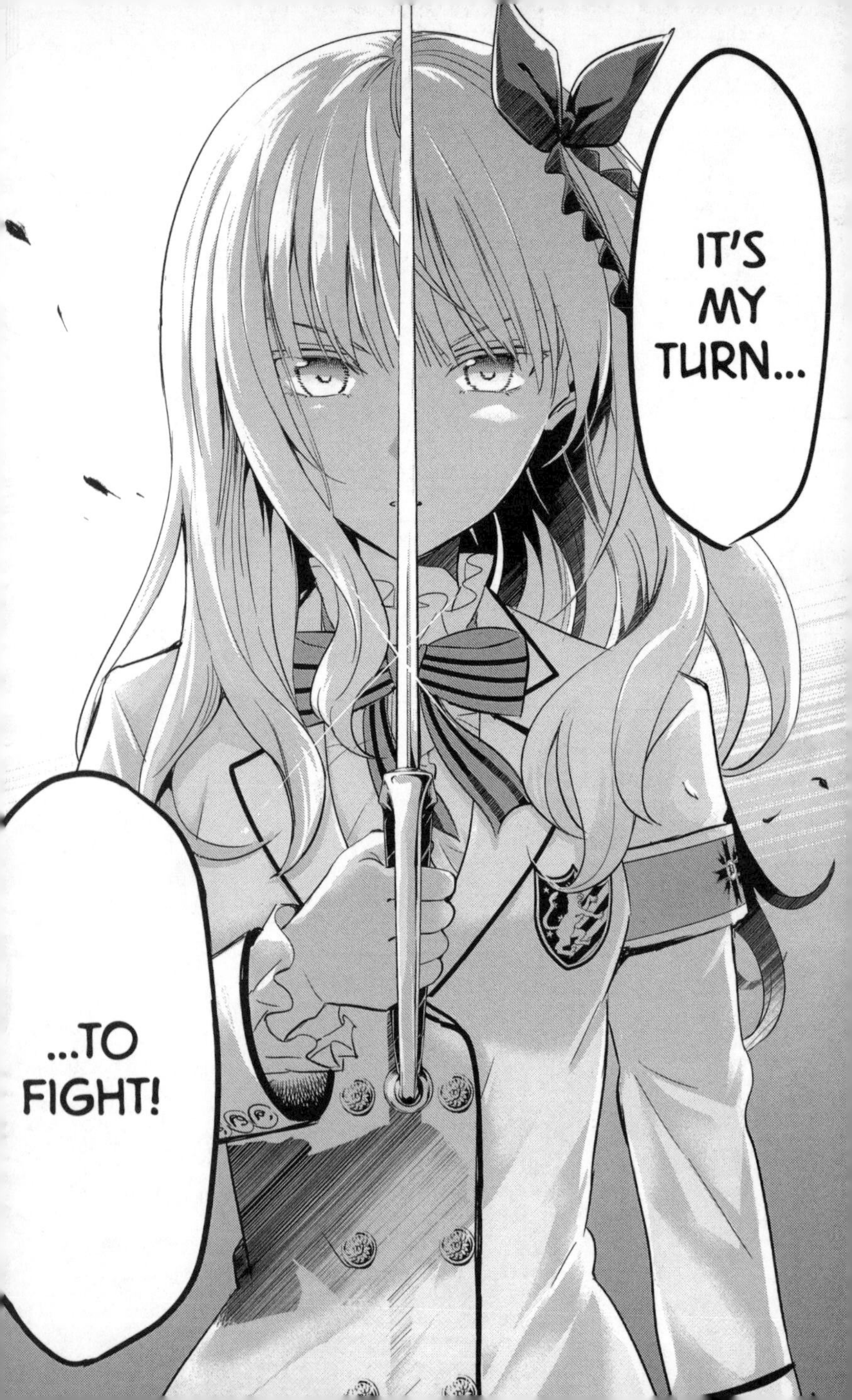
IT'S MY TURN...
...TO FIGHT!

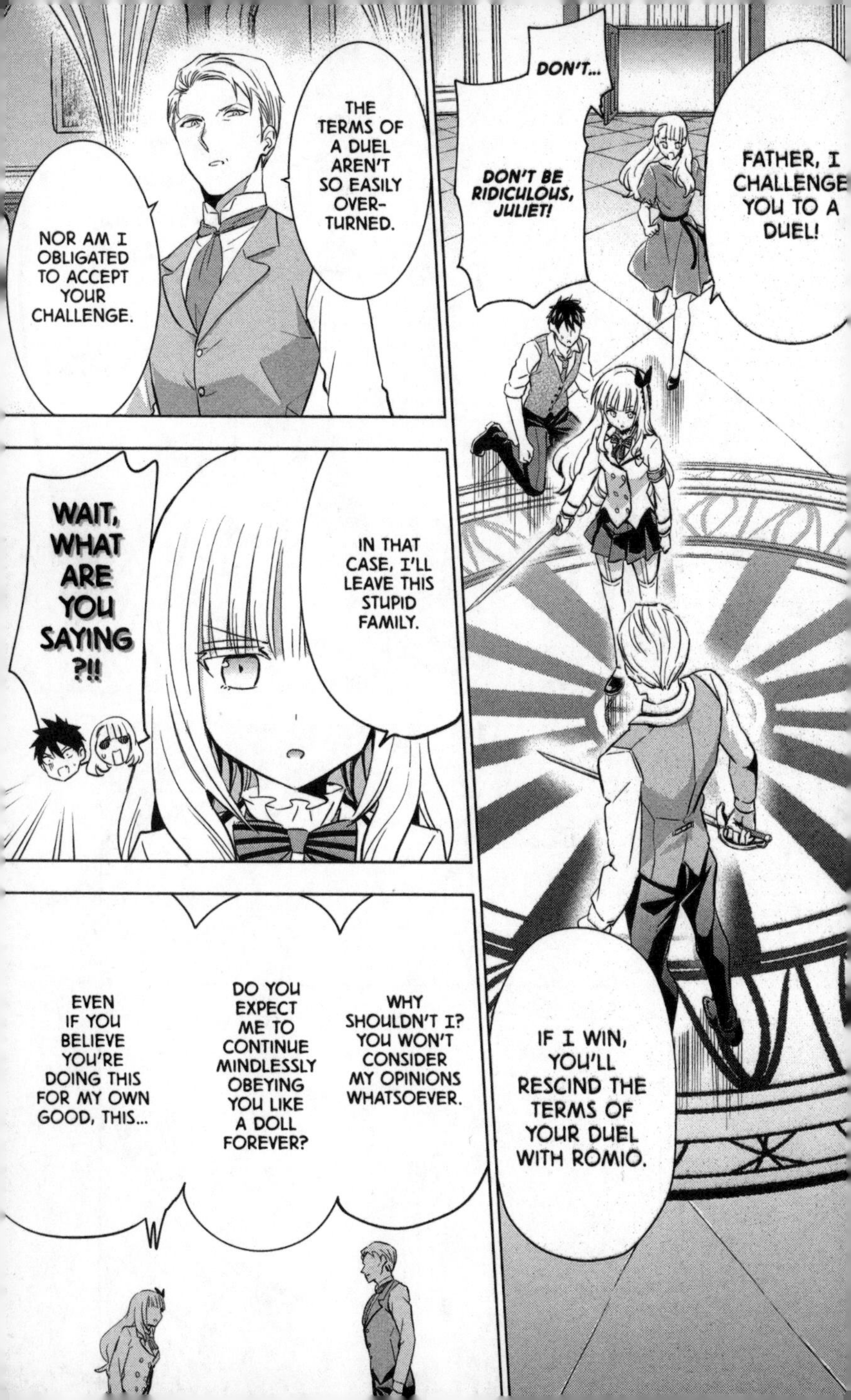
FATHER, I CHALLENGE YOU TO A DUEL!
DON'T...
DON'T BE RIDICULOUS, JULIET!
IF I WIN, YOU'LL RESCIND THE TERMS OF YOUR DUEL WITH ROMIO.
THE TERMS OF A DUEL AREN'T SO EASILY OVER-TURNED.
NOR AM I OBLIGATED TO ACCEPT YOUR CHALLENGE.
IN THAT CASE, I'LL LEAVE THIS STUPID FAMILY.
WAIT, WHAT ARE YOU SAYING?!!
WHY SHOULDN'T I? YOU WON'T CONSIDER MY OPINIONS WHATSOEVER.
DO YOU EXPECT ME TO CONTINUE MINDLESSLY OBEYING YOU LIKE A DOLL FOREVER?
EVEN IF YOU BELIEVE YOU'RE DOING THIS FOR MY OWN GOOD, THIS...

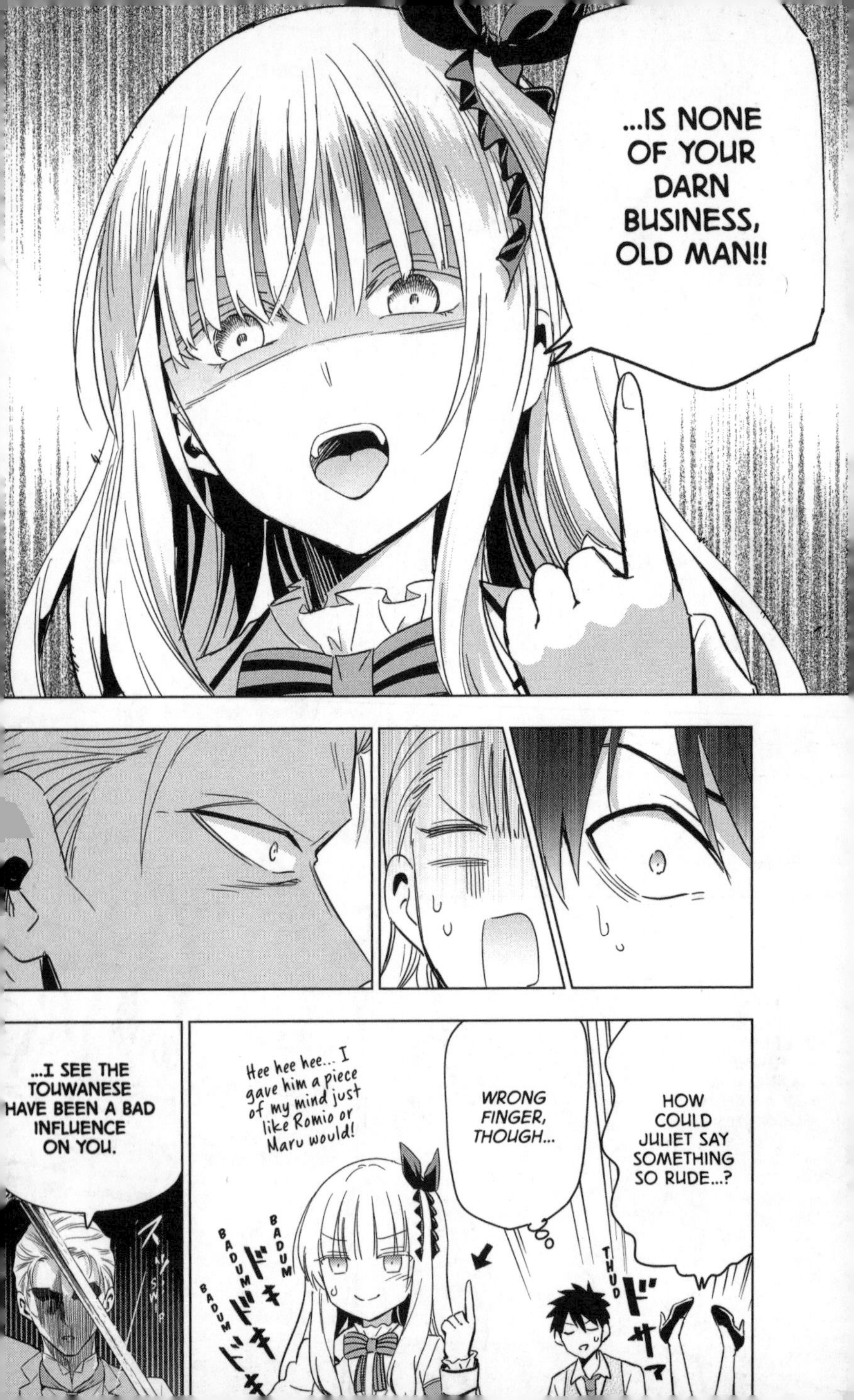
...IS NONE OF YOUR DARN BUSINESS, OLD MAN!!
HOW COULD JULIET SAY SOMETHING SO RUDE...?
WRONG FINGER, THOUGH...
Hee hee hee... I gave him a piece of my mind just like Romio or Maru would!
THUD
BADUM
BADUM
BADUM
...I SEE THE TOUWANESE HAVE BEEN A BAD INFLUENCE ON YOU.
SWIP

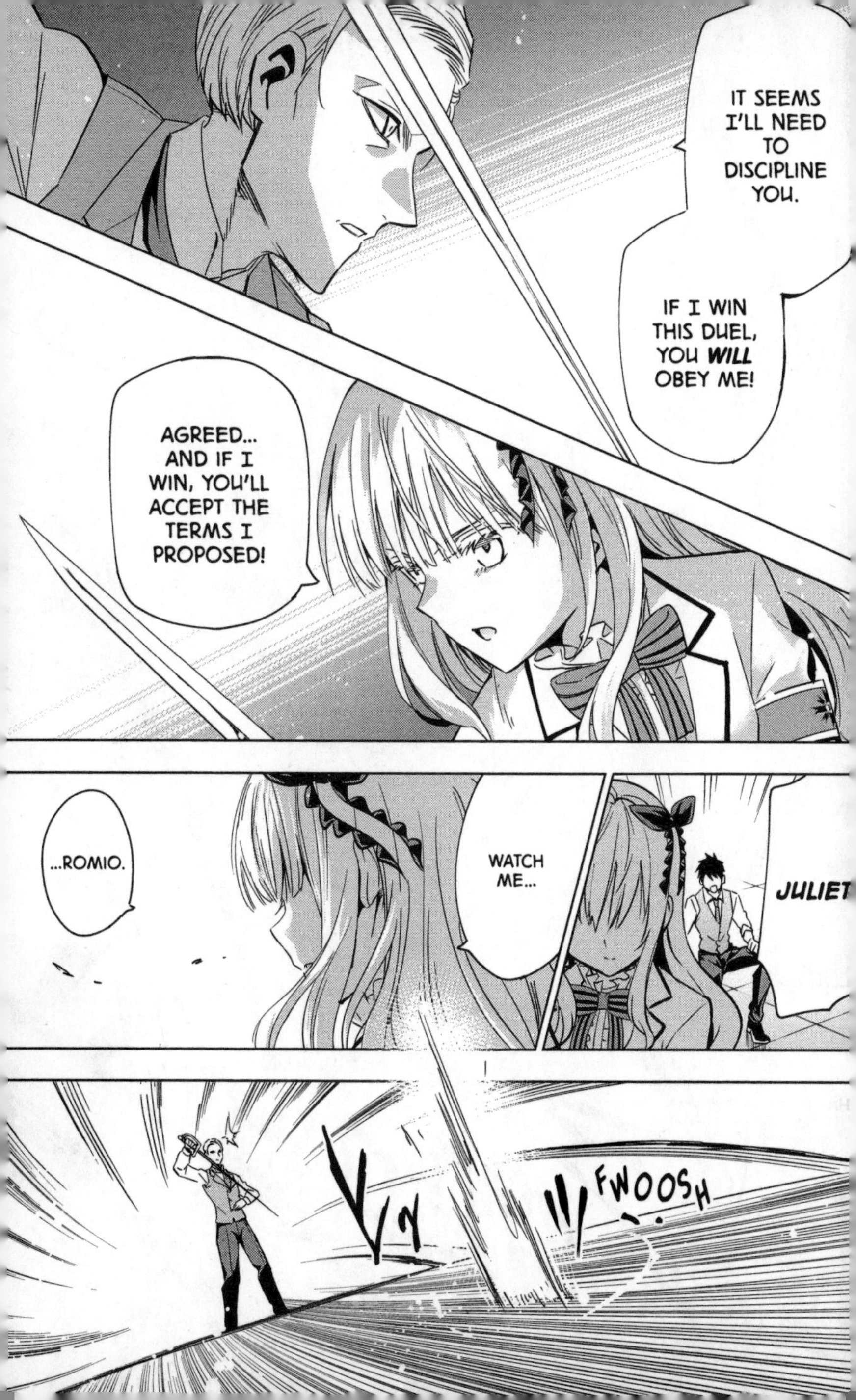
IT SEEMS I'LL NEED TO DISCIPLINE YOU.
IF I WIN THIS DUEL, YOU WILL OBEY ME!
AGREED... AND IF I WIN, YOU'LL ACCEPT THE TERMS I PROPOSED!
JULIET
WATCH ME...
...ROMIO.
FWOOSH

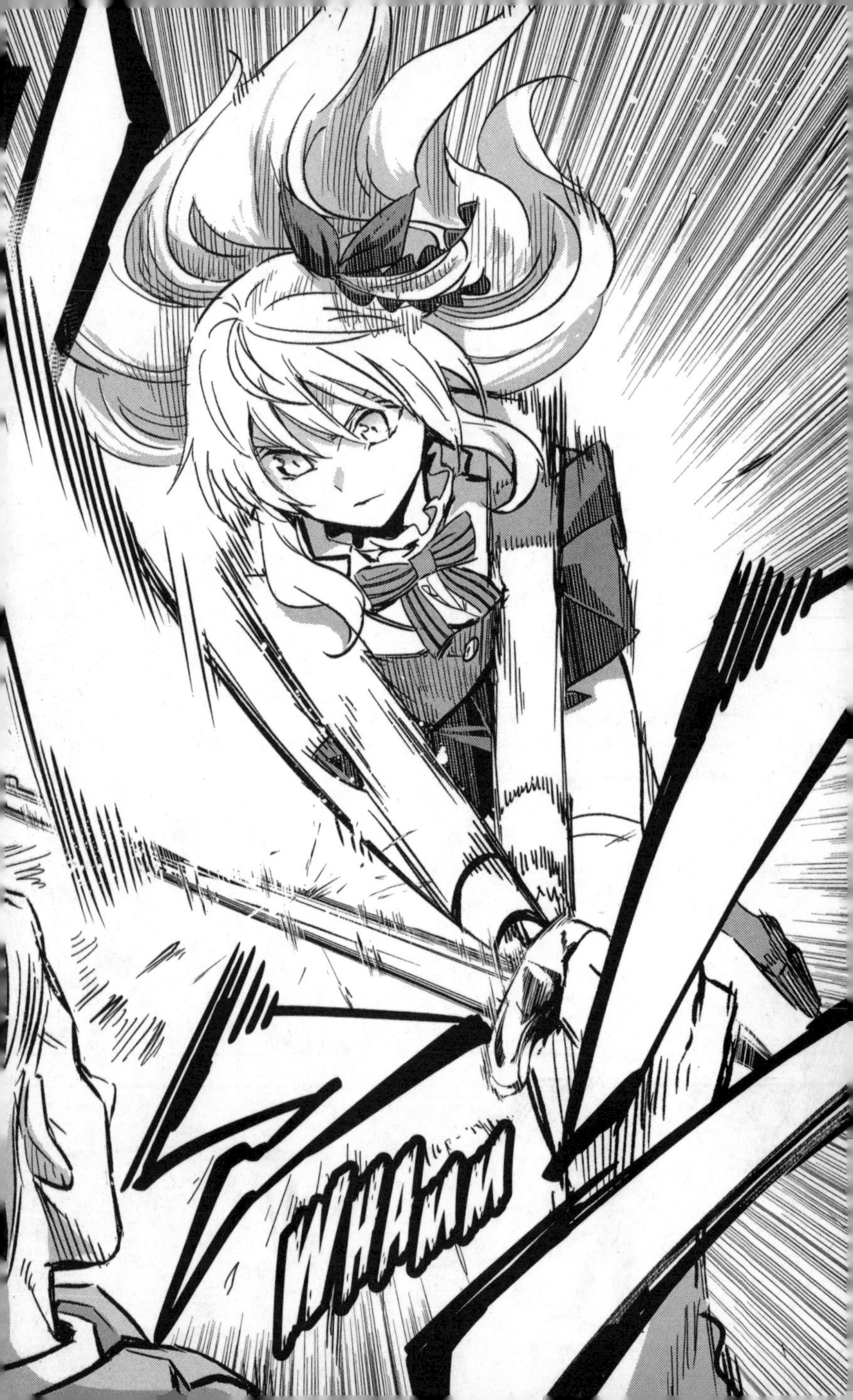
WHAMMM

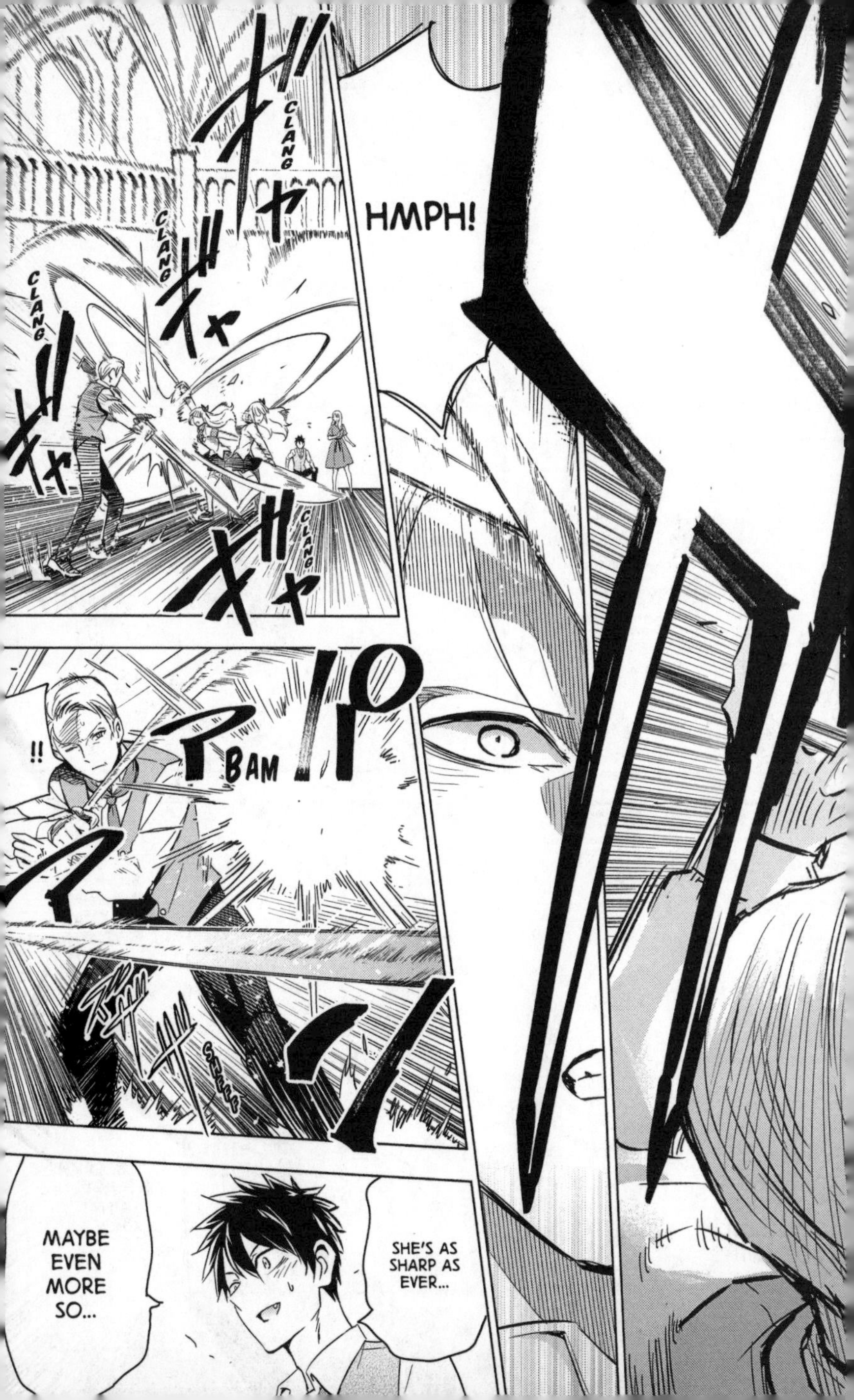
HMPH!
CLANG
CLANG
CLANG
CLANG
BAM
!!
SHFFF
SHE'S AS SHARP AS EVER...
MAYBE EVEN MORE SO...

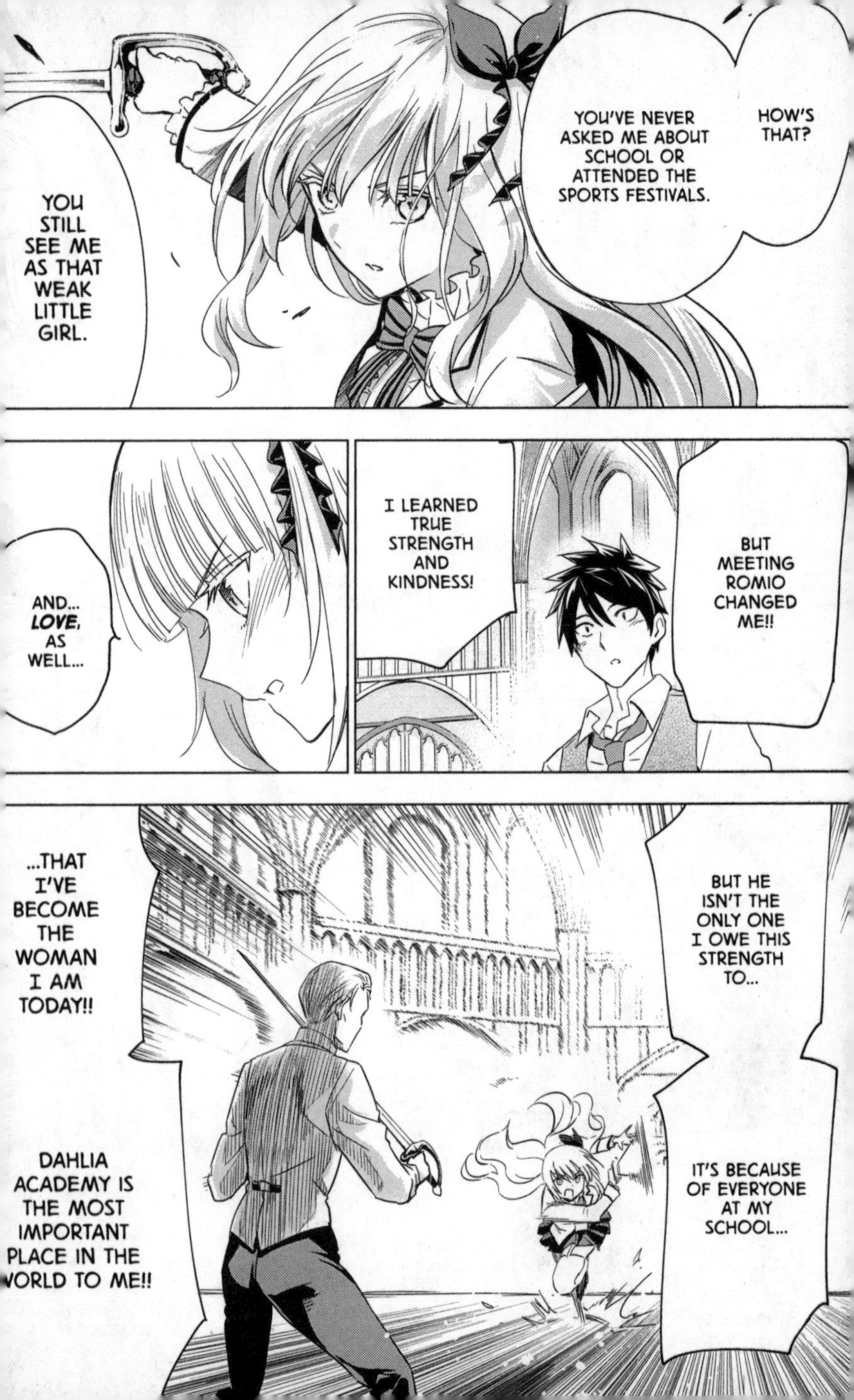
HOW'S THAT?
YOU'VE NEVER ASKED ME ABOUT SCHOOL OR ATTENDED THE SPORTS FESTIVALS.
YOU STILL SEE ME AS THAT WEAK LITTLE GIRL.
BUT MEETING ROMIO CHANGED ME!!
I LEARNED TRUE STRENGTH AND KINDNESS!
AND... *LOVE*, AS WELL...
BUT HE ISN'T THE ONLY ONE I OWE THIS STRENGTH TO...
IT'S BECAUSE OF EVERYONE AT MY SCHOOL...
...THAT I'VE BECOME THE WOMAN I AM TODAY!!
DAHLIA ACADEMY IS THE MOST IMPORTANT PLACE IN THE WORLD TO ME!!

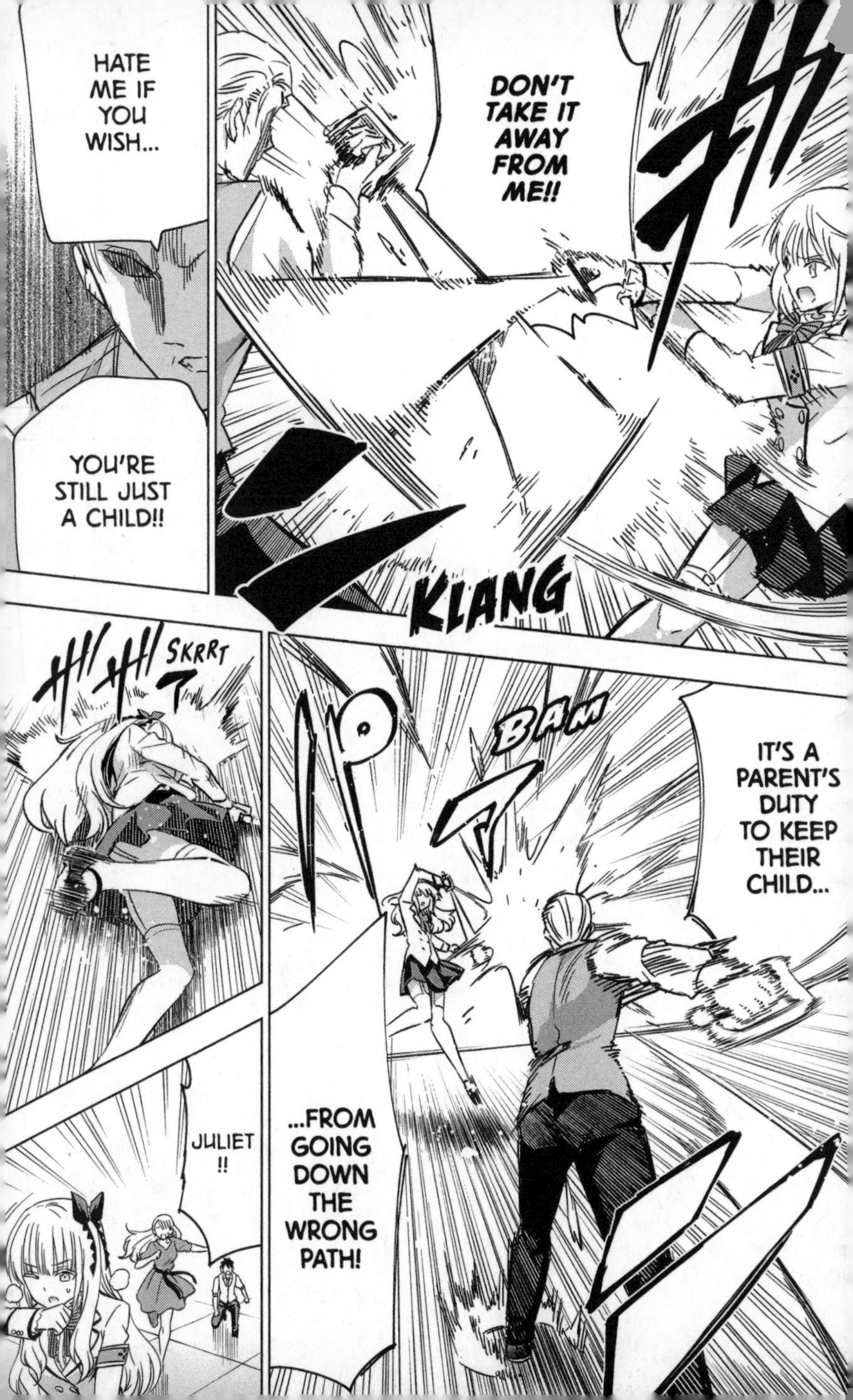
DON'T TAKE IT AWAY FROM ME!!
KLANG
HATE ME IF YOU WISH...
YOU'RE STILL JUST A CHILD!!
BAM
IT'S A PARENT'S DUTY TO KEEP THEIR CHILD...
...FROM GOING DOWN THE WRONG PATH!
SKRRT
JULIET!!

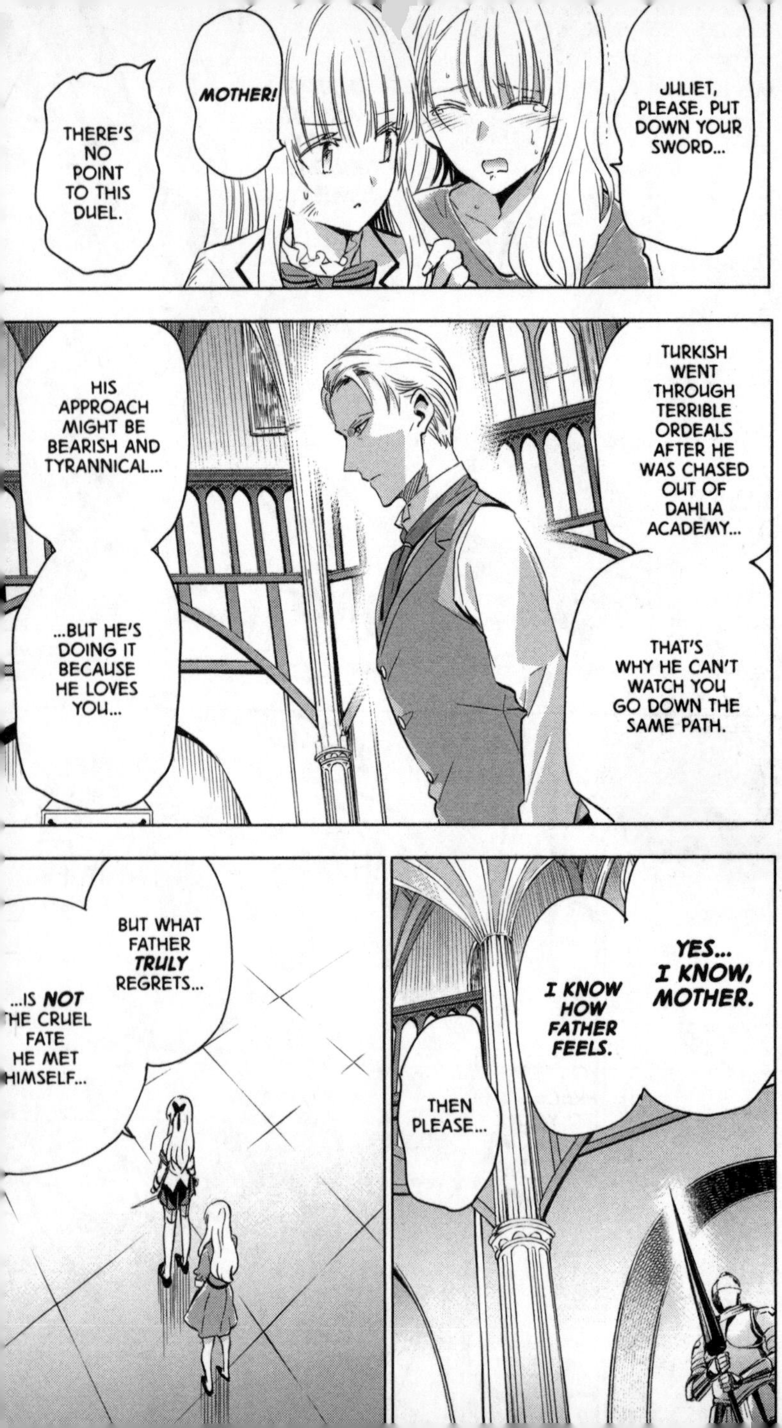
JULIET, PLEASE, PUT DOWN YOUR SWORD...
MOTHER!
THERE'S NO POINT TO THIS DUEL.
TURKISH WENT THROUGH TERRIBLE ORDEALS AFTER HE WAS CHASED OUT OF DAHLIA ACADEMY...
THAT'S WHY HE CAN'T WATCH YOU GO DOWN THE SAME PATH.
HIS APPROACH MIGHT BE BEARISH AND TYRANNICAL...
...BUT HE'S DOING IT BECAUSE HE LOVES YOU...
YES... I KNOW, MOTHER.
I KNOW HOW FATHER FEELS.
THEN PLEASE...
BUT WHAT FATHER TRULY REGRETS...
...IS NOT THE CRUEL FATE HE MET HIMSELF...

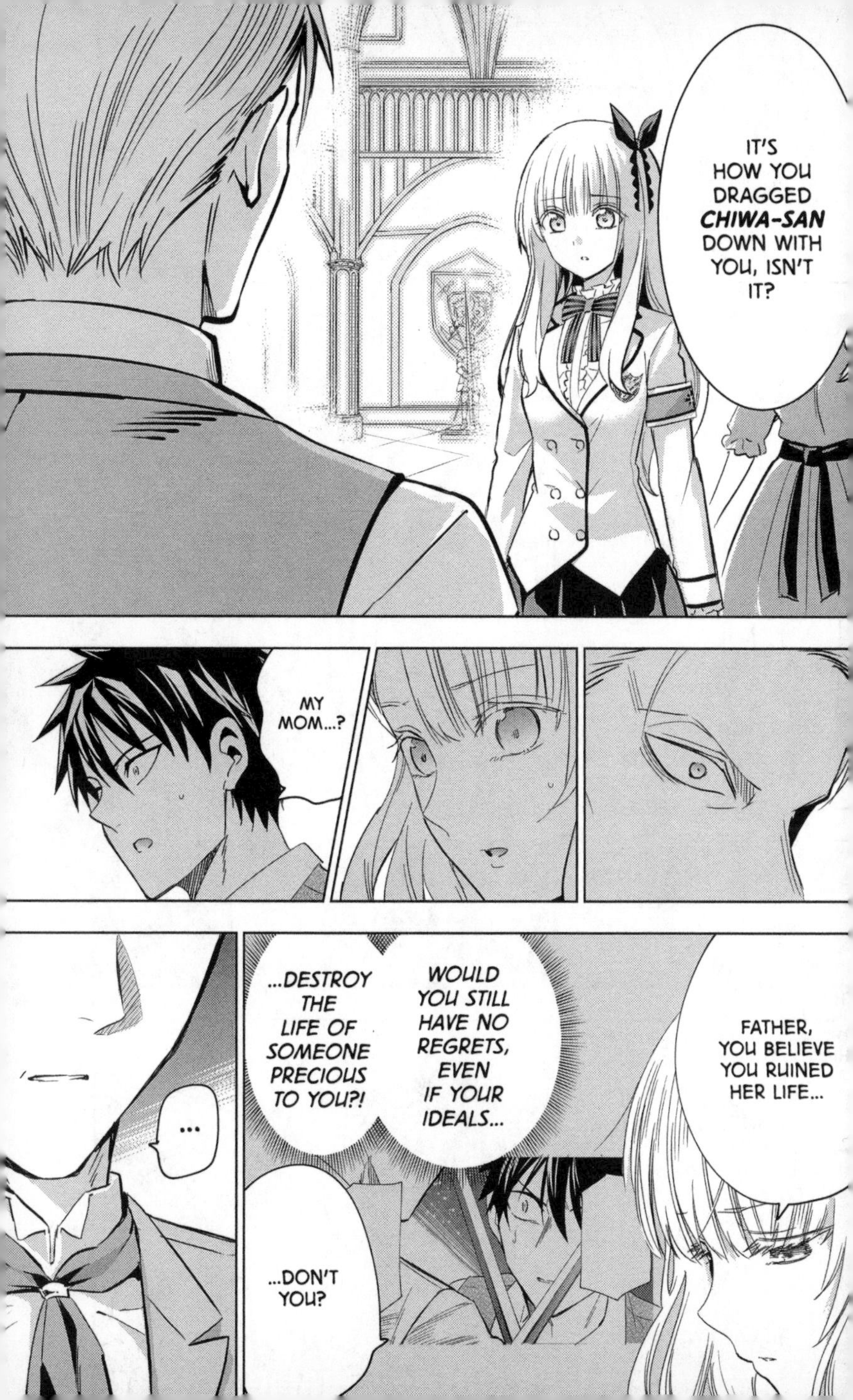
IT'S HOW YOU DRAGGED **CHIWA-SAN** DOWN WITH YOU, ISN'T IT?
MY MOM...?
FATHER, YOU BELIEVE YOU RUINED HER LIFE...
...DON'T YOU?
WOULD YOU STILL HAVE NO REGRETS, EVEN IF YOUR IDEALS...
...DESTROY THE LIFE OF SOMEONE PRECIOUS TO YOU?!
...

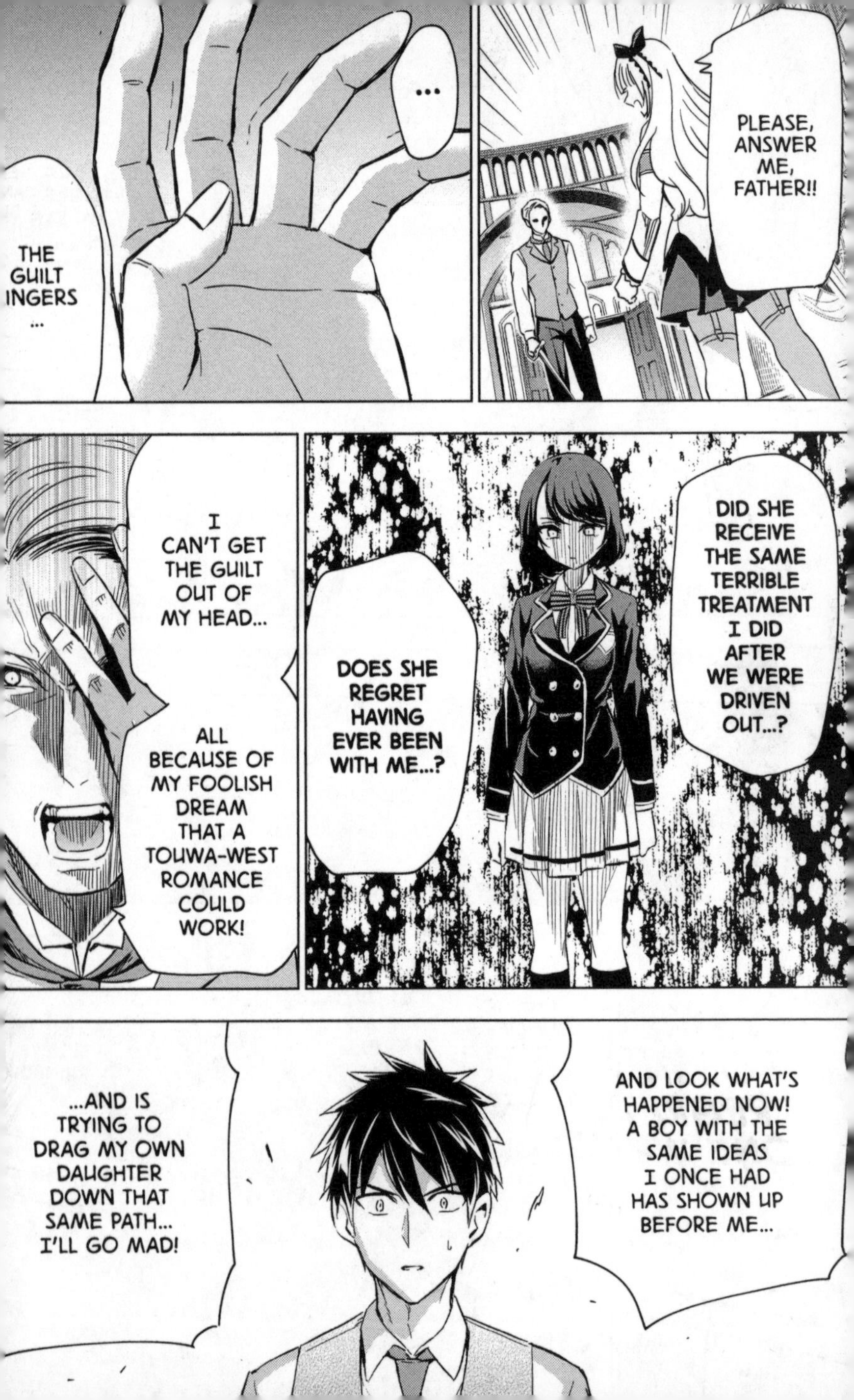
PLEASE, ANSWER ME, FATHER!!
...
THE GUILT INGERS ...
DID SHE RECEIVE THE SAME TERRIBLE TREATMENT I DID AFTER WE WERE DRIVEN OUT...?
DOES SHE REGRET HAVING EVER BEEN WITH ME...?
I CAN'T GET THE GUILT OUT OF MY HEAD...
ALL BECAUSE OF MY FOOLISH DREAM THAT A TOUWA-WEST ROMANCE COULD WORK!
AND LOOK WHAT'S HAPPENED NOW! A BOY WITH THE SAME IDEAS I ONCE HAD HAS SHOWN UP BEFORE ME...
...AND IS TRYING TO DRAG MY OWN DAUGHTER DOWN THAT SAME PATH... I'LL GO MAD!

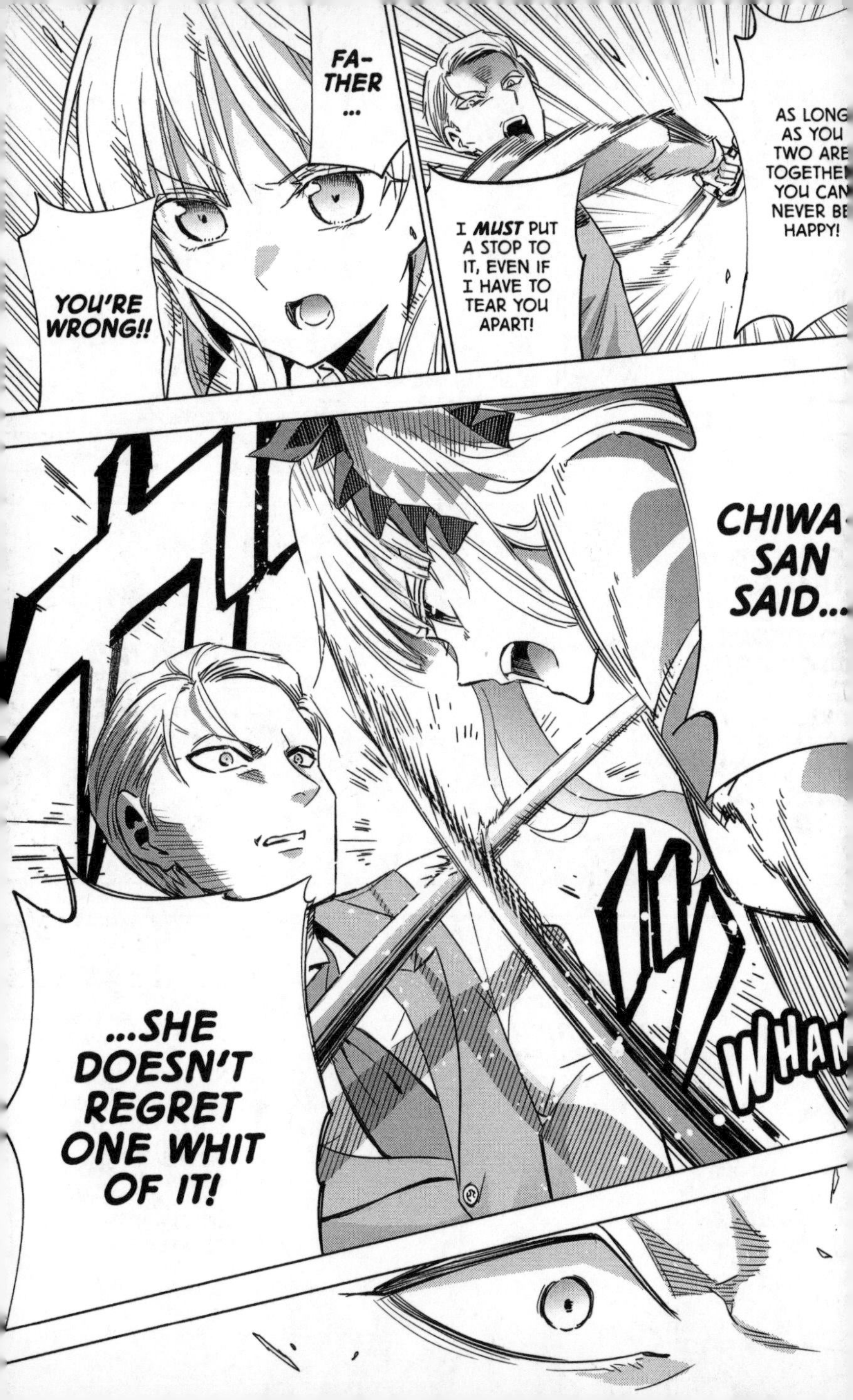
AS LONG AS YOU TWO ARE TOGETHER YOU CAN NEVER BE HAPPY!
I **MUST** PUT A STOP TO IT, EVEN IF I HAVE TO TEAR YOU APART!
FA-THER...
YOU'RE WRONG!!
CHIWA-SAN SAID...
...SHE DOESN'T REGRET ONE WHIT OF IT!
WHAM

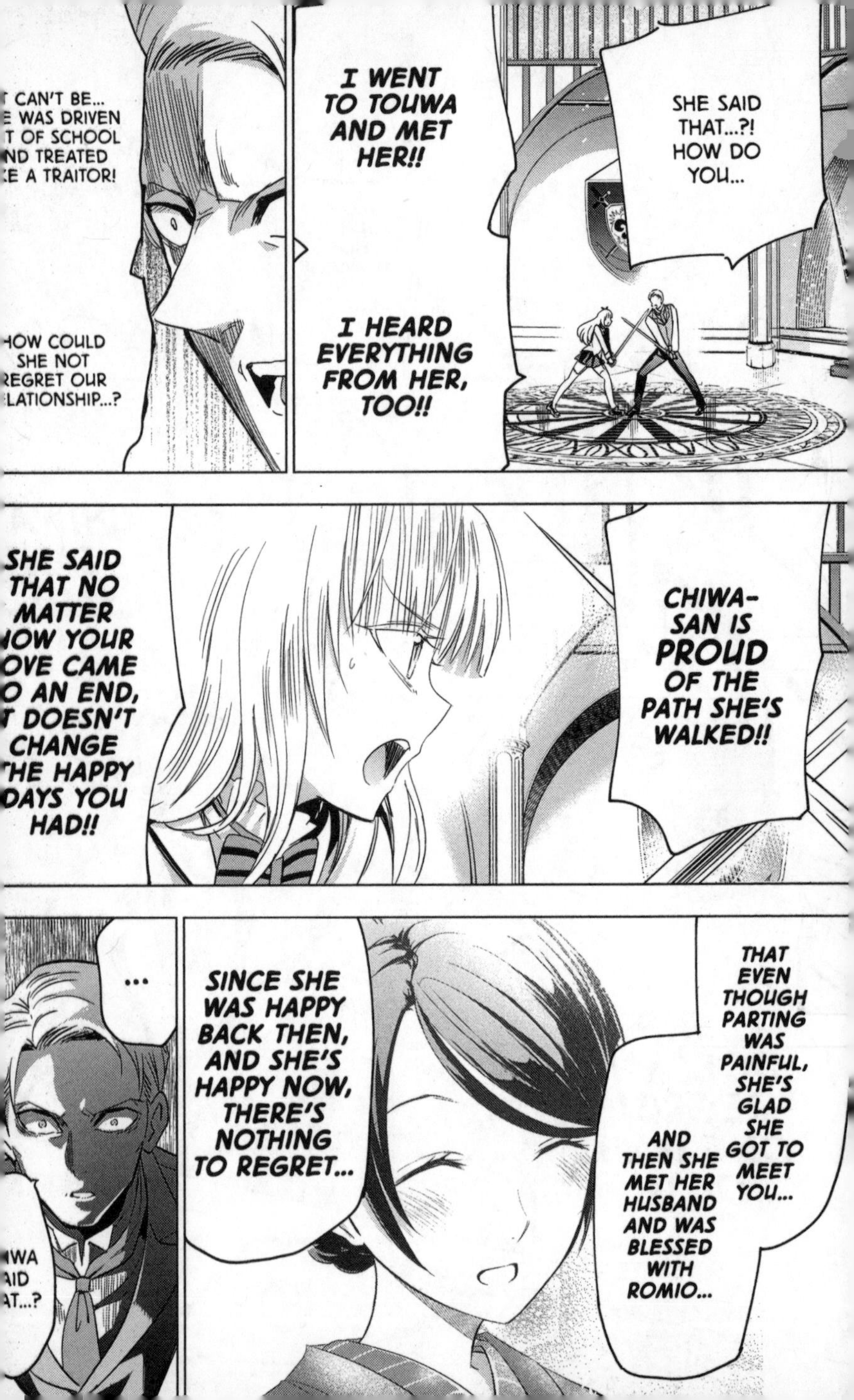
SHE SAID THAT...?! HOW DO YOU...
I WENT TO TOUWA AND MET HER!!
I HEARD EVERYTHING FROM HER, TOO!!
T CAN'T BE... E WAS DRIVEN T OF SCHOOL ND TREATED E A TRAITOR!
HOW COULD SHE NOT REGRET OUR LATIONSHIP...?
CHIWA-SAN IS PROUD OF THE PATH SHE'S WALKED!!
SHE SAID THAT NO MATTER OW YOUR OVE CAME O AN END, T DOESN'T CHANGE HE HAPPY DAYS YOU HAD!!
THAT EVEN THOUGH PARTING WAS PAINFUL, SHE'S GLAD SHE GOT TO MEET YOU...
AND THEN SHE MET HER HUSBAND AND WAS BLESSED WITH ROMIO...
SINCE SHE WAS HAPPY BACK THEN, AND SHE'S HAPPY NOW, THERE'S NOTHING TO REGRET...
...
WA AID AT...?

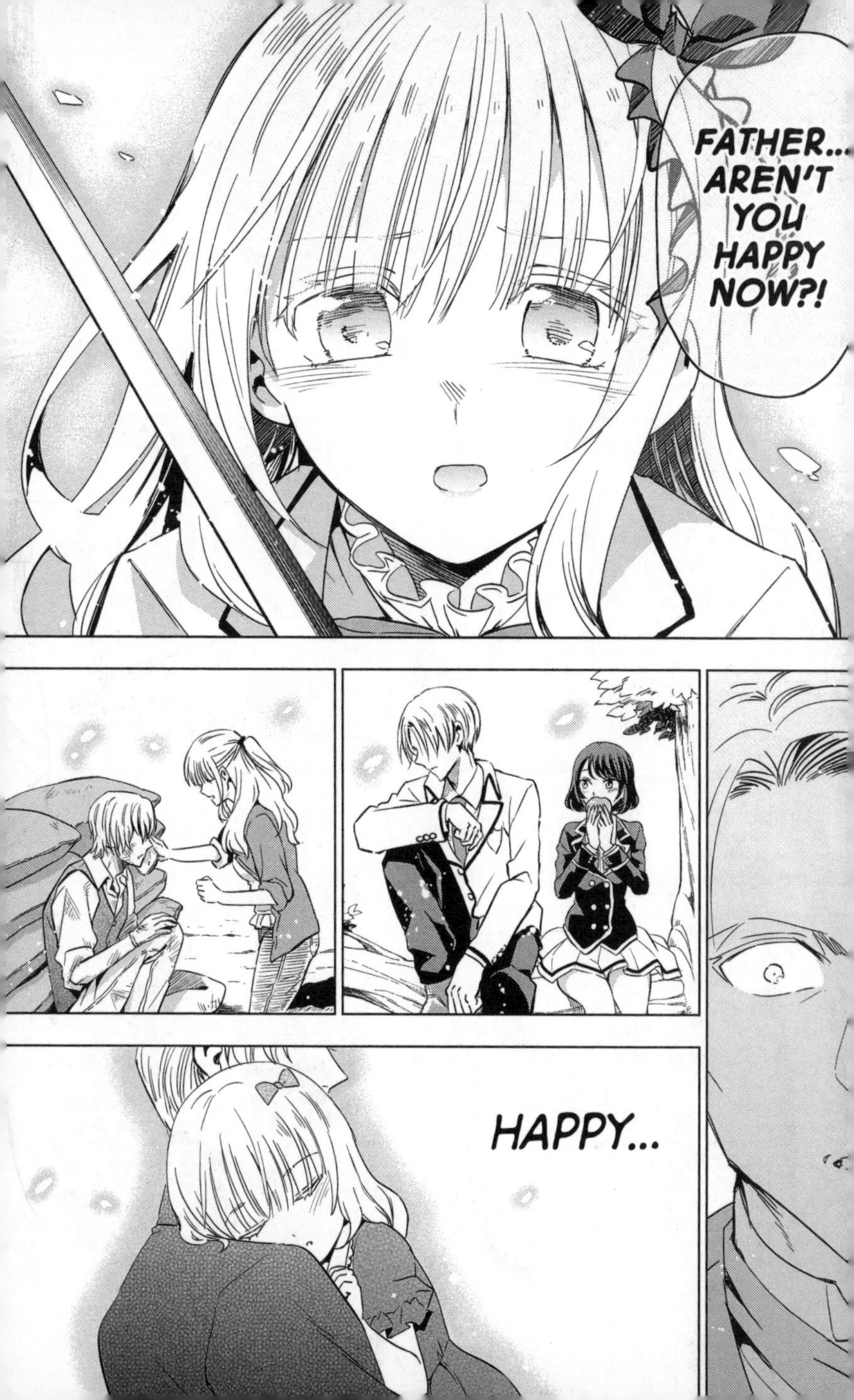
FATHER... AREN'T YOU HAPPY NOW?!
HAPPY...

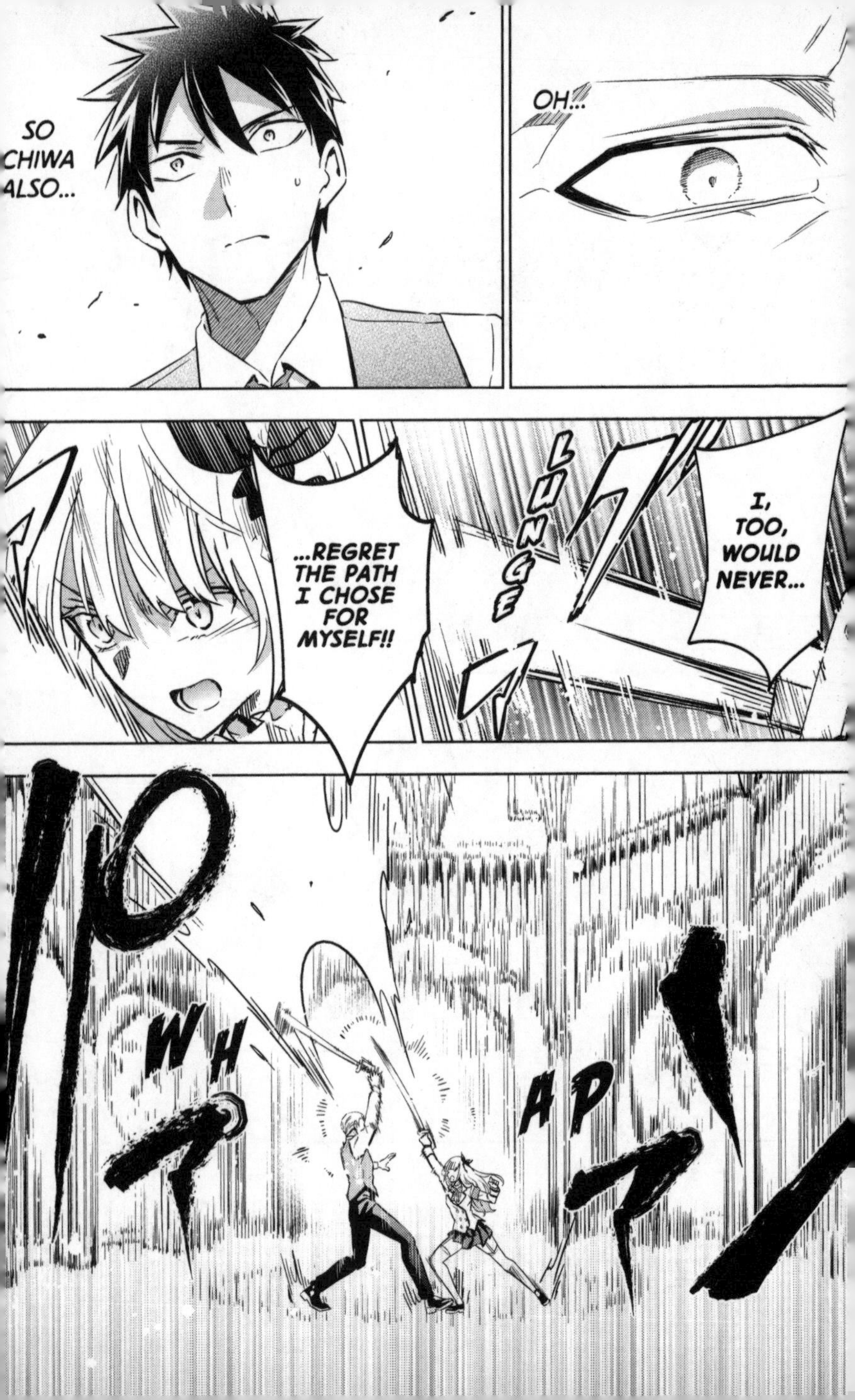
OH...
SO CHIWA ALSO...
I, TOO, WOULD NEVER...
LUNGE
...REGRET THE PATH I CHOSE FOR MYSELF!!
WHAP

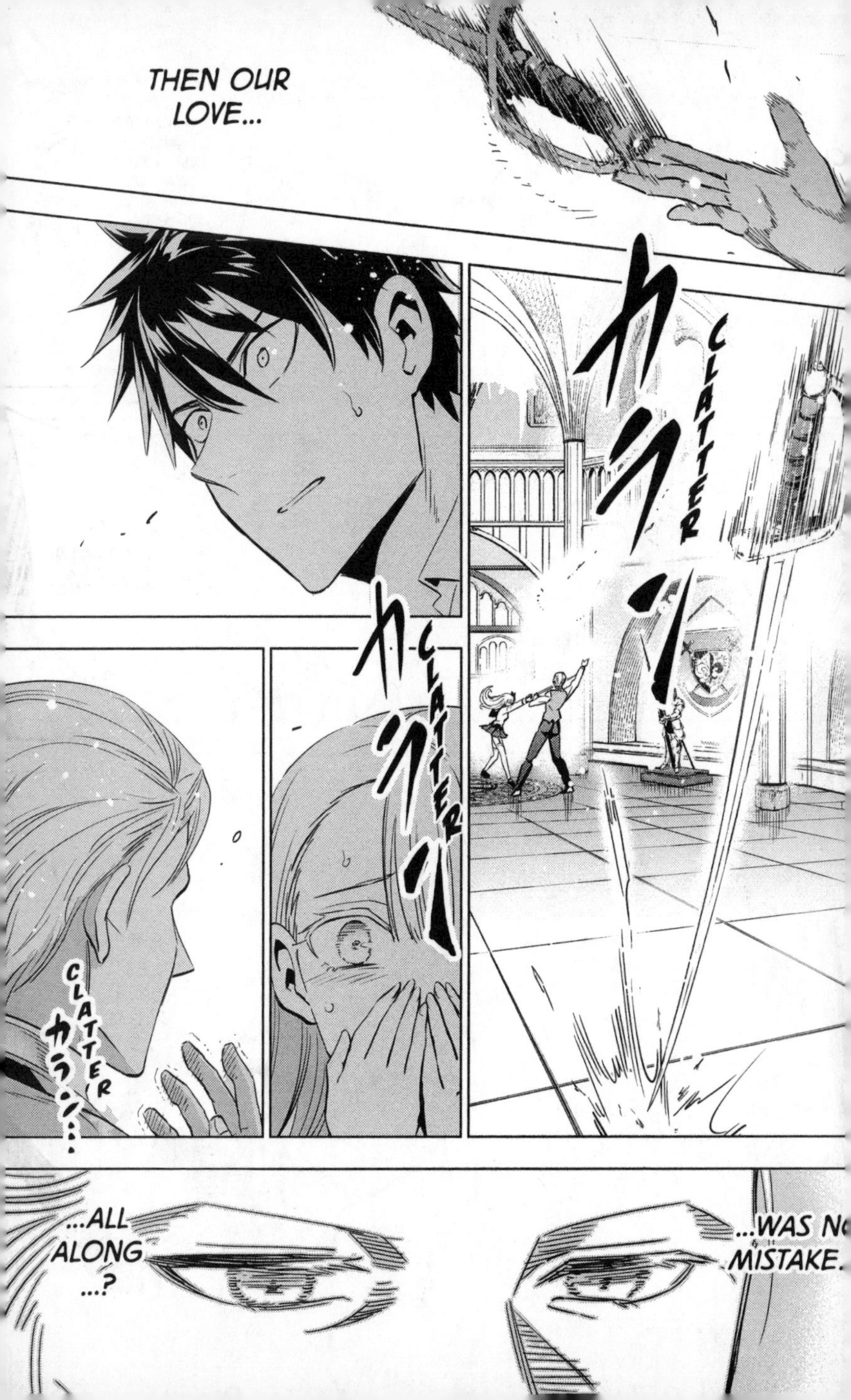
THEN OUR LOVE...
カラン
CLATTER
カラン
CLATTER
CLATTER
カラン…
...WAS NO MISTAKE.
...ALL ALONG ...?

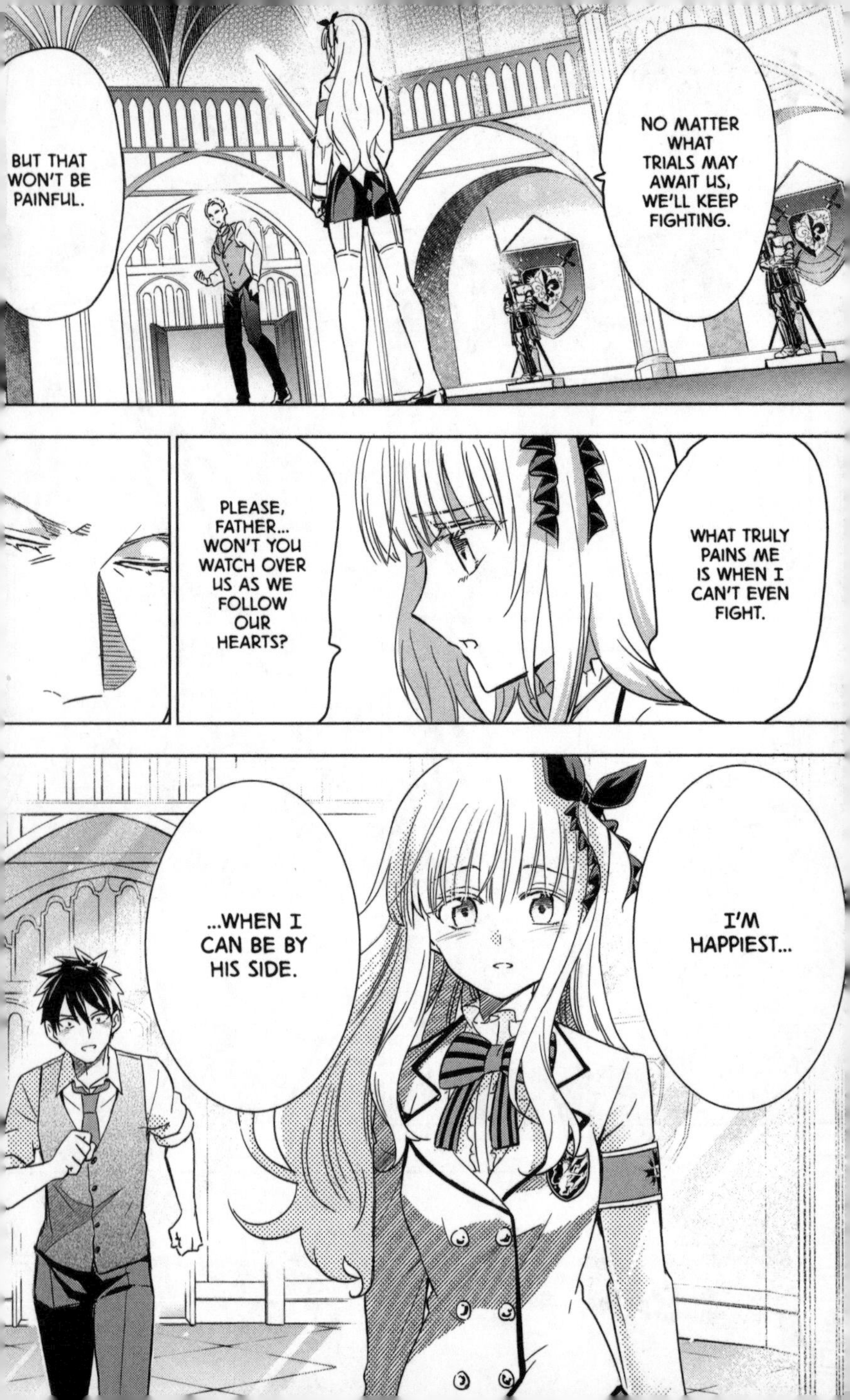
NO MATTER WHAT TRIALS MAY AWAIT US, WE'LL KEEP FIGHTING.
BUT THAT WON'T BE PAINFUL.
WHAT TRULY PAINS ME IS WHEN I CAN'T EVEN FIGHT.
PLEASE, FATHER... WON'T YOU WATCH OVER US AS WE FOLLOW OUR HEARTS?
I'M HAPPIEST...
...WHEN I CAN BE BY HIS SIDE.

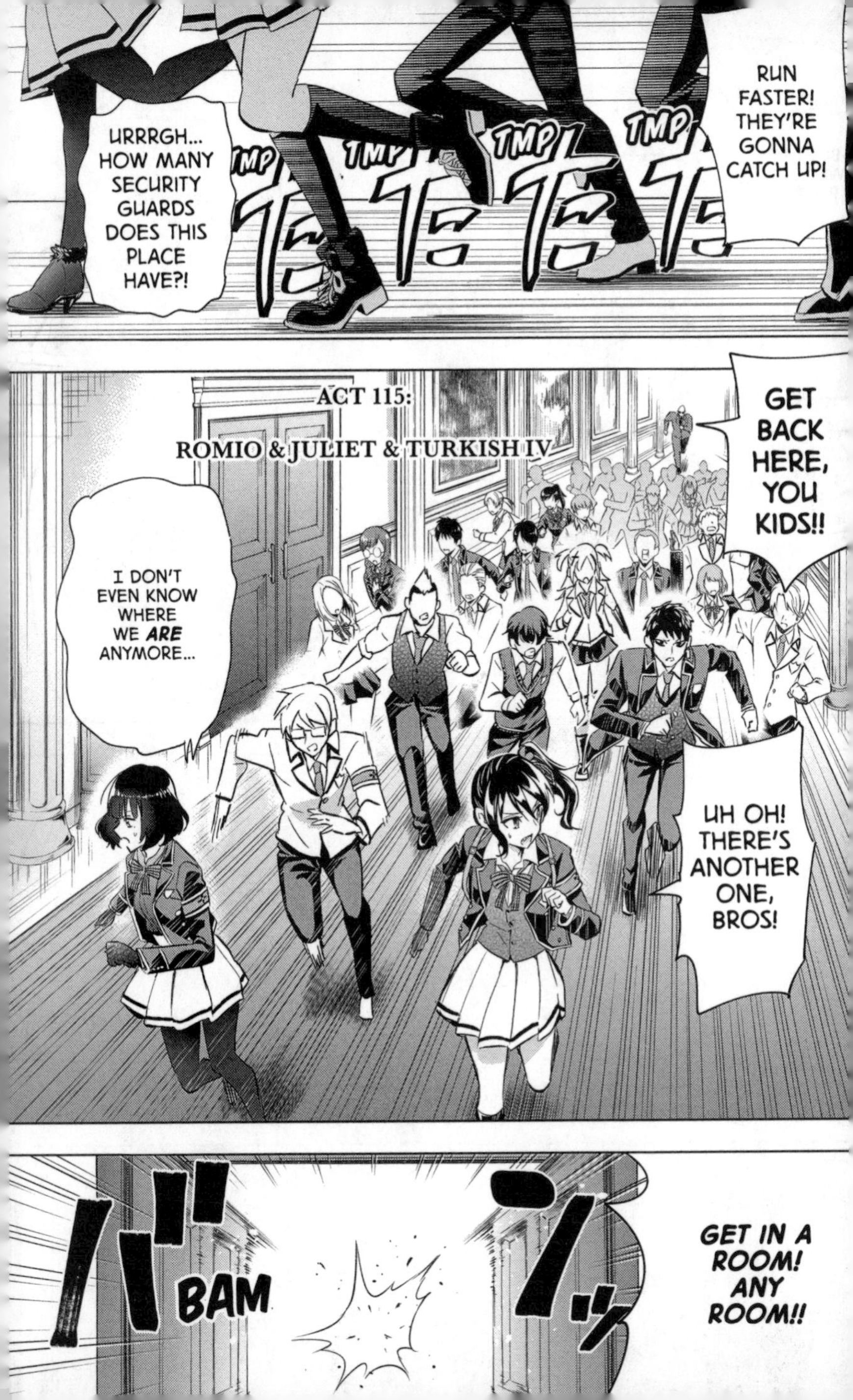
RUN FASTER! THEY'RE GONNA CATCH UP!
TMP
TMP
TMP
TMP
URRRGH... HOW MANY SECURITY GUARDS DOES THIS PLACE HAVE?!
GET BACK HERE, YOU KIDS!!
ACT 115:
ROMIO & JULIET & TURKISH IV
I DON'T EVEN KNOW WHERE WE *ARE* ANYMORE...
UH OH! THERE'S ANOTHER ONE, BROS!
GET IN A ROOM! ANY ROOM!!
BAM

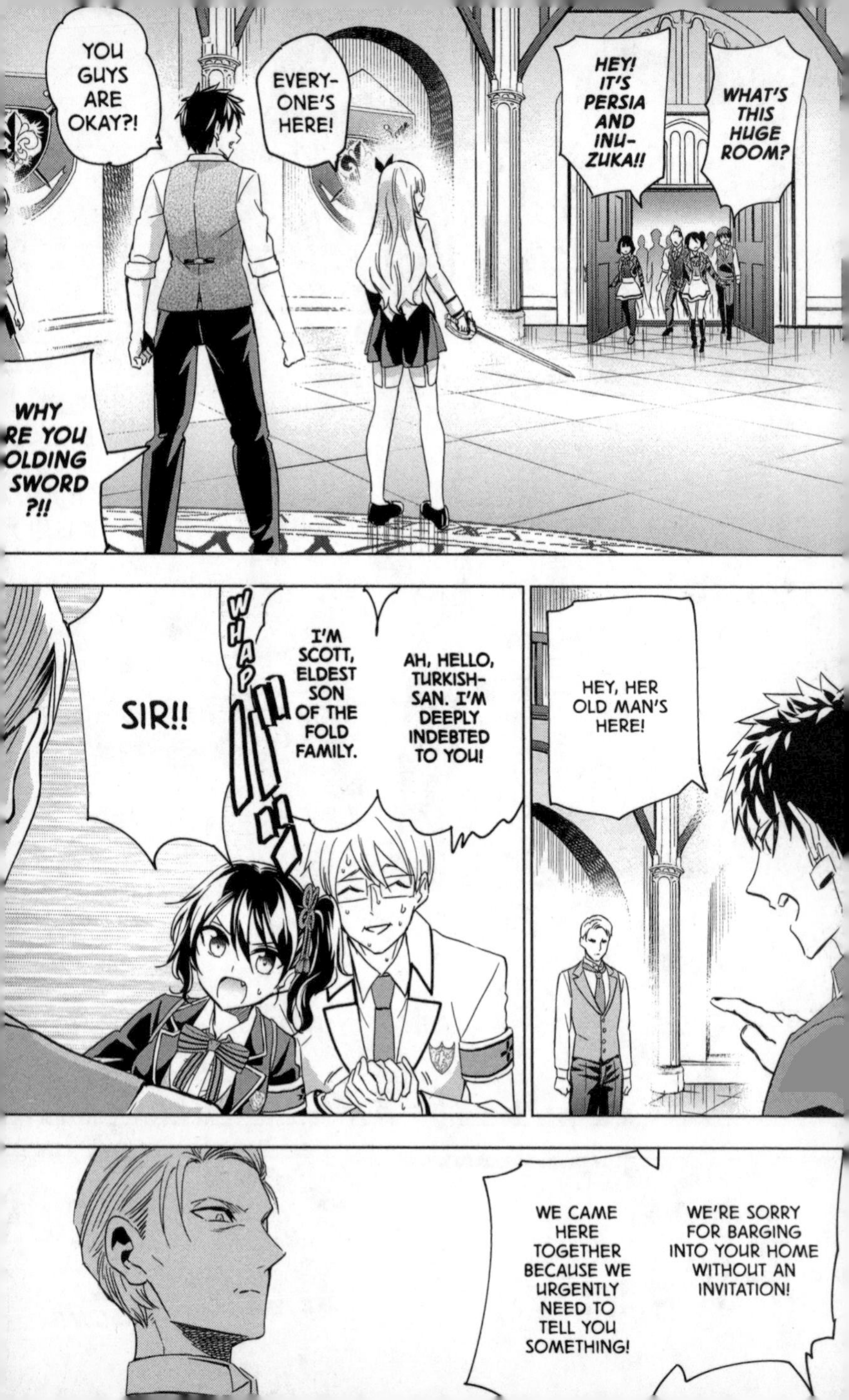
WHAT'S THIS HUGE ROOM?
HEY! IT'S PERSIA AND INU-ZUKA!!
EVERY-ONE'S HERE!
YOU GUYS ARE OKAY?!
WHY RE YOU OLDING SWORD ?!!
HEY, HER OLD MAN'S HERE!
AH, HELLO, TURKISH-SAN. I'M DEEPLY INDEBTED TO YOU!
I'M SCOTT, ELDEST SON OF THE FOLD FAMILY.
WHAP
SIR!!
WE'RE SORRY FOR BARGING INTO YOUR HOME WITHOUT AN INVITATION!
WE CAME HERE TOGETHER BECAUSE WE URGENTLY NEED TO TELL YOU SOMETHING!

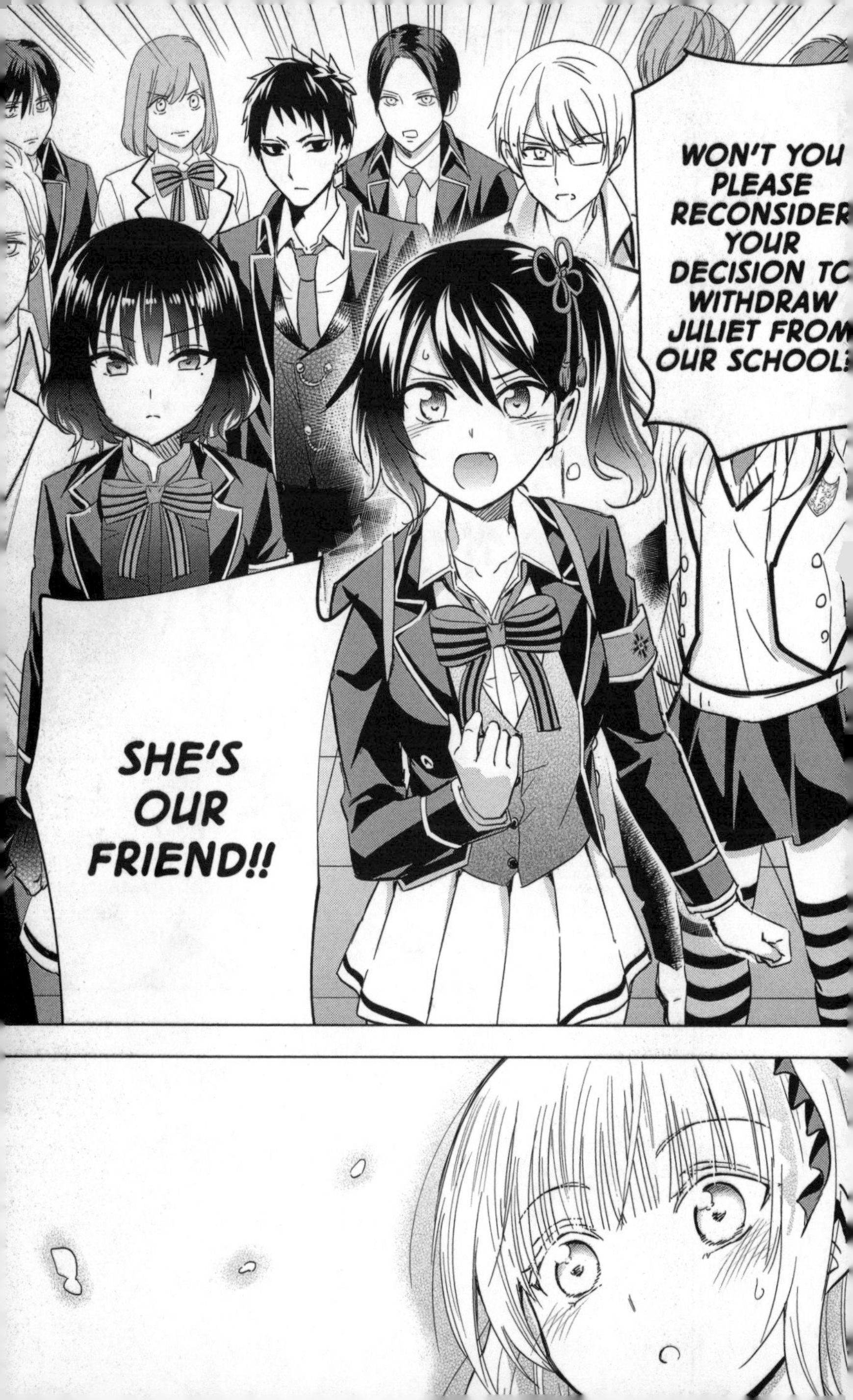
WON'T YOU PLEASE RECONSIDER YOUR DECISION TO WITHDRAW JULIET FROM OUR SCHOOL!?
SHE'S OUR FRIEND!!

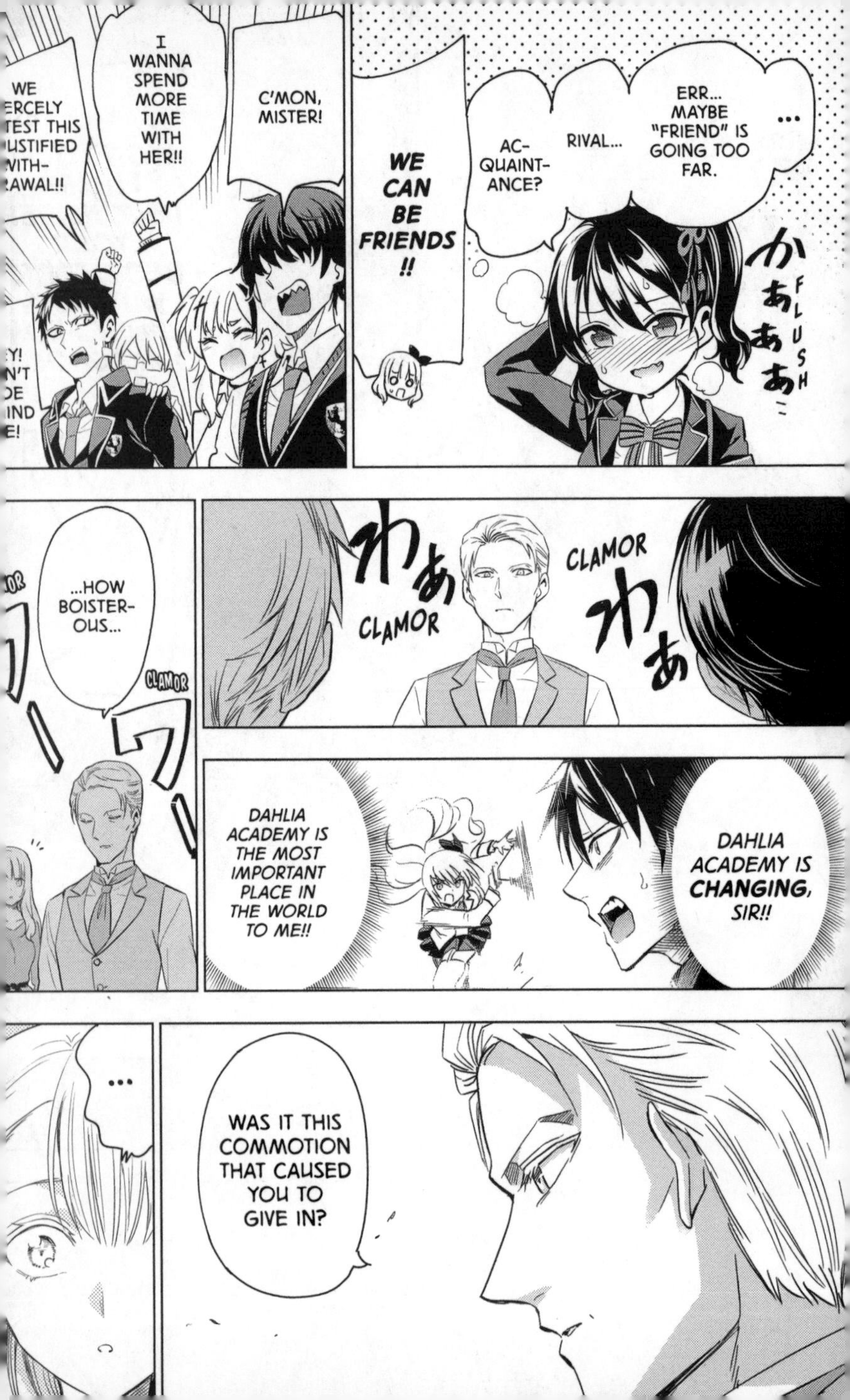
...
ERR... MAYBE "FRIEND" IS GOING TOO FAR.
RIVAL...
AC-QUAINT-ANCE?
かあぁぁ
FLUSH
WE CAN BE FRIENDS!!
C'MON, MISTER!
I WANNA SPEND MORE TIME WITH HER!!
WE ERCELY TEST THIS USTIFIED WITH- AWAL!!
Y! N'T DE IND E!
わあ
CLAMOR
CLAMOR
わあ
...HOW BOISTER-OUS...
CLAMOR
DAHLIA ACADEMY IS CHANGING, SIR!!
DAHLIA ACADEMY IS THE MOST IMPORTANT PLACE IN THE WORLD TO ME!!
WAS IT THIS COMMOTION THAT CAUSED YOU TO GIVE IN?
...

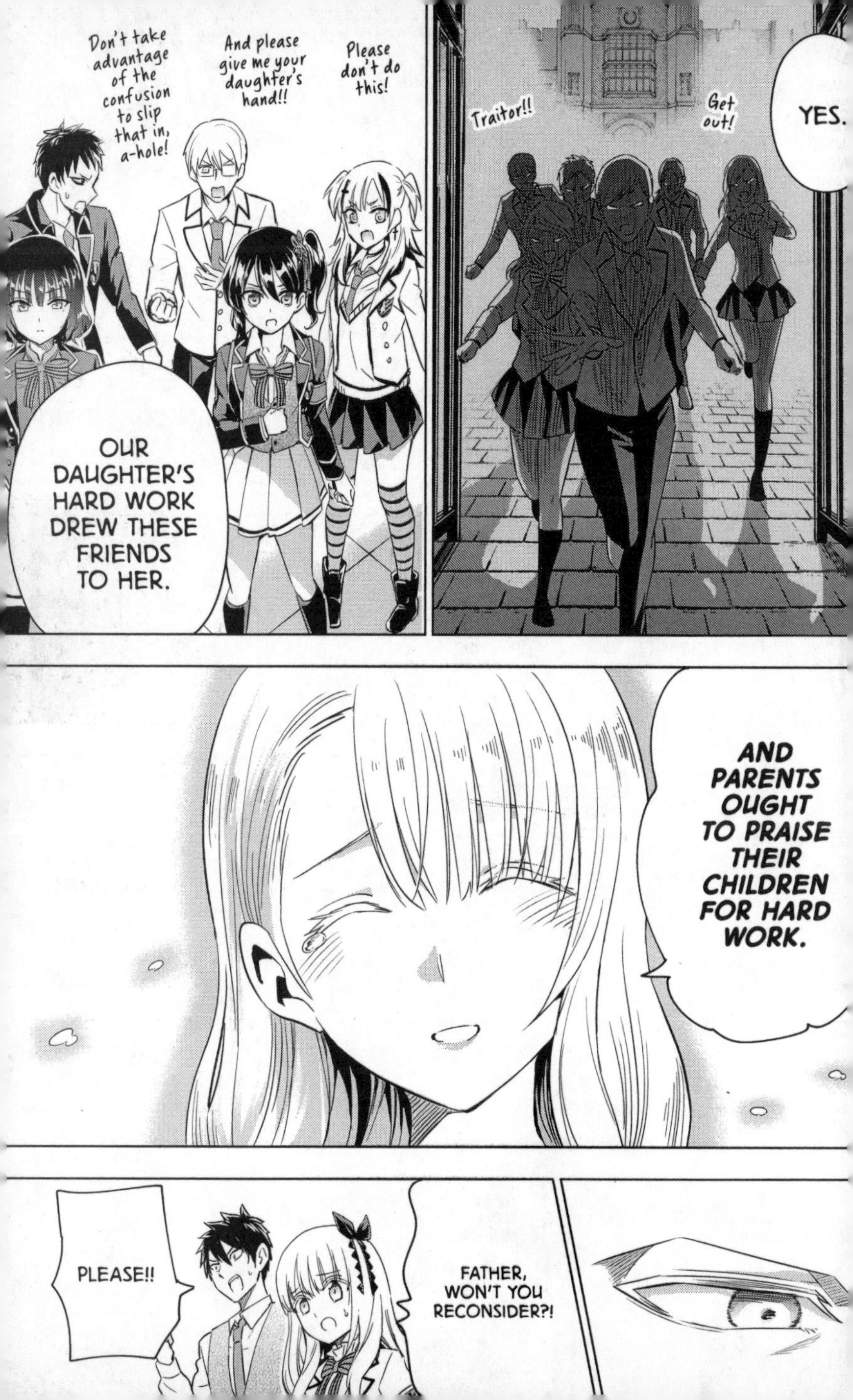
YES.
Get out!
Traitor!!
Please don't do this!
And please give me your daughter's hand!!
Don't take advantage of the confusion to slip that in, a-hole!
OUR DAUGHTER'S HARD WORK DREW THESE FRIENDS TO HER.
AND PARENTS OUGHT TO PRAISE THEIR CHILDREN FOR HARD WORK.
FATHER, WON'T YOU RECONSIDER?!
PLEASE!!

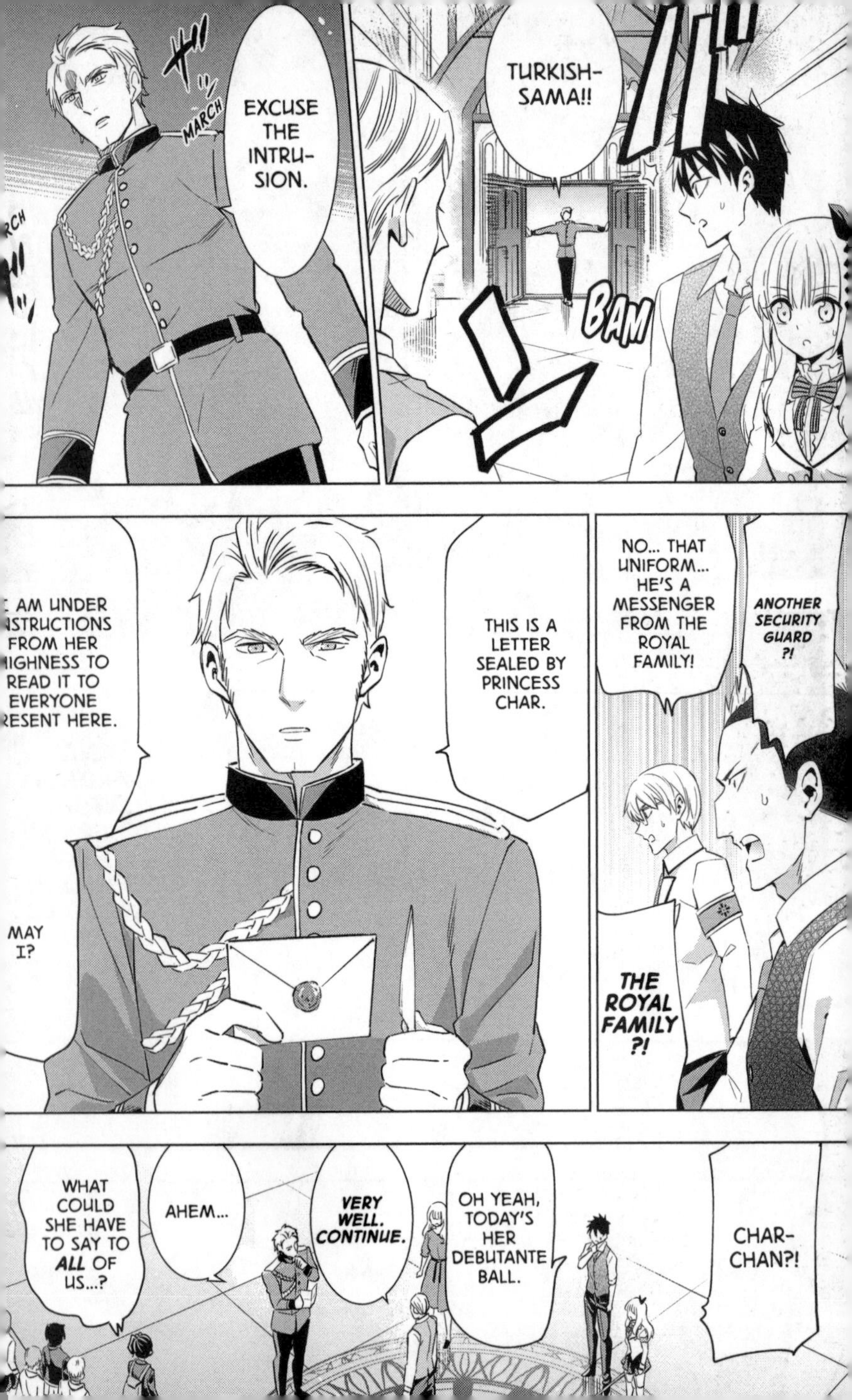
TURKISH-SAMA!!
BAM
MARCH
EXCUSE THE INTRU-SION.
MARCH
ANOTHER SECURITY GUARD?!
NO... THAT UNIFORM... HE'S A MESSENGER FROM THE ROYAL FAMILY!
THE ROYAL FAMILY?!
THIS IS A LETTER SEALED BY PRINCESS CHAR.
I AM UNDER INSTRUCTIONS FROM HER HIGHNESS TO READ IT TO EVERYONE PRESENT HERE.
MAY I?
CHAR-CHAN?!
OH YEAH, TODAY'S HER DEBUTANTE BALL.
VERY WELL. CONTINUE.
AHEM...
WHAT COULD SHE HAVE TO SAY TO ALL OF US...?

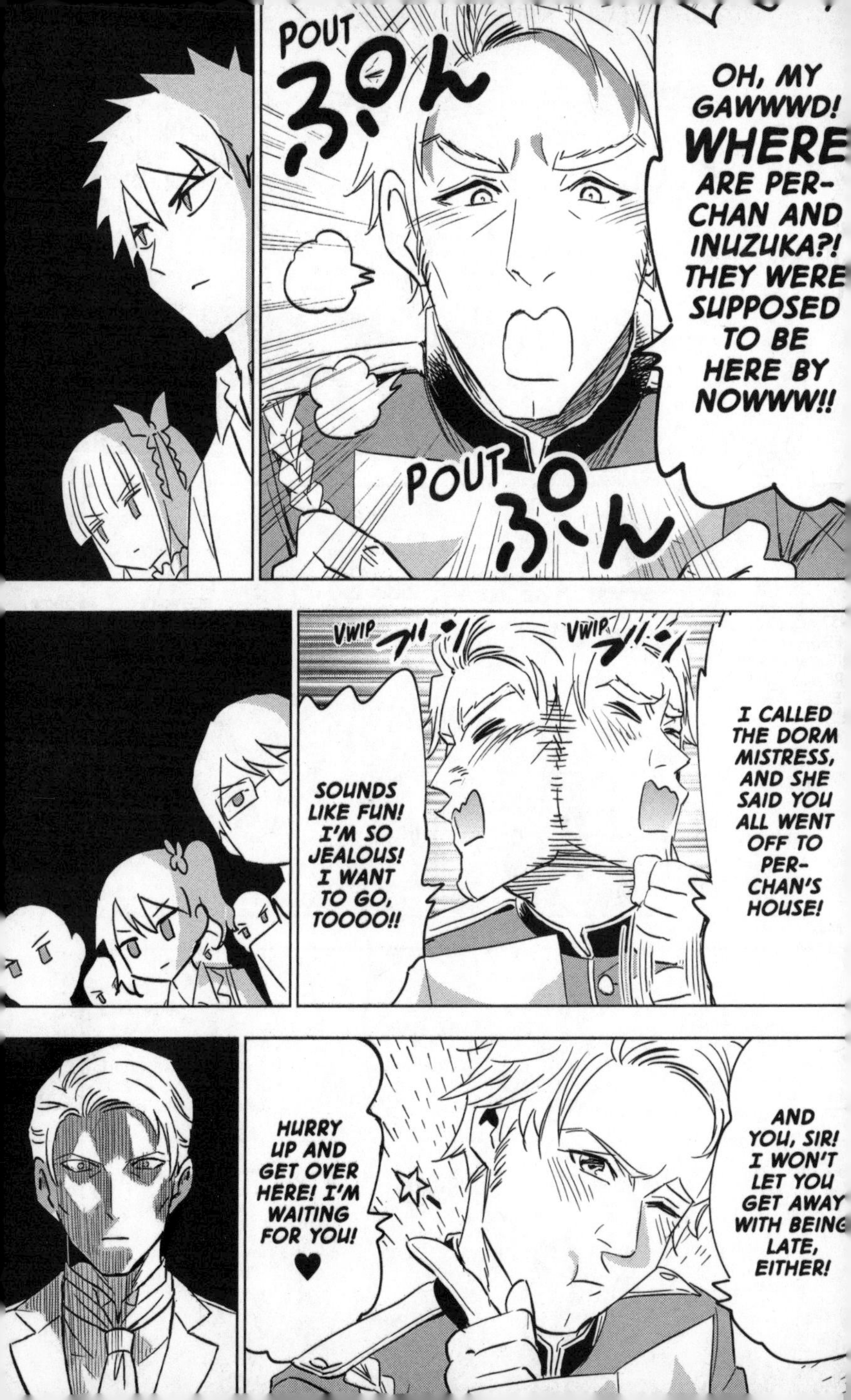
OH, MY GAWWWD! WHERE ARE PER-CHAN AND INUZUKA?! THEY WERE SUPPOSED TO BE HERE BY NOWWW!!
POUT ぷん
POUT ぷん
VWIP
VWIP
I CALLED THE DORM MISTRESS, AND SHE SAID YOU ALL WENT OFF TO PER-CHAN'S HOUSE!
SOUNDS LIKE FUN! I'M SO JEALOUS! I WANT TO GO, TOOOO!!
AND YOU, SIR! I WON'T LET YOU GET AWAY WITH BEING LATE, EITHER!
HURRY UP AND GET OVER HERE! I'M WAITING FOR YOU! ♥

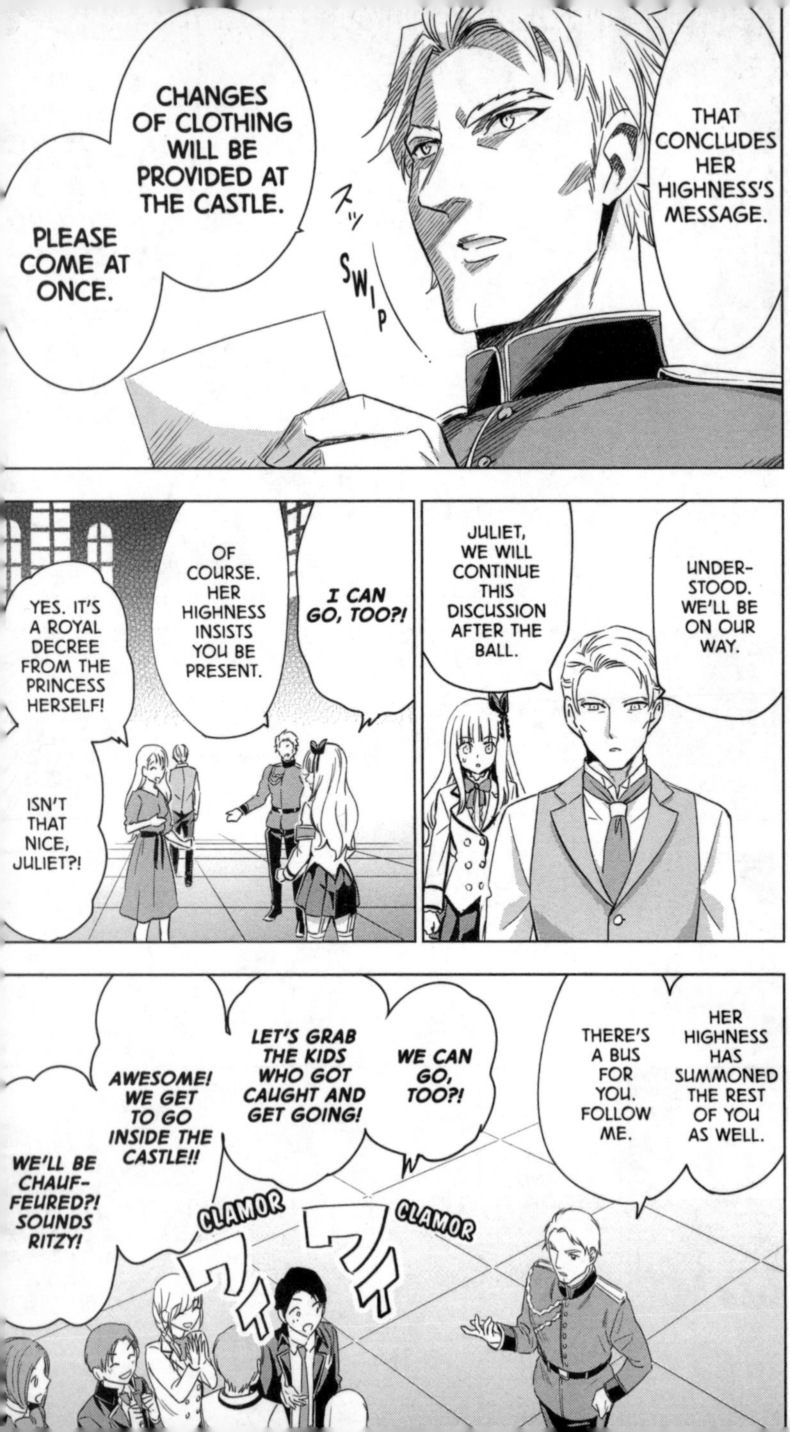

THAT CONCLUDES HER HIGHNESS'S MESSAGE.
スッ
SWIP
CHANGES OF CLOTHING WILL BE PROVIDED AT THE CASTLE.
PLEASE COME AT ONCE.
UNDERSTOOD. WE'LL BE ON OUR WAY.
JULIET, WE WILL CONTINUE THIS DISCUSSION AFTER THE BALL.
I CAN GO, TOO?!
OF COURSE. HER HIGHNESS INSISTS YOU BE PRESENT.
YES. IT'S A ROYAL DECREE FROM THE PRINCESS HERSELF!
ISN'T THAT NICE, JULIET?!
HER HIGHNESS HAS SUMMONED THE REST OF YOU AS WELL.
THERE'S A BUS FOR YOU. FOLLOW ME.
WE CAN GO, TOO?!
LET'S GRAB THE KIDS WHO GOT CAUGHT AND GET GOING!
AWESOME! WE GET TO GO INSIDE THE CASTLE!!
WE'LL BE CHAUFFEURED?! SOUNDS RITZY!
ワイ
CLAMOR
ワイ
CLAMOR

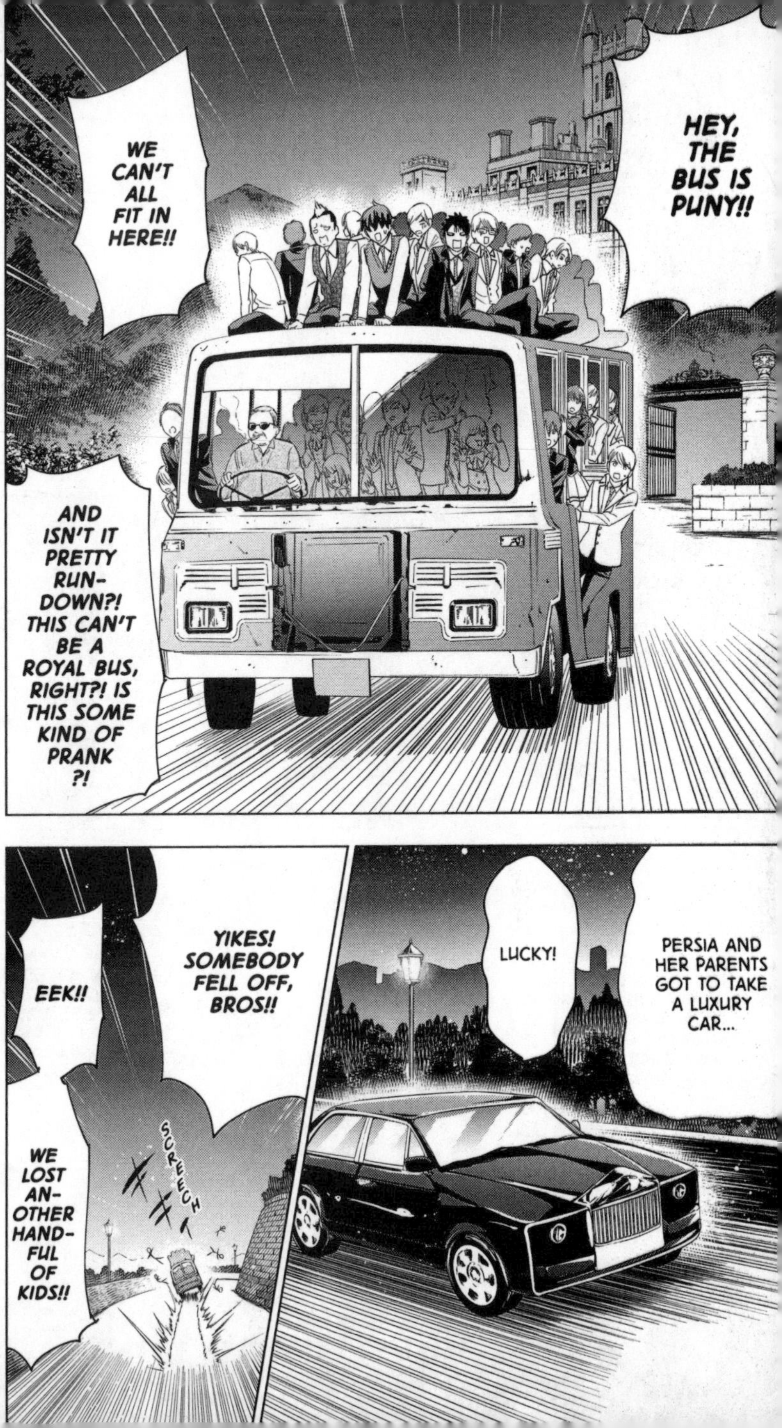
HEY, THE BUS IS PUNY!!
WE CAN'T ALL FIT IN HERE!!
AND ISN'T IT PRETTY RUN-DOWN?! THIS CAN'T BE A ROYAL BUS, RIGHT?! IS THIS SOME KIND OF PRANK ?!
PERSIA AND HER PARENTS GOT TO TAKE A LUXURY CAR...
LUCKY!
YIKES! SOMEBODY FELL OFF, BROS!!
EEK!!
SCREECH
WE LOST AN-OTHER HAND-FUL OF KIDS!!

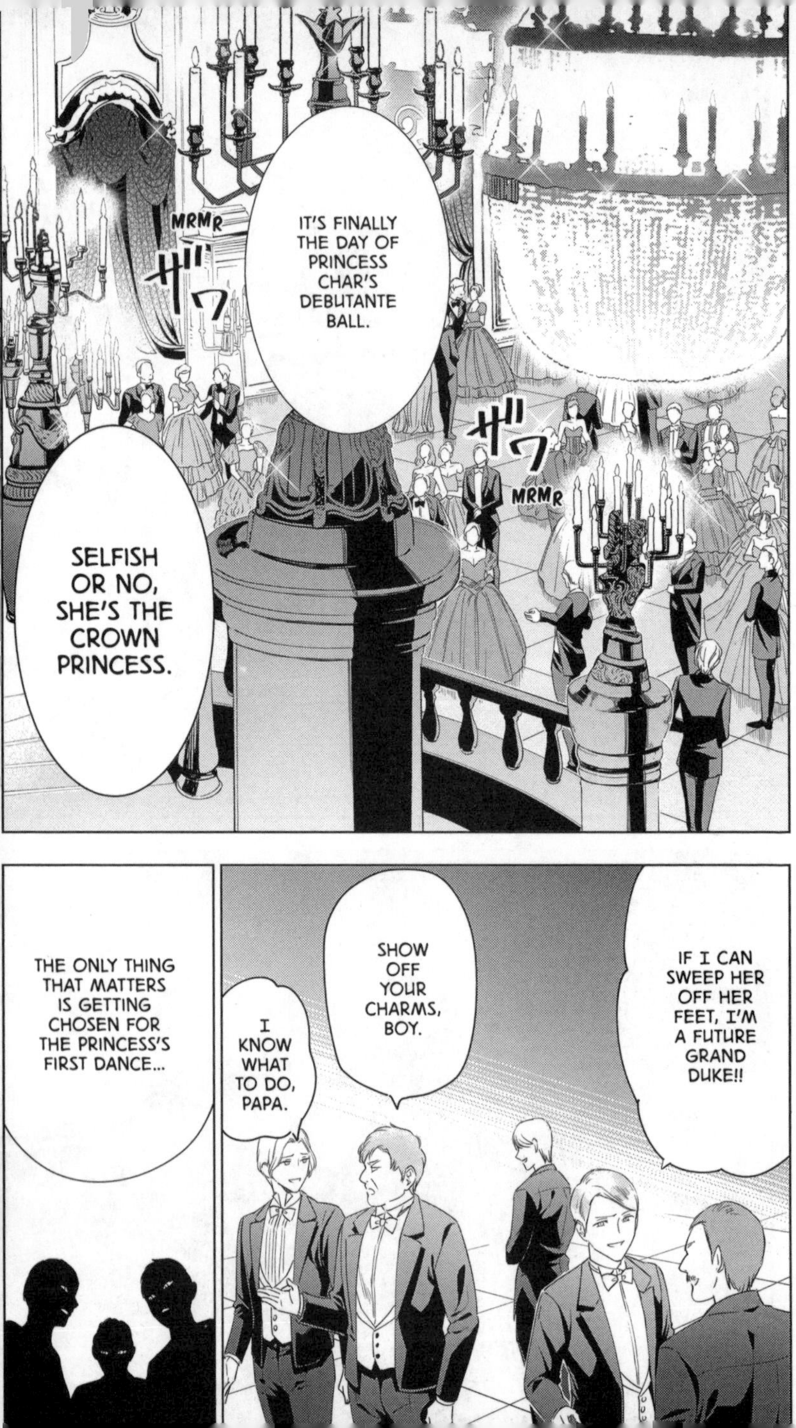
IT'S FINALLY THE DAY OF PRINCESS CHAR'S DEBUTANTE BALL.
ザワ
MRMR
MRMR
ザワ
SELFISH OR NO, SHE'S THE CROWN PRINCESS.
IF I CAN SWEEP HER OFF HER FEET, I'M A FUTURE GRAND DUKE!!
SHOW OFF YOUR CHARMS, BOY.
I KNOW WHAT TO DO, PAPA.
THE ONLY THING THAT MATTERS IS GETTING CHOSEN FOR THE PRINCESS'S FIRST DANCE...

THE PRINCESS'S FIRST CHOICE...

...WILL BE THE MAN SHE WAS INSTANTLY SMITTEN WITH...

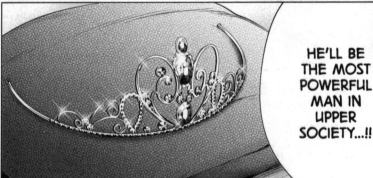

HE'LL BE THE MOST POWERFUL MAN IN UPPER SOCIETY...!!

VROOOOO!!

LOOK! YOU CAN SEE IT NOW!!

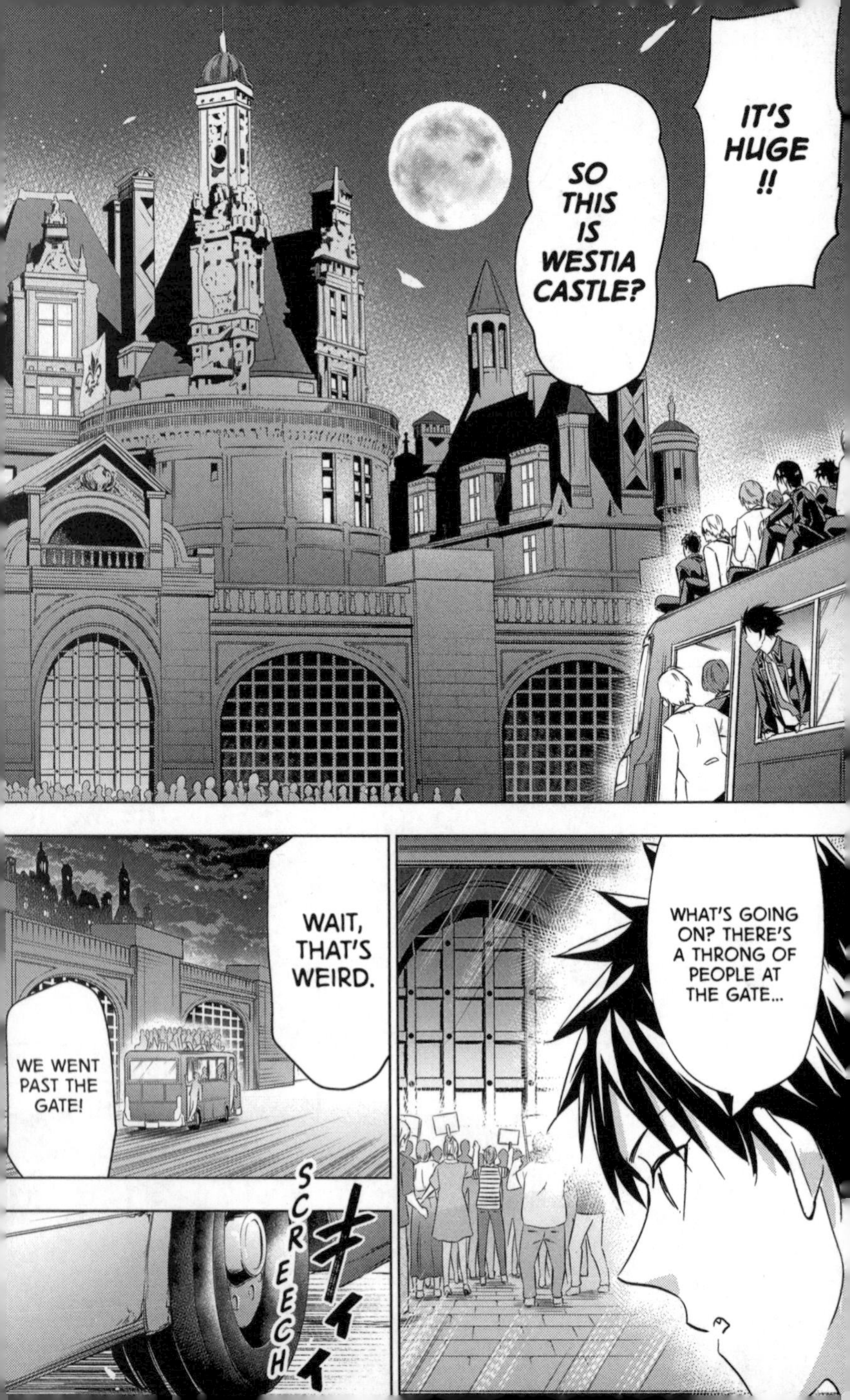
IT'S HUGE !!
SO THIS IS WESTIA CASTLE?
WHAT'S GOING ON? THERE'S A THRONG OF PEOPLE AT THE GATE...
WAIT, THAT'S WEIRD.
WE WENT PAST THE GATE!
SCREECH

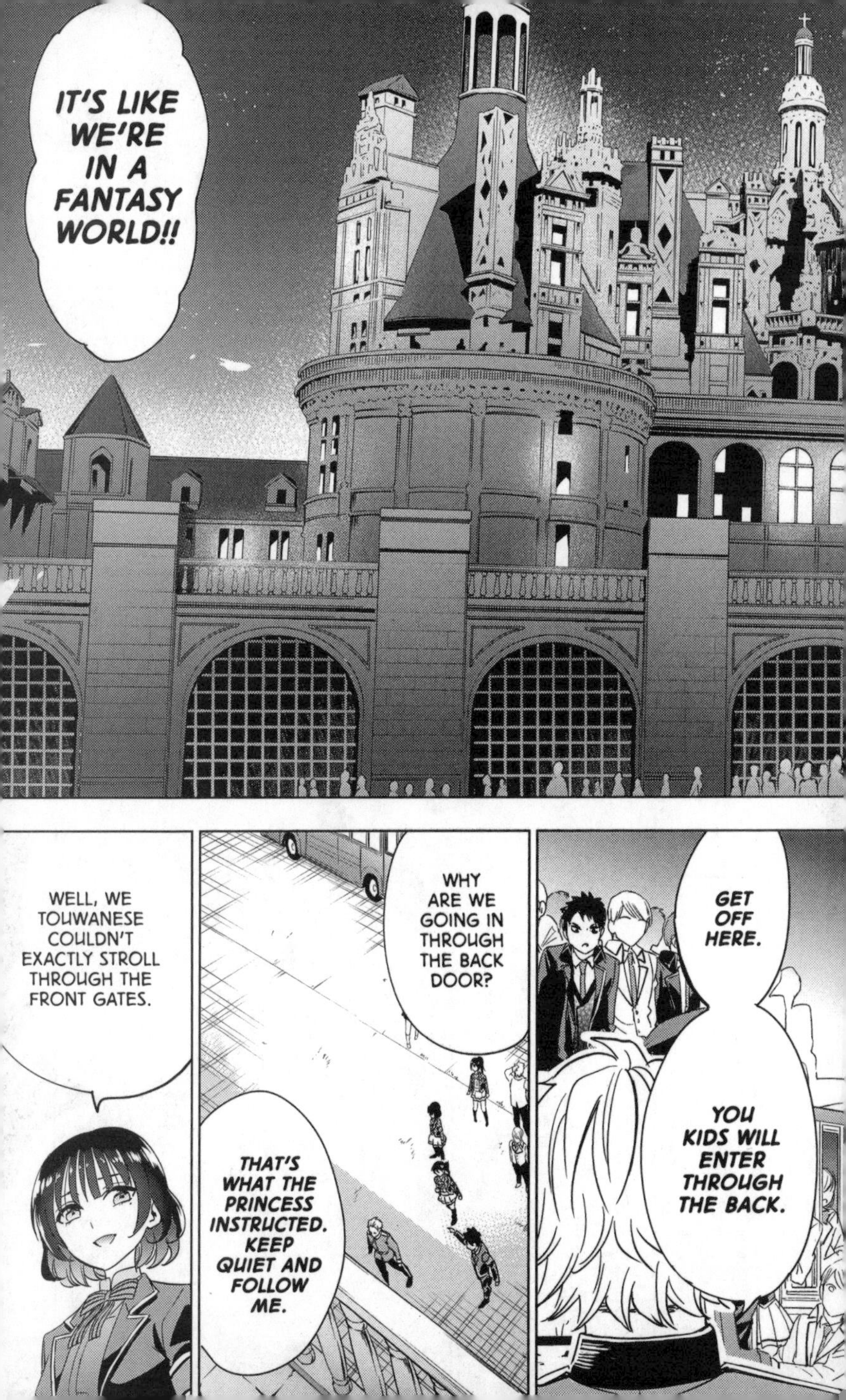
IT'S LIKE WE'RE IN A FANTASY WORLD!!
GET OFF HERE.
YOU KIDS WILL ENTER THROUGH THE BACK.
WHY ARE WE GOING IN THROUGH THE BACK DOOR?
THAT'S WHAT THE PRINCESS INSTRUCTED. KEEP QUIET AND FOLLOW ME.
WELL, WE TOUWANESE COULDN'T EXACTLY STROLL THROUGH THE FRONT GATES.

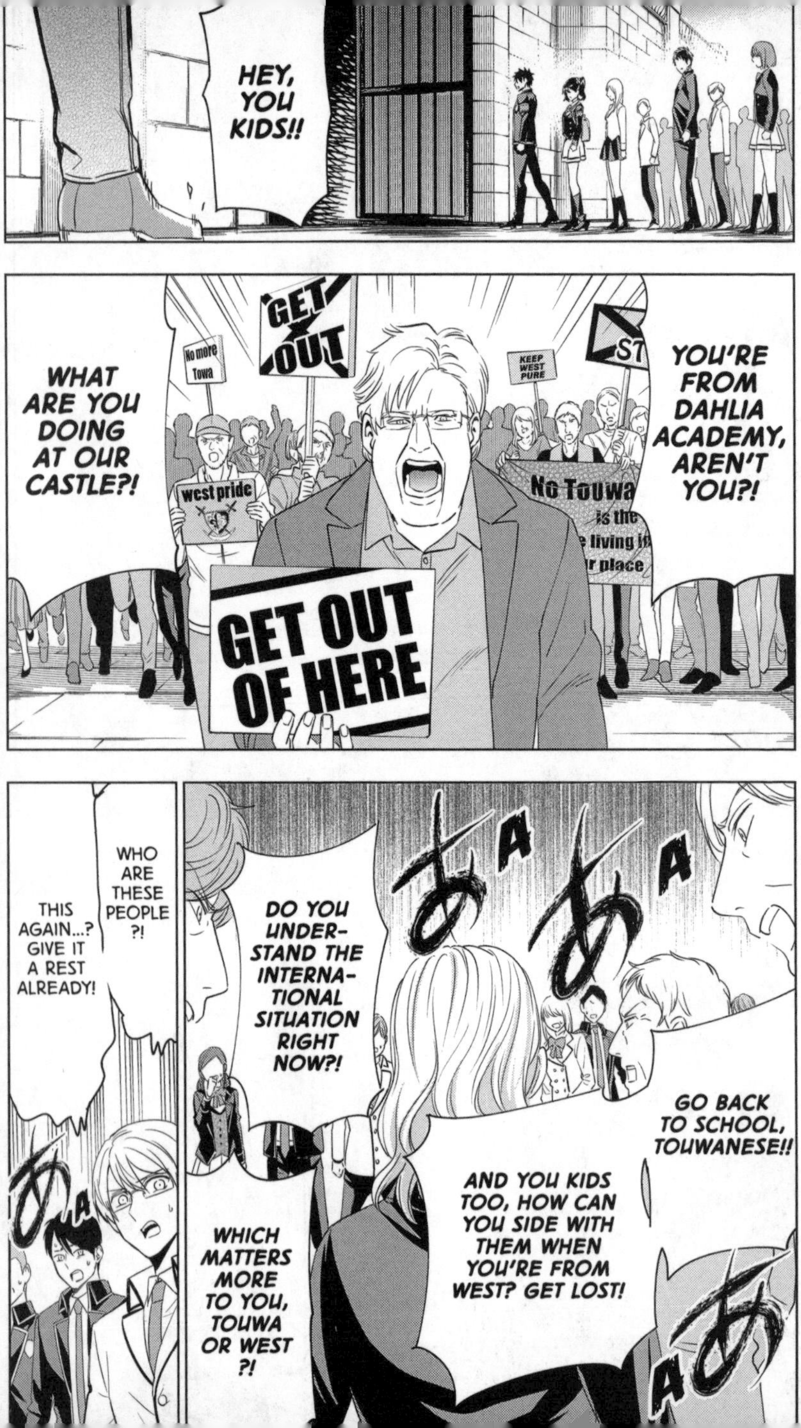
HEY, YOU KIDS!!
YOU'RE FROM DAHLIA ACADEMY, AREN'T YOU?!
WHAT ARE YOU DOING AT OUR CASTLE?!
GET OUT
KEEP WEST PURE
No more Towa
west pride
No Touwa
GET OUT OF HERE
あA
あA
DO YOU UNDER-STAND THE INTERNA-TIONAL SITUATION RIGHT NOW?!
GO BACK TO SCHOOL, TOUWANESE!!
AND YOU KIDS TOO, HOW CAN YOU SIDE WITH THEM WHEN YOU'RE FROM WEST? GET LOST!
WHICH MATTERS MORE TO YOU, TOUWA OR WEST?!
あA
WHO ARE THESE PEOPLE?!
THIS AGAIN...? GIVE IT A REST ALREADY!
あA

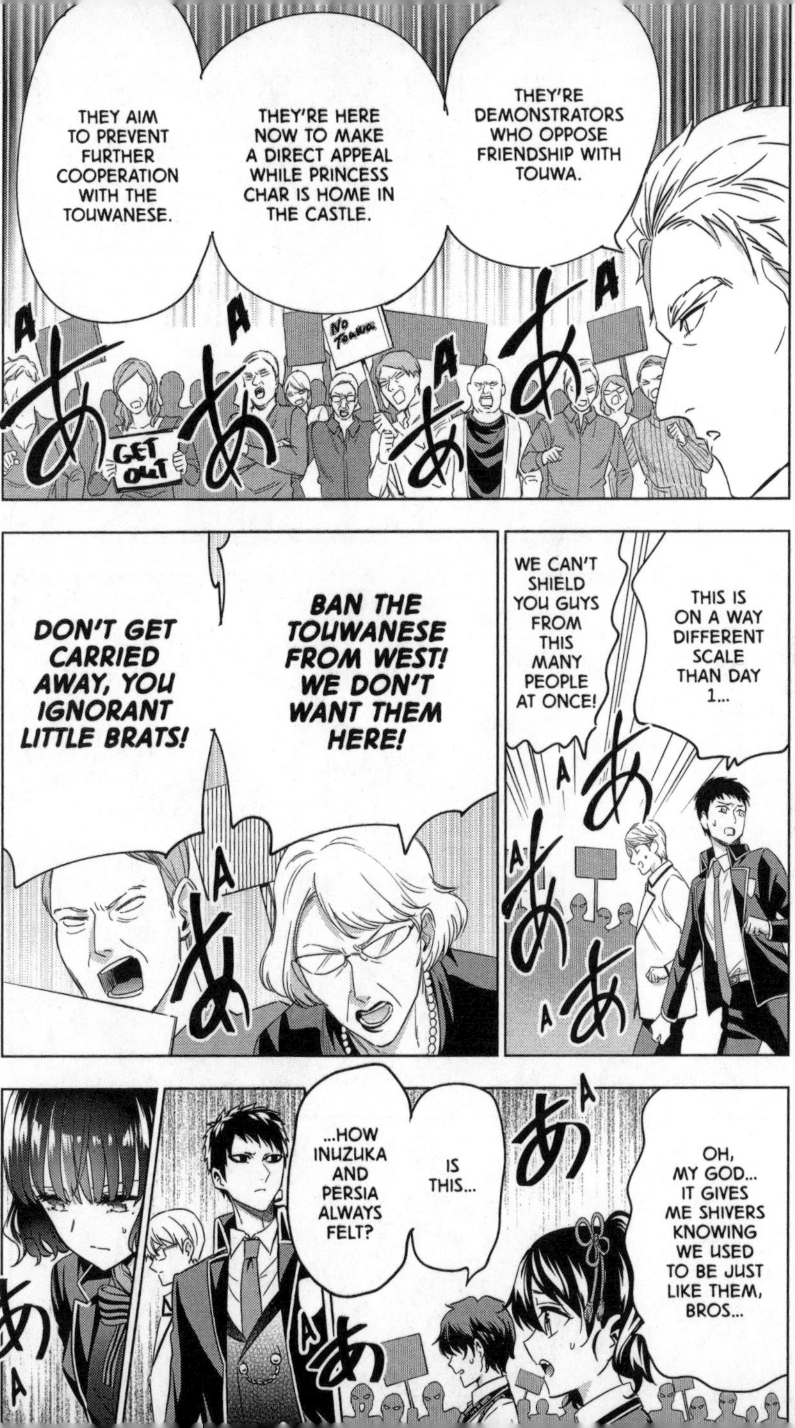
THEY'RE DEMONSTRATORS WHO OPPOSE FRIENDSHIP WITH TOUWA.
THEY'RE HERE NOW TO MAKE A DIRECT APPEAL WHILE PRINCESS CHAR IS HOME IN THE CASTLE.
THEY AIM TO PREVENT FURTHER COOPERATION WITH THE TOUWANESE.
A あ
NO TOUWA
GET OUT
THIS IS ON A WAY DIFFERENT SCALE THAN DAY 1...
WE CAN'T SHIELD YOU GUYS FROM THIS MANY PEOPLE AT ONCE!
A あ
BAN THE TOUWANESE FROM WEST! WE DON'T WANT THEM HERE!
DON'T GET CARRIED AWAY, YOU IGNORANT LITTLE BRATS!
A あ
OH, MY GOD... IT GIVES ME SHIVERS KNOWING WE USED TO BE JUST LIKE THEM, BROS...
IS THIS...
...HOW INUZUKA AND PERSIA ALWAYS FELT?
A あ

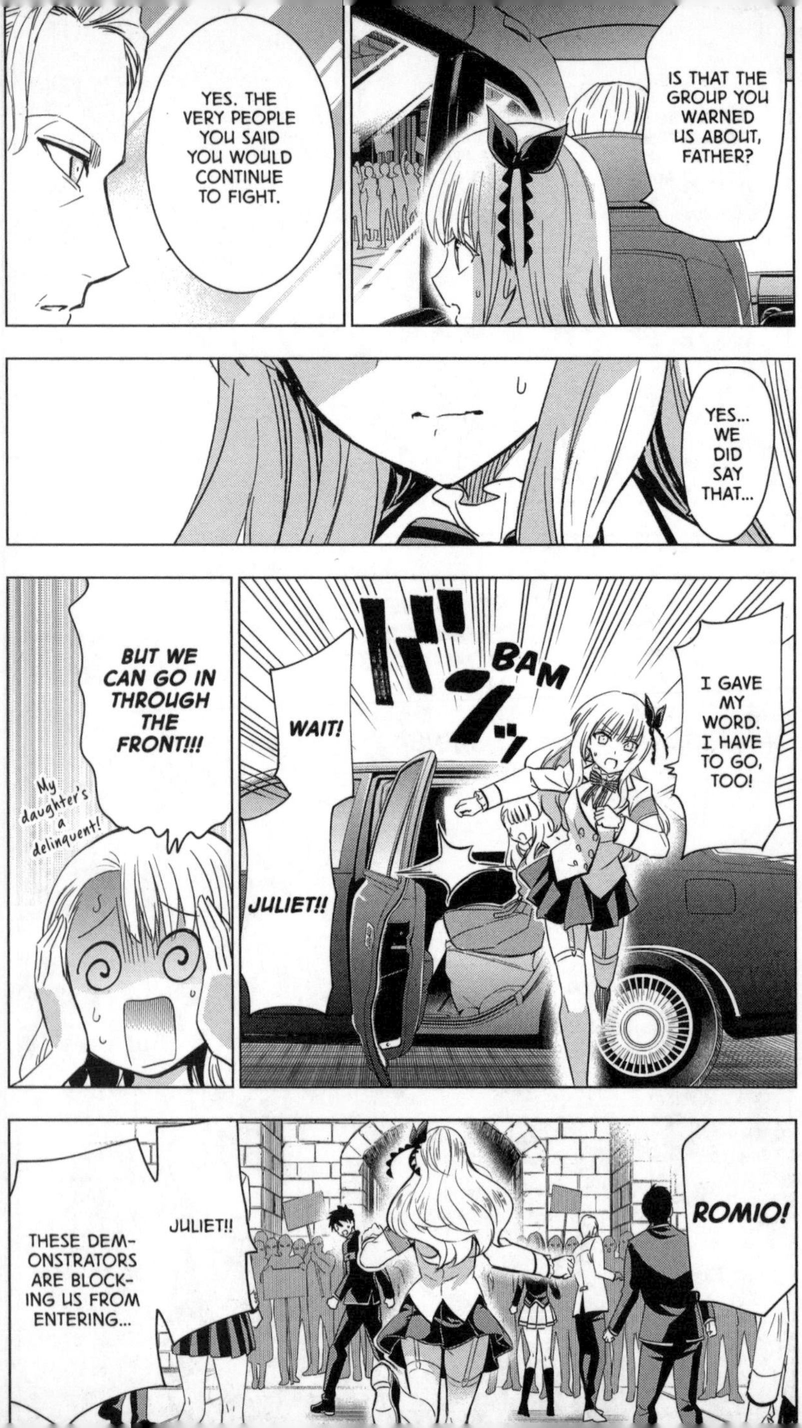
IS THAT THE GROUP YOU WARNED US ABOUT, FATHER?
YES. THE VERY PEOPLE YOU SAID YOU WOULD CONTINUE TO FIGHT.
YES... WE DID SAY THAT...
I GAVE MY WORD. I HAVE TO GO, TOO!
BAM
WAIT!
JULIET!!
BUT WE CAN GO IN THROUGH THE FRONT!!!
My daughter's a delinquent!
ROMIO!
JULIET!!
THESE DEM-ONSTRATORS ARE BLOCK-ING US FROM ENTERING...

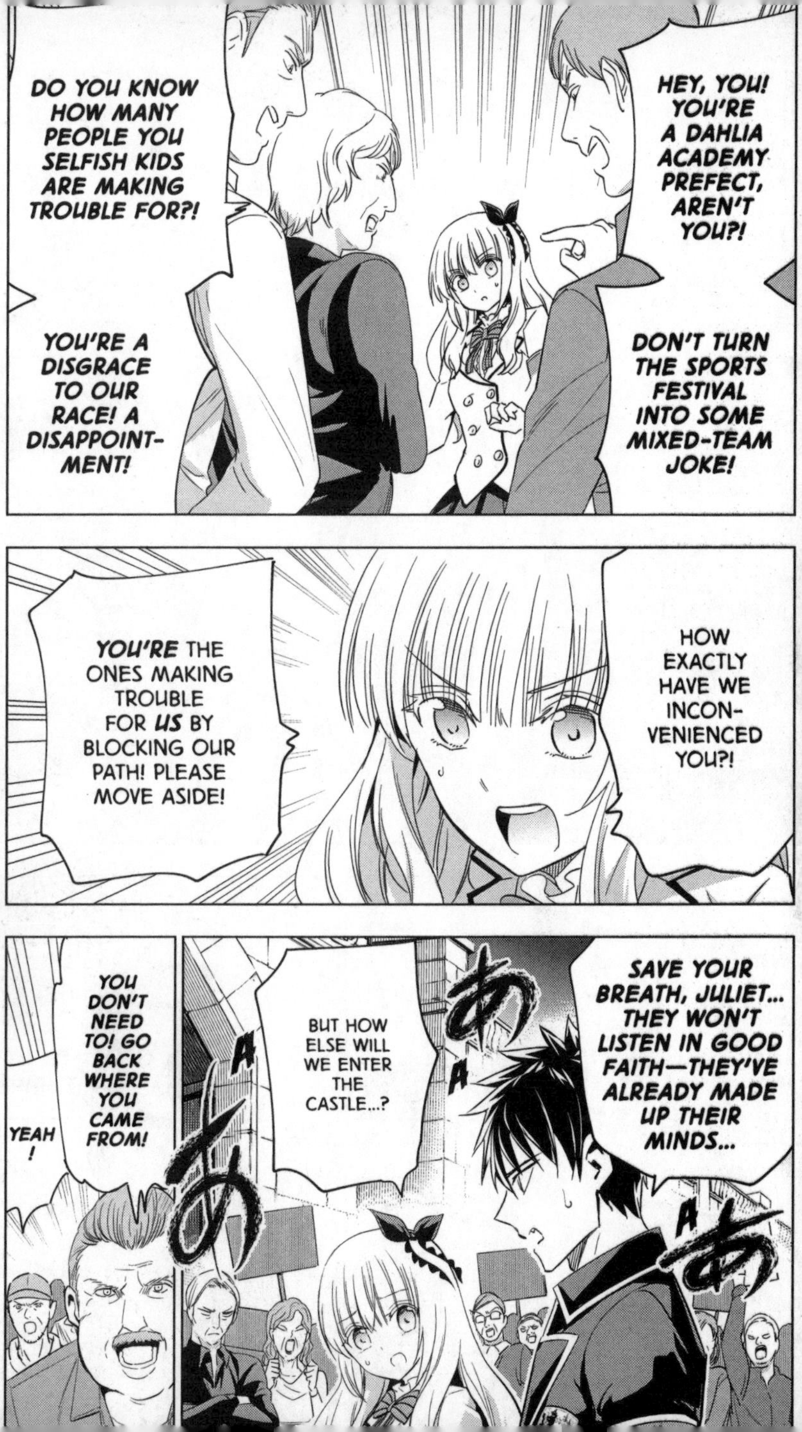
HEY, YOU! YOU'RE A DAHLIA ACADEMY PREFECT, AREN'T YOU?!
DO YOU KNOW HOW MANY PEOPLE YOU SELFISH KIDS ARE MAKING TROUBLE FOR?!
DON'T TURN THE SPORTS FESTIVAL INTO SOME MIXED-TEAM JOKE!
YOU'RE A DISGRACE TO OUR RACE! A DISAPPOINT-MENT!
HOW EXACTLY HAVE WE INCON-VENIENCED YOU?!
YOU'RE THE ONES MAKING TROUBLE FOR US BY BLOCKING OUR PATH! PLEASE MOVE ASIDE!
SAVE YOUR BREATH, JULIET... THEY WON'T LISTEN IN GOOD FAITH—THEY'VE ALREADY MADE UP THEIR MINDS...
A
A
BUT HOW ELSE WILL WE ENTER THE CASTLE...?
A
YOU DON'T NEED TO! GO BACK WHERE YOU CAME FROM!
YEAH!

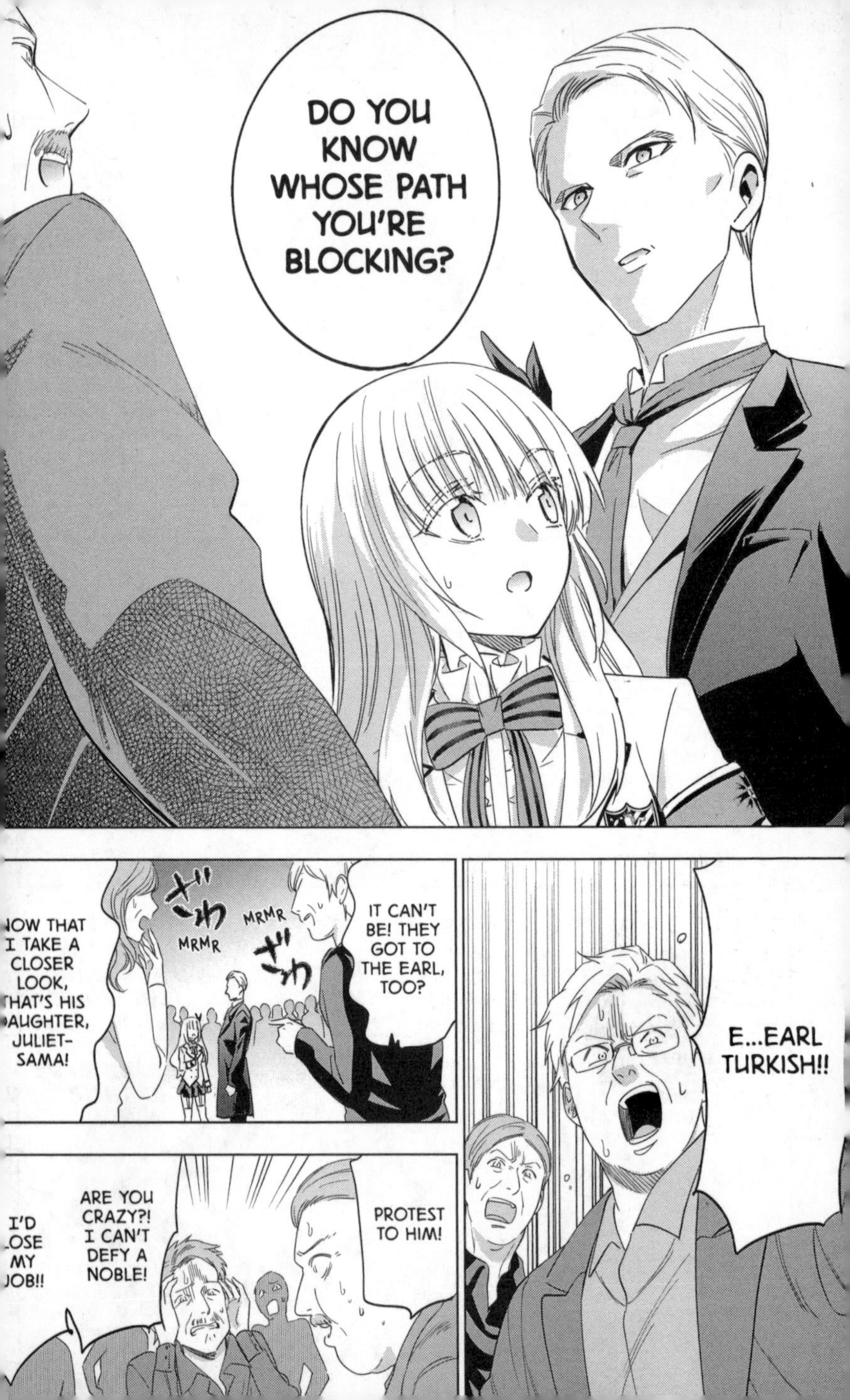
DO YOU KNOW WHOSE PATH YOU'RE BLOCKING?
E...EARL TURKISH!!
IT CAN'T BE! THEY GOT TO THE EARL, TOO?
MRMR
MRMR
NOW THAT I TAKE A CLOSER LOOK, THAT'S HIS DAUGHTER, JULIET-SAMA!
PROTEST TO HIM!
ARE YOU CRAZY?! I CAN'T DEFY A NOBLE!
I'D LOSE MY JOB!!

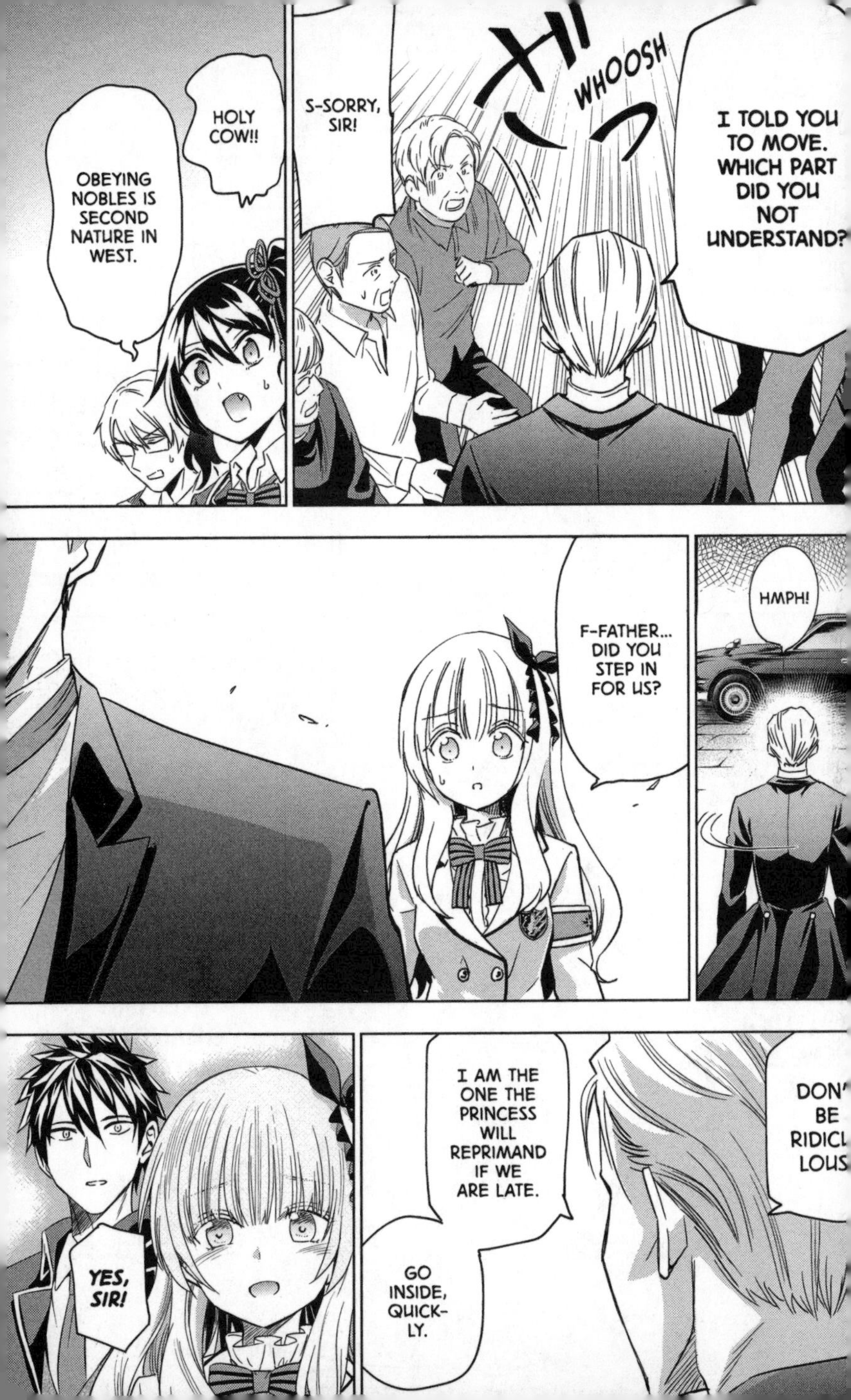
I TOLD YOU TO MOVE. WHICH PART DID YOU NOT UNDERSTAND?
WHOOSH
S-SORRY, SIR!
HOLY COW!!
OBEYING NOBLES IS SECOND NATURE IN WEST.
HMPH!
F-FATHER... DID YOU STEP IN FOR US?
DON' BE RIDICL LOUS
I AM THE ONE THE PRINCESS WILL REPRIMAND IF WE ARE LATE.
GO INSIDE, QUICK-LY.
YES, SIR!

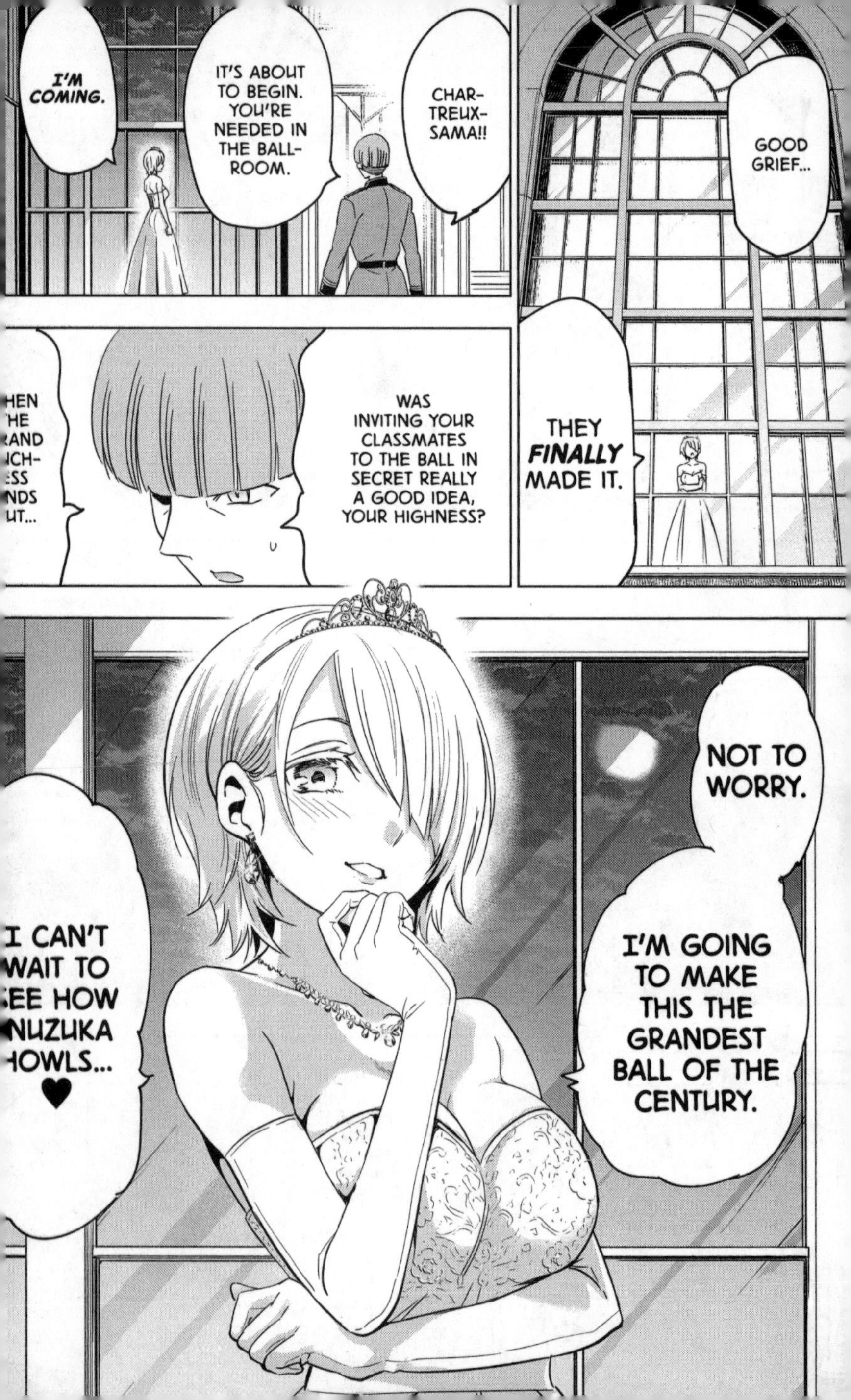
GOOD GRIEF...
THEY *FINALLY* MADE IT.
CHARTREUX-SAMA!!
IT'S ABOUT TO BEGIN. YOU'RE NEEDED IN THE BALLROOM.
I'M COMING.
WAS INVITING YOUR CLASSMATES TO THE BALL IN SECRET REALLY A GOOD IDEA, YOUR HIGHNESS?
HEN THE RAND UCH-ESS NDS UT...
NOT TO WORRY.
I'M GOING TO MAKE THIS THE GRANDEST BALL OF THE CENTURY.
I CAN'T WAIT TO EE HOW NUZUKA HOWLS... ♥

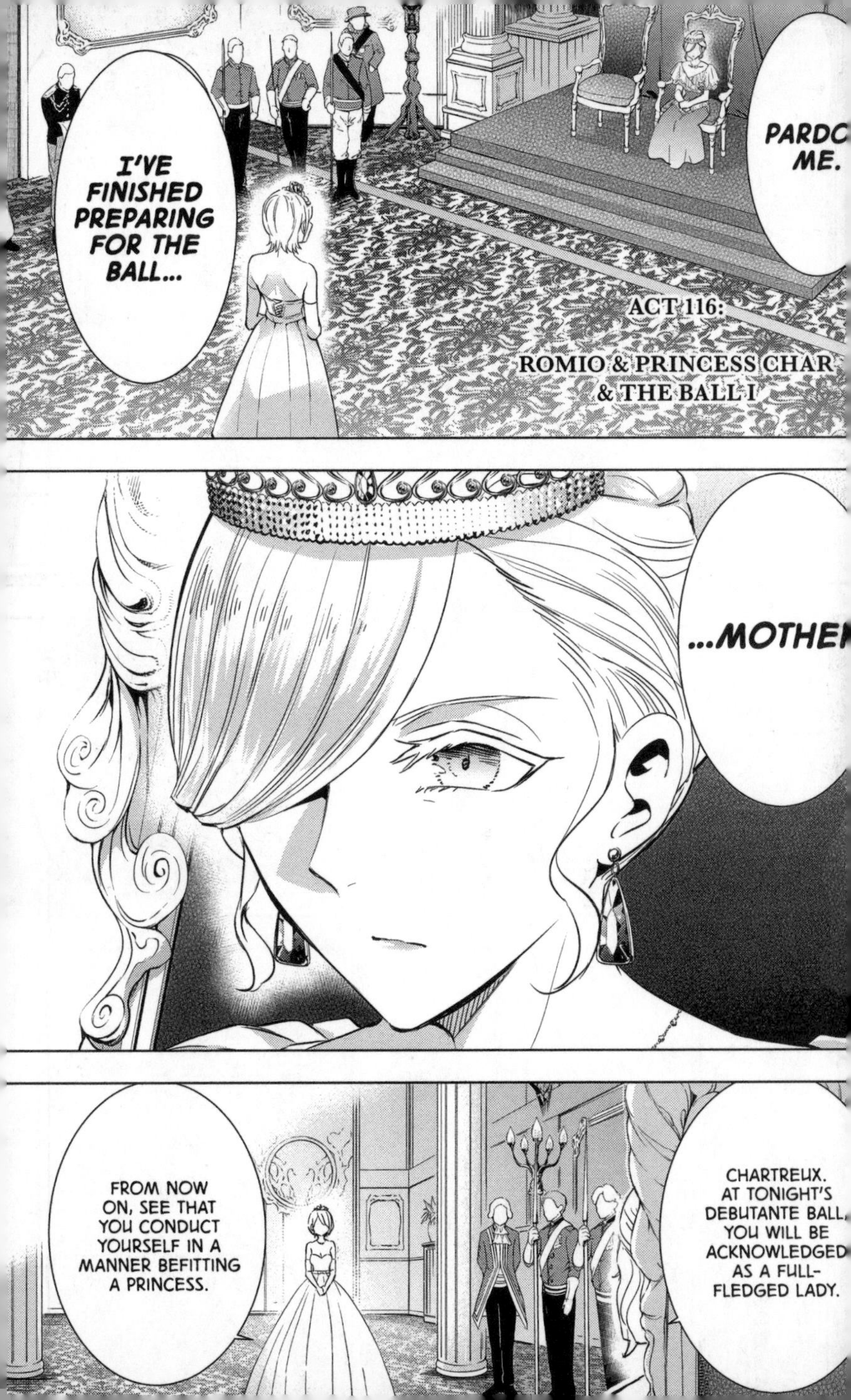
PARDO ME.
I'VE FINISHED PREPARING FOR THE BALL...
ACT 116:
ROMIO & PRINCESS CHAR & THE BALL I
...MOTHE
CHARTREUX. AT TONIGHT'S DEBUTANTE BALL, YOU WILL BE ACKNOWLEDGED AS A FULL-FLEDGED LADY.
FROM NOW ON, SEE THAT YOU CONDUCT YOURSELF IN A MANNER BEFITTING A PRINCESS.

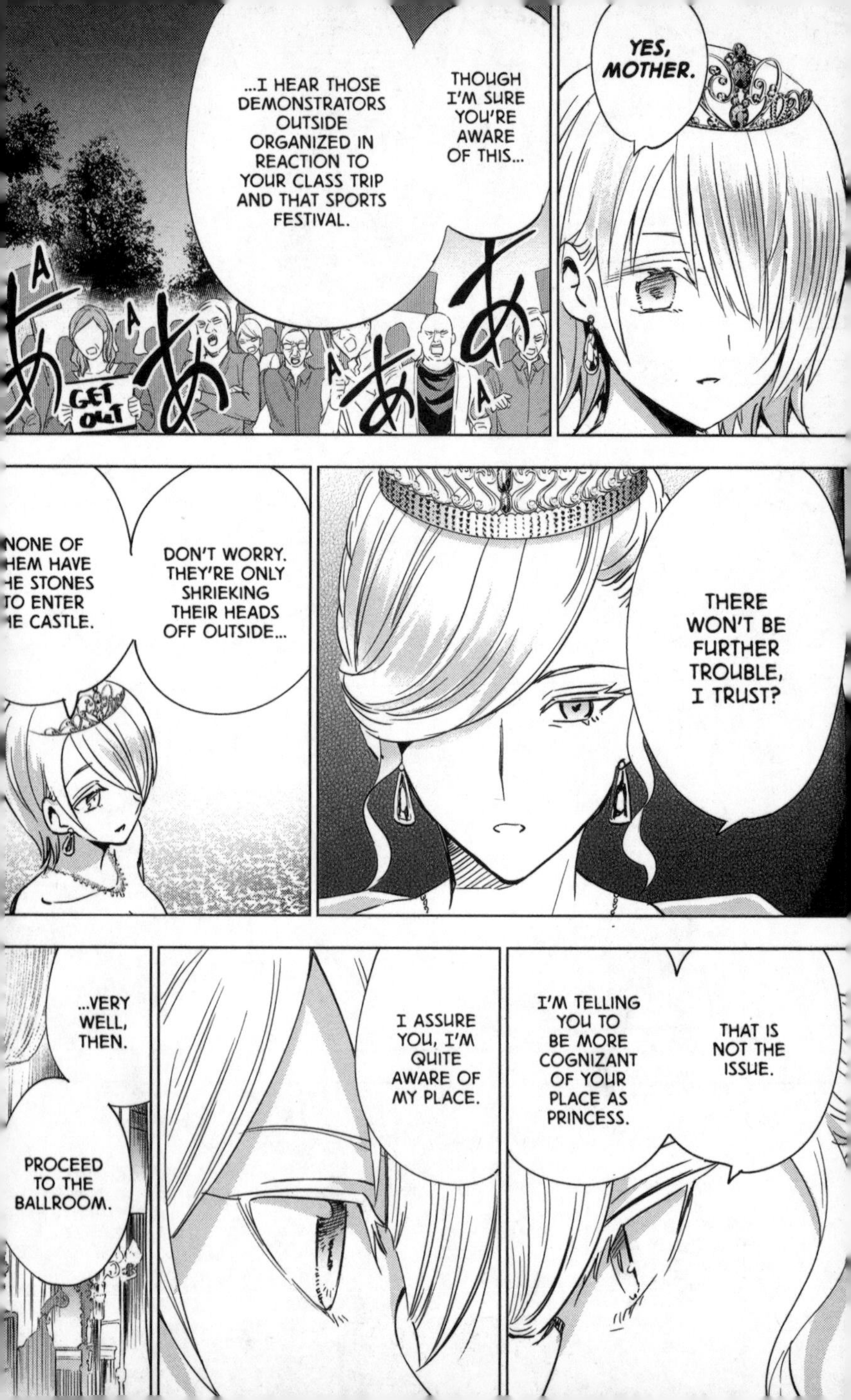
YES, MOTHER.
THOUGH I'M SURE YOU'RE AWARE OF THIS...
...I HEAR THOSE DEMONSTRATORS OUTSIDE ORGANIZED IN REACTION TO YOUR CLASS TRIP AND THAT SPORTS FESTIVAL.
あ
A
あ
A
あ
A
あ
A
GET OUT
THERE WON'T BE FURTHER TROUBLE, I TRUST?
DON'T WORRY. THEY'RE ONLY SHRIEKING THEIR HEADS OFF OUTSIDE...
NONE OF HEM HAVE HE STONES TO ENTER HE CASTLE.
THAT IS NOT THE ISSUE.
I'M TELLING YOU TO BE MORE COGNIZANT OF YOUR PLACE AS PRINCESS.
I ASSURE YOU, I'M QUITE AWARE OF MY PLACE.
...VERY WELL, THEN.
PROCEED TO THE BALLROOM.

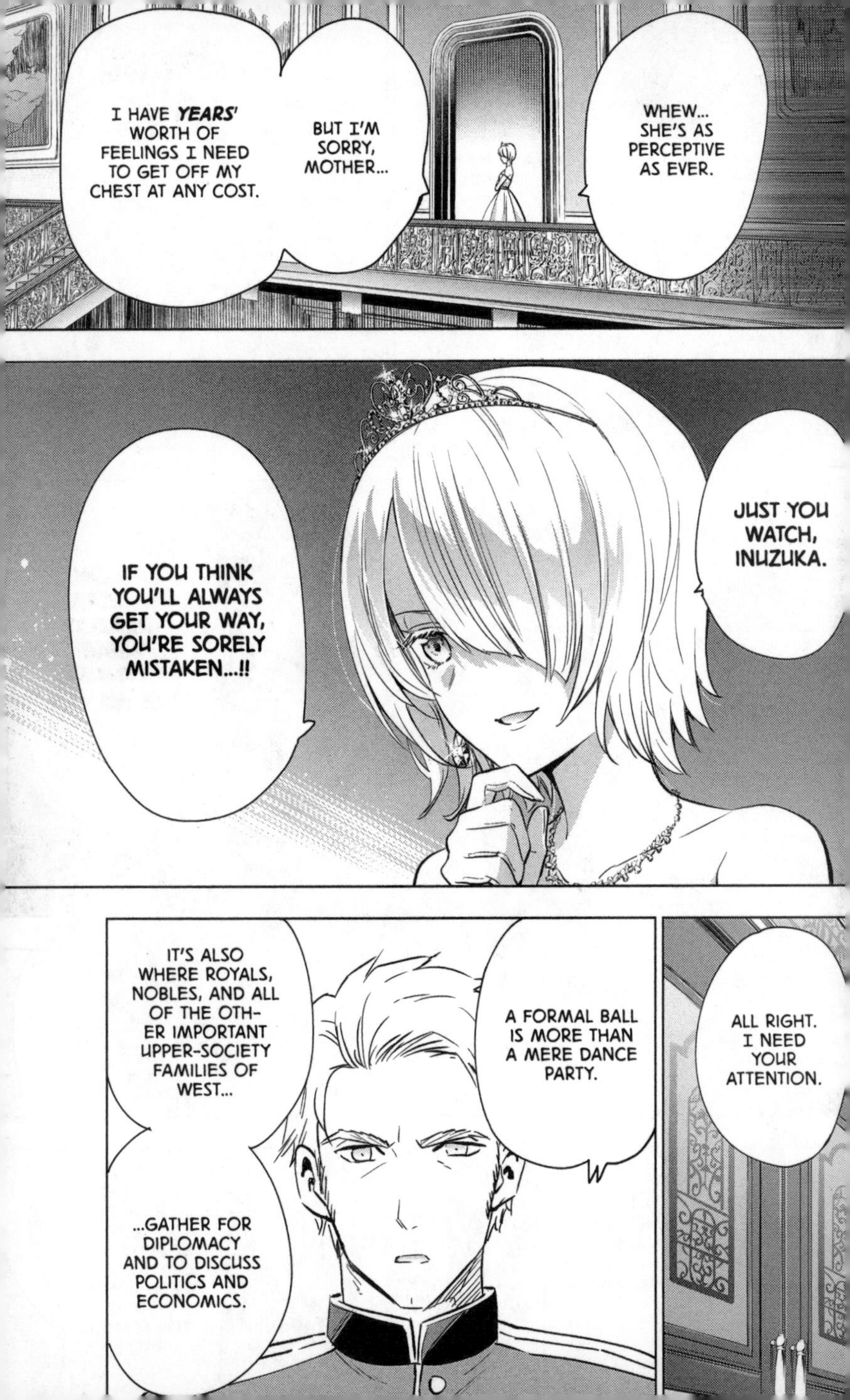
WHEW... SHE'S AS PERCEPTIVE AS EVER.
BUT I'M SORRY, MOTHER...
I HAVE ***YEARS'*** WORTH OF FEELINGS I NEED TO GET OFF MY CHEST AT ANY COST.
JUST YOU WATCH, INUZUKA.
IF YOU THINK YOU'LL ALWAYS GET YOUR WAY, YOU'RE SORELY MISTAKEN...!!
ALL RIGHT. I NEED YOUR ATTENTION.
A FORMAL BALL IS MORE THAN A MERE DANCE PARTY.
IT'S ALSO WHERE ROYALS, NOBLES, AND ALL OF THE OTH-ER IMPORTANT UPPER-SOCIETY FAMILIES OF WEST...
...GATHER FOR DIPLOMACY AND TO DISCUSS POLITICS AND ECONOMICS.

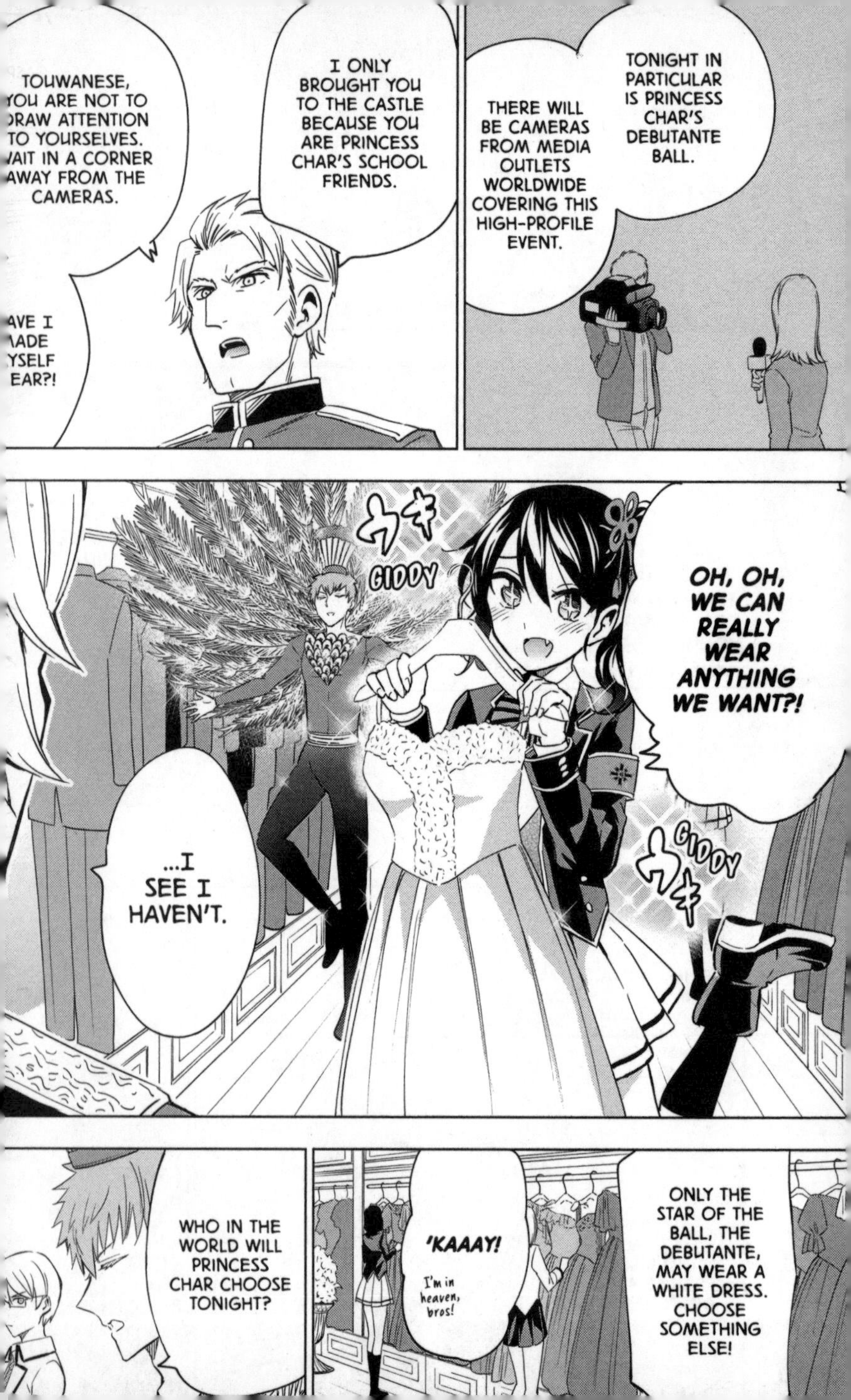
TONIGHT IN PARTICULAR IS PRINCESS CHAR'S DEBUTANTE BALL.
THERE WILL BE CAMERAS FROM MEDIA OUTLETS WORLDWIDE COVERING THIS HIGH-PROFILE EVENT.
I ONLY BROUGHT YOU TO THE CASTLE BECAUSE YOU ARE PRINCESS CHAR'S SCHOOL FRIENDS.
TOUWANESE, YOU ARE NOT TO RAW ATTENTION TO YOURSELVES. AIT IN A CORNER AWAY FROM THE CAMERAS.
AVE I ADE YSELF EAR?!
ウキ
GIDDY
OH, OH, WE CAN REALLY WEAR ANYTHING WE WANT?!
GIDDY
ウキ
...I SEE I HAVEN'T.
ONLY THE STAR OF THE BALL, THE DEBUTANTE, MAY WEAR A WHITE DRESS. CHOOSE SOMETHING ELSE!
'KAAAY!
I'm in heaven, bros!
WHO IN THE WORLD WILL PRINCESS CHAR CHOOSE TONIGHT?

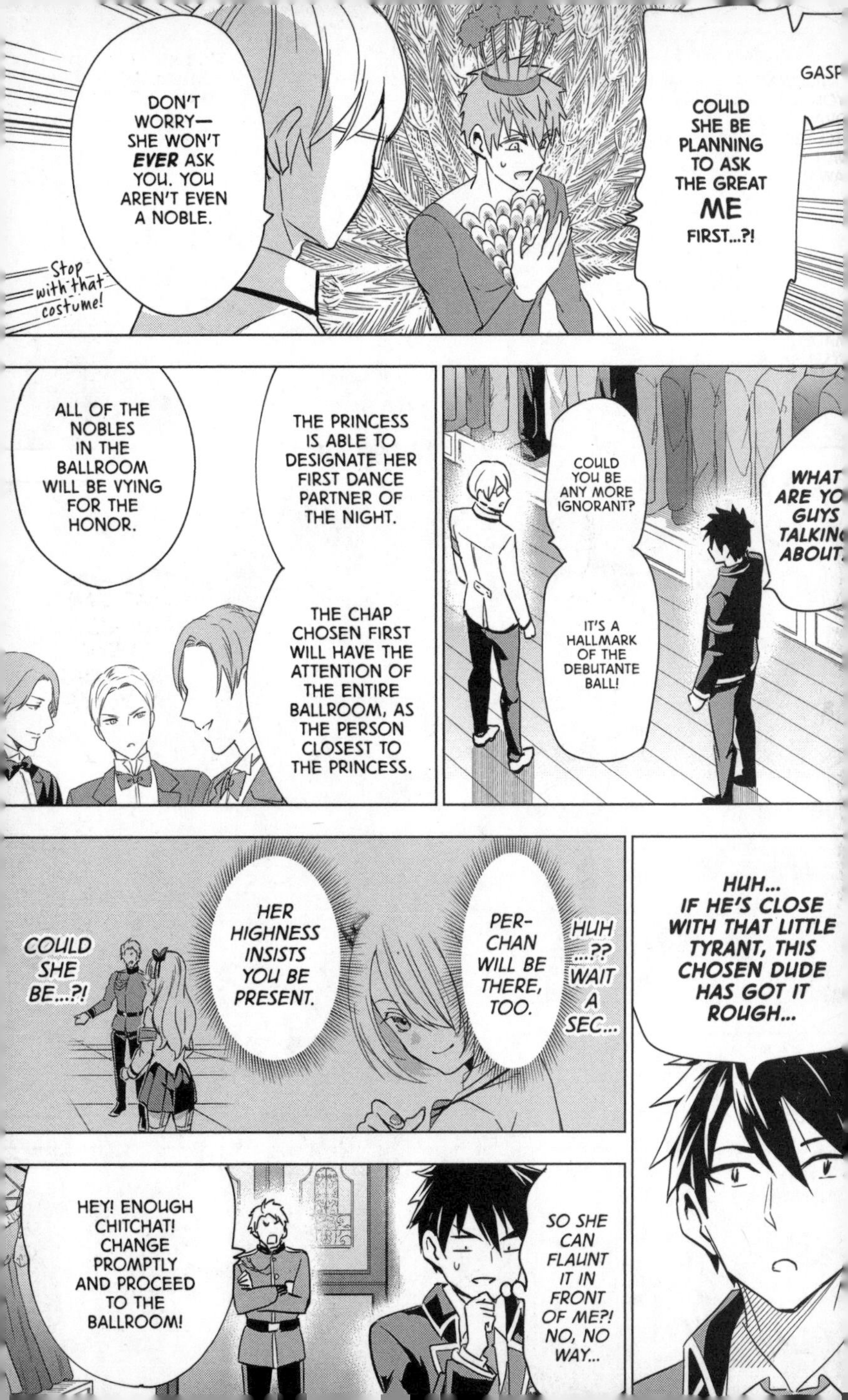
GASP
COULD SHE BE PLANNING TO ASK THE GREAT ME FIRST...?!
DON'T WORRY— SHE WON'T ***EVER*** ASK YOU. YOU AREN'T EVEN A NOBLE.
Stop with that costume!
WHAT ARE YO GUYS TALKIN ABOUT.
COULD YOU BE ANY MORE IGNORANT?
IT'S A HALLMARK OF THE DEBUTANTE BALL!
THE PRINCESS IS ABLE TO DESIGNATE HER FIRST DANCE PARTNER OF THE NIGHT.
THE CHAP CHOSEN FIRST WILL HAVE THE ATTENTION OF THE ENTIRE BALLROOM, AS THE PERSON CLOSEST TO THE PRINCESS.
ALL OF THE NOBLES IN THE BALLROOM WILL BE VYING FOR THE HONOR.
HUH... IF HE'S CLOSE WITH THAT LITTLE TYRANT, THIS CHOSEN DUDE HAS GOT IT ROUGH...
HUH ...?? WAIT A SEC...
PER-CHAN WILL BE THERE, TOO.
HER HIGHNESS INSISTS YOU BE PRESENT.
COULD SHE BE...?!
SO SHE CAN FLAUNT IT IN FRONT OF ME?! NO, NO WAY...
HEY! ENOUGH CHITCHAT! CHANGE PROMPTLY AND PROCEED TO THE BALLROOM!

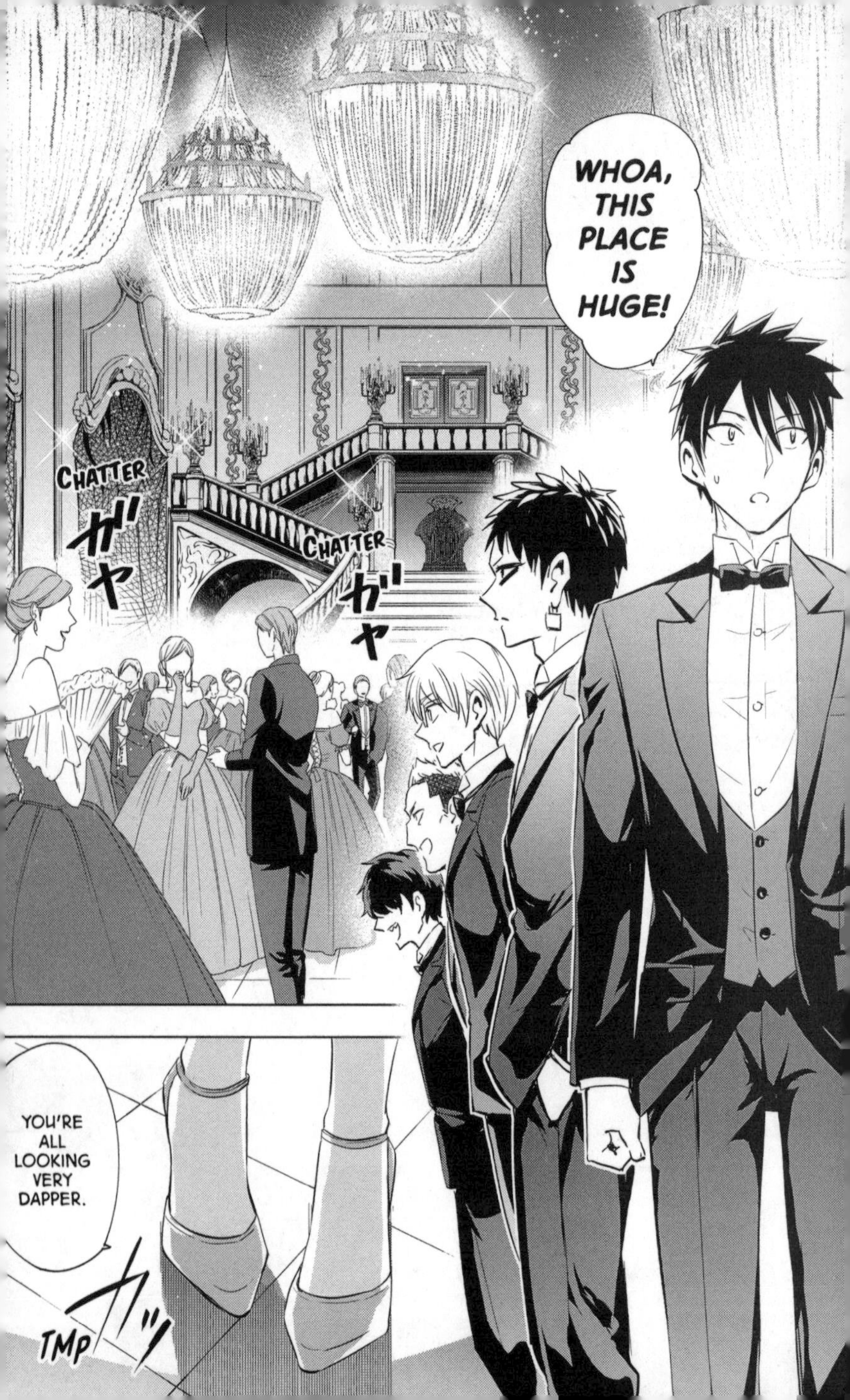
WHOA, THIS PLACE IS HUGE!
CHATTER
ガヤ
CHATTER
ガヤ
YOU'RE ALL LOOKING VERY DAPPER.
TMP
カッ

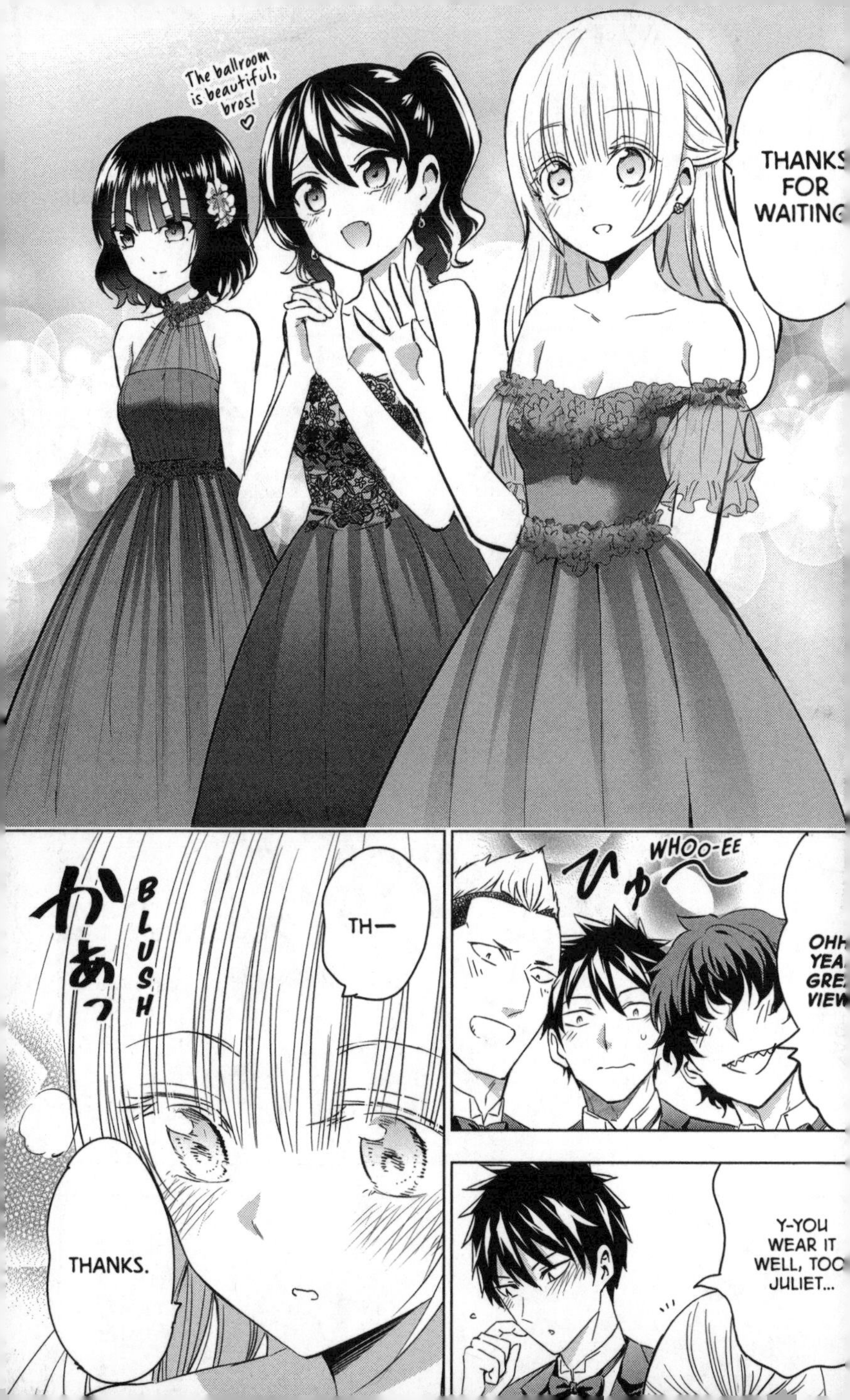
THANKS FOR WAITING
The ballroom is beautiful, bros! ♡
ひゅ〜
WHOO-EE
OHH YEA GRE VIEW
Y-YOU WEAR IT WELL, TOO JULIET...
TH—
かあっ
BLUSH
THANKS.

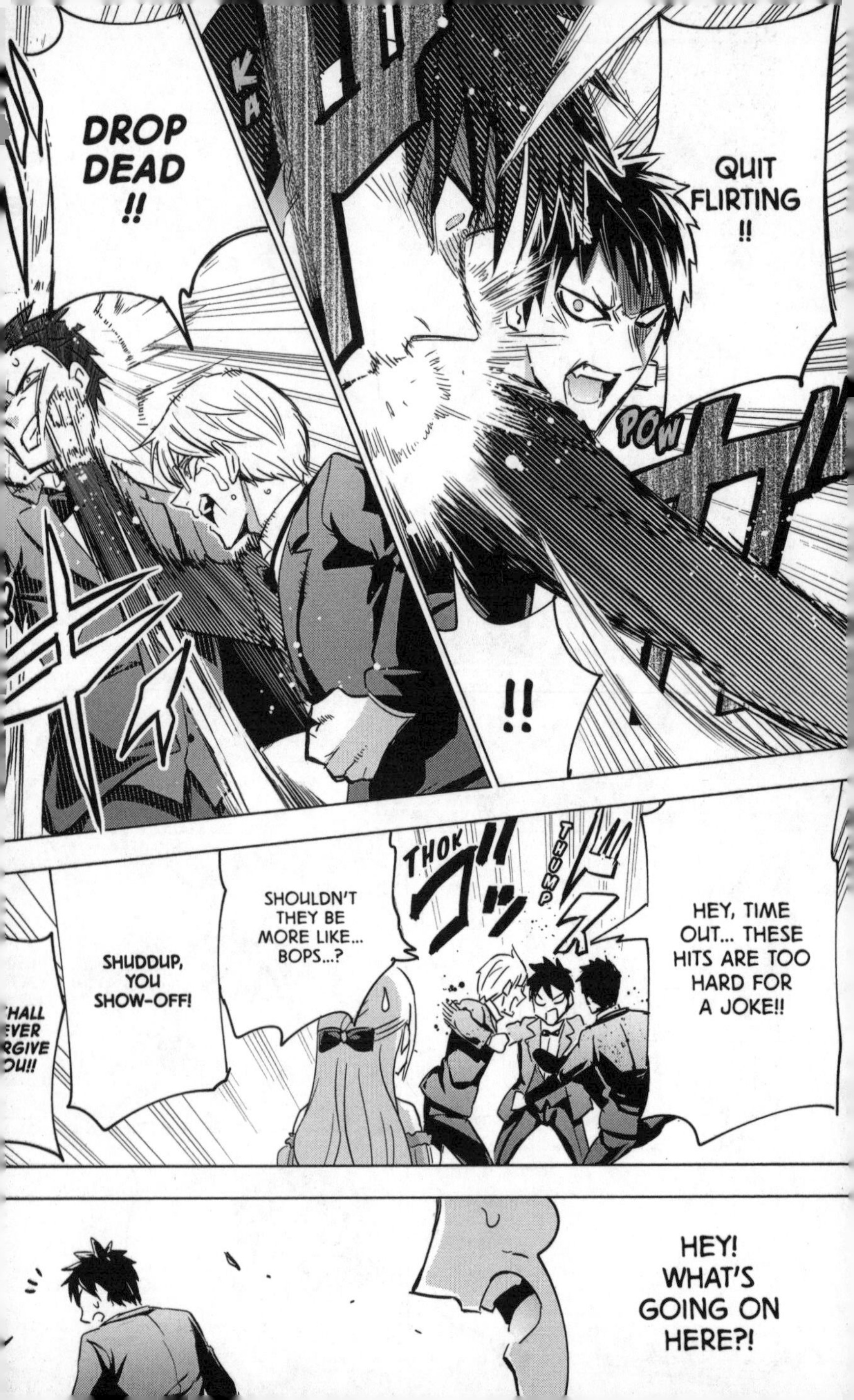
QUIT FLIRTING !!
POW
!!
KA
DROP DEAD !!
HEY, TIME OUT... THESE HITS ARE TOO HARD FOR A JOKE!!
THUMP
THOK
SHOULDN'T THEY BE MORE LIKE... BOPS...?
SHUDDUP, YOU SHOW-OFF!
HEY! WHAT'S GOING ON HERE?!

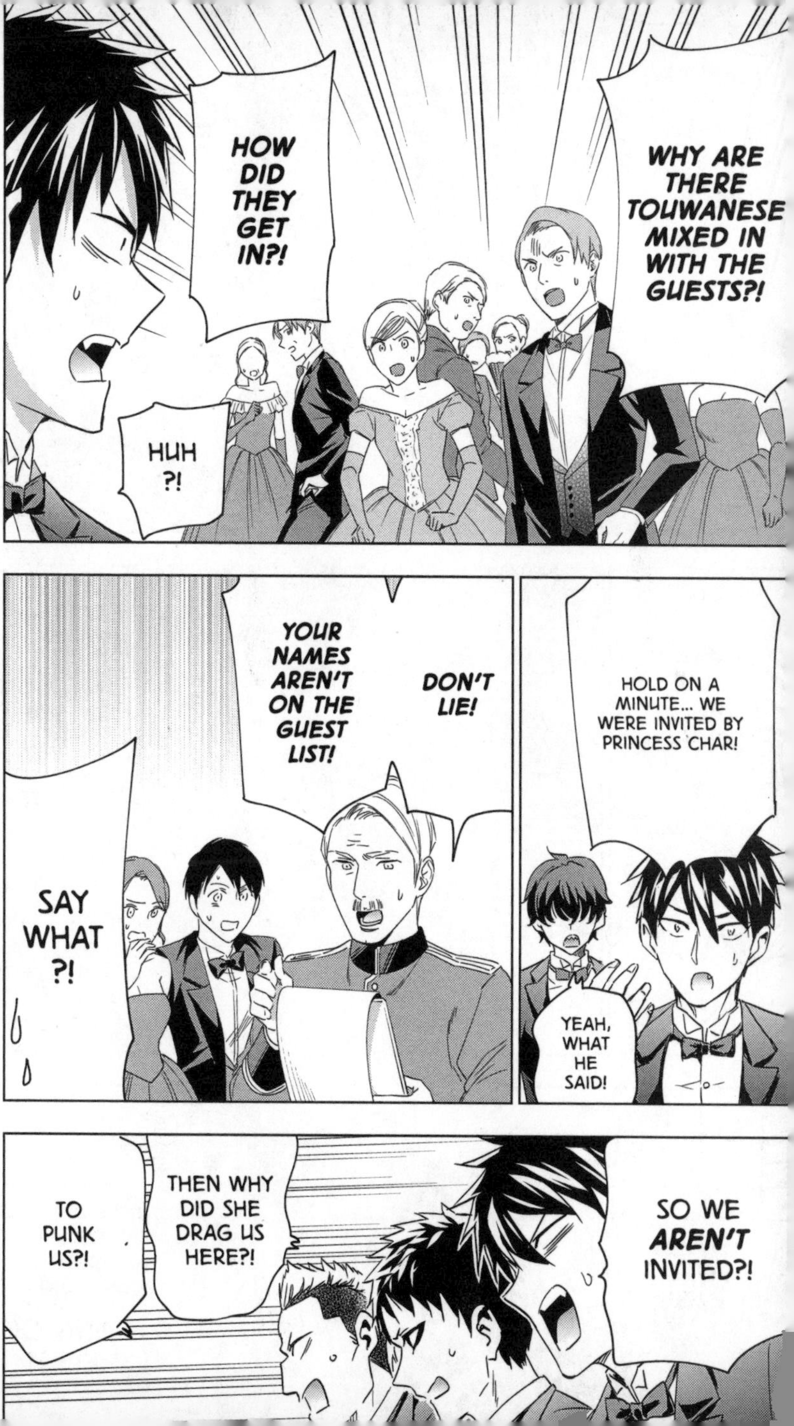
WHY ARE THERE TOUWANESE MIXED IN WITH THE GUESTS?!
HOW DID THEY GET IN?!
HUH ?!
HOLD ON A MINUTE... WE WERE INVITED BY PRINCESS CHAR!
YEAH, WHAT HE SAID!
DON'T LIE!
YOUR NAMES AREN'T ON THE GUEST LIST!
SAY WHAT ?!
SO WE AREN'T INVITED?!
THEN WHY DID SHE DRAG US HERE?!
TO PUNK US?!

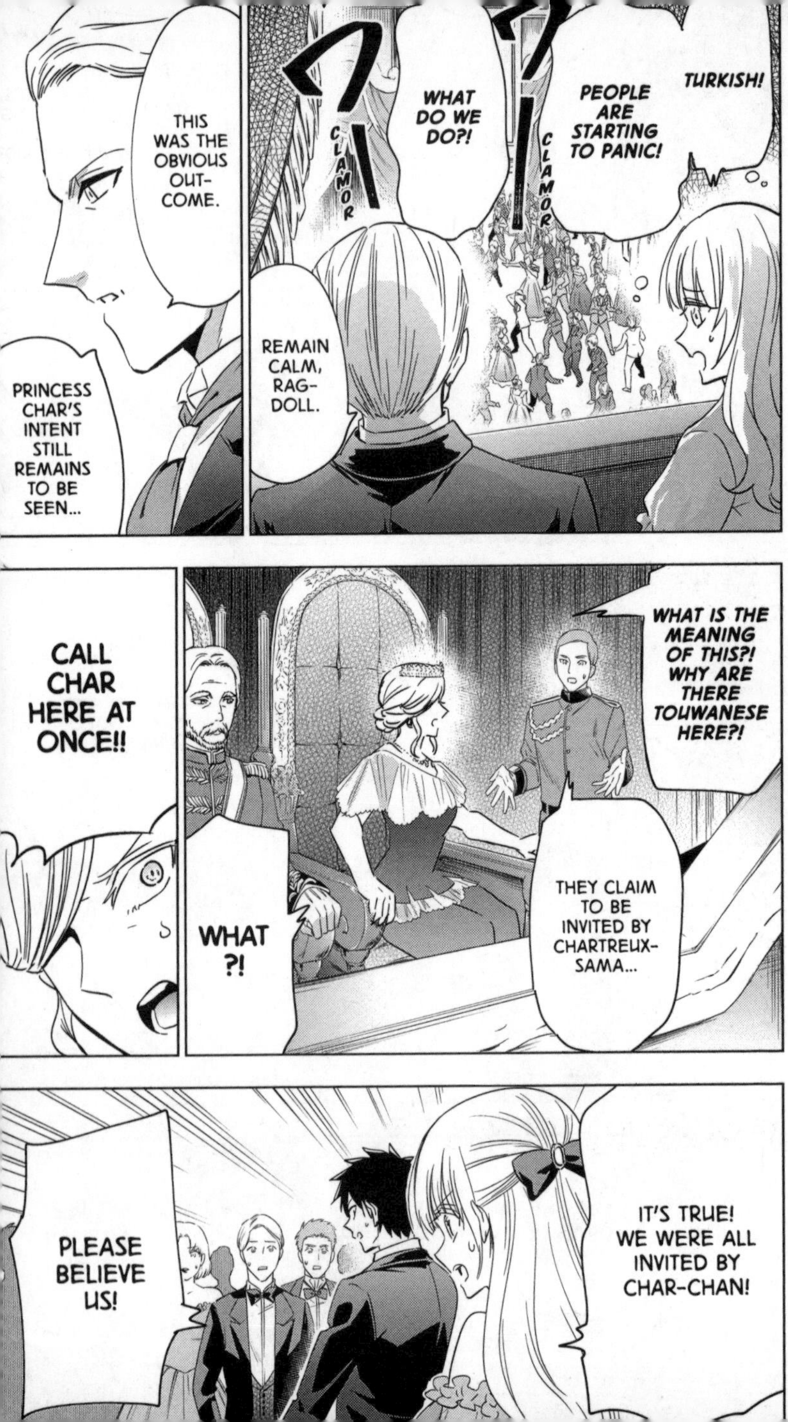
TURKISH!
PEOPLE ARE STARTING TO PANIC!
CLAMOR
WHAT DO WE DO?!
CLAMOR
REMAIN CALM, RAG-DOLL.
THIS WAS THE OBVIOUS OUT-COME.
PRINCESS CHAR'S INTENT STILL REMAINS TO BE SEEN...
WHAT IS THE MEANING OF THIS?! WHY ARE THERE TOUWANESE HERE?!
THEY CLAIM TO BE INVITED BY CHARTREUX-SAMA...
WHAT ?!
CALL CHAR HERE AT ONCE!!
IT'S TRUE! WE WERE ALL INVITED BY CHAR-CHAN!
PLEASE BELIEVE US!

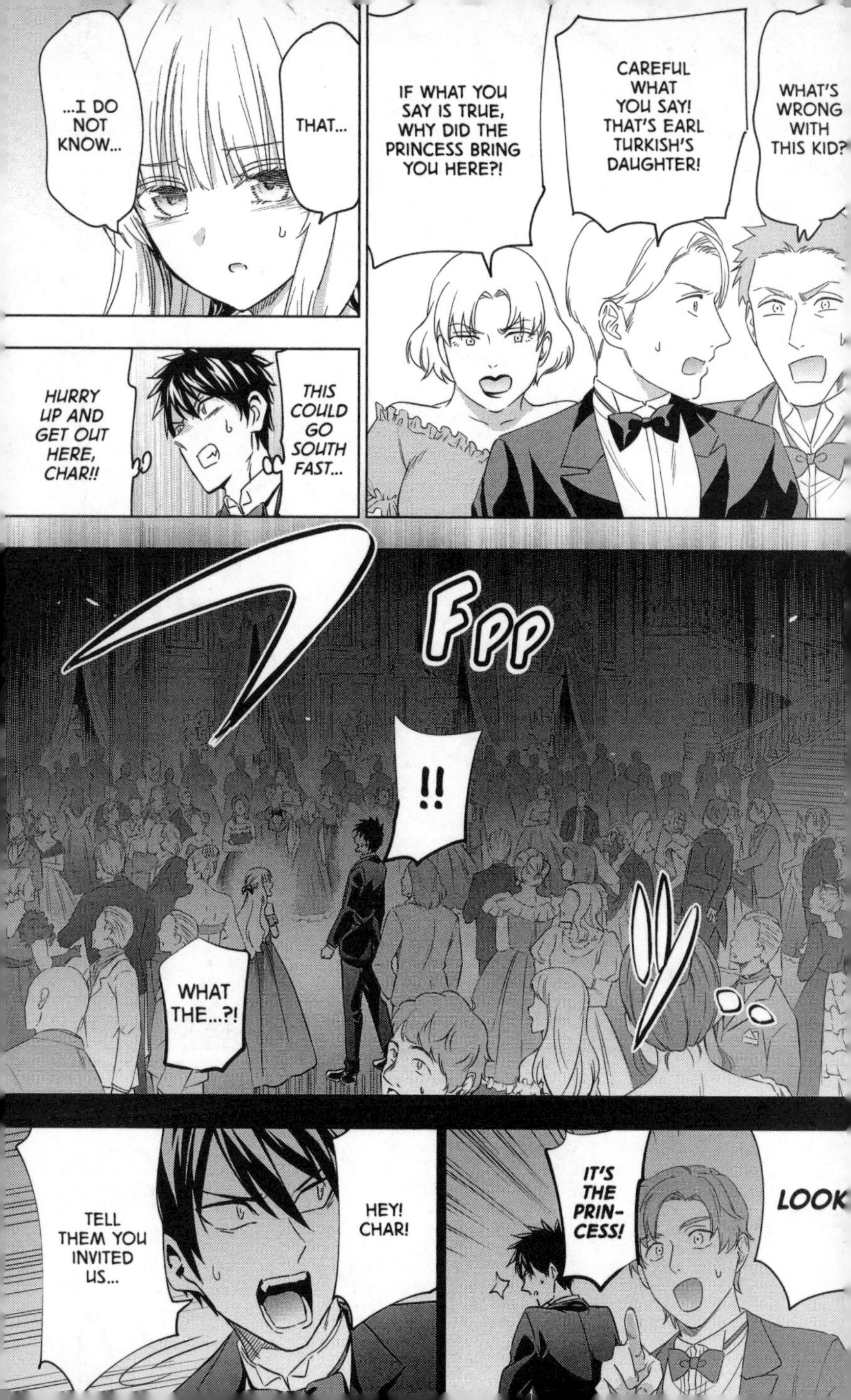
WHAT'S WRONG WITH THIS KID?
CAREFUL WHAT YOU SAY! THAT'S EARL TURKISH'S DAUGHTER!
IF WHAT YOU SAY IS TRUE, WHY DID THE PRINCESS BRING YOU HERE?!
THAT...
...I DO NOT KNOW...
THIS COULD GO SOUTH FAST...
HURRY UP AND GET OUT HERE, CHAR!!
FPP
!!
WHAT THE...?!
LOOK
IT'S THE PRIN-CESS!
HEY! CHAR!
TELL THEM YOU INVITED US...

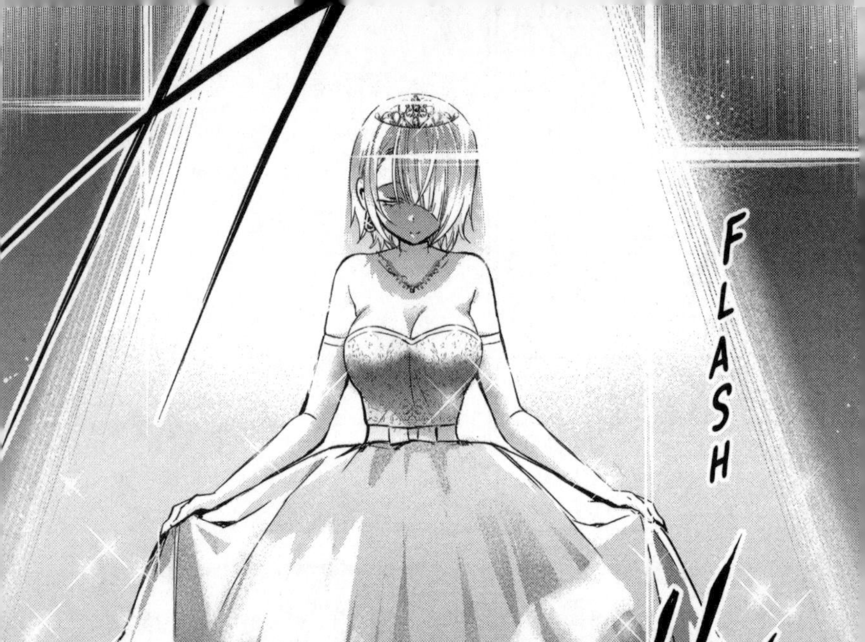
FLASH
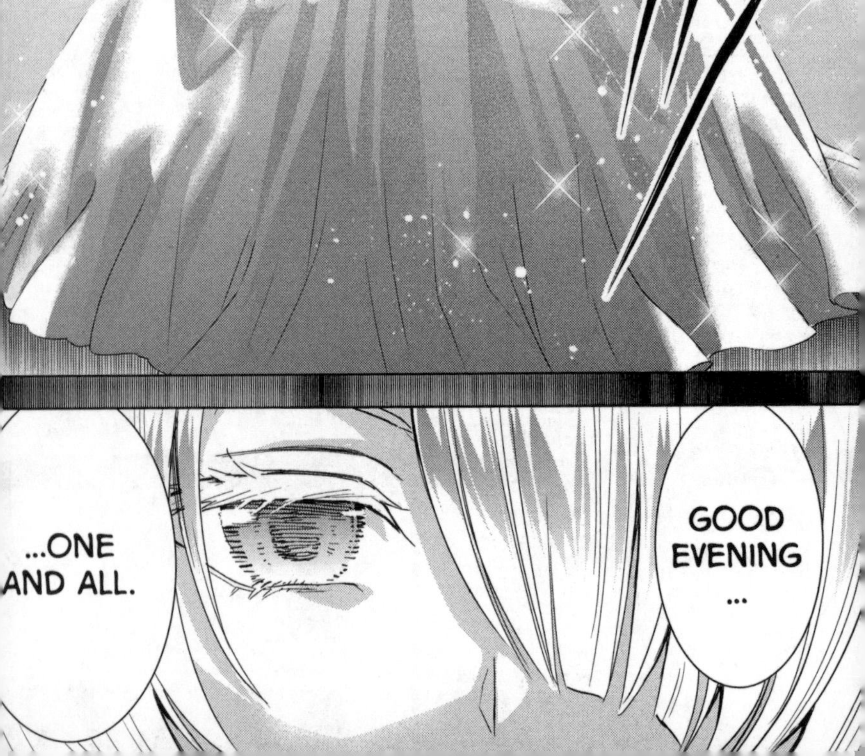
GOOD EVENING ...
...ONE AND ALL.

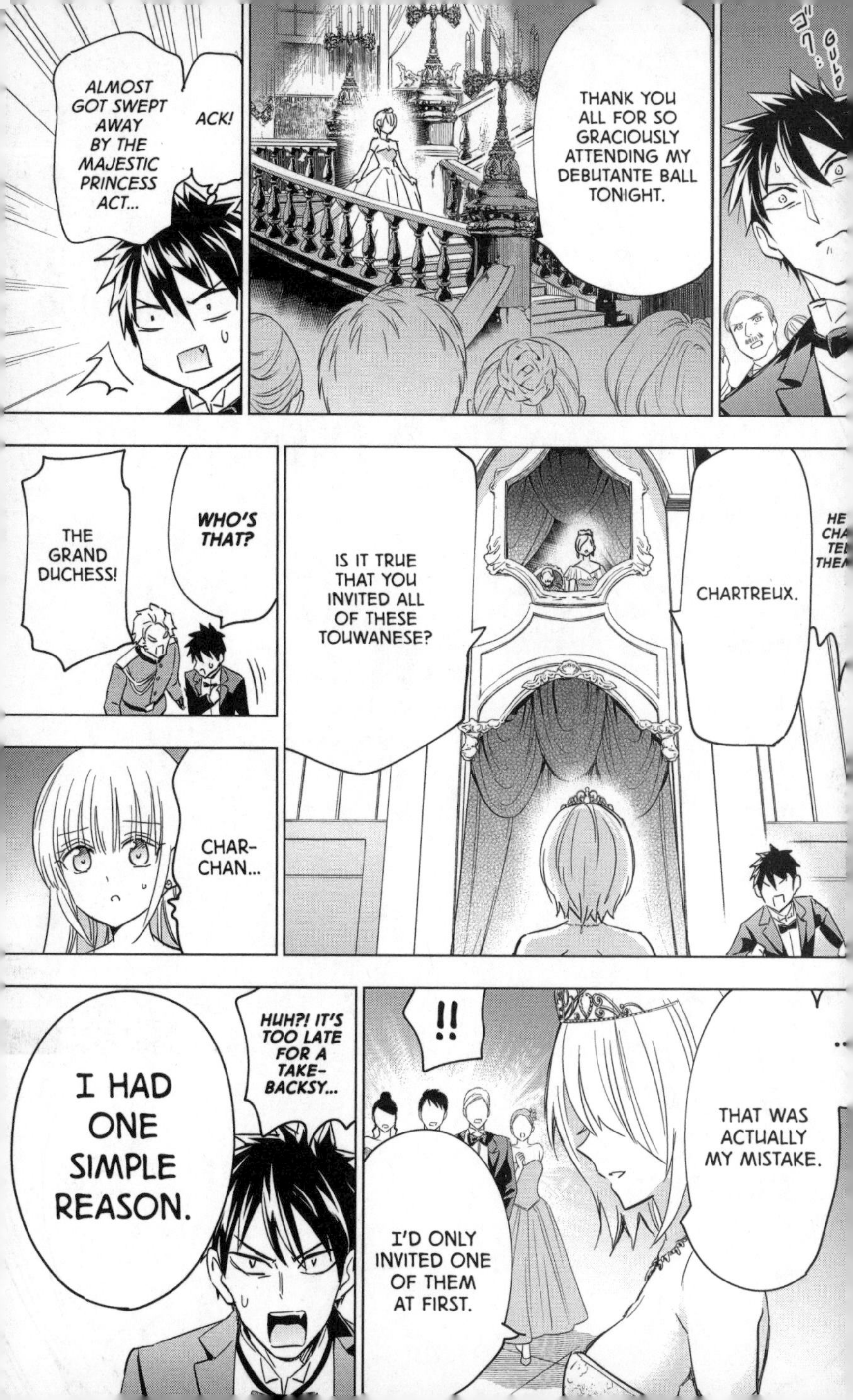
GULP
THANK YOU ALL FOR SO GRACIOUSLY ATTENDING MY DEBUTANTE BALL TONIGHT.
ACK!
ALMOST GOT SWEPT AWAY BY THE MAJESTIC PRINCESS ACT...
CHARTREUX.
IS IT TRUE THAT YOU INVITED ALL OF THESE TOUWANESE?
WHO'S THAT?
THE GRAND DUCHESS!
CHAR-CHAN...
THAT WAS ACTUALLY MY MISTAKE.
!!
I'D ONLY INVITED ONE OF THEM AT FIRST.
HUH?! IT'S TOO LATE FOR A TAKE-BACKSY...
I HAD ONE SIMPLE REASON.

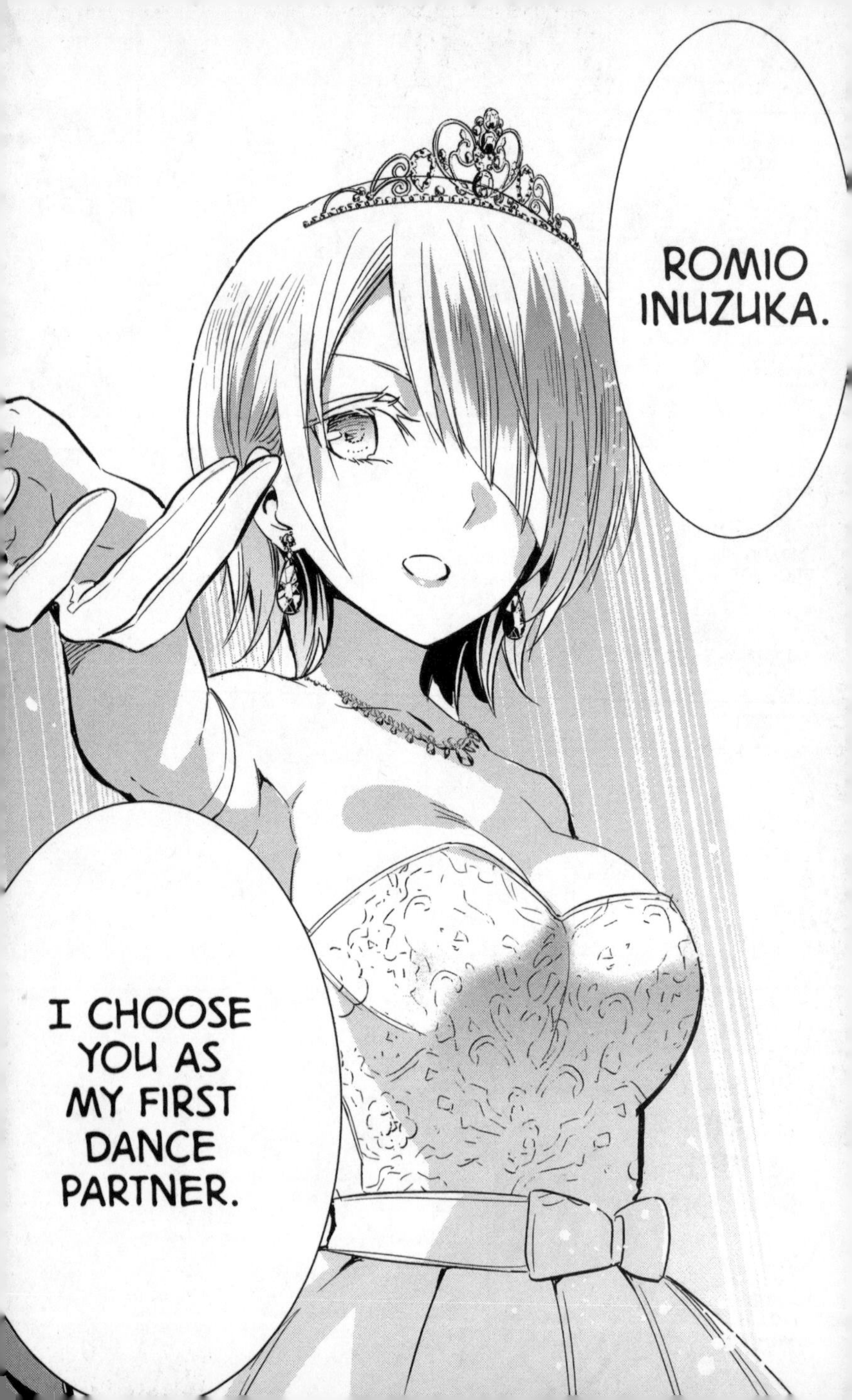
ROMIO INUZUKA.
I CHOOSE YOU AS MY FIRST DANCE PARTNER.

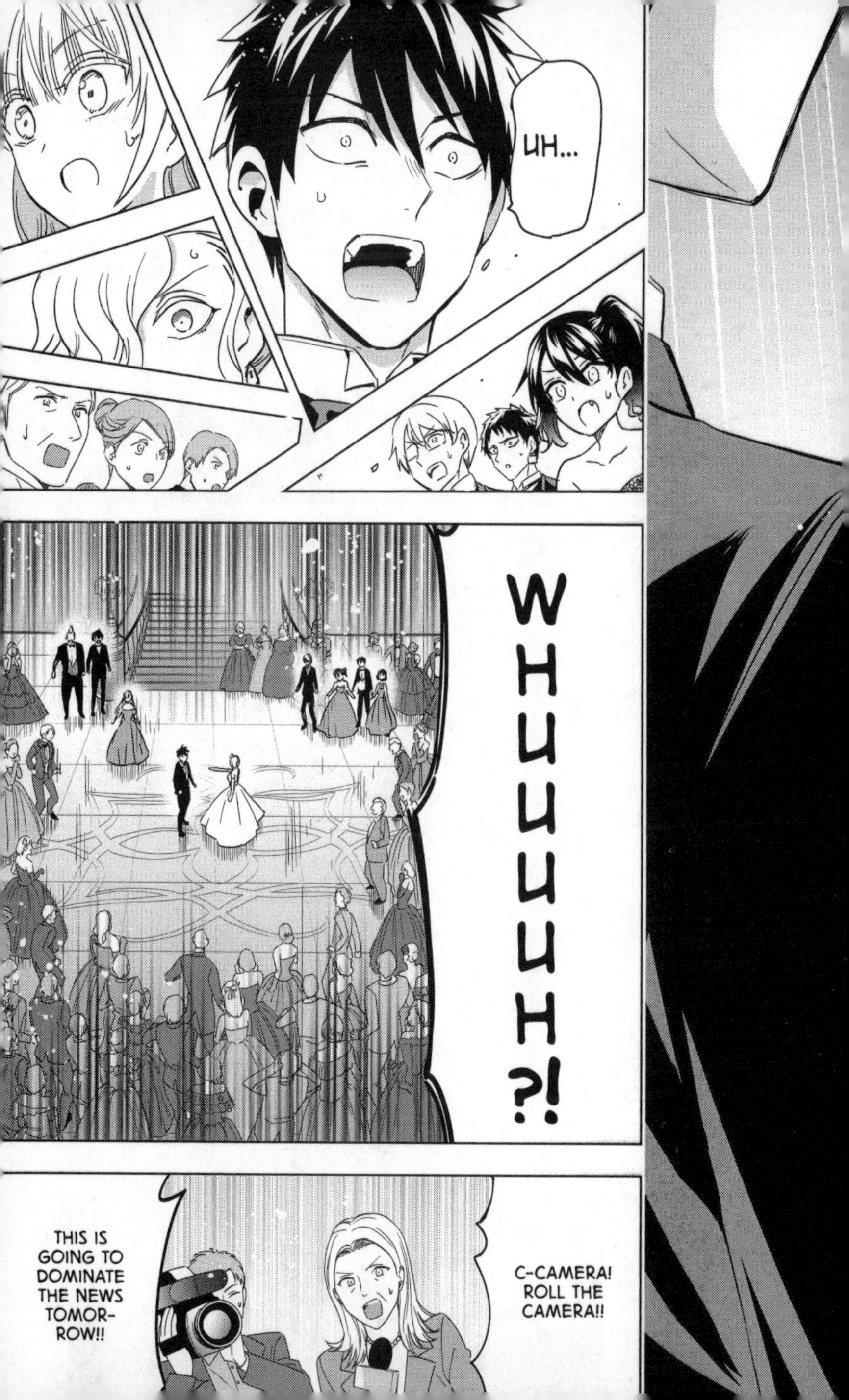
UH...
WHUUUUH?!
C-CAMERA! ROLL THE CAMERA!!
THIS IS GOING TO DOMINATE THE NEWS TOMOR-ROW!!

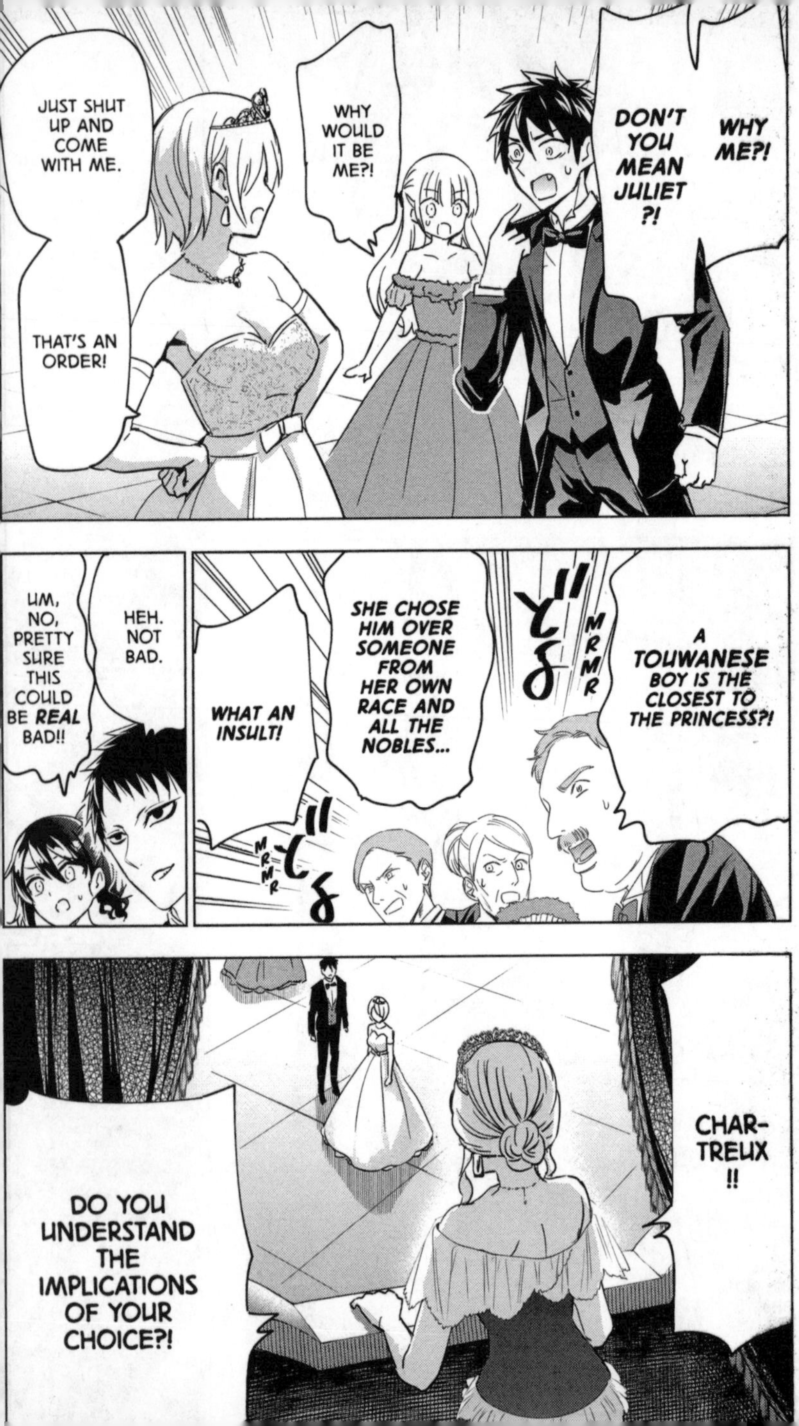
WHY ME?!
DON'T YOU MEAN JULIET?!
WHY WOULD IT BE ME?!
JUST SHUT UP AND COME WITH ME.
THAT'S AN ORDER!
A TOUWANESE BOY IS THE CLOSEST TO THE PRINCESS?!
MRMR
SHE CHOSE HIM OVER SOMEONE FROM HER OWN RACE AND ALL THE NOBLES...
WHAT AN INSULT!
MRMR
HEH. NOT BAD.
UM, NO, PRETTY SURE THIS COULD BE *REAL* BAD!!
CHARTREUX!!
DO YOU UNDERSTAND THE IMPLICATIONS OF YOUR CHOICE?!

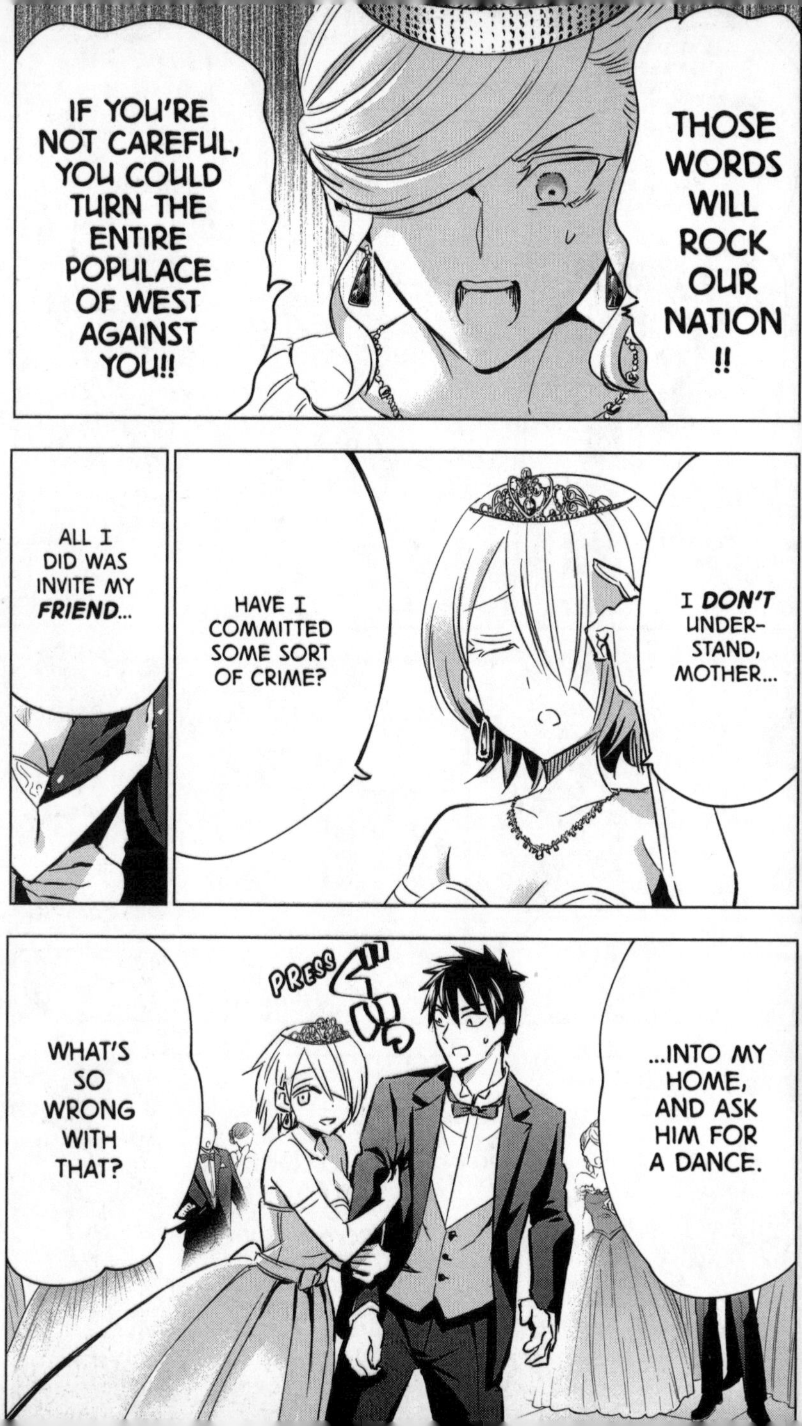
THOSE WORDS WILL ROCK OUR NATION!!
IF YOU'RE NOT CAREFUL, YOU COULD TURN THE ENTIRE POPULACE OF WEST AGAINST YOU!!
I *DON'T* UNDERSTAND, MOTHER...
HAVE I COMMITTED SOME SORT OF CRIME?
ALL I DID WAS INVITE MY *FRIEND*...
...INTO MY HOME, AND ASK HIM FOR A DANCE.
PRESS
WHAT'S SO WRONG WITH THAT?

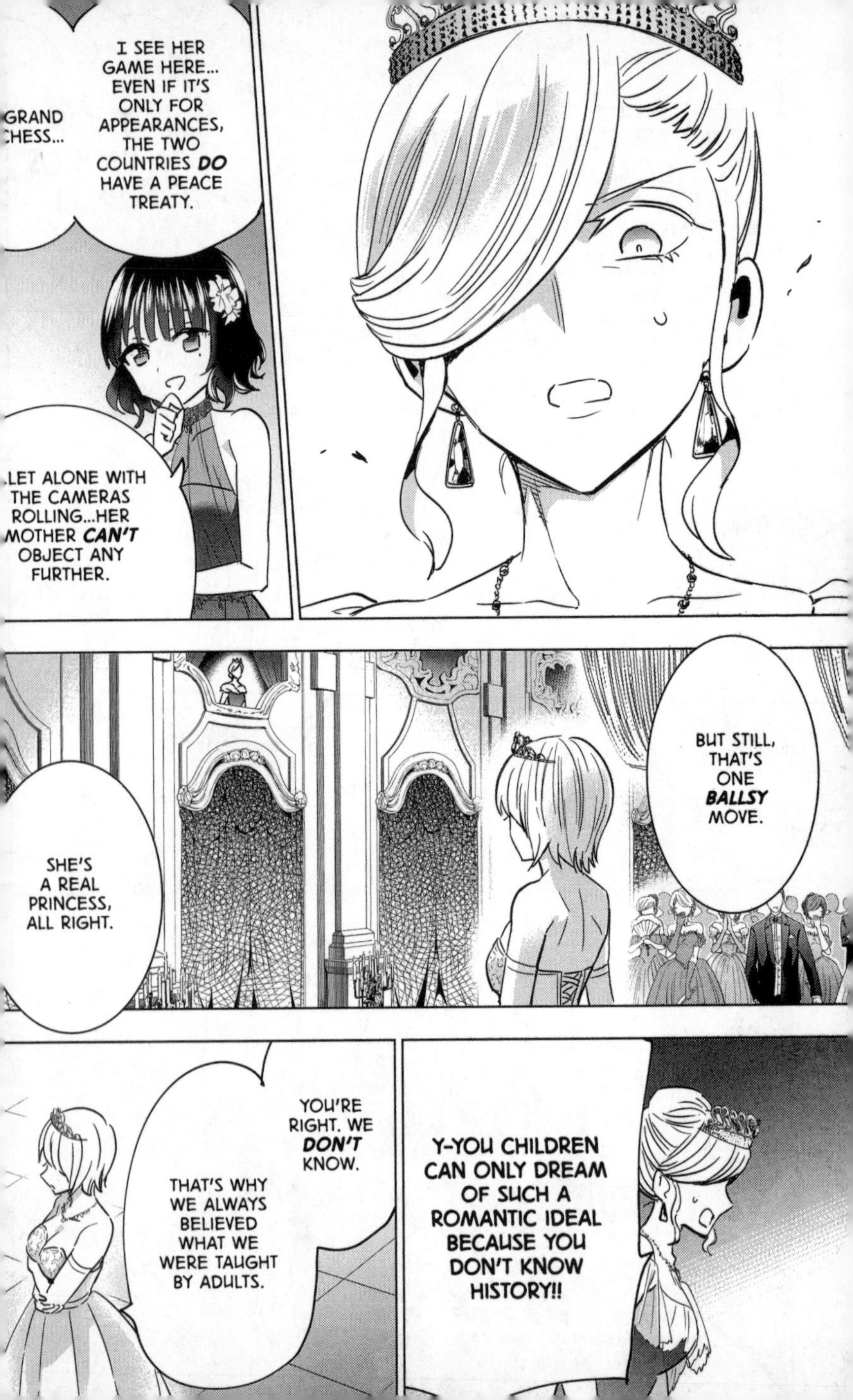
I SEE HER GAME HERE... EVEN IF IT'S ONLY FOR APPEARANCES, THE TWO COUNTRIES *DO* HAVE A PEACE TREATY.
GRAND CHESS...
LET ALONE WITH THE CAMERAS ROLLING...HER MOTHER *CAN'T* OBJECT ANY FURTHER.
BUT STILL, THAT'S ONE *BALLSY* MOVE.
SHE'S A REAL PRINCESS, ALL RIGHT.
Y-YOU CHILDREN CAN ONLY DREAM OF SUCH A ROMANTIC IDEAL BECAUSE YOU DON'T KNOW HISTORY!!
YOU'RE RIGHT. WE *DON'T* KNOW.
THAT'S WHY WE ALWAYS BELIEVED WHAT WE WERE TAUGHT BY ADULTS.

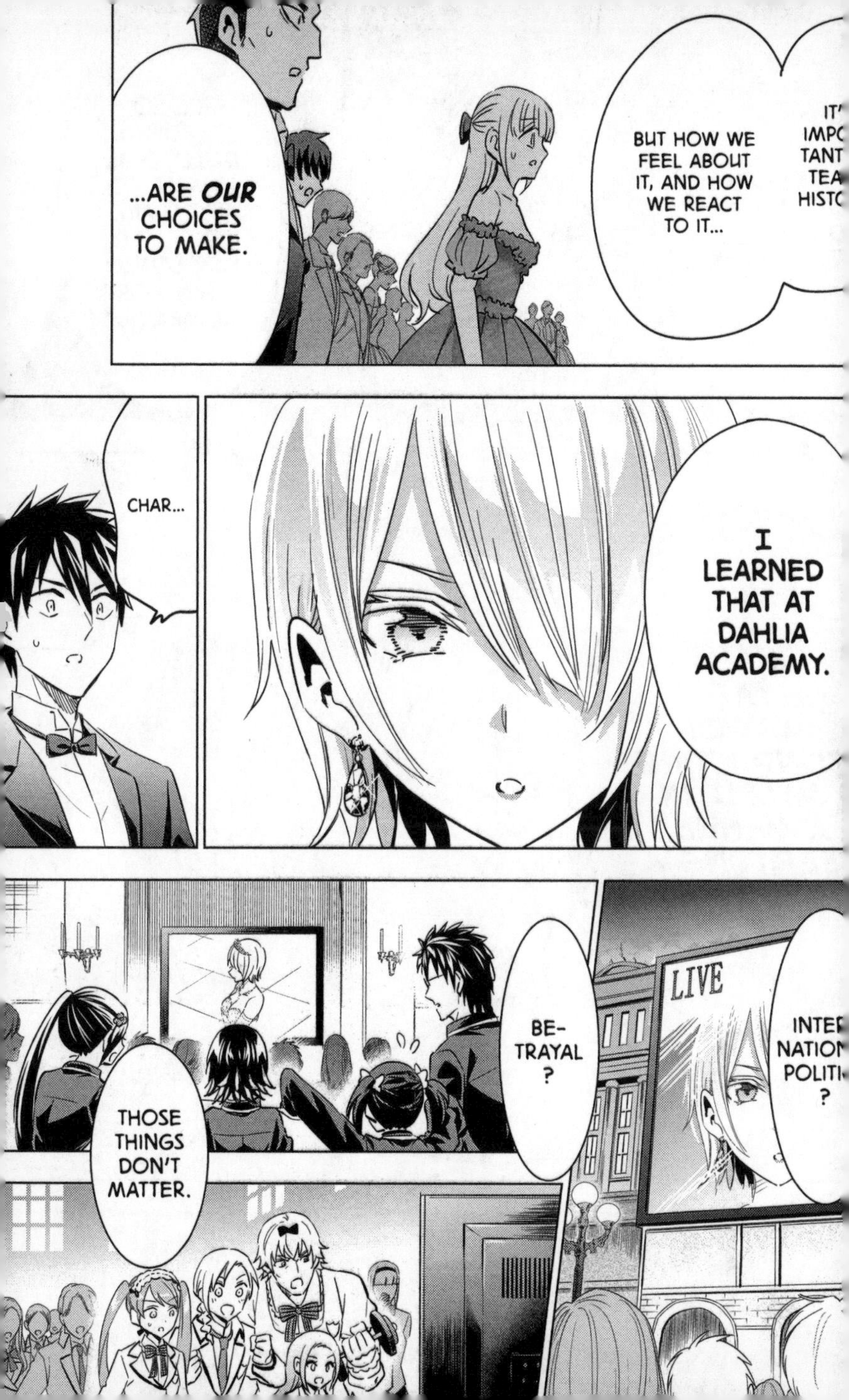
IT' IMPO TANT TEA HISTO
BUT HOW WE FEEL ABOUT IT, AND HOW WE REACT TO IT...
...ARE *OUR* CHOICES TO MAKE.
I LEARNED THAT AT DAHLIA ACADEMY.
CHAR...
LIVE
INTER NATIO POLITI ?
BE-TRAYAL ?
THOSE THINGS DON'T MATTER.

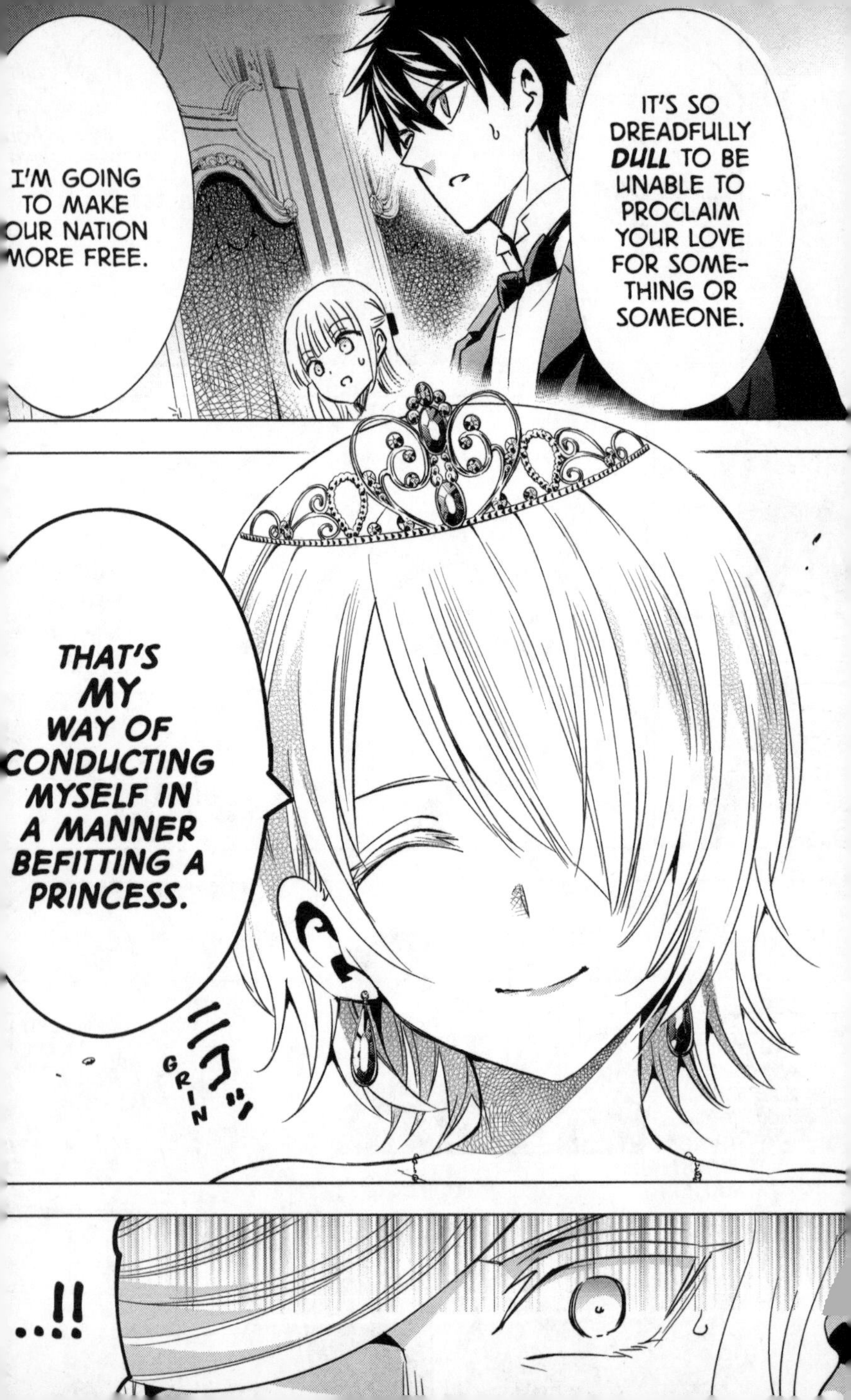
IT'S SO DREADFULLY DULL TO BE UNABLE TO PROCLAIM YOUR LOVE FOR SOME-THING OR SOMEONE.
I'M GOING TO MAKE OUR NATION MORE FREE.
THAT'S MY WAY OF CONDUCTING MYSELF IN A MANNER BEFITTING A PRINCESS.
GRIN
..!!

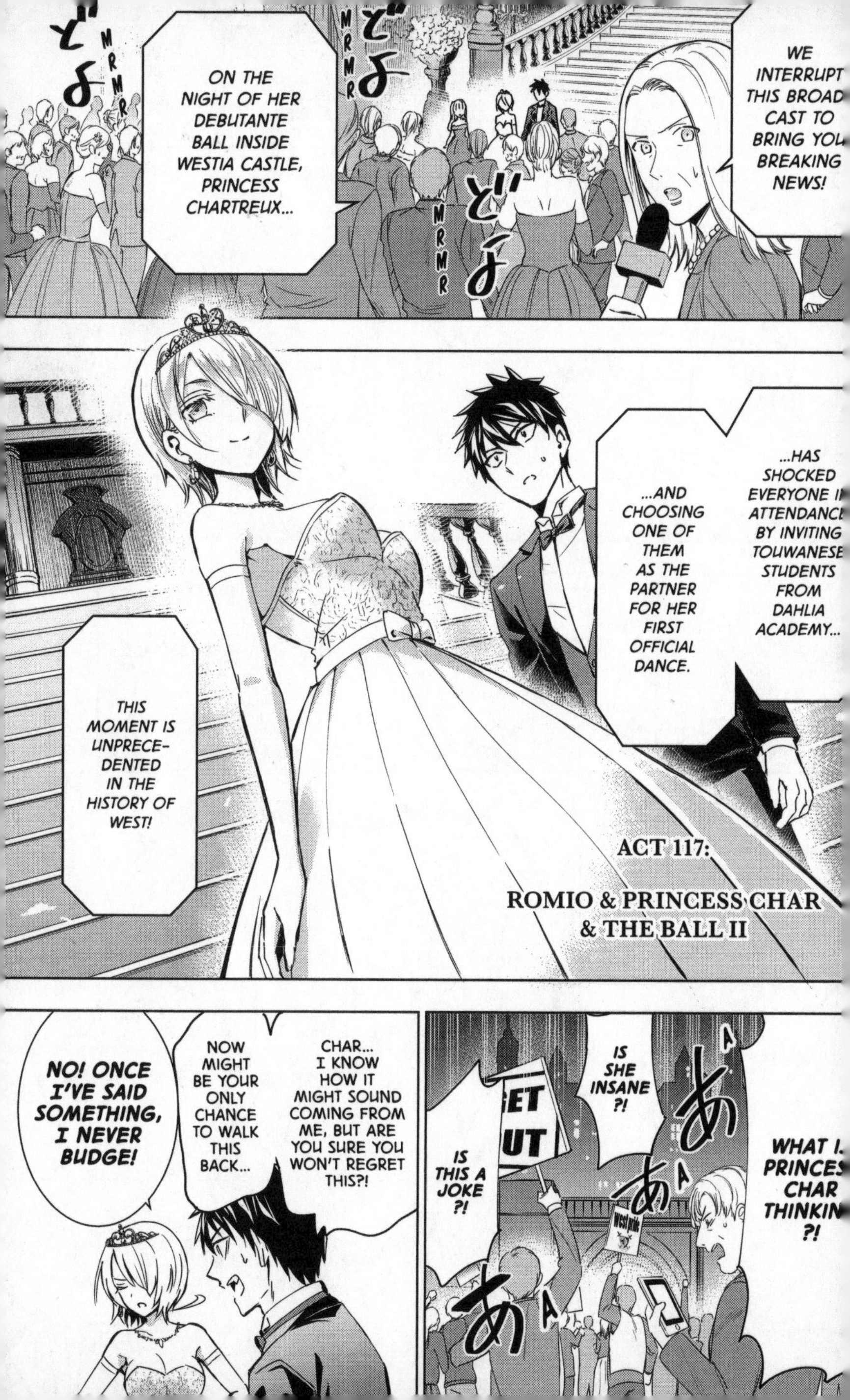
WE INTERRUPT THIS BROAD CAST TO BRING YOU BREAKING NEWS!
ざわ MRMR
ざわ MRMR
ざわ MRMR
ON THE NIGHT OF HER DEBUTANTE BALL INSIDE WESTIA CASTLE, PRINCESS CHARTREUX...
...HAS SHOCKED EVERYONE IN ATTENDANCE BY INVITING TOUWANESE STUDENTS FROM DAHLIA ACADEMY...
...AND CHOOSING ONE OF THEM AS THE PARTNER FOR HER FIRST OFFICIAL DANCE.
THIS MOMENT IS UNPRECEDENTED IN THE HISTORY OF WEST!
ACT 117:
ROMIO & PRINCESS CHAR & THE BALL II
WHAT IS PRINCESS CHAR THINKING?!
あ A
IS SHE INSANE?!
あ A
IS THIS A JOKE?!
あ A
CHAR... I KNOW HOW IT MIGHT SOUND COMING FROM ME, BUT ARE YOU SURE YOU WON'T REGRET THIS?!
NOW MIGHT BE YOUR ONLY CHANCE TO WALK THIS BACK...
NO! ONCE I'VE SAID SOMETHING, I NEVER BUDGE!

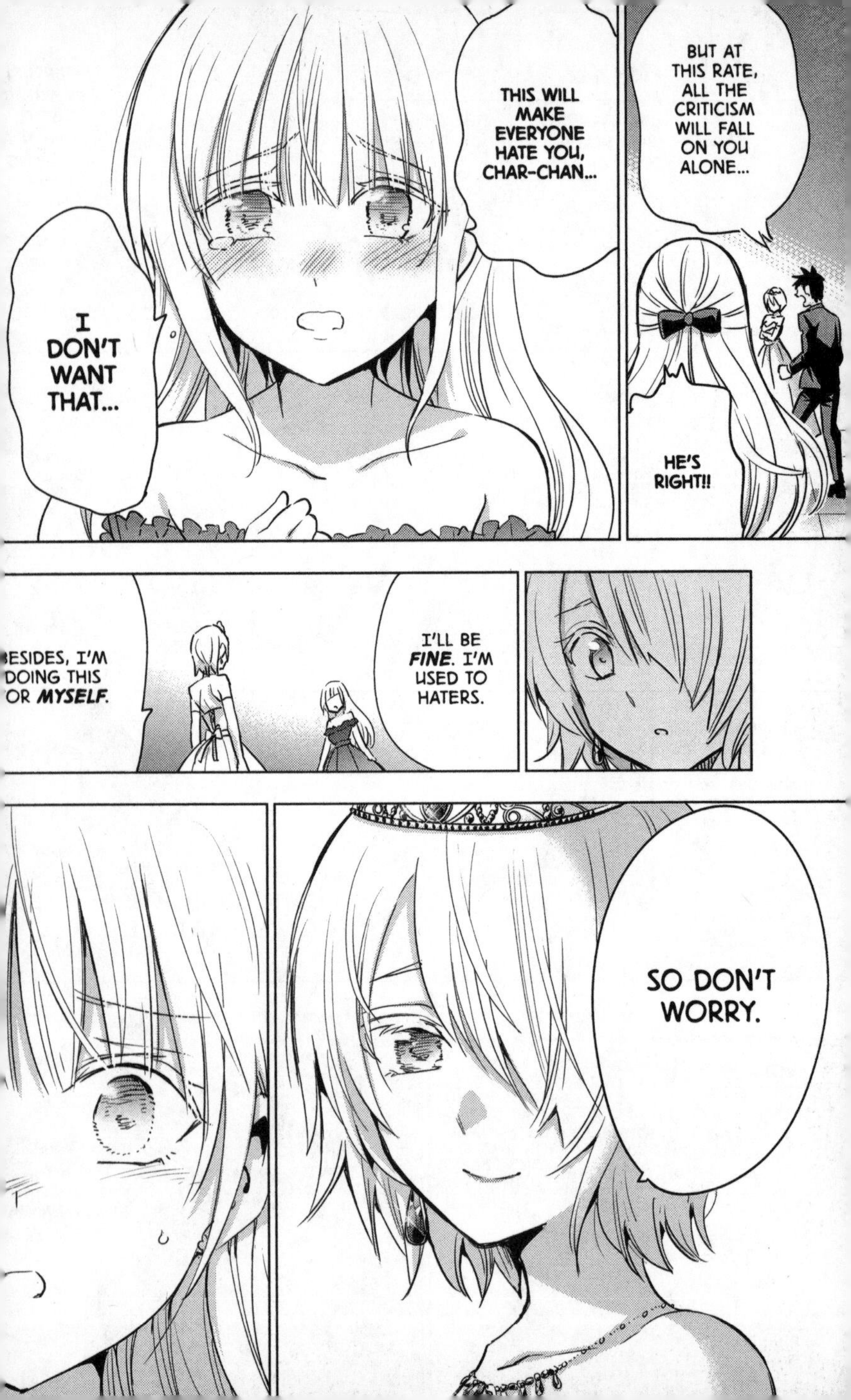
BUT AT THIS RATE, ALL THE CRITICISM WILL FALL ON YOU ALONE...
HE'S RIGHT!!
THIS WILL MAKE EVERYONE HATE YOU, CHAR-CHAN...
I DON'T WANT THAT...
I'LL BE *FINE*. I'M USED TO HATERS.
ESIDES, I'M DOING THIS OR *MYSELF*.
SO DON'T WORRY.

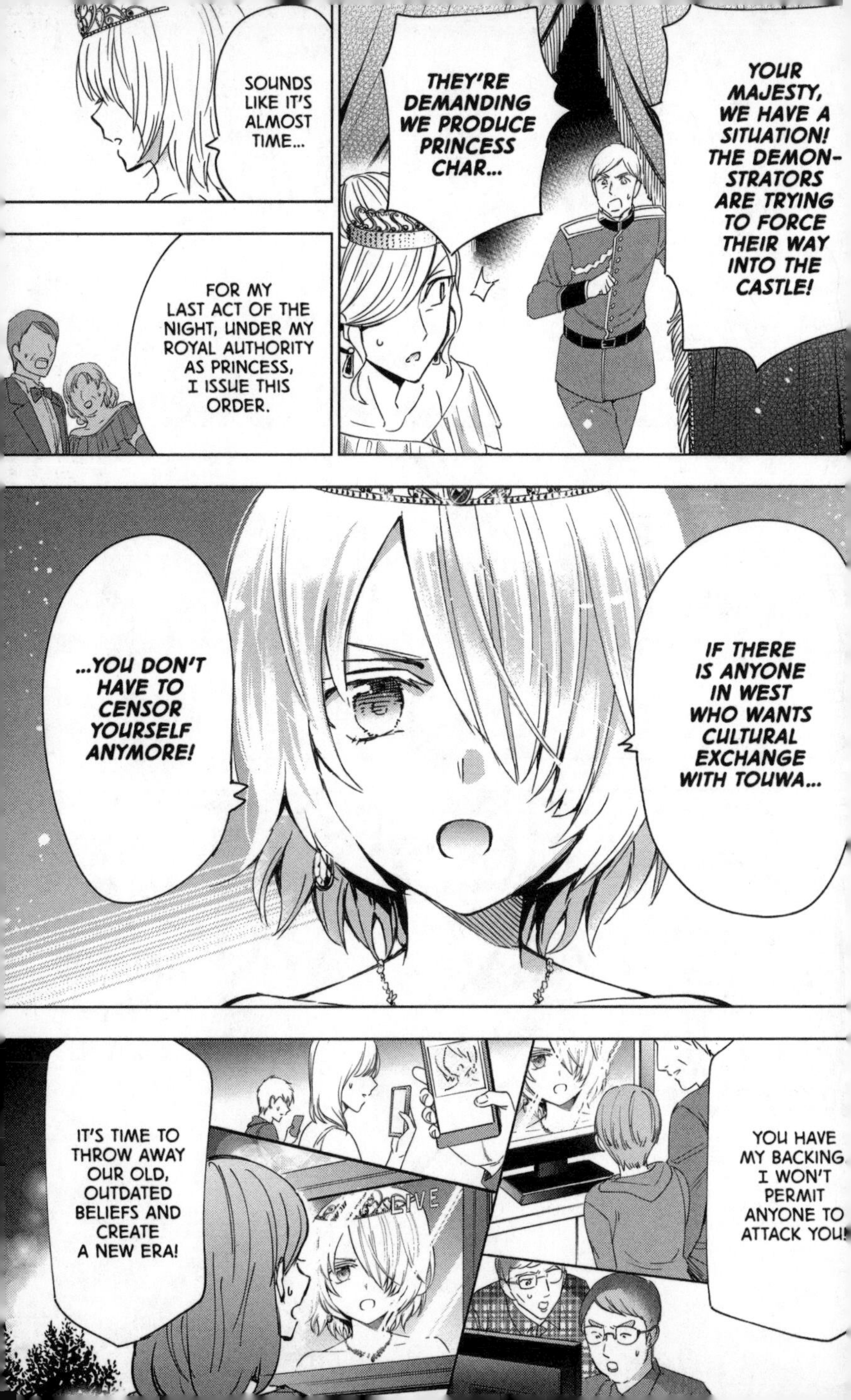
YOUR MAJESTY, WE HAVE A SITUATION! THE DEMON-STRATORS ARE TRYING TO FORCE THEIR WAY INTO THE CASTLE!
THEY'RE DEMANDING WE PRODUCE PRINCESS CHAR...
SOUNDS LIKE IT'S ALMOST TIME...
FOR MY LAST ACT OF THE NIGHT, UNDER MY ROYAL AUTHORITY AS PRINCESS, I ISSUE THIS ORDER.
IF THERE IS ANYONE IN WEST WHO WANTS CULTURAL EXCHANGE WITH TOUWA...
...YOU DON'T HAVE TO CENSOR YOURSELF ANYMORE!
YOU HAVE MY BACKING. I WON'T PERMIT ANYONE TO ATTACK YOU!
IT'S TIME TO THROW AWAY OUR OLD, OUTDATED BELIEFS AND CREATE A NEW ERA!

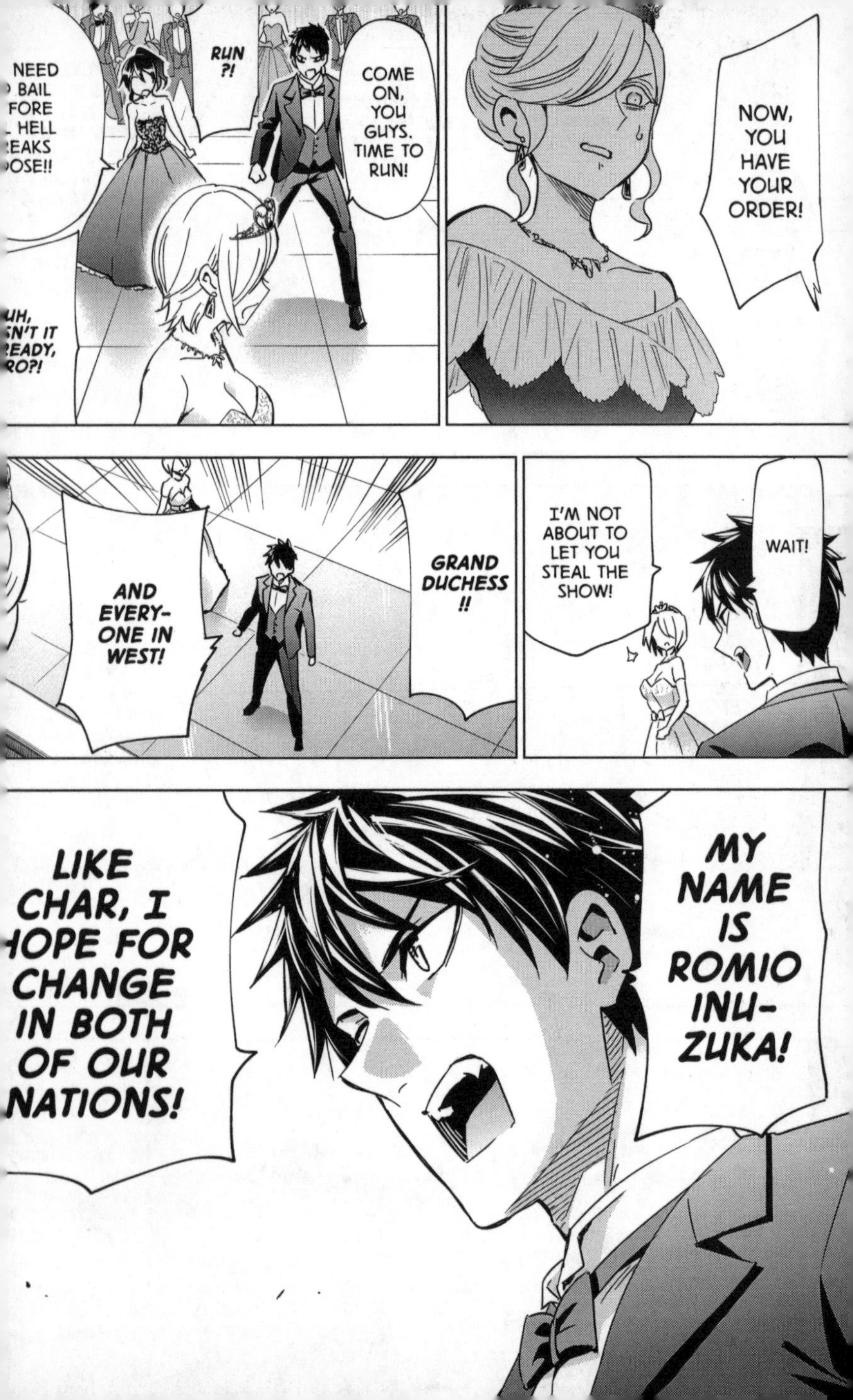
NOW, YOU HAVE YOUR ORDER!
COME ON, YOU GUYS. TIME TO RUN!
RUN ?!
NEED
BAIL
FORE
HELL
EAKS
OSE!!
UH,
SN'T IT
EADY,
RO?!
WAIT!
I'M NOT ABOUT TO LET YOU STEAL THE SHOW!
GRAND DUCHESS !!
AND EVERY-ONE IN WEST!
MY NAME IS ROMIO INU-ZUKA!
LIKE CHAR, I
OPE FOR CHANGE IN BOTH OF OUR NATIONS!

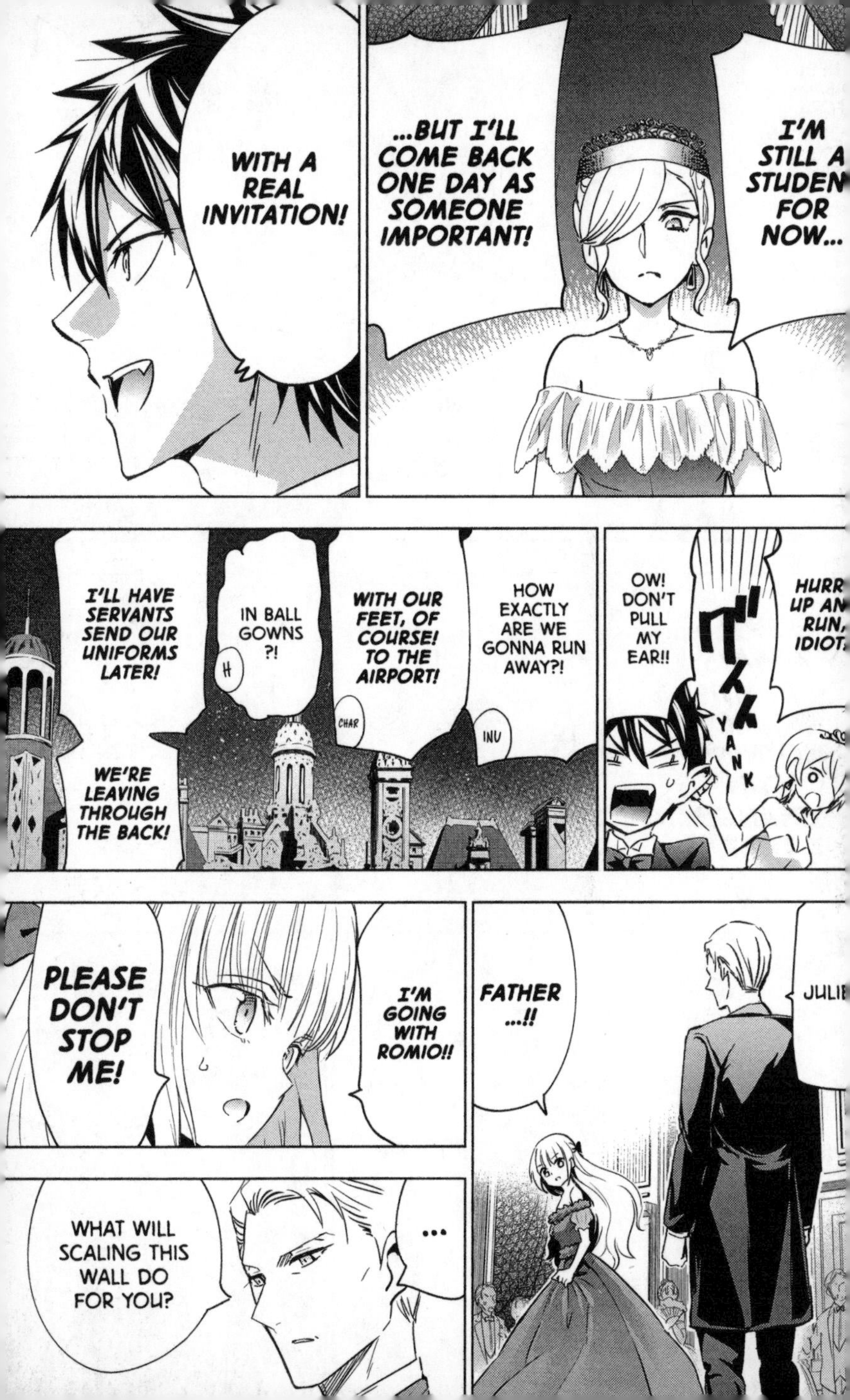
I'M STILL A STUDEN FOR NOW...
...BUT I'LL COME BACK ONE DAY AS SOMEONE IMPORTANT!
WITH A REAL INVITATION!
HURR UP AN RUN, IDIOT
YANK
OW! DON'T PULL MY EAR!!
HOW EXACTLY ARE WE GONNA RUN AWAY?!
INU
WITH OUR FEET, OF COURSE! TO THE AIRPORT!
CHAR
IN BALL GOWNS?!
H
I'LL HAVE SERVANTS SEND OUR UNIFORMS LATER!
WE'RE LEAVING THROUGH THE BACK!
JULI
FATHER ...!!
I'M GOING WITH ROMIO!!
PLEASE DON'T STOP ME!
...
WHAT WILL SCALING THIS WALL DO FOR YOU?

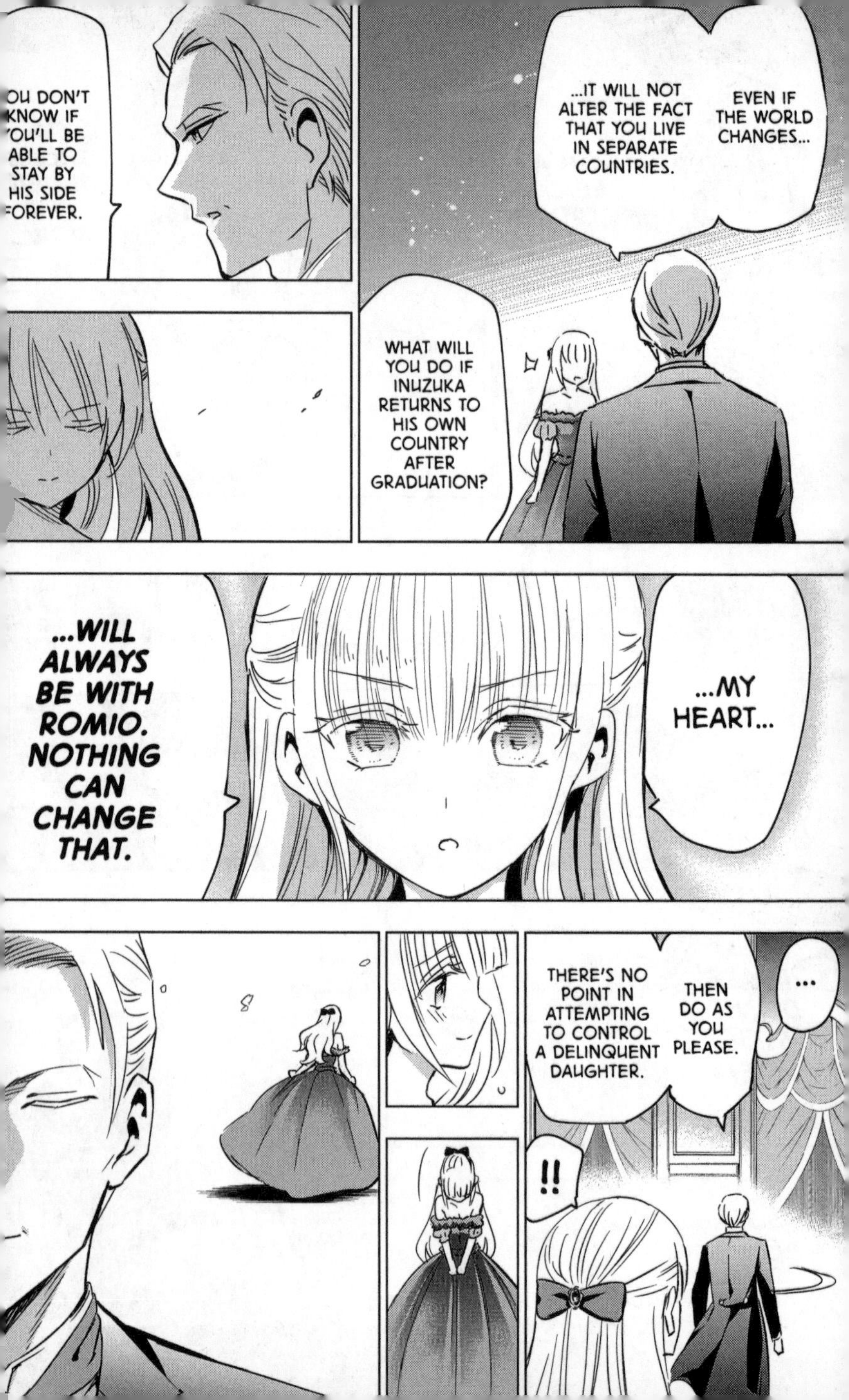
EVEN IF THE WORLD CHANGES...
...IT WILL NOT ALTER THE FACT THAT YOU LIVE IN SEPARATE COUNTRIES.
WHAT WILL YOU DO IF INUZUKA RETURNS TO HIS OWN COUNTRY AFTER GRADUATION?
OU DON'T KNOW IF 'OU'LL BE ABLE TO STAY BY HIS SIDE FOREVER.
...MY HEART...
...WILL ALWAYS BE WITH ROMIO. NOTHING CAN CHANGE THAT.
...
THEN DO AS YOU PLEASE.
THERE'S NO POINT IN ATTEMPTING TO CONTROL A DELINQUENT DAUGHTER.
!!

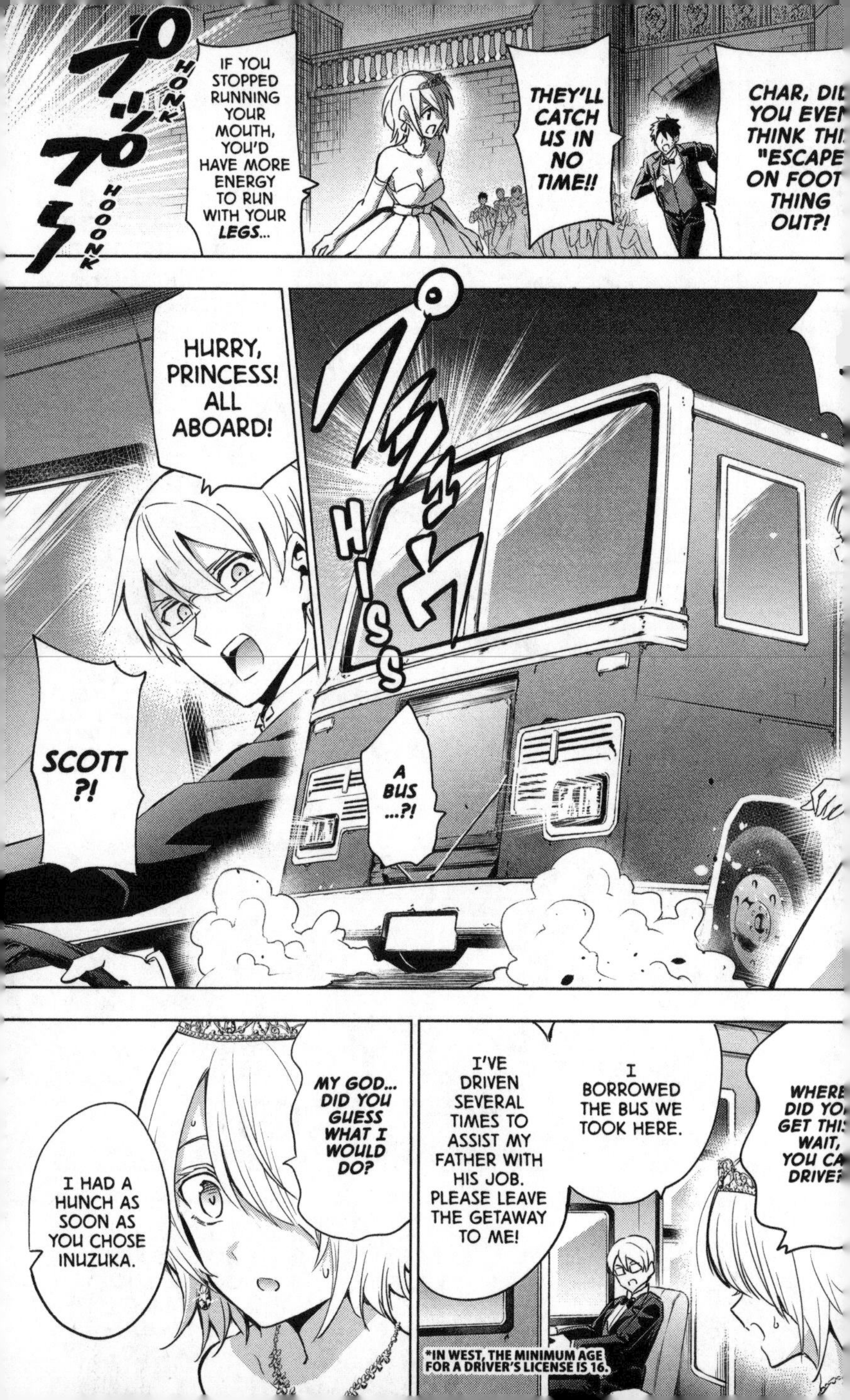

CHAR, DI YOU EVE THINK THI "ESCAPE ON FOOT THING OUT?!
THEY'LL CATCH US IN NO TIME!!
IF YOU STOPPED RUNNING YOUR MOUTH, YOU'D HAVE MORE ENERGY TO RUN WITH YOUR *LEGS*...
HONK
HOOONK
HISS
HURRY, PRINCESS! ALL ABOARD!
A BUS ...?!
SCOTT ?!
WHERE DID YO GET THIS WAIT, YOU CA DRIVE
I BORROWED THE BUS WE TOOK HERE.
I'VE DRIVEN SEVERAL TIMES TO ASSIST MY FATHER WITH HIS JOB. PLEASE LEAVE THE GETAWAY TO ME!
*IN WEST, THE MINIMUM AGE FOR A DRIVER'S LICENSE IS 16.
MY GOD... DID YOU GUESS WHAT I WOULD DO?
I HAD A HUNCH AS SOON AS YOU CHOSE INUZUKA.

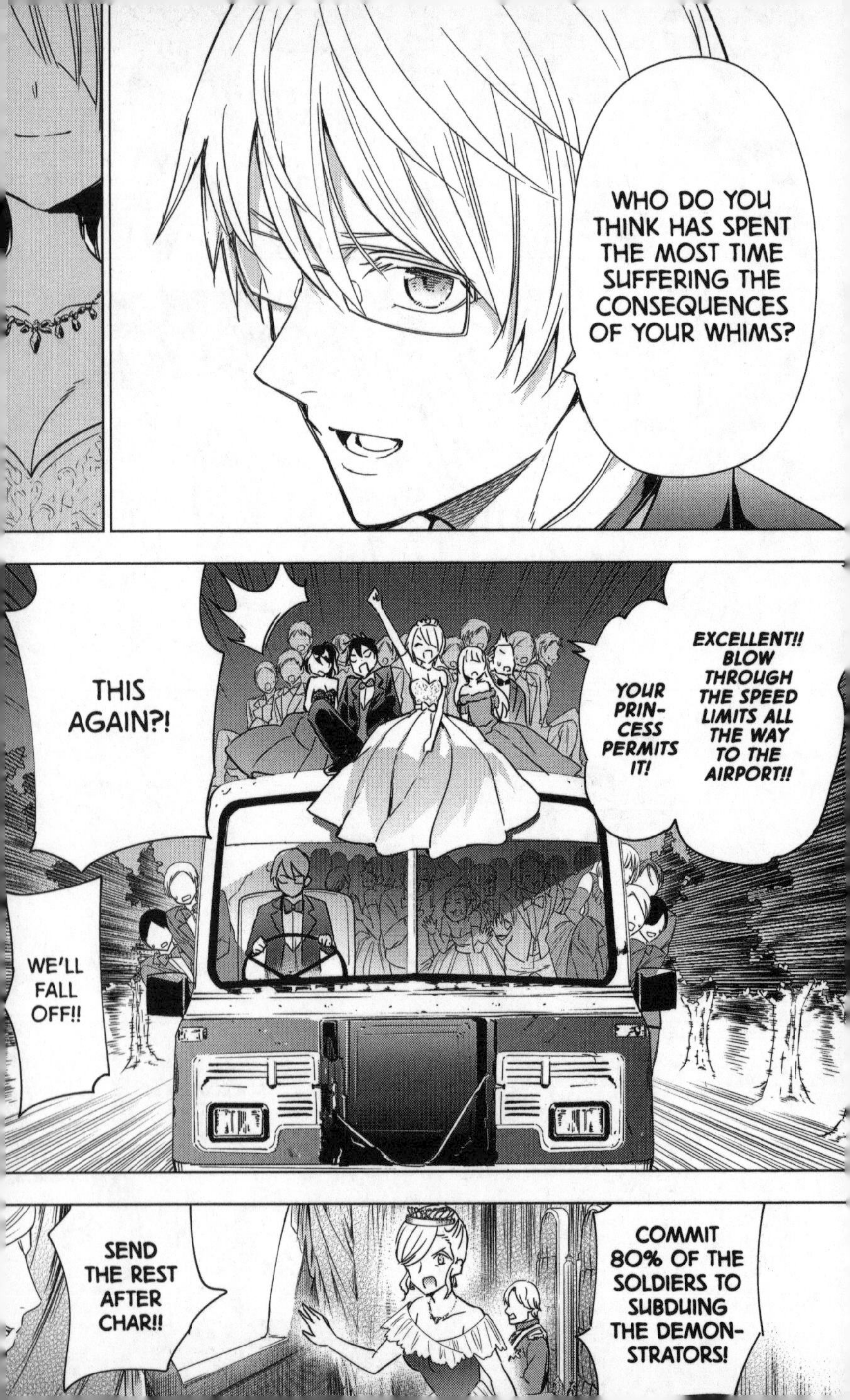
WHO DO YOU THINK HAS SPENT THE MOST TIME SUFFERING THE CONSEQUENCES OF YOUR WHIMS?
EXCELLENT!! BLOW THROUGH THE SPEED LIMITS ALL THE WAY TO THE AIRPORT!!
YOUR PRIN-CESS PERMITS IT!
THIS AGAIN?!
WE'LL FALL OFF!!
COMMIT 80% OF THE SOLDIERS TO SUBDUING THE DEMON-STRATORS!
SEND THE REST AFTER CHAR!!

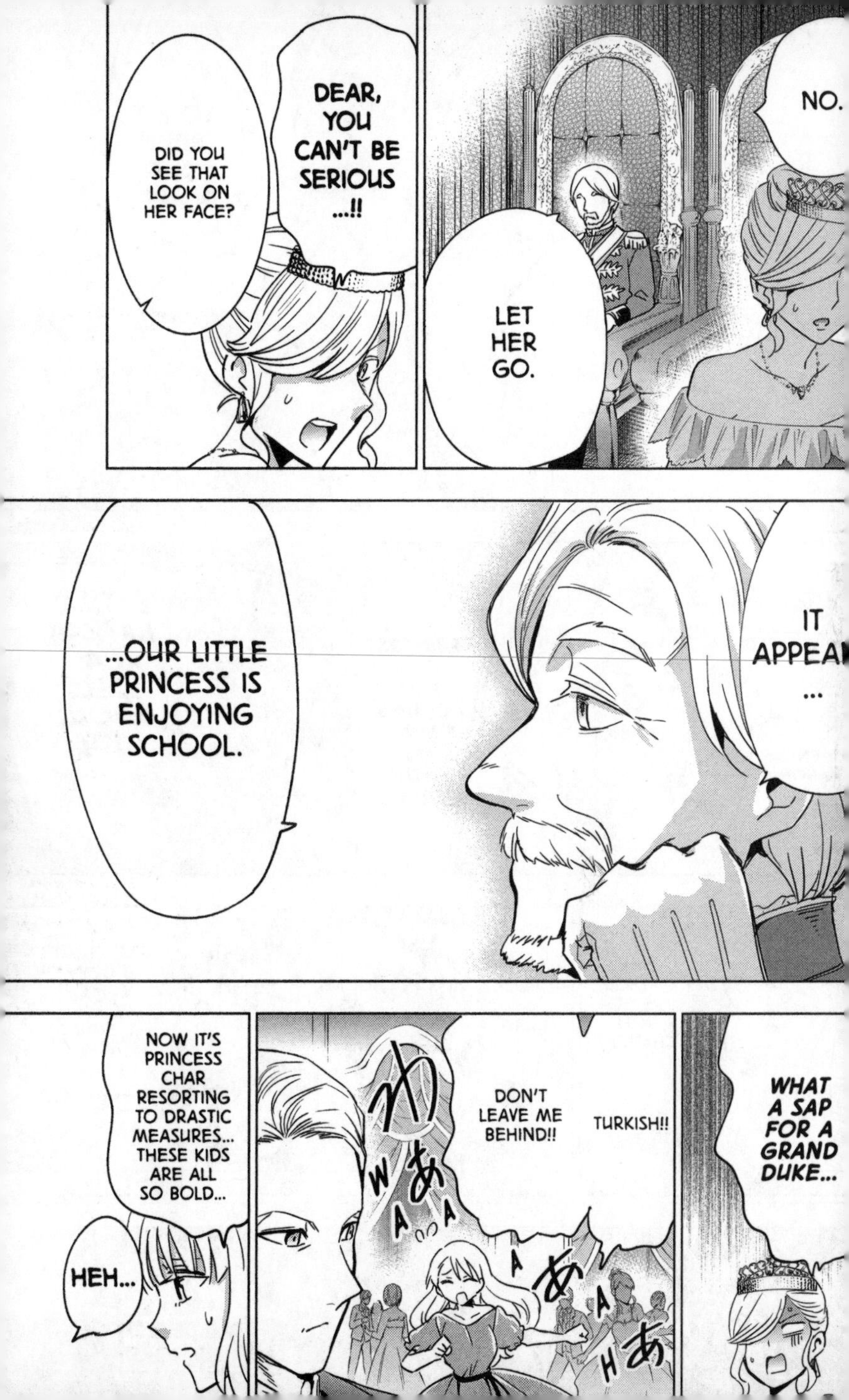
NO.
LET HER GO.
DEAR, YOU CAN'T BE SERIOUS ...!!
DID YOU SEE THAT LOOK ON HER FACE?
IT APPEA ...
...OUR LITTLE PRINCESS IS ENJOYING SCHOOL.
WHAT A SAP FOR A GRAND DUKE...
TURKISH!!
DON'T LEAVE ME BEHIND!!
WAAAH
NOW IT'S PRINCESS CHAR RESORTING TO DRASTIC MEASURES... THESE KIDS ARE ALL SO BOLD...
HEH...

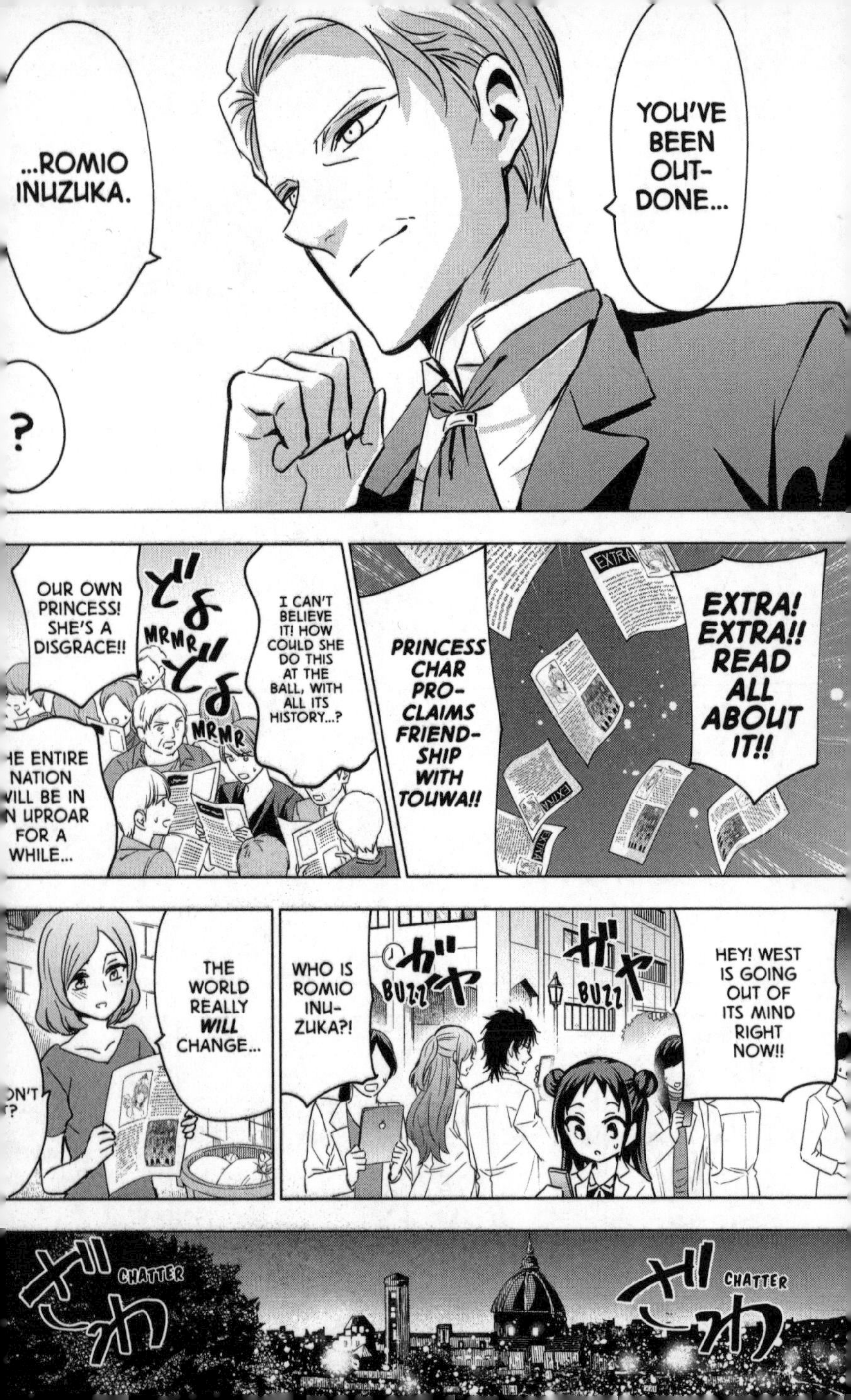
YOU'VE BEEN OUT-DONE...
...ROMIO INUZUKA.
?
EXTRA! EXTRA!! READ ALL ABOUT IT!!
PRINCESS CHAR PRO-CLAIMS FRIEND-SHIP WITH TOUWA!!
I CAN'T BELIEVE IT! HOW COULD SHE DO THIS AT THE BALL, WITH ALL ITS HISTORY...?
MRMR
MRMR
OUR OWN PRINCESS! SHE'S A DISGRACE!!
HEY! WEST IS GOING OUT OF ITS MIND RIGHT NOW!!
BUZZ
BUZZ
WHO IS ROMIO INU-ZUKA?!
THE WORLD REALLY WILL CHANGE...
CHATTER
CHATTER

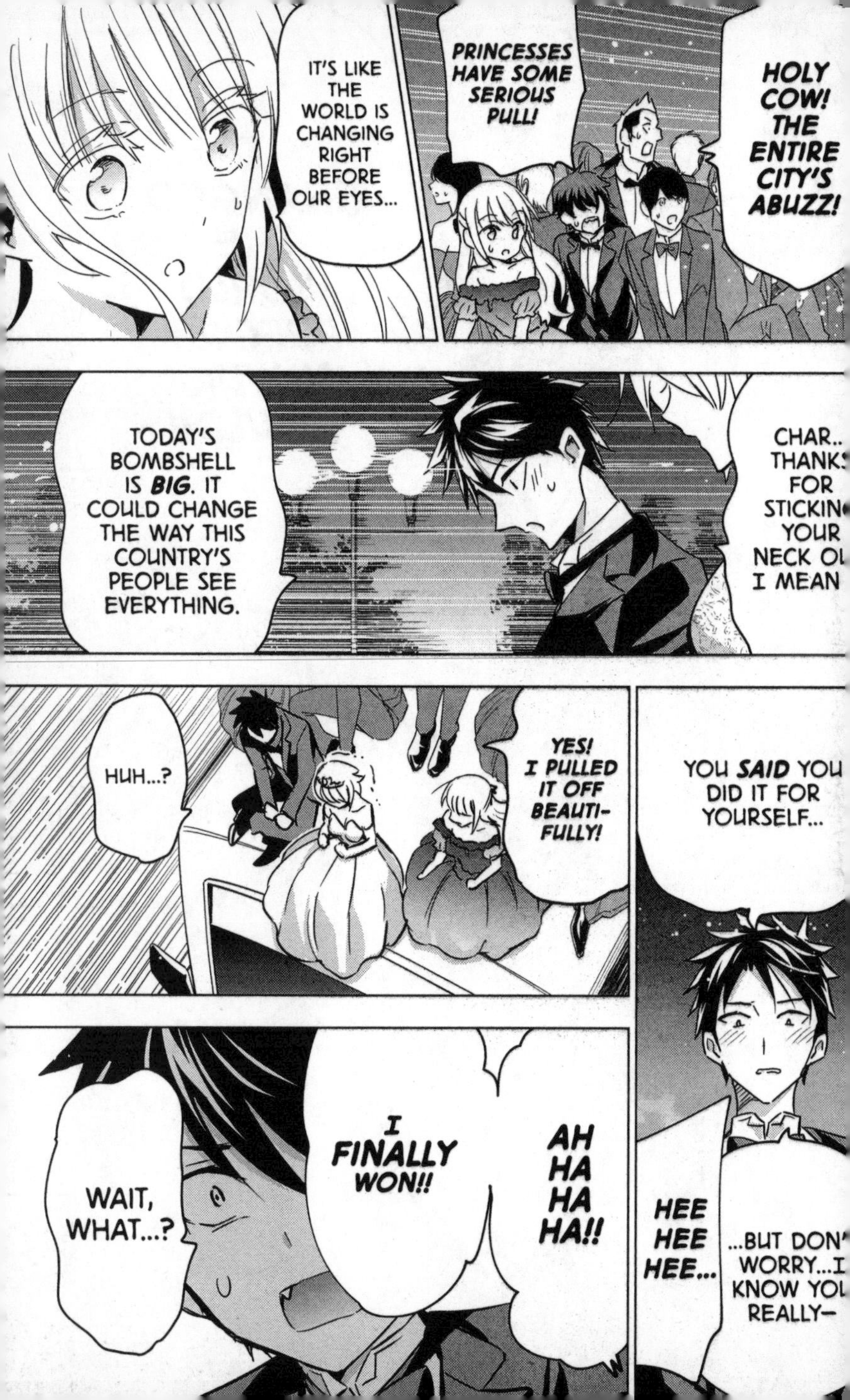

HOLY COW! THE ENTIRE CITY'S ABUZZ!
PRINCESSES HAVE SOME SERIOUS PULL!
IT'S LIKE THE WORLD IS CHANGING RIGHT BEFORE OUR EYES...
CHAR.. THANKS FOR STICKIN YOUR NECK O I MEAN
TODAY'S BOMBSHELL IS BIG. IT COULD CHANGE THE WAY THIS COUNTRY'S PEOPLE SEE EVERYTHING.
YOU SAID YOU DID IT FOR YOURSELF...
...BUT DON' WORRY...I KNOW YO REALLY—
HEE HEE HEE...
YES! I PULLED IT OFF BEAUTIFULLY!
HUH...?
AH HA HA HA!!
I FINALLY WON!!
WAIT, WHAT...?

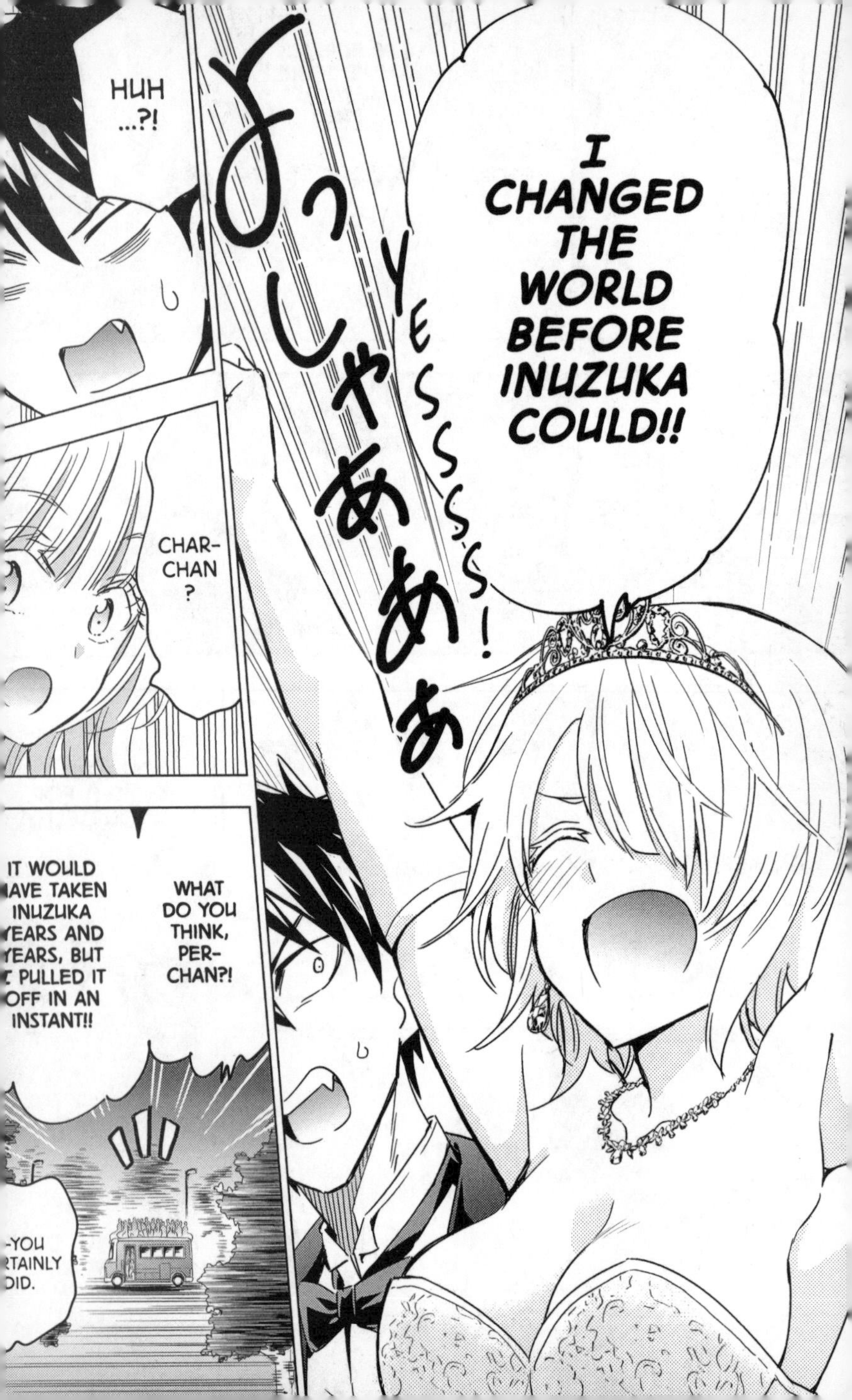
I CHANGED THE WORLD BEFORE INUZUKA COULD!!
よっしゃあああぁ
YESSSS!
HUH ...?!
CHAR-CHAN ?
WHAT DO YOU THINK, PER-CHAN?!
IT WOULD AVE TAKEN INUZUKA YEARS AND YEARS, BUT PULLED IT OFF IN AN INSTANT!!
-YOU RTAINLY DID.

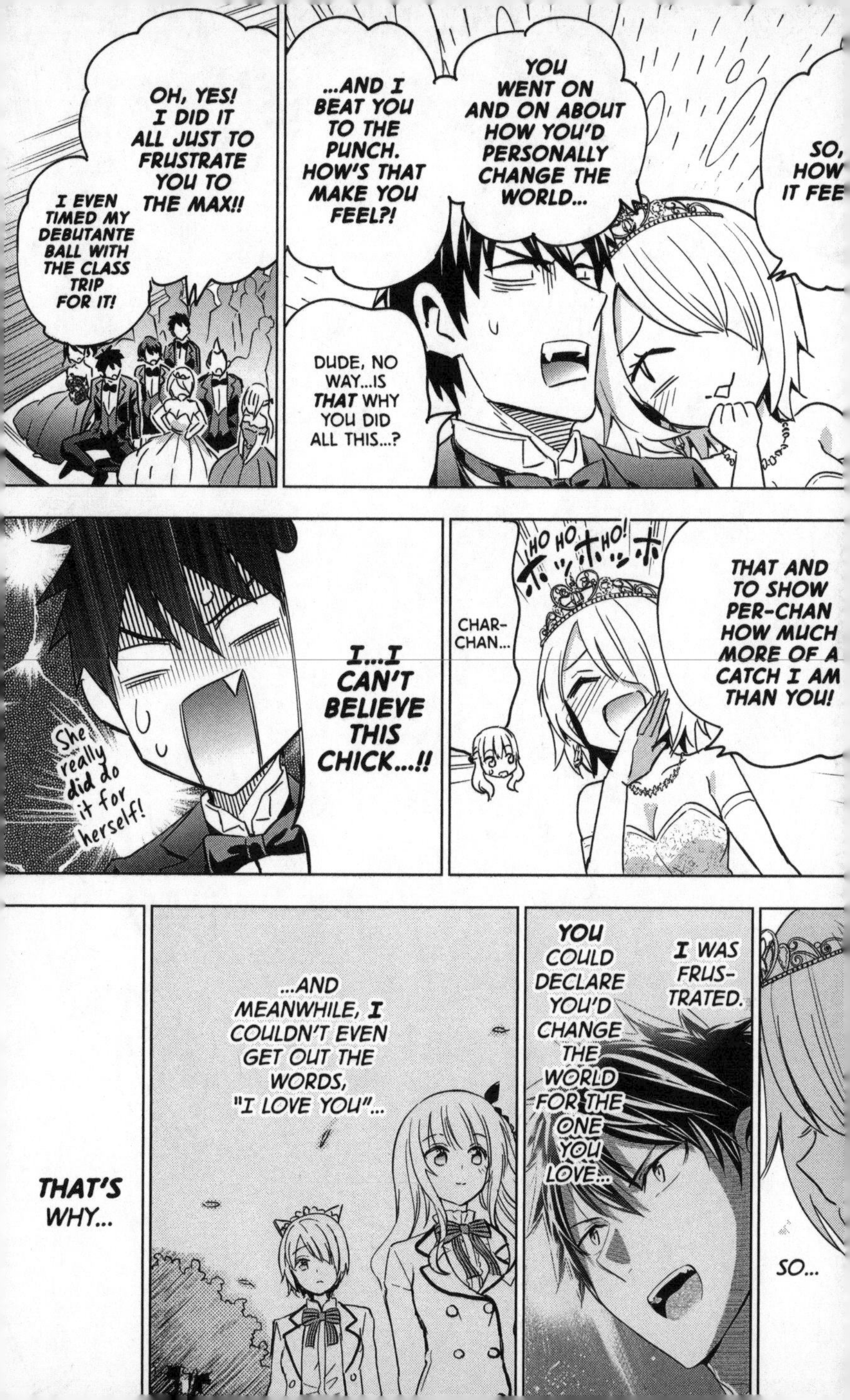

SO, HOW IT FEE
YOU WENT ON AND ON ABOUT HOW YOU'D PERSONALLY CHANGE THE WORLD...
...AND I BEAT YOU TO THE PUNCH. HOW'S THAT MAKE YOU FEEL?!
DUDE, NO WAY...IS *THAT* WHY YOU DID ALL THIS...?
OH, YES! I DID IT ALL JUST TO FRUSTRATE YOU TO THE MAX!!
I EVEN TIMED MY DEBUTANTE BALL WITH THE CLASS TRIP FOR IT!
HO HO HO!
THAT AND TO SHOW PER-CHAN HOW MUCH MORE OF A CATCH I AM THAN YOU!
CHAR-CHAN...
I...I CAN'T BELIEVE THIS CHICK...!!
She really did do it for herself!
SO...
I WAS FRUS-TRATED.
YOU COULD DECLARE YOU'D CHANGE THE WORLD FOR THE ONE YOU LOVE...
...AND MEANWHILE, I COULDN'T EVEN GET OUT THE WORDS, "I LOVE YOU"...
THAT'S WHY...

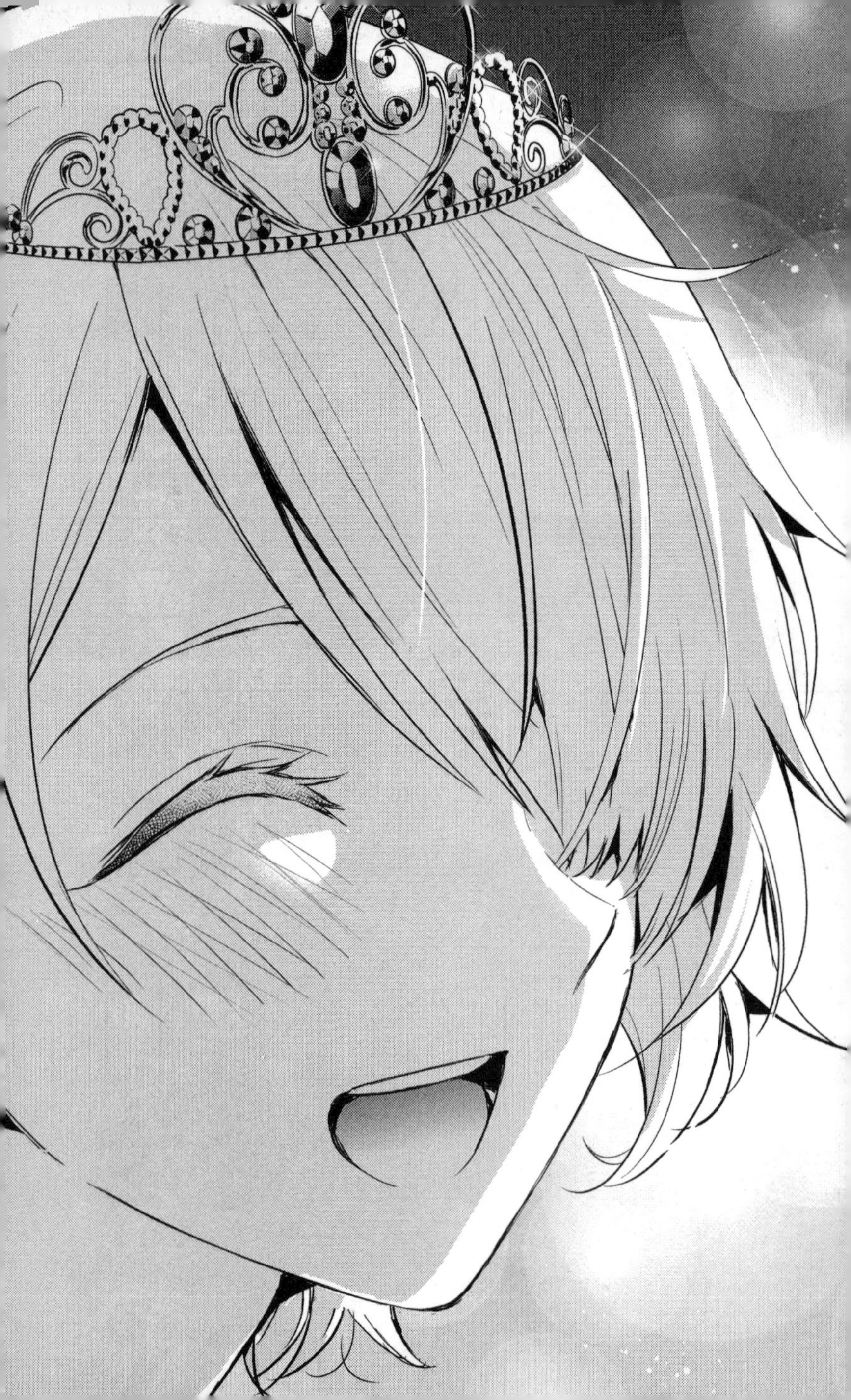

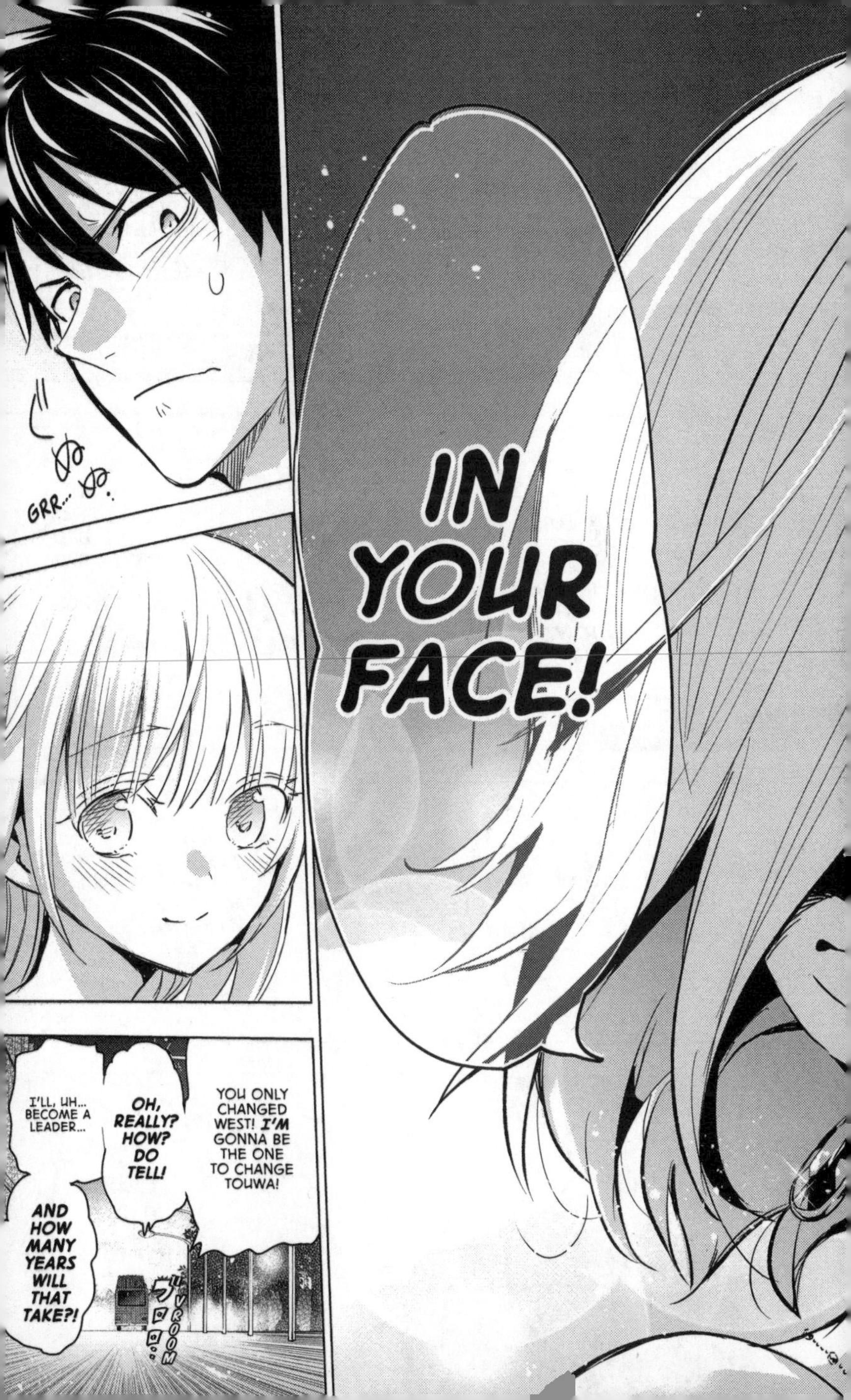
IN YOUR FACE!
GRR...
YOU ONLY CHANGED WEST! **I'M** GONNA BE THE ONE TO CHANGE TOUWA!
OH, REALLY? HOW? DO TELL!
I'LL, UH... BECOME A LEADER...
AND HOW MANY YEARS WILL THAT TAKE?!
VROOM

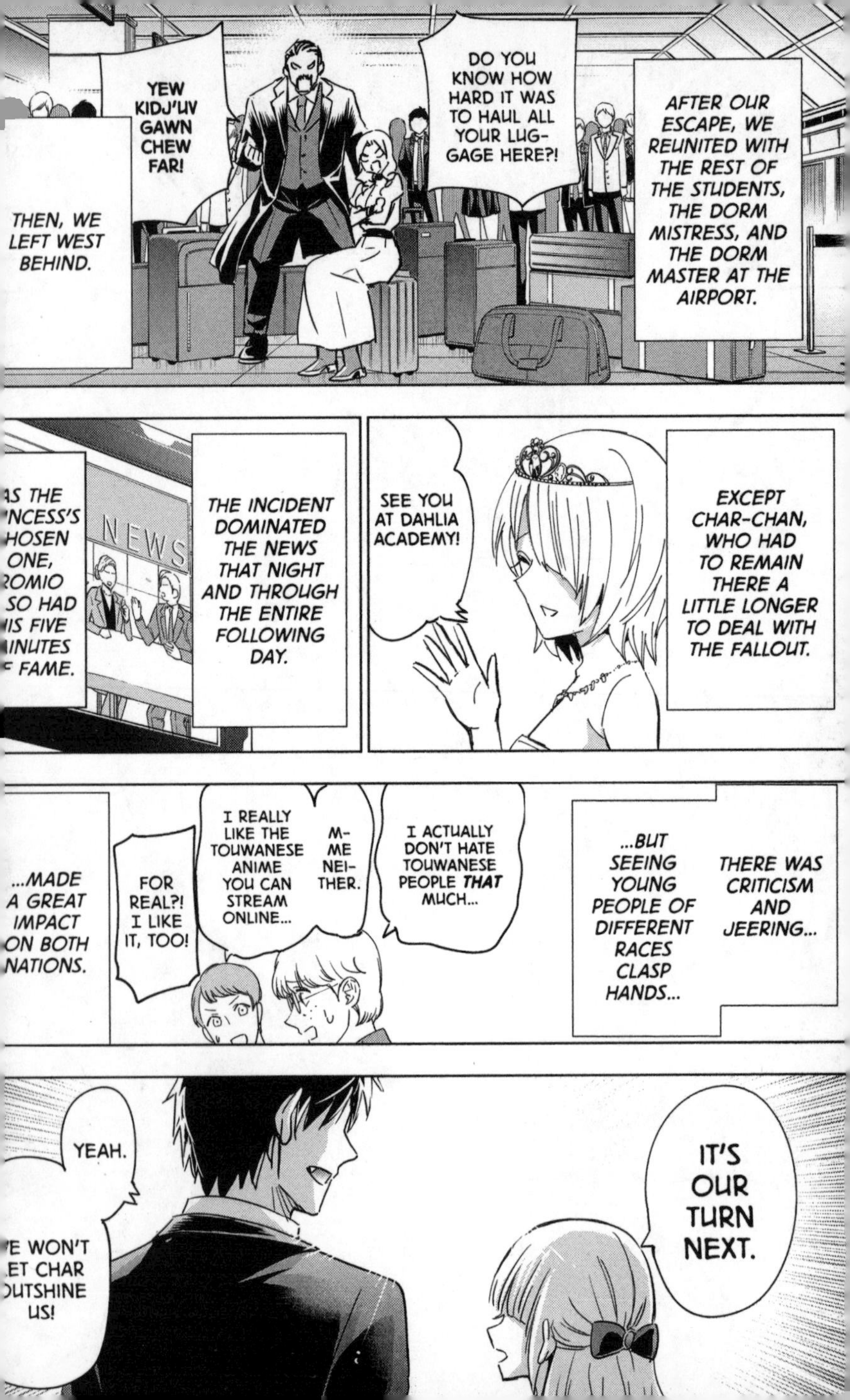
AFTER OUR ESCAPE, WE REUNITED WITH THE REST OF THE STUDENTS, THE DORM MISTRESS, AND THE DORM MASTER AT THE AIRPORT.
DO YOU KNOW HOW HARD IT WAS TO HAUL ALL YOUR LUG-GAGE HERE?!
YEW KIDJ'UV GAWN CHEW FAR!
THEN, WE LEFT WEST BEHIND.
EXCEPT CHAR-CHAN, WHO HAD TO REMAIN THERE A LITTLE LONGER TO DEAL WITH THE FALLOUT.
SEE YOU AT DAHLIA ACADEMY!
THE INCIDENT DOMINATED THE NEWS THAT NIGHT AND THROUGH THE ENTIRE FOLLOWING DAY.
NEWS
AS THE NCESS'S HOSEN ONE, ROMIO SO HAD IS FIVE INUTES FAME.
THERE WAS CRITICISM AND JEERING...
...BUT SEEING YOUNG PEOPLE OF DIFFERENT RACES CLASP HANDS...
I ACTUALLY DON'T HATE TOUWANESE PEOPLE **THAT** MUCH...
M-ME NEI-THER.
I REALLY LIKE THE TOUWANESE ANIME YOU CAN STREAM ONLINE...
FOR REAL?! I LIKE IT, TOO!
...MADE A GREAT IMPACT ON BOTH NATIONS.
IT'S OUR TURN NEXT.
YEAH.
E WON'T ET CHAR UTSHINE US!

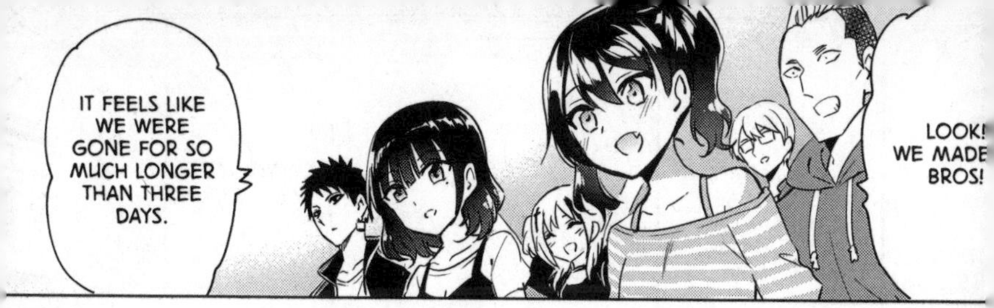
LOOK! WE MADE BROS!
IT FEELS LIKE WE WERE GONE FOR SO MUCH LONGER THAN THREE DAYS.

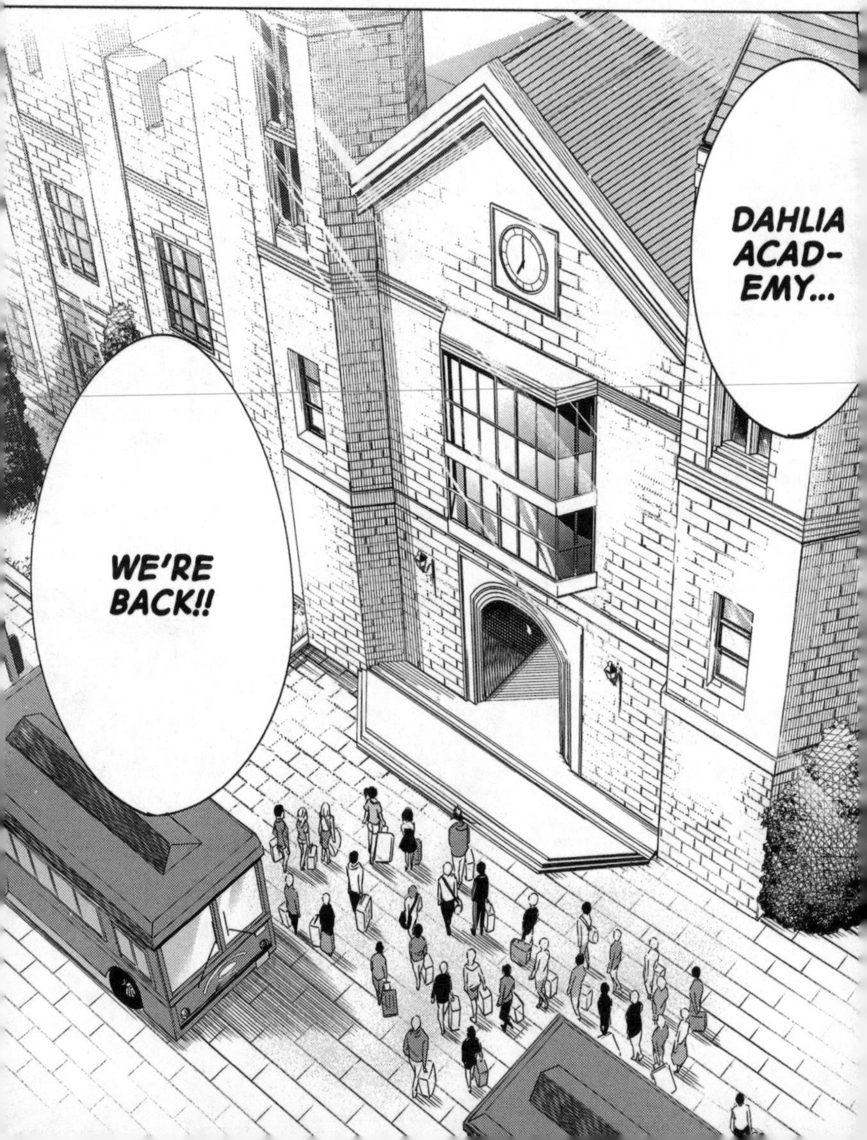
DAHLIA ACAD-EMY...
WE'RE BACK!!

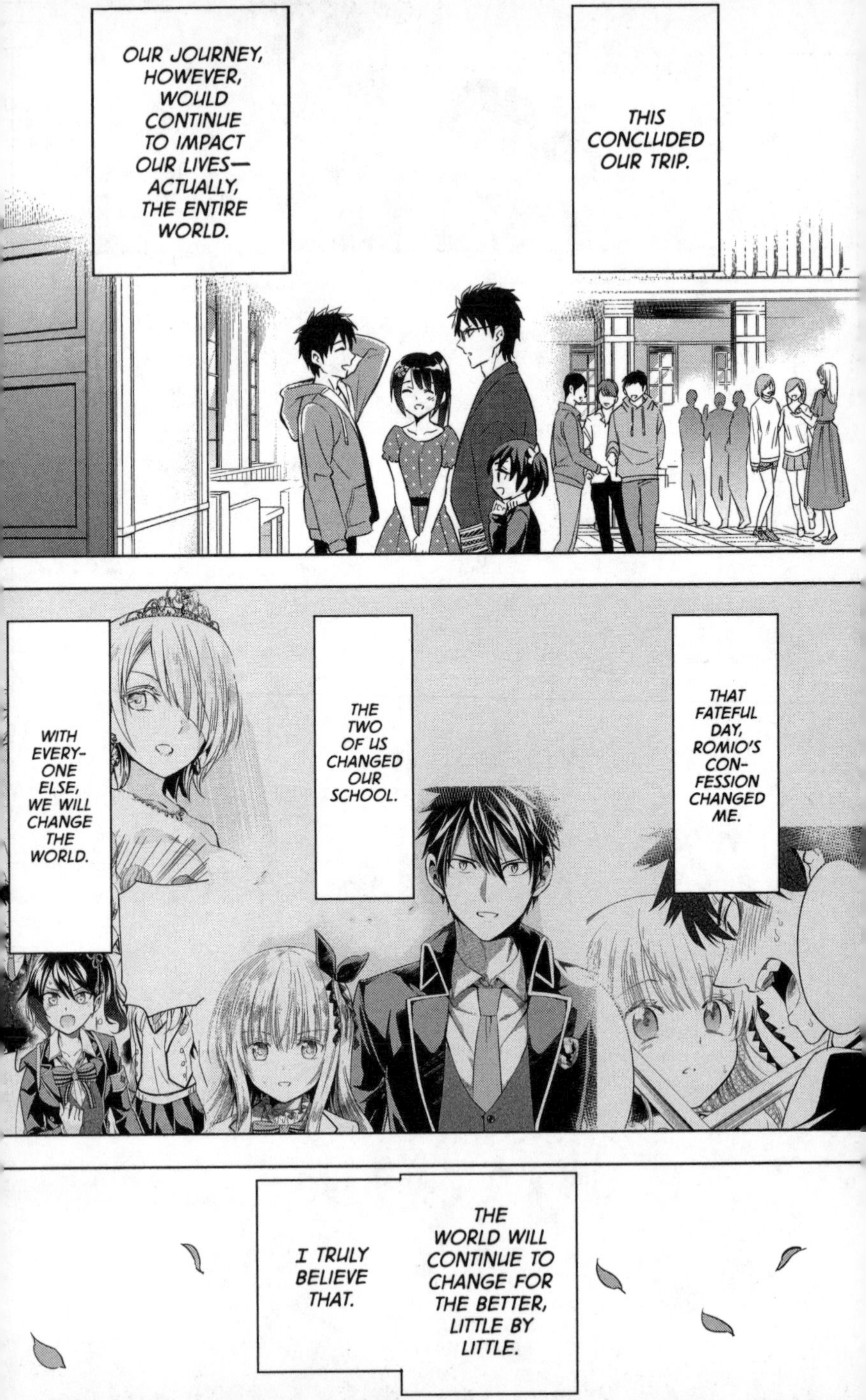
THIS CONCLUDED OUR TRIP.
OUR JOURNEY, HOWEVER, WOULD CONTINUE TO IMPACT OUR LIVES—ACTUALLY, THE ENTIRE WORLD.
THAT FATEFUL DAY, ROMIO'S CONFESSION CHANGED ME.
THE TWO OF US CHANGED OUR SCHOOL.
WITH EVERYONE ELSE, WE WILL CHANGE THE WORLD.
THE WORLD WILL CONTINUE TO CHANGE FOR THE BETTER, LITTLE BY LITTLE.
I TRULY BELIEVE THAT.

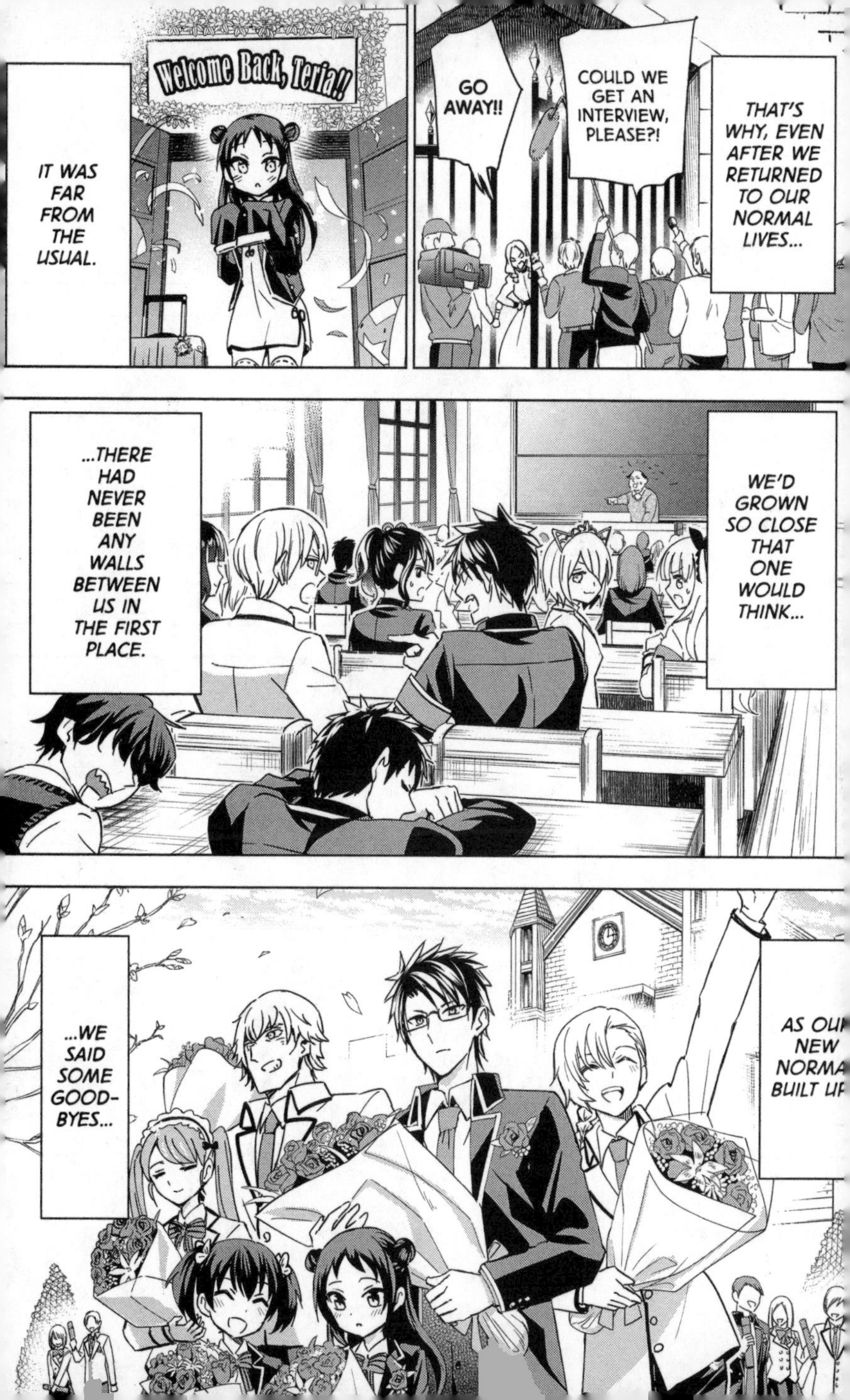
THAT'S WHY, EVEN AFTER WE RETURNED TO OUR NORMAL LIVES...
COULD WE GET AN INTERVIEW, PLEASE?!
GO AWAY!!
Welcome Back, Teria!!
IT WAS FAR FROM THE USUAL.
WE'D GROWN SO CLOSE THAT ONE WOULD THINK...
...THERE HAD NEVER BEEN ANY WALLS BETWEEN US IN THE FIRST PLACE.
AS OU NEW NORMA BUILT UP
...WE SAID SOME GOOD-BYES...

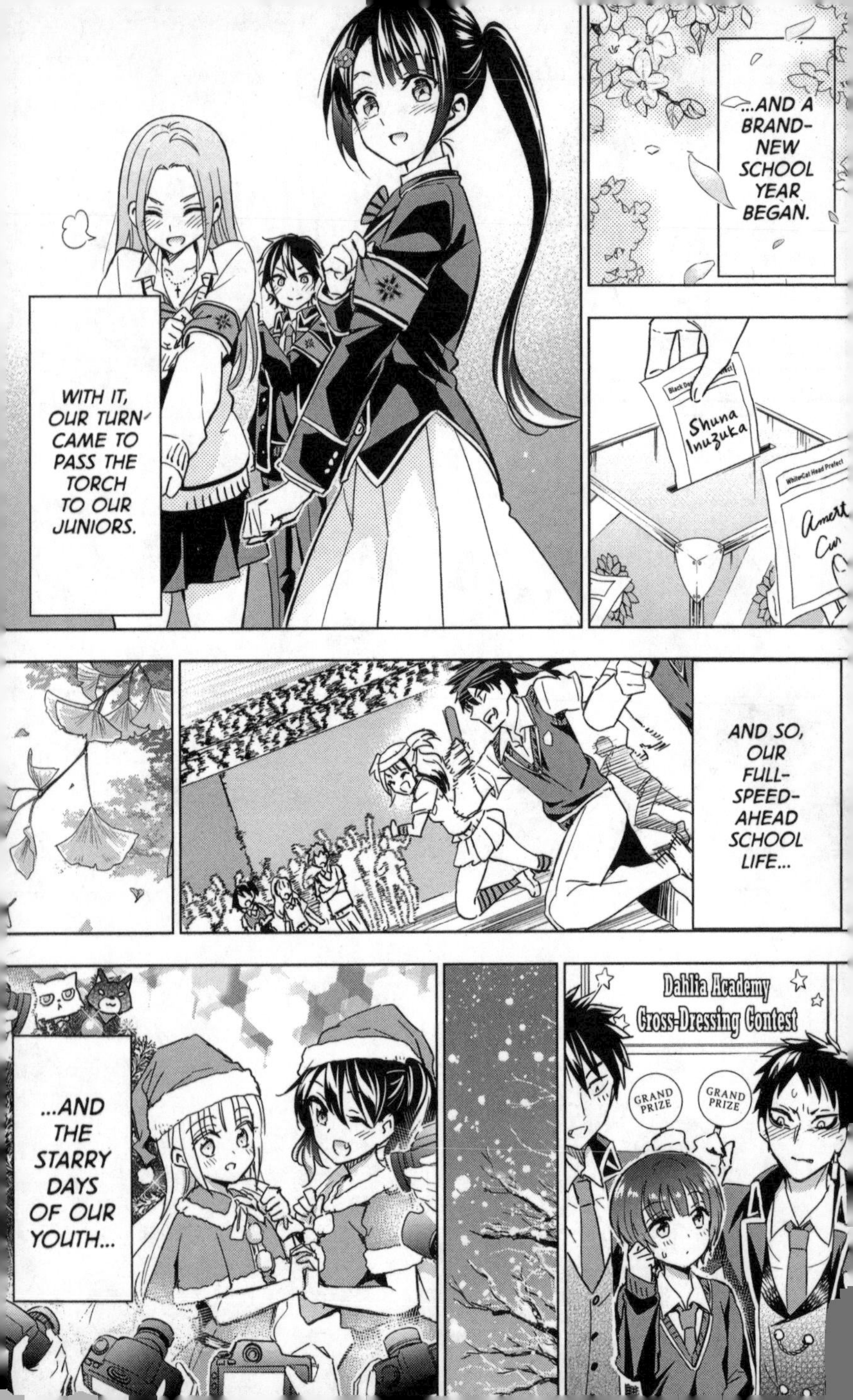
...AND A BRAND-NEW SCHOOL YEAR BEGAN.
Shuna Inuzuka
White Cat Head Prefect
WITH IT, OUR TURN CAME TO PASS THE TORCH TO OUR JUNIORS.
AND SO, OUR FULL-SPEED-AHEAD SCHOOL LIFE...
Dahlia Academy Cross-Dressing Contest
GRAND PRIZE
GRAND PRIZE
...AND THE STARRY DAYS OF OUR YOUTH...

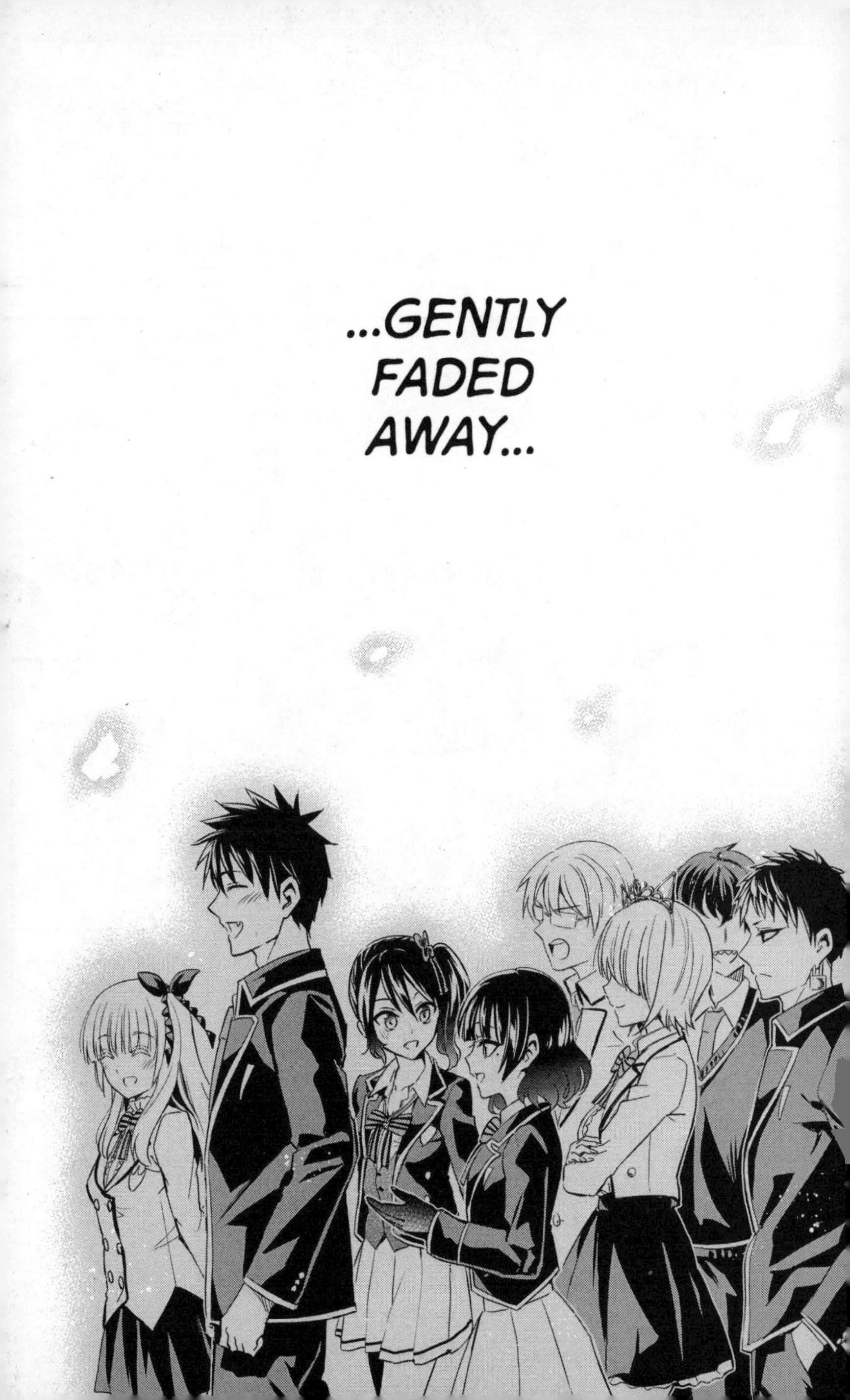
...GENTLY FADED AWAY...

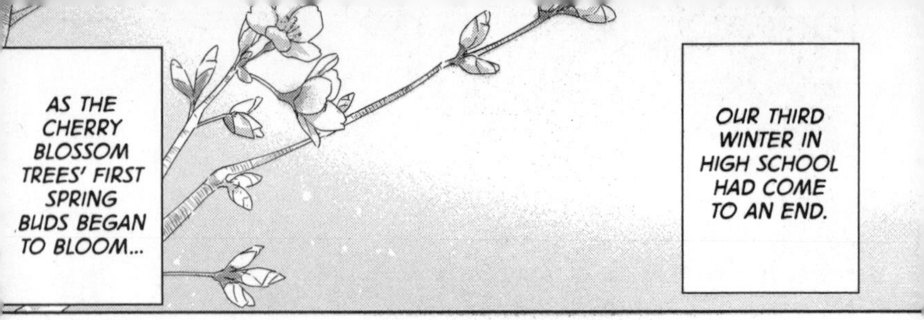
OUR THIRD WINTER IN HIGH SCHOOL HAD COME TO AN END.
AS THE CHERRY BLOSSOM TREES' FIRST SPRING BUDS BEGAN TO BLOOM...
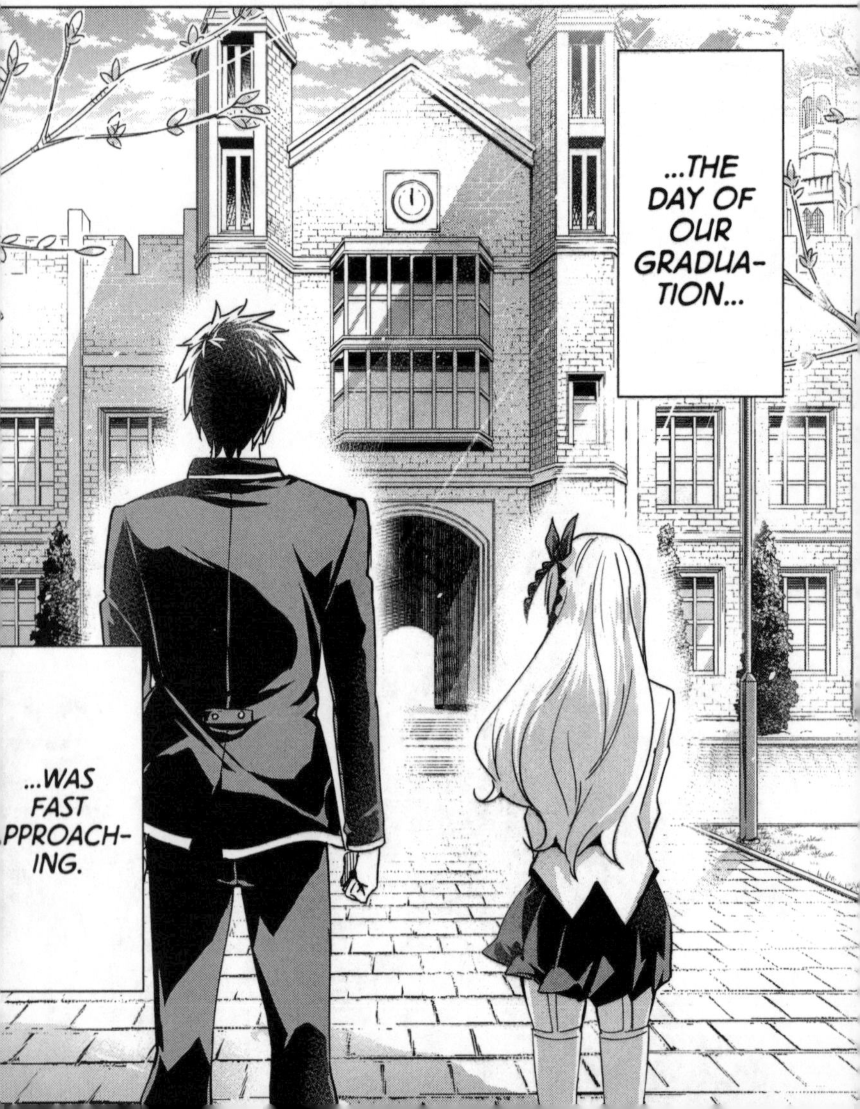
...THE DAY OF OUR GRADUA-TION...
...WAS FAST PPROACH-ING.

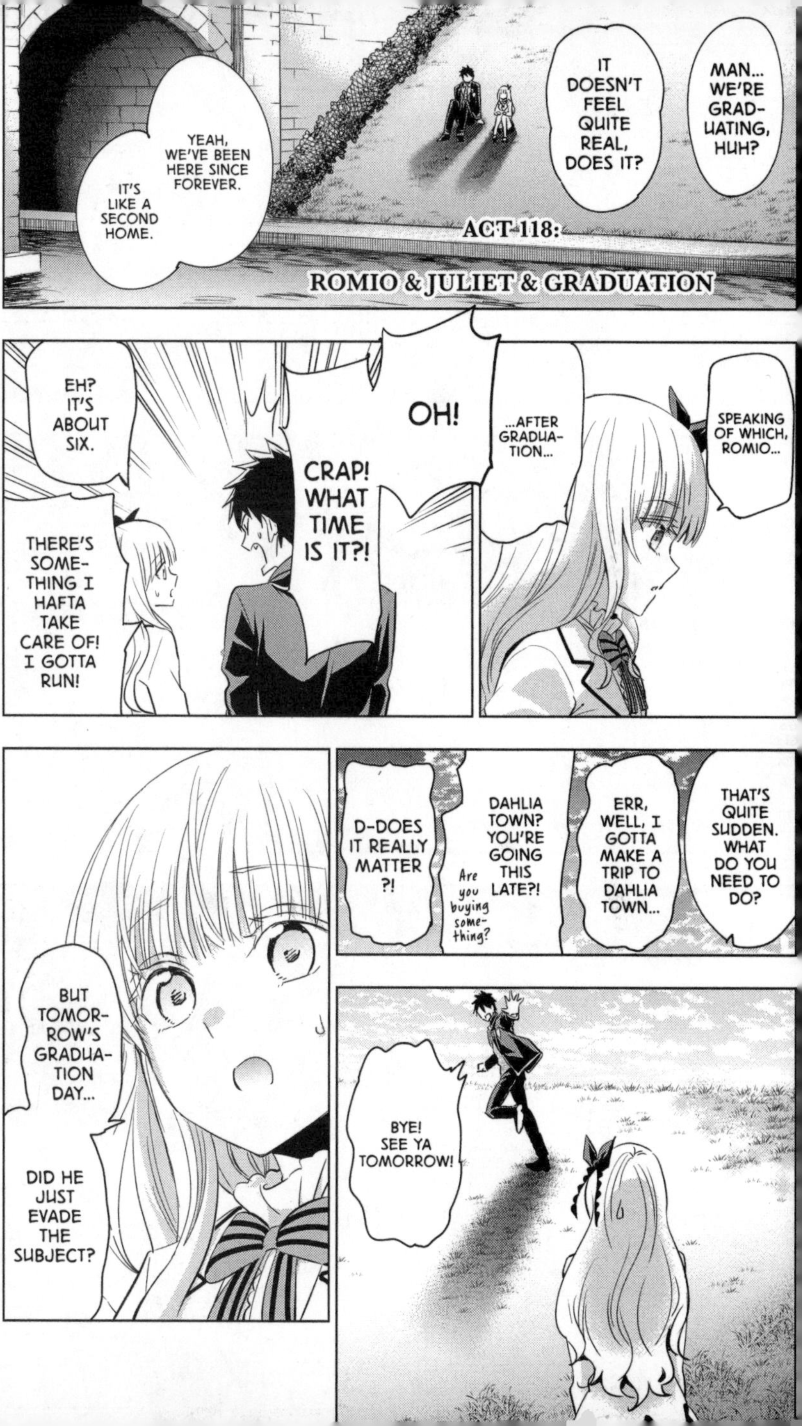
MAN... WE'RE GRADUATING, HUH?
IT DOESN'T FEEL QUITE REAL, DOES IT?
YEAH, WE'VE BEEN HERE SINCE FOREVER.
IT'S LIKE A SECOND HOME.
ACT 118:
ROMIO & JULIET & GRADUATION
SPEAKING OF WHICH, ROMIO...
...AFTER GRADUATION...
OH!
CRAP! WHAT TIME IS IT?!
EH? IT'S ABOUT SIX.
THERE'S SOMETHING I HAFTA TAKE CARE OF! I GOTTA RUN!
THAT'S QUITE SUDDEN. WHAT DO YOU NEED TO DO?
ERR, WELL, I GOTTA MAKE A TRIP TO DAHLIA TOWN...
DAHLIA TOWN? YOU'RE GOING THIS LATE?!
Are you buying something?
D-DOES IT REALLY MATTER?!
BYE! SEE YA TOMORROW!
BUT TOMORROW'S GRADUATION DAY...
DID HE JUST EVADE THE SUBJECT?

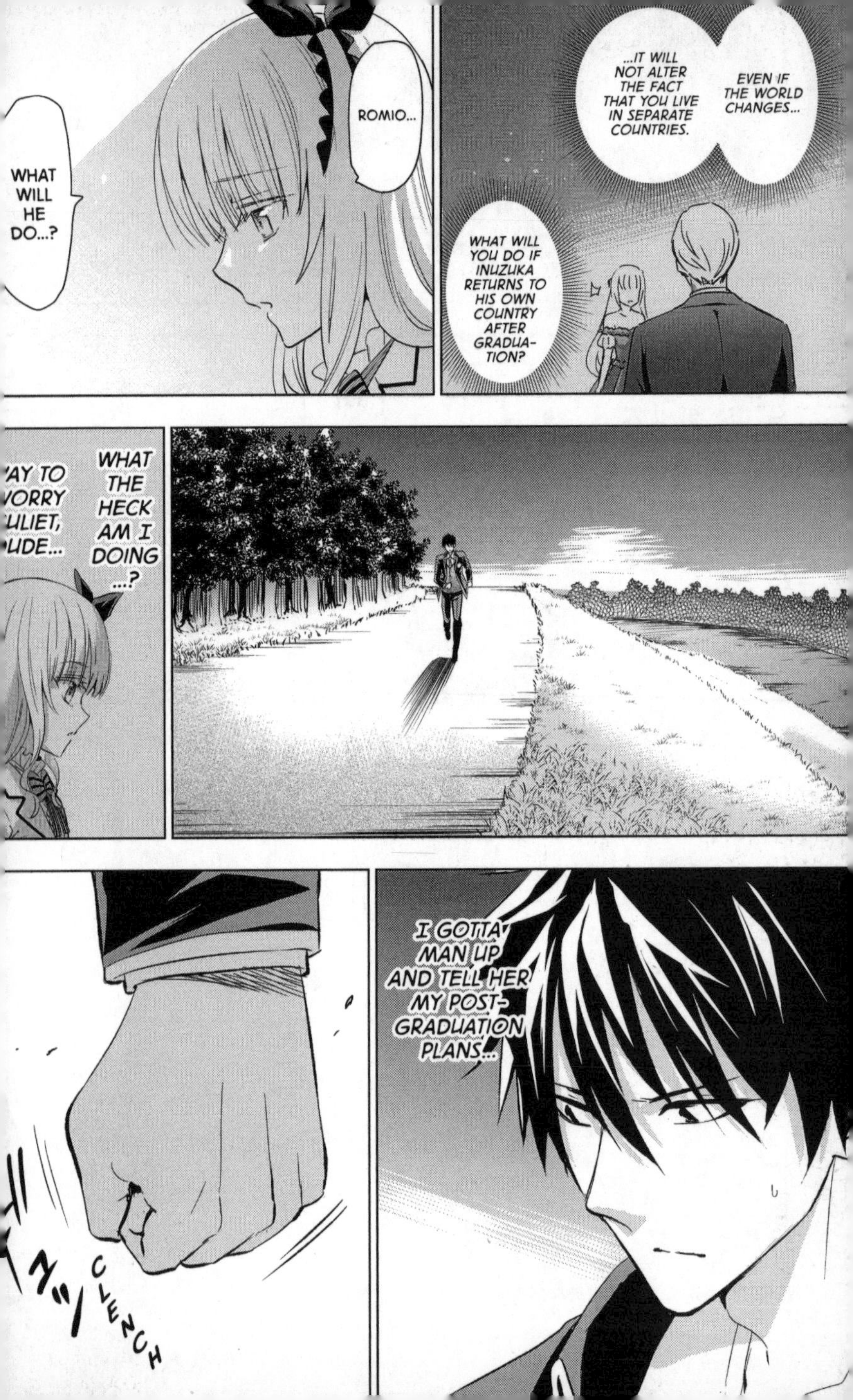
EVEN IF THE WORLD CHANGES...
...IT WILL NOT ALTER THE FACT THAT YOU LIVE IN SEPARATE COUNTRIES.
WHAT WILL YOU DO IF INUZUKA RETURNS TO HIS OWN COUNTRY AFTER GRADUA-TION?
ROMIO...
WHAT WILL HE DO...?
WHAT THE HECK AM I DOING ...?
AY TO ORRY ULIET, UDE...
I GOTTA MAN UP AND TELL HER MY POST-GRADUATION PLANS...
CLENCH

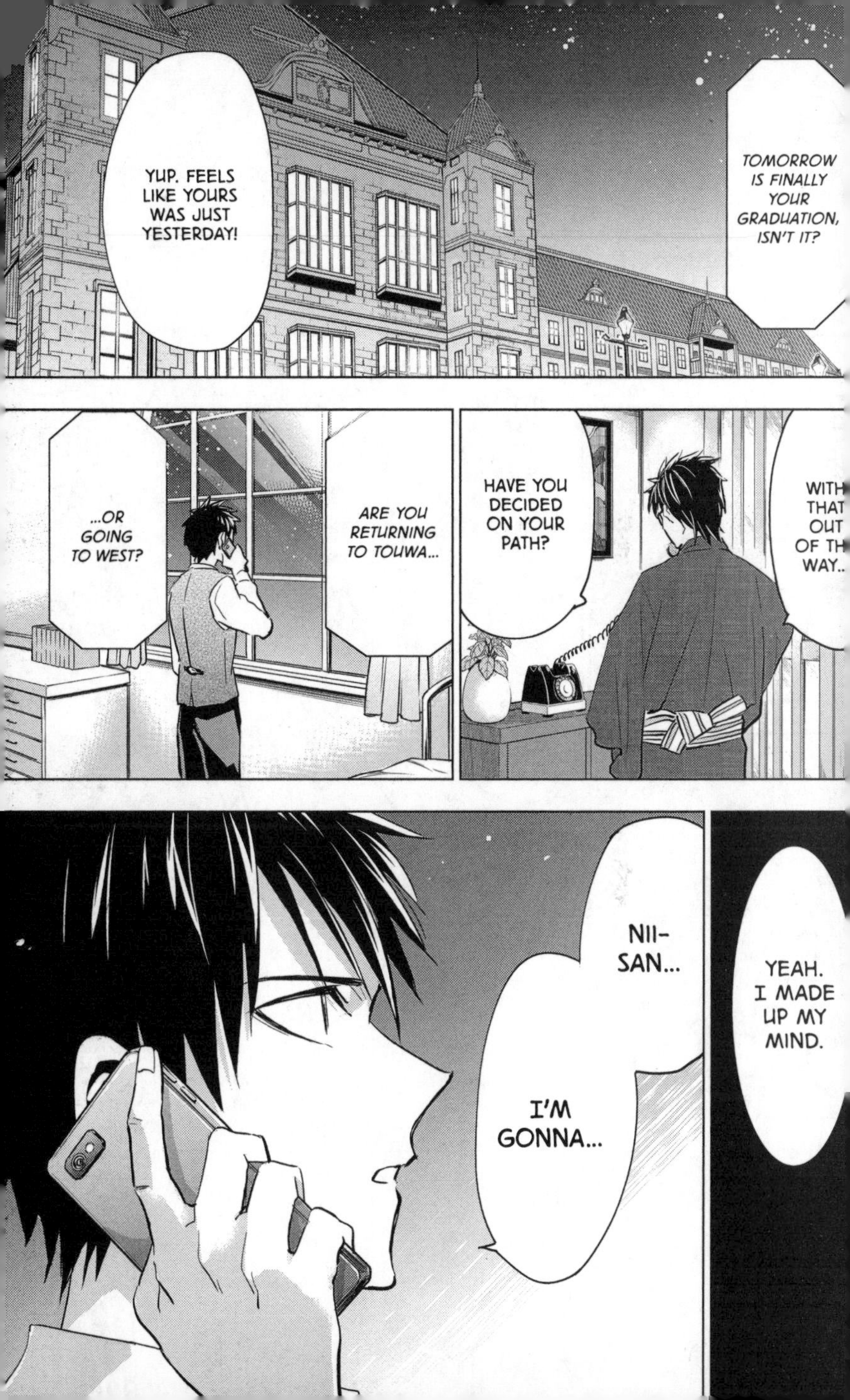
TOMORROW IS FINALLY YOUR GRADUATION, ISN'T IT?
YUP. FEELS LIKE YOURS WAS JUST YESTERDAY!
WITH THAT OUT OF TH WAY..
HAVE YOU DECIDED ON YOUR PATH?
ARE YOU RETURNING TO TOUWA...
...OR GOING TO WEST?
YEAH. I MADE UP MY MIND.
NII-SAN...
I'M GONNA...

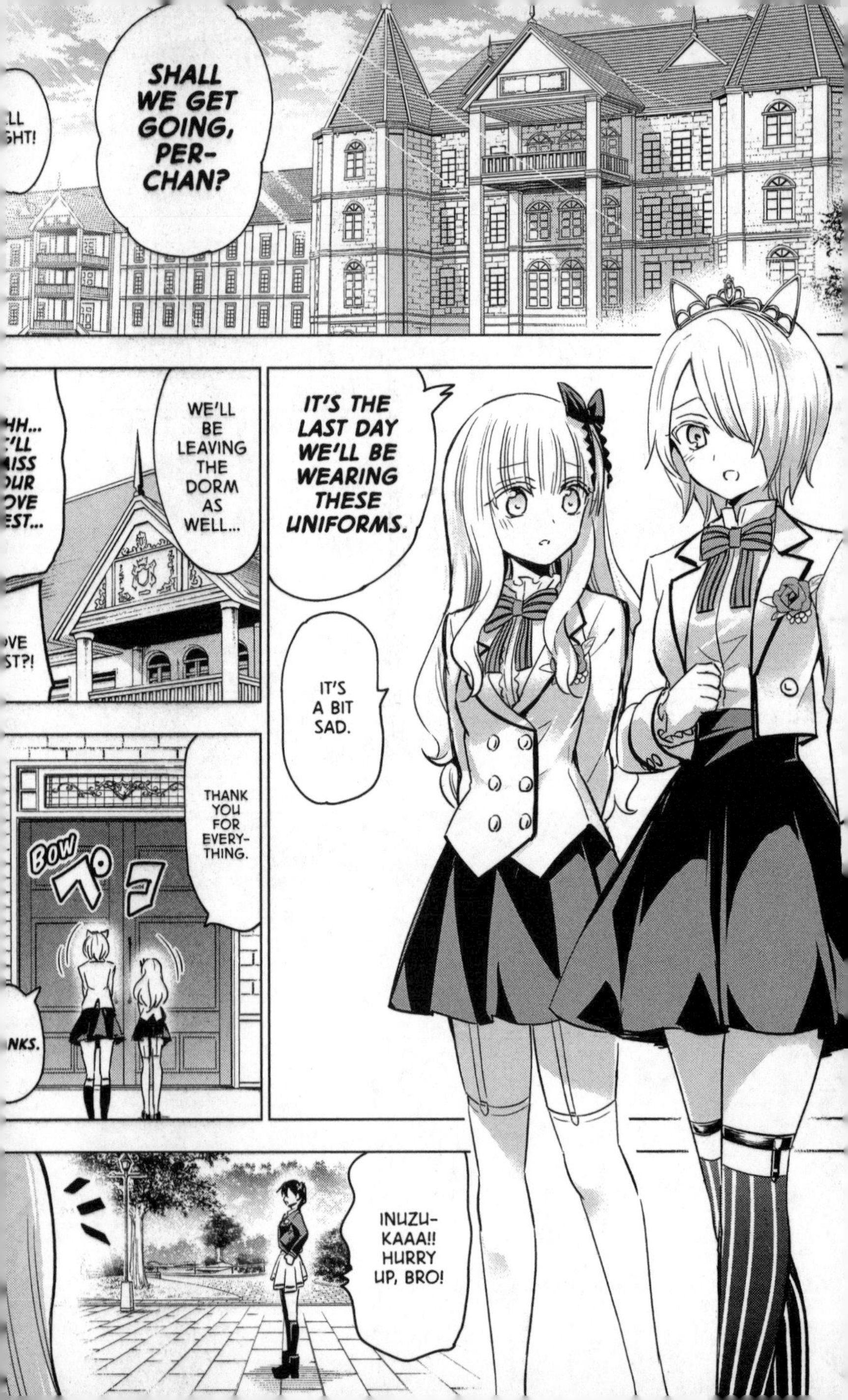
SHALL WE GET GOING, PER-CHAN?
IT'S THE LAST DAY WE'LL BE WEARING THESE UNIFORMS.
IT'S A BIT SAD.
WE'LL BE LEAVING THE DORM AS WELL...
THANK YOU FOR EVERYTHING.
BOW
INUZU-KAAA!! HURRY UP, BRO!

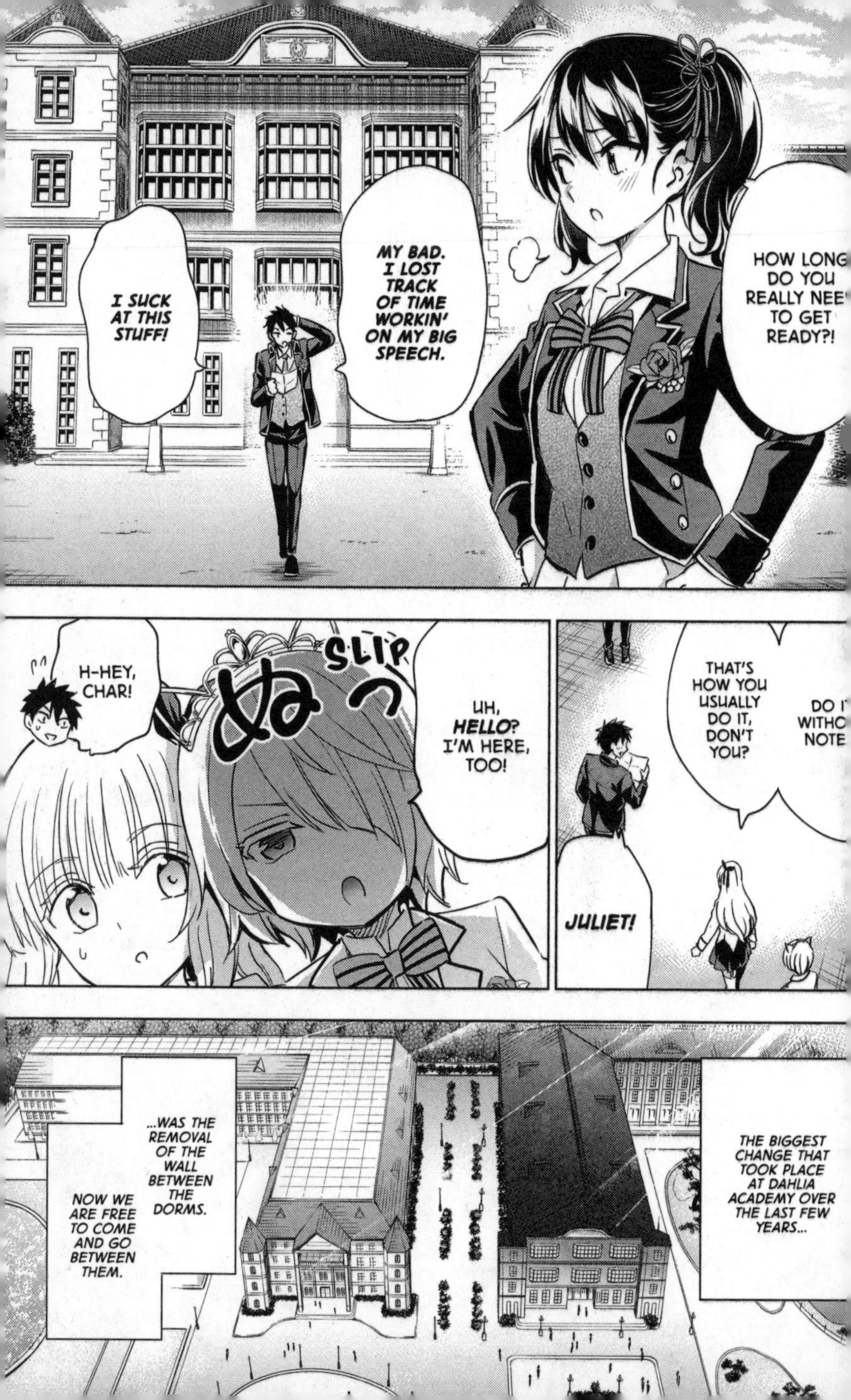
HOW LONG DO YOU REALLY NEE TO GET READY?!
MY BAD. I LOST TRACK OF TIME WORKIN' ON MY BIG SPEECH.
I SUCK AT THIS STUFF!
DO I WITHO NOTE
THAT'S HOW YOU USUALLY DO IT, DON'T YOU?
JULIET!
UH, HELLO? I'M HERE, TOO!
SLIP
ぬっ
H-HEY, CHAR!
THE BIGGEST CHANGE THAT TOOK PLACE AT DAHLIA ACADEMY OVER THE LAST FEW YEARS...
...WAS THE REMOVAL OF THE WALL BETWEEN THE DORMS.
NOW WE ARE FREE TO COME AND GO BETWEEN THEM.

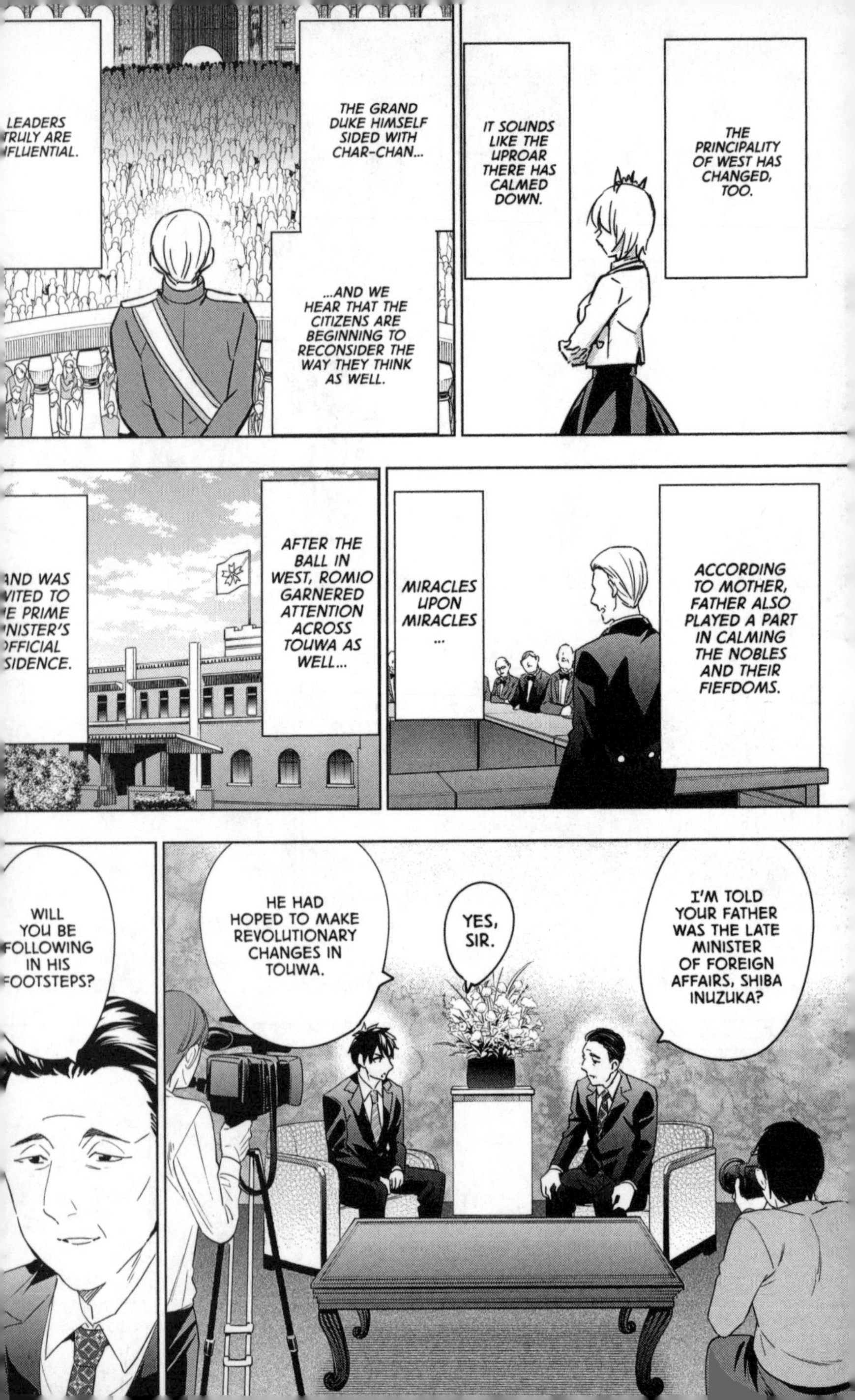
THE PRINCIPALITY OF WEST HAS CHANGED, TOO.
IT SOUNDS LIKE THE UPROAR THERE HAS CALMED DOWN.
THE GRAND DUKE HIMSELF SIDED WITH CHAR-CHAN...
...AND WE HEAR THAT THE CITIZENS ARE BEGINNING TO RECONSIDER THE WAY THEY THINK AS WELL.
LEADERS TRULY ARE INFLUENTIAL.
ACCORDING TO MOTHER, FATHER ALSO PLAYED A PART IN CALMING THE NOBLES AND THEIR FIEFDOMS.
MIRACLES UPON MIRACLES...
AFTER THE BALL IN WEST, ROMIO GARNERED ATTENTION ACROSS TOUWA AS WELL...
AND WAS INVITED TO THE PRIME MINISTER'S OFFICIAL RESIDENCE.
I'M TOLD YOUR FATHER WAS THE LATE MINISTER OF FOREIGN AFFAIRS, SHIBA INUZUKA?
YES, SIR.
HE HAD HOPED TO MAKE REVOLUTIONARY CHANGES IN TOUWA.
WILL YOU BE FOLLOWING IN HIS FOOTSTEPS?

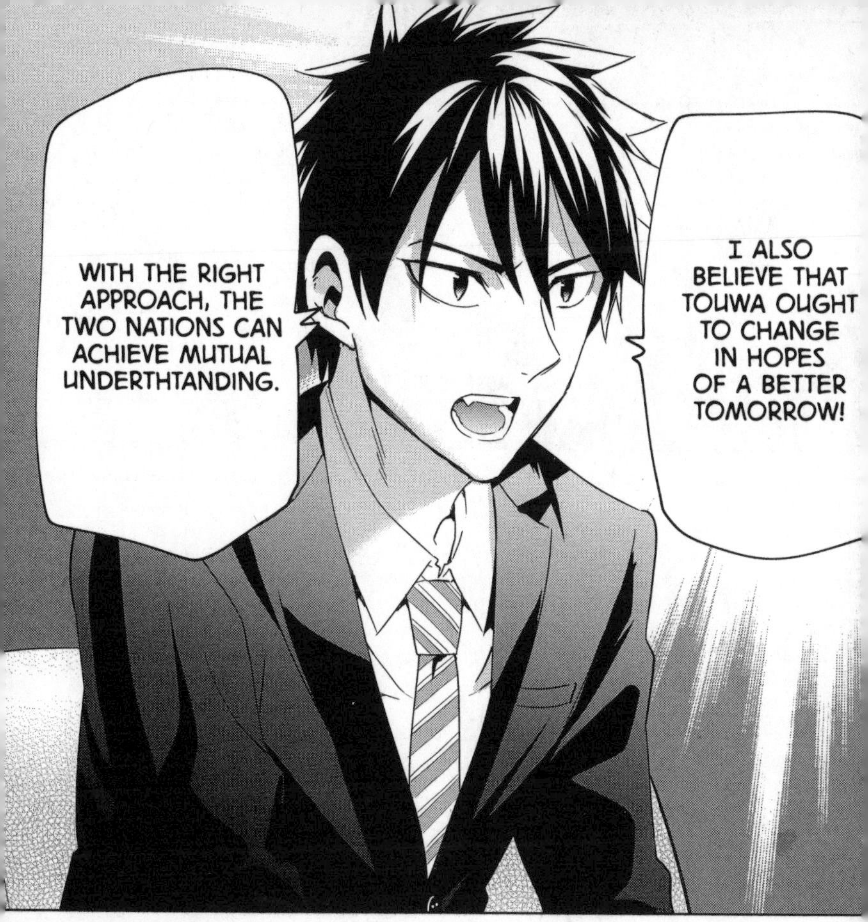
I ALSO BELIEVE THAT TOUWA OUGHT TO CHANGE IN HOPES OF A BETTER TOMORROW!
WITH THE RIGHT APPROACH, THE TWO NATIONS CAN ACHIEVE MUTUAL UNDERTHTANDING.

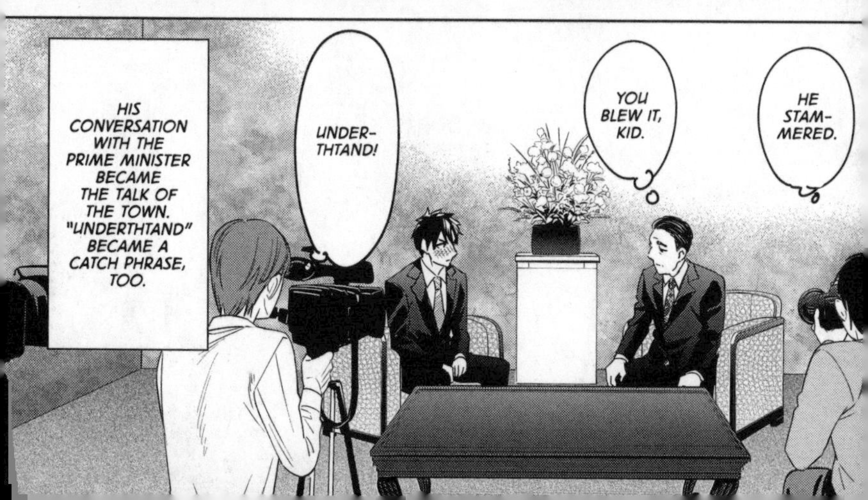
HE STAM-MERED.
YOU BLEW IT, KID.
UNDER-THTAND!
HIS CONVERSATION WITH THE PRIME MINISTER BECAME THE TALK OF THE TOWN. "UNDERTHTAND" BECAME A CATCH PHRASE, TOO.

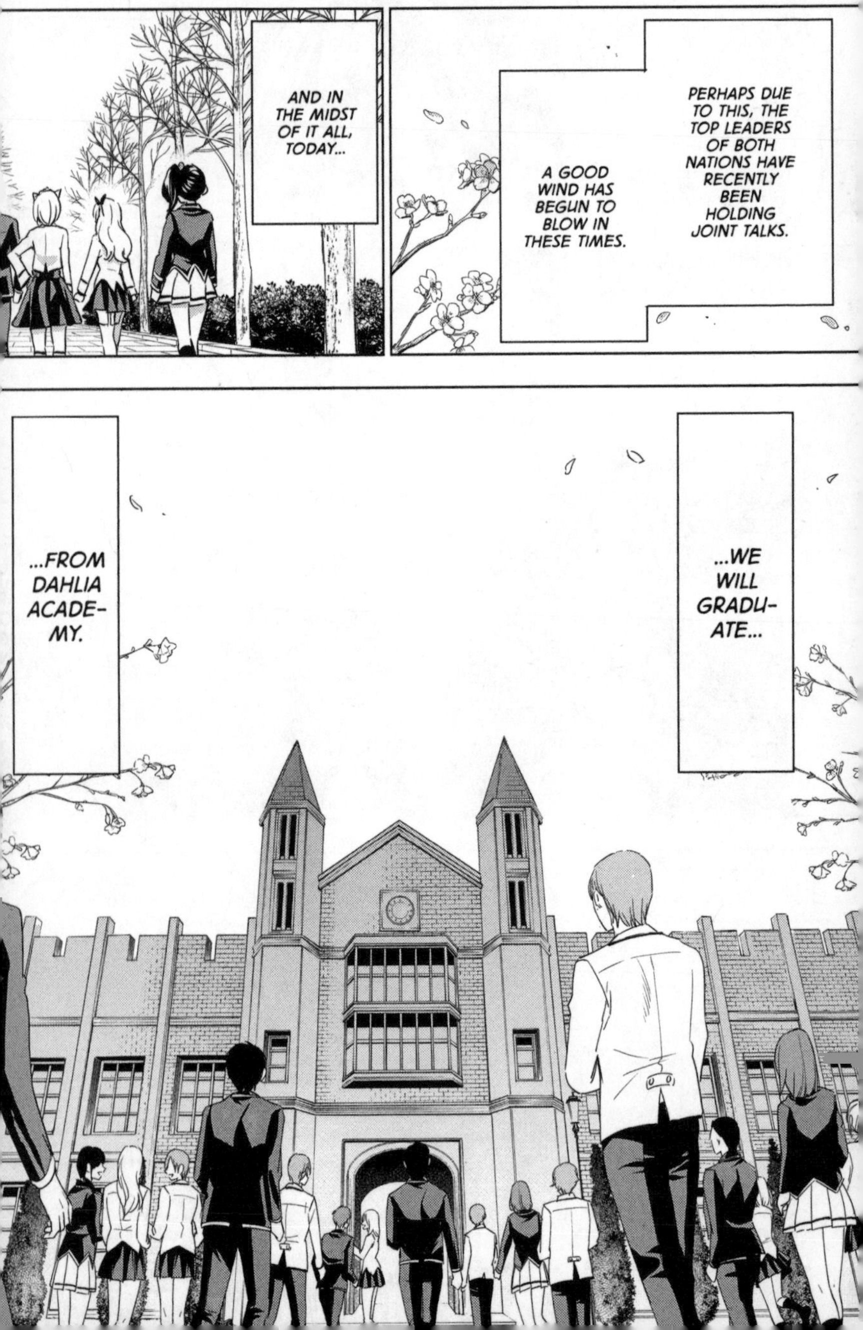
PERHAPS DUE TO THIS, THE TOP LEADERS OF BOTH NATIONS HAVE RECENTLY BEEN HOLDING JOINT TALKS.
A GOOD WIND HAS BEGUN TO BLOW IN THESE TIMES.
AND IN THE MIDST OF IT ALL, TODAY...
...WE WILL GRADU-ATE...
...FROM DAHLIA ACADE-MY.

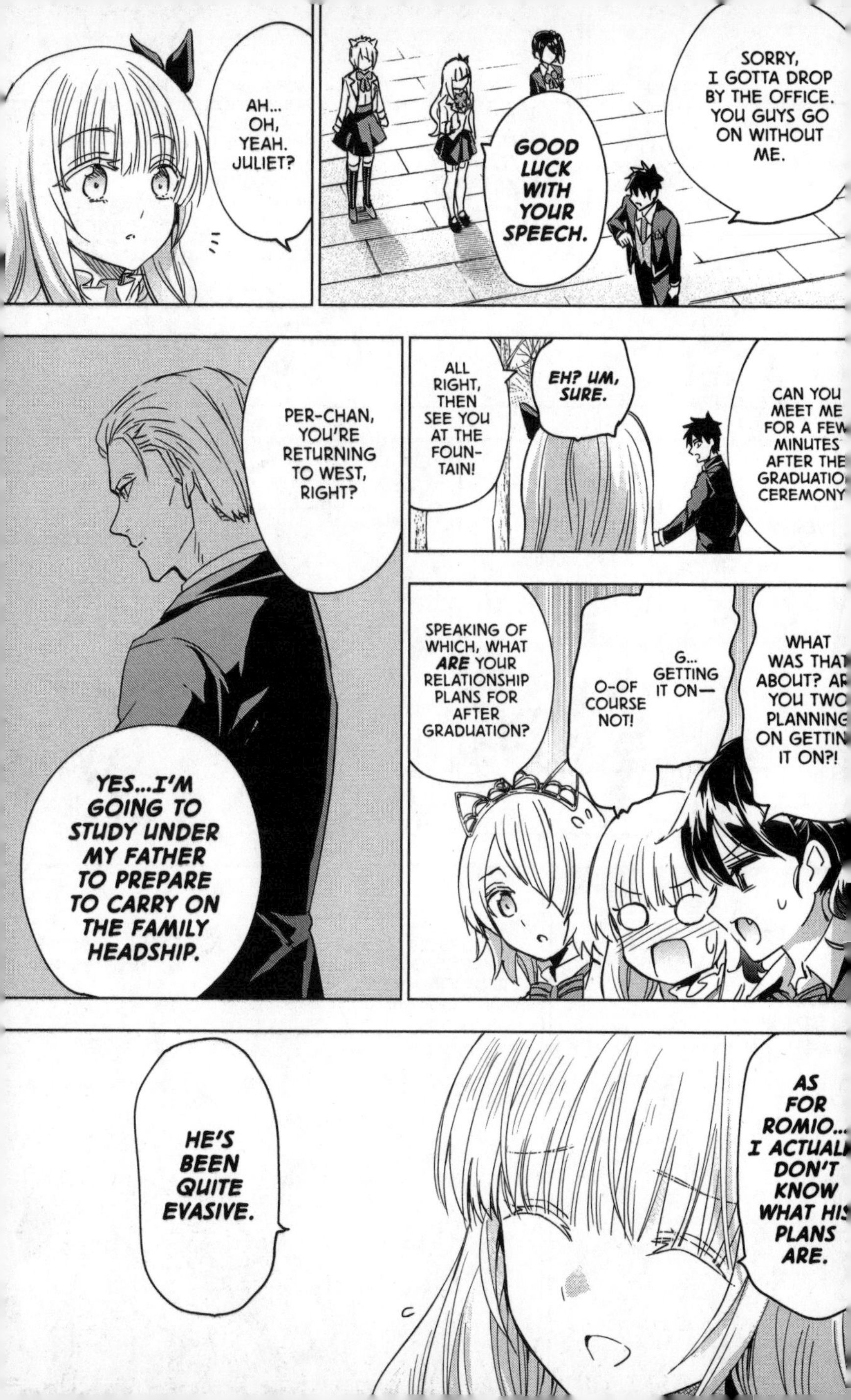
SORRY, I GOTTA DROP BY THE OFFICE. YOU GUYS GO ON WITHOUT ME.
GOOD LUCK WITH YOUR SPEECH.
AH... OH, YEAH. JULIET?
CAN YOU MEET ME FOR A FEW MINUTES AFTER THE GRADUATIO CEREMONY
EH? UM, SURE.
ALL RIGHT, THEN SEE YOU AT THE FOUN-TAIN!
WHAT WAS THAT ABOUT? AR YOU TWO PLANNING ON GETTIN IT ON?!
G... GETTING IT ON—
O-OF COURSE NOT!
SPEAKING OF WHICH, WHAT ARE YOUR RELATIONSHIP PLANS FOR AFTER GRADUATION?
PER-CHAN, YOU'RE RETURNING TO WEST, RIGHT?
YES...I'M GOING TO STUDY UNDER MY FATHER TO PREPARE TO CARRY ON THE FAMILY HEADSHIP.
AS FOR ROMIO... I ACTUAL DON'T KNOW WHAT HIS PLANS ARE.
HE'S BEEN QUITE EVASIVE.

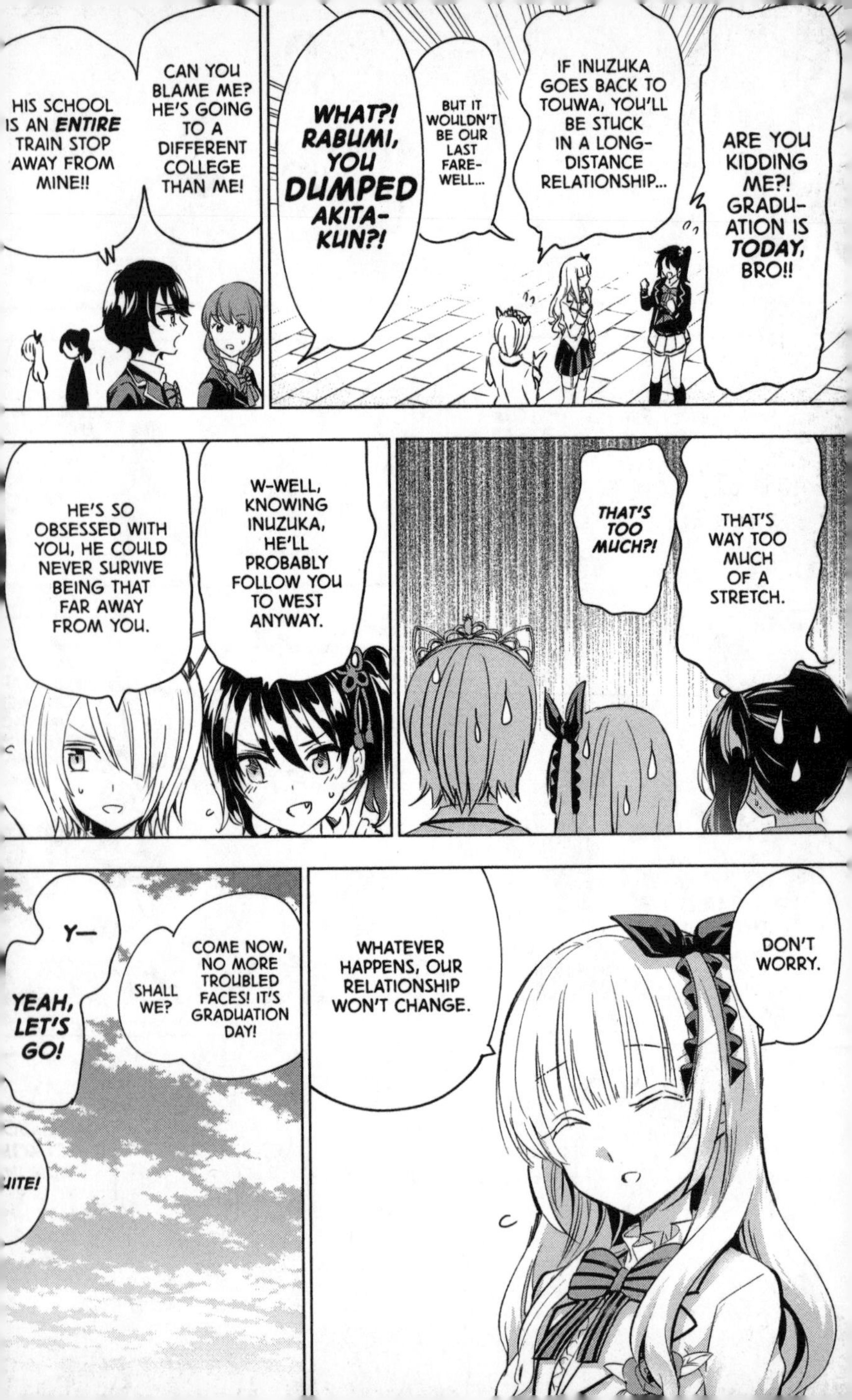
ARE YOU KIDDING ME?! GRADUATION IS *TODAY,* BRO!!
IF INUZUKA GOES BACK TO TOUWA, YOU'LL BE STUCK IN A LONG-DISTANCE RELATIONSHIP...
BUT IT WOULDN'T BE OUR LAST FAREWELL...
WHAT?! RABUMI, YOU **DUMPED** *AKITA-KUN?!*
CAN YOU BLAME ME? HE'S GOING TO A DIFFERENT COLLEGE THAN ME!
HIS SCHOOL IS AN ***ENTIRE*** TRAIN STOP AWAY FROM MINE!!
THAT'S WAY TOO MUCH OF A STRETCH.
THAT'S TOO MUCH?!
W-WELL, KNOWING INUZUKA, HE'LL PROBABLY FOLLOW YOU TO WEST ANYWAY.
HE'S SO OBSESSED WITH YOU, HE COULD NEVER SURVIVE BEING THAT FAR AWAY FROM YOU.
DON'T WORRY.
WHATEVER HAPPENS, OUR RELATIONSHIP WON'T CHANGE.
COME NOW, NO MORE TROUBLED FACES! IT'S GRADUATION DAY!
SHALL WE?
Y—
YEAH, LET'S GO!

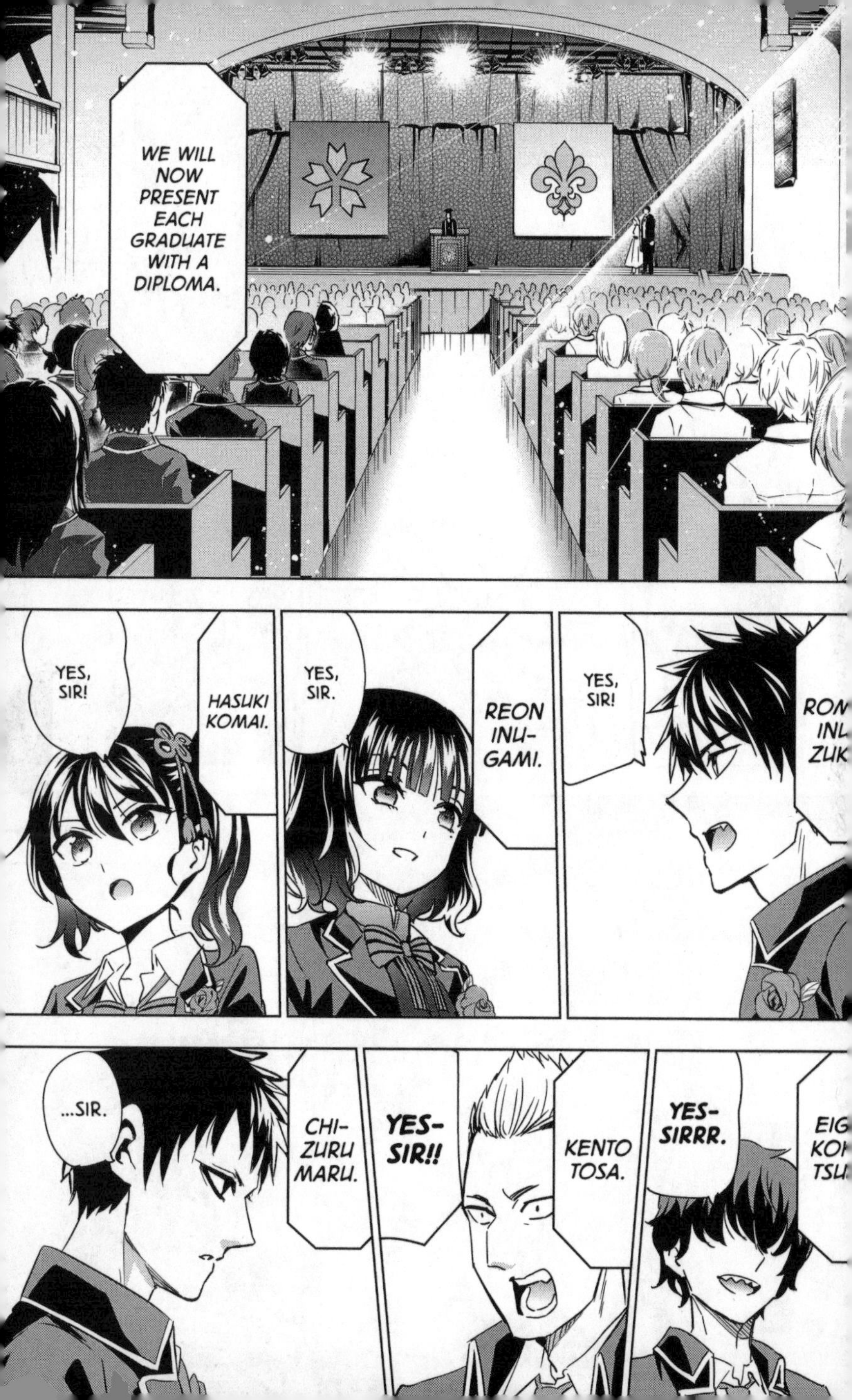
WE WILL NOW PRESENT EACH GRADUATE WITH A DIPLOMA.
RON INL ZUK
YES, SIR!
REON INU-GAMI.
YES, SIR.
HASUKI KOMAI.
YES, SIR!
EIG KO TSU
YES-SIRRR.
KENTO TOSA.
YES-SIR!!
CHI-ZURU MARU.
...SIR.

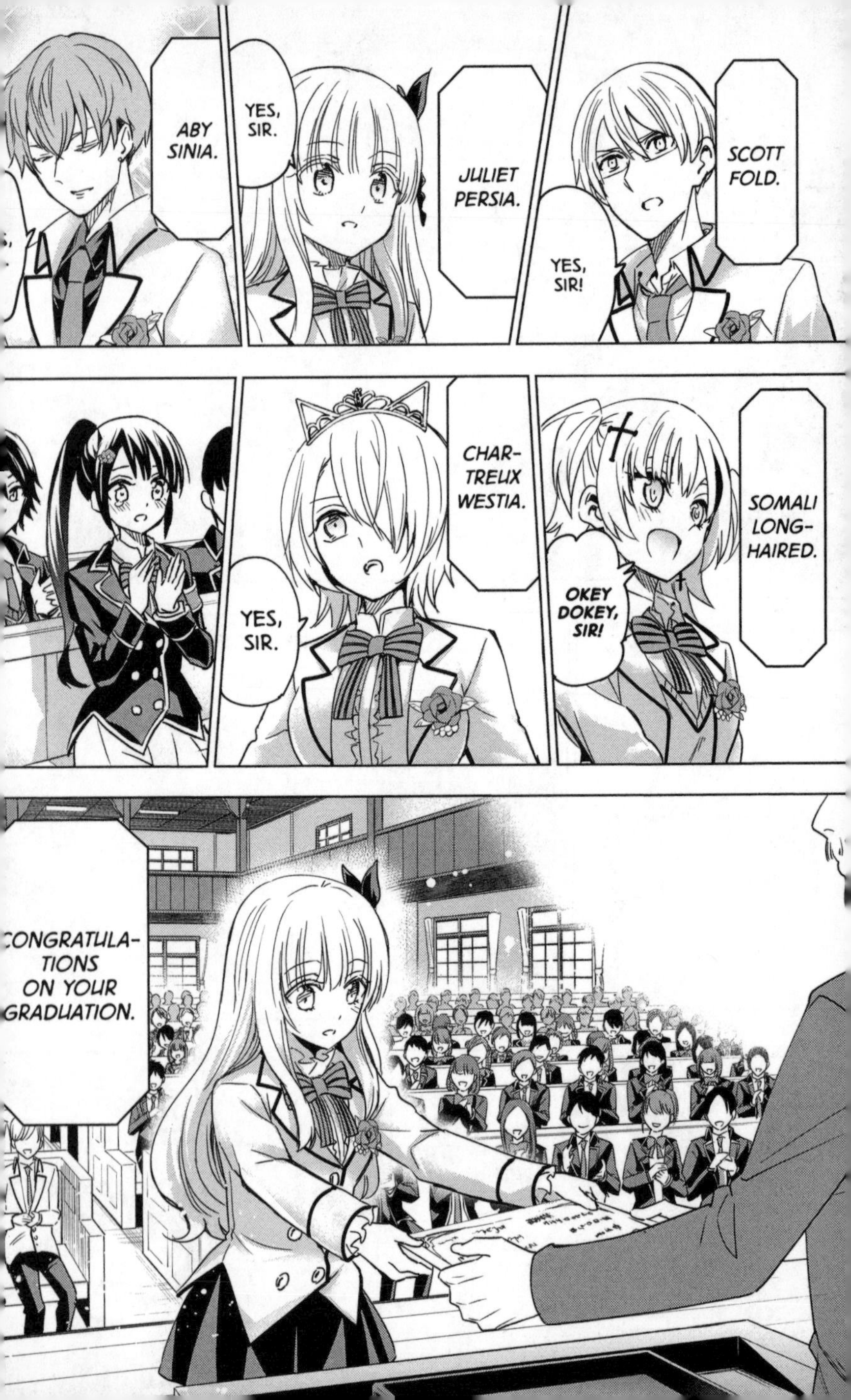
SCOTT FOLD.
YES, SIR!
JULIET PERSIA.
YES, SIR.
ABY SINIA.
SOMALI LONG-HAIRED.
OKEY DOKEY, SIR!
CHAR-TREUX WESTIA.
YES, SIR.
CONGRATULATIONS ON YOUR GRADUATION.

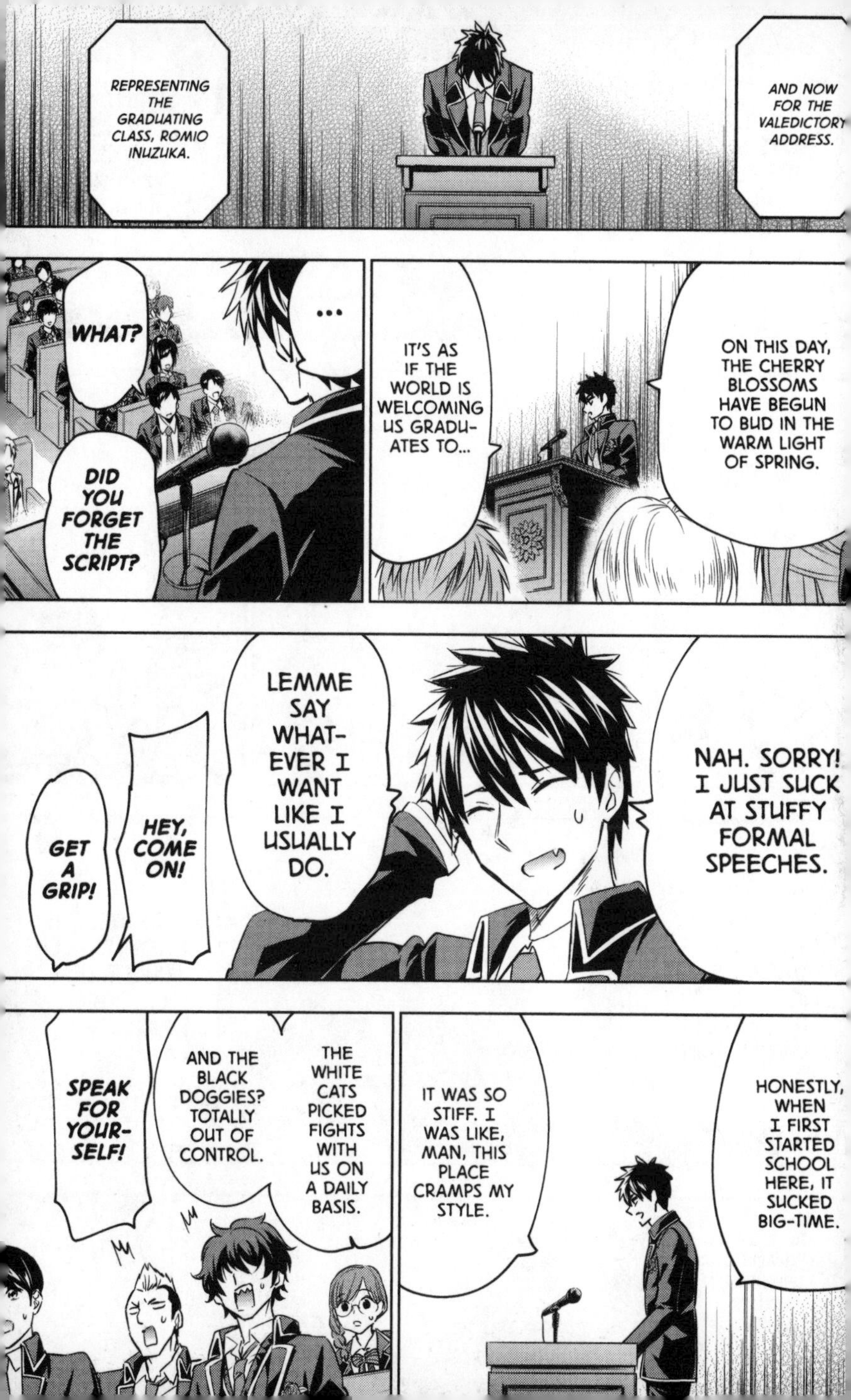
AND NOW FOR THE VALEDICTORY ADDRESS.
REPRESENTING THE GRADUATING CLASS, ROMIO INUZUKA.
ON THIS DAY, THE CHERRY BLOSSOMS HAVE BEGUN TO BUD IN THE WARM LIGHT OF SPRING.
IT'S AS IF THE WORLD IS WELCOMING US GRADU-ATES TO...
...
WHAT?
DID YOU FORGET THE SCRIPT?
NAH. SORRY! I JUST SUCK AT STUFFY FORMAL SPEECHES.
LEMME SAY WHAT-EVER I WANT LIKE I USUALLY DO.
HEY, COME ON!
GET A GRIP!
HONESTLY, WHEN I FIRST STARTED SCHOOL HERE, IT SUCKED BIG-TIME.
IT WAS SO STIFF. I WAS LIKE, MAN, THIS PLACE CRAMPS MY STYLE.
THE WHITE CATS PICKED FIGHTS WITH US ON A DAILY BASIS.
AND THE BLACK DOGGIES? TOTALLY OUT OF CONTROL.
SPEAK FOR YOUR-SELF!

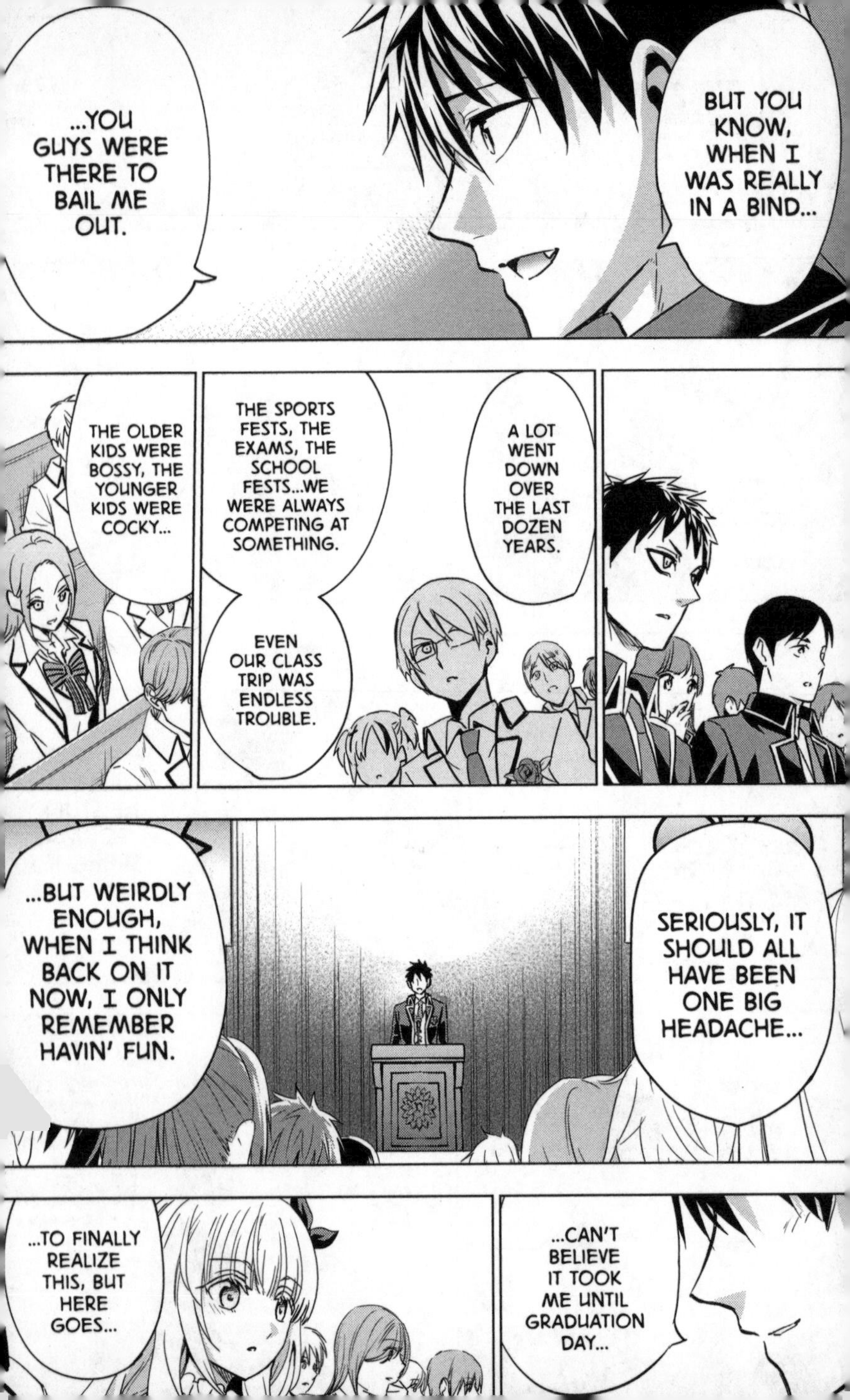
BUT YOU KNOW, WHEN I WAS REALLY IN A BIND...
...YOU GUYS WERE THERE TO BAIL ME OUT.
A LOT WENT DOWN OVER THE LAST DOZEN YEARS.
THE SPORTS FESTS, THE EXAMS, THE SCHOOL FESTS...WE WERE ALWAYS COMPETING AT SOMETHING.
EVEN OUR CLASS TRIP WAS ENDLESS TROUBLE.
THE OLDER KIDS WERE BOSSY, THE YOUNGER KIDS WERE COCKY...
SERIOUSLY, IT SHOULD ALL HAVE BEEN ONE BIG HEADACHE...
...BUT WEIRDLY ENOUGH, WHEN I THINK BACK ON IT NOW, I ONLY REMEMBER HAVIN' FUN.
...CAN'T BELIEVE IT TOOK ME UNTIL GRADUATION DAY...
...TO FINALLY REALIZE THIS, BUT HERE GOES...

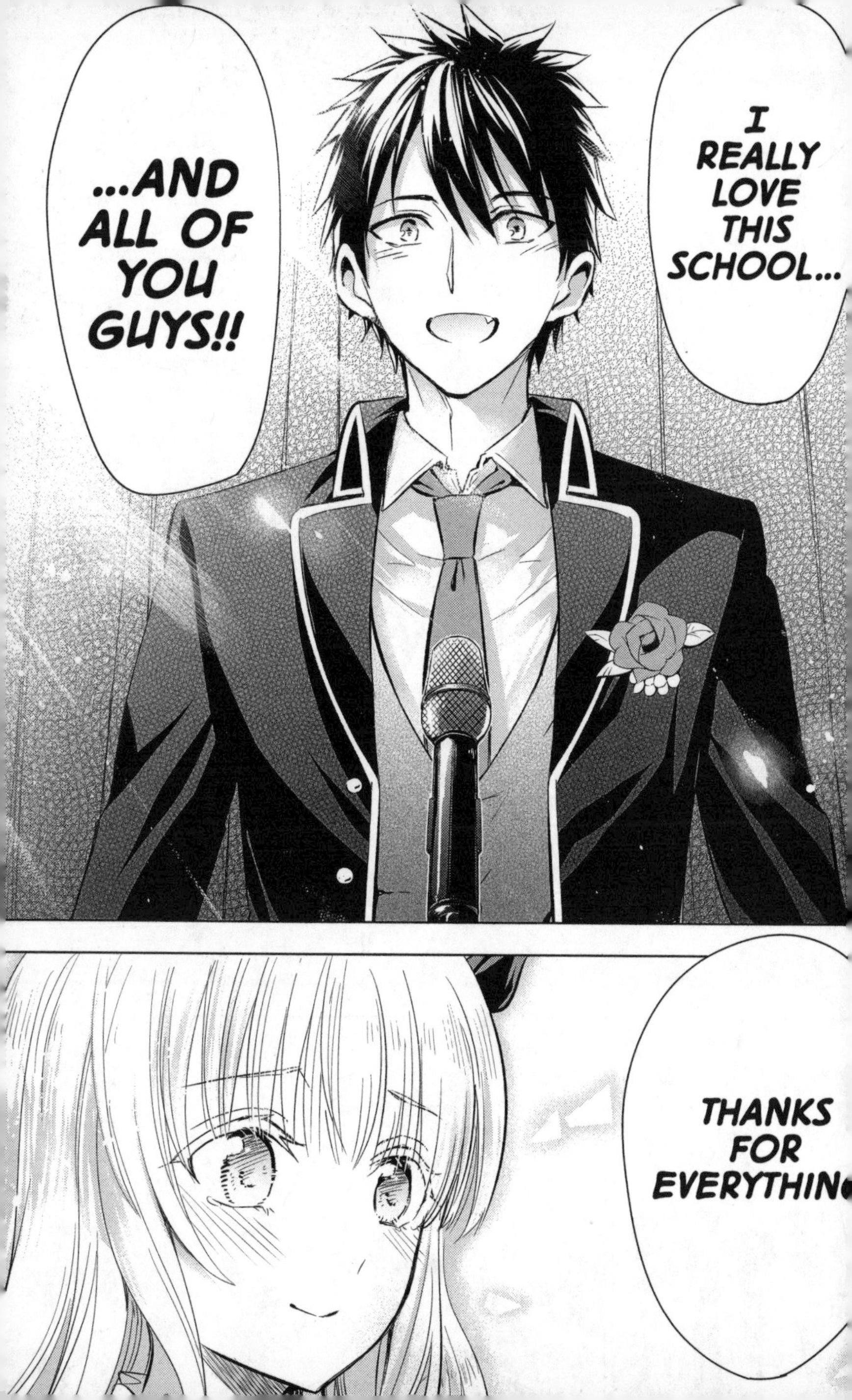
I REALLY LOVE THIS SCHOOL...
...AND ALL OF YOU GUYS!!
THANKS FOR EVERYTHIN

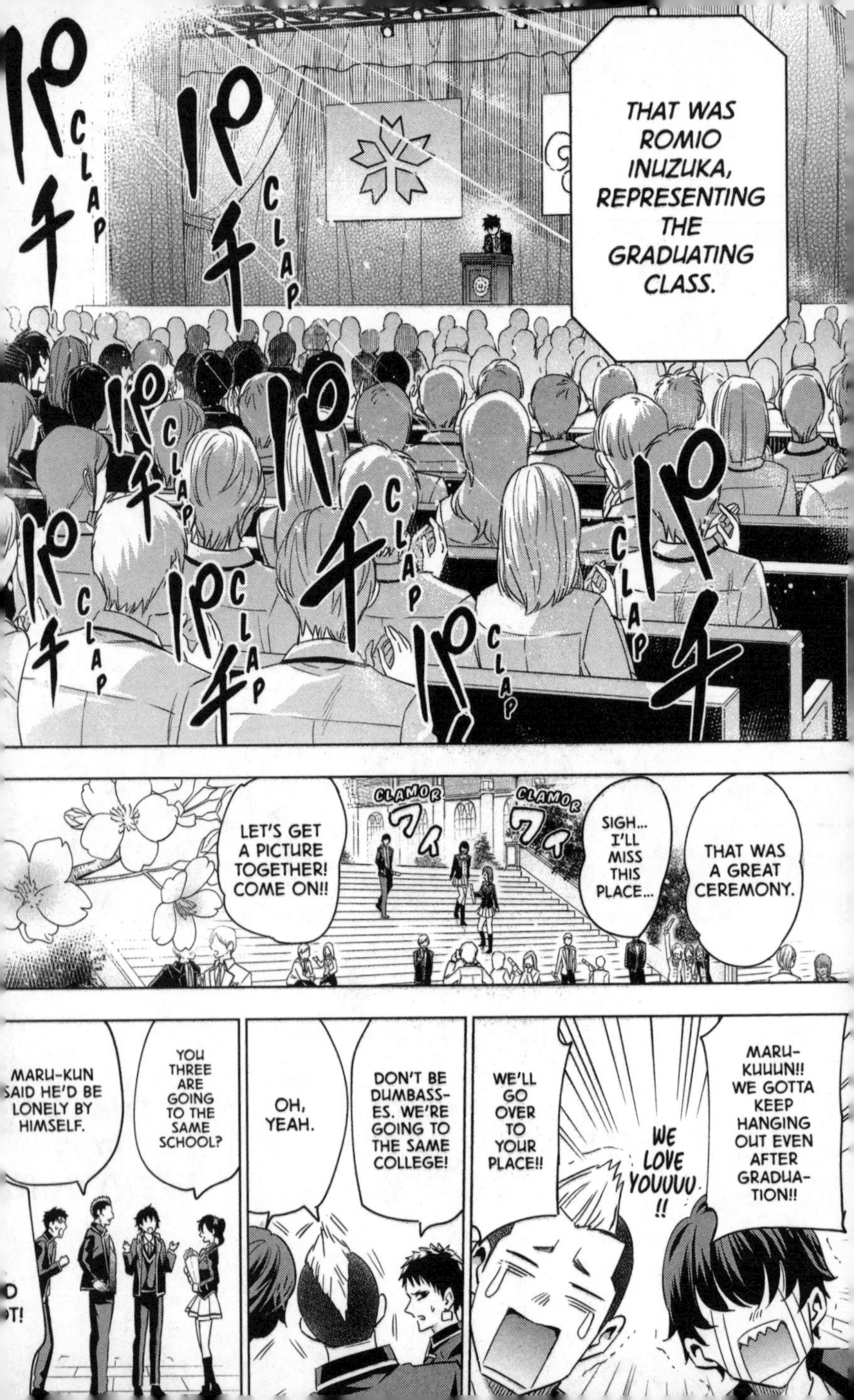
THAT WAS ROMIO INUZUKA, REPRESENTING THE GRADUATING CLASS.
パチ CLAP
パチ CLAP
パチ CLAP
パチ CLAP
パチ CLAP
パチ CLAP
パチ CLAP
パチ CLAP
THAT WAS A GREAT CEREMONY.
SIGH... I'LL MISS THIS PLACE...
ワイ CLAMOR
ワイ CLAMOR
LET'S GET A PICTURE TOGETHER! COME ON!!
MARU-KUUUN!! WE GOTTA KEEP HANGING OUT EVEN AFTER GRADUATION!!
WE LOVE YOUUUU!!
WE'LL GO OVER TO YOUR PLACE!!
DON'T BE DUMBASSES. WE'RE GOING TO THE SAME COLLEGE!
OH, YEAH.
YOU THREE ARE GOING TO THE SAME SCHOOL?
MARU-KUN SAID HE'D BE LONELY BY HIMSELF.

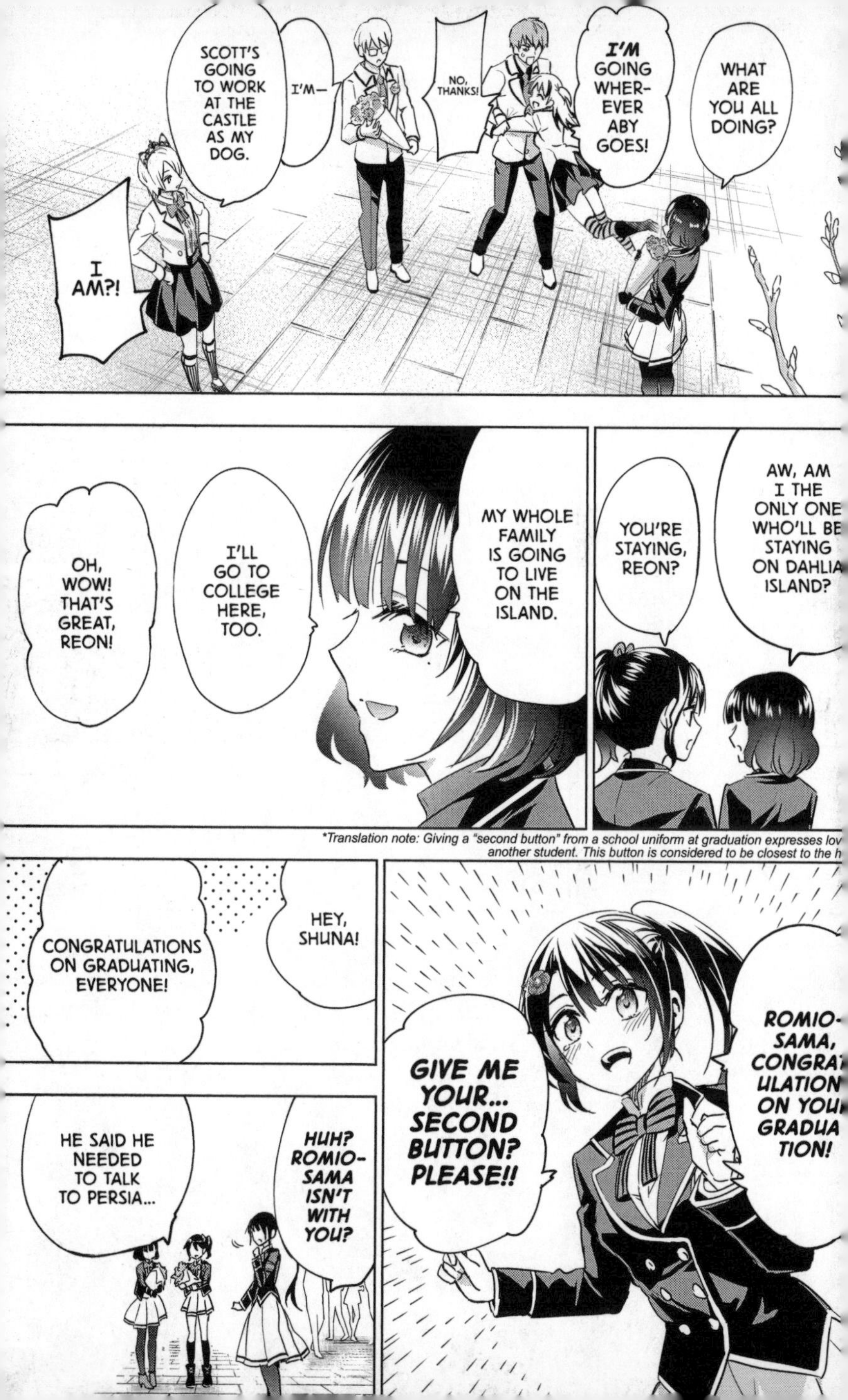
WHAT ARE YOU ALL DOING?
I'M GOING WHEREVER ABY GOES!
NO, THANKS!
I'M—
SCOTT'S GOING TO WORK AT THE CASTLE AS MY DOG.
I AM?!
AW, AM I THE ONLY ONE WHO'LL BE STAYING ON DAHLIA ISLAND?
YOU'RE STAYING, REON?
MY WHOLE FAMILY IS GOING TO LIVE ON THE ISLAND.
I'LL GO TO COLLEGE HERE, TOO.
OH, WOW! THAT'S GREAT, REON!
*Translation note: Giving a "second button" from a school uniform at graduation expresses lov another student. This button is considered to be closest to the h
ROMIO-SAMA, CONGRAT ULATION ON YOU GRADUA TION!
GIVE ME YOUR... SECOND BUTTON? PLEASE!!
HEY, SHUNA!
CONGRATULATIONS ON GRADUATING, EVERYONE!
HUH? ROMIO-SAMA ISN'T WITH YOU?
HE SAID HE NEEDED TO TALK TO PERSIA...

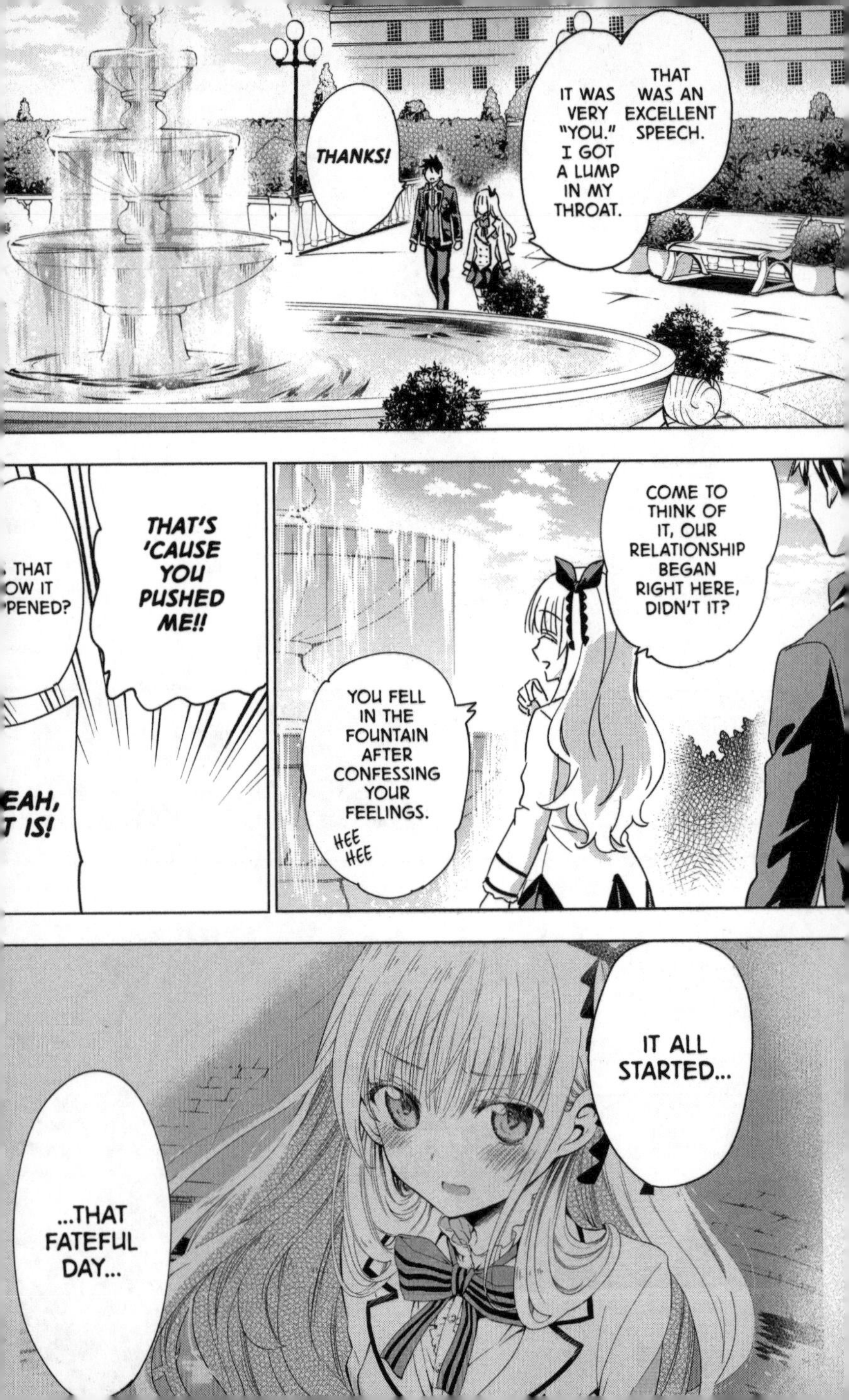
THAT WAS AN EXCELLENT SPEECH.
IT WAS VERY "YOU." I GOT A LUMP IN MY THROAT.
THANKS!
COME TO THINK OF IT, OUR RELATIONSHIP BEGAN RIGHT HERE, DIDN'T IT?
YOU FELL IN THE FOUNTAIN AFTER CONFESSING YOUR FEELINGS.
HEE HEE
THAT'S 'CAUSE YOU PUSHED ME!!
IT ALL STARTED...
...THAT FATEFUL DAY...

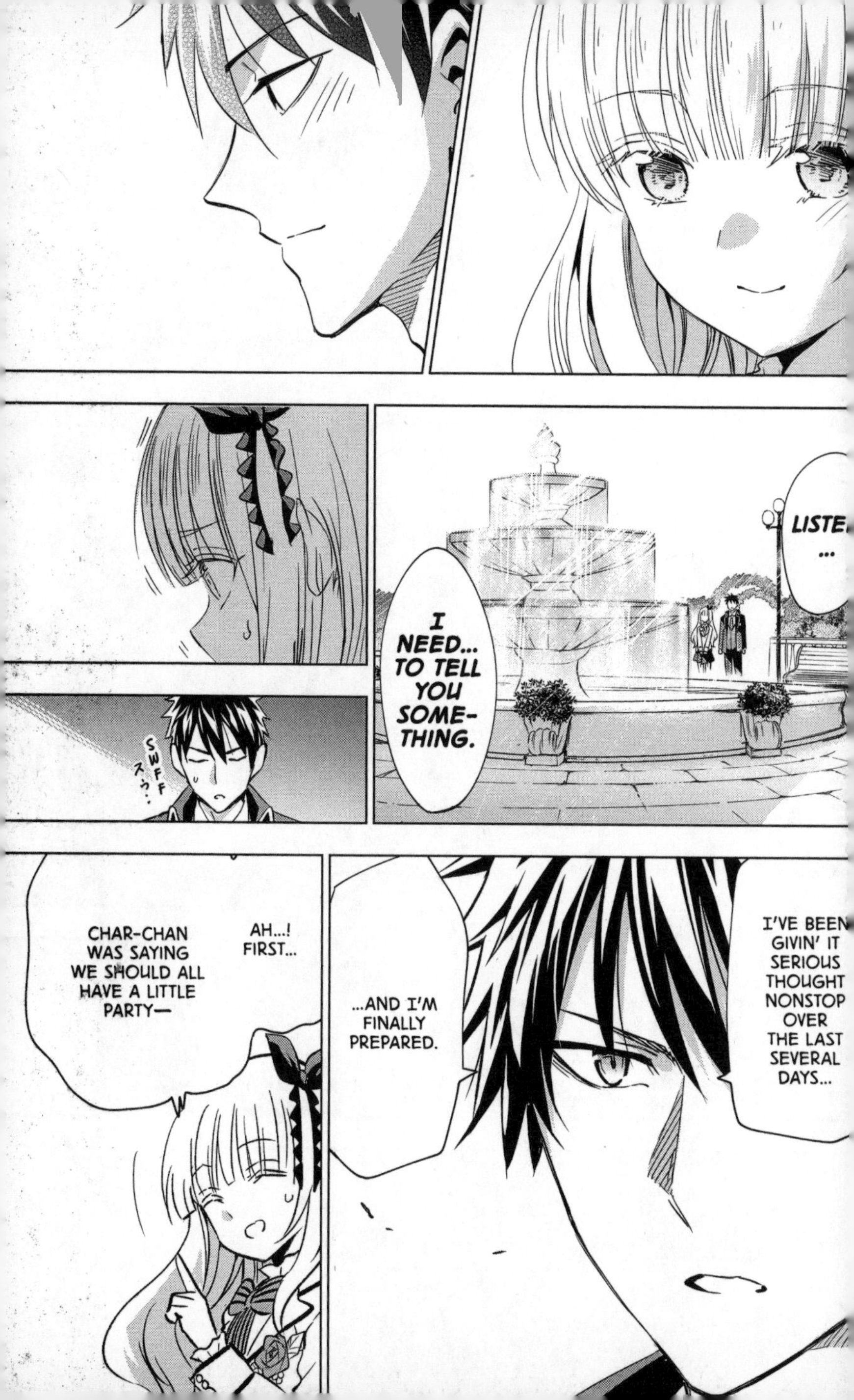
LISTE ...
I NEED... TO TELL YOU SOMETHING.
SWFF
スゥ..
I'VE BEEN GIVIN' IT SERIOUS THOUGHT NONSTOP OVER THE LAST SEVERAL DAYS...
...AND I'M FINALLY PREPARED.
AH...! FIRST...
CHAR-CHAN WAS SAYING WE SHOULD ALL HAVE A LITTLE PARTY—

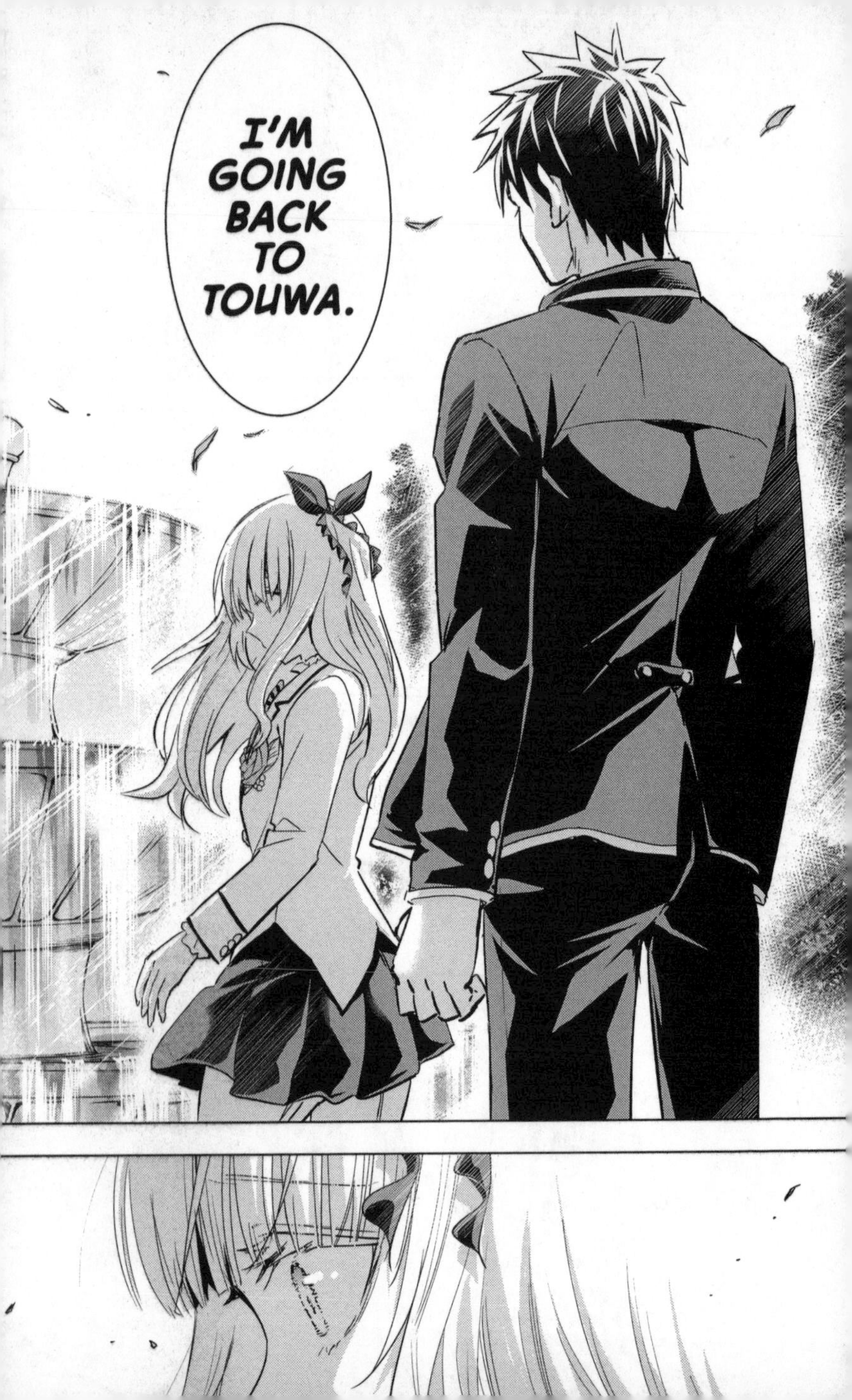
I'M GOING BACK TO TOUWA.

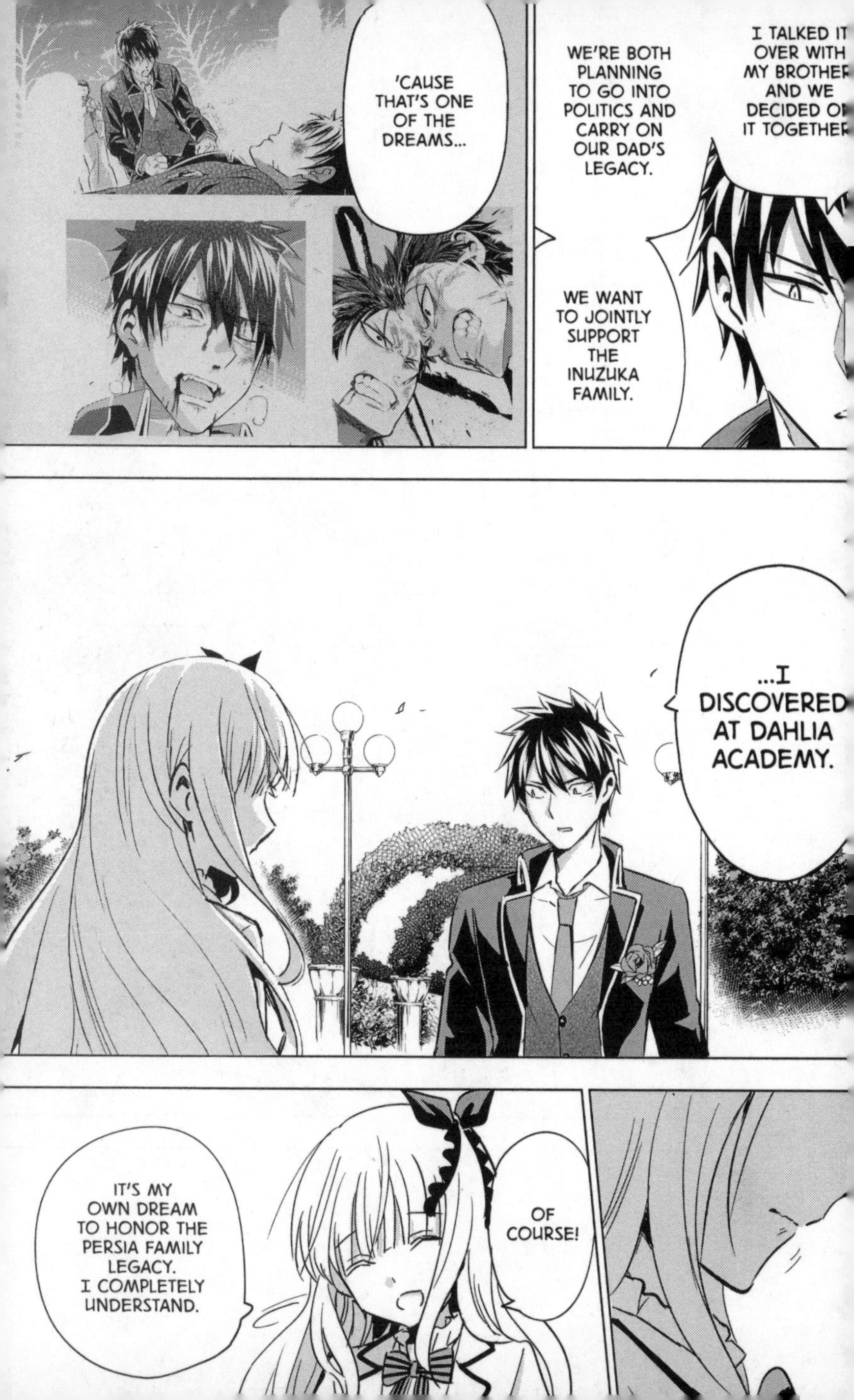
I TALKED IT OVER WITH MY BROTHER AND WE DECIDED ON IT TOGETHER
WE'RE BOTH PLANNING TO GO INTO POLITICS AND CARRY ON OUR DAD'S LEGACY.
WE WANT TO JOINTLY SUPPORT THE INUZUKA FAMILY.
'CAUSE THAT'S ONE OF THE DREAMS...
...I DISCOVERED AT DAHLIA ACADEMY.
OF COURSE!
IT'S MY OWN DREAM TO HONOR THE PERSIA FAMILY LEGACY. I COMPLETELY UNDERSTAND.

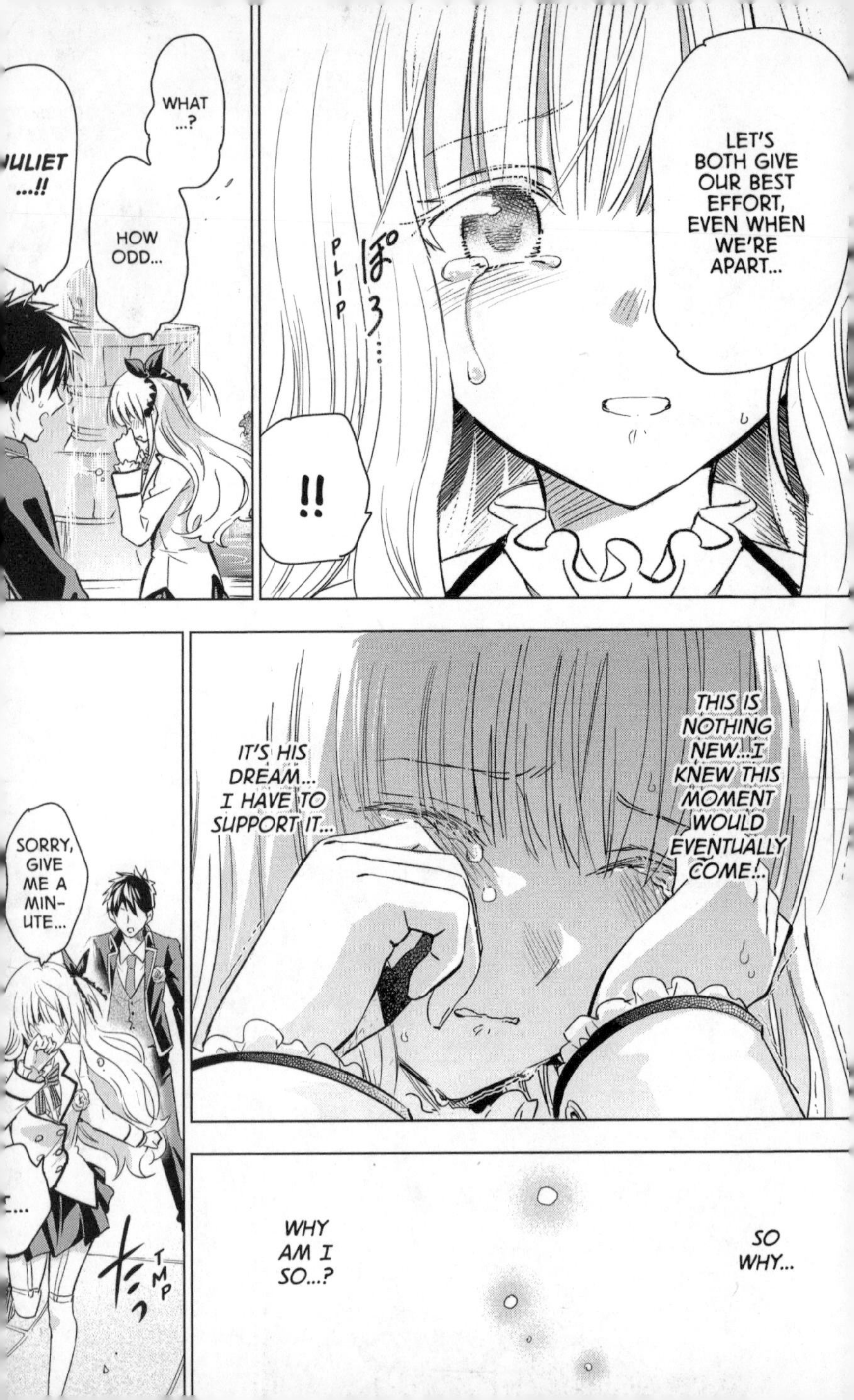
LET'S BOTH GIVE OUR BEST EFFORT, EVEN WHEN WE'RE APART...
PLIP
!!
WHAT ...?
HOW ODD...
ULIET ...!!
THIS IS NOTHING NEW...I KNEW THIS MOMENT WOULD EVENTUALLY COME...
IT'S HIS DREAM... I HAVE TO SUPPORT IT...
SO WHY...
WHY AM I SO...?
SORRY, GIVE ME A MIN-UTE...
TMP

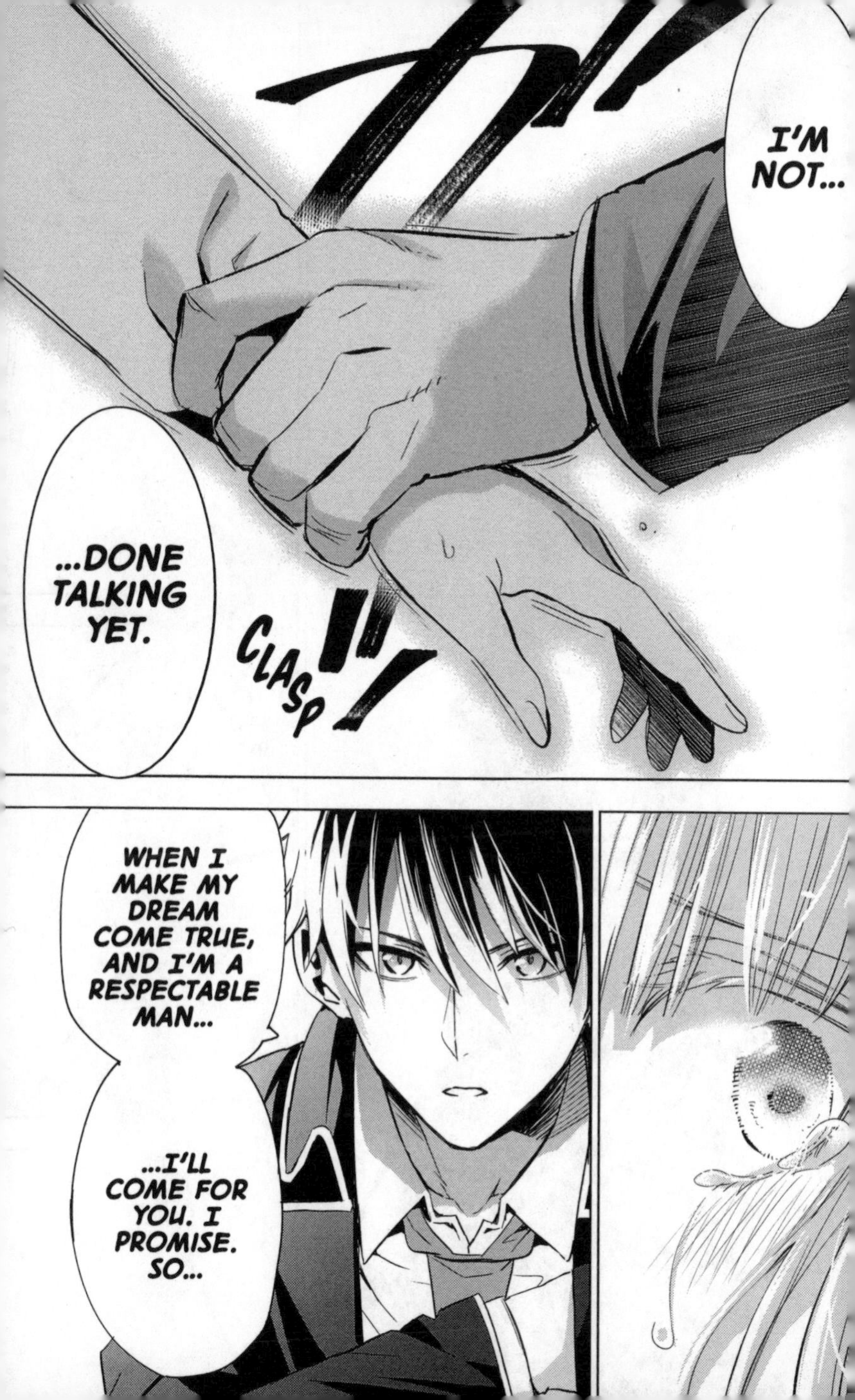

I'M NOT...
...DONE TALKING YET.
CLASP
WHEN I MAKE MY DREAM COME TRUE, AND I'M A RESPECTABLE MAN...
...I'LL COME FOR YOU. I PROMISE. SO...

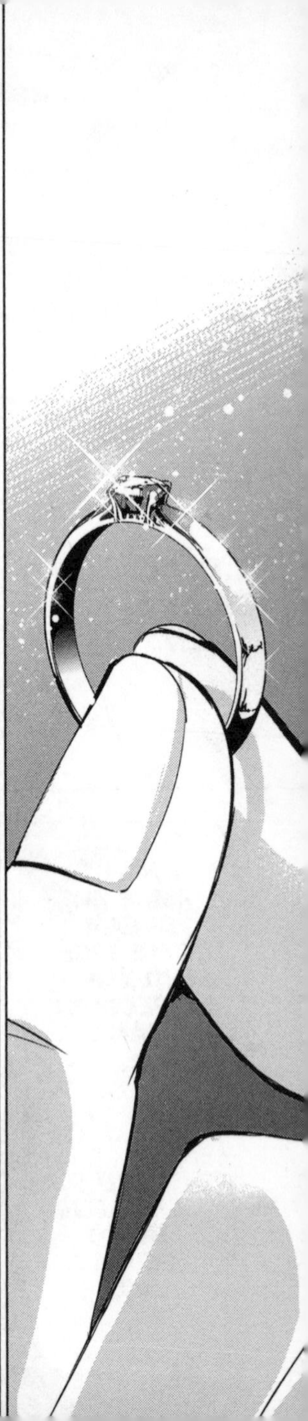

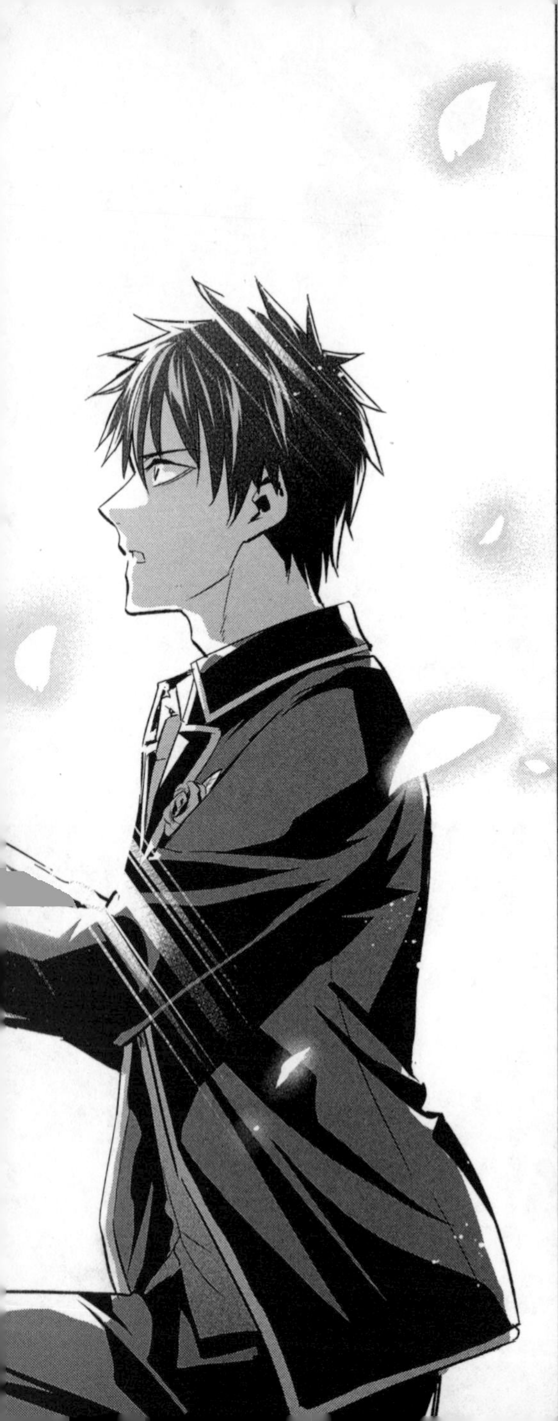

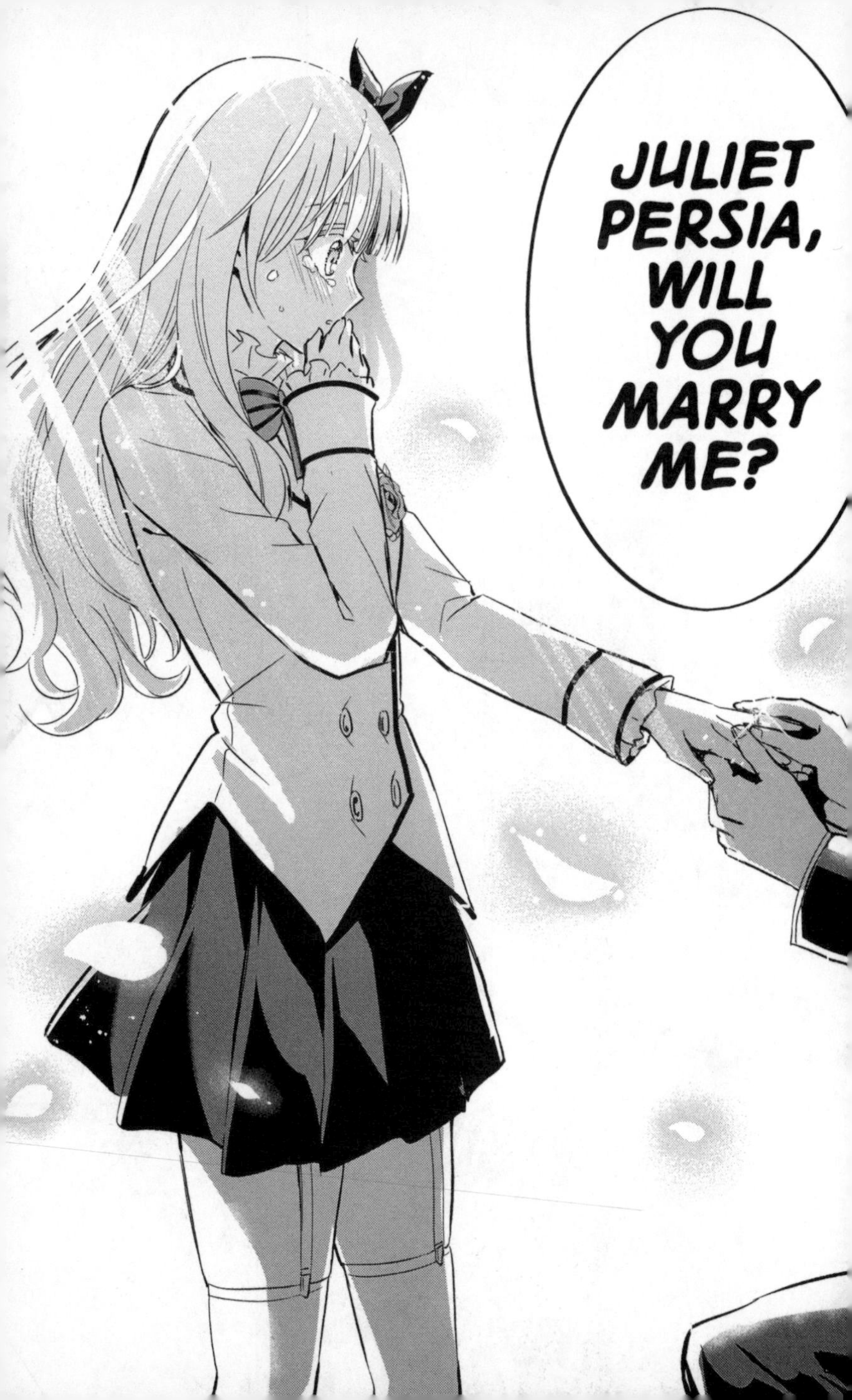
JULIET PERSIA, WILL YOU MARRY ME?

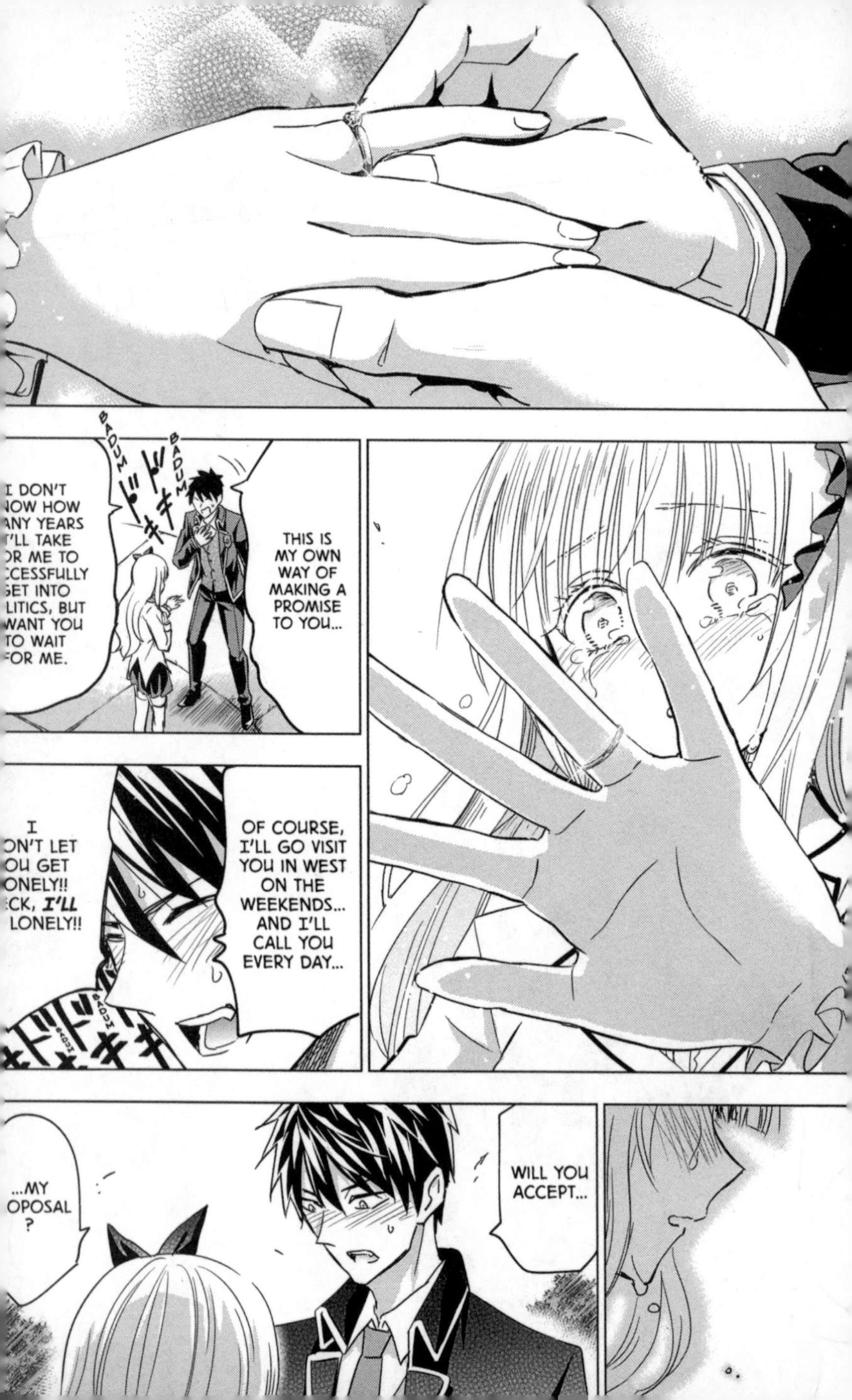
THIS IS MY OWN WAY OF MAKING A PROMISE TO YOU...
I DON'T NOW HOW ANY YEARS I'LL TAKE OR ME TO CCESSFULLY GET INTO LITICS, BUT WANT YOU TO WAIT FOR ME.
BADUM
BADUM
OF COURSE, I'LL GO VISIT YOU IN WEST ON THE WEEKENDS... AND I'LL CALL YOU EVERY DAY...
I ON'T LET OU GET ONELY!! ECK, I'LL LONELY!!
BADUM
WILL YOU ACCEPT...
...MY OPOSAL ?

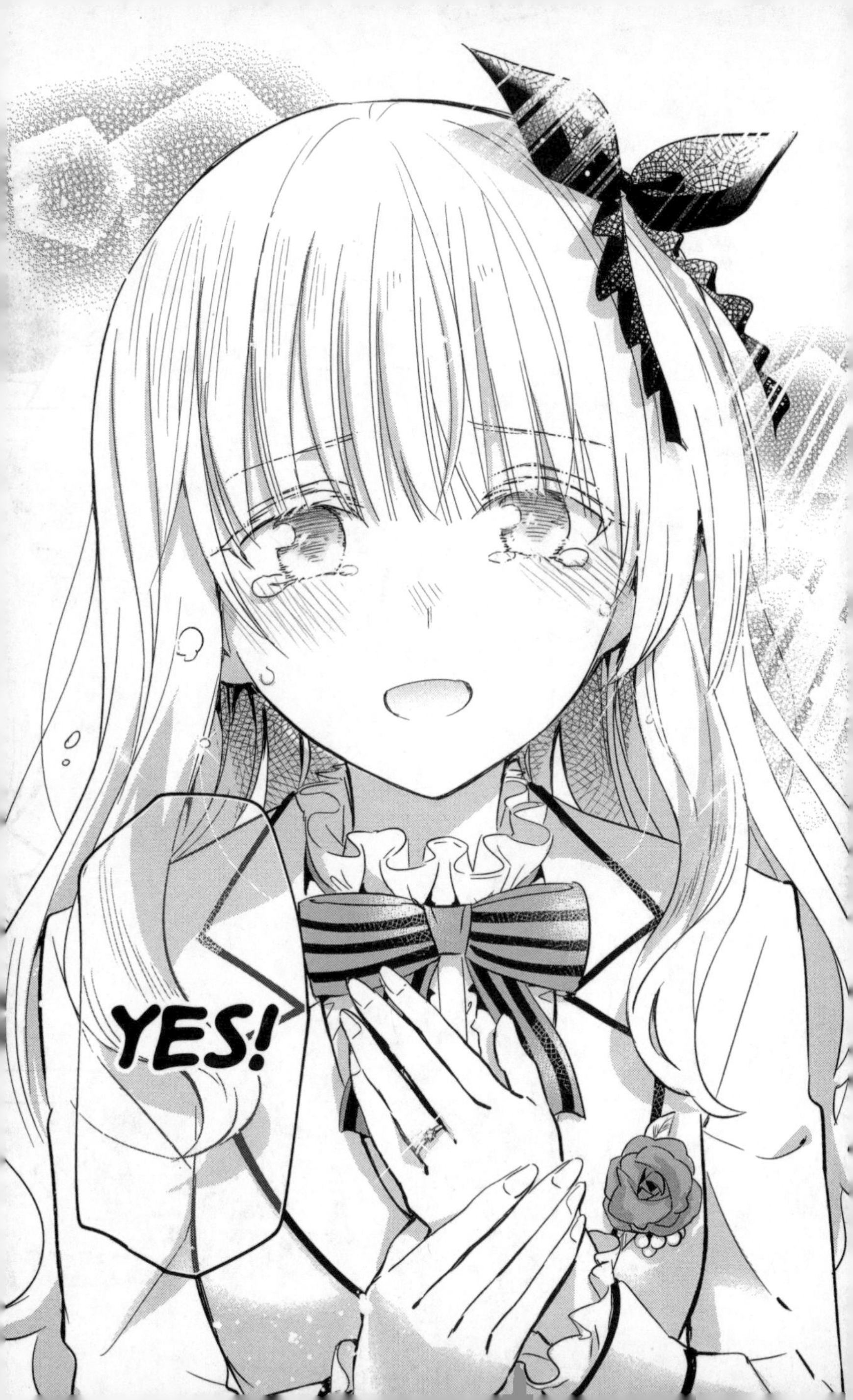
YES!

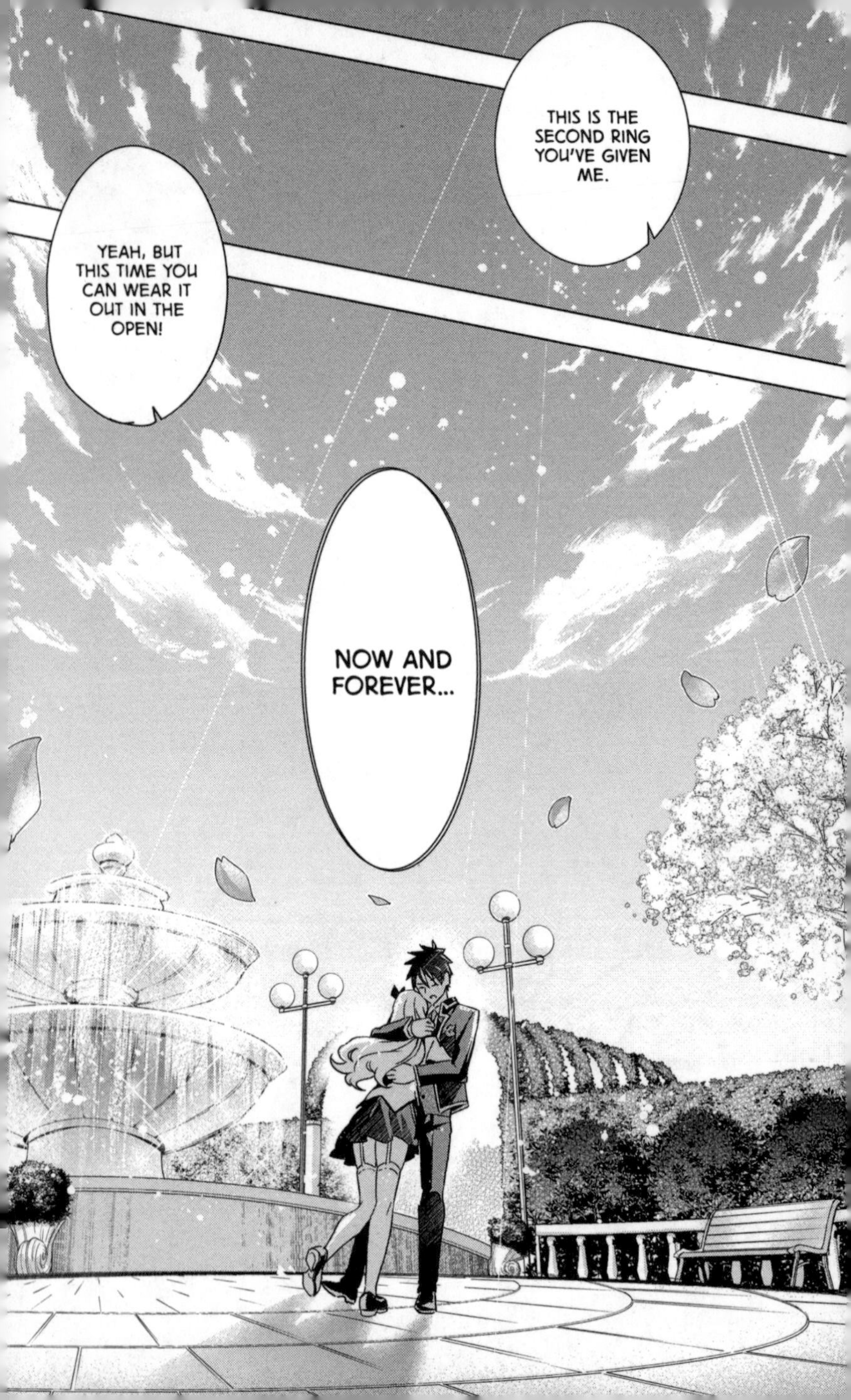
THIS IS THE SECOND RING YOU'VE GIVEN ME.
YEAH, BUT THIS TIME YOU CAN WEAR IT OUT IN THE OPEN!
NOW AND FOREVER...

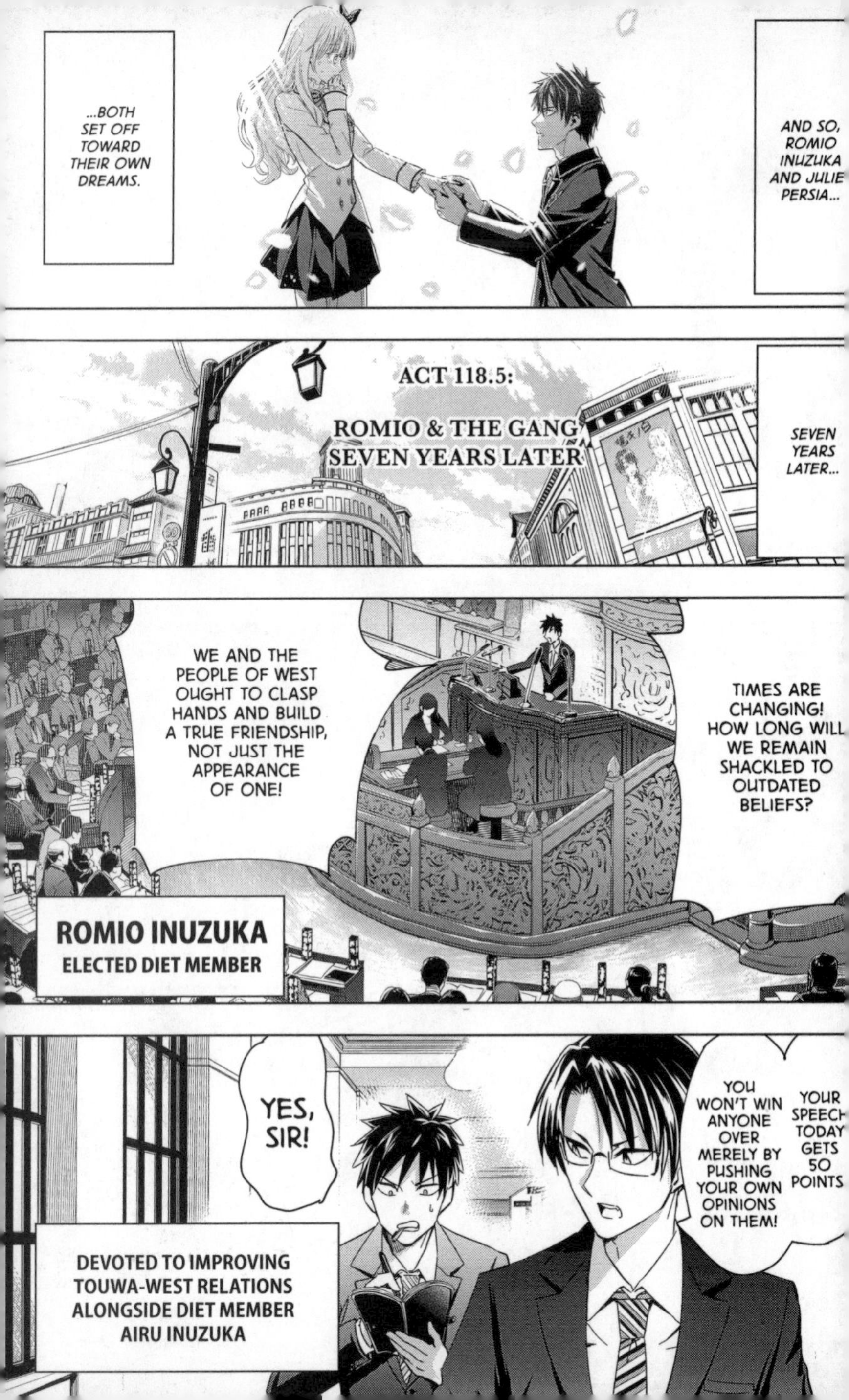
AND SO, ROMIO INUZUKA AND JULIE PERSIA...
...BOTH SET OFF TOWARD THEIR OWN DREAMS.
SEVEN YEARS LATER...
ACT 118.5:
ROMIO & THE GANG SEVEN YEARS LATER
TIMES ARE CHANGING! HOW LONG WILL WE REMAIN SHACKLED TO OUTDATED BELIEFS?
WE AND THE PEOPLE OF WEST OUGHT TO CLASP HANDS AND BUILD A TRUE FRIENDSHIP, NOT JUST THE APPEARANCE OF ONE!
ROMIO INUZUKA
ELECTED DIET MEMBER
YOUR SPEECH TODAY GETS 50 POINTS
YOU WON'T WIN ANYONE OVER MERELY BY PUSHING YOUR OWN OPINIONS ON THEM!
YES, SIR!
DEVOTED TO IMPROVING TOUWA-WEST RELATIONS ALONGSIDE DIET MEMBER AIRU INUZUKA

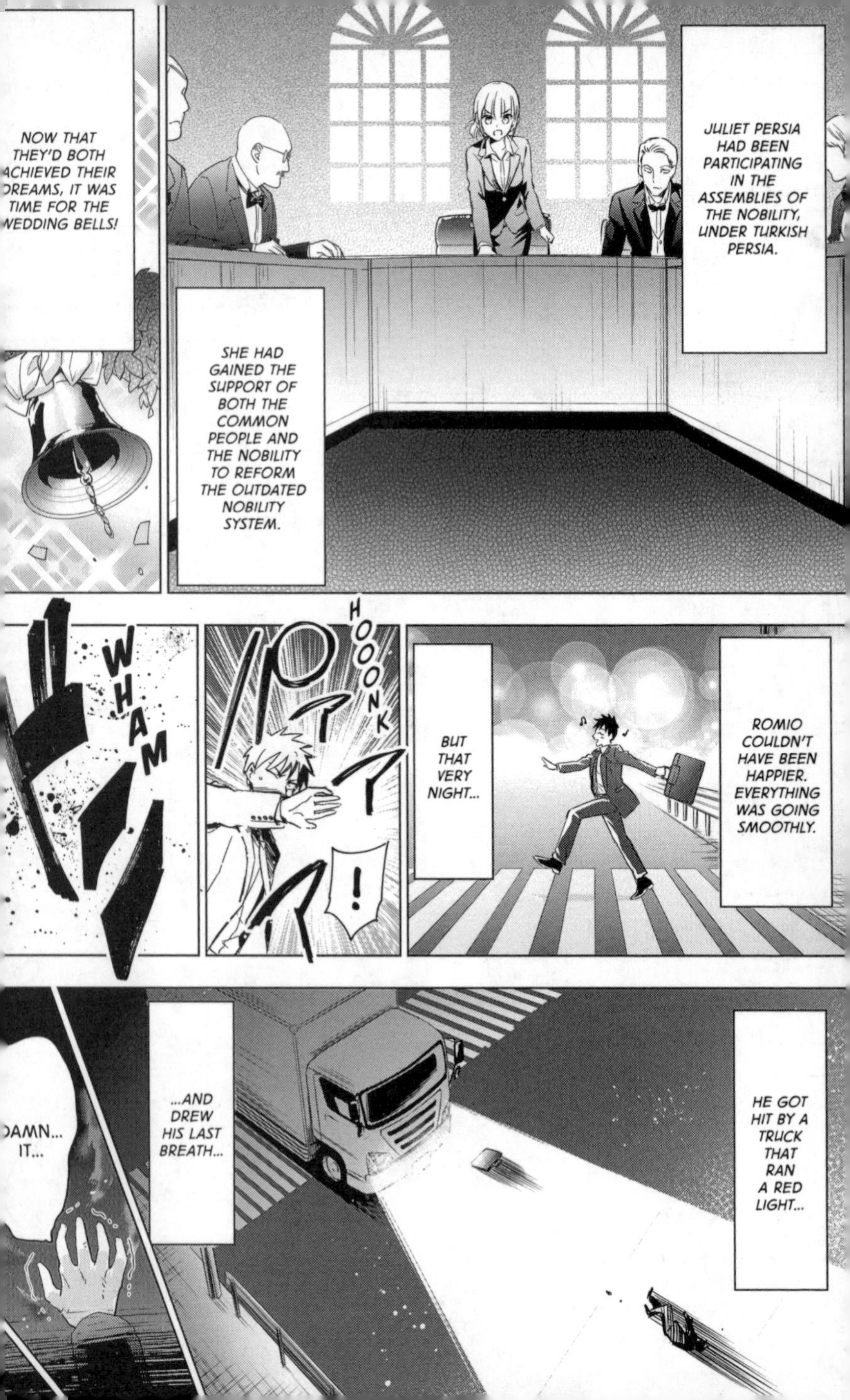
JULIET PERSIA HAD BEEN PARTICIPATING IN THE ASSEMBLIES OF THE NOBILITY, UNDER TURKISH PERSIA.
SHE HAD GAINED THE SUPPORT OF BOTH THE COMMON PEOPLE AND THE NOBILITY TO REFORM THE OUTDATED NOBILITY SYSTEM.
NOW THAT THEY'D BOTH ACHIEVED THEIR DREAMS, IT WAS TIME FOR THE WEDDING BELLS!
ROMIO COULDN'T HAVE BEEN HAPPIER. EVERYTHING WAS GOING SMOOTHLY.
BUT THAT VERY NIGHT...
HOOONK
!
WHAM
HE GOT HIT BY A TRUCK THAT RAN A RED LIGHT...
...AND DREW HIS LAST BREATH...
DAMN... IT...

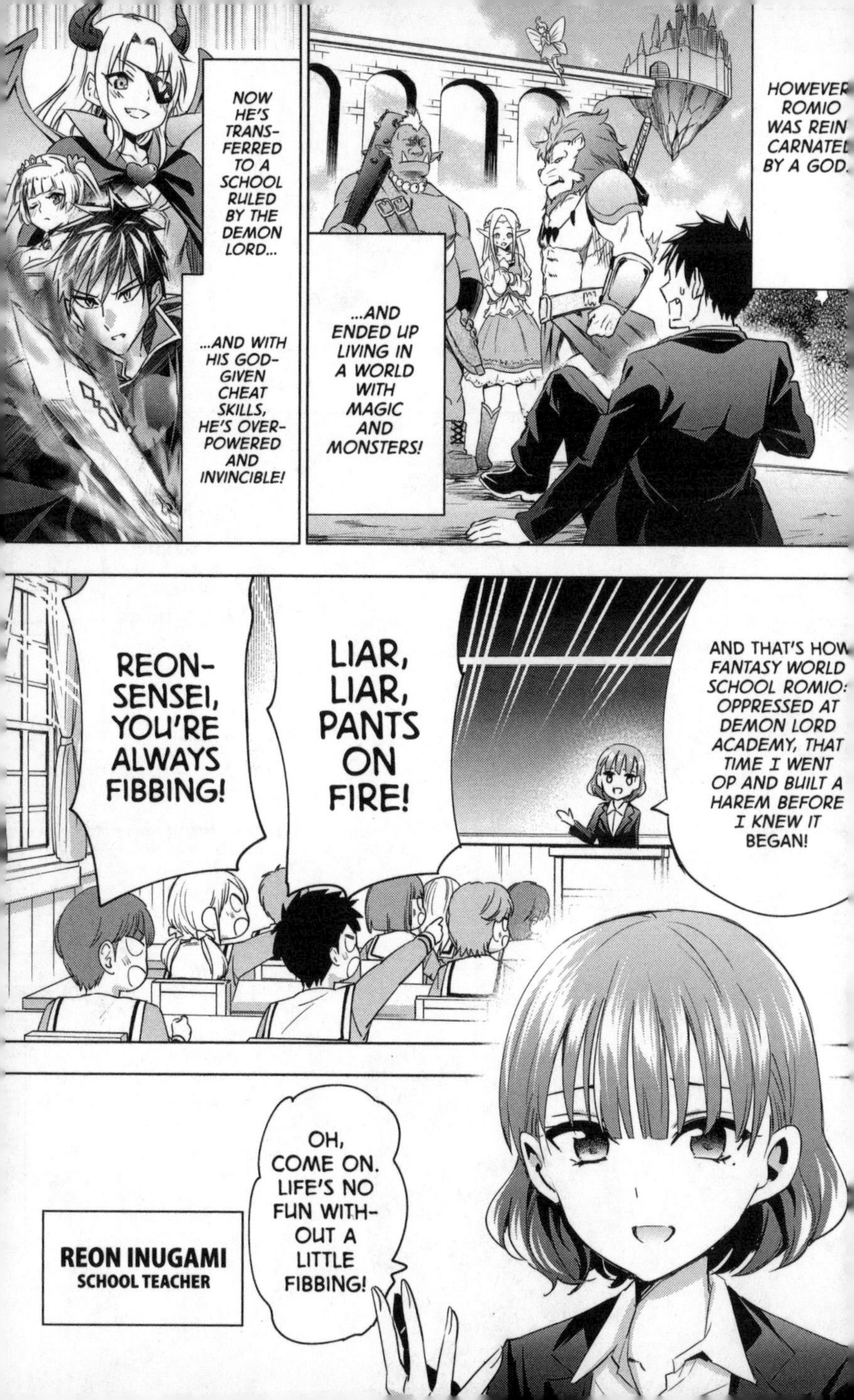
HOWEVER ROMIO WAS REIN CARNATED BY A GOD.
...AND ENDED UP LIVING IN A WORLD WITH MAGIC AND MONSTERS!
NOW HE'S TRANS-FERRED TO A SCHOOL RULED BY THE DEMON LORD...
...AND WITH HIS GOD-GIVEN CHEAT SKILLS, HE'S OVER-POWERED AND INVINCIBLE!
AND THAT'S HOW FANTASY WORLD SCHOOL ROMIO: OPPRESSED AT DEMON LORD ACADEMY, THAT TIME I WENT OP AND BUILT A HAREM BEFORE I KNEW IT BEGAN!
LIAR, LIAR, PANTS ON FIRE!
REON-SENSEI, YOU'RE ALWAYS FIBBING!
OH, COME ON. LIFE'S NO FUN WITH-OUT A LITTLE FIBBING!
REON INUGAMI
SCHOOL TEACHER

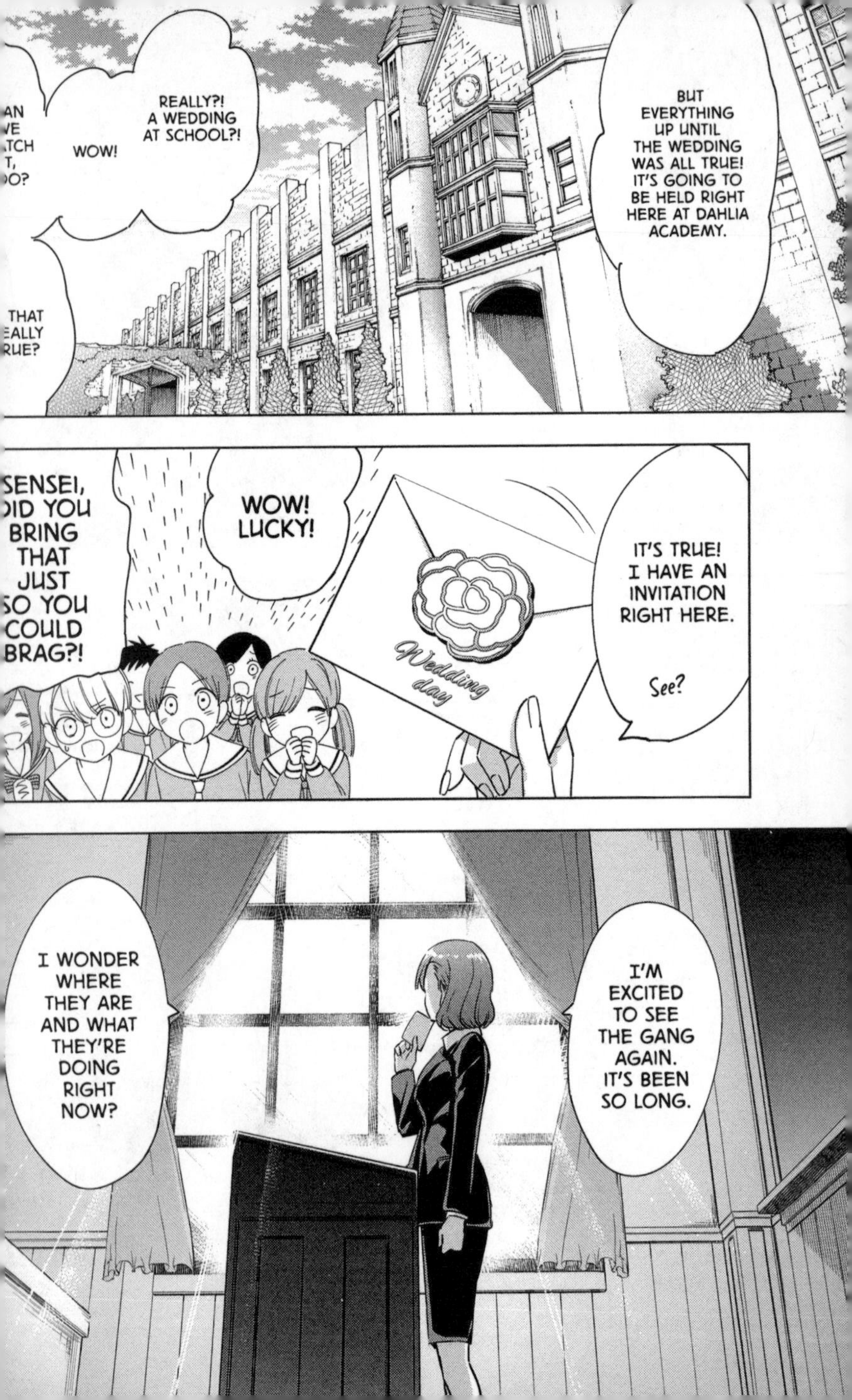

BUT EVERYTHING UP UNTIL THE WEDDING WAS ALL TRUE! IT'S GOING TO BE HELD RIGHT HERE AT DAHLIA ACADEMY.
REALLY?! A WEDDING AT SCHOOL?!
WOW!
IT'S TRUE! I HAVE AN INVITATION RIGHT HERE.
See?
Wedding day
WOW! LUCKY!
SENSEI, DID YOU BRING THAT JUST SO YOU COULD BRAG?!
I'M EXCITED TO SEE THE GANG AGAIN. IT'S BEEN SO LONG.
I WONDER WHERE THEY ARE AND WHAT THEY'RE DOING RIGHT NOW?

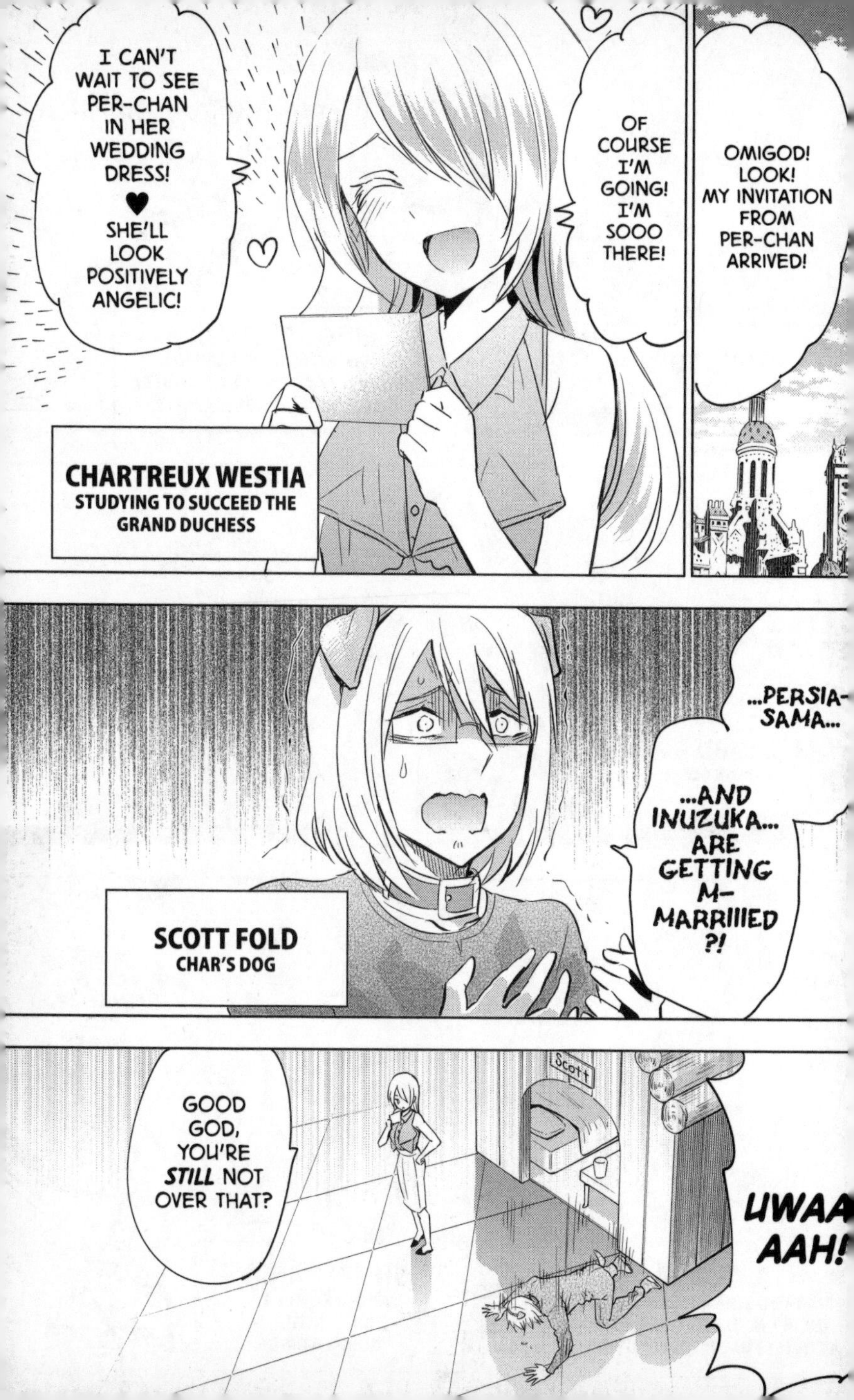
OMIGOD! LOOK! MY INVITATION FROM PER-CHAN ARRIVED!
OF COURSE I'M GOING! I'M SOOO THERE!
I CAN'T WAIT TO SEE PER-CHAN IN HER WEDDING DRESS! ♥ SHE'LL LOOK POSITIVELY ANGELIC!
CHARTREUX WESTIA
STUDYING TO SUCCEED THE GRAND DUCHESS
...PERSIA-SAMA...
...AND INUZUKA... ARE GETTING M-MARRIIIED?!
SCOTT FOLD
CHAR'S DOG
Scott
UWAAAAH!
GOOD GOD, YOU'RE *STILL* NOT OVER THAT?

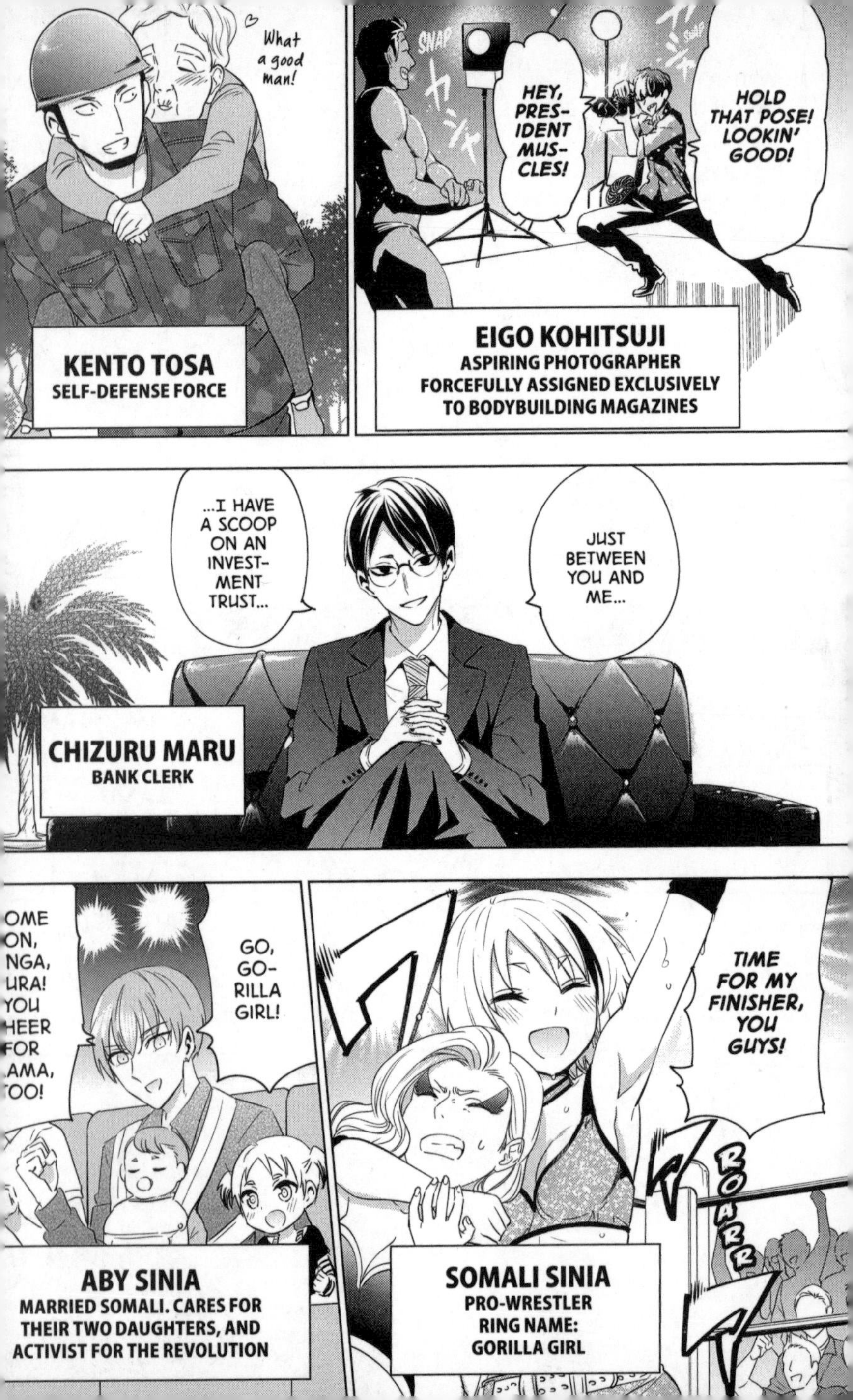
SNAP
SNAP
HOLD THAT POSE! LOOKIN' GOOD!
HEY, PRES- IDENT MUS- CLES!
EIGO KOHITSUJI
ASPIRING PHOTOGRAPHER
FORCEFULLY ASSIGNED EXCLUSIVELY TO BODYBUILDING MAGAZINES
What a good man!
KENTO TOSA
SELF-DEFENSE FORCE
JUST BETWEEN YOU AND ME...
...I HAVE A SCOOP ON AN INVEST- MENT TRUST...
CHIZURU MARU
BANK CLERK
TIME FOR MY FINISHER, YOU GUYS!
ROARR
SOMALI SINIA
PRO-WRESTLER
RING NAME: GORILLA GIRL
GO, GO- RILLA GIRL!
OME ON, NGA, URA! YOU HEER FOR AMA, TOO!
ABY SINIA
MARRIED SOMALI. CARES FOR THEIR TWO DAUGHTERS, AND ACTIVIST FOR THE REVOLUTION

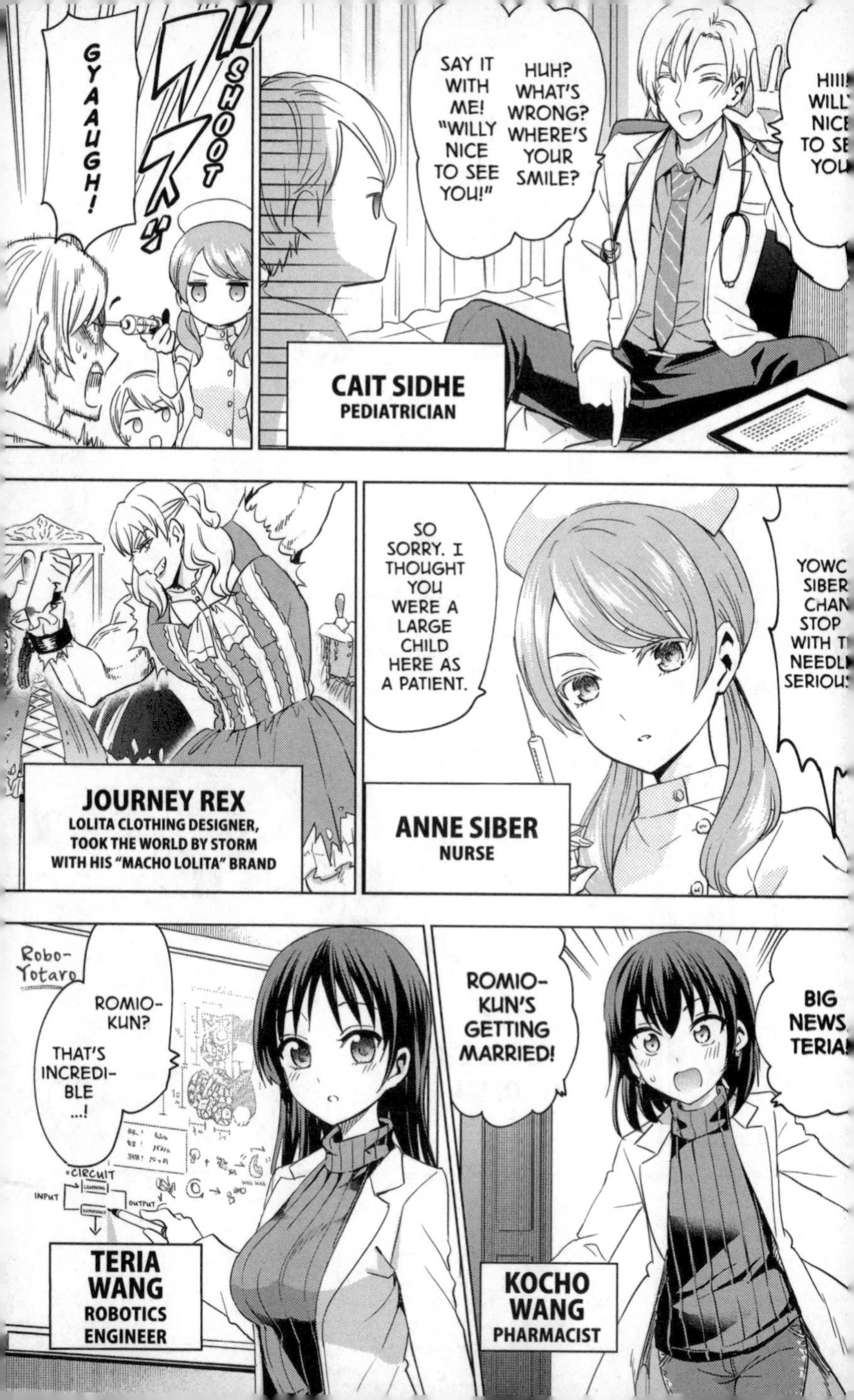
HIII! WILLY NICE TO SE YOU
HUH? WHAT'S WRONG? WHERE'S YOUR SMILE?
SAY IT WITH ME! "WILLY NICE TO SEE YOU!"
CAIT SIDHE
PEDIATRICIAN
SHOOT
GYAAUGH!
YOWC SIBER CHAN STOP WITH T NEEDL SERIOUS
SO SORRY. I THOUGHT YOU WERE A LARGE CHILD HERE AS A PATIENT.
ANNE SIBER
NURSE
JOURNEY REX
LOLITA CLOTHING DESIGNER, TOOK THE WORLD BY STORM WITH HIS "MACHO LOLITA" BRAND
BIG NEWS, TERIA
ROMIO-KUN'S GETTING MARRIED!
KOCHO WANG
PHARMACIST
Robo-Yotaro
ROMIO-KUN?
THAT'S INCREDIBLE...!
CIRCUIT
INPUT
OUTPUT
WAG WAG
TERIA WANG
ROBOTICS ENGINEER

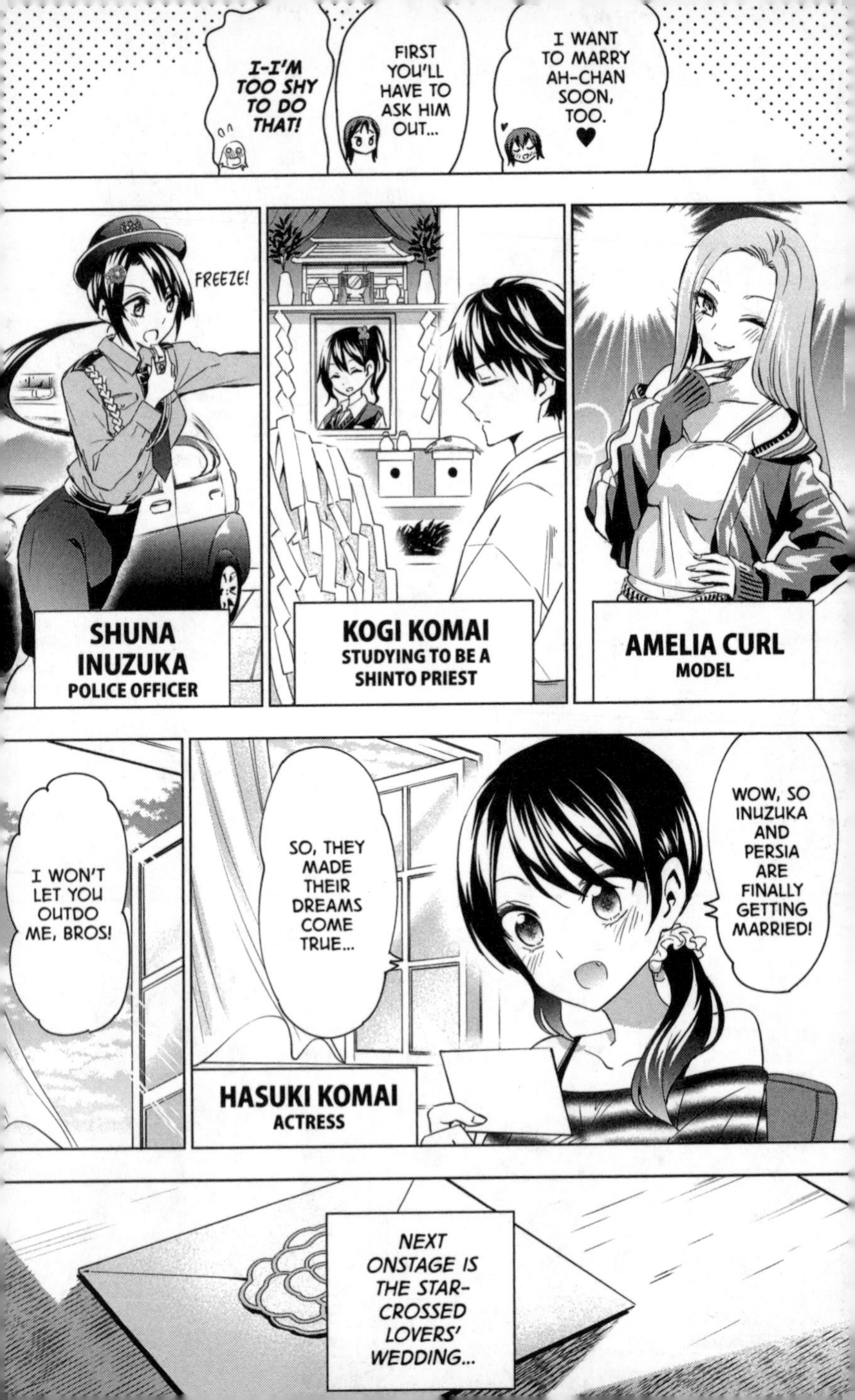

I WANT TO MARRY AH-CHAN SOON, TOO. ♥
FIRST YOU'LL HAVE TO ASK HIM OUT...
I-I'M TOO SHY TO DO THAT!
AMELIA CURL
MODEL
KOGI KOMAI
STUDYING TO BE A SHINTO PRIEST
FREEZE!
SHUNA INUZUKA
POLICE OFFICER
WOW, SO INUZUKA AND PERSIA ARE FINALLY GETTING MARRIED!
SO, THEY MADE THEIR DREAMS COME TRUE...
HASUKI KOMAI
ACTRESS
I WON'T LET YOU OUTDO ME, BROS!
NEXT ONSTAGE IS THE STAR-CROSSED LOVERS' WEDDING...

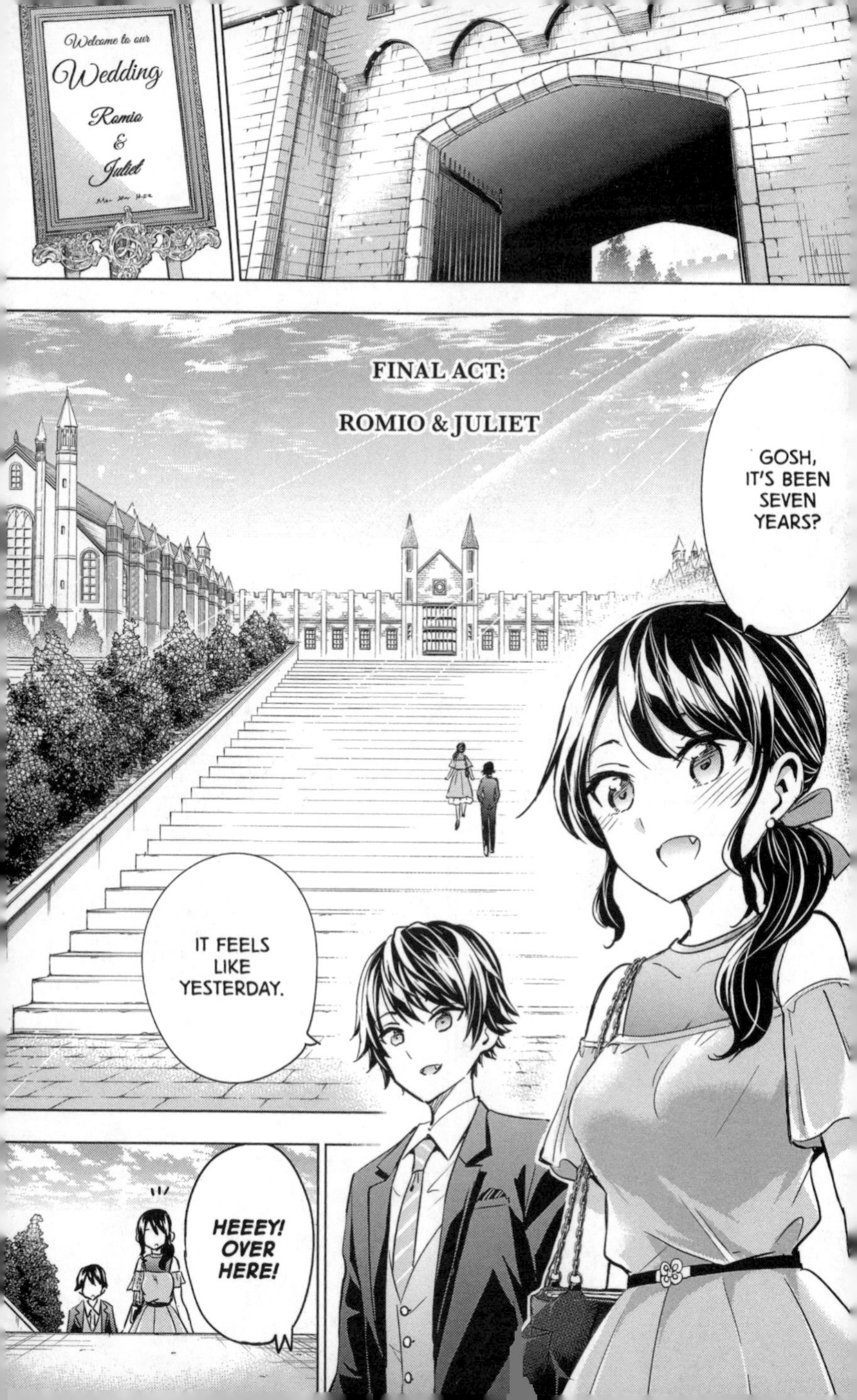
Welcome to our
Wedding
Romio
&
Juliet
FINAL ACT:
ROMIO & JULIET
GOSH, IT'S BEEN SEVEN YEARS?
IT FEELS LIKE YESTERDAY.
HEEEY! OVER HERE!

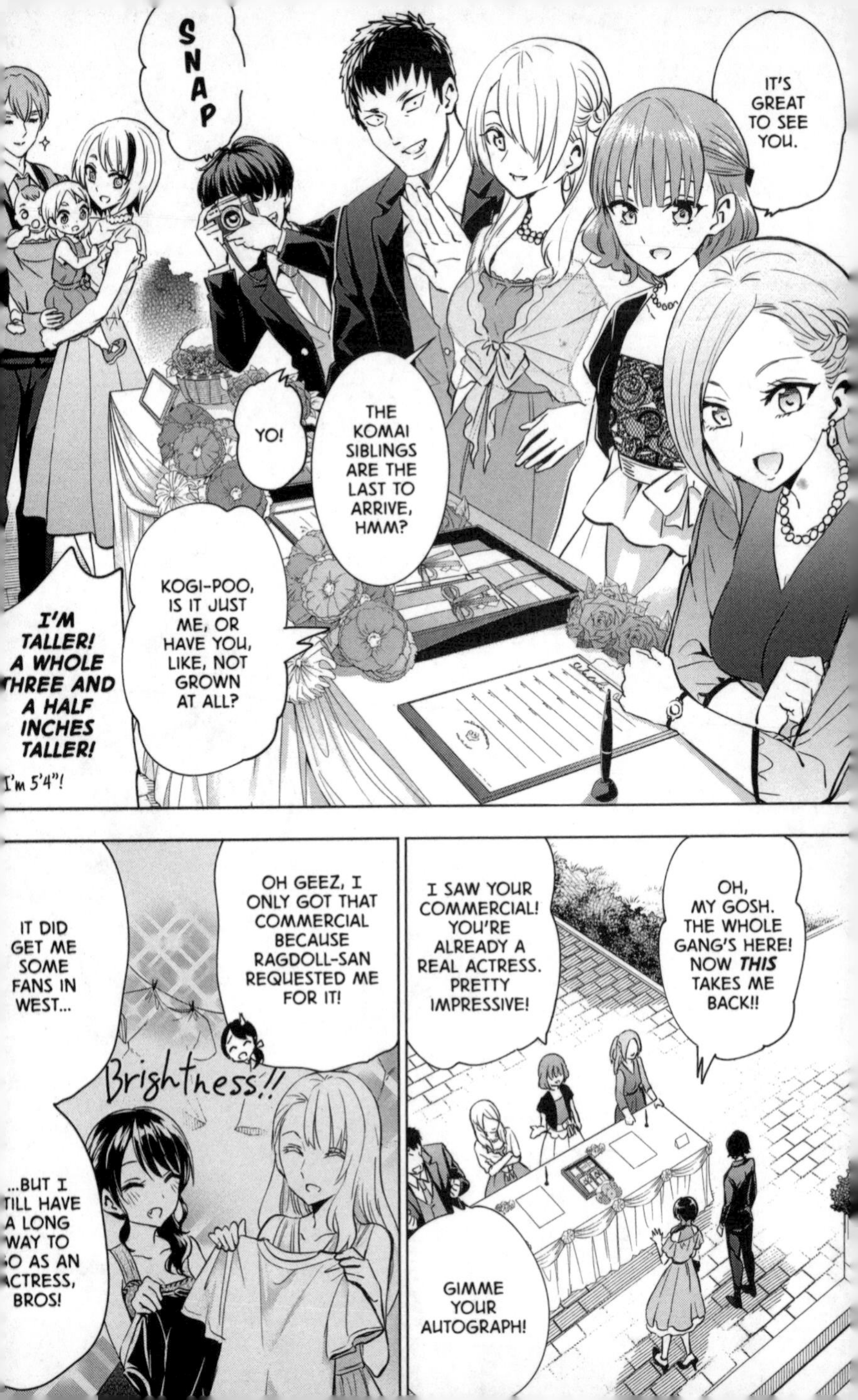
IT'S GREAT TO SEE YOU.
SNAP
THE KOMAI SIBLINGS ARE THE LAST TO ARRIVE, HMM?
YO!
KOGI-POO, IS IT JUST ME, OR HAVE YOU, LIKE, NOT GROWN AT ALL?
I'M TALLER! A WHOLE THREE AND A HALF INCHES TALLER!
I'm 5'4"!
OH, MY GOSH. THE WHOLE GANG'S HERE! NOW THIS TAKES ME BACK!!
I SAW YOUR COMMERCIAL! YOU'RE ALREADY A REAL ACTRESS. PRETTY IMPRESSIVE!
GIMME YOUR AUTOGRAPH!
OH GEEZ, I ONLY GOT THAT COMMERCIAL BECAUSE RAGDOLL-SAN REQUESTED ME FOR IT!
IT DID GET ME SOME FANS IN WEST...
Brightness!!
...BUT I TILL HAVE A LONG WAY TO O AS AN CTRESS, BROS!

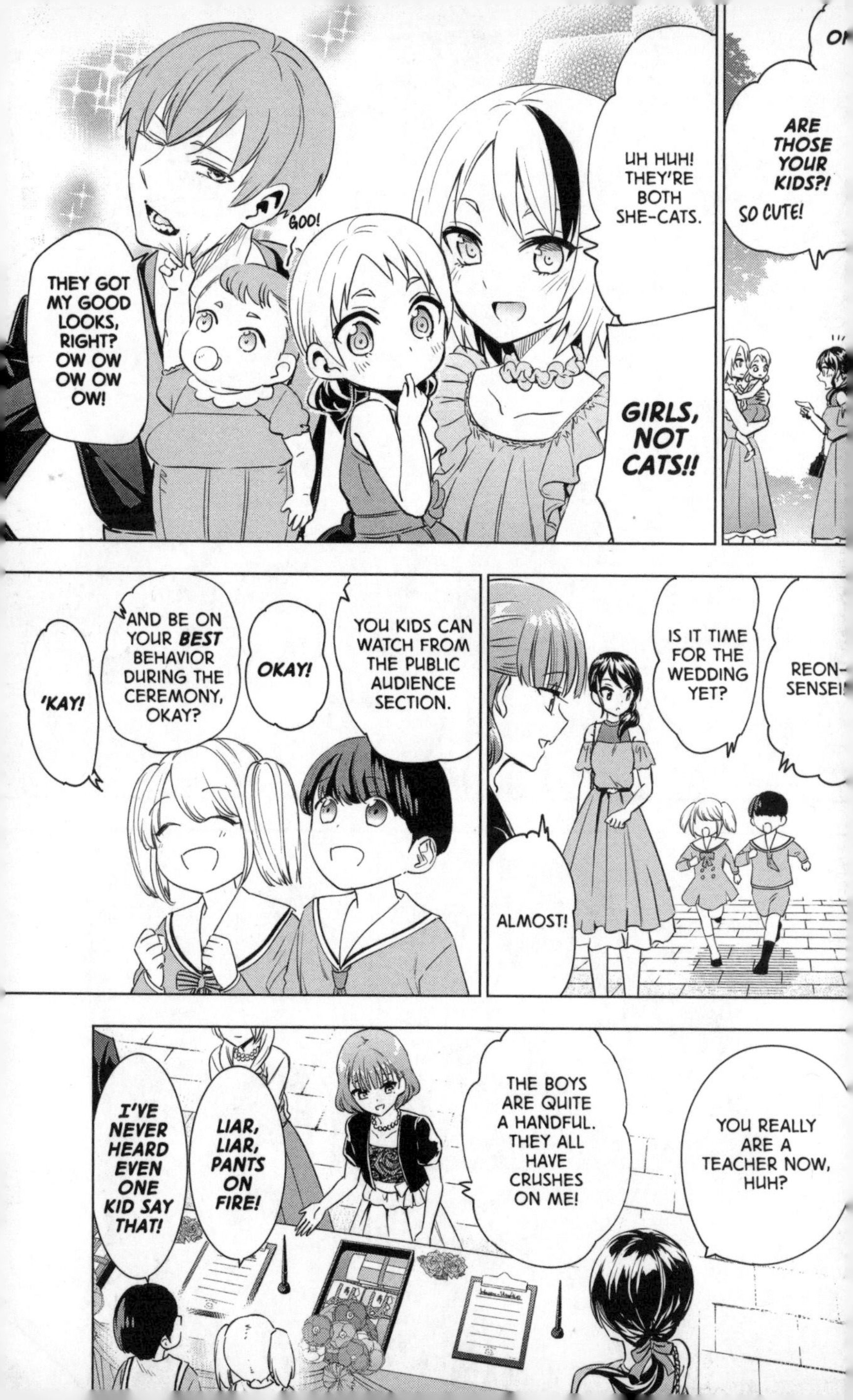
ARE THOSE YOUR KIDS?!
SO CUTE!
UH HUH! THEY'RE BOTH SHE-CATS.
GIRLS, NOT CATS!!
GOO!
THEY GOT MY GOOD LOOKS, RIGHT? OW OW OW OW OW!
REON-SENSEI!
IS IT TIME FOR THE WEDDING YET?
ALMOST!
YOU KIDS CAN WATCH FROM THE PUBLIC AUDIENCE SECTION.
OKAY!
AND BE ON YOUR BEST BEHAVIOR DURING THE CEREMONY, OKAY?
'KAY!
YOU REALLY ARE A TEACHER NOW, HUH?
THE BOYS ARE QUITE A HANDFUL. THEY ALL HAVE CRUSHES ON ME!
LIAR, LIAR, PANTS ON FIRE!
I'VE NEVER HEARD EVEN ONE KID SAY THAT!

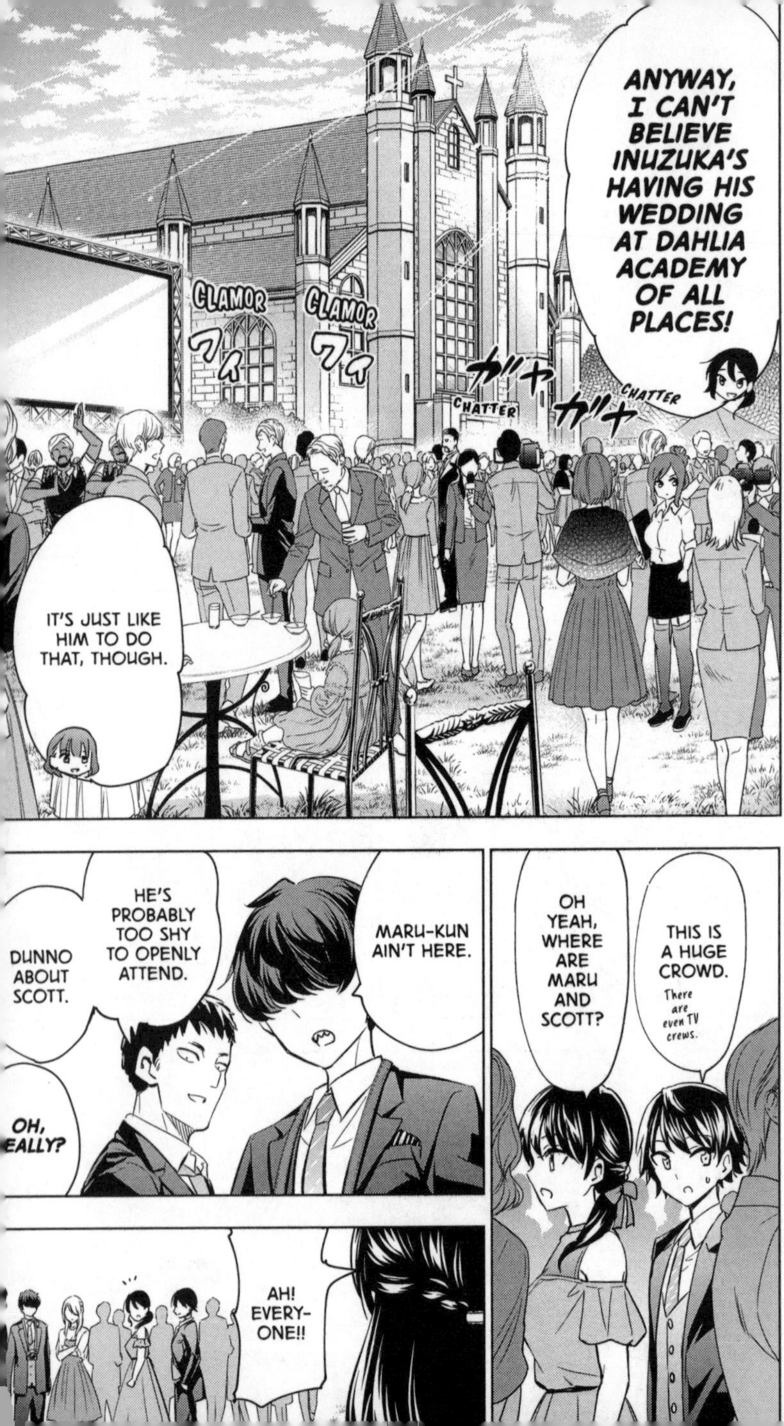
ANYWAY, I CAN'T BELIEVE INUZUKA'S HAVING HIS WEDDING AT DAHLIA ACADEMY OF ALL PLACES!
CLAMOR
ワイ
CLAMOR
ワイ
ガヤ
CHATTER
ガヤ
CHATTER
IT'S JUST LIKE HIM TO DO THAT, THOUGH.
THIS IS A HUGE CROWD.
There are even TV crews.
OH YEAH, WHERE ARE MARU AND SCOTT?
MARU-KUN AIN'T HERE.
HE'S PROBABLY TOO SHY TO OPENLY ATTEND.
DUNNO ABOUT SCOTT.
OH, EALLY?
AH! EVERYONE!!

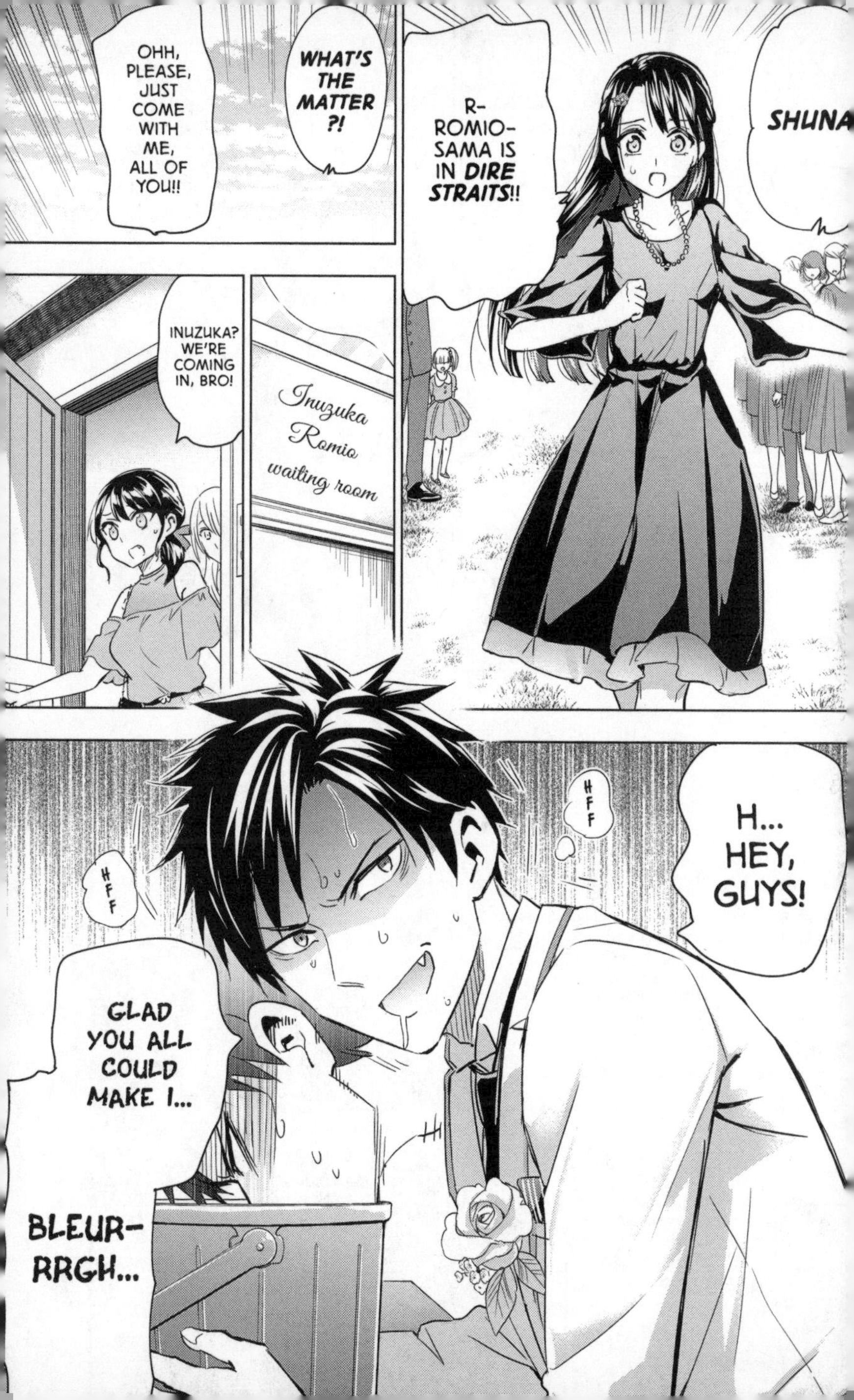
SHUNA
R-ROMIO-SAMA IS IN DIRE STRAITS!!
WHAT'S THE MATTER?!
OHH, PLEASE, JUST COME WITH ME, ALL OF YOU!!
Inuzuka Romio waiting room
INUZUKA? WE'RE COMING IN, BRO!
HFF
H... HEY, GUYS!
HFF
GLAD YOU ALL COULD MAKE I...
BLEUR-RRGH...

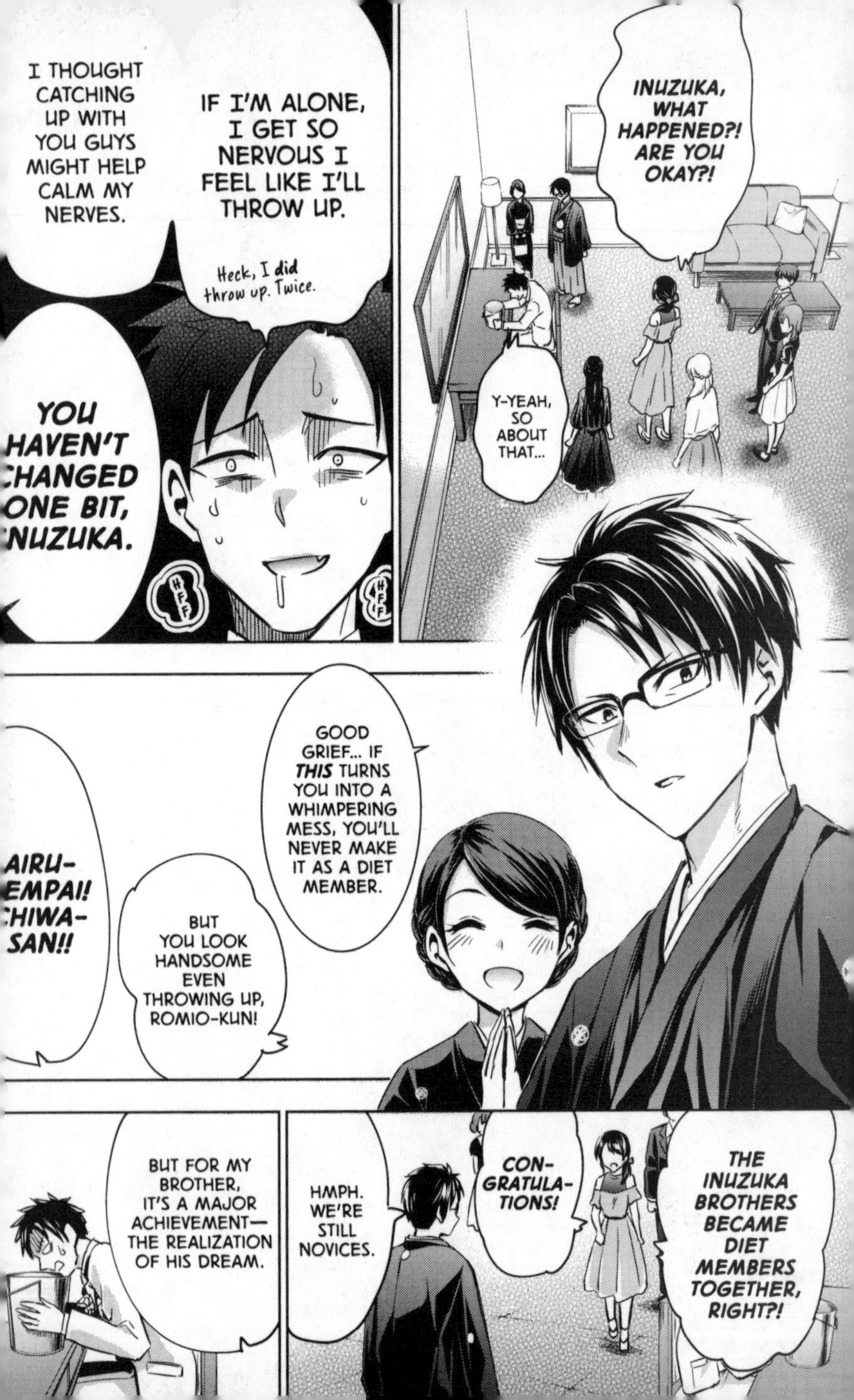
INUZUKA, WHAT HAPPENED?! ARE YOU OKAY?!
Y-YEAH, SO ABOUT THAT...
IF I'M ALONE, I GET SO NERVOUS I FEEL LIKE I'LL THROW UP.
I THOUGHT CATCHING UP WITH YOU GUYS MIGHT HELP CALM MY NERVES.
Heck, I did throw up. Twice.
YOU HAVEN'T CHANGED ONE BIT, INUZUKA.
HFF
HFF
GOOD GRIEF... IF THIS TURNS YOU INTO A WHIMPERING MESS, YOU'LL NEVER MAKE IT AS A DIET MEMBER.
BUT YOU LOOK HANDSOME EVEN THROWING UP, ROMIO-KUN!
AIRU-EMPAI! HIWA-SAN!!
THE INUZUKA BROTHERS BECAME DIET MEMBERS TOGETHER, RIGHT?!
CON-GRATULA-TIONS!
HMPH. WE'RE STILL NOVICES.
BUT FOR MY BROTHER, IT'S A MAJOR ACHIEVEMENT—THE REALIZATION OF HIS DREAM.

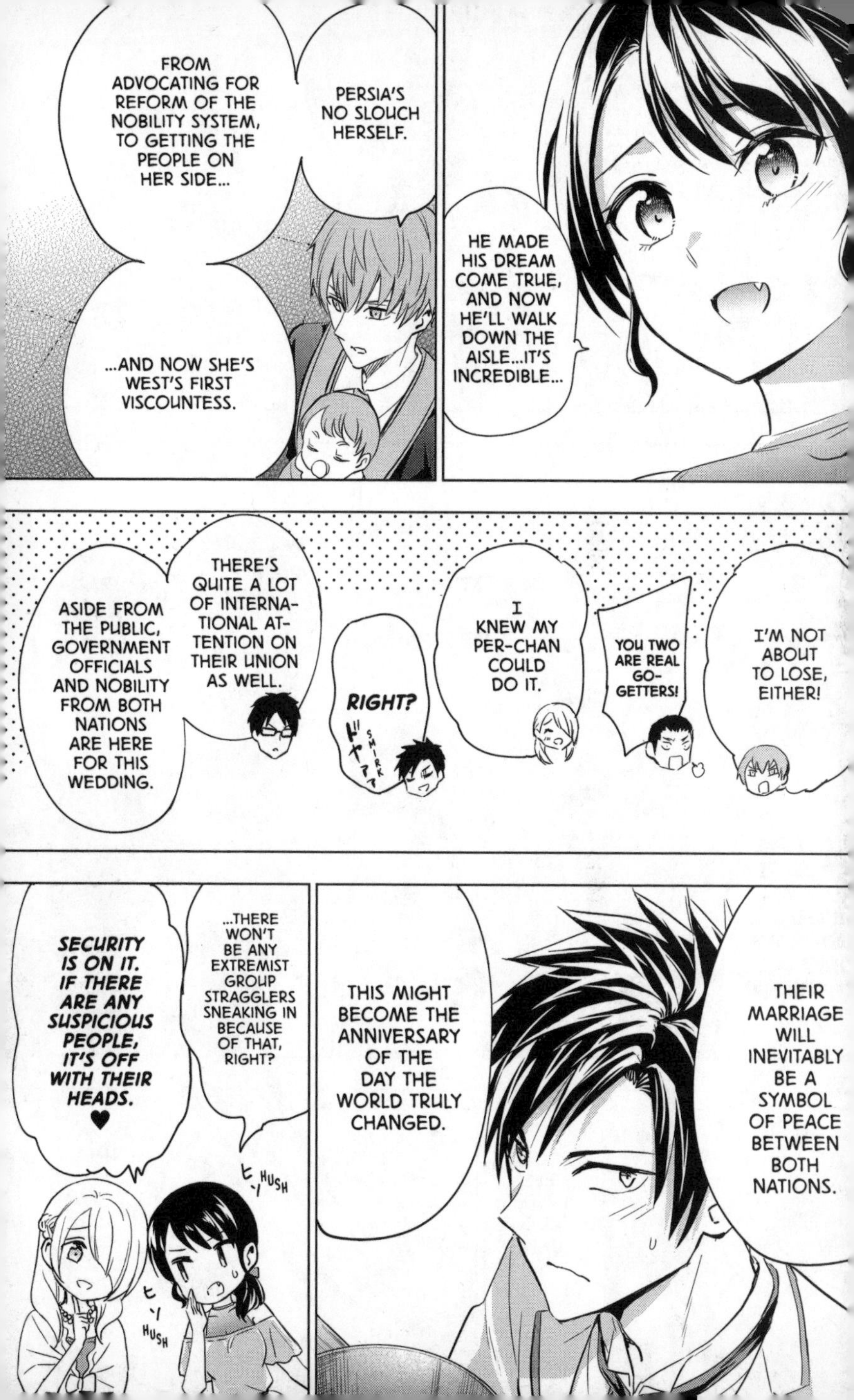
HE MADE HIS DREAM COME TRUE, AND NOW HE'LL WALK DOWN THE AISLE...IT'S INCREDIBLE...
PERSIA'S NO SLOUCH HERSELF.
FROM ADVOCATING FOR REFORM OF THE NOBILITY SYSTEM, TO GETTING THE PEOPLE ON HER SIDE...
...AND NOW SHE'S WEST'S FIRST VISCOUNTESS.
I'M NOT ABOUT TO LOSE, EITHER!
YOU TWO ARE REAL GO-GETTERS!
I KNEW MY PER-CHAN COULD DO IT.
RIGHT?
SMIRK
THERE'S QUITE A LOT OF INTERNATIONAL ATTENTION ON THEIR UNION AS WELL.
ASIDE FROM THE PUBLIC, GOVERNMENT OFFICIALS AND NOBILITY FROM BOTH NATIONS ARE HERE FOR THIS WEDDING.
THEIR MARRIAGE WILL INEVITABLY BE A SYMBOL OF PEACE BETWEEN BOTH NATIONS.
THIS MIGHT BECOME THE ANNIVERSARY OF THE DAY THE WORLD TRULY CHANGED.
...THERE WON'T BE ANY EXTREMIST GROUP STRAGGLERS SNEAKING IN BECAUSE OF THAT, RIGHT?
SECURITY IS ON IT. IF THERE ARE ANY SUSPICIOUS PEOPLE, IT'S OFF WITH THEIR HEADS. ♥
HUSH
HUSH

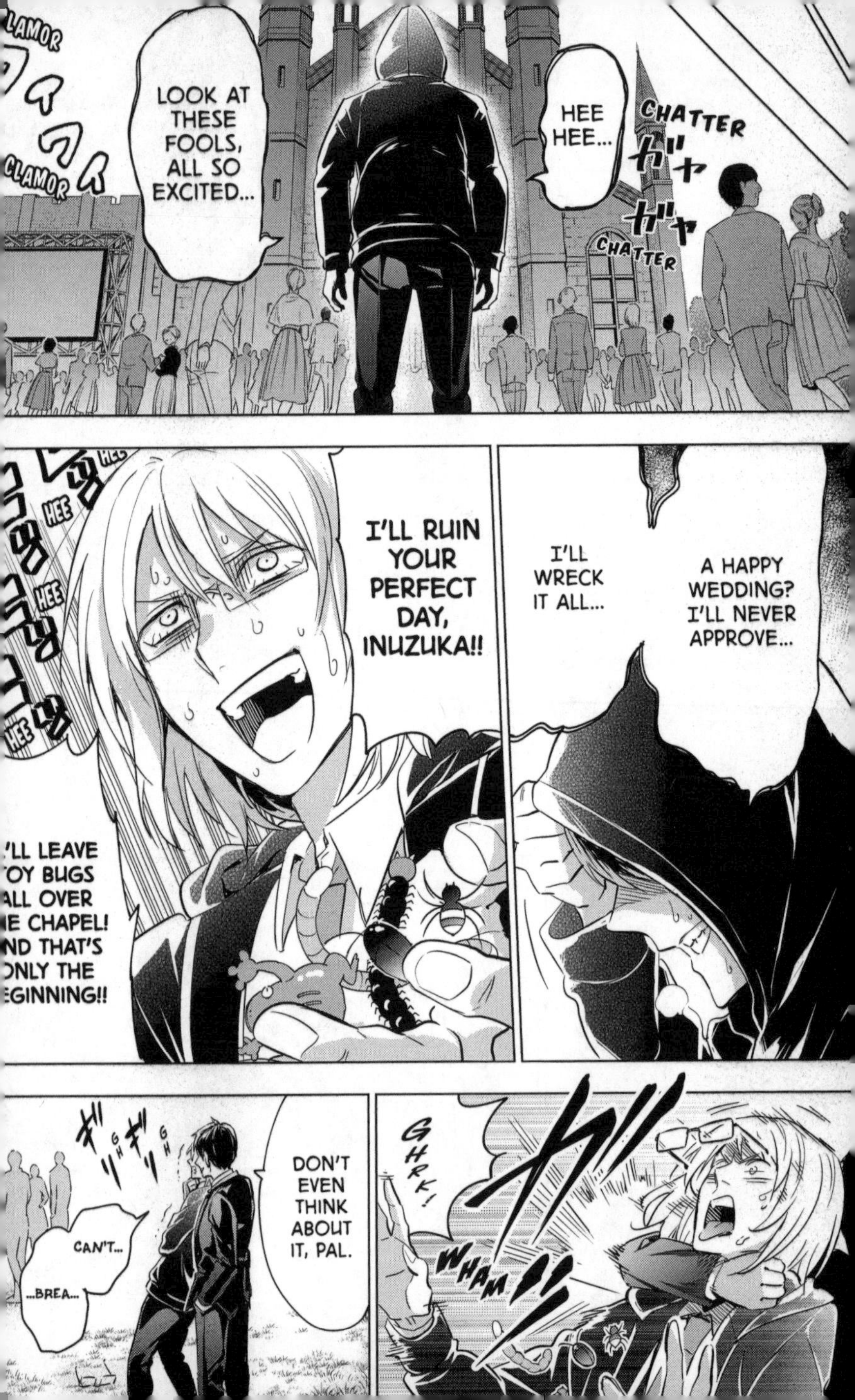
CHATTER
HEE HEE...
LOOK AT THESE FOOLS, ALL SO EXCITED...
CLAMOR
CHATTER
CLAMOR
A HAPPY WEDDING? I'LL NEVER APPROVE...
I'LL WRECK IT ALL...
I'LL RUIN YOUR PERFECT DAY, INUZUKA!!
HEE
HEE
HEE
HEE
'LL LEAVE OY BUGS ALL OVER IE CHAPEL! ND THAT'S ONLY THE EGINNING!!
GHRK!
WHAM!!
DON'T EVEN THINK ABOUT IT, PAL.
GH
GH
CAN'T...
...BREA...

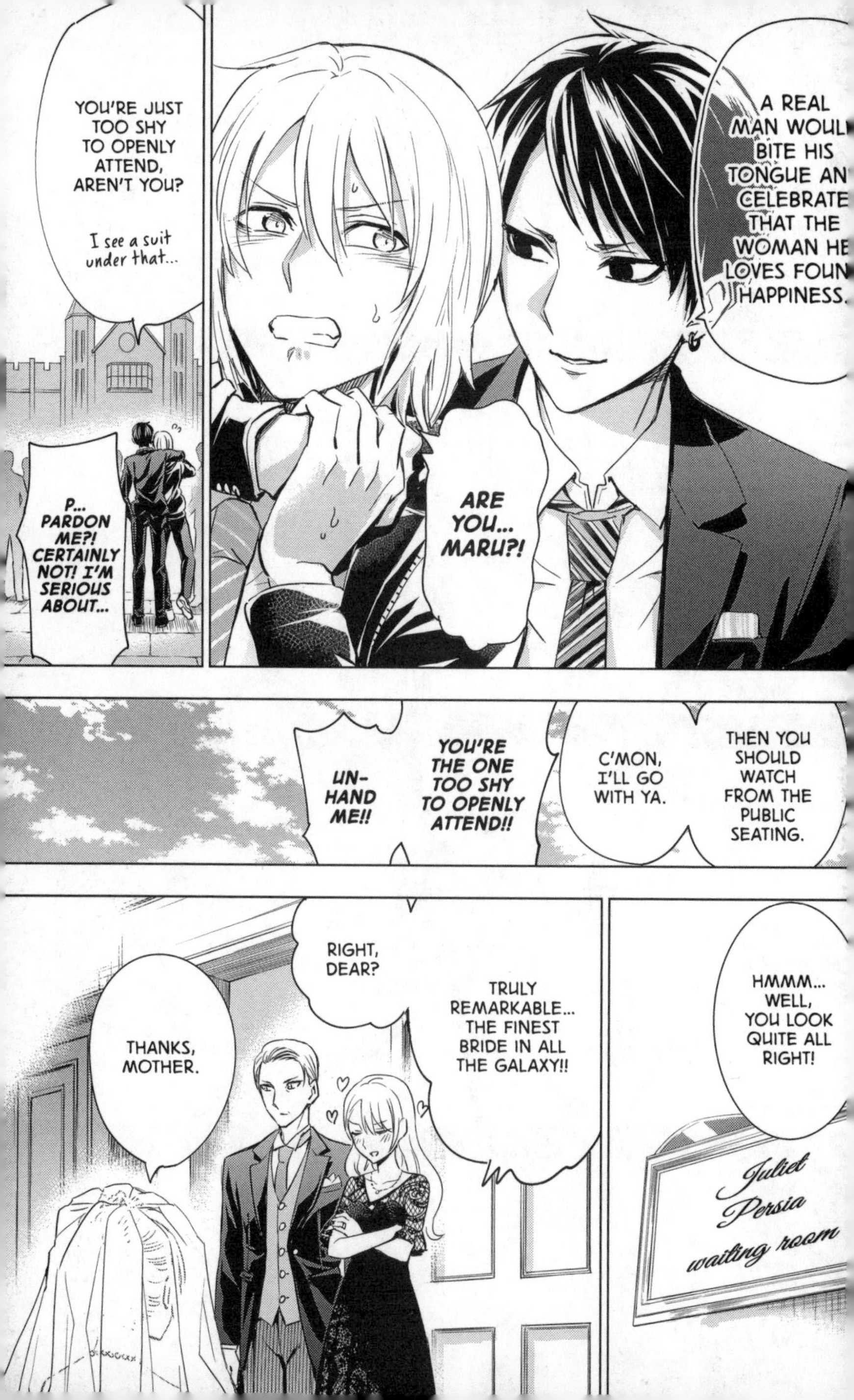
A REAL MAN WOUL BITE HIS TONGUE AN CELEBRATE THAT THE WOMAN HE LOVES FOUN HAPPINESS.
ARE YOU... MARU?!
YOU'RE JUST TOO SHY TO OPENLY ATTEND, AREN'T YOU?
I see a suit under that...
P... PARDON ME?! CERTAINLY NOT! I'M SERIOUS ABOUT...
THEN YOU SHOULD WATCH FROM THE PUBLIC SEATING.
C'MON, I'LL GO WITH YA.
YOU'RE THE ONE TOO SHY TO OPENLY ATTEND!!
UN-HAND ME!!
HMMM... WELL, YOU LOOK QUITE ALL RIGHT!
Juliet Persia waiting room
TRULY REMARKABLE... THE FINEST BRIDE IN ALL THE GALAXY!!
RIGHT, DEAR?
THANKS, MOTHER.

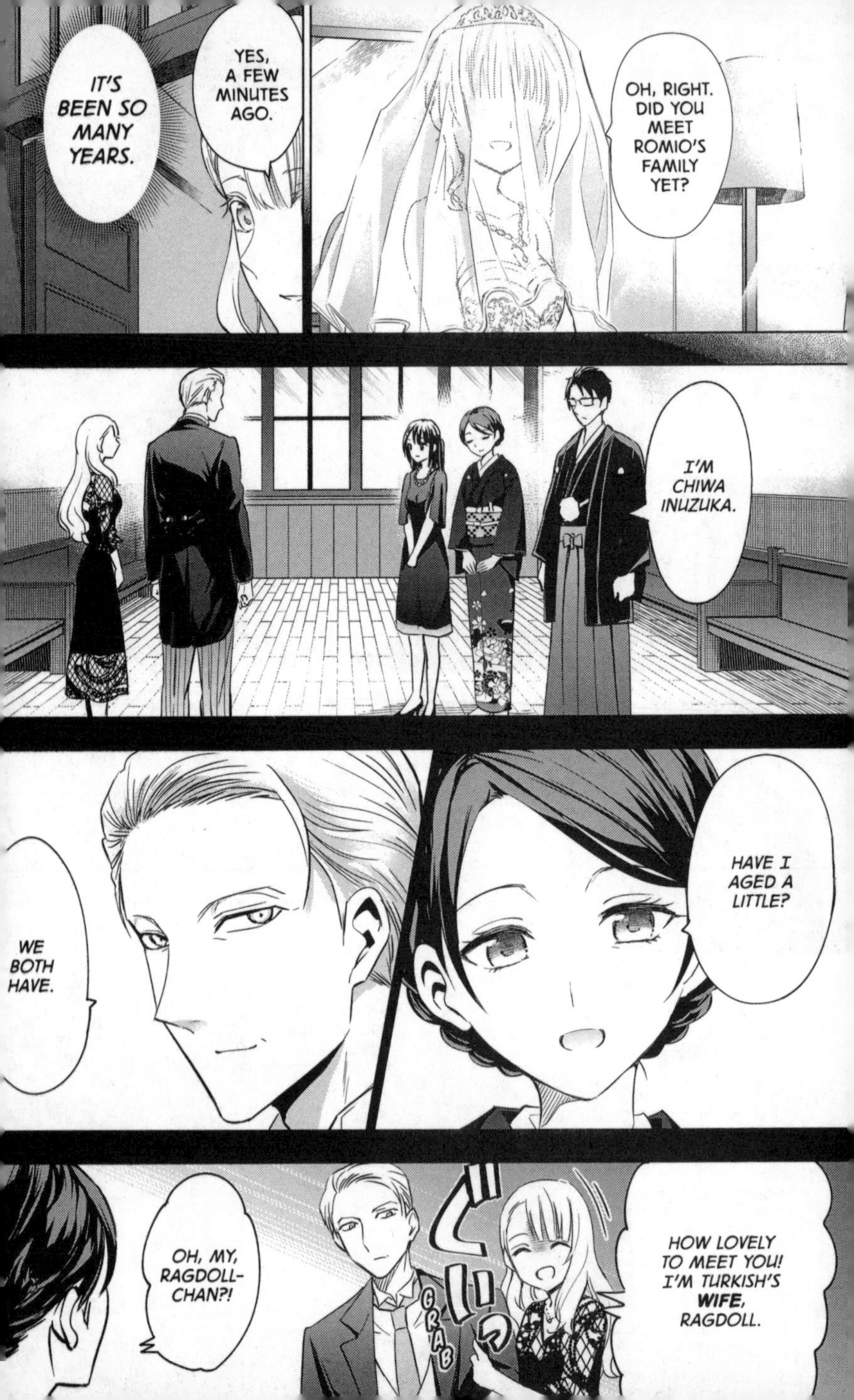
OH, RIGHT. DID YOU MEET ROMIO'S FAMILY YET?
YES, A FEW MINUTES AGO.
IT'S BEEN SO MANY YEARS.
I'M CHIWA INUZUKA.
HAVE I AGED A LITTLE?
WE BOTH HAVE.
HOW LOVELY TO MEET YOU! I'M TURKISH'S **WIFE**, RAGDOLL.
GRAB
OH, MY, RAGDOLL-CHAN?!

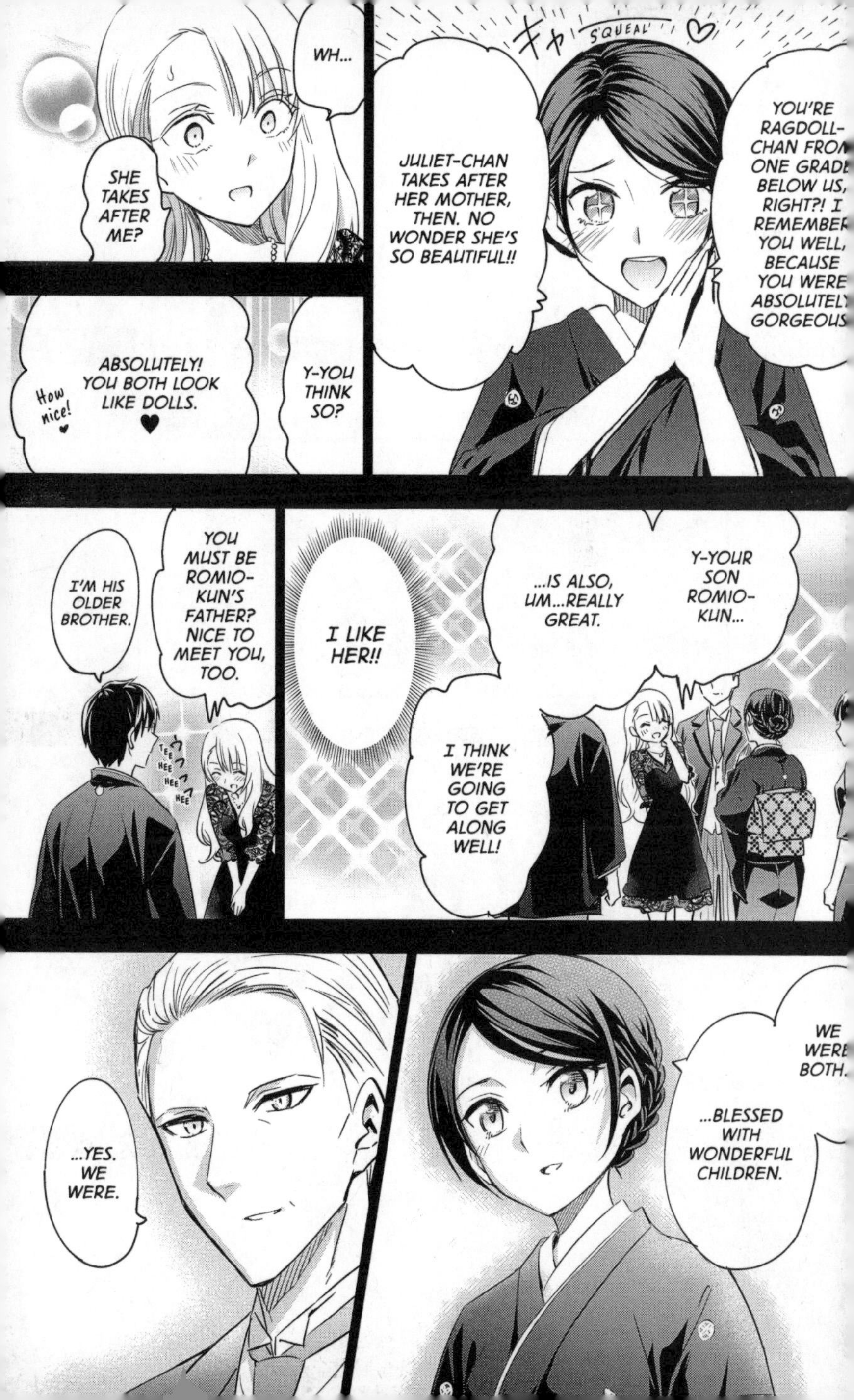
キャ SQUEAL ♡
YOU'RE RAGDOLL-CHAN FROM ONE GRADE BELOW US, RIGHT?! I REMEMBER YOU WELL, BECAUSE YOU WERE ABSOLUTELY GORGEOUS
JULIET-CHAN TAKES AFTER HER MOTHER, THEN. NO WONDER SHE'S SO BEAUTIFUL!!
WH...
SHE TAKES AFTER ME?
Y-YOU THINK SO?
ABSOLUTELY! YOU BOTH LOOK LIKE DOLLS. ♥
How nice! ♥
Y-YOUR SON ROMIO-KUN...
...IS ALSO, UM...REALLY GREAT.
I THINK WE'RE GOING TO GET ALONG WELL!
I LIKE HER!!
YOU MUST BE ROMIO-KUN'S FATHER? NICE TO MEET YOU, TOO.
I'M HIS OLDER BROTHER.
TEE HEE HEE HEE
WE WERE BOTH...
...BLESSED WITH WONDERFUL CHILDREN.
...YES. WE WERE.

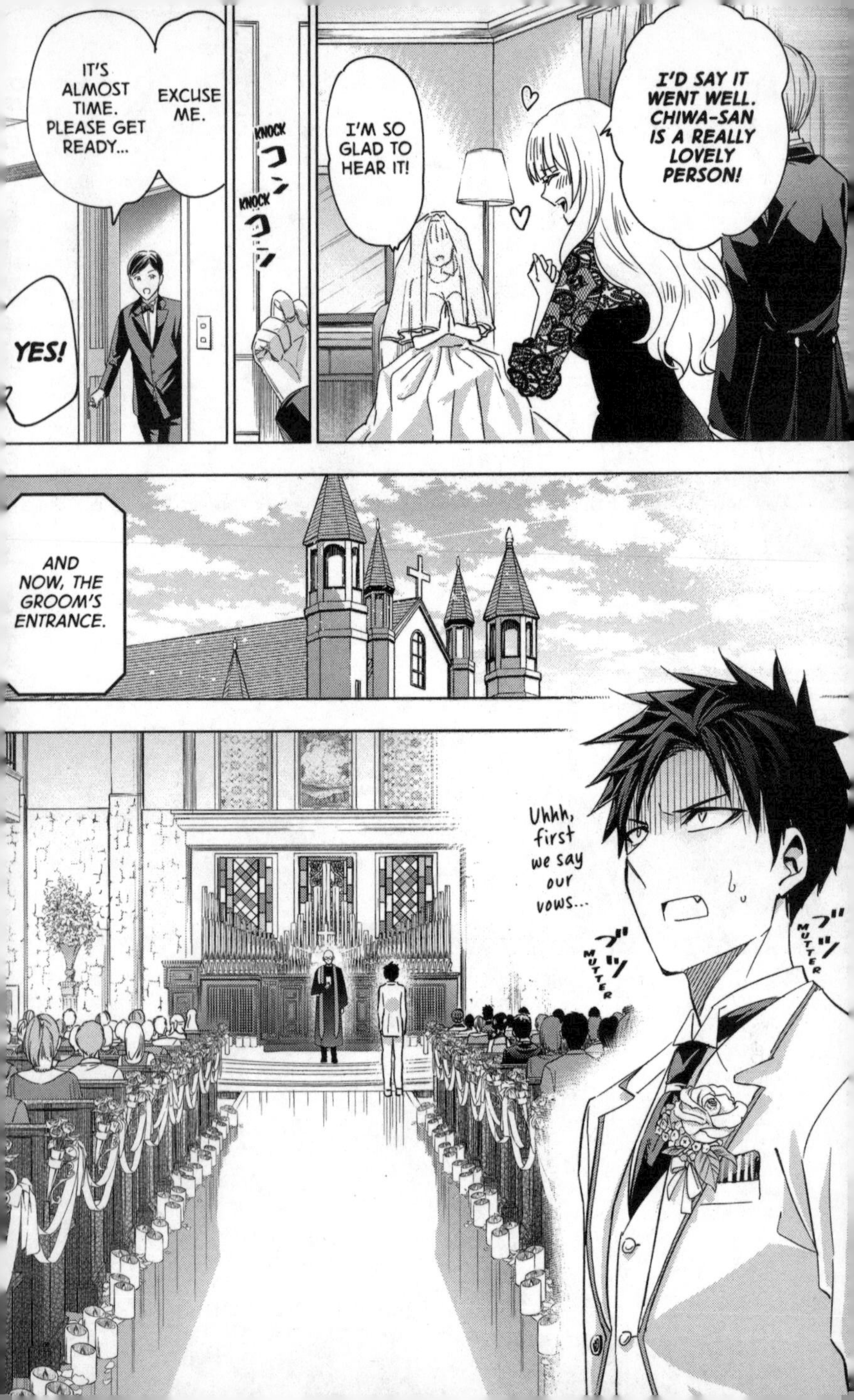
I'D SAY IT WENT WELL. CHIWA-SAN IS A REALLY LOVELY PERSON!
I'M SO GLAD TO HEAR IT!
KNOCK
KNOCK
EXCUSE ME.
IT'S ALMOST TIME. PLEASE GET READY...
YES!
AND NOW, THE GROOM'S ENTRANCE.
Uhhh, first we say our vows...
MUTTER
MUTTER

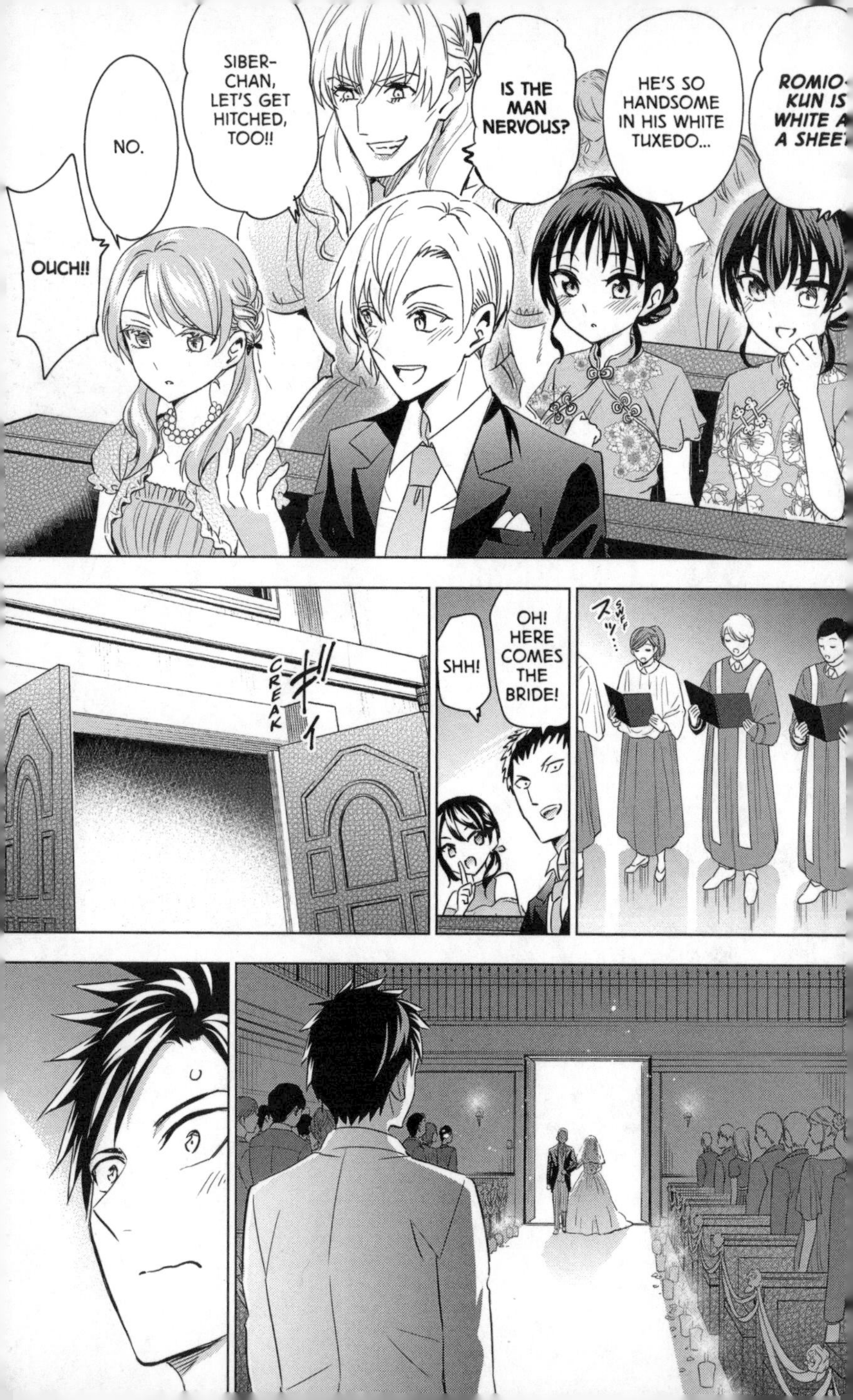
ROMIO-KUN IS WHITE A A SHEE
HE'S SO HANDSOME IN HIS WHITE TUXEDO...
IS THE MAN NERVOUS?
SIBER-CHAN, LET'S GET HITCHED, TOO!!
NO.
OUCH!!
SWEE
OH! HERE COMES THE BRIDE!
SHH!
CREAK

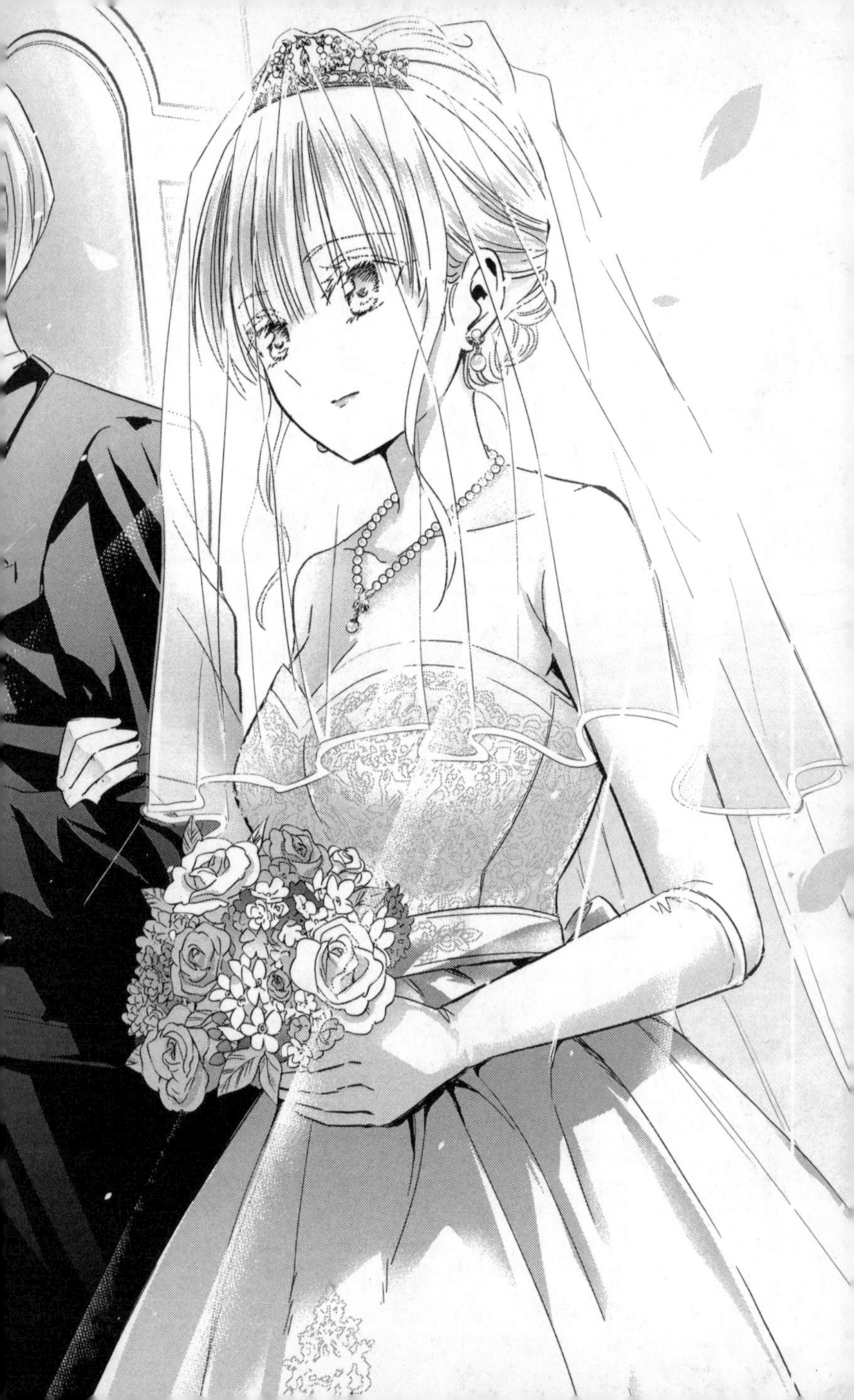

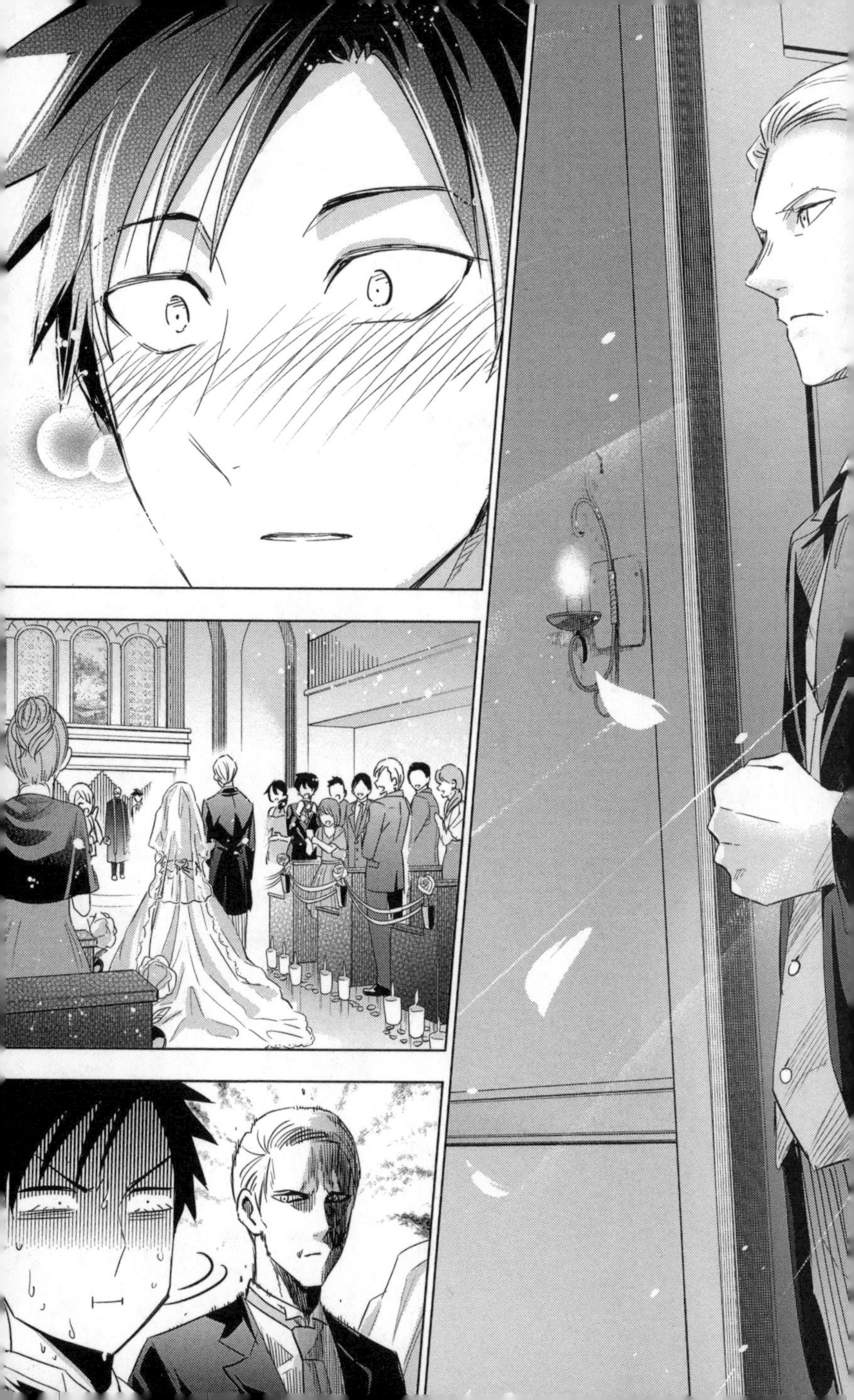

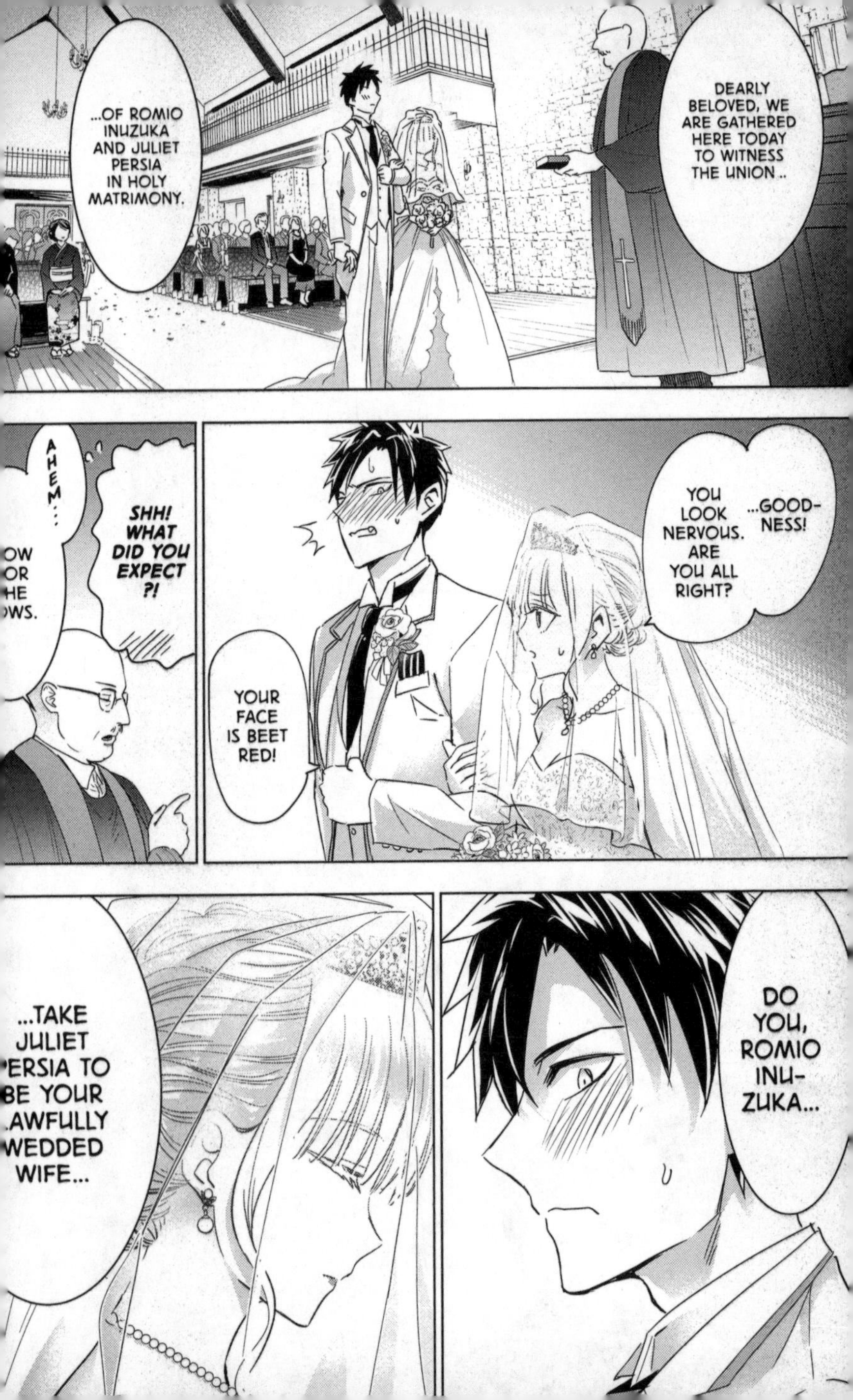
DEARLY BELOVED, WE ARE GATHERED HERE TODAY TO WITNESS THE UNION...
...OF ROMIO INUZUKA AND JULIET PERSIA IN HOLY MATRIMONY.
...GOODNESS!
YOU LOOK NERVOUS. ARE YOU ALL RIGHT?
YOUR FACE IS BEET RED!
SHH! WHAT DID YOU EXPECT?!
AHEM...
DO YOU, ROMIO INU-ZUKA...
...TAKE JULIET ERSIA TO BE YOUR AWFULLY WEDDED WIFE...

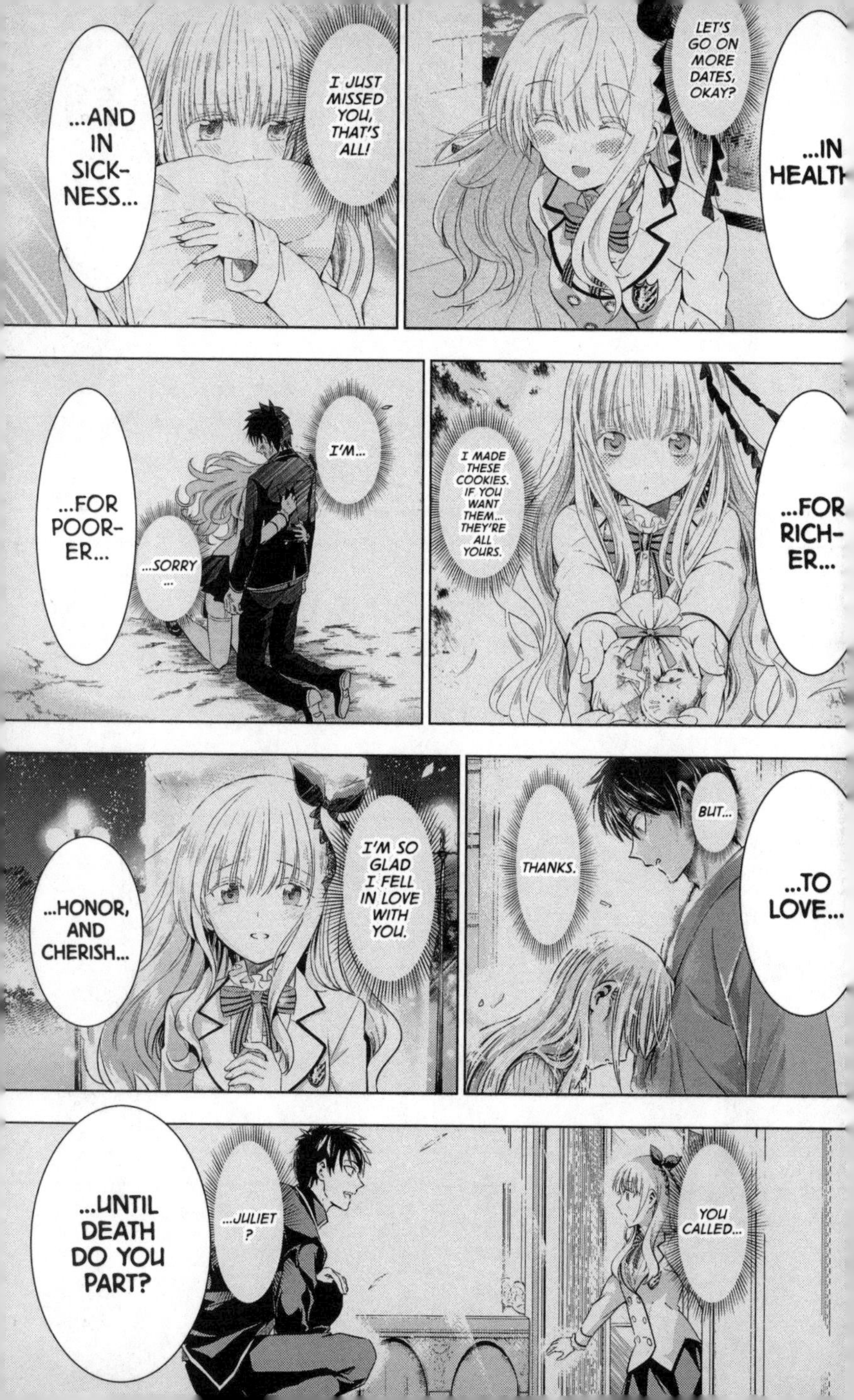
LET'S GO ON MORE DATES, OKAY?
...IN HEALTH
I JUST MISSED YOU, THAT'S ALL!
...AND IN SICKNESS...
...FOR RICHER...
I MADE THESE COOKIES. IF YOU WANT THEM... THEY'RE ALL YOURS.
I'M...
...SORRY ...
...FOR POORER...
...TO LOVE...
BUT...
THANKS.
I'M SO GLAD I FELL IN LOVE WITH YOU.
...HONOR, AND CHERISH...
YOU CALLED...
...JULIET ?
...UNTIL DEATH DO YOU PART?

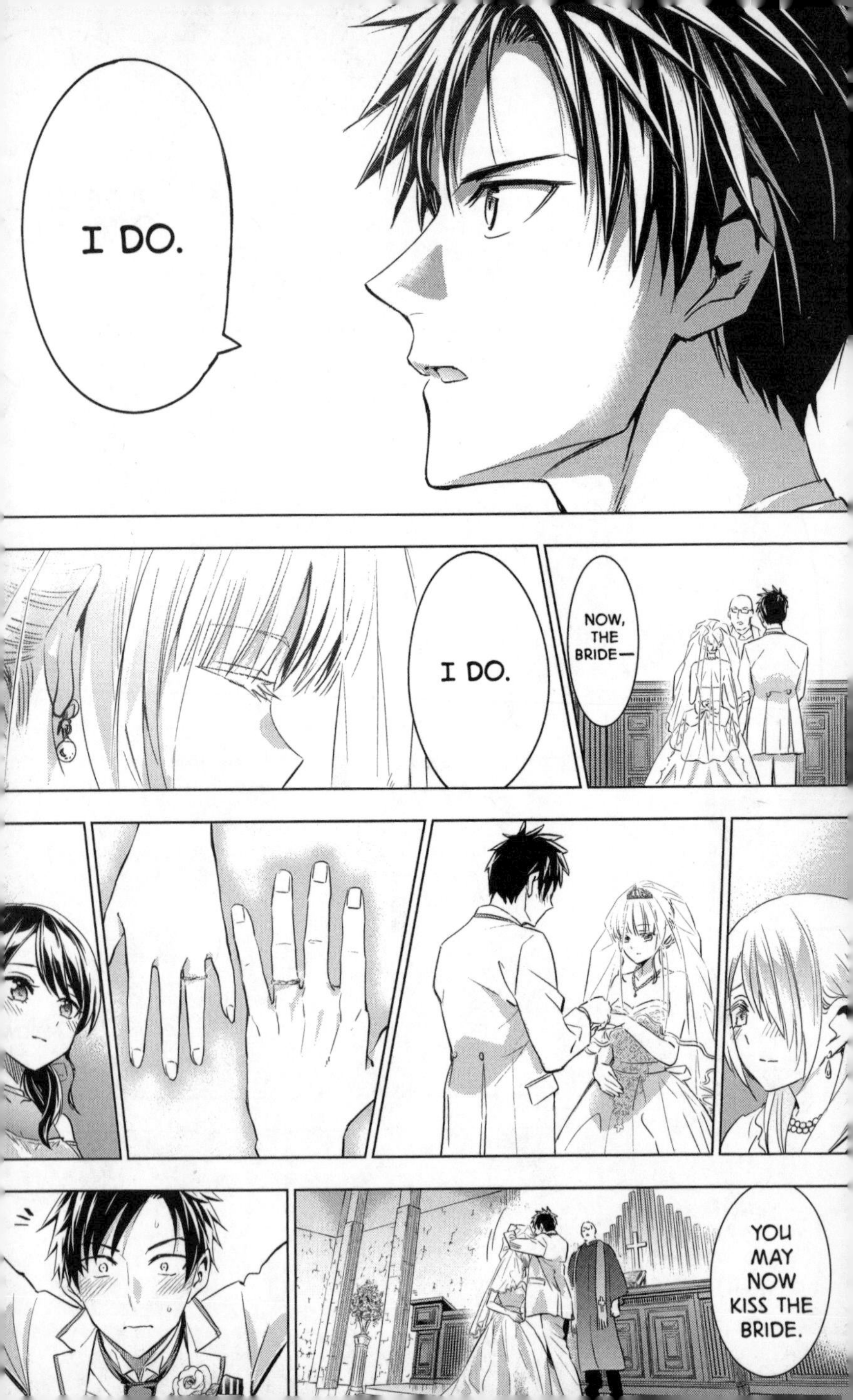
I DO.
NOW, THE BRIDE—
I DO.
YOU MAY NOW KISS THE BRIDE.

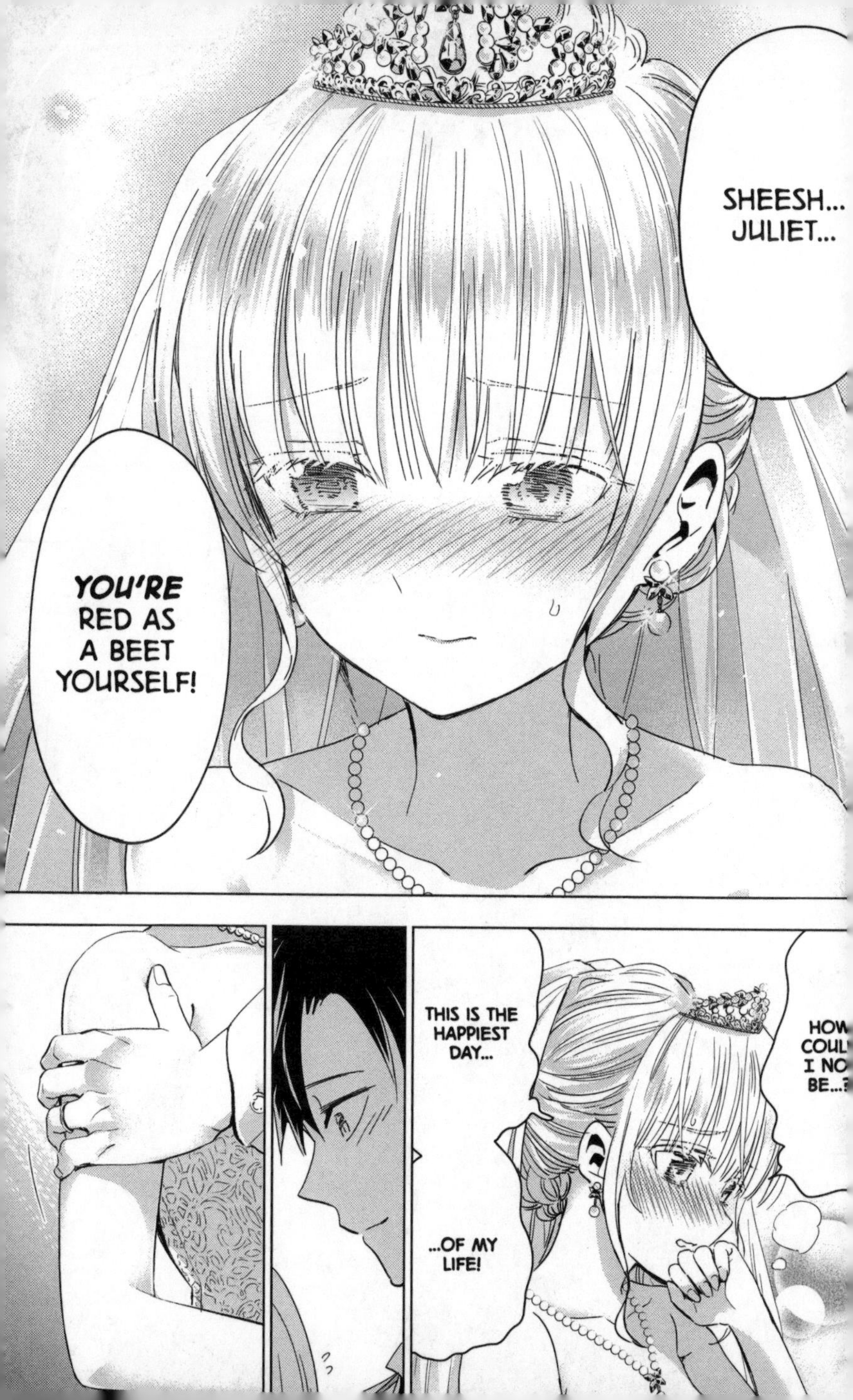
SHEESH... JULIET...
YOU'RE RED AS A BEET YOURSELF!
HOW COUL I NO BE...?
THIS IS THE HAPPIEST DAY...
...OF MY LIFE!

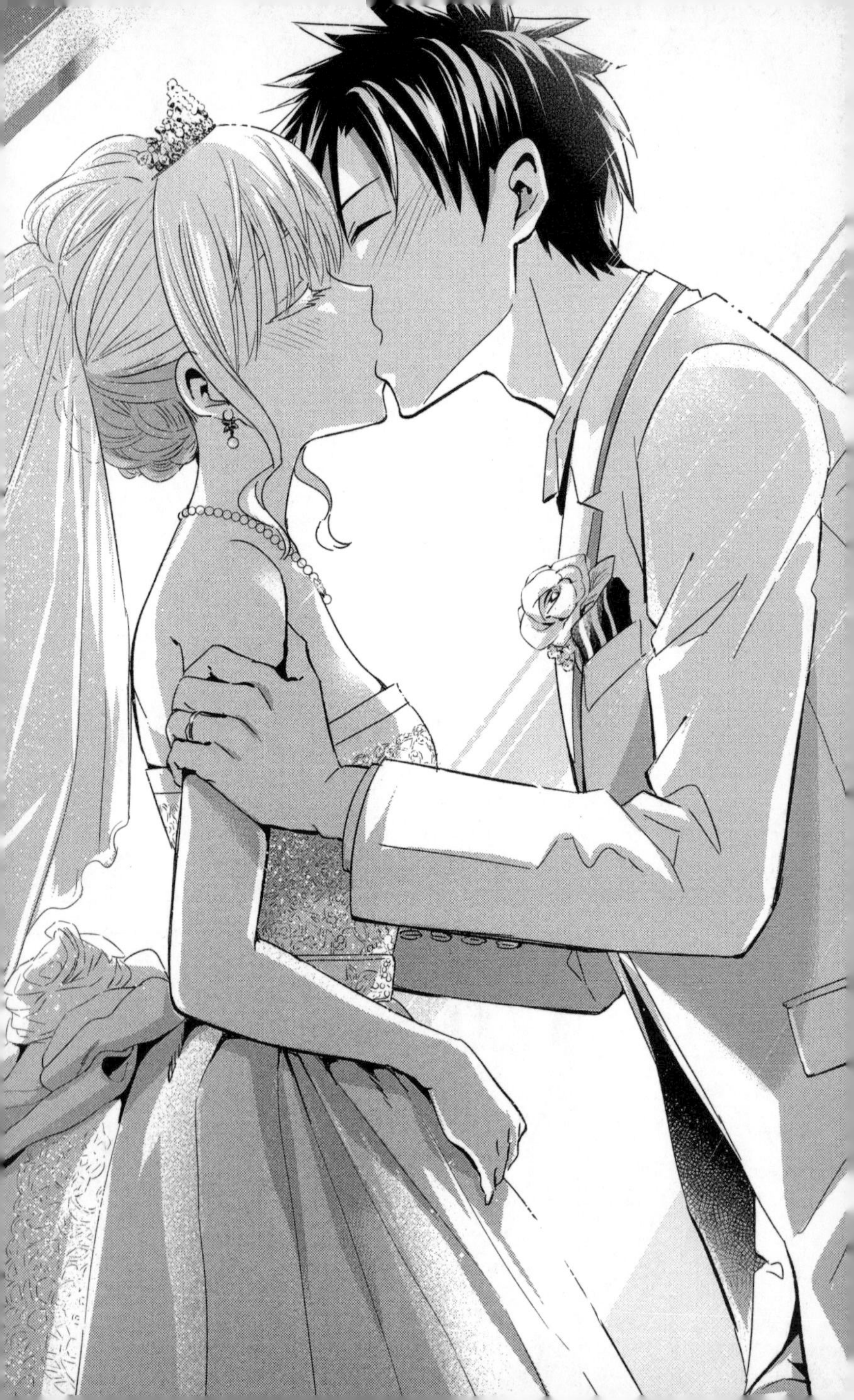

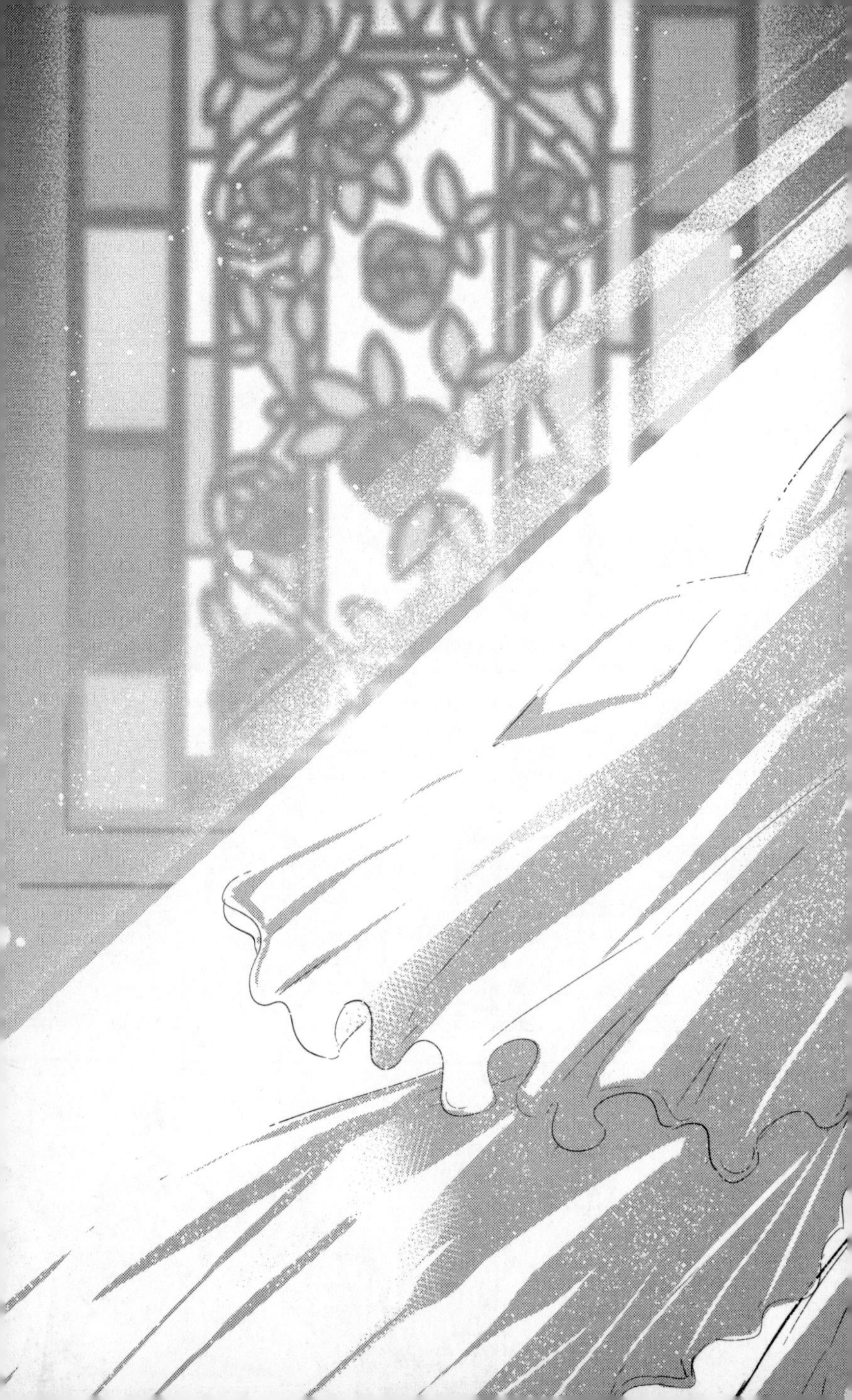

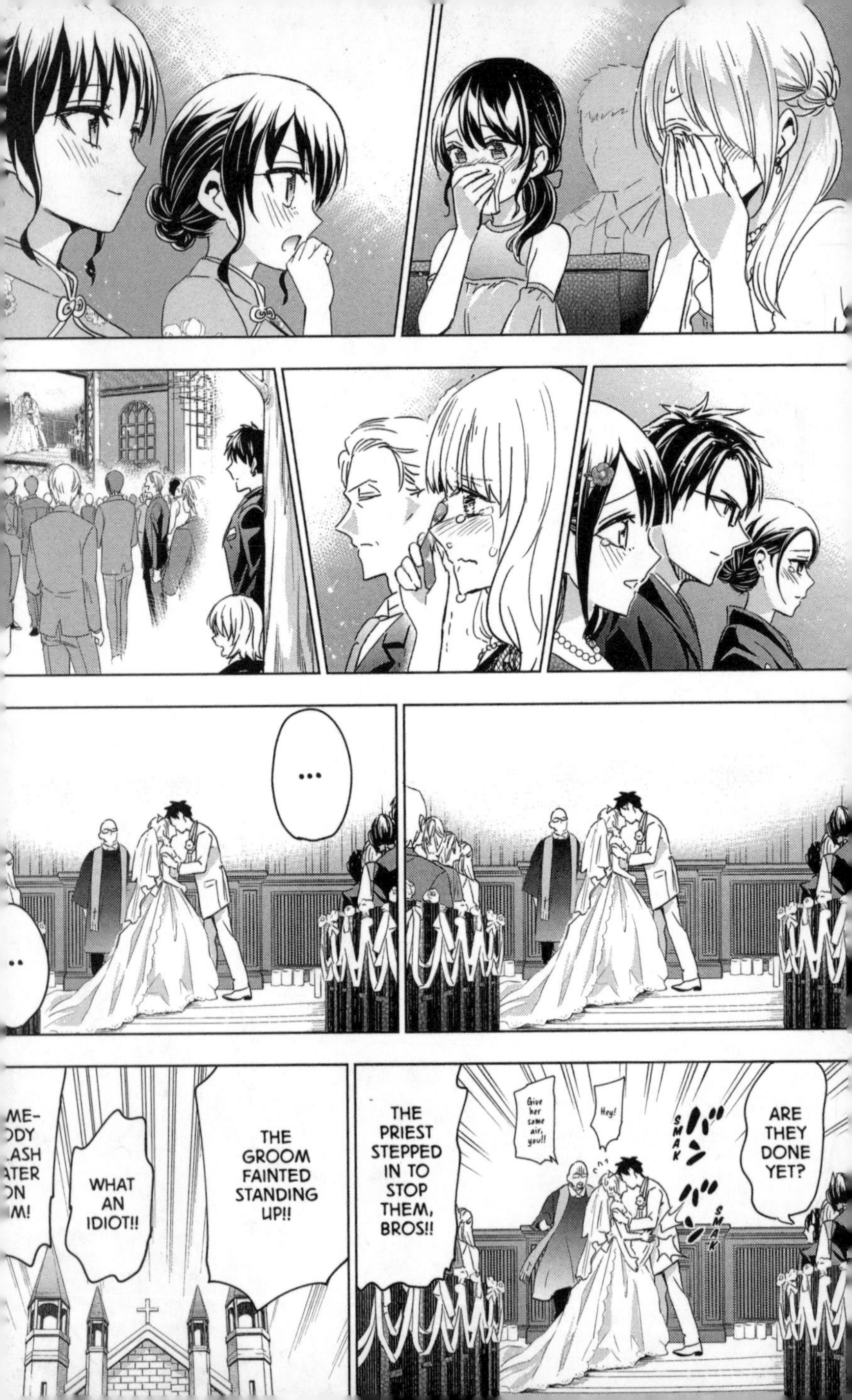
...
ARE THEY DONE YET?
Hey!
Give her some air, you!!
SMAK
SMAK
THE PRIEST STEPPED IN TO STOP THEM, BROS!!
THE GROOM FAINTED STANDING UP!!
WHAT AN IDIOT!!

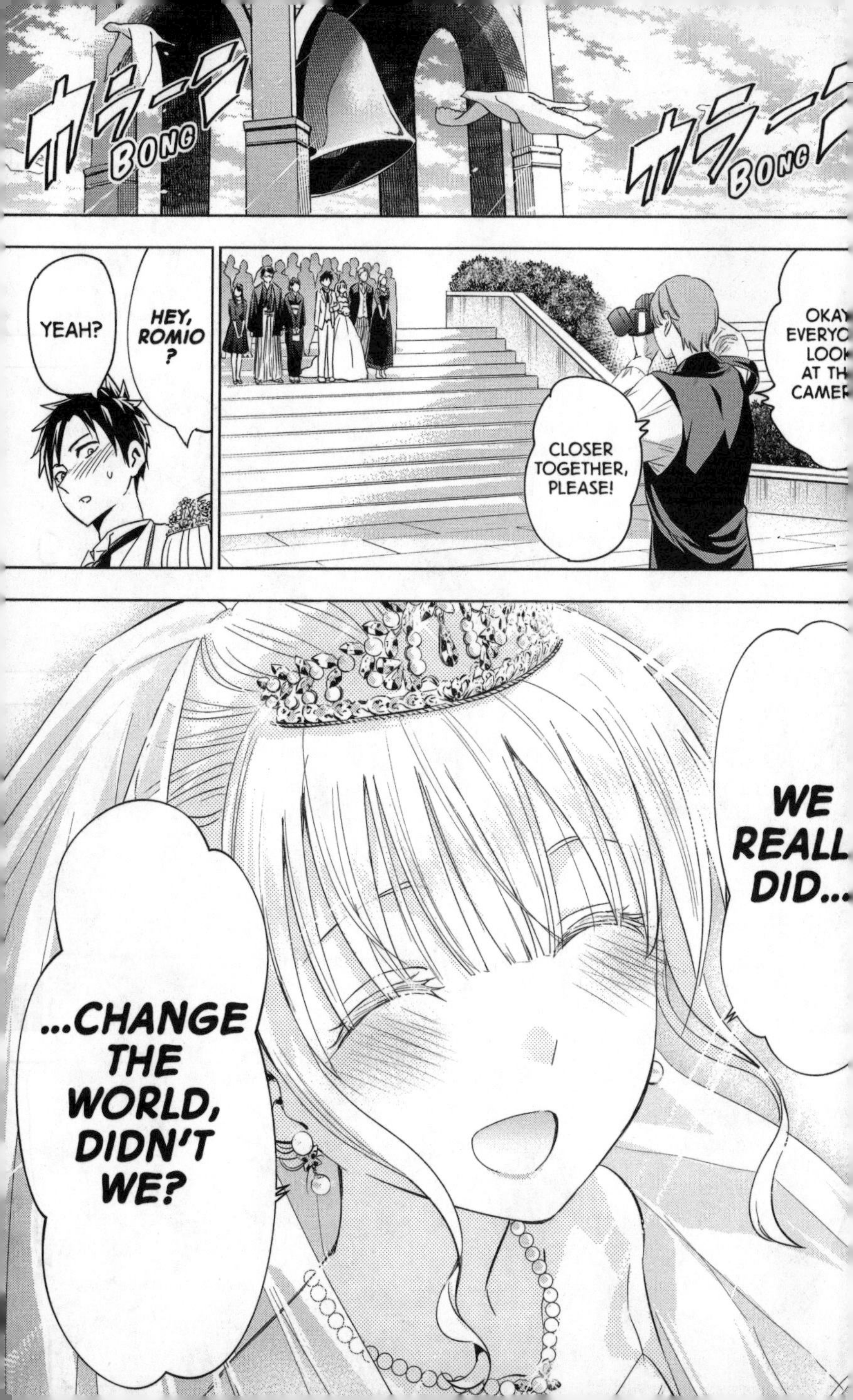
ウラ～ン
BONG
ウラ～ン
BONG
OKAY EVERYO LOOK AT THE CAMER
CLOSER TOGETHER, PLEASE!
HEY, ROMIO ?
YEAH?
WE REALL DID...
...CHANGE THE WORLD, DIDN'T WE?

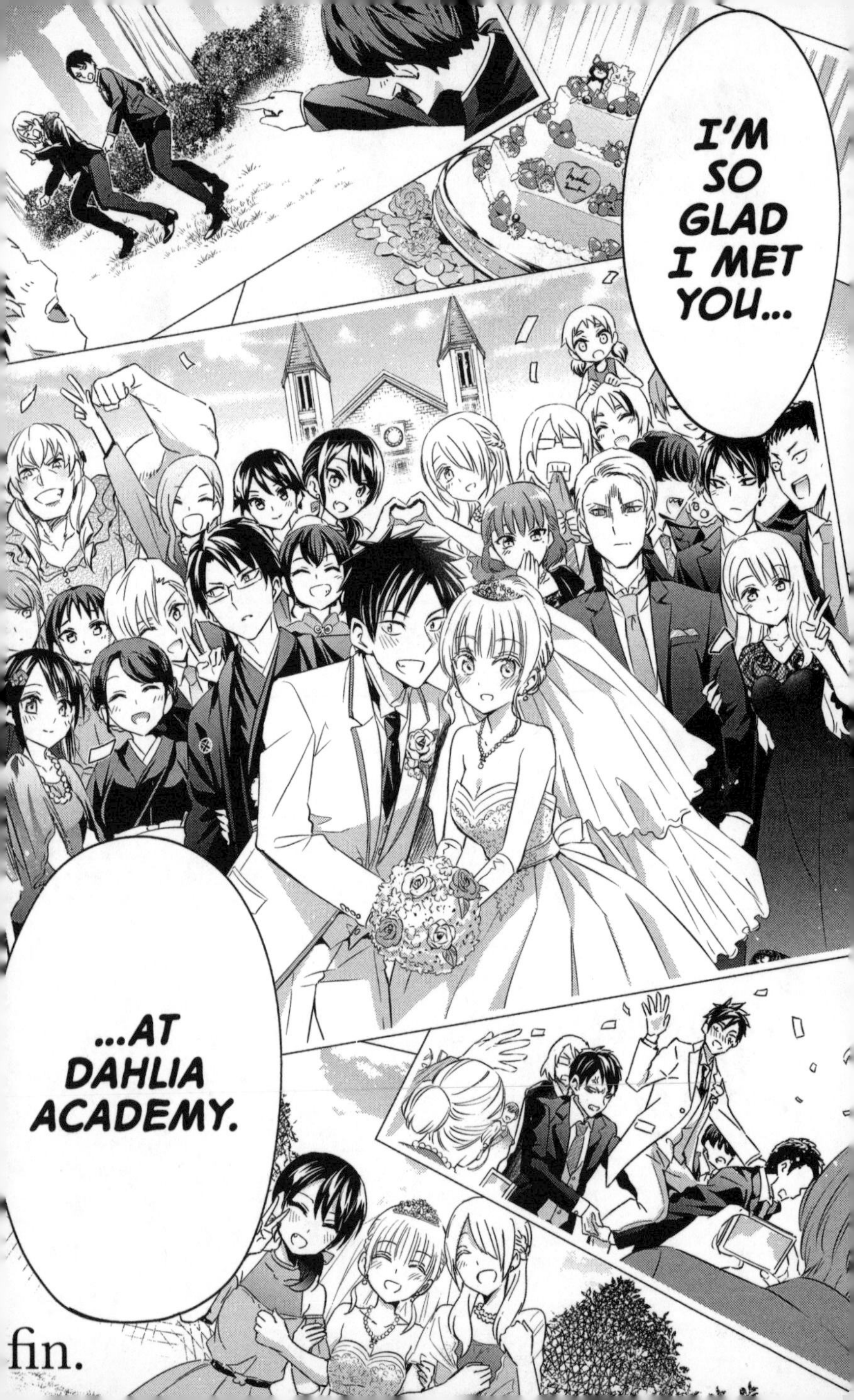
I'M SO GLAD I MET YOU...
...AT DAHLIA ACADEMY.
fin.

STAFF
TARO KUROKI
YAGAMI
REIJI
SHIBA

EDITORS
SHU HASHIMOTO
YUTO KIKUCHI
YUIKO TORIUMI

COMIC DESIGNERS
HIVE, SEIKO DOBASHI, TAKASHI OSOKO

SPECIAL THANKS
ASUKA KANEDA

and You!

BONUS 1: **SIBER & CAIT**

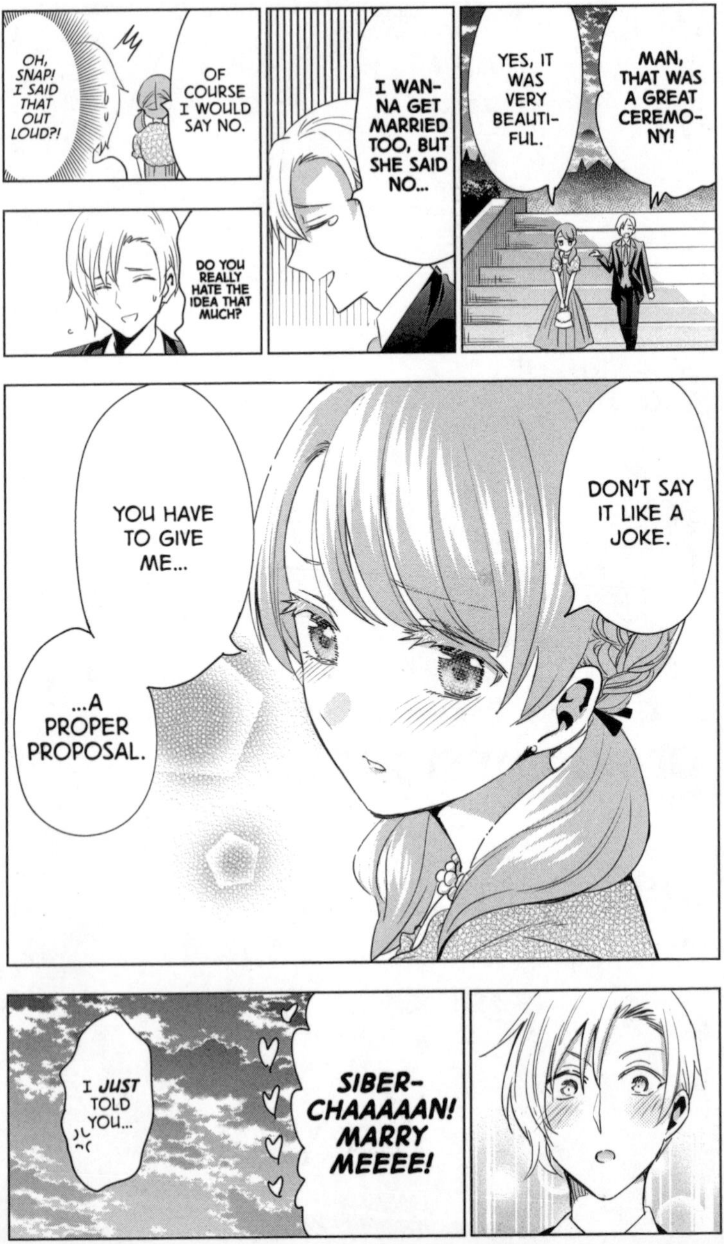
MAN, THAT WAS A GREAT CEREMONY!
YES, IT WAS VERY BEAUTIFUL.
I WANNA GET MARRIED TOO, BUT SHE SAID NO...
OF COURSE I WOULD SAY NO.
OH, SNAP! I SAID THAT OUT LOUD?!
DO YOU REALLY HATE THE IDEA THAT MUCH?
DON'T SAY IT LIKE A JOKE.
YOU HAVE TO GIVE ME...
...A PROPER PROPOSAL.
SIBER-CHAAAAAN! MARRY MEEEE!
I *JUST* TOLD YOU...

BONUS 2: NEWLYWED LIFE

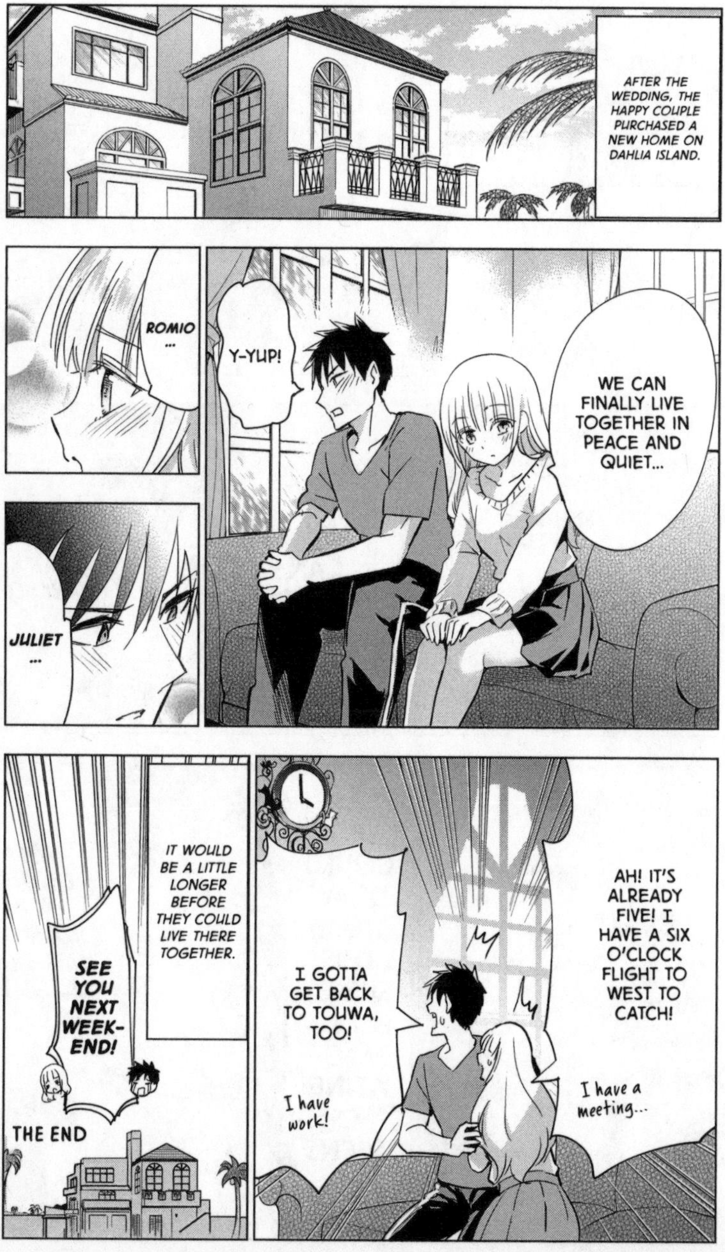
AFTER THE WEDDING, THE HAPPY COUPLE PURCHASED A NEW HOME ON DAHLIA ISLAND.
WE CAN FINALLY LIVE TOGETHER IN PEACE AND QUIET...
Y-YUP!
ROMIO...
JULIET...
AH! IT'S ALREADY FIVE! I HAVE A SIX O'CLOCK FLIGHT TO WEST TO CATCH!
I have a meeting...
I GOTTA GET BACK TO TOUWA, TOO!
I have work!
IT WOULD BE A LITTLE LONGER BEFORE THEY COULD LIVE THERE TOGETHER.
SEE YOU NEXT WEEK-END!
THE END

AFTERWORD

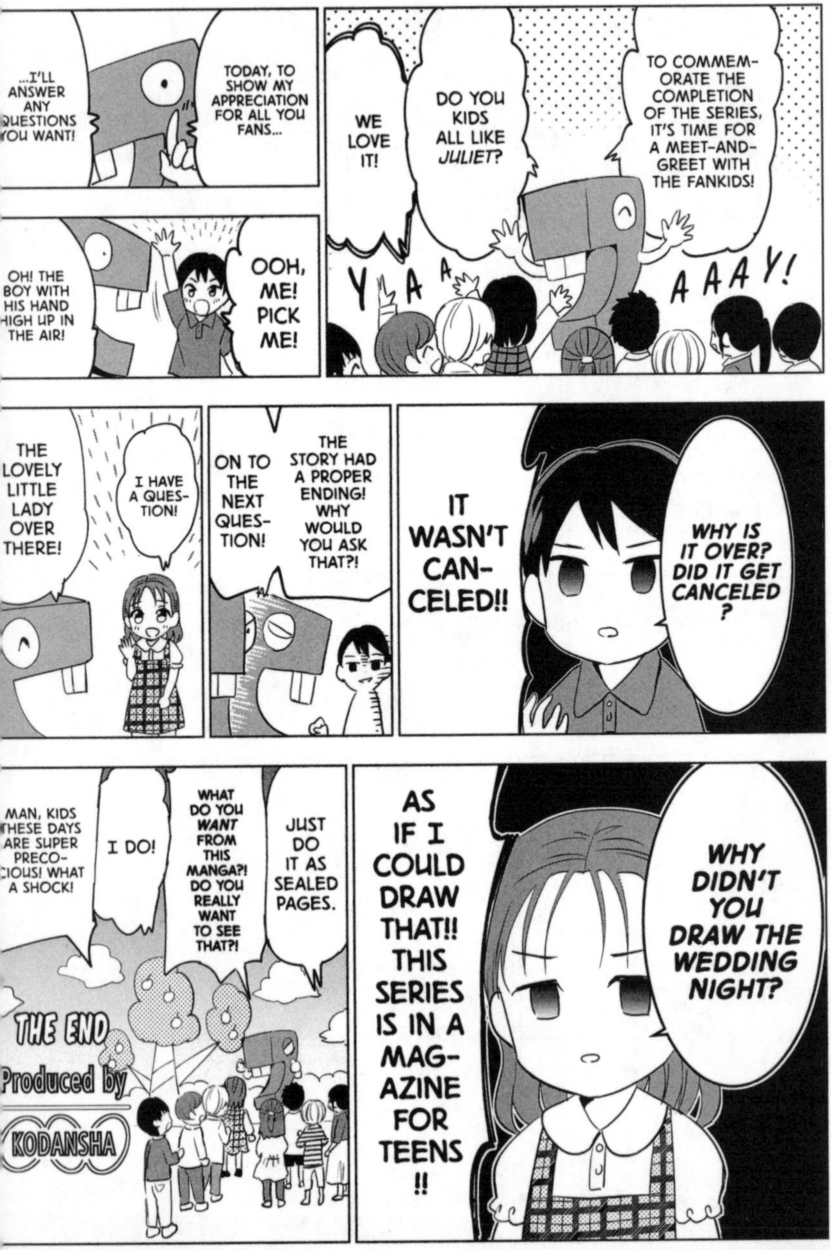

TO COMMEMORATE THE COMPLETION OF THE SERIES, IT'S TIME FOR A MEET-AND-GREET WITH THE FANKIDS!
DO YOU KIDS ALL LIKE *JULIET*?
WE LOVE IT!
YAAAAAY!
TODAY, TO SHOW MY APPRECIATION FOR ALL YOU FANS...
...I'LL ANSWER ANY QUESTIONS YOU WANT!
OOH, ME! PICK ME!
OH! THE BOY WITH HIS HAND HIGH UP IN THE AIR!
WHY IS IT OVER? DID IT GET CANCELED?
IT WASN'T CANCELED!!
THE STORY HAD A PROPER ENDING! WHY WOULD YOU ASK THAT?!
ON TO THE NEXT QUESTION!
I HAVE A QUESTION!
THE LOVELY LITTLE LADY OVER THERE!
WHY DIDN'T YOU DRAW THE WEDDING NIGHT?
AS IF I COULD DRAW THAT!! THIS SERIES IS IN A MAGAZINE FOR TEENS!!
JUST DO IT AS SEALED PAGES.
WHAT DO YOU *WANT* FROM THIS MANGA?! DO YOU REALLY WANT TO SEE THAT?!
I DO!
MAN, KIDS THESE DAYS ARE SUPER PRECOCIOUS! WHAT A SHOCK!
THE END
Produced by
KODANSHA

Afterword

All right, if I'm drawing, I'll inevitably screw around, so this is the real afterword.

Thank you so much for sticking with the series to the end.

Boarding School Juliet came to be from me cramming all of my favorite things into one manga. I wanted to do a Romeo and Juliet story! And a story with school dorms! And I wanted to draw blonde babes!

Because of that, I had an incredibly fun time drawing it. I'd feel like I had become a student, too. Then I'd look in the mirror and realize, "That's right, I was just some adult dude all along…" Then I'd come back to my senses. That's how the days went by.

To have had so many people say they wanted to read more when the final act was published is a blessing as an author.

For me, this story was all about secret love and Romio's growth, so I felt that dragging it out beyond the West arc would be superfluous. I discussed it with my editor and was allowed to conclude the story the way I wanted. This series really was blessed.

In the four or so years of serialization, it started off from a pilot chapter in a monthly magazine, then moved to a weekly magazine, and even got an anime adaptation. It's all thanks to your support.

There was actually one time when the hectic schedule of weekly serialization almost broke me, and I thought about quitting. What kept me going then were the reader reactions in fan letters, Twitter replies, etc.

When my readers are excited, I get excited, too. As long as there were people looking forward to my manga, I could buckle down and stay positive. You really reinvigorated me every week. I can't thank you enough.

My biggest thanks also to my editors, my assistants, my wife, the bookstores, the designers, and everyone else involved, who saved me again and again!

I'll keep striving to be a win-win style manga artist who gets energy from the readers while giving energy to them in return, so keep an eye out for me! Hope to see you in my next manga! Thank you very much!

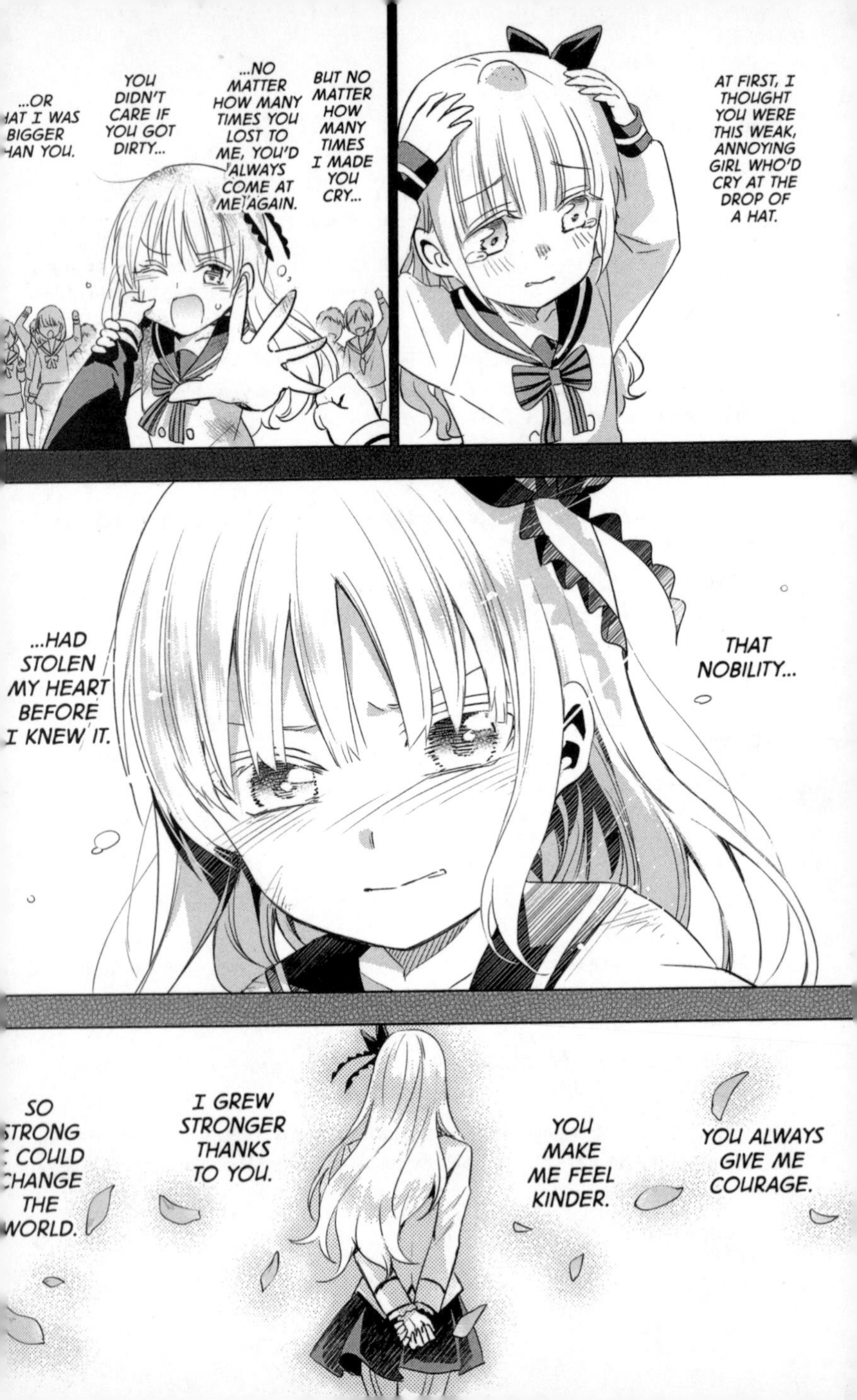
AT FIRST, I THOUGHT YOU WERE THIS WEAK, ANNOYING GIRL WHO'D CRY AT THE DROP OF A HAT.
BUT NO MATTER HOW MANY TIMES I MADE YOU CRY...
...NO MATTER HOW MANY TIMES YOU LOST TO ME, YOU'D ALWAYS COME AT ME AGAIN.
YOU DIDN'T CARE IF YOU GOT DIRTY...
...OR HAT I WAS BIGGER HAN YOU.
THAT NOBILITY...
...HAD STOLEN MY HEART BEFORE I KNEW IT.
YOU ALWAYS GIVE ME COURAGE.
YOU MAKE ME FEEL KINDER.
I GREW STRONGER THANKS TO YOU.
SO TRONG COULD HANGE THE WORLD.

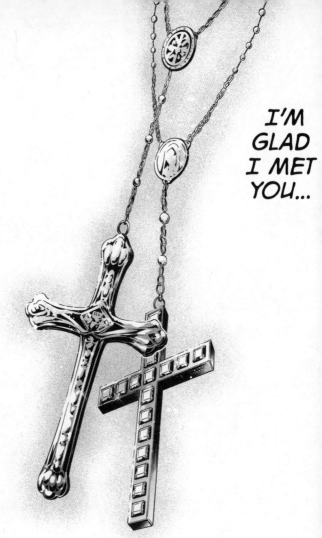

I'M GLAD I MET YOU...

...AT DAHLIA ACADEMY.

Boarding
School *Juliet*

On the following pages is a special Volume 0 of *Boarding School Juliet*, originally included as a bonus booklet with the final volume in Japan. Enjoy another perspective on the origins of Romio and Juliet's star-crossed love story!

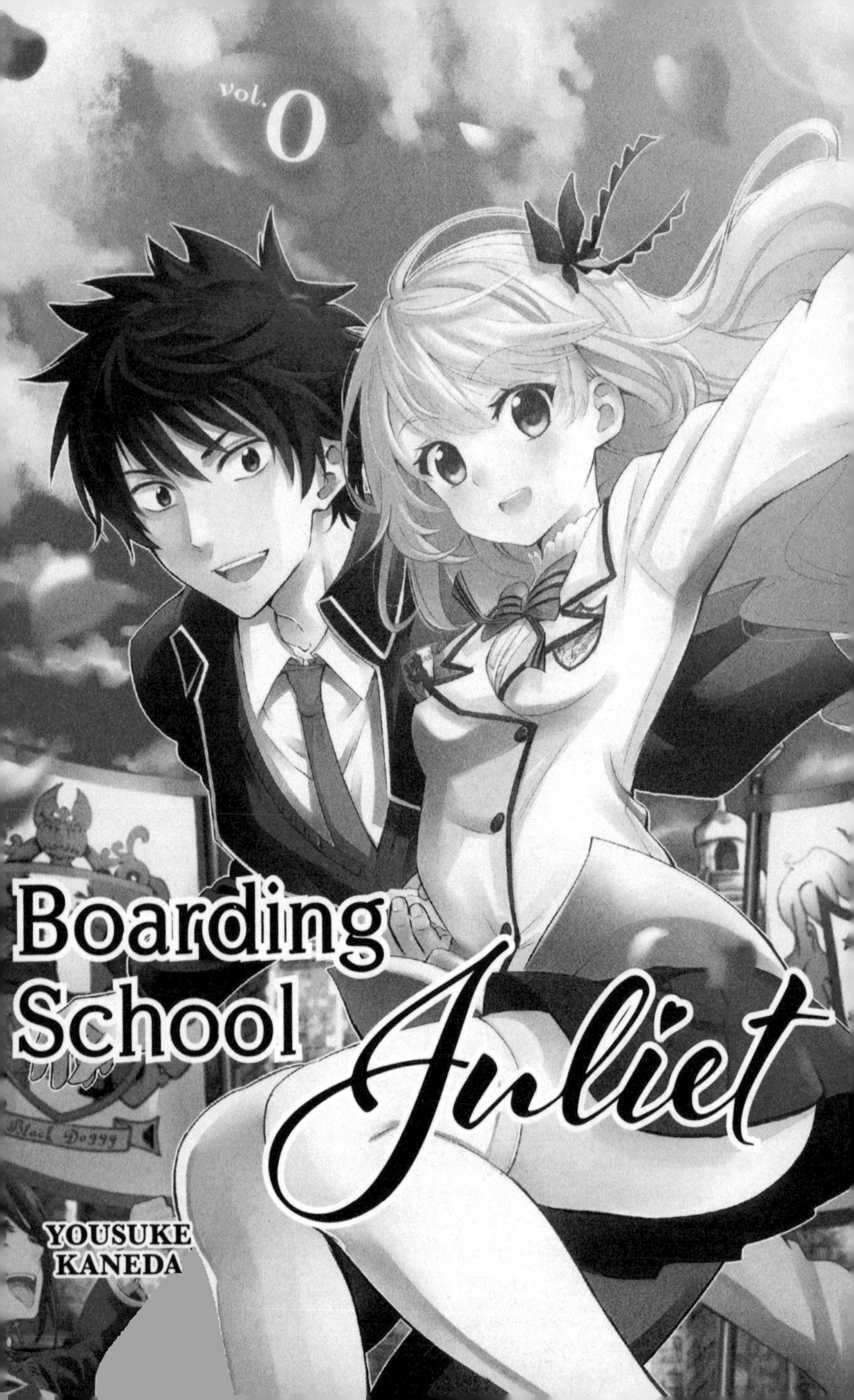
vol. 0
Boarding School Juliet
YOUSUKE KANEDA
Black Doggy

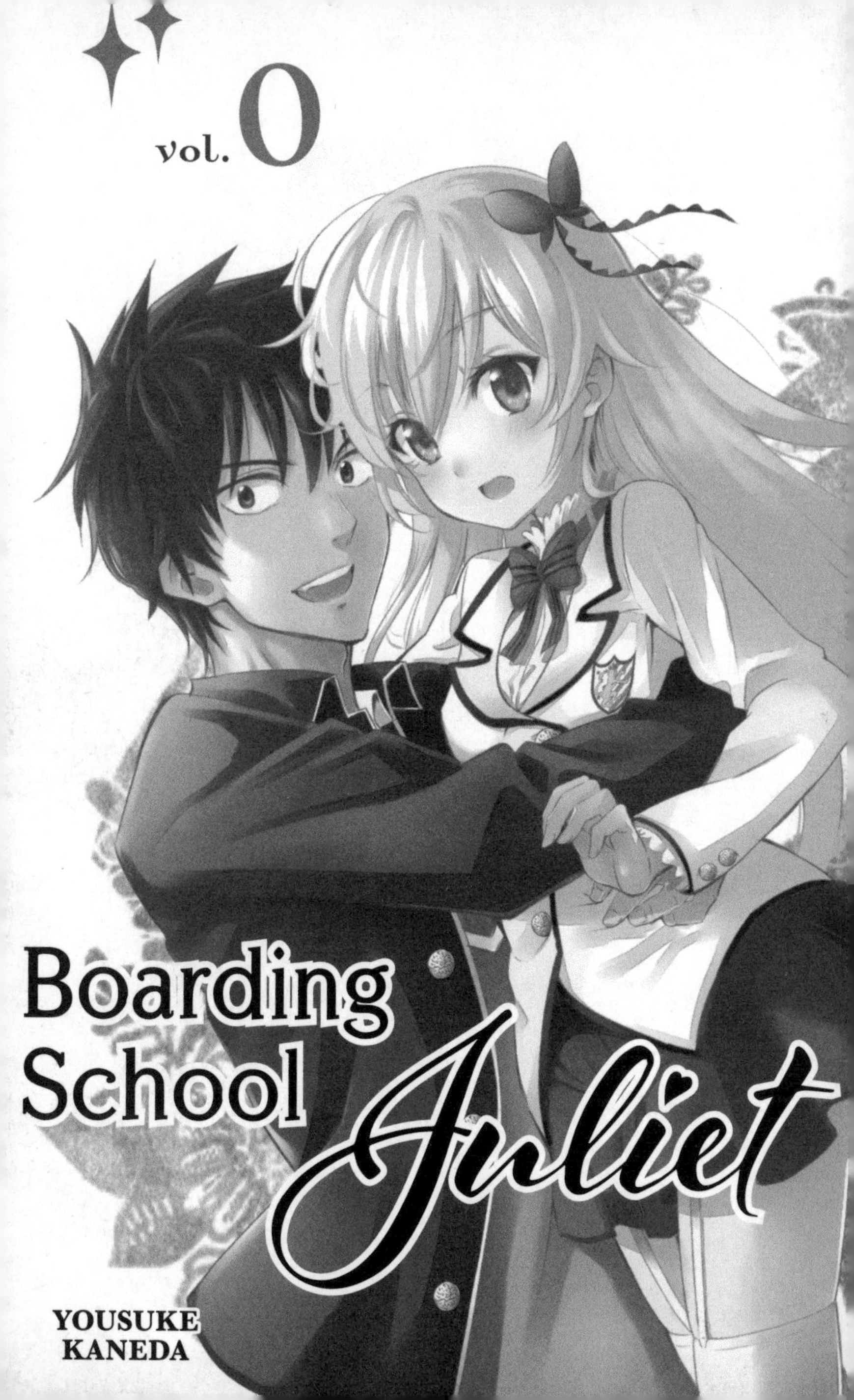
vol. 0
Boarding School
Juliet
YOUSUKE KANEDA

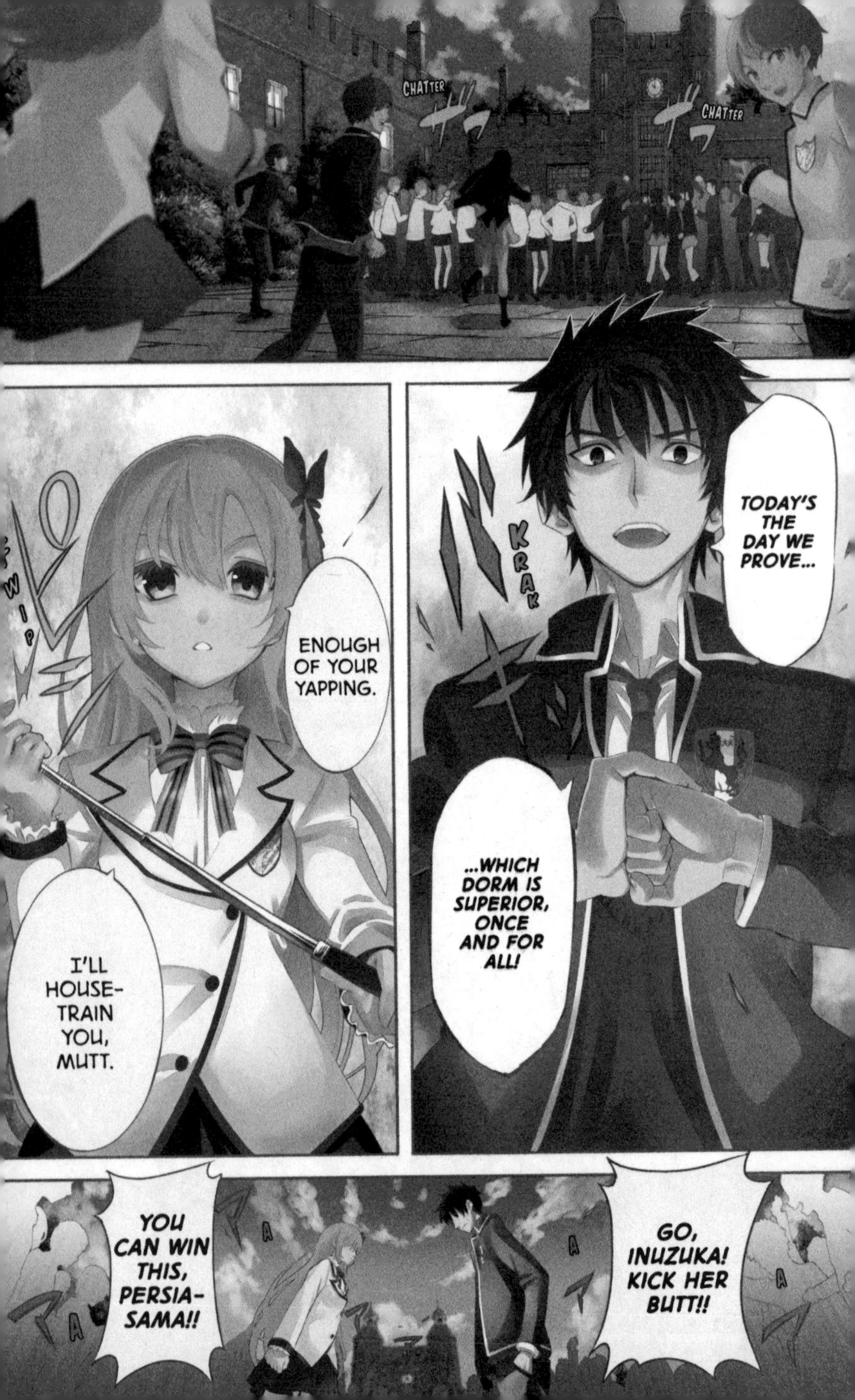
CHATTER
CHATTER
KRAK
TODAY'S THE DAY WE PROVE...
...WHICH DORM IS SUPERIOR, ONCE AND FOR ALL!
ENOUGH OF YOUR YAPPING.
I'LL HOUSE-TRAIN YOU, MUTT.
GO, INUZUKA! KICK HER BUTT!!
YOU CAN WIN THIS, PERSIA-SAMA!!

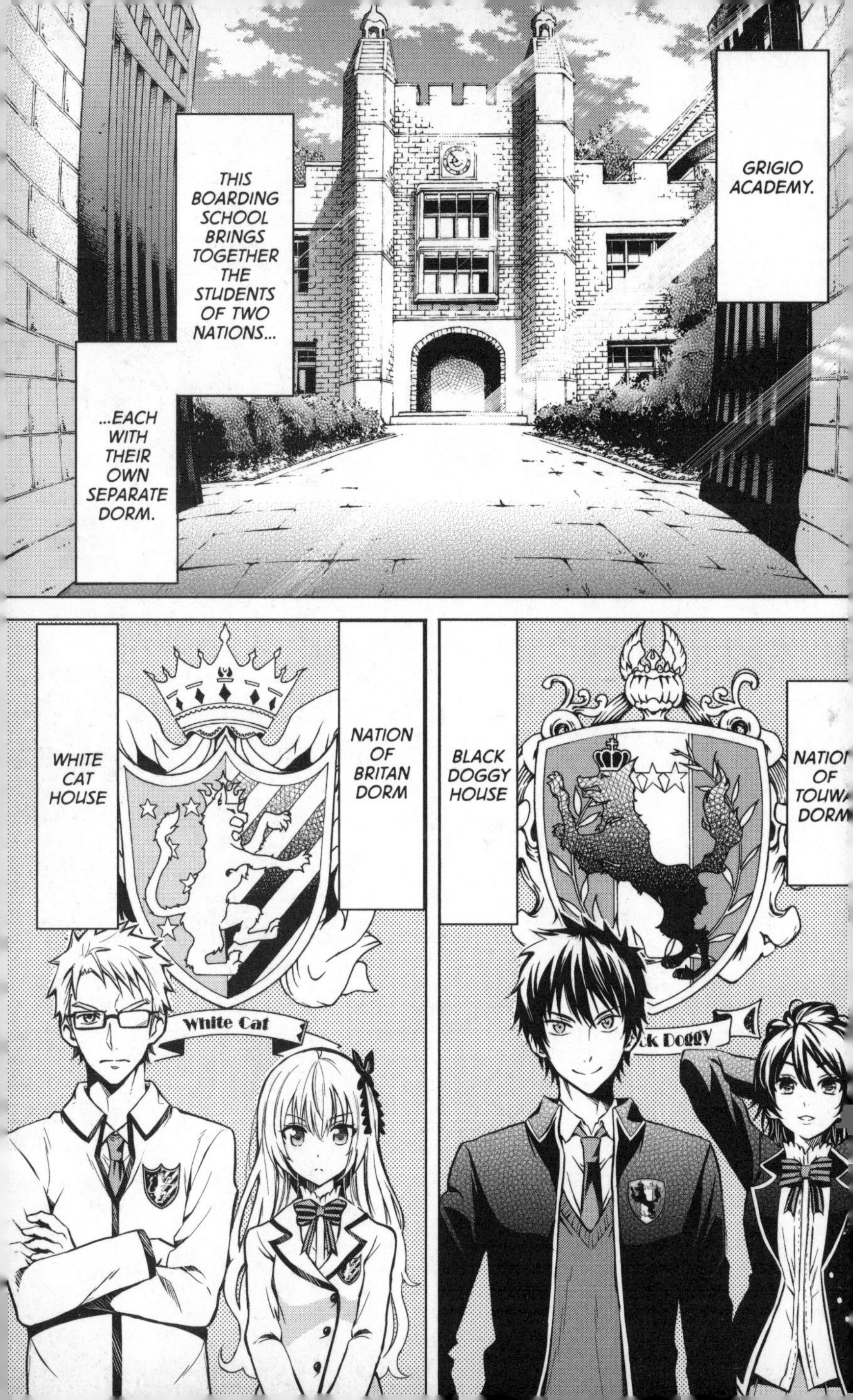
GRIGIO ACADEMY.
THIS BOARDING SCHOOL BRINGS TOGETHER THE STUDENTS OF TWO NATIONS...
...EACH WITH THEIR OWN SEPARATE DORM.
NATIO OF TOUW DORM
BLACK DOGGY HOUSE
ck Doggy
NATION OF BRITAN DORM
WHITE CAT HOUSE
White Cat

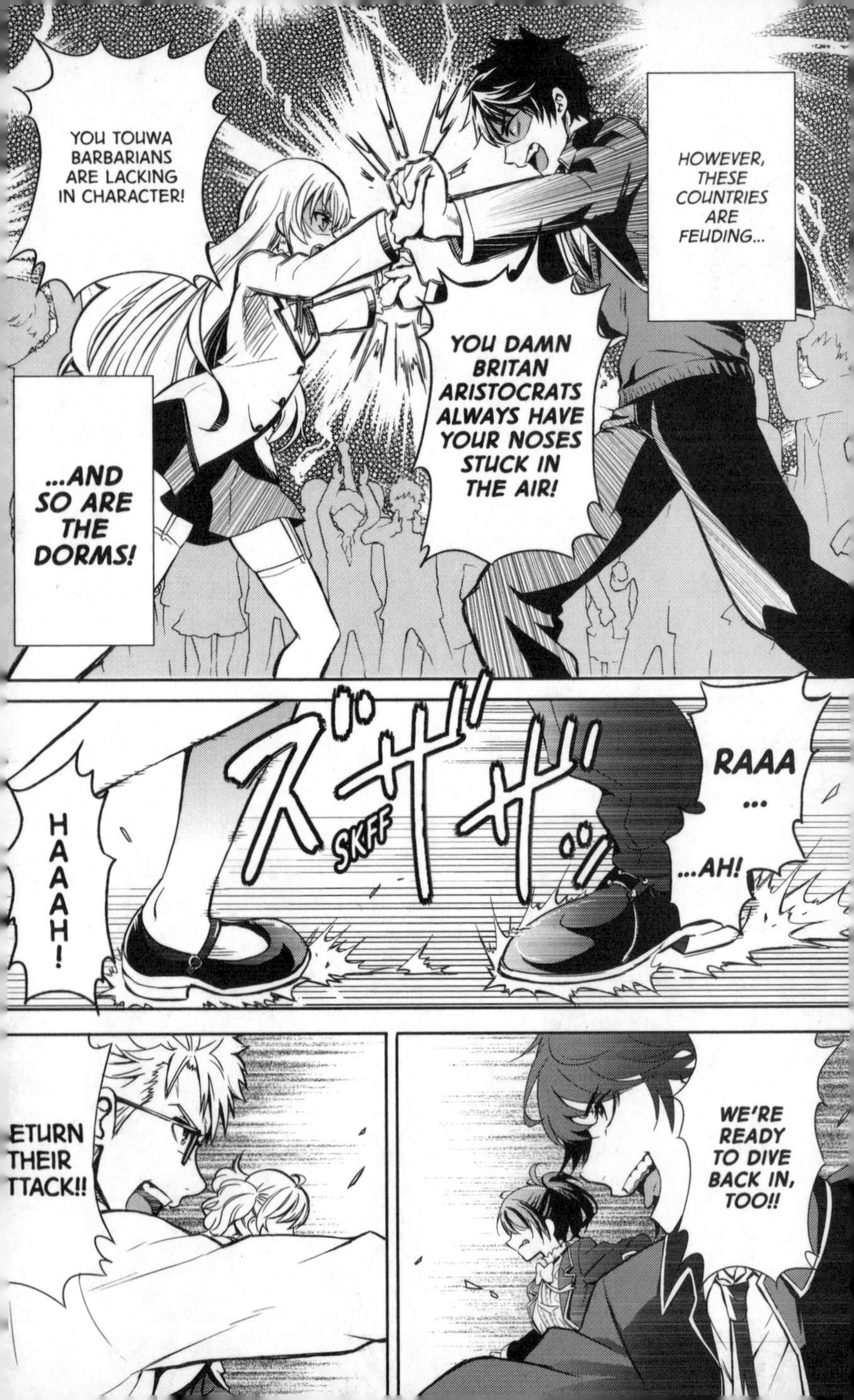
HOWEVER, THESE COUNTRIES ARE FEUDING...
YOU TOUWA BARBARIANS ARE LACKING IN CHARACTER!
YOU DAMN BRITAN ARISTOCRATS ALWAYS HAVE YOUR NOSES STUCK IN THE AIR!
...AND SO ARE THE DORMS!
RAAA ... ...AH!
ズザザッ
SKFF
HAAAAH!
WE'RE READY TO DIVE BACK IN, TOO!!
ETURN THEIR TTACK!!

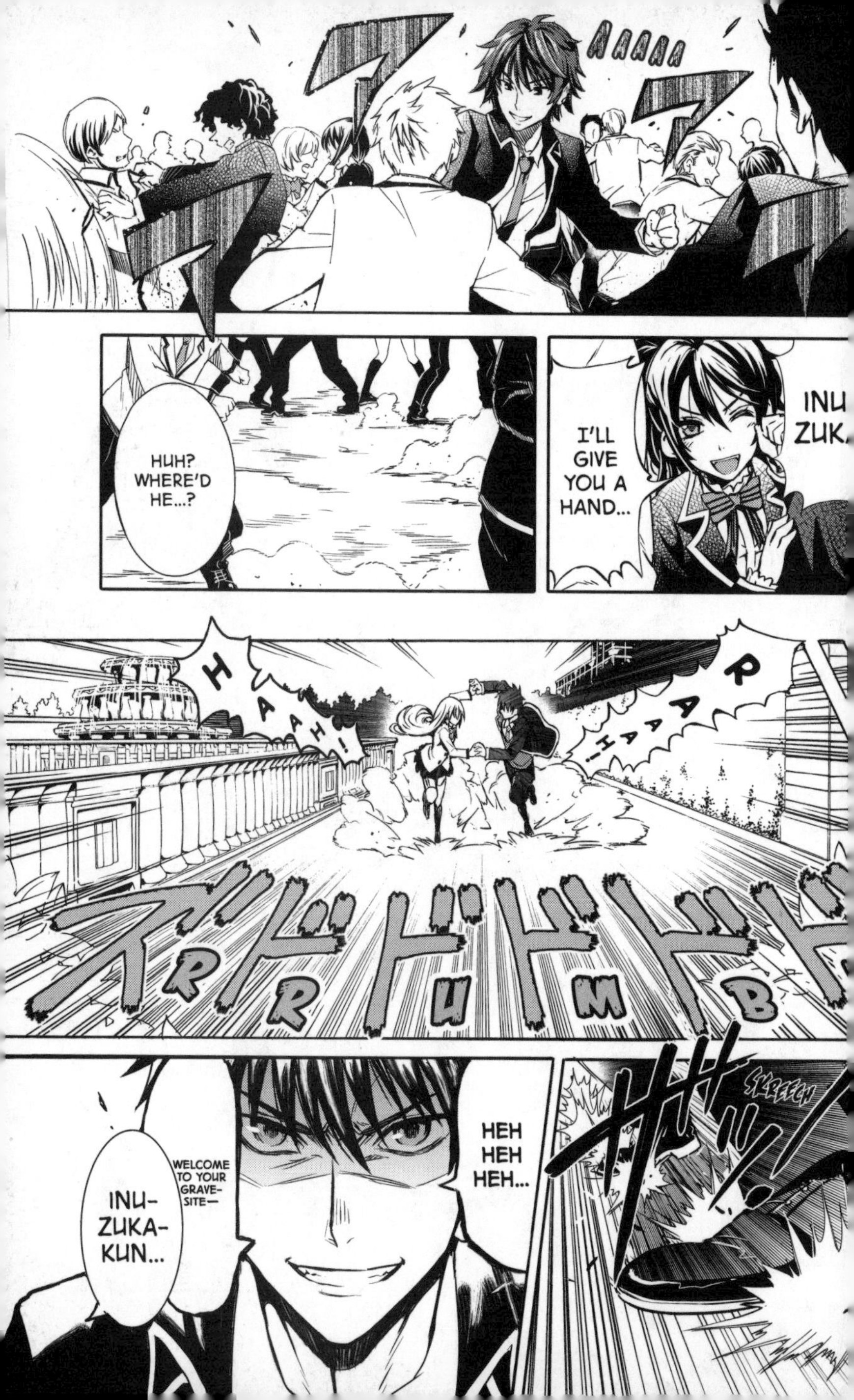
AAAAA
INU ZUK...
I'LL GIVE YOU A HAND...
HUH? WHERE'D HE...?
RAAHAA!
HAAH!
RRUMB
SKREECH
HEH HEH HEH...
WELCOME TO YOUR GRAVE-SITE—
INU-ZUKA-KUN...

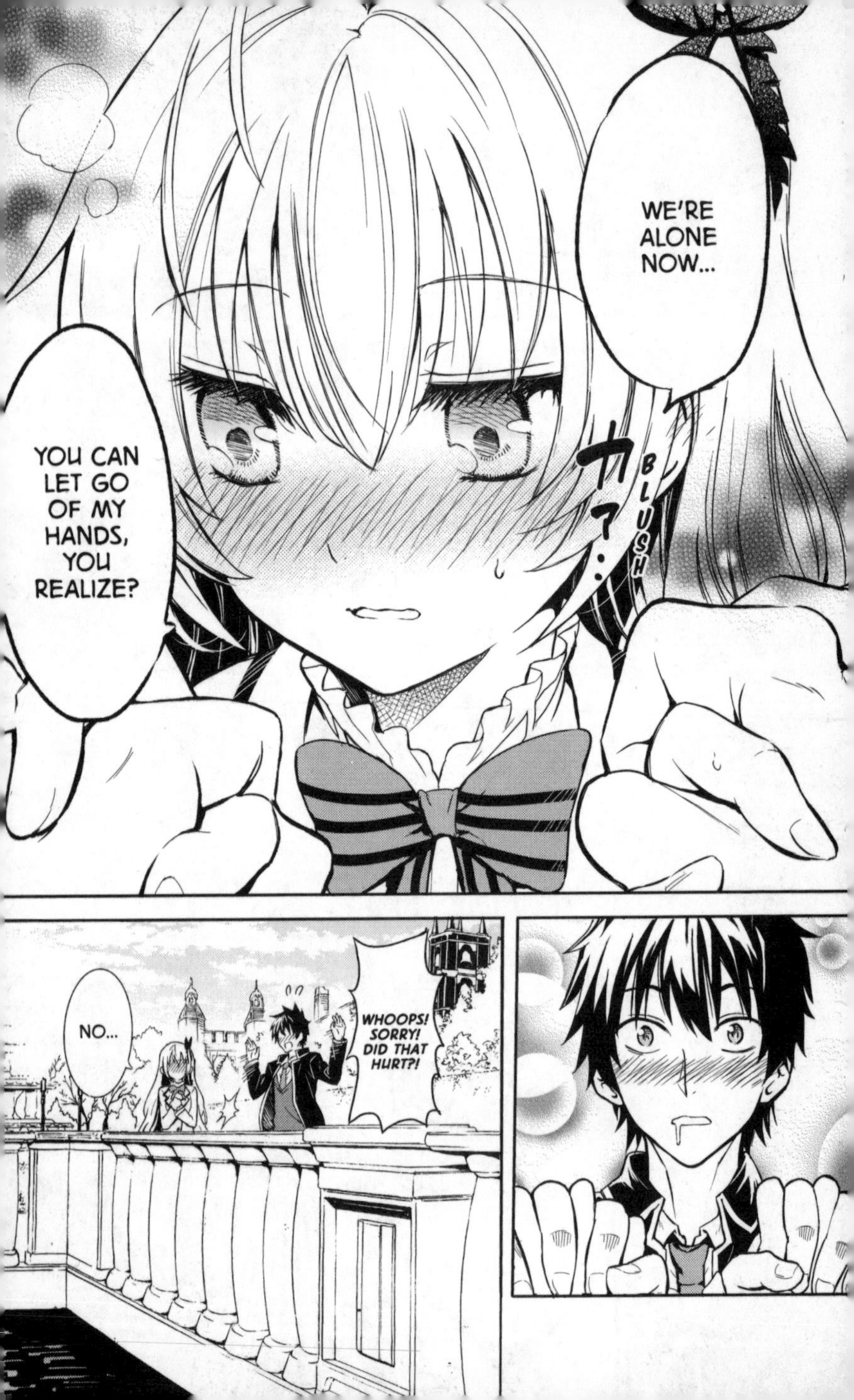
WE'RE ALONE NOW...
カァ…
BLUSH
YOU CAN LET GO OF MY HANDS, YOU REALIZE?
WHOOPS! SORRY! DID THAT HURT?!
NO...

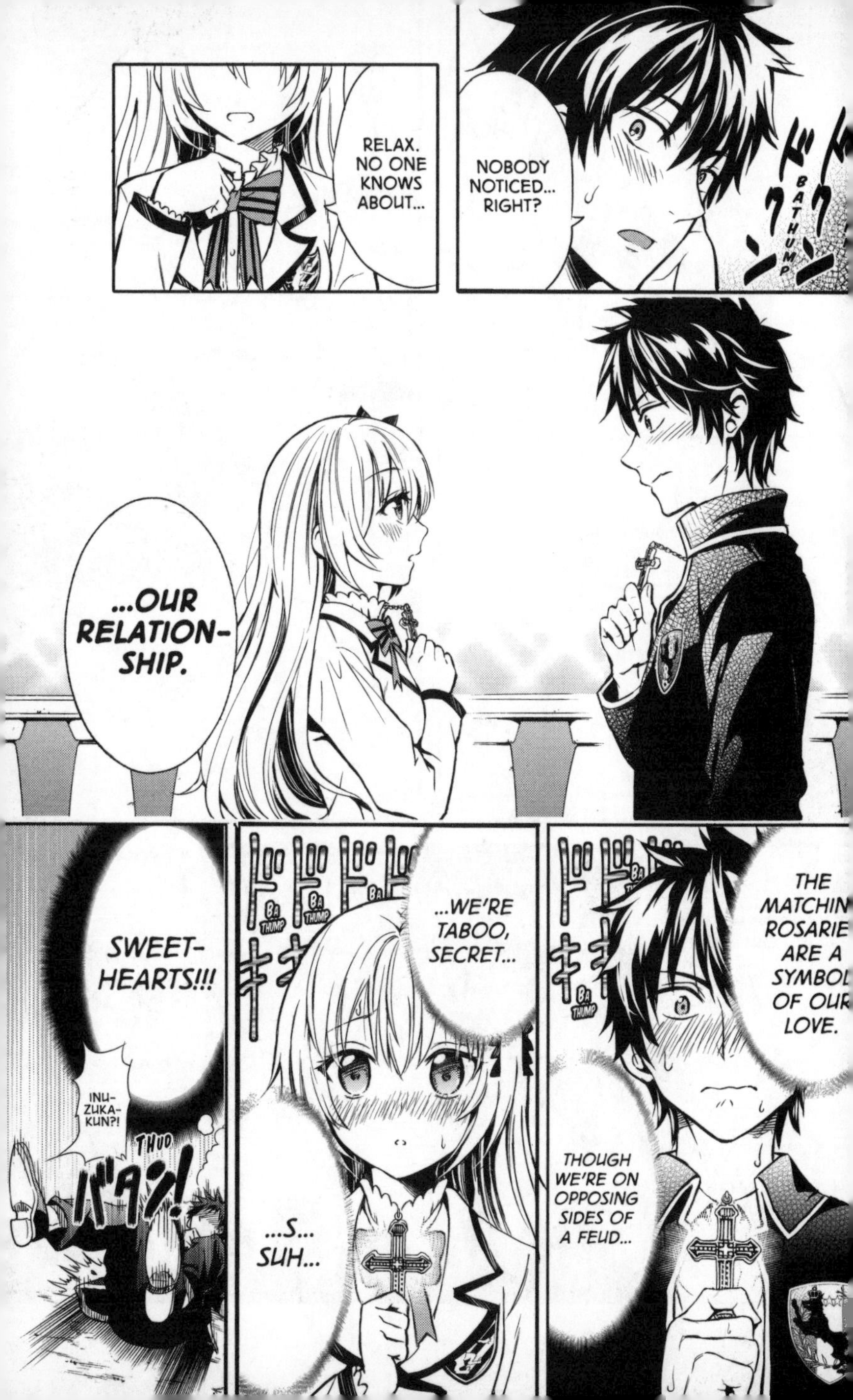
NOBODY NOTICED... RIGHT?
BATHUMP
RELAX. NO ONE KNOWS ABOUT...
...OUR RELATION-SHIP.
THE MATCHIN ROSARIE ARE A SYMBOL OF OUR LOVE.
BA THUMP
THOUGH WE'RE ON OPPOSING SIDES OF A FEUD...
...WE'RE TABOO, SECRET...
BA THUMP
BA THUMP
BA
...S... SUH...
SWEET-HEARTS!!!
INU-ZUKA-KUN?!
THUD
バタン!

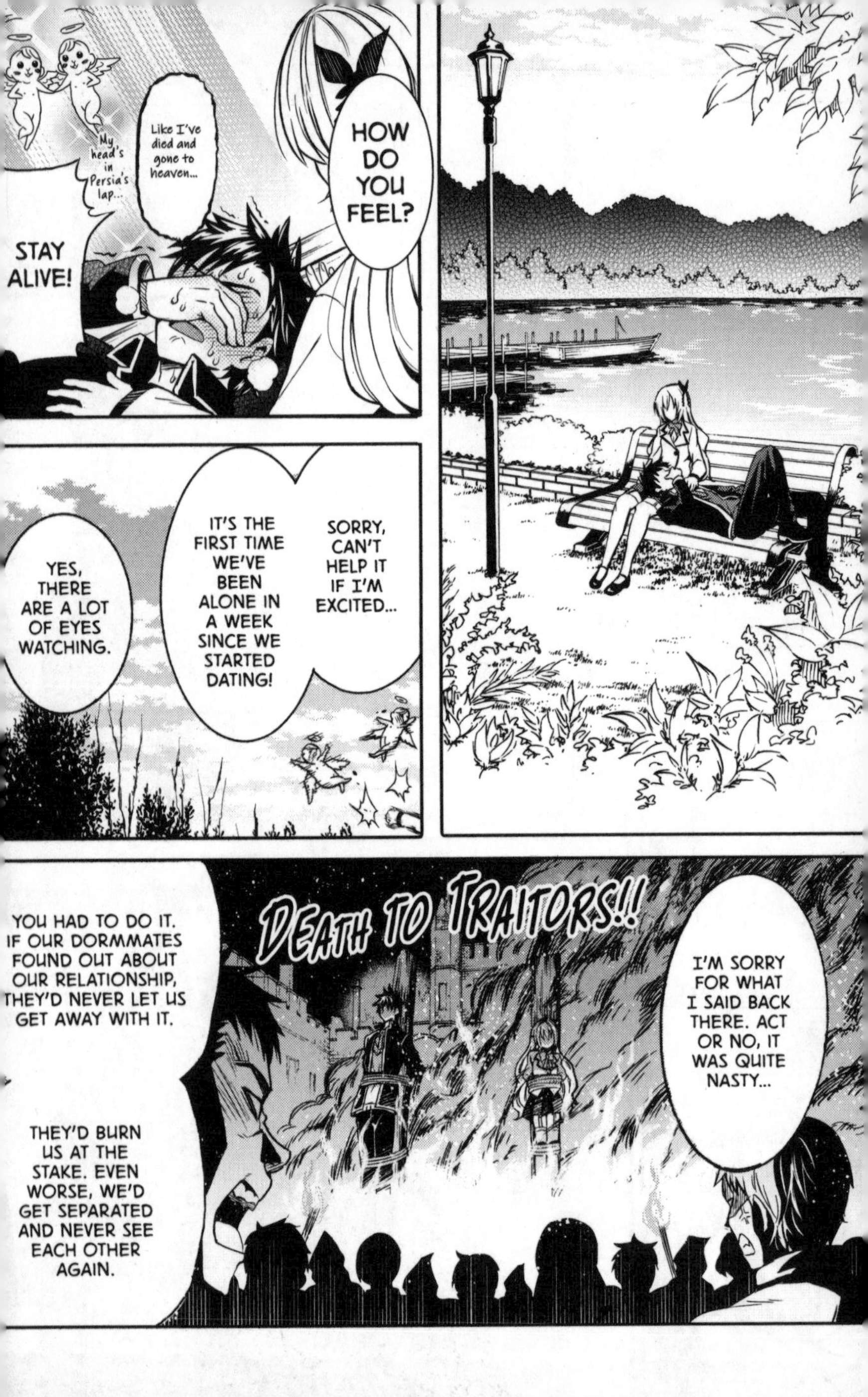
HOW DO YOU FEEL?
Like I've died and gone to heaven...
My head's in Persia's lap...
STAY ALIVE!
SORRY, CAN'T HELP IT IF I'M EXCITED...
IT'S THE FIRST TIME WE'VE BEEN ALONE IN A WEEK SINCE WE STARTED DATING!
YES, THERE ARE A LOT OF EYES WATCHING.
I'M SORRY FOR WHAT I SAID BACK THERE. ACT OR NO, IT WAS QUITE NASTY...
DEATH TO TRAITORS!!
YOU HAD TO DO IT. IF OUR DORMMATES FOUND OUT ABOUT OUR RELATIONSHIP, THEY'D NEVER LET US GET AWAY WITH IT.
THEY'D BURN US AT THE STAKE. EVEN WORSE, WE'D GET SEPARATED AND NEVER SEE EACH OTHER AGAIN.

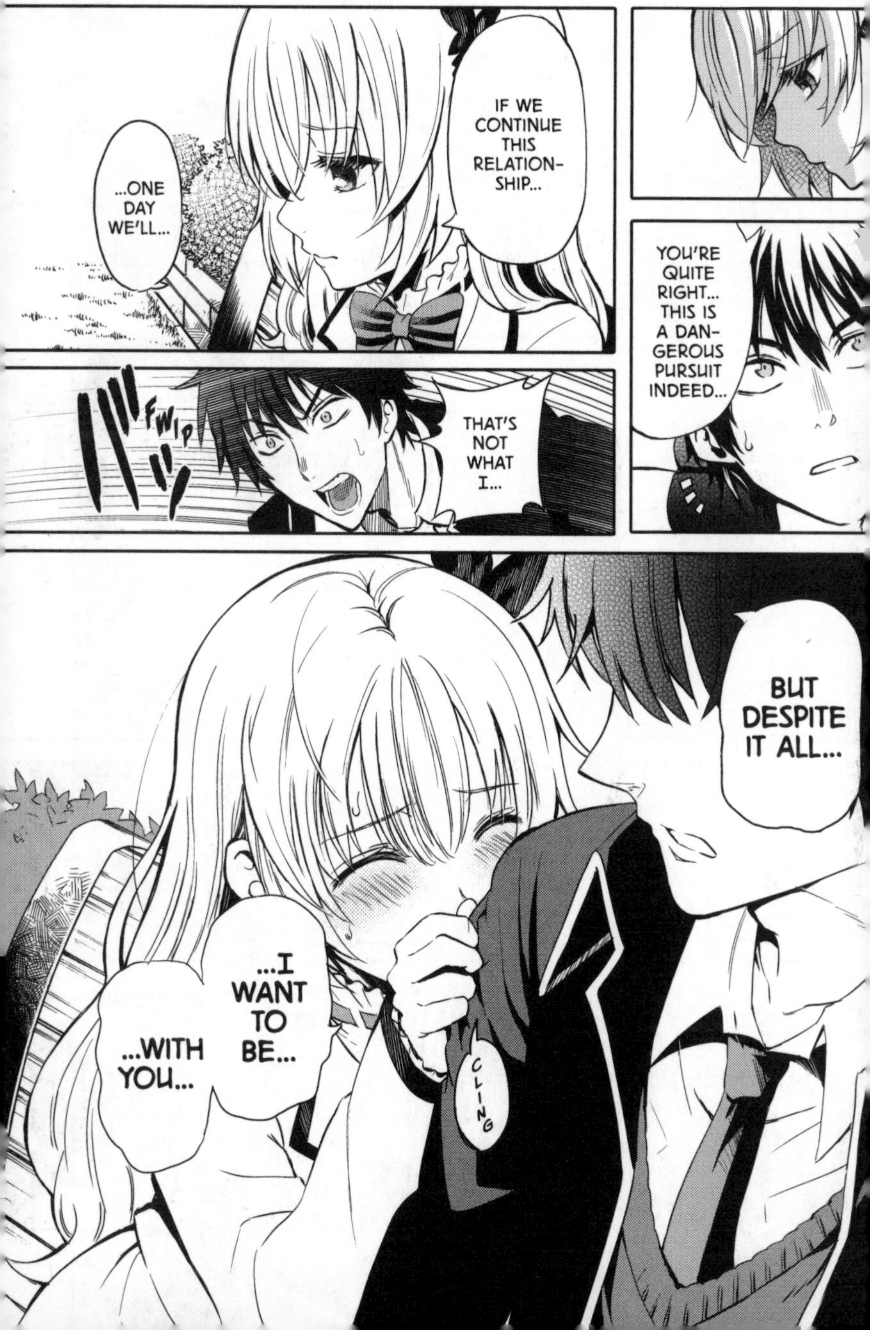
IF WE CONTINUE THIS RELATION-SHIP...
...ONE DAY WE'LL...
YOU'RE QUITE RIGHT... THIS IS A DAN-GEROUS PURSUIT INDEED...
FWIP
THAT'S NOT WHAT I...
BUT DESPITE IT ALL...
...I WANT TO BE...
...WITH YOU...
CLING

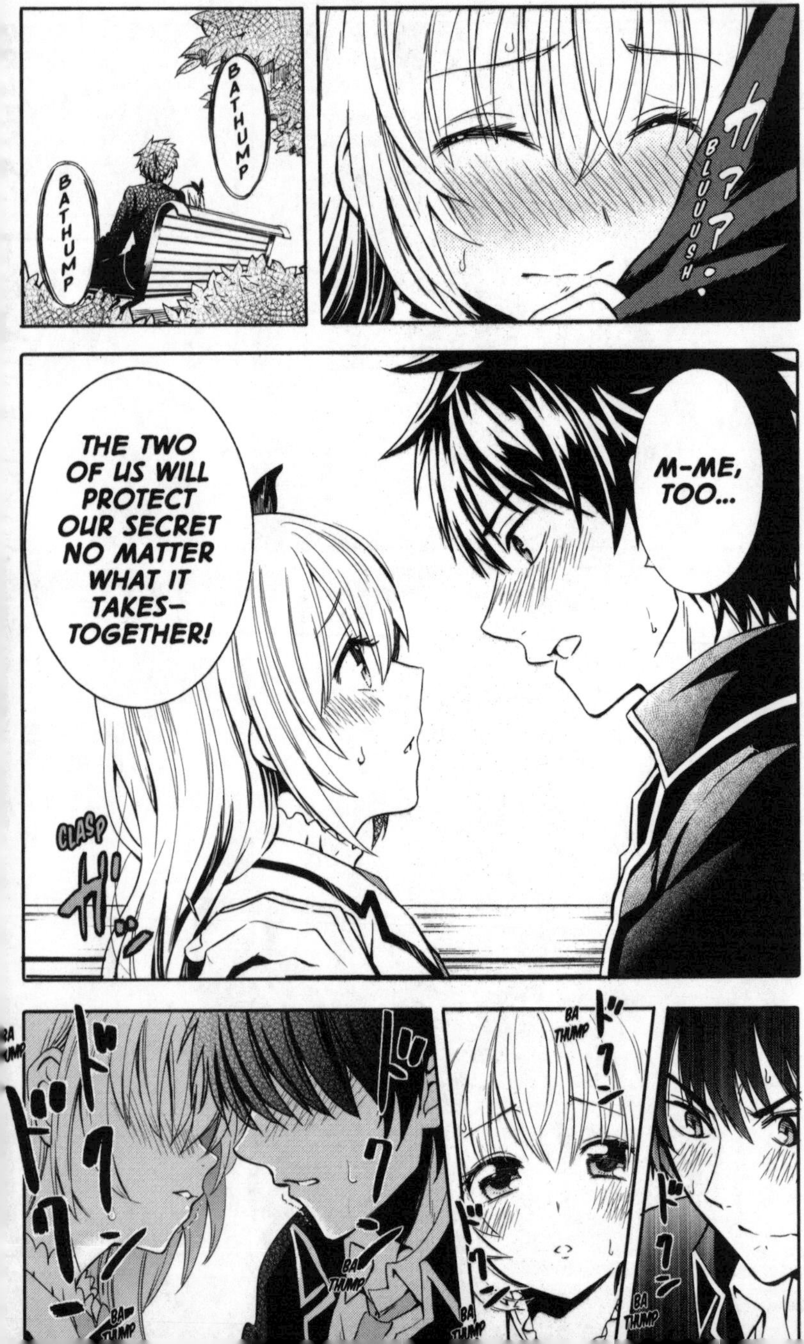

BLUUUSH
BATHUMP
BATHUMP
M-ME, TOO...
THE TWO OF US WILL PROTECT OUR SECRET NO MATTER WHAT IT TAKES—TOGETHER!
CLASP
BA THUMP
BA THUMP
BA THUMP
BA THUMP
BA THUMP

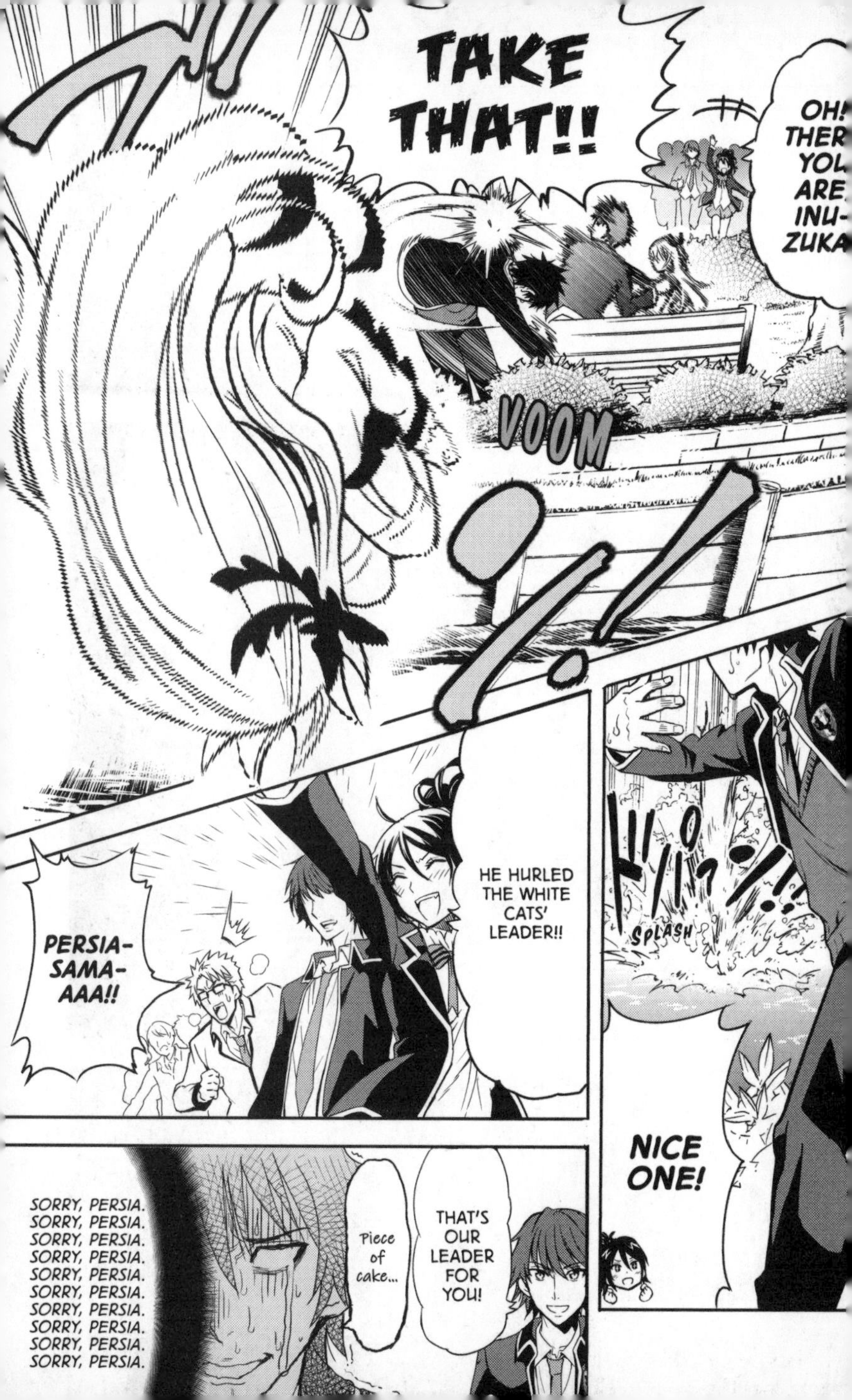
OH! THER YOU ARE, INU-ZUKA
TAKE THAT!!
VOOM
SPLASH
NICE ONE!
HE HURLED THE WHITE CATS' LEADER!!
PERSIA-SAMA-AAA!!
THAT'S OUR LEADER FOR YOU!
Piece of cake...
SORRY, PERSIA. SORRY, PERSIA. SORRY, PERSIA. SORRY, PERSIA. SORRY, PERSIA. SORRY, PERSIA. SORRY, PERSIA. SORRY, PERSIA. SORRY, PERSIA. SORRY, PERSIA.

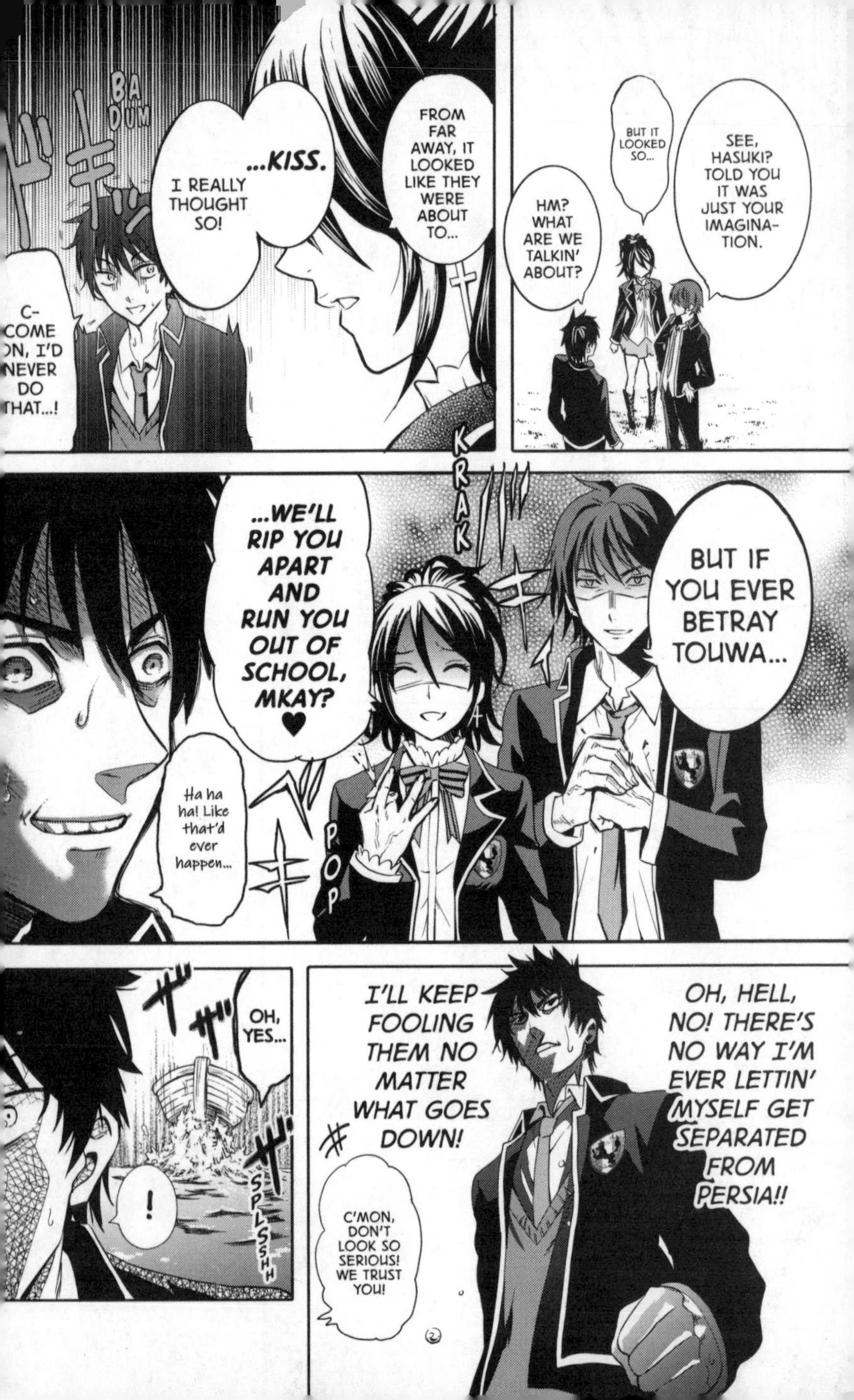
SEE, HASUKI? TOLD YOU IT WAS JUST YOUR IMAGINATION.
BUT IT LOOKED SO...
HM? WHAT ARE WE TALKIN' ABOUT?
FROM FAR AWAY, IT LOOKED LIKE THEY WERE ABOUT TO...
...KISS. I REALLY THOUGHT SO!
BA DUM
C- COME ON, I'D NEVER DO THAT...!
BUT IF YOU EVER BETRAY TOUWA...
KRAK
...WE'LL RIP YOU APART AND RUN YOU OUT OF SCHOOL, MKAY? ♥
POP
Ha ha ha! Like that'd ever happen...
OH, HELL, NO! THERE'S NO WAY I'M EVER LETTIN' MYSELF GET SEPARATED FROM PERSIA!!
I'LL KEEP FOOLING THEM NO MATTER WHAT GOES DOWN!
C'MON, DON'T LOOK SO SERIOUS! WE TRUST YOU!
OH, YES...
SPLSSHH
!

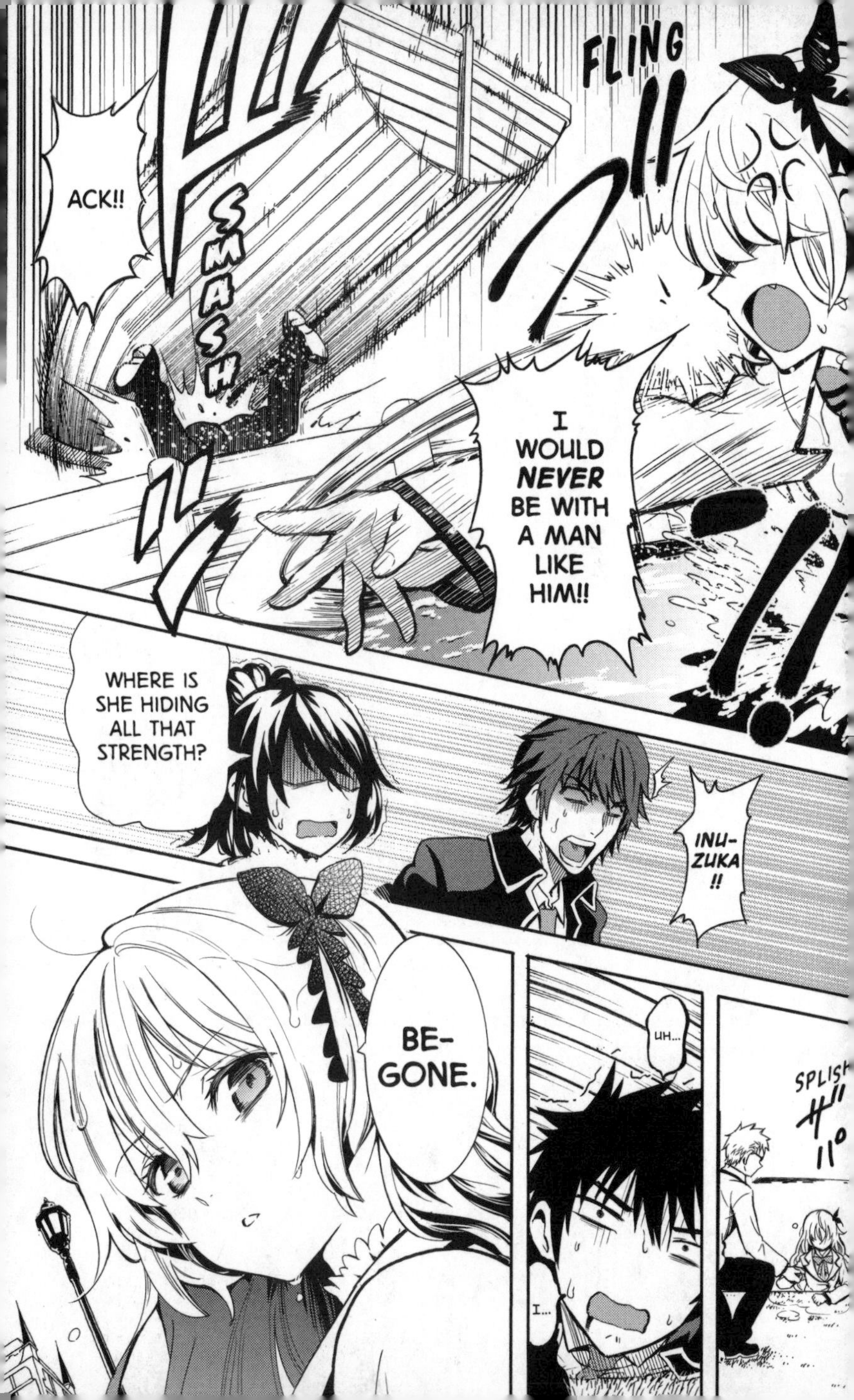
FLING
I WOULD NEVER BE WITH A MAN LIKE HIM!!
SMASH
ACK!!
INU-ZUKA!!
WHERE IS SHE HIDING ALL THAT STRENGTH?
SPLISH
UH...
I...
BE-GONE.

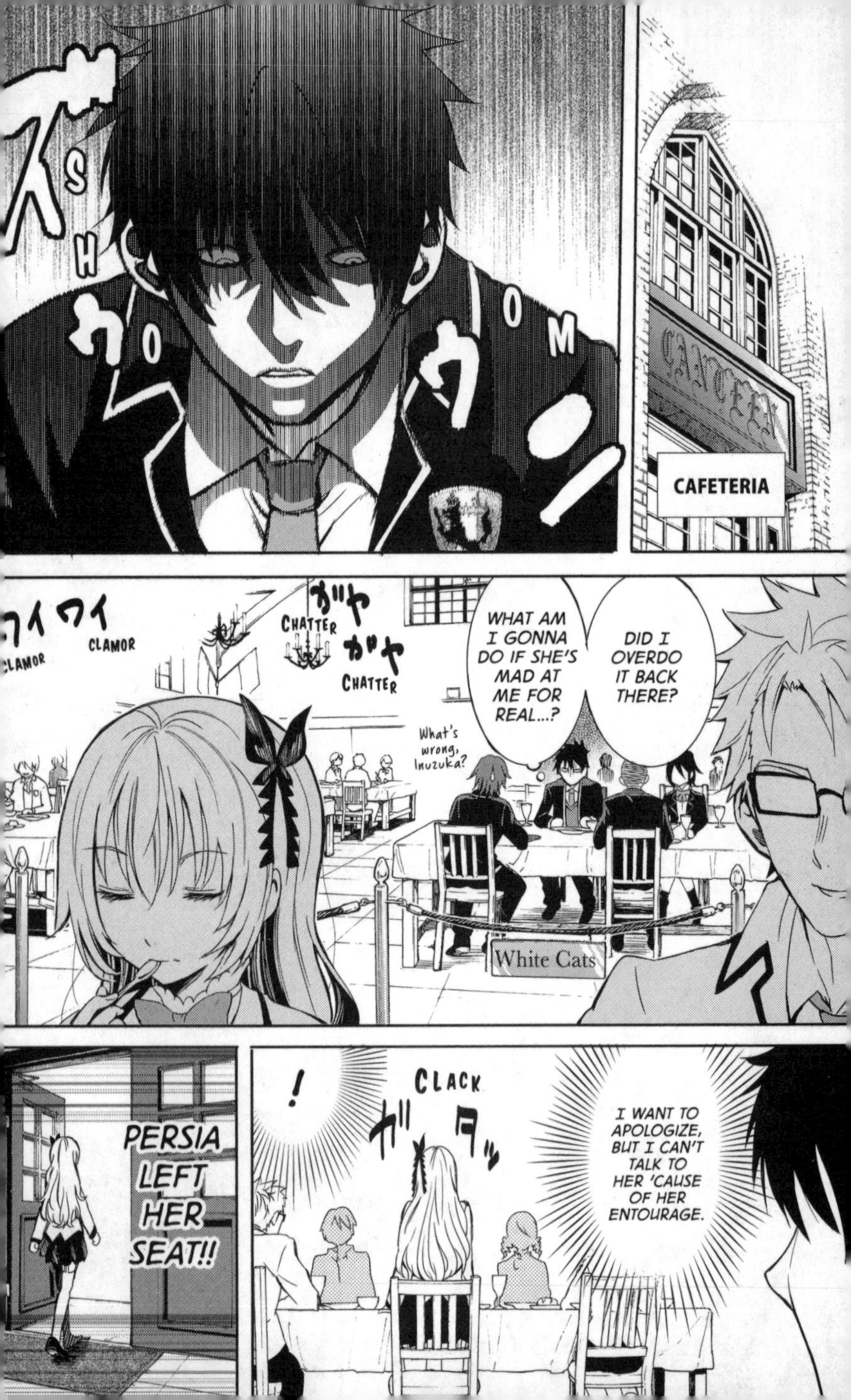

CANTEEN
CAFETERIA
SHOOM
DID I OVERDO IT BACK THERE?
WHAT AM I GONNA DO IF SHE'S MAD AT ME FOR REAL...?
What's wrong, Inuzuka?
ガヤガヤ
CHATTER CHATTER
ワイワイ
CLAMOR CLAMOR
White Cats
I WANT TO APOLOGIZE, BUT I CAN'T TALK TO HER 'CAUSE OF HER ENTOURAGE.
ガタッ
CLACK
!
PERSIA LEFT HER SEAT!!

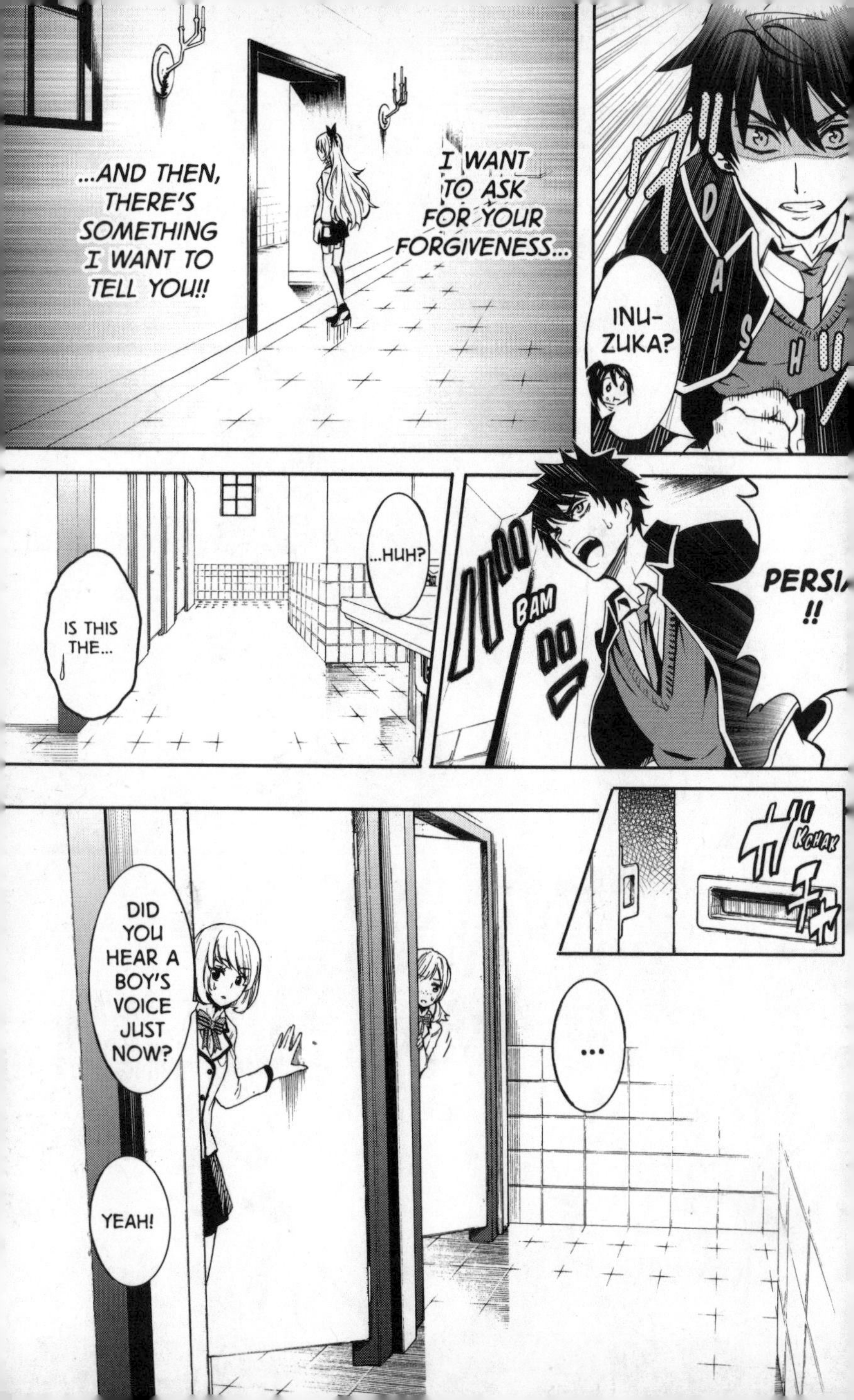
DASHIII
INU-ZUKA?
I WANT TO ASK FOR YOUR FORGIVENESS...
...AND THEN, THERE'S SOMETHING I WANT TO TELL YOU!!
PERSI!!
BAM
...HUH?
IS THIS THE...
KCHAK
DID YOU HEAR A BOY'S VOICE JUST NOW?
...
YEAH!

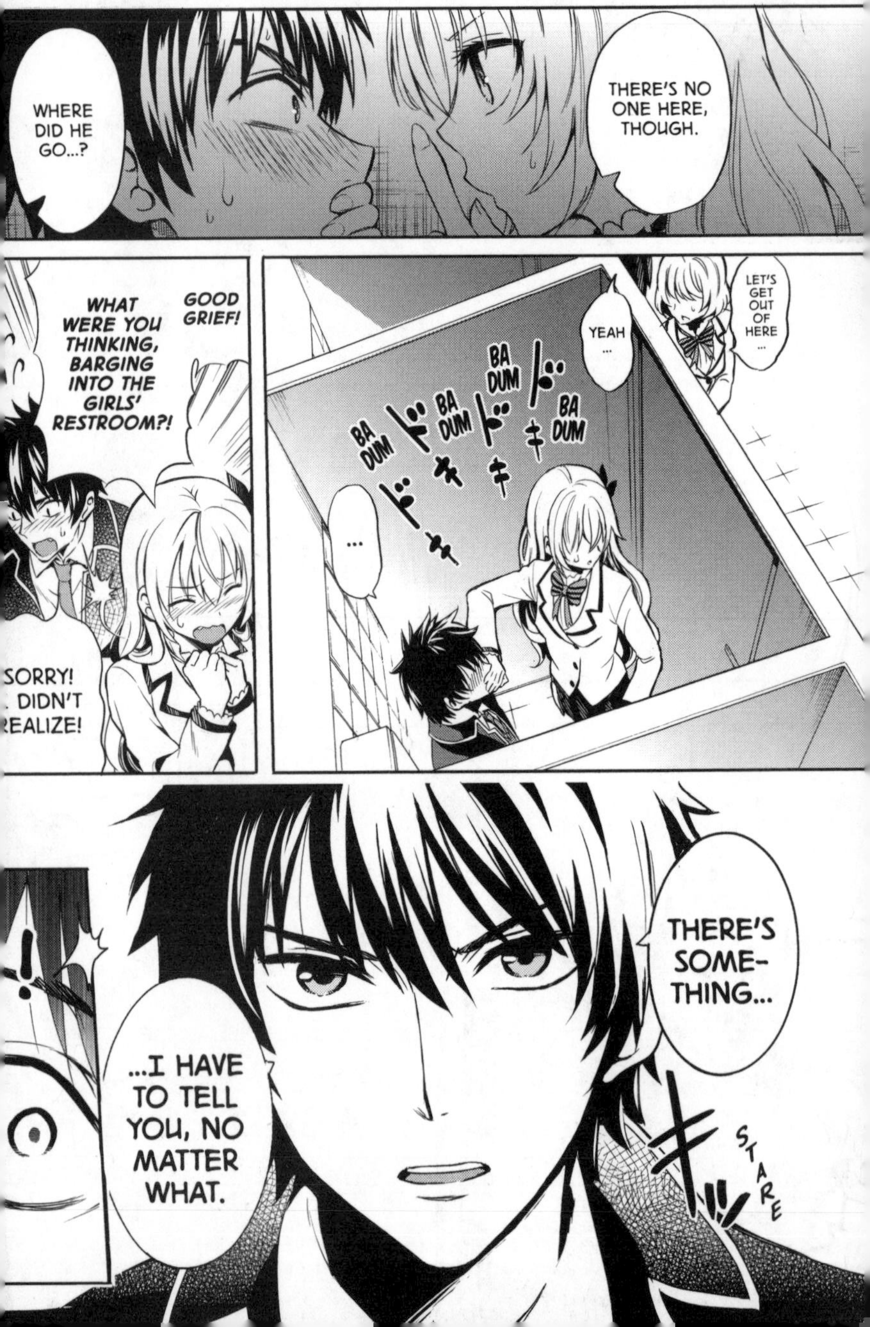
THERE'S NO ONE HERE, THOUGH.
WHERE DID HE GO...?
LET'S GET OUT OF HERE ...
YEAH ...
BA DUM BA DUM BA DUM BA DUM
...
GOOD GRIEF!
WHAT WERE YOU THINKING, BARGING INTO THE GIRLS' RESTROOM?!
SORRY! DIDN'T REALIZE!
THERE'S SOME-THING...
...I HAVE TO TELL YOU, NO MATTER WHAT.
!
STARE

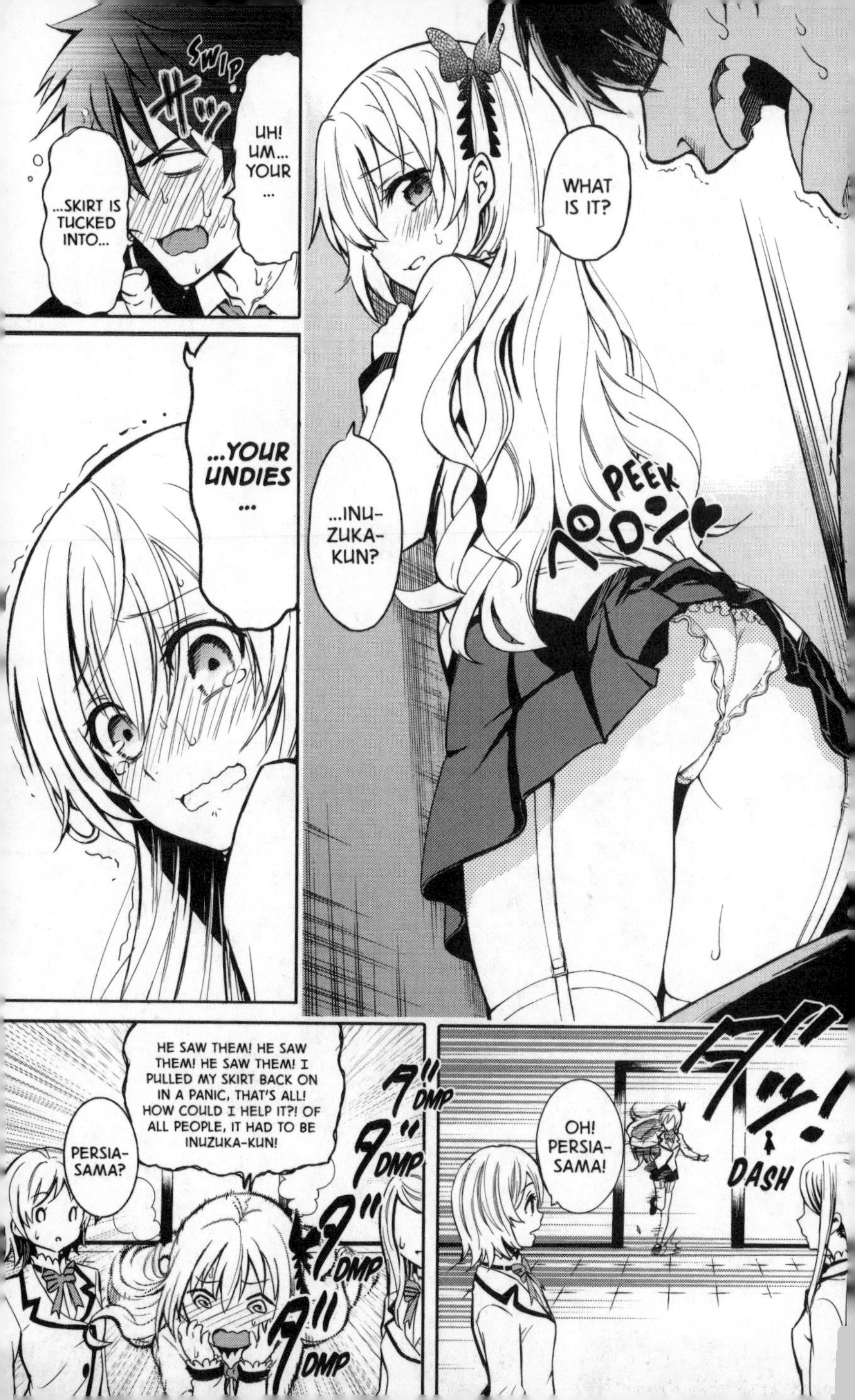
WHAT IS IT?
PEEK
...INUZUKA-KUN?
SWIP
UH! UM... YOUR ...
...SKIRT IS TUCKED INTO...
...YOUR UNDIES ...
DASH
OH! PERSIA-SAMA!
HE SAW THEM! HE SAW THEM! HE SAW THEM! I PULLED MY SKIRT BACK ON IN A PANIC, THAT'S ALL! HOW COULD I HELP IT?! OF ALL PEOPLE, IT HAD TO BE INUZUKA-KUN!
DMP
DMP
DMP
DMP
PERSIA-SAMA?

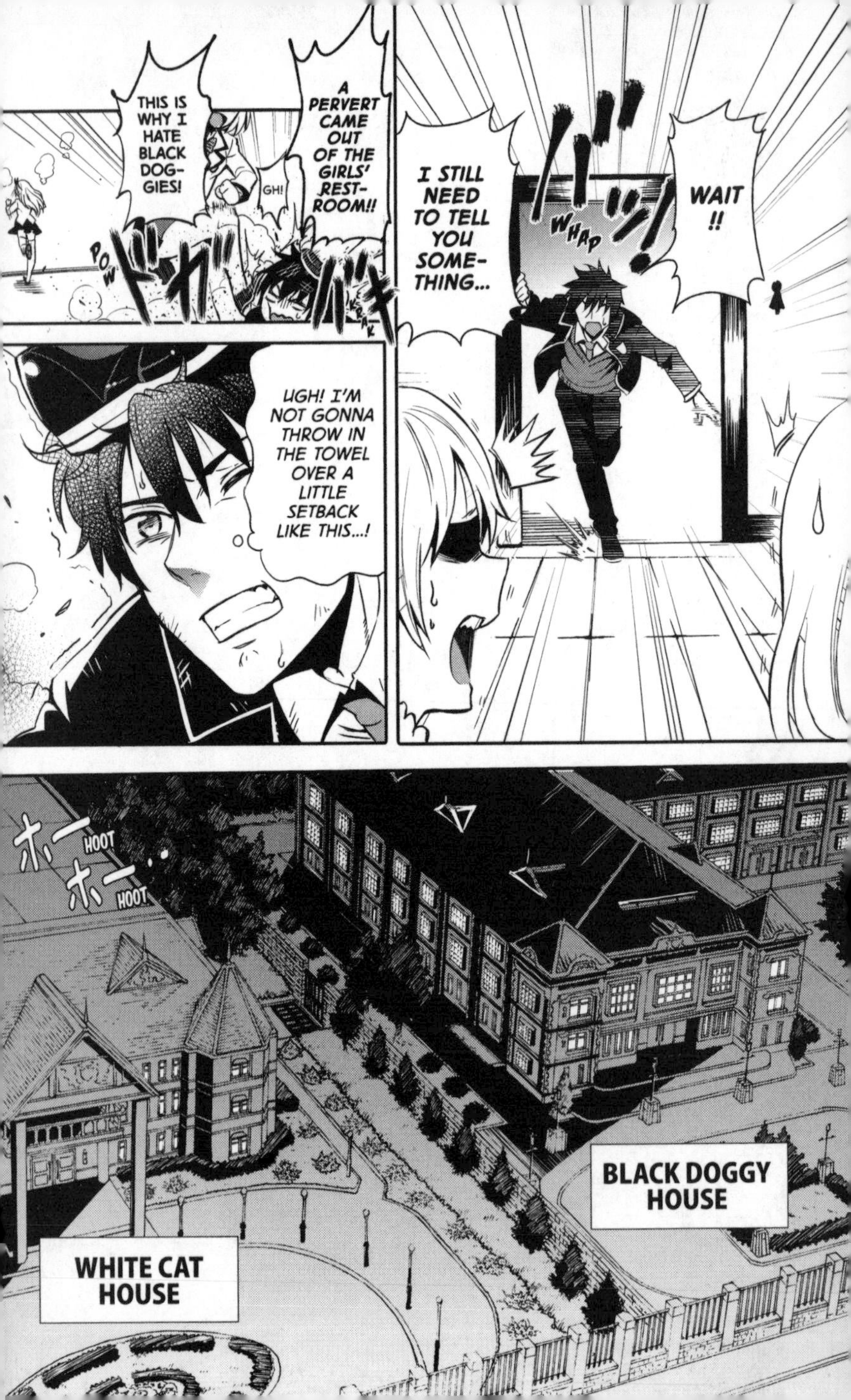
WAIT!!
I STILL NEED TO TELL YOU SOMETHING...
WHAP
A PERVERT CAME OUT OF THE GIRLS' RESTROOM!!
GH!
THIS IS WHY I HATE BLACK DOGGIES!
POW
KRAK
UGH! I'M NOT GONNA THROW IN THE TOWEL OVER A LITTLE SETBACK LIKE THIS...!
ホー HOOT
ホー HOOT
BLACK DOGGY HOUSE
WHITE CAT HOUSE

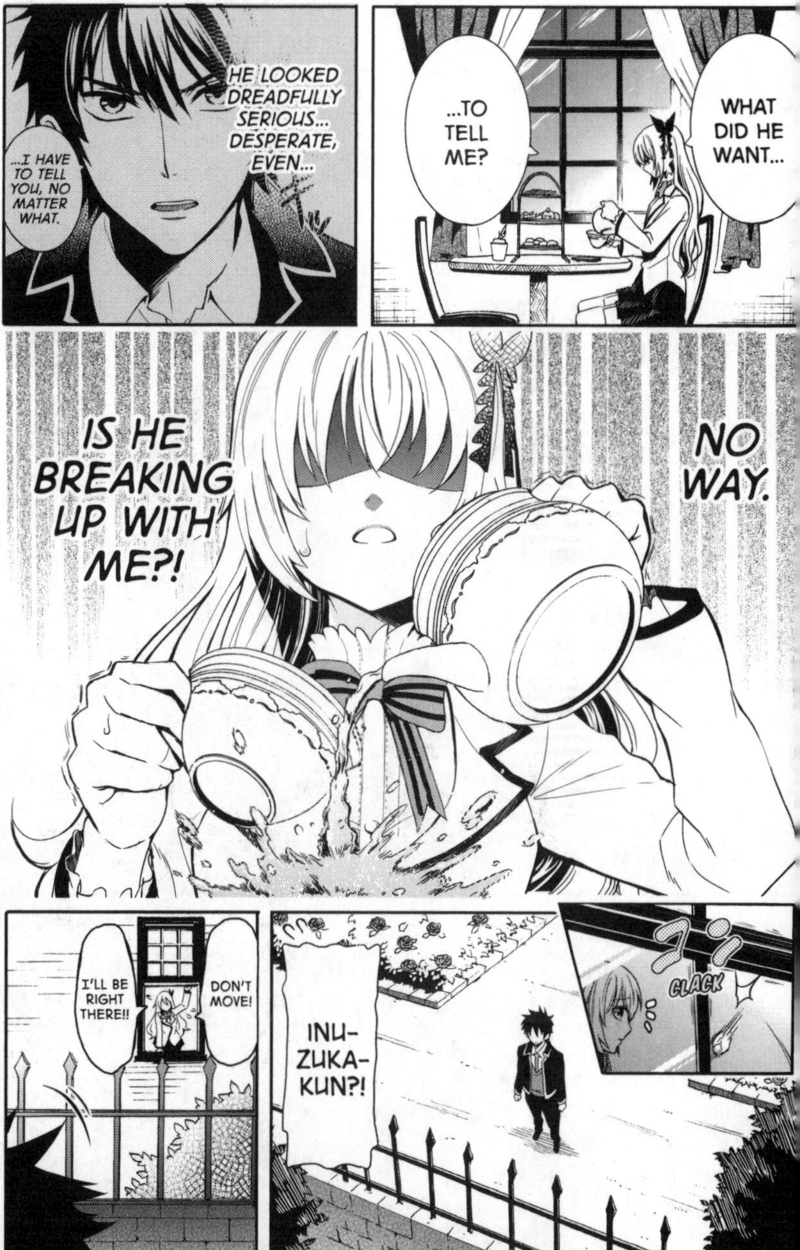
WHAT DID HE WANT...
...TO TELL ME?
HE LOOKED DREADFULLY SERIOUS... DESPERATE, EVEN...
...I HAVE TO TELL YOU, NO MATTER WHAT.
NO WAY.
IS HE BREAKING UP WITH ME?!
CLACK
INU-ZUKA-KUN?!
DON'T MOVE!
I'LL BE RIGHT THERE!!

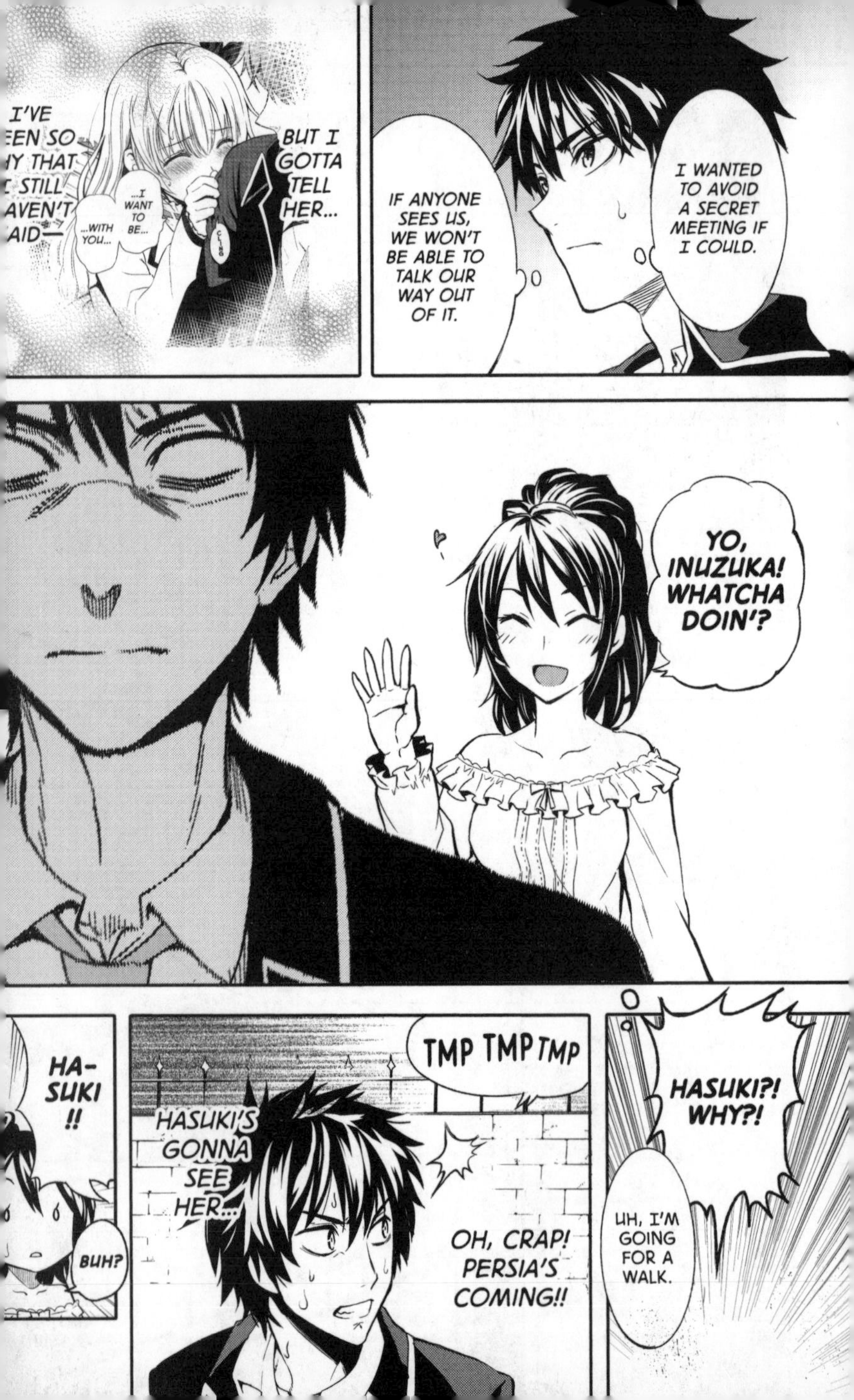
I WANTED TO AVOID A SECRET MEETING IF I COULD.
IF ANYONE SEES US, WE WON'T BE ABLE TO TALK OUR WAY OUT OF IT.
BUT I GOTTA TELL HER...
...I WANT TO BE...
...WITH YOU...
CLING
I'VE EEN SO IY THAT STILL AVEN'T AID—
YO, INUZUKA! WHATCHA DOIN'?
HASUKI?! WHY?!
UH, I'M GOING FOR A WALK.
TMP TMP TMP
HASUKI'S GONNA SEE HER...
OH, CRAP! PERSIA'S COMING!!
HA-SUKI!!
BUH?

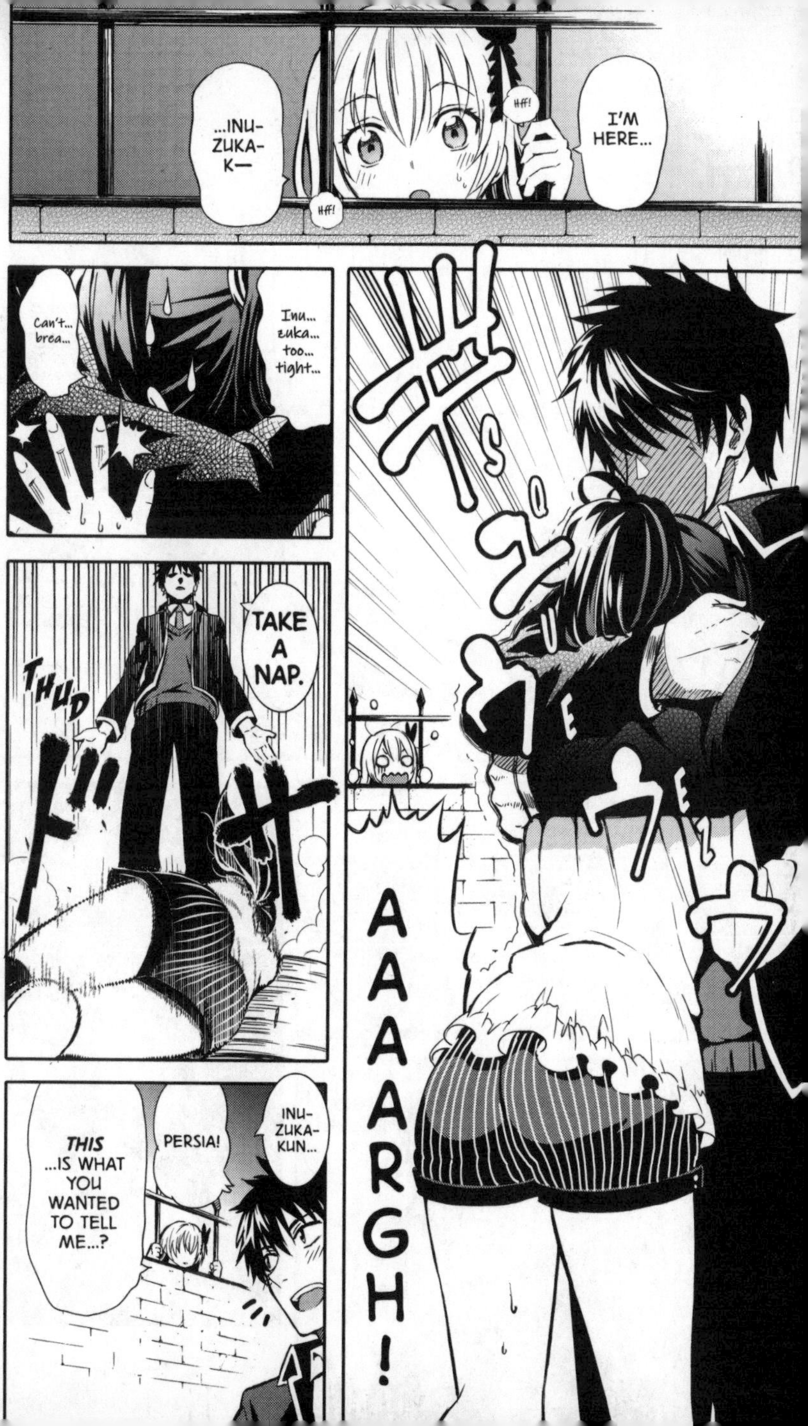

Hff!
I'M HERE...
...INU-ZUKA-K—
Hff!
SQUEEZE
AAAARGH!
Inu... zuka... too... tight...
Can't... brea...
TAKE A NAP.
THUD
INU-ZUKA-KUN...
PERSIA!
THIS ...IS WHAT YOU WANTED TO TELL ME...?

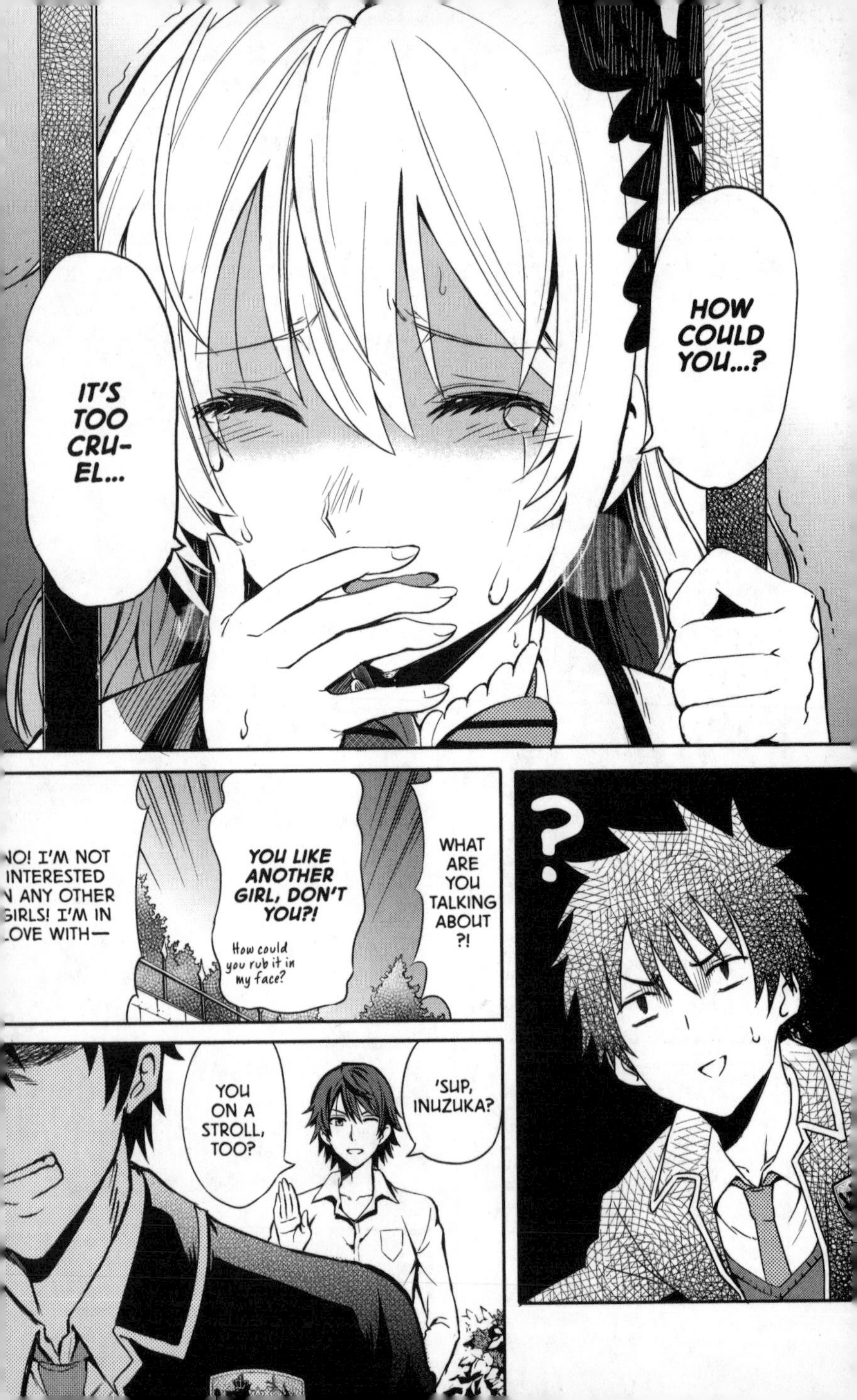
HOW COULD YOU...?
IT'S TOO CRU-EL...
?
WHAT ARE YOU TALKING ABOUT?!
YOU LIKE ANOTHER GIRL, DON'T YOU?!
How could you rub it in my face?
NO! I'M NOT INTERESTED IN ANY OTHER GIRLS! I'M IN LOVE WITH—
'SUP, INUZUKA?
YOU ON A STROLL, TOO?

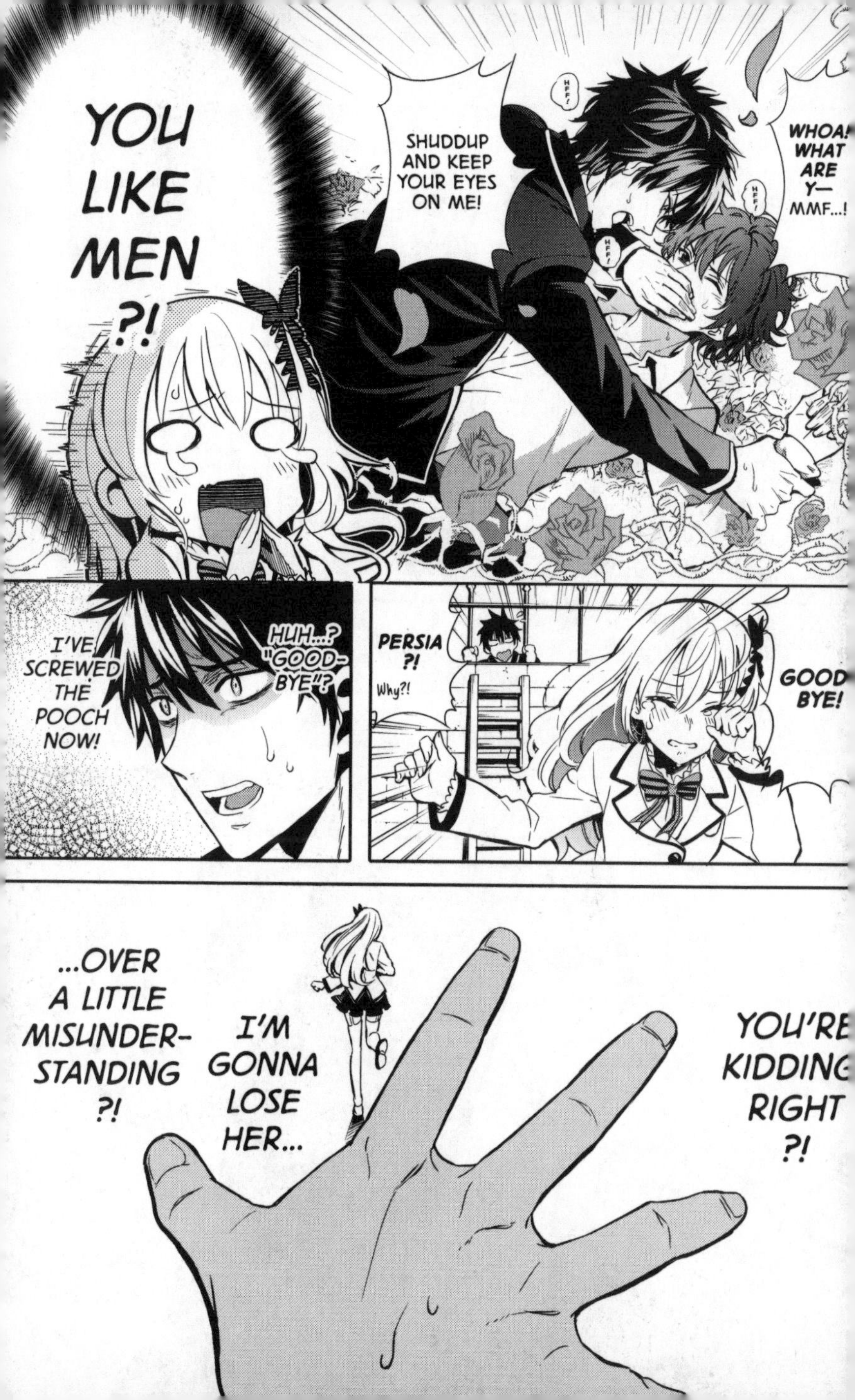
WHOA! WHAT ARE Y— MMF...!
HFF!
HFF!
HFF!
SHUDDUP AND KEEP YOUR EYES ON ME!
YOU LIKE MEN ?!
GOOD BYE!
PERSIA ?!
Why?!
HUH...? "GOOD-BYE"?
I'VE SCREWED THE POOCH NOW!
YOU'RE KIDDING RIGHT ?!
I'M GONNA LOSE HER...
...OVER A LITTLE MISUNDERSTANDING ?!

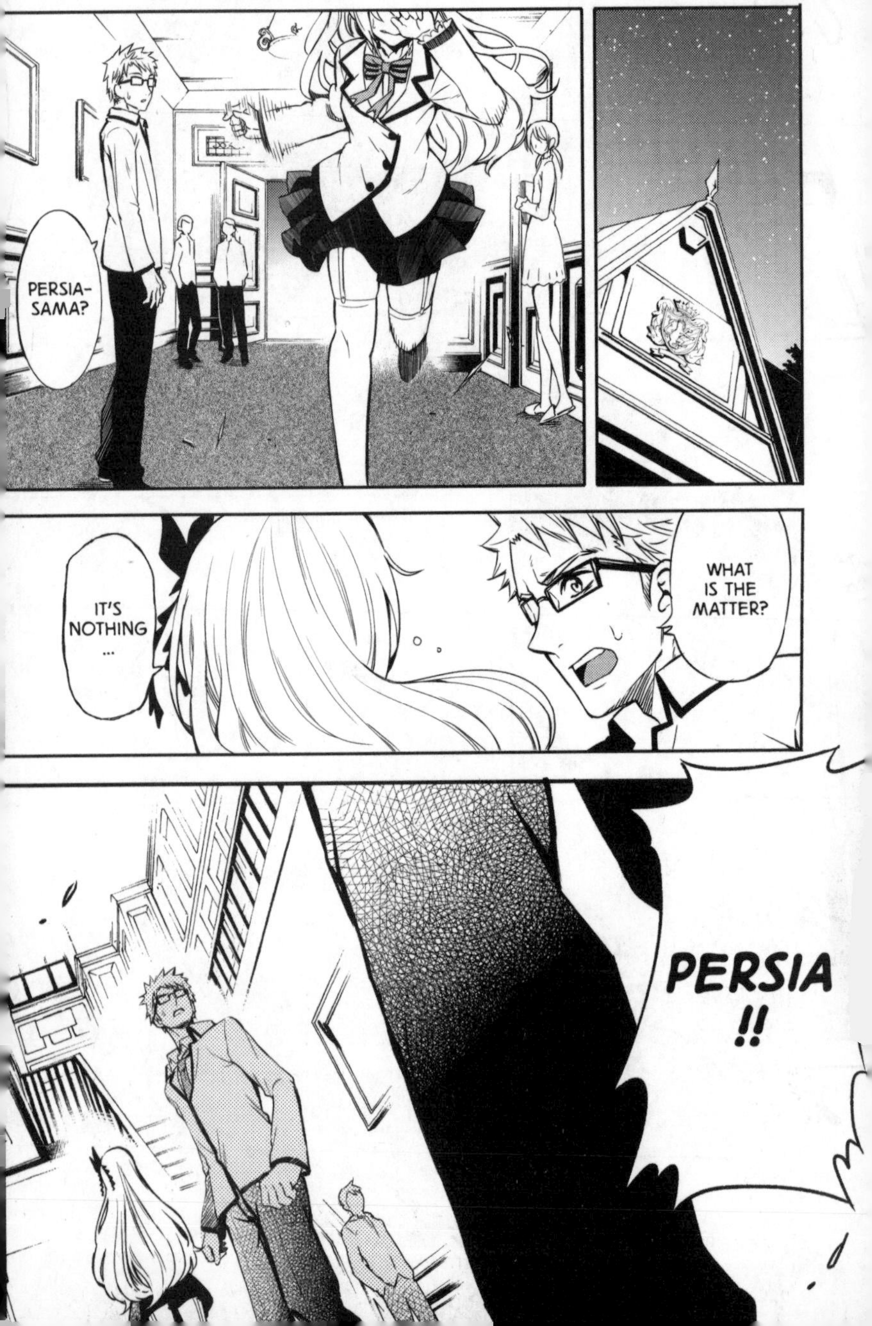
PERSIA-SAMA?
WHAT IS THE MATTER?
IT'S NOTHING ...
PERSIA !!

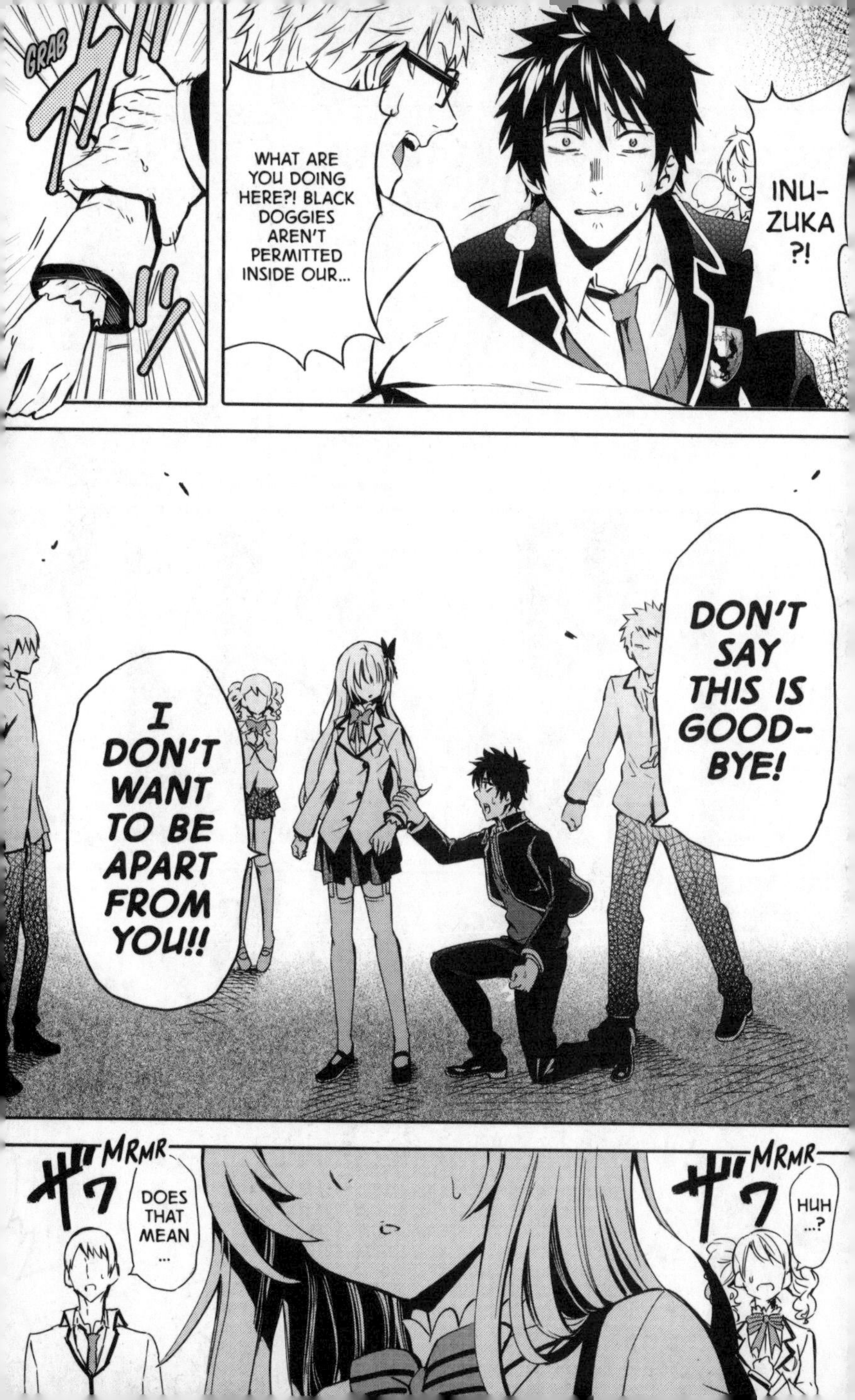
INU-ZUKA ?!
WHAT ARE YOU DOING HERE?! BLACK DOGGIES AREN'T PERMITTED INSIDE OUR...
GRAB
DON'T SAY THIS IS GOOD-BYE!
I DON'T WANT TO BE APART FROM YOU!!
MRMR
HUH ...?
MRMR
DOES THAT MEAN ...

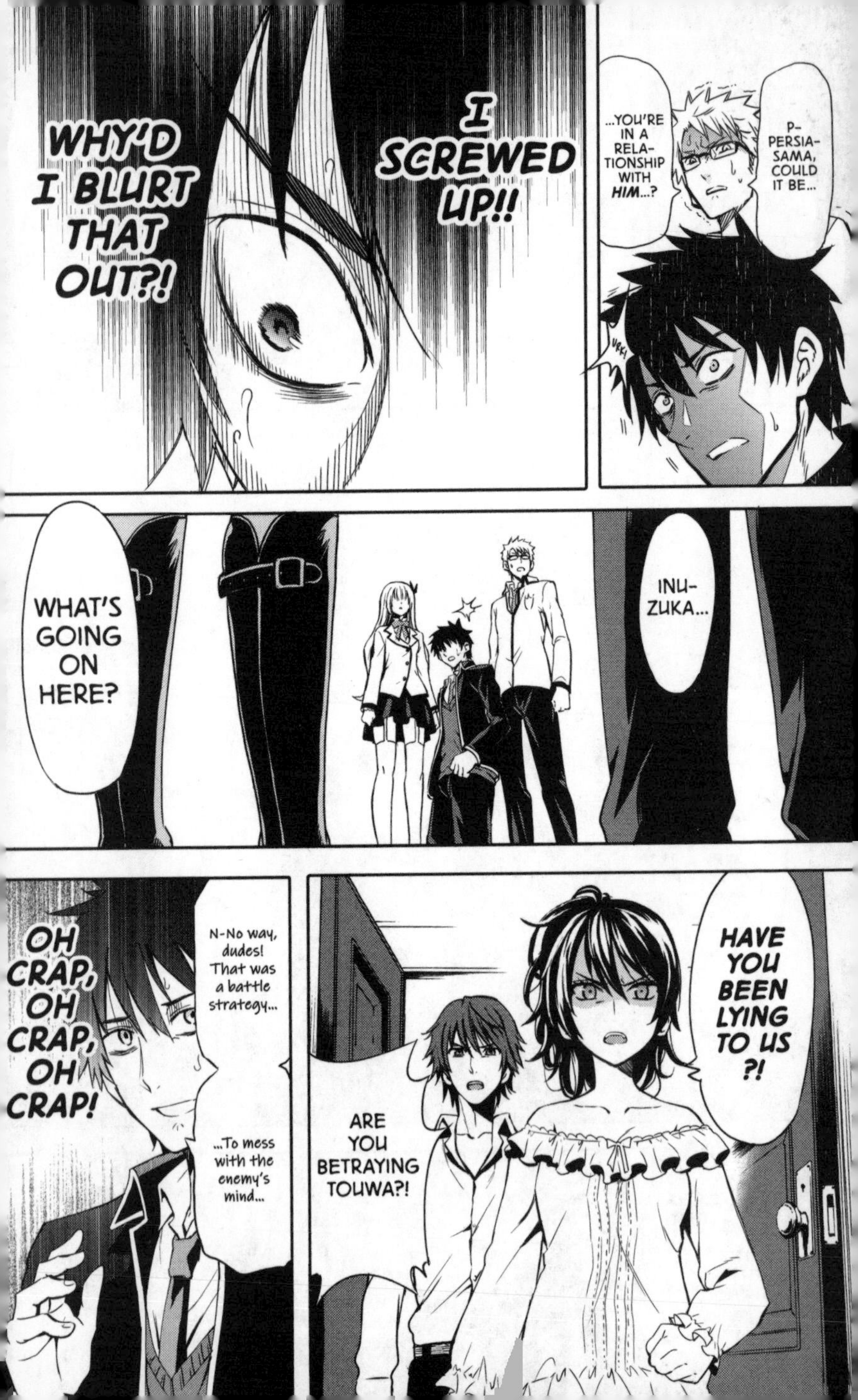
P-PERSIA-SAMA, COULD IT BE...
...YOU'RE IN A RELATIONSHIP WITH HIM...?
URK!
I SCREWED UP!!
WHY'D I BLURT THAT OUT?!
INU-ZUKA...
WHAT'S GOING ON HERE?
HAVE YOU BEEN LYING TO US?!
ARE YOU BETRAYING TOUWA?!
N-No way, dudes! That was a battle strategy...
...To mess with the enemy's mind...
OH CRAP, OH CRAP, OH CRAP!

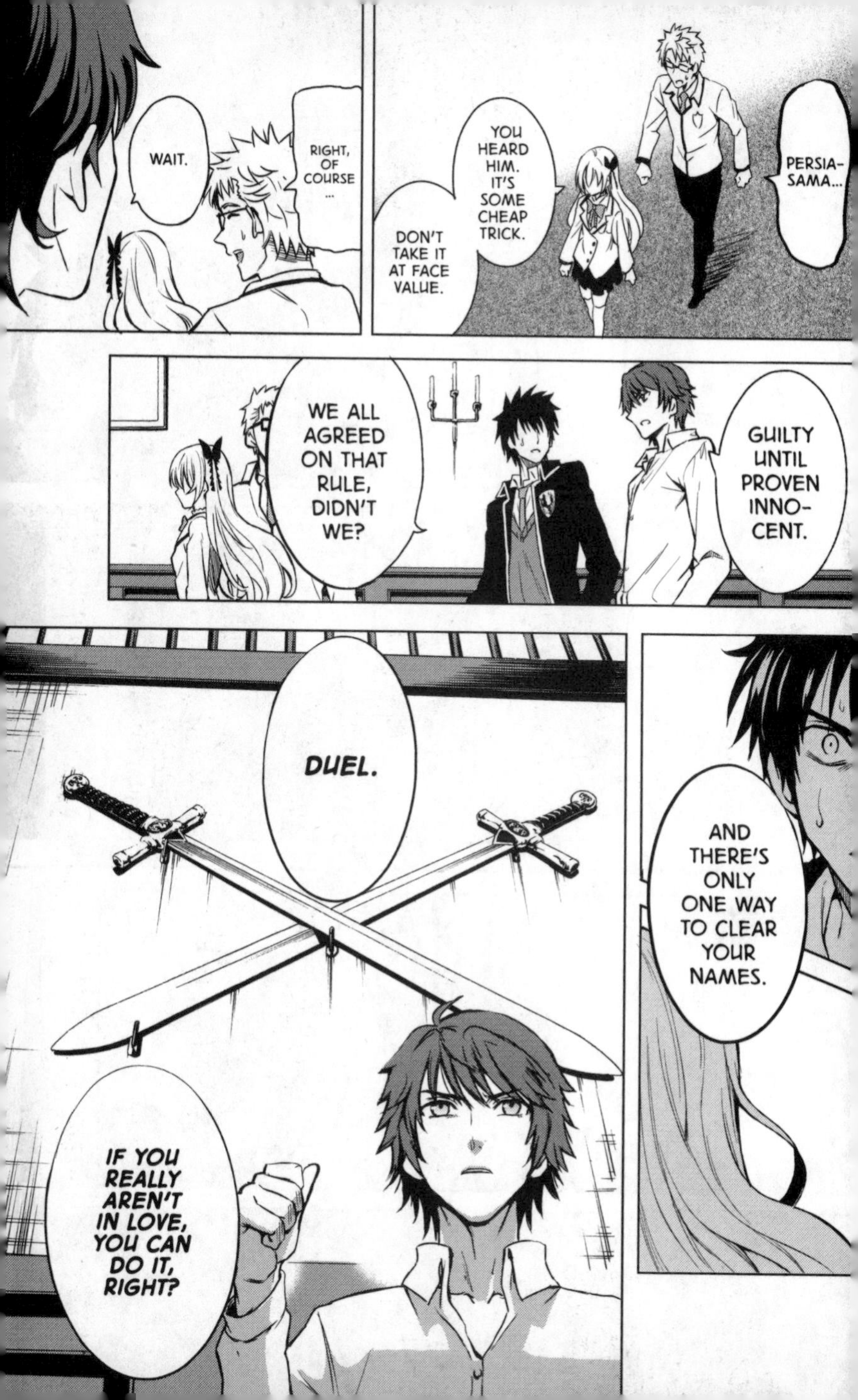
PERSIA-SAMA...
YOU HEARD HIM. IT'S SOME CHEAP TRICK.
DON'T TAKE IT AT FACE VALUE.
RIGHT, OF COURSE ...
WAIT.
GUILTY UNTIL PROVEN INNO-CENT.
WE ALL AGREED ON THAT RULE, DIDN'T WE?
AND THERE'S ONLY ONE WAY TO CLEAR YOUR NAMES.
DUEL.
IF YOU REALLY AREN'T IN LOVE, YOU CAN DO IT, RIGHT?

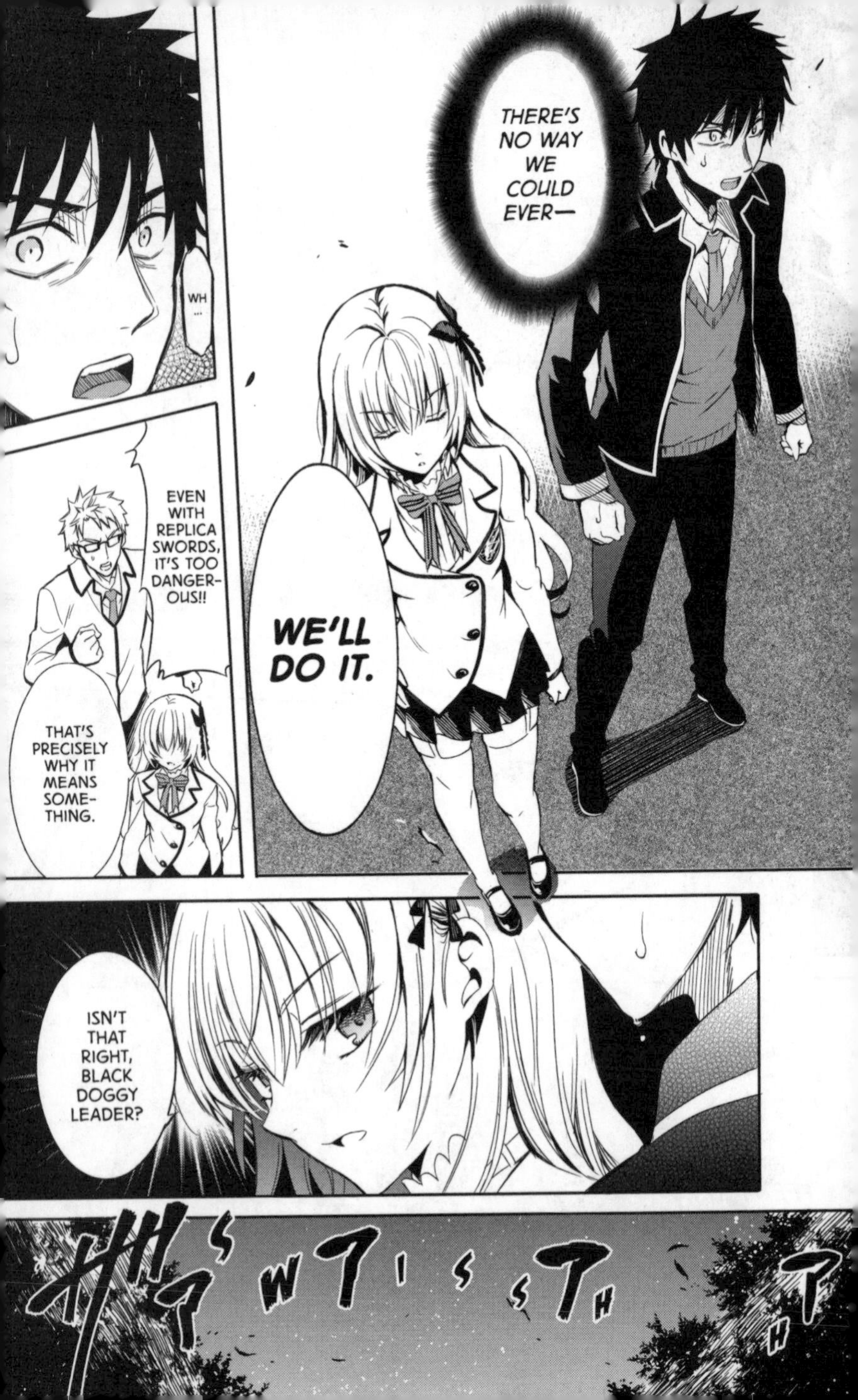
THERE'S NO WAY WE COULD EVER—
WE'LL DO IT.
WH...
EVEN WITH REPLICA SWORDS, IT'S TOO DANGER-OUS!!
THAT'S PRECISELY WHY IT MEANS SOME-THING.
ISN'T THAT RIGHT, BLACK DOGGY LEADER?

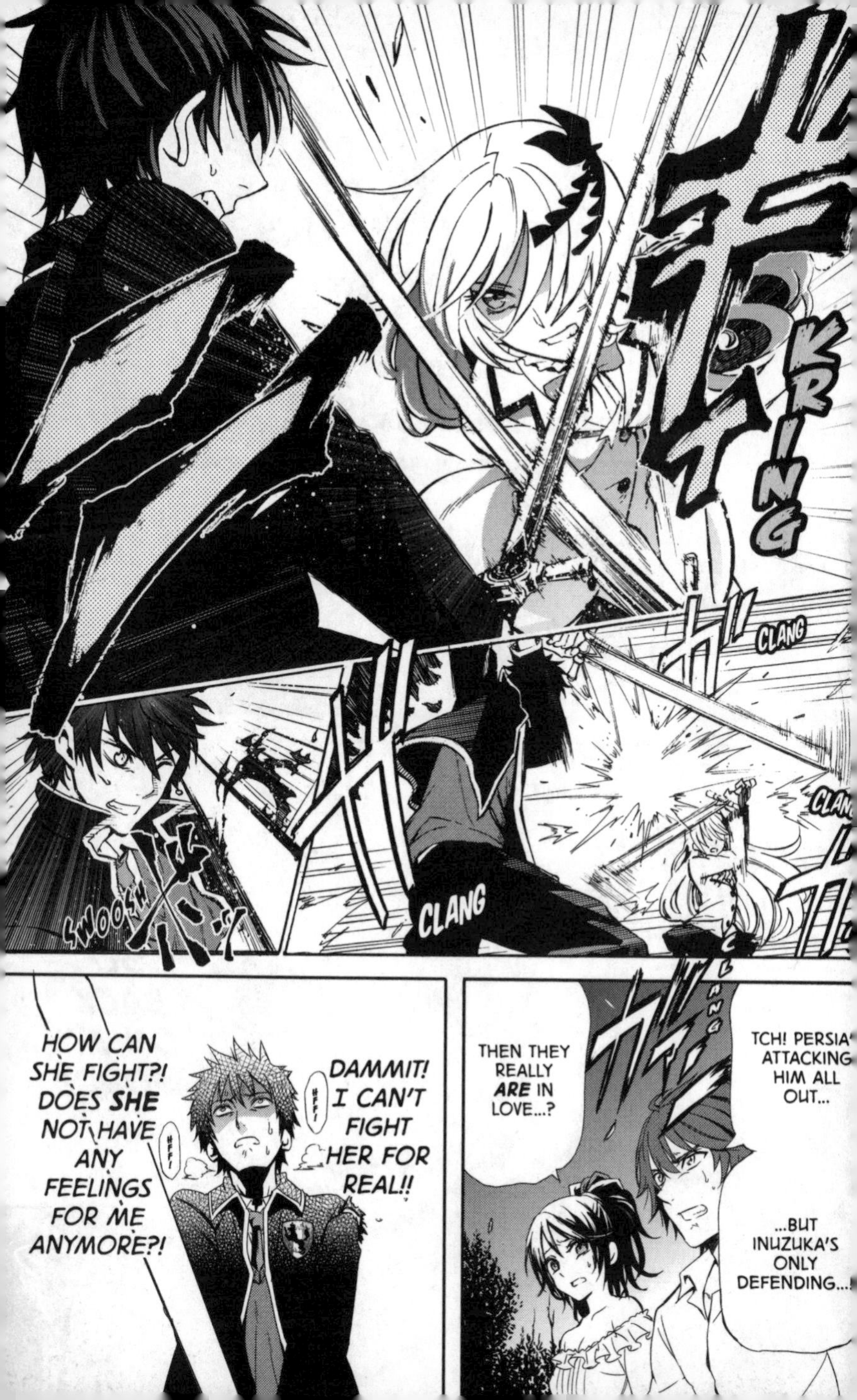
KRING
CLANG
CLANG
SWOOSH
TCH! PERSIA'S ATTACKING HIM ALL OUT...
THEN THEY REALLY ARE IN LOVE...?
...BUT INUZUKA'S ONLY DEFENDING...
CLANG
DAMMIT! I CAN'T FIGHT HER FOR REAL!!
HFF
HFF
HOW CAN SHE FIGHT?! DOES SHE NOT HAVE ANY FEELINGS FOR ME ANYMORE?!

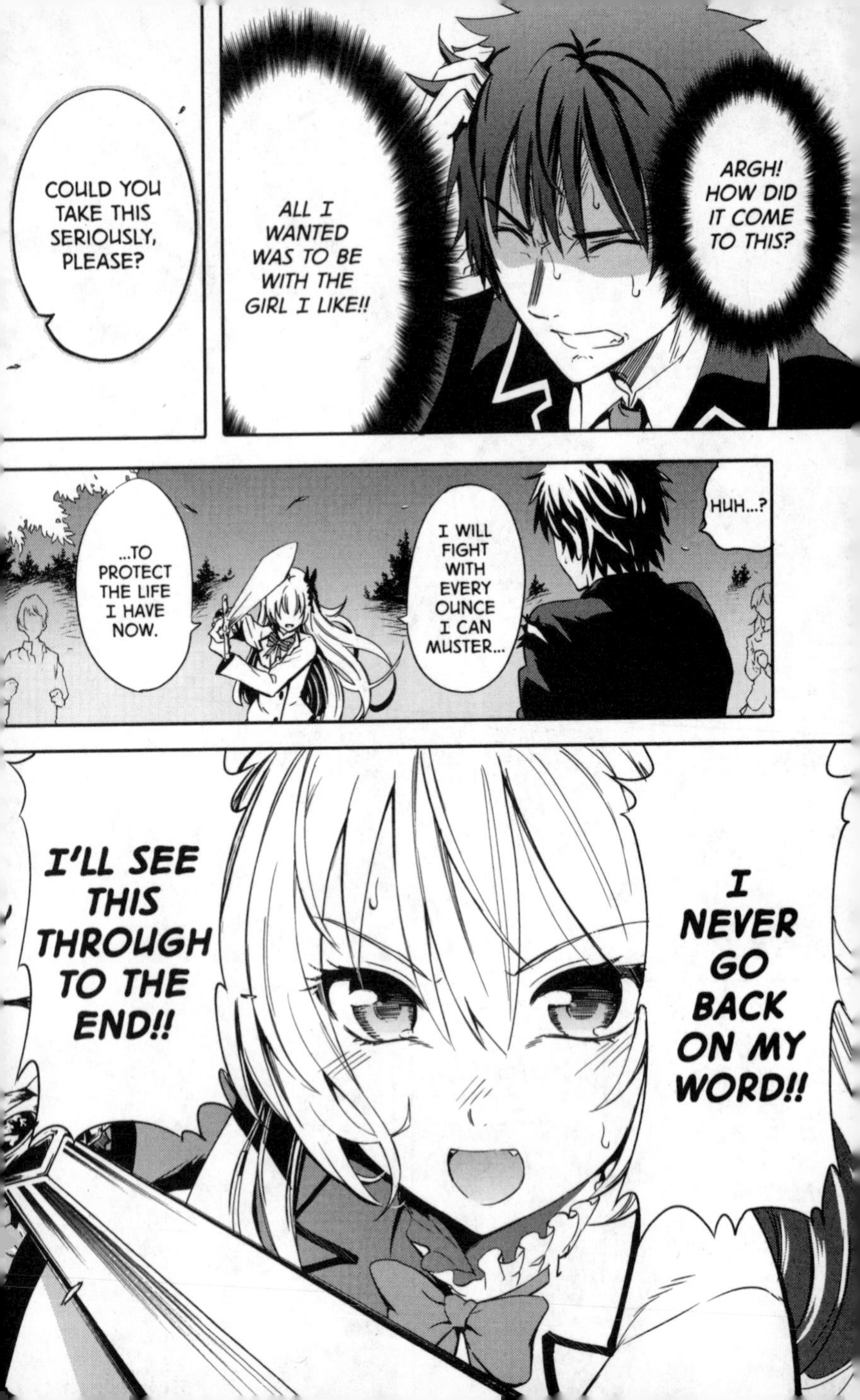
ARGH! HOW DID IT COME TO THIS?
ALL I WANTED WAS TO BE WITH THE GIRL I LIKE!!
COULD YOU TAKE THIS SERIOUSLY, PLEASE?
HUH...?
I WILL FIGHT WITH EVERY OUNCE I CAN MUSTER...
...TO PROTECT THE LIFE I HAVE NOW.
I NEVER GO BACK ON MY WORD!!
I'LL SEE THIS THROUGH TO THE END!!

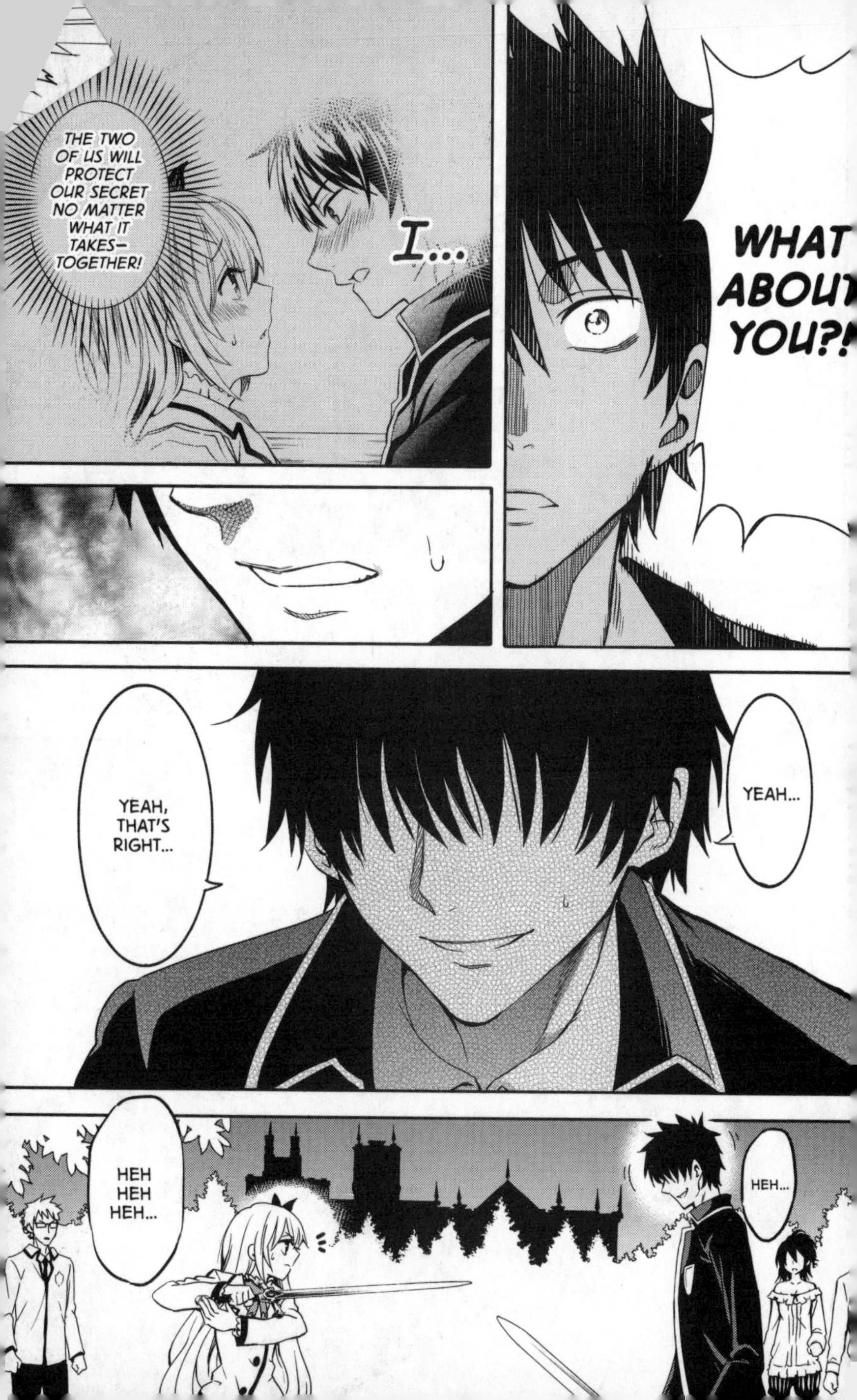
WHAT ABOUT YOU?!
THE TWO OF US WILL PROTECT OUR SECRET NO MATTER WHAT IT TAKES—TOGETHER!
I...
YEAH...
YEAH, THAT'S RIGHT...
HEH...
HEH HEH HEH...

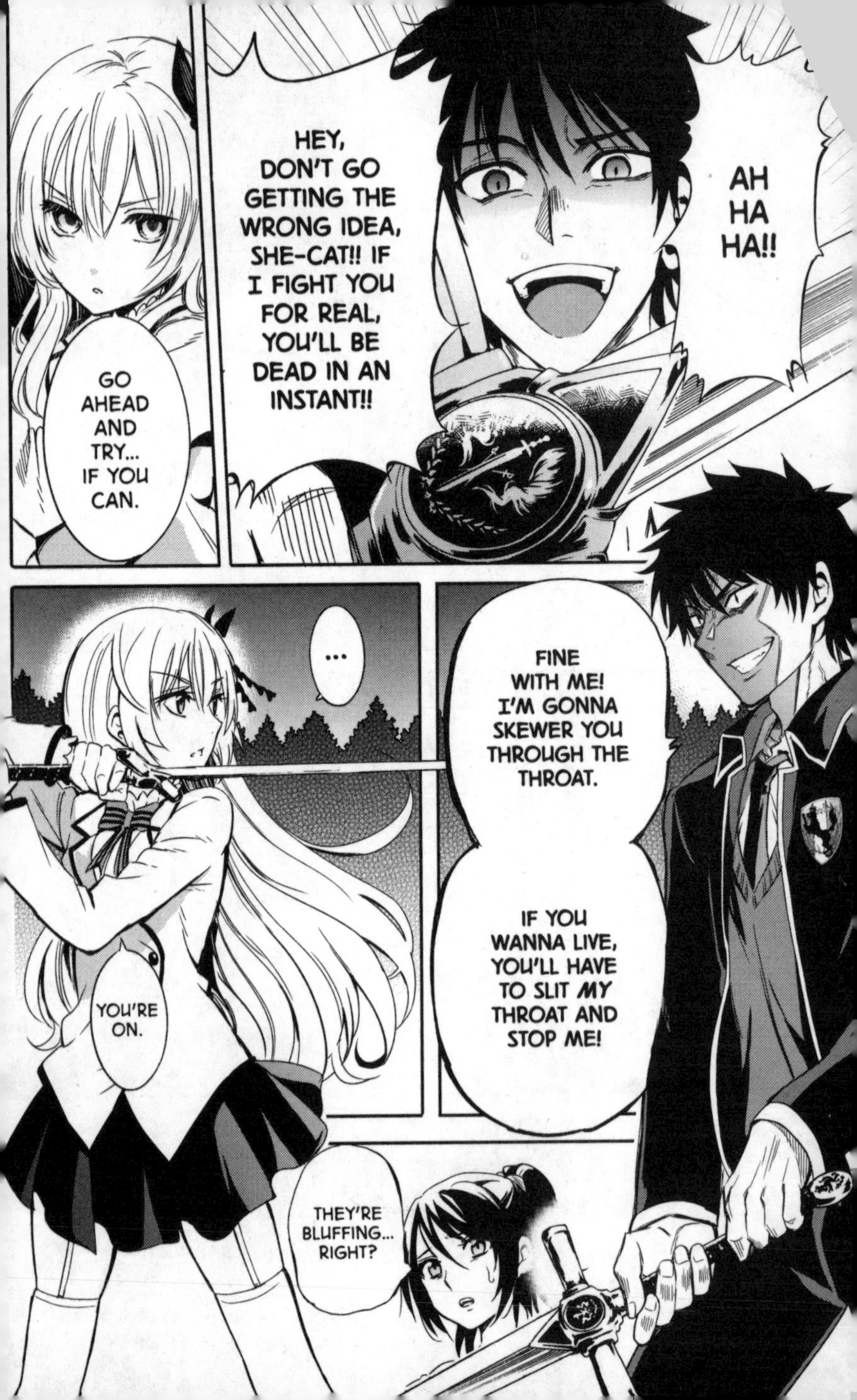
AH HA HA!!
HEY, DON'T GO GETTING THE WRONG IDEA, SHE-CAT!! IF I FIGHT YOU FOR REAL, YOU'LL BE DEAD IN AN INSTANT!!
GO AHEAD AND TRY... IF YOU CAN.
FINE WITH ME! I'M GONNA SKEWER YOU THROUGH THE THROAT.
IF YOU WANNA LIVE, YOU'LL HAVE TO SLIT *MY* THROAT AND STOP ME!
THEY'RE BLUFFING... RIGHT?
...
YOU'RE ON.

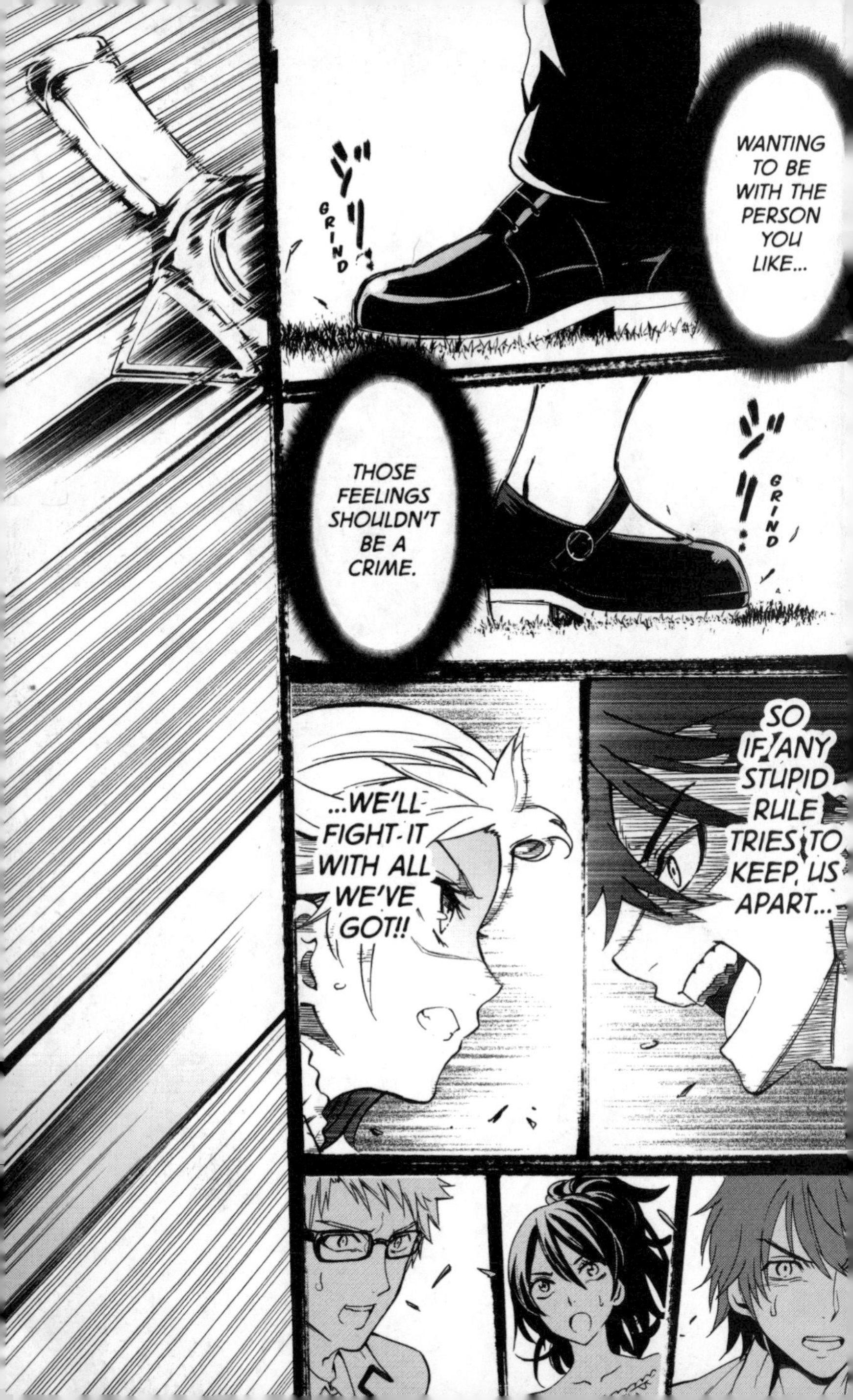
WANTING TO BE WITH THE PERSON YOU LIKE...
GRIND
THOSE FEELINGS SHOULDN'T BE A CRIME.
GRIND
SO IF ANY STUPID RULE TRIES TO KEEP US APART...
...WE'LL FIGHT IT WITH ALL WE'VE GOT!!

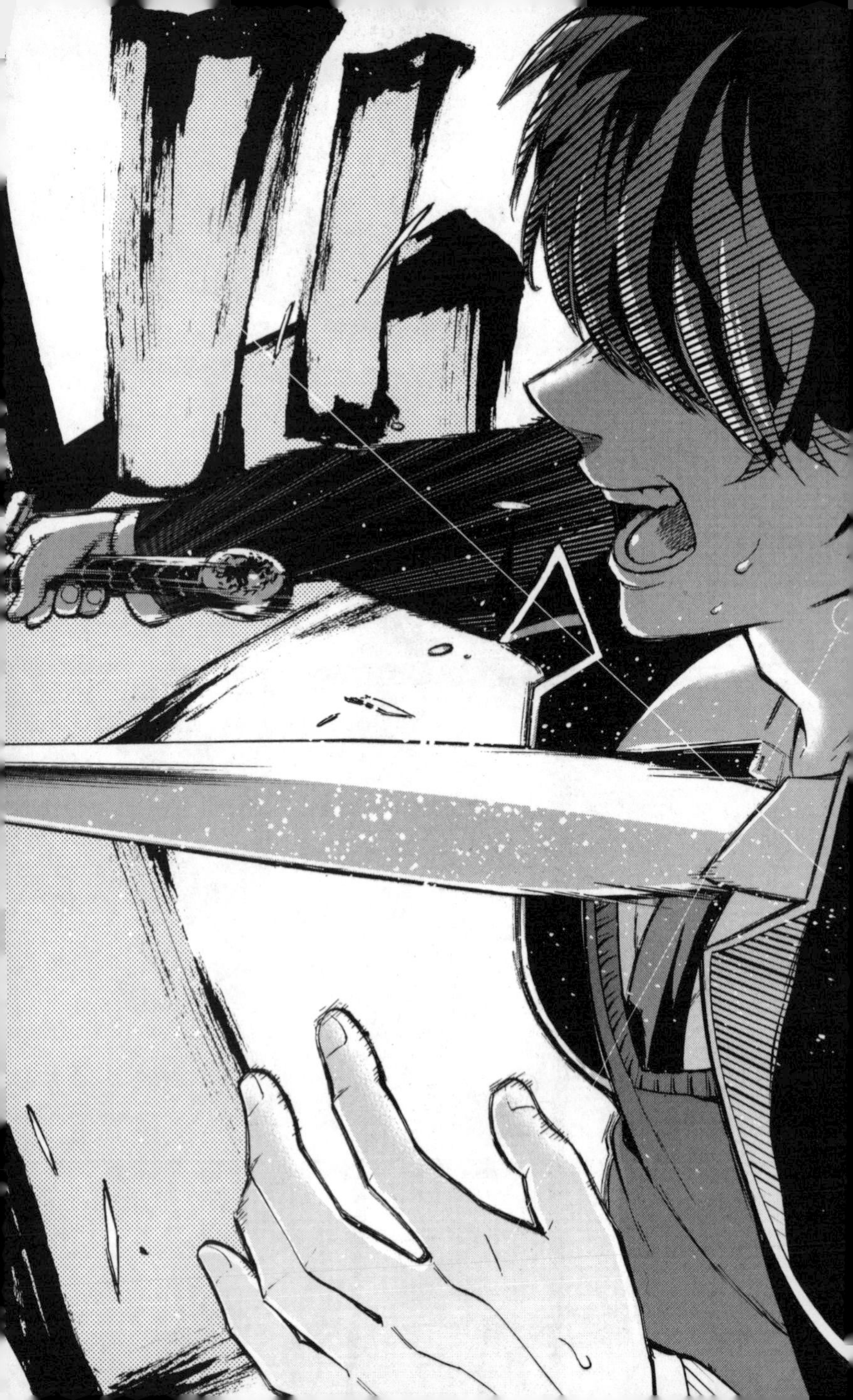

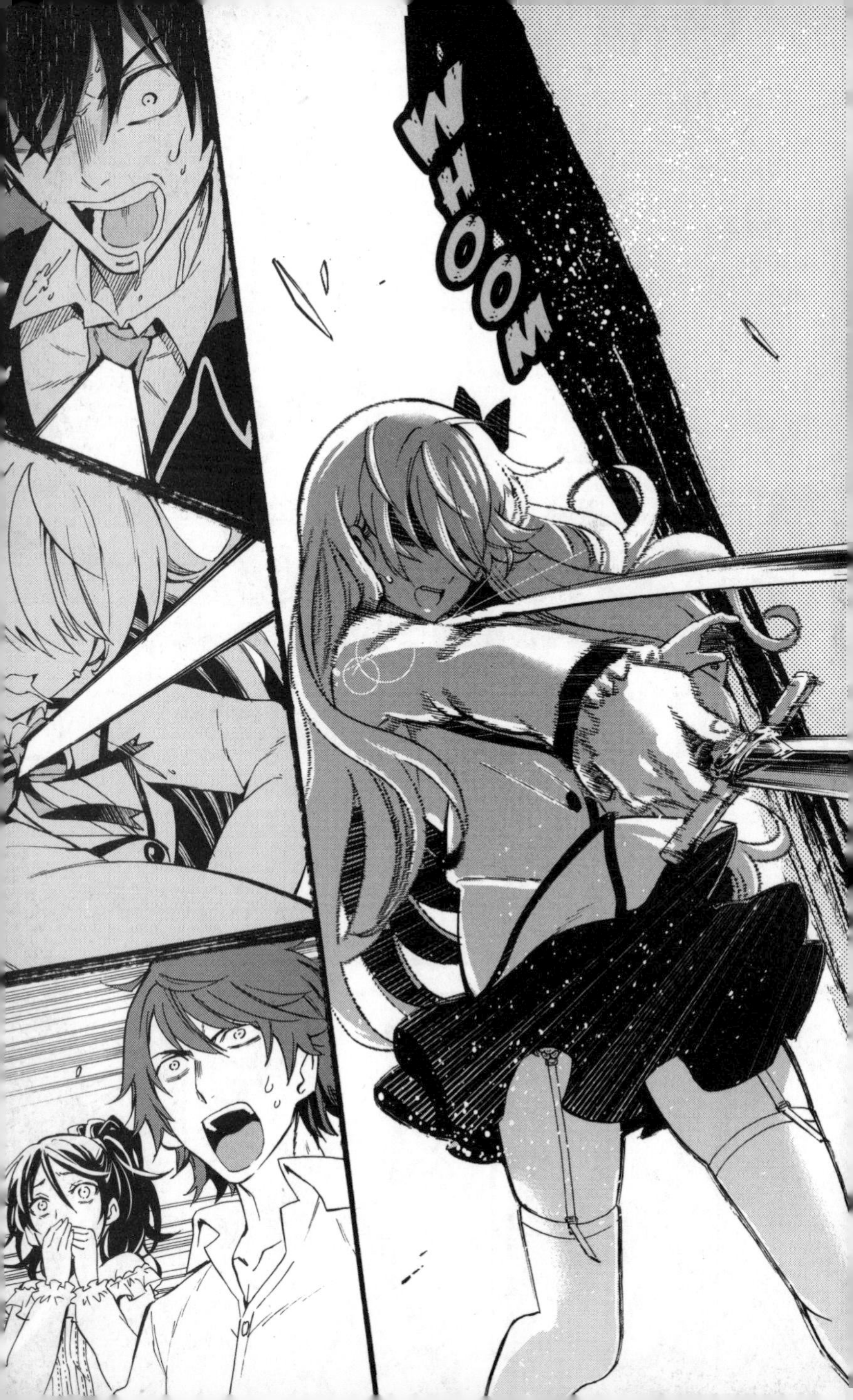
WHOOM

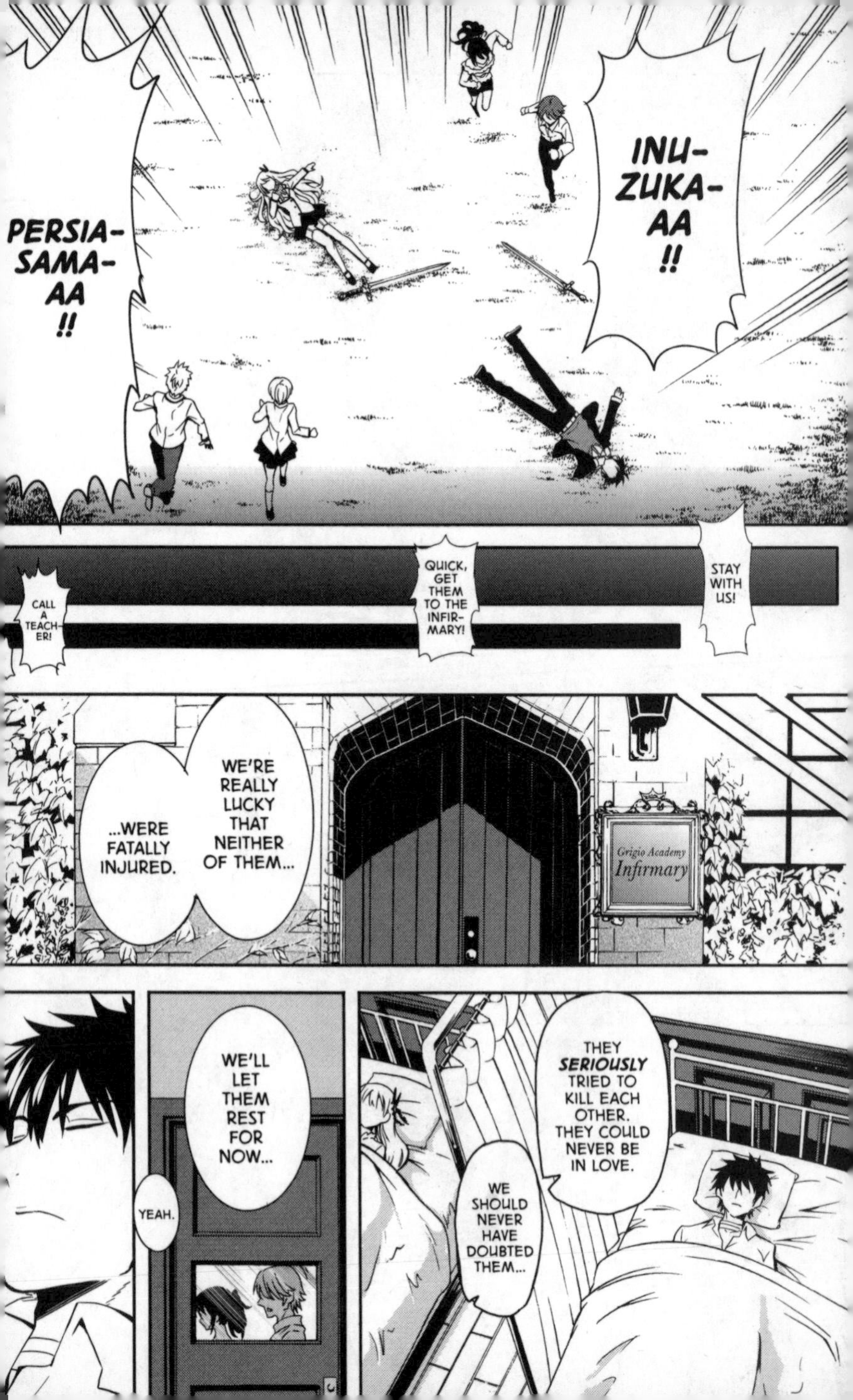
INUZUKA-AA!!
PERSIA-SAMA-AA!!
STAY WITH US!
QUICK, GET THEM TO THE INFIRMARY!
CALL A TEACHER!
Grigio Academy Infirmary
WE'RE REALLY LUCKY THAT NEITHER OF THEM...
...WERE FATALLY INJURED.
THEY ***SERIOUSLY*** TRIED TO KILL EACH OTHER. THEY COULD NEVER BE IN LOVE.
WE SHOULD NEVER HAVE DOUBTED THEM...
WE'LL LET THEM REST FOR NOW...
YEAH.

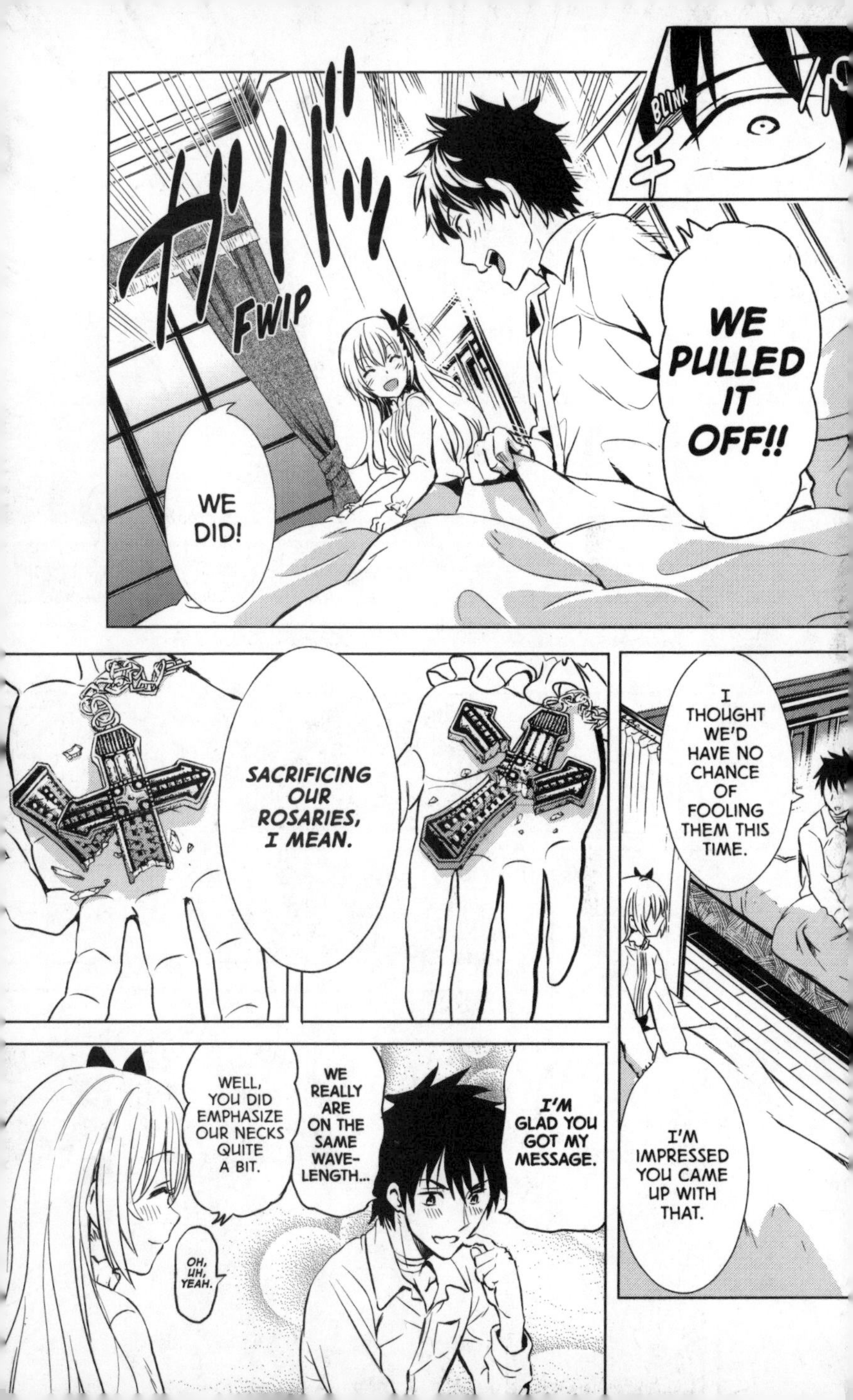
BLINK
WE PULLED IT OFF!!
ガバッ
FWIP
WE DID!
I THOUGHT WE'D HAVE NO CHANCE OF FOOLING THEM THIS TIME.
I'M IMPRESSED YOU CAME UP WITH THAT.
SACRIFICING OUR ROSARIES, I MEAN.
I'M GLAD YOU GOT MY MESSAGE.
WE REALLY ARE ON THE SAME WAVE-LENGTH...
WELL, YOU DID EMPHASIZE OUR NECKS QUITE A BIT.
OH, UH, YEAH.

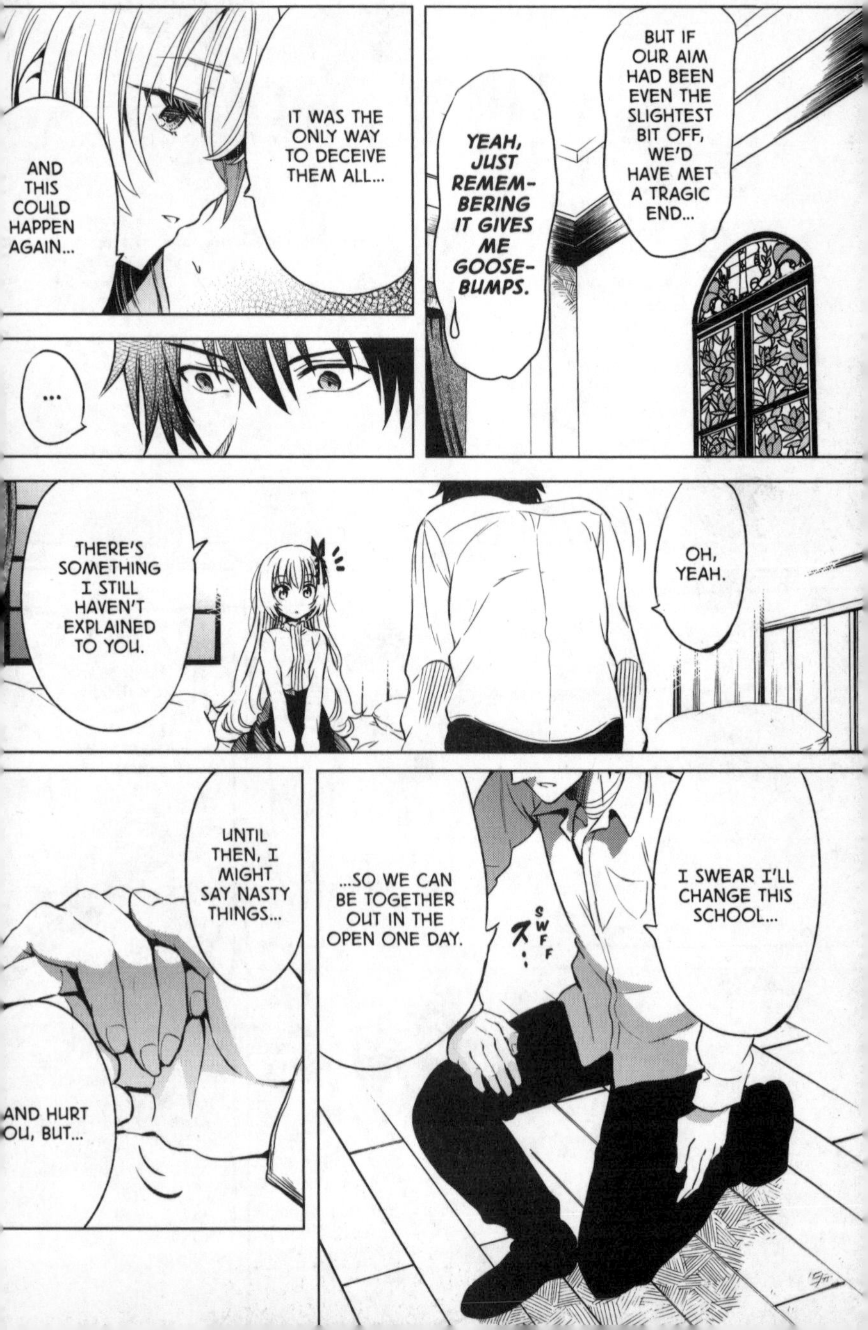
BUT IF OUR AIM HAD BEEN EVEN THE SLIGHTEST BIT OFF, WE'D HAVE MET A TRAGIC END...
YEAH, JUST REMEMBERING IT GIVES ME GOOSEBUMPS.
IT WAS THE ONLY WAY TO DECEIVE THEM ALL...
AND THIS COULD HAPPEN AGAIN...
...
OH, YEAH.
THERE'S SOMETHING I STILL HAVEN'T EXPLAINED TO YOU.
I SWEAR I'LL CHANGE THIS SCHOOL...
ス SWFF
...SO WE CAN BE TOGETHER OUT IN THE OPEN ONE DAY.
UNTIL THEN, I MIGHT SAY NASTY THINGS...
AND HURT OU, BUT...

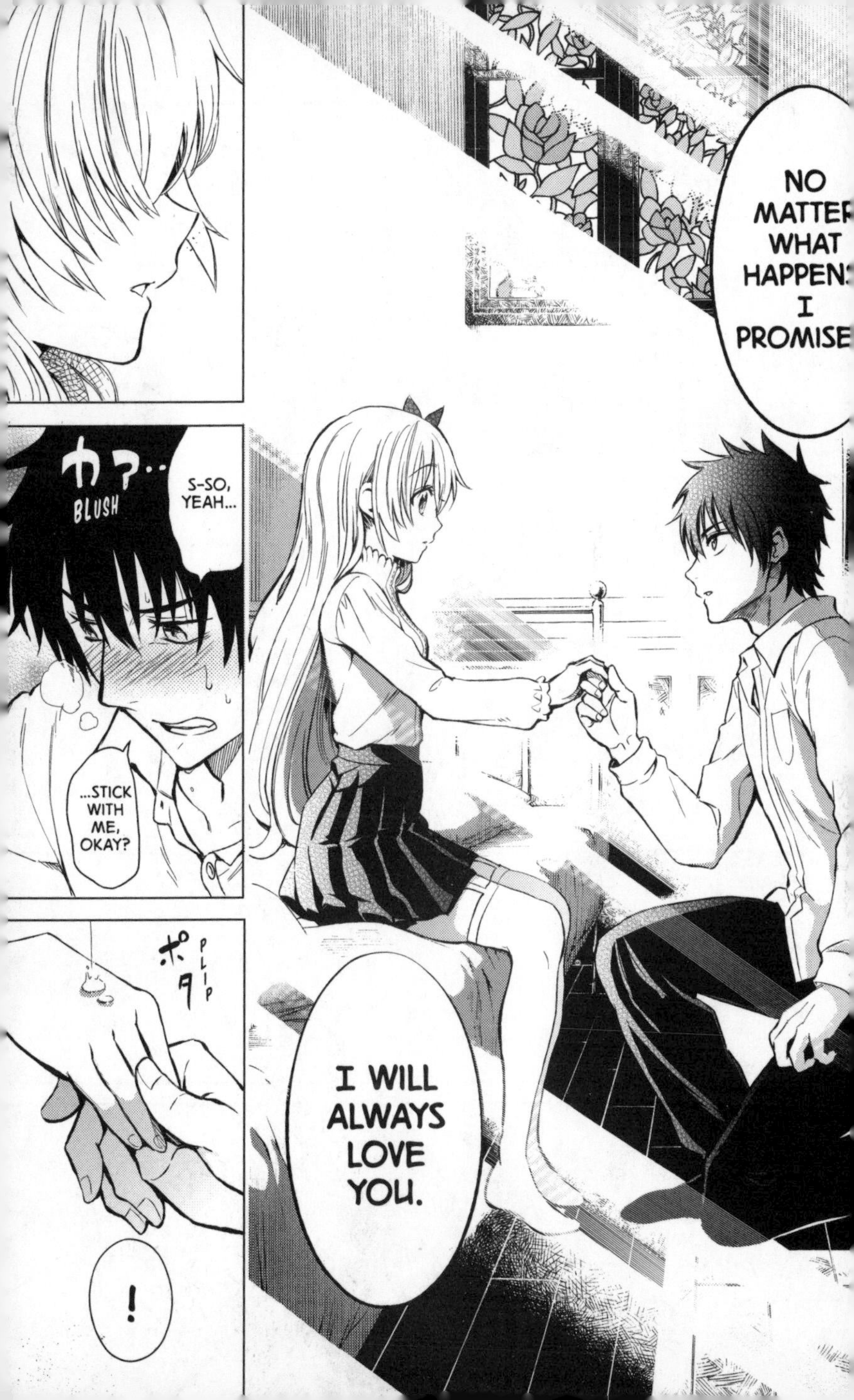
NO MATTER WHAT HAPPEN I PROMISE
I WILL ALWAYS LOVE YOU.
カァ…
BLUSH
S-SO, YEAH...
...STICK WITH ME, OKAY?
ポタ
PLIP
!

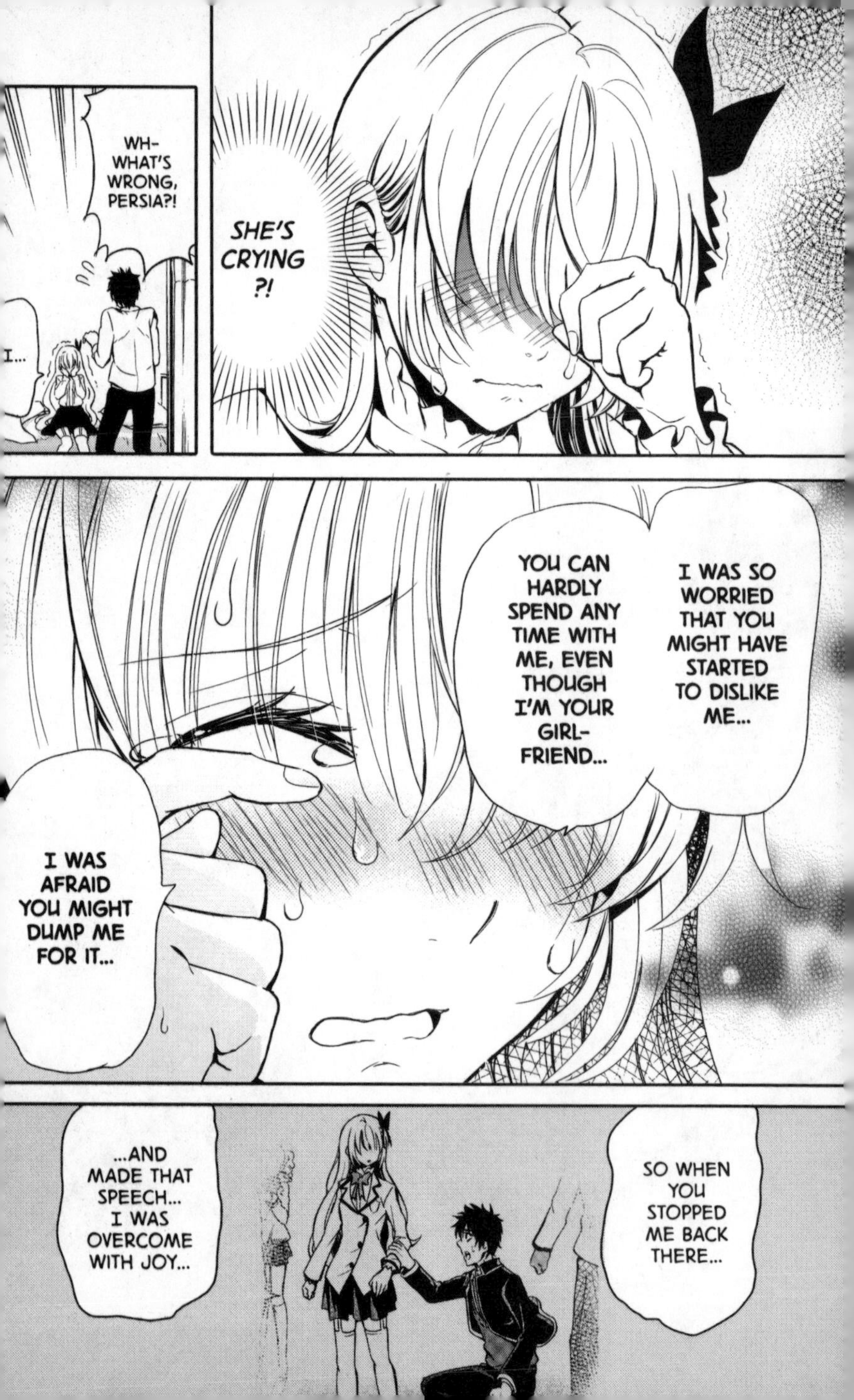
SHE'S CRYING ?!
WH- WHAT'S WRONG, PERSIA?!
I...
I WAS SO WORRIED THAT YOU MIGHT HAVE STARTED TO DISLIKE ME...
YOU CAN HARDLY SPEND ANY TIME WITH ME, EVEN THOUGH I'M YOUR GIRL-FRIEND...
I WAS AFRAID YOU MIGHT DUMP ME FOR IT...
SO WHEN YOU STOPPED ME BACK THERE...
...AND MADE THAT SPEECH... I WAS OVERCOME WITH JOY...

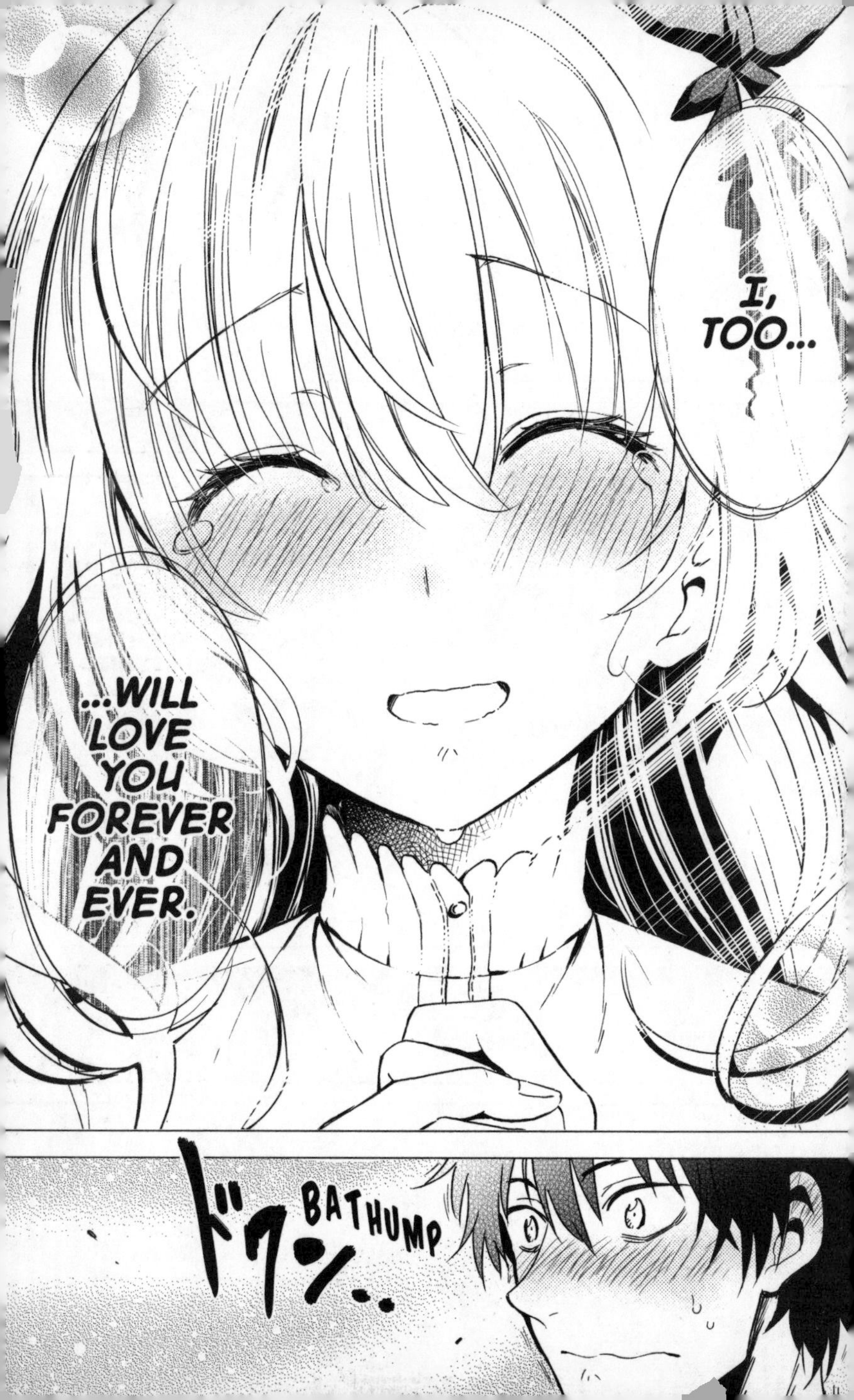
I, TOO...
...WILL LOVE YOU FOREVER AND EVER.
ドクン…
BATHUMP

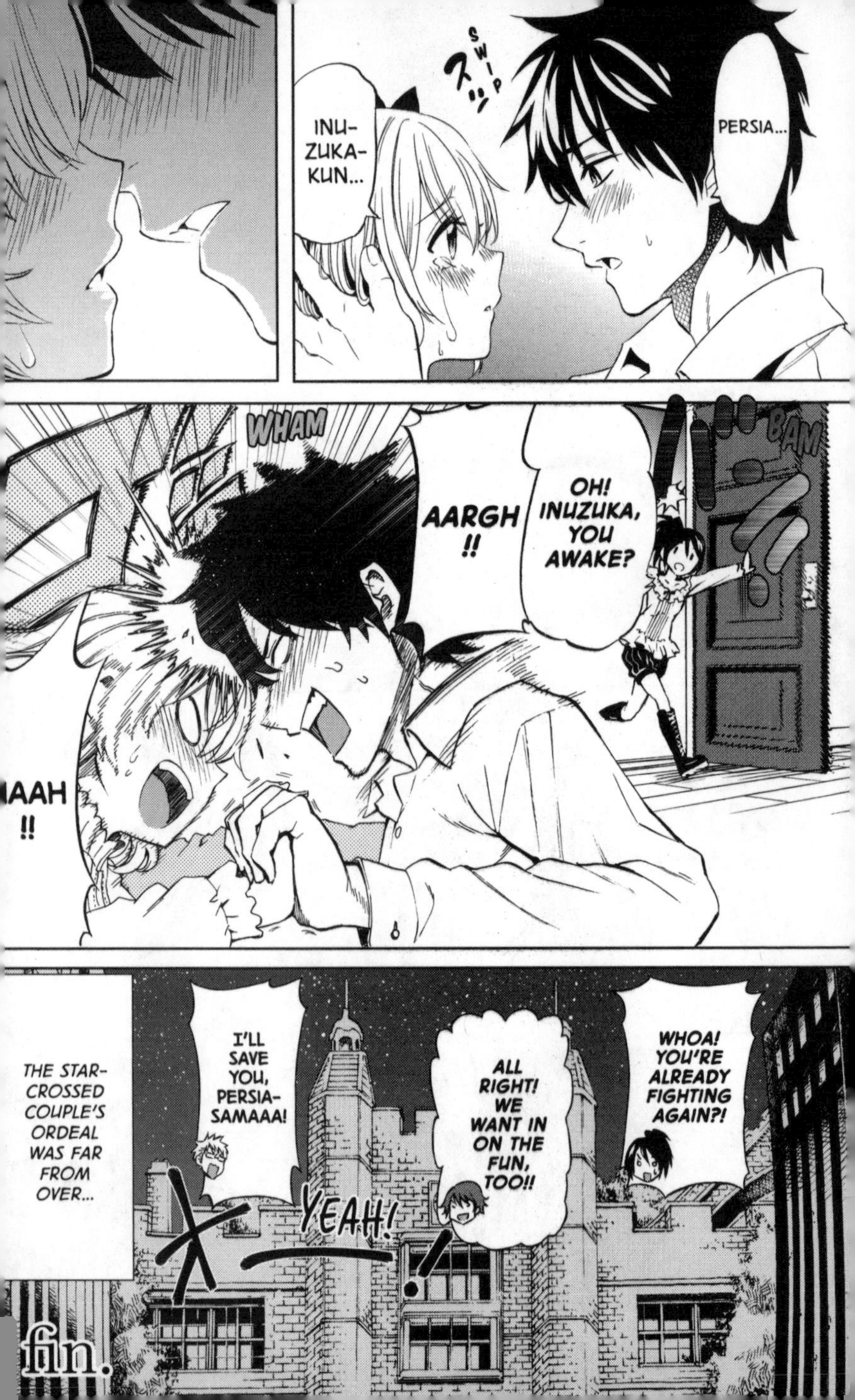

PERSIA...
SWIP
スッ
INUZUKA-KUN...
BAM
OH! INUZUKA, YOU AWAKE?
WHAM
AARGH!!
AAH!!
WHOA! YOU'RE ALREADY FIGHTING AGAIN?!
ALL RIGHT! WE WANT IN ON THE FUN, TOO!!
I'LL SAVE YOU, PERSIA-SAMAAA!
YEAH!
THE STAR-CROSSED COUPLE'S ORDEAL WAS FAR FROM OVER...
fin.

Boarding
School *Juliet*

PERFECT WORLD

Rie Aruga

A TOUCHING NEW SERIES ABOUT LOVE AND COPING WITH DISABILITY

An office party reunites Tsugumi with her high school crush Itsuki. He's realized his dream of becoming an architect, but along the way, he experienced a spinal injury that put him in a wheelchair. Now Tsugumi's rekindled feelings will butt up against prejudices she never considered — and Itsuki will have to decide if he's ready to let someone into his heart...

"Depicts with great delicacy and courage the difficulties some with disabilities experience getting involved in romantic relationships... Rie Aruga refuses to romanticize, pushing her heroine to face the reality of disability. She invites her readers to the same tasks of empathy, knowledge and recognition."
—Slate.fr

"An important entry [in manga romance]... The emotional core of both plot and characters indicates thoughtfulness... [Aruga's] research is readily apparent in the text and artwork, making this feel like a real story."
—Anime News Network

Perfect World © Rie Aruga/Kodansha Ltd.

Knight of the Ice ©Yayoi Ogawa

Yayoi Ogawa

SKATING THRILLS AND ICY CHILLS WITH THIS NEW TINGLY ROMANCE SERIES!

A rom-com on ice, perfect for fans of *Princess Jellyfish* and *Wotakoi*. Kokoro is the talk of the figure-skating world, winning trophies and hearts. But little do they know... he's actually a huge nerd! From the beloved creator of *You're My Pet* (*Tramps Like Us*).

Chitose is a serious young woman, working for the health magazine *SASSO*. Or at least, she would be, if she wasn't constantly getting distracted by her childhood friend, international figure skating star Kokoro Kijinami! In the public eye and on the ice, Kokoro is a gallant, flawless knight, but behind his glittery costumes and breathtaking spins lies a secret: He's actually a hopelessly romantic otaku, who can only land his quad jumps when Chitose is on hand to recite a spell from his favorite magical girl anime!

KC KODANSHA COMICS

Boarding School Juliet 16 is a work of fiction. Names, characters, places, and incidents are the products of the author's imagination or are used fictitiously. Any resemblance to actual events, locales, or persons, living or dead, is entirely coincidental.

Boarding School Juliet 16 copyright © 2019 Yousuke Kaneda
English translation copyright © 2021 Yousuke Kaneda

All rights reserved.

Published in the United States by Kodansha Comics, an imprint of Kodansha USA Publishing, LLC, New York.

Publication rights for this English edition arranged through Kodansha Ltd., Tokyo.

First published in Japan in 2019 by Kodansha Ltd., Tokyo as *Kishuku Gakkou no Jurietto*, volume 16.

Original cover design by Seiko Tsuchihashi (hive & co., Ltd.)

ISBN 978-1-64651-132-7

Printed in the United States of America.

www.kodansha.us

9 8 7 6 5 4 3 2 1
Translation: Amanda Haley
Lettering: James Dashiell
Editing: Erin Subramanian, Tomoko Nagano
Kodansha Comics edition cover design by Phil Balsman

Publisher: Kiichiro Sugawara

Director of publishing services: Ben Applegate
Associate director of operations: Stephen Pakula
Publishing services managing editors: Alanna Ruse, Madison Salters
Production managers: Emi Lotto, Angela Zurlo